Ashok Liu

Computercare's
LAPTOP
Repair Workbook

THE 300 CASES OF CLASSIC NOTEBOOK COMPUTERS TROUBLESHOOTING AND REPAIR

E-Version 2.2

authorHOUSE®

AuthorHouse™
1663 Liberty Drive
Bloomington, IN 47403
www.authorhouse.com
Phone: 1-800-839-8640

Published by AuthorHouse   05/10/2013

ISBN: 978-1-4772-0540-2 (sc)

Library of Congress Control Number: 2012909020

Version 2.2
Edit with Microsoft standard flow chart
Technical text verifier: Grahame Fournier
Proofread: Joe Akinwale
Copyright: Ashok Liu

CONTENTS

1.   Laptop, notebook Common Questions

1.1   Notices for using a laptop   Page 1

1.1.1   Should we let laptops run uninterrupted for a 24 hour period?   Page 1
1.1.2   What is the most pivotal factor influencing a laptops life expectancy?   Page 2
1.1.3   What're the environmental factors causing laptop problems?   Page 5
1.1.4   Transporting and carrying Your Laptop.   Page 7

1.2   Laptop for daily use and maintenance   Page 9

1.2.1   Factors affecting laptop battery life and discharge time.   Page 9
1.2.2   LCD—little tips for liquid crystal screen usage and maintenance   Page 11
1.2.3   Usage tips and maintenance for your hard drive   Page 15
1.2.4   How to prolong your power adapter's useful life?   Page 17
1.2.5   Taboos for keyboard: humidity, dust and pull drag   Page 19

This is a practical reference book which uses simple testing methods to confirm if a laptop's failure is software or hardware-related. The testing methods presented here can provide a diagnostic accuracy of ninety-nine percent within minutes.

Another highlight of this book is that the reader is able to follow a typical repair shortcut, thereby saving considerable 'swap test' time (i.e. avoiding the trial and error system). For the majority of readers, this book will provide most of the failure status information needed to diagnose and resolve an issue. There are thirteen diagnostic flowcharts at the core of this book which are marked with the percentage (probability) of failed components. By checking the components listed on the diagnosis flowcharts one by one starting with components marked as having a high failure rate then gradually inspecting each component with a lower percentage of failure, most individuals will be able to find a resolution.

There are also three hundred classic repair cases and dozens of fault detecting methods with application skills available within these pages. Also adopted here is a unique mode of operation to repair laptops with simple steps in which the reader can refer to the eight articles in the "Analysis and Diagnostic" table to find information matching their particular case.

The experience and advice provided within this text will assist you diagnose and repair numerous software and hardware problems, and perhaps aid you on your way to becoming your own laptop repair expert.

FOREWORD

The knowledge you cannot learn from a college "computer repair" course is contained here-in. It is based on the real experience of a computer repair professional. Many of those who graduate from a college course are not yet capable of offering competent repair services; they need to work under the tutelage of an experienced professional for a period of time.

There are many books available on Laptop repair but few of them will offer the depth and detail of the repair process that this book does. A laptop is an extremely complex device requiring a knowledge of analog and digital electronics, data protocol, video, audio, electricity, software, and cooling systems all integrated together. This book does not replace the need for a thorough understanding of the theory needed for an in depth understanding of the device, but it will guide you through dealing with many common problems and avoiding the expense of a computer repair service.

This book will teach you the first rule to identify laptop failures successfully, does the failure originate in the hardware or software or both? If you use the wrong method to test your laptop or the electronic components, I can ensure that you will not be able to repair or solve these computer problems. I've already been engaged in an electronic maintenance career for more than 35 years, and more than 25 years for computer maintenance. I have repaired thousands of laptops and electronic equipment successfully, and quite a few of these laptops were the so-called "beyond repair" by other "experts". My own unique approach to the repair process was developed over many years and enabled me to solve many problems that were considered "beyond repair".

I find that when testing and repairing laptops, many beginners have no idea how to decide whether the problem is from the hardware or software with accuracy. They have to be very lucky to hit on the failure cause and successfully carry out the repair. I try to eliminate the luck factor and provide a logical approach to resolving a laptop failure.

If your success rate in providing competent repair services is not what it should be because your techniques are not sufficiently developed, then you may be declaring computers "beyond repair" that can be repaired. You will lose credibility and customers will be going elsewhere. Your competition may have already learned the techniques presented in this manual. If that is your situation, you need this book.

This e-book is for beginners, amateurs, technology institutes or college students and enthusiasts of laptop repair. Even some computer repair services with an abundance of experience can find it a useful reference. I spent countless hours carrying out' test and analysis, and have found the best way to deal with most common laptop failures, which has resulted in the successful repair of thousands of repair cases. The techniques offered apply to most standard laptops but they are not for some special brands or models. This point has already been approved by most other people of the same occupation. Now let my experience work for you.

By repair practices, this book summarizes an abundance of classic repair cases, failure test methods, and application techniques, especially for hardware failures where there is a deep and intensive analysis.

It's difficult to truly learn about repair without practice, in this book I offer classic 300 HP laptop repair cases, hardware test and repair methods. Practising according to these cases will enable readers to learn the repair methods and also build on their repair experience. This is a full-scale professional laptop repair book with original contents!

Disclaimer

Therefore, each advice, information, suggestion, technique, method and product should be used only as a general guide and not as the ultimate truth and/or source about laptop repair and related subjects.

The authors shall have neither liability nor responsibility to any person or entity with respect to any loss or damage caused, or alleged to be caused, directly or indirectly by the information contained in this book. This information is for you to use at your own risk.

CHAPTER 1

Frequently asked questions
with the methods to repair laptop

1.1 Notes on using a laptop

1.1.1 Should we let laptops run uninterrupted for a 24 hour period?

All laptops are designed and manufactured to meet an operating life expectancy requirement. The longer the design life, the more expensive the laptop. For example, a light-bulb can be rated to operate for 1000 hours of use before it fails. It may last longer or sometimes less, but on average it will be 1000 hrs. A more expensive light bulb might be rated for 2000hrs.

Laptops are considerably more complex than a light bulb but the same principles do apply. Obviously turning off a laptop when not in use will prolong its life expectancy.

Most manufacturers set their standard (home-use) laptops to operate uninterrupted for 8 hours. Keeping the device running for a longer period of time may result in damage to the internal components due to lengthy exposure to heat.

Cooling fans are a mechanical device and will wear out over time. The less it runs, the longer it will last. The fan will also tend to clog up with dust and dirt over time causing your laptop to overheat and thus degrade components.

Do not obstruct the air flow vents on your computer. Avoid smoking tobacco when using your laptop. These will accelerate the aging of your laptop.

Avoid using your laptop in a high temperature, or damp environment. This can drastically reduce the life expectancy of your laptop.

Commercial laptops are built to be run continuously, but are much more expensive to buy. You will not likely have one of these.

Personal laptops are not commercial laptops. Don't let them run continuously. Even if you use a commercial laptop, it is still good practice to turn it off at night unless it must remain active for a 24 hour period.

The laptop view screen is also affected by overheating. The LCD (liquid crystal display) degrades over time, and the image quality will deteriorate until there is nothing but a blank screen. Prolonged usage of the laptop without the recommended cool down time will cause the breakdown of the LCD, thus shortening the life span of the laptop.

The battery is probably the most dangerous component of the laptop when allowed to overheat due to reduced ventilation or any other reason. In extreme conditions it might explode. Shut your laptop off and let it cool if your laptop feels too hot.

In conclusion, the laptops of today are not intended to run continuously. Shortening the time that you use the laptop, and remembering to give the laptop a cool down period, will greatly improve and prolong the life span of your laptop.

1.1.2   What is the most pivotal factor influencing a laptops life expectancy?

Over the years there has been much discussion on the relationship between laptop useful life vs. accumulated operating time (AOT). Useful life or life expectancy is often defined as the point at which the manufacturer ceases to support the product. For our purpose we will define it as the point at which unit repair is no longer cost effective. We will concern ourselves only with hardware and not software.

It has been said that a factor affecting electrical apparatus' life expectancy is AOT. The more the laptop is used, the more durable it would be, and the less you use it, the shorter its life would be. This is an opposing view to the accepted theory. You might also hear this argument. At my work place, the computers have been running for 4 to 5 years without interruption, and we have never suffered a failure. Our family computer was finished within 2 years even though we did not use it continuously. I can only conclude that the more the computer is operating, the longer will its life expectancy will be.

Of course this is not exactly true. The computers referred to were operating in a highly controlled environment where temperature, dust, and humidity were all controlled.

Your laptop will not likely be used in this kind of environment but there is something to be learned from this story.

What is the most vital factor influencing laptop life expectancy?

The environment it lives in is the most important factor that will influence life expectancy. The importance of the environment in which your computer operates, cannot be over stressed. Ambient temperature, humidity and clean environment are decisive factors that determine laptop life expectancy. An environmentally controlled computer room would be the ideal place to use your laptop if you want to run it continuously. Unfortunately our laptops have to be operated in much less controlled environments. It is important to be aware of this scenario and do your best to use your laptop in conditions that will prolong its life expectancy.

When storing your laptop for long periods of time, especially during humid weather, you need to run the laptop occasionally for a minimum of 1 hr but not more than 12, to allow the heat to dry it out. This will prevent the electronic components inside from being corrupted.

Do not store your laptop in a damp environment such as your basement, or in your automobile or a place where the sun will hit it and heat it. Keep it in a case and store it in a cool, clean, and dry environment in your house or office. Even a short period of 7 to 10 days improper storage is enough to degrade the laptop. You might find a perfectly good computer will not boot up when you bring it out of a bad storage situation. You need to be aware of, and avoid this bad practice that can shorten the life of your computer.

When a computer is run continuously in a poor environment its life expectancy will be greatly reduced. Dust accumulation inside the computer will inhibit proper cooling and the unit will run too hot. The fan and hard disc have rotating parts that wear out, and the more you operate, the shorter their lifespan and more so in a poor environment.

Power surges or spikes from your utility source are another condition that can cause your laptop to be degraded or fail. Your external power supply and internal battery will buffer out most of these, but strong surges such as generated by lightening, can get through by being radiated and travelling on the surface of the incoming power cable, it can link in by many ways. It is advisable to unplug your power supply and run on battery during a lightening storm. If your battery is fully charged, shut your computer off and disconnect the power supply when you are not using it. This will protect your laptop from surges and prolong the battery life.

Surges can also arrive via your internet connection if it is not wireless. Disconnecting the internet cable and working off line using your battery, would be the ultimate precaution for you and your laptop during a storm. Also disconnect the internet cable when you are not using the laptop.

Hardware maintenance for your laptop is just as important as your daily software maintenance. It does not have to be on a daily basis but needs to be occasionally done. The most important maintenance is of the preventive variety that we have been discussing. After that, periodic hands-on maintenance should be performed. The following tips will extend the life of your laptop.

Never restrict the laptop cooling

- A laptop radiator is an inexpensive device that can greatly enhance you laptop cooling. It will contain fans and is USB powered. You place your laptop on top of it. This device will make your laptop run cooler, and therefore increase its useful life span. It can even improve the computers performance. A good investment.
- Using your laptop on your lap is a bad practice. It will interfere with the cooling. Keep your laptop on a hard, flat surface. Not directly on your legs or lap,

- Never put your laptop on a carpet or on a bed, or other fabric surface. It will block the cooling and allow dust to be drawn in. This is a very bad practice.
- After turning off the laptop completely, put it into your brief case or backpack. Never put a laptop in a running or hibernation state in a case or in a small confined space. It can overheat and damage or ruin your laptop.

Keeping Your Laptop Clean.

How to Clean Your Screen

Cloth—Only use a 100%-cotton cloth that is soft and absorbent, either an old T-shirt, sock, or Turkish towel. Make sure you're not using a cotton/polyester blend that contains stiff filaments which can scratch an LCD's surface.

Paper towel or facial tissue should never be used because they contain wood fibers, also hazardous to LCDs, and definitely are not how to clean a laptop screen.

Also remember to never use a dry cloth on your LCD monitor. Dust particles moved around with even the softest cloth could create scratches.

Liquid—The best way to get a really clean laptop screen is to use 70% isopropyl alcohol, readily available at any drugstore or supermarket. It's perfectly safe for use on electronic equipment and LCD screens because it evaporates quickly and does not leave a residue. This lesser strength 70% isopropyl alcohol is used primarily for massages and muscle pain.

Certain household liquids should never be used on LCDs. These include ammonia and tap or mineral water, which leave permanent white spots and streaks. Household window cleaners should be avoided because they might contain ammonia, or other harmful chemicals which also can cause irreparable damage.

Another caution is to never spray a solution directly onto an LCD. Always spray the liquid on a cloth, only enough to moisten it slightly, and then apply to the screen in gentle, counter-clockwise motions.

How Clean Your Keyboard

One method is to use a can of compressed air. Be aware that a can of compressed air does not simply contain air but contains a toxic chemical. So be careful when handling it and never hold the bottle upside down. Just tilt it at an angle two or three inches away from your key board as you direct the air between the keys. The good thing about having a laptop is that if it is too difficult to tilt the can of air you can always tilt your computer. Just be careful not to drop it.

If you feel comfortable doing it, you can also hold your laptop upside down over a trash can and tap on it lightly to dislodge any remaining debris that might be hiding in there once you're done spraying.

4

There are many methods on the internet. Just Google and you will find them.

How to Clean a Laptop Fan and Heat sink

Cleaning a Laptop fan and heat sink requires taking the laptop apart. Do not use a vacuum cleaner, it can create static. Using compressed air to blow into the vents simply blows dirt into the interior of the laptop. This task should normally be carried out by a qualified technician, however, if you elect to do it yourself there are many good procedures published on the internet.

Cleaning needs to be done periodically but you should develop good habits when using your computer to keep it clean.

Do not eat or drink in the proximity of your computer. Take a break and do it elsewhere.

Do not smoke while using your computer.

Keep your hands clean.

Clean the external surfaces of your computer regularly. Weekly if you are using the computer often or for long periods.

Good habits will do much to extend the life expectancy of your laptop.

Do not use your computer in direct sunlight for long periods.

Use "SpeedFan" monitoring software to monitor and track your laptop temperature, hard drives and other parts. Check the voltage, fan speed, temperature and other data to see whether everything is OK. If not, diagnose the problem immediately. Adjust your power settings to help you get rid of unnecessary heat.

Your laptop BIOS controls many of the hardware functions in your computer. This includes the fan and automatic shutdown functions should your computer be overheating or developing other fatal faults that can cause damage. The manufacturer provides BIOS updates to improve the performance of your computer or correct bugs that are discovered. Check the manufacturer's web page occasionally for these updates and install them. This will provide you with additional protection against problems that can shorten the life of your computer.

1.1.3 What're the environmental factors causing laptop problems?

Keeping your laptop in good running condition requires you to develop good habits and knowledge of what will negatively affect its performance and life expectancy. You will avoid the repair shop and catastrophic losses of data if you follow a few simple guidelines to provide the optimum environment for your computer. Get the most from your investment. These guidelines will provide the optimum environment that is needed. The following environmental factors affect the performance and reliability of your laptop:

Shock and Vibration—Treat your computer gently. Don't drop or knock it. Don't use it on an unstable, uneven, or vibrating surface. Place it in a secure location when being transported in your automobile. Don't let it be jarred, slide around, or fall. When operating, your computer it is even more susceptible to damage by vibration or hard knocks. The hard disc and CD/DVD drive have a low tolerance to this kind of abuse. It is easy to break the shell or screen by bad handling. Always be mindful of these unhealthy situations and avoid them.

Humidity—a humid environment can be very detrimental to your laptop. Components become degraded. Wire connections and connectors can oxidize and create intermittent problems. You should avoid operating or storing in a humid environment such as found in your basement.

Air Quality—It is very important to use the laptop in an environment that is as dust free as possible Dust is drawn into the computer through the intake vents where it will coat the fan and heatsink and lead to overheating, failure or degraded performance. Dust on the circuit boards or components can cause short circuits. Use of the laptop on a fabric surface such as your bed or your lap, not only blocks the ventilation, but draws in dust and dirt from the fabric. Smoking in the room with your computer or while using it, is a bad habit that can coat your screen and cause impurities to be drawn into the computer with resulting negative affects.

Temperature—the ambient temperature in which you are using your computer is an important consideration. Too hot or too cold can affect performance and accelerate aging. Rapid temperature changes when moving the computer can cause dew to form inside the computer, and lead to serious damage. A rapid 10 degree transition is sufficient to cause this to happen. It is important to be aware of these conditions and avoid them s much as possible.

Electromagnetism interference—strong electromagnetism interference will cause damage to your laptop. Keep your laptop away from appliances or entertainment systems by at least 15cm. keep it well away from a microwave oven. Please take a look at figure 1-1; 1-2; 1-3.

Figure 1-1 Don't put your coffee cup on the laptop

Figure1-2 Dust is drawn in through the ventilation openings.

Figure 1-3 Please don't put your laptop on a bed, sofa, desk or any other fabric surface

And here is the best laptop working environment (recommended)

Environment parameters	
Temperature	25 °C
Comparative humidity (maximum)	70 %
Altitude height	-15.2-3,048 m (-50-10,000ft)

Notice: the environmental parameters above are typical and recommended, for optimum performance and long life. Please also refer to your user manual for parameters specific to your unit.

1.1.4 Transporting and carrying Your Laptop.

Your laptop can be damaged when you are carrying it with you.

Suggestions:

a) Use a properly fitting laptop bag to transport your unit.
b) Fully power off your laptop before placing it in your laptop bag. Do not close the laptop screen before it is fully shut down. That can prevent the laptop from completing the

shutdown process. Placing your laptop in your bag while still running, will overheat it and possibly damage it.

c) Avoid packing items unrelated to your laptop in the bag. It should contain your laptop and essential accessories only. Be careful not to arrange the items in a manner that might scratch or damage the laptop. Take extra care not to place items on top of the cover that would stress it and damage the LCD screen.

d) Do not check your laptop when you are flying. Carry it with you. Make sure it is in a safe position in the overhead bins and nothing heavy is placed on top of it. It is best to place it under the seat in front of you.

e) Temperature variations and extreme high or low temperatures can occur during transport. Allow sufficient time for your laptop to stabilize its internal temperature to room temperature before you power it up. Temperatures changes greater than +/-10C when entering the room you will operate in, is sufficient for you to take this precaution. Please take a look at Figure 1-4; 1-5; 1-6.

Figure 1-4 Don't put laptop together with other stuffs

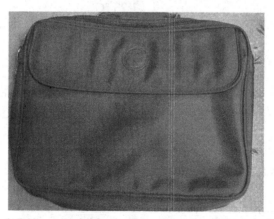

Figure 1-5 Use special bag when carry on laptop with you

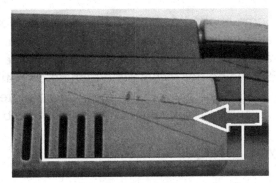

Figure 1-6 Laptop has been scratches

1.2   Usage tips, maintenance and repair for Laptops

1.2.1   Factors affecting laptop battery life and discharge time.

1.   How to prolong your Notebook battery run time.

1)   Adjusting the processor speed—Enhanced Intel Speedstep (EIST) is provide with Microsoft XP and later versions. There are no EIST drivers available for earlier Windows versions unless provided by the computer manufacturer. Under Microsoft Windows XP, Speedstep support is built into the power management console in the control panel. In Windows XP a user can regulate the processor's speed indirectly by changing power schemes. The laptop power scheme enables Speed Step, and the "Max Battery" uses Speedstep to slow the processor to minimal power levels as the battery weakens. This will extend the time your laptop will run on battery to the maximum possible . . .

2)   CD, DVD, CD-RW—The CD/DVD drive consumes considerable power and dramatically shortens the time you can run on battery. Avoid using it when running on battery power.

3)   Power management and Speedstep setup—in your control panel, open power options, and set the Power Plan, to decrease or increase battery time to suit your needs

4)   LCD Brightness—lowering LCD brightness will help to prolong battery time, by using the function keys on your laptop, FN key plus the up or down key (or left right on some units) will adjust the brightness. Most laptops some have a sun sign to indicate the keys to use.

5)   Wireless devices and Bluetooth devices use considerable battery power; Turn off your wireless when you don't need it by using the function key to save power.

6)   Applications—When on battery power close all applications you do not need after you boot up, and during use. The more applications running, the more power you will consume, and the shorter the time available on battery. The more applications open, the more disk space will be occupied for file exchange (virtual memory); your hard disc is thus more frequently used for read/write sequences. By closing all unnecessary programs after start-up, more memory will be freed up, and read/write operations reduced, thus conserving battery power.

7) Other software—Some application software increase CPU loading when running in the background, and will speed up battery power consumption—We suggest you close those programs and leave only the ones you need open

8) DVD & 3D GAMES—We do not recommend running on battery when viewing DVD movies or playing 3D games. Use your external power adapter. You will consume too much battery power and your run time will be too short to be useful.

2. How to maximize your battery life.

The average life of a battery should be 1 year but can be extended to 3 years with proper battery care.

The aging process varies depending on the chemical composition of the battery and how it is used . . . Lithium-ion is commonly used for laptops and it will age even when not in use. Don't purchase a new battery until you need it and make sure it has not been on the shelf long. Remove the battery and keep it in your fridge (not freezer) if you are not using you laptop for an extended period. Partially discharge your battery (not fully) occasionally and do not leave it continually charging when not using your laptop. Unplug the external supply. Charge/discharge cycles also reduce your battery life expectancy. It is a complicated process and optimum care is somewhat of an art that you will learn with experience.

In summary the factors that reduce battery life expectancy are these:

1) Battery charging/discharging cycles. The more this happens the less the battery life expectancy although occasional cycles can extend life. Total discharges have a greater influence.

2) Environment—Extreme high or low environment temperature will affect the activation of the chemical material in the battery core, thus lowering its life. Storage in a cool temperature is beneficial.

3) Battery Usage: Even though you mostly use the external power as opposed to the battery, as time passes, battery's aging is ongoing. Rarely using the battery may prolong the aging process, but aging is still inevitable.

4) Vibration and impact and similar abuse accelerate the battery aging process.

5) Continual charging if your external power supply is left on when the unit is not in use reduces life expectancy. Please take a look at Figure 1-7; 1-8; 1-9.

Figure 1-7 Cracks by dropping

Figure 1-8 broken by crashing

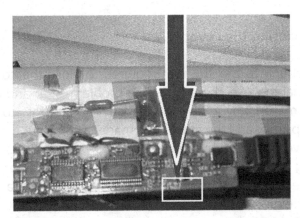

Figure 1-9 the crashing damaged an electric circuit.

1.2.2 LCD—little tips for liquid crystal screen usage and maintenance

An LCD is a primary part of a laptop. Good habits and periodic maintenance can enhance its performance and prolong its useful life. Keeping your LCD in good condition requires good habits and periodic maintenance to achieve a long life. This is very important.

1. Don't exert pressure on your laptop LCD

1). Direct impact or pressure exerted by articles such as a pen, ruler, your finger, and any other stiff implement can cause permanent physical damage to the screen and affect its performance. Never wipe the LCD directly with your palm or fingers. You should be aware that the LCD is not designed to withstand pressure put on it, with your palms or fingers or anything else. It is quite difficult to build a screen with the strength to withstand this. If you exert undue pressure on it, you can cause the LCD crystal molecules to be permanently damaged, White spots can occur or other abnormal symptoms would begin to appear on some areas of the screen. Therefore never wipe the LCD screen directly with your hand.

2). When transporting or carrying the laptop, never exert pressure on the screen top cover. That pressure may cause interconnecting wiring problems, and may in the extreme disintegrate the LCD screen.

11

Avoid exposing the screen to strong light & high humidity

a). Strong light shining on the screen will accelerate LCD aging. Avoid using your laptop where the screen will not be exposed to direct sunlight or strong light as much as possible.

b). If you notice moisture on the screen after a period of inactivity or at any time, wipe it away with a soft cloth, before applying power to the unit. If possible, keep the LCD turned on for 1 hour or more each day. This will drive away moisture by the heat generated by the LCD. If there seems to be too much moisture, already present inside or on the LCD, you will need to place the laptop while opened, in a warm location to evaporate the moisture after you have wiped it clean. If you power on the LCD with moisture on it, you might erode the liquid crystal electrodes, thus causing permanent damage.

2. be careful when closing the cover

1). Please pay attention to the strength required to close the cover. If it seems to be harder than usual to close, there may be a problem. Stop and examine the cover to determine the reason why it is resisting you. The laptops' connection axis (hinge) between the top cover and the machine is made of compound materials, which might be broken or even deviated by previous use. The liquid crystal screen, or hinges, or interconnecting wiring might be damaged if you need to apply to much pressure to close it. To correctly close or open the cover, use the center part of the front edge of the cover, and be gentle.

2). Always close the cover when you carry the laptop with you. Please don't close the top cover too hard, or allow anything to remain between the keyboard and display that will result in breakage when you close it.

3. Notices about cleaning screen

1). Because of static, dust attaches to the surface of the liquid crystal screen; just clean it away with a dry soft brush.

2). Paper of all kinds is not recommended to use to wipe an LCD screen. In actual practice, this is the most common cleaning method used for LCD screens. If you have to use paper to clean it, my suggestion is to fold the paper towel keeping it flat, and wipe the screen gently.

3). Please do not use chemical cleanser, organic solvent, soap or any·general cleanser to wipe the screen, and definitely not water. The liquid crystal screen has strong permeability, and moisture penetration will have detrimental affects on the LCD.

4). we recommend buying special screen cleanser and special cloth for wiping and cleaning up the screen. Please don't touch it with your fingers, in case fingerprints are left. Please don't clean the screen when the laptop is running. Always wipe it gently.

5). When cleaning up external parts, please wipe with a small soft dampened cloth. Please take a look at Figure 1-10; 1-11; 1-12; 1-13; 1-14; 1-15; 1-16; 1-17.

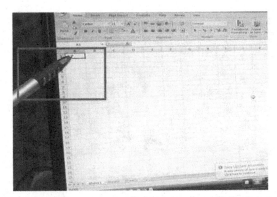

Figure 1-10 don't directly touch the screen with something hard

Figure 1-11 don't put something heavy like books on top cover

Figure 1-12 don't put anything between the screen and the keyboard

Figure 1-13 don't lift laptop with only one hand

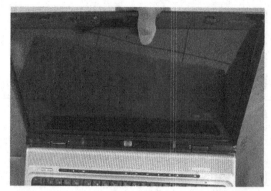

Figure 1-14 Please don't lift the laptop only by its top cover

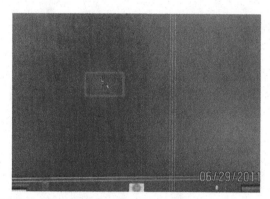

Figure 1-15 The trace left by heavy stuffs pressing on the screen

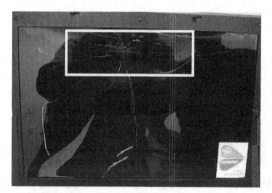

Figure 1-16 Cracked LCD screen

Figure 1-17 broken axes (hinges) by lifting screen top cover

4.   A few things you should remember when using your LCD in daily life.

1).   Do not let LCD work 24 hours continually day and night.

Many users think that LCD power consumption is much less than of a CRT, so they frequently let it work continuously, 24 hrs. A day. In fact this is quite wrong. It is pointed out by experts that after the LCD run continually for 48 hours without a break, it ages dramatically faster than if used intermittently by turning it off when not in use.

2).   Do not use highlight and high contrast for long periods.

Many LCD products have the highlight function. Highlight and high contrast really enhance the vision effect for games and movies, but the negative affects are not small. It is not good for the LCD to use the highlight feature for too long. It will accelerate LCD aging process. Also, for human health, having the brightness too high negatively affects human eyes.

3).   An LCD should be kept clear of strong magnetic fields

4).   Do not allow the undertone cannon in a sound box, speakers, or any other equipment producing a strong magnetic field close to the LCD. Exposure to a strong magnetic field is very harmful for an LCD monitor. It can accelerate the aging process or even cause a display abnormality.

1.2.3   Usage tips and maintenance for your hard drive

1.   Keep your laptop working environment clean

The hard drive interior air is drawn in from the computer through super extract filtration paper with spiracles, allowing it to be used in a normal room environment without air purifier devices. If it is in a very dusty environment, dust can be absorbed on the surface of the PCBA, migrate into the inside of the primary axis motor, and block the breathing filter. It is designed to be dustproof but there are limits to the dust it can filter.

Additionally, environment, humidity, and unstable voltage may all cause hard drive damage.

2.   Always shut down properly

Suddenly cutting off power when the disk is working, may damage the disk because of fierce attrition between the magnetic head and disc, and may also disable the magnetic head from resetting correctly, which may scratch the disk. With a laptop, you should avoid exerting too much pressure on the location where the disk is, when you are carrying the laptop with one hand. When turning it off, you should pay attention to the disk indicator light on the board, whether it is still flashing. You can carry it or transport it only when the disk indicator light stops flashing and the disk stops reading/writing.

3. Do not use your laptop on an unstable surface.

    Do not use your laptop when driving your car, or drop, strike, or otherwise impact it, or place it on a surface with large vibrations when the system is running. External vibration can cause harm to the hard drive and may damage it.

    Notice: The so-called "Anti-bump ability" or "Shockproof system" specified by the manufacturer does not mean while the unit is running. It means when the laptop is properly powered down and the lid closed.

4. Users should not remove the hard disk cover.

    The hard disk manufacturing and assembling processes are carried out in a special dust free room. Keep this in mind: general computer users should not remove the hard disk cover on his/her own. Dust in the air in normal room environments can contaminate the hard disk when attracted by the magnetic head component. This can damage the magnetic head or the disc, and even ruin the entire hard drive.

5. Preventing interference from high temperature, humidity and electromagnetism.

    The hard drive working condition is affected by temperature. The disk temperature should be between 20 ~ 25°C when working. Excessive high or low temperature can change the clock primary frequency of the crystal oscillator and disable the functionality of disk circuitry components. The magnetic medium can impair the recording process and cause errors because of the effects of Thermal Expansion. If the temperature is too low, the moisture in the air can condense on the integrated circuitry components, and cause a short circuit.

    The unstable condition caused by overheating can cause incorrect data reading/writing.

    When the temperature is too high, moisture may condense on an overheated electronic component surface. This will oxidize and erode the circuitry, finally causing a poor connection or even a short circuit.

    When the temperature is too low, a high level of static charge produced by the disc rotation can easily accumulate, and these static charges may burn the CMOS chip internal circuitry, attract dust, damage the magnetic head and scratch the disk.

    Avoid leaving a laptop close to a strong magnetic field such as a sound box or speaker etc. to prevent the data the disk has recorded, from being corrupted by the external magnetic field.

More than 12 hrs of continuous running of the hard disc is not recommended.

6.   Defrag the hard drive periodically

Periodic cleaning of the File fragmentation in the drive disk can increase speed, but if data fragments collect randomly on the drive, not only the read/write process will slow down, but also the magnetic track might be deteriorated or damaged. However, not defragging the disk often might reduce disk lift.

7.   Correct way to hold a hard drive

When removing a hard drive, hold the two sides of the hard drive with your fingers, avoiding direct contact with the circuit board on the back side. Remove it carefully avoiding bumping it, or hitting it with your tools, or any other hard object. Do not touch the circuit board on the back side of the hard drive with your hands. There might be static on your hands, which would damage the electrical components on the drive and stop it from running normally. Shutdown and power off your laptop before carrying out hard drive maintenance.

8.   Let hard drive rest

Letting the hard drive automatically enter the "Off state" when not in use can control the hard disk working temperature, and extend the useful life. First enter "My Computer", double click "Control panel" with left mouse, and then choose "Power management", set the option "Turn off hard drive" 15 minutes, apply and then exit.

9.   Limit your use of low level format operations as much as possible. Avoid frequent advanced level formatting operations

Do not low format the disk if it can be avoided as it will degrade the hard disc performance. Similarly, advanced format also affects disc performance, when not repartitioned; you could add the parameter "Q" quick format command.

1.2.4   How to prolong your power adapter's useful life?

Power adapter

The power adapter is an essential part of your laptop and should be treated with care in order to avoid damaging it, and losing the use of your laptop while you search for a replacement. Normally it should outlast the life of your laptop. Take special care with the cable connected to the adapter through a stress relief cover. Damage to the cable where it attaches to the adapter, can end the life of the adapter even though it is still working. The male jack that plugs into your laptop as well as the female end in the laptop often wears out or is broken because of careless use. Replacing the female end in the laptop is a difficult and expensive repair, Avoid stressing it while plugging in or during laptop use. Be careful when packing the power adapter cable to avoid damaging the insulation or the stress relief connection. Coil the cable without bending the stress relief and place it beside the adapter in the case.

Do not pack sharp objects in the case with the adapter to avoid damaging the cable. Avoid dropping or hitting it. When laptop is off and unused, disconnect the power and unplug the jack.

Recommended practices to prolong your power adapter's useful life:

1.   How to insure your power adapter will not prematurely fail?

Your power adapter is not easily damaged but you should still treat it with care in order to insure it does not fail during the life of your laptop. The following suggestions will help to avoid unnecessary failures:

1)   Avoid stresses on the cables such as by stepping on it or being tripped by it, as you can seriously damage the cables or your laptop. Position your cables so this cannot happen. Do not set objects on the cables or the adapter unit.

2)   Avoid spilling food, oil, or drink on the cable or adapter that can cause deterioration, and make sure infants, pets, insects, or mice etc. cannot chew on the cables.

3)   Do not use your cables as a means to tie or secure anything.

4)   Avoid dropping or striking the adapter as it can, cause internal damage or crack the case of the adapter and cause it to fail.

5)   When the laptop is turned off and unused, disconnect the power adapter and jack and store it in a safe place.

In the manual for your adapter generally, there will be a notice stating "Only to be used indoors and for its intended purpose." It is important to not use the power adapter outdoors or in a damp environment. Do not leave the adapter outdoors or exposed to sunlight for long periods of time this also applies to any other electrical product not designed for that purpose. Insulation hardens and cracks leading to a short circuit when the device is left outdoors. Moisture can also migrate into the cable and adapter. Degradation can be partial or total depending on the length of exposure. The adapter might then run hotter than designed with eventual failure.

Please pull off the adapter energised when you are not using it. Because long times keep the AC adapter working, which would affect its use life. The connection of the output cable to the adapter is protected by a molded stress relief covering. Bending the stress release cover is not recommended nor the cable where it enters the stress relief covers.

Although adapters are specified to operate over a wide voltage range from 100V to 240V, voltage spikes and surges might cause damage. These cannot be avoided however the surge and interference filter near the jack end of the cable does filter most abnormalities, and you can provide additional protection by not leaving the unit energised when you don't need it.

2. What is the most common adapter failure?

Generally speaking, it will be the adapter circuitry or the connection of the output cable to the adapter. Wear and tear on the jack connection to the computer comes a close second. Sometimes the problem can be repaired but mostly replacement is necessary.

Please take a look Figure 1-18; 1-19.

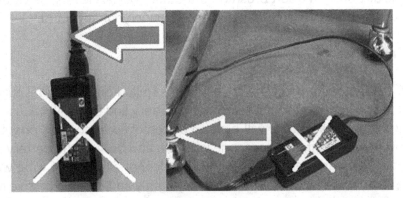

Figure 1-18. Please don't hang power adapter Please don't press or cover the power cable

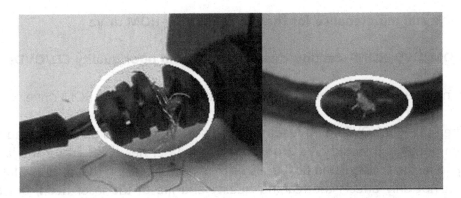

Figure 1-19. Broken cable caused by hanging adapter Cable damage after impact.

1.2.5 Taboos for keyboard: humidity, dust and pull drag

Keyboard—your worst taboos are: Moisture, dust and wiping action.

1. Avoid accidents that can cause spillage on your keyboard.

    Most keyboards today use a plastic film switch. The switch is composed of a three-thread thin film, the middle insulated one with holes in it, and the two side films are plated with metal circuitry and contact points. Moisture, wear, dust, and dirt can all cause a bad connection, and loss or degradation of key functions. Be especially careful that you do not accidentally damage your keyboard by liquid spillage on the keyboard. That is probably the worst thing you can do.

2. Do not use your computer in a dusty environment and do not smoke while using the computer. Dust, ashes, and smoke can all accelerate erosion of the insulation and contacts in the keyboard. Keep your work place, as clean and unobstructed as you can. Especially near your keyboard,

3. Do not eat while using your computer. Keep the food away from it. Not just food, but avoid spilling or dropping anything that can damage or contaminate your keyboard. If this situation happens, and it is not a liquid spill, do not remove the keyboard. Clean the dirt off with a soft brush or anti-static special cleaner. Be careful. Dragging a cloth across the keys can easily damage keys on your keyboard.

Keyboard Maintenance

1. Turn off the laptop immediately once liquid is spilled on it. Do not shut it down first. Unplug the power adapter, and remove the battery and dry it. Never use a hot blower to blow it dry. The keyboard will have to be removed as soon as possible. If you do not know how to do it, find someone who can and be sure the battery is removed.

2. Clean your keyboard periodically with pure alcohol and do not wipe with a cloth. A cotton swab should be used. Wipe each key lightly and avoid excessive force that can knock off or break a key mechanism. Compressed air is useful to remove dust and dirt between the keys.

1.2.6   Usage and maintenance for the CD-ROM/DVD-ROM drive

1.   CD-ROM/DVD-ROM—taboos: dust, vibration and poor quality CD/DVDs.

a) Do not touch the internal components of the CD-ROM/DVD-ROM drive.

When CD-ROM/DVD-ROM reading speed slows down or is unable to read the disc, then primarily it would be a problem with the laser head. Except for the laser head aging factor, accumulated dust is also a main factor causing the lift of the laser head. Dust not only affects the reading quality and life of the laser head, but also the precision of all internal mechanical parts. Therefore it is important to keep CD-ROM/ DVD-ROM drive clean.

Generally we can wipe the mechanical parts with cotton and alcohol, but the laser head should not be touched, nor should alcohol or any other cleaner be used on the laser head. Use a dry compressed air bottle to blow the dust off of the laser head. Do not touch the laser head with your hands, and do not blow from your mouth to clean the dust off of the laser head.

b) When CD-ROM/DVD-ROM is reading, do not open the tray by force. Support the tray when inserting/removing a CD/DVD.

From the above we realize that dust is a "Killer" of the laser head, but vibrations also can cause damage to the laser head when it touches the disc. Therefore, when we repair a CD-ROM/DVD-ROM drive, reduction of vibration is an important factor we should consider. Make certain that all screws used to assemble and secure the drive are present and tightened. No screws should be missing.

Finally you should never open the drive forcibly or otherwise until the disc stops rotating. This can cause the disc to hit the laser head and damage it.

c) Use higher quality CD/DVDs to prolong the life of your disc drive.

A cheap CD/DVD is another big enemy of your drive, It will increase the burden to the laser head servo-circuitry, accelerate the abrasion of the machine core and aging of the laser tube. Now on the market, the popular DVCD is a most dangerous enemy of your DVD-ROM drive. The spot distance will be much less than the standard DVD-ROM's spot distance. The DVCD is quite difficult to read, and it won't take long to damage the DVD-ROM drive.

2. Port—bad taboo: plug-and-pull with power on

a) Do not pull or plug serial ports, parallel ports, PS/2 and other ports with the power on. These accessories are cheap and convenient to use, but there is a big problem with them. They easily get dirty and cease to operate. To compensate or troubleshoot, a user may pull on the defective device cable connection to the laptop and damage a port of the laptop. Be careful to keep your cables from being pulled tight, and secure the connector at the laptop with the screws or clamps provided.

b) Do not mistakenly try to insert the power cable port into another port

Although it is not really possible, the power pin might contact a pin in the port and may cause a power short circuit, and burn the power adapter or the laptop port, or internal circuitry of the laptop.

c) Plug and pull USB connectors straight out,

When you use a USB port, you should plug or pull a USB connector as straight out as possible, without twisting or pulling towards the sides. Grasp and pull the connector body and not the cable. Clean up your USB ports periodically, to remove dust or dirt that can makes it difficult to pull or plug a USB cable or flash drive, and possibly loosen the port.

3. Influence of sweat and skin oil to the laptop shell

As temperature is high in summer, people tend to sweat and excrete oil from their body. If the laptop shell often gets wet and greasy from your body, it will cause certain problems with the shell, especially with some of the lower price laptops with an inexpensive plastic shell. Bad anti-causticity is the common fault of all plastic products. The affect of sweat and grease on plastic can cause unattractive discolouration. To avoid this, periodic cleaning of the shell is recommended using cleaners that are appropriate.

1.3   What to do when your laptop has an accident

1.3.1   What to do when you spill liquid on the laptop?

The first step: when liquid enters a laptop is to immediately remove the power cable from the laptop, and then remove the battery. This should all be done as fast as possible. Do not go through the normal shutdown process or use the OFF button to turn off the computer. Finally remove all device cables from the laptop.

The second step: You need to intelligently remove as much liquid from the laptop as you can without letting it spread any further into the laptop. Visually identify where the liquid was spilled and if it entered the laptop. If the spill is on the keyboard, do not touch the keyboard at this point, as the rubber tray under the key buttons plays a certain role in sealing the keyboard. First, blot up any liquid on the surface and keyboard with a dry cloth and wipe carefully without depressing the keys. If you know how to remove the keyboard, do so now. If not, skip the rest of this instruction. You should bring your laptop to a professional repair centre for further preventive maintenance. Remove the keyboard and wipe the water on the back side, and let it dry in a warm area not exposed to sunlight. Do not use a hot air blower as it may cause some tiny plastic components to be distorted and ruin the keyboard. With the keyboard removed, let the laptop sit for a full day or two to allow the inside to dry thoroughly to prevent further damage. Inspect the visible internal components for any signs of moisture before attempting to use the laptop.

The third step: after you have completed the cleaning and drying process, you might find that some of the keys are not working. You will have to remove the keyboard once more and inspect the faulty keys on the underside of the board for damage or moisture. Further drying may solve your problem. Check the keyboard connector for moisture or damage as well. Generally speaking, most laptop keyboards would not need replacement just because of a water spill. There's a good chance of saving it if you have properly cleaned and dried it . . .

The fourth step: if there's a large amount of water that entered your machine or the spill was with let's say a soft drink or coffee, then you will need to take apart the machine and clean the liquid inside. Liquids other than water will leave residue that is difficult to clean and will likely cause failure if it is not all removed. You need to open the laptop and make sure not to use it for a minimum of 72 hours at least. During this period, it'll be better to use a low-configured cold air blower and use it to dry the waterish area inside the laptop. Cleaning residue from liquids other than water may require complete disassembly of the laptop and close examination and cleaning of each board in the laptop.

This would normally be done by a qualified repair facility.

The fifth step: Once you find the laptop to be completely dried, then you attempt to start your laptop and install the cleaned system battery. If your laptop doesn't start up, even after executing the steps above, then wait a couple more days and try it again.

If it still fails, then you need to seek support from a computer repair company.

It's quite important to contact one as soon as possible.

If your keyboard is quite dirty it will require thorough cleaning, you can purchase a good brush where the fibres won't come apart along with a cold air bottle. Turn off the laptop and stand it sideways, and then clean up the apertures of the keyboard carefully. Keep the brush dry and away from any water! Or you could use a little dust collector to absorb the dust at the connection joint and keyboard apertures.

1.3.2 What to do when the Laptop is dropped or falls to the ground

The first step: if the machine was on when dropped, turn it off. This is the first and foremost thing to do. Do not wait for a normal shutdown.

The second step: after the machine is turned off, visually look for any damage that may have occurred from the fall. Either a crack or scratch on the shell. After careful examination of the notebook, verify that the metal shell around the screen is OK and make sure there is no damage to the hinges. Make sure the screen itself and the bottom or top of the notebook is intact. If there's no apparent visual damage then go to the third step. If there is physical damage to the shell skips to the fourth step to solve the problem.

The third step: Check the internal components of the laptop for damage. Fold the laptop, shake it and listen for any loose object or abnormal sound.

The fourth step: If you hear loose pieces or parts or notice serious shell distortion, you'll need to take it apart and check the damage. Before disassembling it, check your warranty if any, don't take it apart yourself, which would void your warranty. If you have none, you will need to locate the loose parts and where they came from as well as repair any damage before using the computer.

Remove all devices and covers accessible on the bottom of the computer. Battery, DVD/CD drive and hard drives are easily removed and inspected. When doing this watch for loose parts that might fall out. Shake the laptop to see if something falls out. If nothing, next remove the keyboard if you know how. Visually look at the parts under the keyboard to try to find loose or broken parts. Turn the computer over and shake it to see if something falls out. You will need to check the thermal system to make sure it's ok. And check whether the screws used to fasten the thermal system are still in place.

If you still have not located loose parts or found damage and you still hear the loose parts when you shake the unit, full disassembly will be necessary. If you are not experienced with any of these procedures and are hesitant to try it yourself, take the unit to a repair shop.

The fifth step: after finishing checking the machine and conducting any necessary repairs turn the power on and test the start-up. At this time do not install the battery. It will make it easier to turn it off in case there is a problem. After starting up, listen closely with your ear near the hard drive. Listen to it running. Ensure it is running and there is no abnormal sound. Then check whether the laptop starts normally and you can enter the system successfully.

The sixth step: The LCD screen and hard disk drive are the two areas most likely to be damaged from a dropped laptop. Usually the likelihood is above 80% if these two accessories fall directly from 1 meter or higher. Although the hard disk may be repaired from a fall, it is best to then use it as an external hard disk drive as it will probably be no longer reliable and data would easily be lost.

1.3.3   What should I do if my Notebook overheats?

System freezing and shutdown messages often occur when a laptop is working. Normally the underside of a laptop is hot to the touch. A laptop has many internal components that generate heat and are enclosed in a small space making it difficult to cool properly. The heat builds up quite easily, and serious overheating may damage the CPU or motherboard or even completely ruin the laptop. When using a laptop, to avoid overheating, please follow these simple steps.

1. Avoid using in a high temperature environment (direct sunshine) for long periods, Keep your laptop clean and free of dust to avoid any obstruction to the intake of clean air and the exhaust of hot air.
2. Laptops need to be used on a stable, hard, and flat operating surface. Such as a desk or table that is clean and bare for at least 6 in. around the periphery of the laptop. No litter underneath the laptop or within the 6in periphery.
3. Never use your laptop on a carpet, bed, your lap, or any other area with a soft surface, which will result in blocking the fan intake of the laptop and stopping effective cooling. You can place a piece of plywood or even a bread board between the soft surface and the computer, to use it in these locations. It should be larger than the laptop surface, and you still need to take care not to block the laptop ventilation.
4. Please make sure your laptop is turned off completely before putting it away inside a case or backpack. Never put a running or hibernating laptop in any non-ventilated, tight space that will restrict the cooling or allow heat build up around the computer.
5. I recommend purchasing a USB thermal base (fan) for your laptop which will allow it to function at its optimum temperature. Also use monitoring software (SpeedFan is recommended) to monitor and track the temperature of the processor, hard disk and other components. Please read this article I wrote previously: How to detect an overheating problem? http://www.computercare.ca/forum/showthread.php?t=3890
6. Adjust your power settings. Some applications (Games) can and will lead to the temperature of your laptop rising, and the longer the laptop is in this state, the more harm it will do. By setting the power management, the laptop will automatically slow down the CPU speed, to protect it from high temperature, by reducing its heat rejection.
7. Update your laptop BIOS periodically as improvements often occur that will more efficiently control the laptop cooling system if the laptop temperature becomes noticeably high when working, you should quickly save your current files, turn off and cut off power, and change the working environment you are in. If the problem above still occurs, then send your laptop to a professional repair department.

1.3.4 How to disassemble a laptop in an emergency

First of all, we should get to know the general structure of a laptop. It can be divided into five parts: liquid crystal screen, keyboard, top panel, motherboard, bottom panel. Before we disassemble it, we need to get the necessary tools such as a flat screwdriver, Phillips screwdriver, and inner hexagon screwdriver of different sizes but mainly small ones, to deal with screws of different types. The Laptop structures are largely identical but with minor differences, so the take-down steps are basically similar.

1. Disassemble the parts of the laptop which are easily removed from the bottom of the laptop or the side.

    Generally, components in a laptop which can be upgraded such as a hard disk, CD / DVD-ROM drive, RAM, and battery are easily removed . . . Start with the battery, and then remove the rest of the components mentioned above. The position marked "HDD" on the bottom is the hard disk. The DVD drive unlocks from the bottom and is removed from the side. Remove any other covers from the bottom and remove any other devices that plug in to a connector. This should include the RAM but it can also be under the keyboard which you will have to remove. Do not lose your screws and remember where they go. Keep them together in a small container. There are usually screws as well as a latch that holds these devices in place.

2. Removing the keyboard

    You should next remove the keyboard since many of the assembly screws and possibly the RAM are underneath the keyboard. Once you remove the keyboard, you can continue to the next step to separate the LCD display and the host computer. Uninstall tip: there is a group of soft line cables between keyboard and motherboard, you must take care when you uninstall it, be sure to pay attention to avoid damaging the cable or connectors.

    For more details about this aspect, please refer to my previous articles about replacing keyboard "How to take down and replace a keyboard?"
    http://www.computercare.ca/forum/showthread.php?t=4035

3. Removing the LCD screen

    Before uninstalling an LCD screen, we need to separate the top panel from the bottom panel. Locating the screws that need to be removed is a difficult process. There can also be pressure fittings holding the panel in place. Again, you should pay attention to the cables and connectors. Don't stress them and disconnect them carefully. There is a group of cables between the panel and motherboard.

    Uninstall tip: before removing the LCD bracket bolts, you should keep the LCD display unfolded and at a 90° angle from the top. This will make it easier to remove the screws on the bottom panel and will avoid sliding the screw sleeve out of position. Note how they go together for future reference when you are re-assembling the unit. For more details on this aspect, please check my previous articles about LCD replacement http://www.computercare.ca/forum/showthread.php?t=3400

1.3.5 Notebook disassembly steps and precautions

1) First before uninstalling, remove the power cable and battery to avoid any damage that might occur if the power is still on. Remove all peripheral equipment, such as printer, external hard drive and any others. If you can make a backup of your data, do so before starting to disassemble, then shutdown normally and power off by pressing the power button until it turns off.

2) A laptop has four parts:

    a) LCD Rear Cover: This is the top cover when the laptop is folded.
    b) LCD Bezel: The frame surrounding the LCD when the laptop is unfolded.
    c) Upper Motherboard Case: The part that contains the keyboard.
    d) Bottom Motherboard Case: The bottom section of the laptop.

3) The first step of the disassembly is to shutdown, power off and removes the power cable and battery to avoid electrical damage. Beside the battery there is generally a latch. Pull back the latch and remove the battery at the same time. Before you remove the power cable and battery, press the power switch and hold, 5 seconds later, it shuts down. Then the power of the internal DC circuitry will be OFF

4) Remove the bottom motherboard case screws, and keep them together, separating them from other screws. It is very important to remember the positions of the long screws and special screws. Do not make a mistake when you re-install them since the long ones may penetrate the motherboard and damage it.

5) Remove the CD/DVD-ROM, hard disk and RAM memory. For some machines, you may have to first remove Upper Motherboard Case to do this. To remove CD/DVD-ROM: find a clip or latch on Bottom Motherboard Case. Pull or push the latch to release the CD/DVD-ROM. For some machines, such as IBM and DELL, there will be a button besides CD/DVD-ROM, press the button to remove the CD/DVD-ROM.

    Often there may also be screws holding the device. Do not force or pry the disk, floppy drive or CD/DVD-ROM with a screwdriver. They come out easily when done correctly.

6) Now you can remove the keyboard. It has to be carefully pried out with a flat head screw driver. First pry out the decorative strip running along the upper part of the keyboard. There may be screws underneath the strip to remove. Next lift the keyboard enough to disconnect the cable underneath. Never use too much force. If something is still holding the keyboard, look for the cause and remedy it. After removing the

keyboard, pack it singly in a plastic or bubbled bag if possible. Avoid impact with other accessories, which may break a key cap or clip.

Note on some laptops (Compaq) you must first remove 1 or 2 screws from underneath the laptop to fully release it.

7) After removing the keyboard, loosen the screws on screen axis, and then you can take the entire screen off. The LCD Rear Cover, LCD Bezel and the LCD do not need to be taken apart, except if the problem is with the LCD itself such as the inverter, backlight, an LCD cracked screen, or a broken cable. Only then would we disassemble them. If the laptop has an internal wireless network card, you may have to first pull out the antenna of the wireless network card in order to remove the LCD.

8) Next you can remove the Upper Motherboard Case. Most laptop parts are made of plastic, so when you uninstall them, be gentle and do not use force. Remove all the necessary remaining screws that are holding the top and bottom covers together, and then try to separate the press fittings. Be careful, you may have missed a screw or two. Trial and observation of how the top bends when you try to remove it will provide clues where more screws are located. Do not stress any of the interconnecting cables. They will need to be disconnected before the top can be fully removed. Some connectors can be pulled out and some are held by a latch mechanism. If there is a latch mechanism, the latch can be pried back and then the cable released. Be gentle with this, it is easy to break the latch tabs which is a disaster not easily repaired. Once separated, the circuitry inside is completely visible to your eyes. The motherboard is still attached to the bottom panel of the laptop.

9) Next you can disassemble the Bottom Motherboard Case: Before separating the motherboard and bottom panel, you will need to remove the cooling system of the laptop. It is a fan and heat sink assembly fastened on top of the CPU. When removing the CPU screws you need to loosen them evenly so that an unbalanced force does not damage the CPU. Loosen each one a half revolution at a time until they are no longer putting pressure on the CPU. Then remove all of the screws. (Simply uninstalling one bolt at a time can easily cause unbalanced force on the surface of CPU, may damage the sides of the CPU. Now you can lift the cooling system off of the CPU, and unplug its cable. Lastly, uninstall the screws on the motherboard and bottom panel and remove the Motherboard.

10) After removing the motherboard, if you need BGA repair (machine repair) then you should remove the PC base from the motherboard, COM battery on motherboard should also be removed, since it can cause further damage. Remove insulating mucus paper. High temperature may have caused the paper to curl up and some electronic components such as tiny capacitors and resistors may loosen. When removing the insulated mucus paper, remember their positions on the motherboard and shapes, so you won't make a mistake or miss something when reinstalling them. When you take down the motherboard, you should pack it in an anti-static bag, to avoid contact with other accessories and avoid further damage.

11) When re-assembling the machine, first clean your area of debris, take the motherboard out, and install the insulated mucus paper. This avoids static damage or short circuits that would result in the computer failing to start.

   Keeping track of the position where parts, screws, springs etc were installed, will allow you to properly re-assemble the computer. There are many ways including writing it down. Choose one that suits you but do so, because it is very easy to make a mistake

12) When re-assembling the machine, the most common problem are the longer screws that can penetrate too far if in the wrong hole, and can contact the motherboard or shell. If you feel the screw becoming harder to turn, remove it as it is probably too long. Try a shorter one

13) Often detailed disassembly instructions with photos can be found on the internet. These can be used in conjunction with this instruction. Simply search with your make and model number

1.4   Basic rules you should follow when repairing laptops:

1.4.1   Observe and repair, the simple way

A.   The simplest way:

   Is refers to the direct observation and use the "trial and error" method with the "minimum system mode"; the simplest method is to pay close attention to:

1.   The way it's used: The climate, the position, the power supply, the connection and the environment (Such as temperature and humidity) the laptop is in and any other devices connected to it are important.
2.   Abnormal symptoms of the laptop: The status of the indicator lights, rotating sound of the fan, any other sounds, no display on screen, or the content displayed has changed are important clues.
3.   Internal laptop conditions such as dust, connections, discolour of parts, and the temperatures of CPU/GPU are symptoms.

4.   Laptop software and hardware configuration: Includes all hardware involved and resource occupation situation; operating system used, applications installed, hardware configuration, and the version of the drivers installed.

B.   Minimum system mode:

This method uses the most basic hardware and software environment which merely ensures the laptop can start up and run. In the "minimum system mode", you can observe and locate the failure by "trial and error". After the initial power on, you can then swap or add suspected faulty components. Pay close attention, you must observe carefully and repeatedly until you can ensure the failure cause in order to determine the repair needed.

The "minimum system mode" are includes "minimum hardware system" and "smallest of the software system".

1.   Minimum hardware system

Hardware test: This test is done by using the very basic hardware components to prove system functionality; with only the power adapter, motherboard, CPU, and no other onboard wire connections, except the power wires between power adapter and the motherboard. During this test we verify whether the core components are working by listening for the fan or any other sounds that are normal or unusual.

2.   Smallest of the software system.

Software test: power adapter, motherboard, CPU, memory, display card/monitor, keyboard and optical drive (no hard drive include). Insert a DOS start up disk or other compatible start up disc, (note: not OS installer CD). This tests whether the system is capable of finishing a normal start up cycle.

C.   Test and determine the causes, then repair accordingly.

Here are few things to consider:

1.   Refer to the relevant chapter material as much as possible. Check whether they are in accordance with the failure symptoms of your laptop, and then according to the informational you referenced, start the repair process. During the repair process pay attention to the technical requirement and decide whether you are able to tackle the task on hand with your knowledge and experience. If you feel you can't, consult with a skilled technician first and ask for help.
2.   One of the most important initial steps in your troubleshooting process is to determine whether the issue comes from software or hardware. Try not to be tempted to follow the popular repair method of "First software then hardware". To save time and your sanity, refer to section 1.4.2 Laptop Repair—The 6 hard-ways
3.   Know your priorities, always start from the component with the highest failure rate and work your way down:

In a complex situation, there can often be more than one failure on a machine, with two or more failure symptoms. Refer to the material in this book as much as possible, pay attention to the statistical failure rates such as item X has Y% of the failure rate. For hardware failure, first check the components with the highest failure rate by replacing them with known working substitute. Then proceed to the components with lower failure rate, until the problem is solved. For example, laptop with a dark screen or red screen is a pure hardware issue. The repair flow chart states that the high voltage inverter and backlight has 90% failure rate and the switch or cable has only 6% failure rate. Therefore it makes sense and saves time that we start with the testing of inverter and backlight. If that does not solve it, then check the switch and cable which has lower failure rates.

4.   Always assume "First hardware then software"

Consider a case where Windows does not load, and blue screen after repeated restarts. The problem might be hardware, software or both. The repair flow chart indicates that hard disk and memory has 65% failure rate. Laptop overheating, virus and the operating system has 30% failure rate, by using the minimum system mode explained above, check and confirm whether the problem comes from hardware or software. If it is caused by both, then you should first tackle the main faulty hardware, sometimes minor software issues are self-resolved by hardware fix.

1.4.2   6 "hard" methods to repair laptop

A)   Observation

Observation is an important an important aspect of the repair process. Observation isn't just about observing but also not overlooking important clues. Sometimes, you need to compare it to a good working laptop of the same make and model. Carefully and repeatedly, pulls out a suspected power adapter jack and the RAM memory. Plug them in again, observing the affect. Observation also includes:

1.   Surrounding environment, temperature and humidity etc;
2.   Hardware environment, including dust, connection pins, jack and slot connections, discoloration of components, and CPU/GPU humidity etc.
3.   Software environment, including resource usage, operating system usage, and user operation habits.

B)   Minimum system judgment

Minimum system judgment is mainly seeing whether the system works normally with the most basic software and hardware installed. If there is a problem in that mode, then we can be sure the issue is with the hardware these components and not the rest. We can then pin point where the problem is by elimination. Cleaning these components is a good starting point, and may eliminate the problem without further effort.

1.   Remove the battery, wireless network card, network card, modem, card reader, external devices, and disk drive. If under minimum system the laptop still doesn't start up or there is a black screen error, then we can be sure there is something wrong with the basic hardware.
2.   Put a pure DOS disc in the DVD-ROM/CD-ROM to start with, during the start up process, if there are symptoms like laptop auto restarts or automatic shut down, error prompt or system freeze, then it means there is definitely a problem with the

hardware. At this moment, the source of failure will be within connections, memory RAM, motherboard, CPU/GPU temperature and so on.

3. After the laptop finishes DOS start-up, tap any key on the keyboard to do the typing test. If it displays characters that were not typed or keys that do not work or worse the whole keyboard doesn't respond, then you are sure there is a hardware issue. The next step is the connections, keyboard, memory stick, and motherboard

4. After finishing DOS start-up, and doing the typing test in DOS system, if everything is OK, and no system crash symptom occurs, then it means the failure is not with the running hardware. Now you can proceed to the operating system, applications, viruses, hacker software, hard disk and drivers needed for the hardware contained in the unit . . .

Prompt

1). Preserve the user's original software environment on hard disk, keep original applications, do not uninstall applications or delete files, and do not try repairing the operating system, which can jeopardize the security of data. If you suspect that the laptop failure has nothing to do with the working hardware, and if you are able, first make a backup of the data;

2). The hard disk is a combination of hardware and software, therefore, during the repair process we have to test the disk twice to ensure it's working well. Tests for the hardware and software are done separately. First test the hardware and then if OK, re-install the OS. If this is successful, applications are loaded or uninstalled and loaded again. During this process, the main job is to confirm the hardware; in minimum system state is OK, by checking the conflicts within the software, and the conflicts between hardware and software.

C) Cleaning

Many laptops have overheating problems, which are caused by too much dust inside the machine. This requires us to open, verify and clean components before continuing the repair process. Remember to pay close attention to the following areas:

1. Regularly clean the dust from laptop air intake, to allow the air to flow without any obstruction

2. The fan is one of the most important parts that control the temperature. When fan ages, and slows down or stops rotating, overheating occurs. The computer will shut down when the auto start protection system is activated. If this happens and cleaning does not clear up the problem, replace the CPU fan assembly.

3. When replacing the fan assembly, check the silicone gel compound on the top of the CPU. It is used to conduct the heat away from the CPU efficiently. If it is dry, the computer will overheat. Remove the old silica gel on the CPU and the fan assembly carefully with a cue tip, and recoat with a fresh silica gel, being careful to only apply on the thermal strip. Clean off any excess.

4. Disk drive overheating or bad tracking can all cause an auto shutdown. If this problem occurs, use an additional external USB cooling fan to dissipate the heat.

5. The cleaning of connectors in the laptop is important. Flat gold fingers can be cleaned with an eraser or with cotton and alcohol. Pin connectors cannot so simply unplug, inspect, and plug them back in. Discoloured pins indicate a problem on either side of the connector or on the devices connected. Connector or device replacement may be necessary

6. Motherboard cleaning. When cleaning up the motherboard, first cut off all power, including removing the motherboard battery. You must prevent static damage occurring by insuring you are properly grounded and discharged. It is best to use a ground strap on your wrist and fasten the alligator clip to an unpainted part of the laptop. Usually where the power jack plugs in. Do not work with your feet on a rug. Some technicians simply remove their shoes and socks or just touch the bare metal on the computer case before doing anything. Use a brush made of natural material, never use a plastic brush or dust collector to get rid of dust. Observe whether there is bad soldering or moisture symptoms on LSI (Large Scale Integration), components and pins, and whether the motherboard is distorted or there is discolouring or signs of liquid.

7. Tools used for cleaning: small brush, bottled air blower, small knife, screwdriver, cleaning paper, and alcohol.

D) Addition and subtraction for system reconstruction

After completing all minimum system tests, the next step is to determine whether you have a software failure possibly in the operating system or a hardware failure by using a process of addition and subtraction for system reconstruction. The method has two components: the first step is to rebuild the system; the second step is to add or subtract software or hardware gradually while reconstructing the system to find the defective component.

1. During the process of reconstructing the system, preserve the user's disk drive data.
2. To keep the system clean, before installation, execute Frisk /MBR command. When necessary, execute "format <drive> /u[/s]" command after that. Make sure to check whether there are bad tracks on the disk medium. If it's a brand new disk, then you can totally skip this procedure.
3. Directly use a valid or OEM version of the operating system for installation. Try it to see whether it can't be installed and used. If not, then the problem is still in the basic hardware environment. You will have to reconfirm and locate the defective hardware.
4. If the rebuilt system passes, then you should only add one hardware or one software component at a time, while restarting the laptop to check whether the failure symptom disappears or changes. This will provide important clues to judge and locate the failed part. If you suspect the added component or installed software, then you should remove and try it again. Add to the minimum system state logically. Subtract or change one hardware at a time or uninstall and reinstall one software at a time. Addition and subtraction for system reconstruction is a very important method

and measure to repair laptops. It can quickly locate the hardware and/or software problem, and in turn quickly increase your repair efficiency.

5. After rebuilding the system, you should gradually recover the user's original disk state and determine complex failures. For instance, for onboard network failures, you need to add or disable the network card on the minimum system, integrated on motherboard in BIOS, and then add a USB network card. Gradually add or subtract software and make a judgment. Make sure the driver for the network card installed won't conflict with other software or hardware. Generally this method of replacement, can easily and accurately locate the failure part.

E)   Replacement

Replacement is to replace the suspected issued parts with good ones, and then restart the laptop to check whether the failure disappears or changes. Good components for replacement could be the same model or different, but they have to be completely compatible with the original accessory and have the proper driver, generally, here's the replacement sequence:

1. Find out failure type according to the laptop failure symptom, and then according to the repair flow chart of this chapter, consider which parts should be replaced.
2. Each chapter's repair flow chart states that XXX component occupies XX failure rate. If it's a failure purely caused by hardware, then you should consider the first component to replace according to the failure rate. Components wit high failure rates should first be replaced and checked. If the repair flow chart indicates that software and hardware both could cause the failure, then you will have to first determine and confirm if the problem comes from the hardware. If the software environment is OK, but the failure still exists, then proceed by the hardware replacement process.
3. Before replacing components, you should first replace the power adapter; ensure it is rated properly to handle the power and voltage required. Next check the connection parts of suspected components or connection cable and signal cable. Clean the memory sticks and the slots, uninstall and reinstall the CPU, and at lastly replace the component you suspect.
4. Replace by sequence of "simple first and complex second". To repair a sound card failure, verify that the sound card interface is OK, whether the external speaker and microphone are working, and then the internal speaker, cable and sound card. Consider changing the motherboard or adding a USB sound card as a final test.

F)   Knocking

Sometimes, there might be bad connection happening to some components in a laptop, which makes the symptom appear and disappear. It is very inconvenient to repair. Usually vibrating or knocking gently will identify the problem if it is an intermittent connection. This method is quite easy and feasible. Repair can be more difficult. Inspect with a magnifying glass to locate bad solder connections or other irregularities. Repair or replace if necessary.

1.4.3   4 "Soft" methods to repair laptop

A). Comparison

The comparison method of identifying problems requires an identical fully functional computer to compare with the defective computer. Comparisons are made between start up and shutdown processes and between Bios settings and hardware drivers. It is a very effective way to deal with complex failures.

B). Temperature related failures

A laptop failure can be caused by internal temperature that is too high or low. At a certain temperature the failures begin appearing. If this failure mechanism is suspected, you can artificially create high and low temperatures in the unit to create a failure and confirm your suspicion.

Method to raise temperature:

1. When the computer is shutdown, remove all power including the main battery and motherboard battery, then heat up the area around the memory and the hard disk to around 45 degrees with an electric heat source. Then quickly re-install batteries, power on, and test.

Method to drop temperature:

2. Remove batteries and power again, cool the unit with a fan for at least an hour
3. Exposed the unit to a cold environment to reduce its internal temperature to 15 deg. Then install batteries, power up, and test.

C)   Isolation and shield

The isolation and shield method requires that the suspected hardware or software be removed to see if it eliminates the problem. There are two ways to proceed with isolation and shield, software shield, and hardware shield.

For software shield, stop it from running by Start->Run->msconfig->startup->disable software or enter the Control Panel to uninstall the software.

For hardware, disable or uninstall the driver in the device manager, or delete the hardware from the BIOS. The isolation and shield method is very effective in solving the conflicts between software components or software and hardware.

D)   Ultimate repair for soft failures

1. Preserve the software environment of the original disk. Do not try repairing the operating system, it can jeopardize the security of your data, unless you have already done a backup for the data or the owner does not require a backup.

2. For some troublesome software problems, the ultimate repair is the most thorough and easiest solution. It primarily focuses on a one-key (F11) recovery, including recover installation and complete reinstallation. There are two choices. The first is to backup all data and then carry out complete reinstallation. The second choice is a one-key (F11) recovery which directly calls up the recovery disk or partition, and includes drivers for all devices like the display card, sound card, wireless network card and camera. Don't worry that all the laptop drivers needed aren't installed. You can either go to the manufacturer's website and download them, or find a laptop of the same make and model and copy the (recovery disk) data on a disk, and copy it on the troubled notebook

3. When you update drivers, if there's some problem updating, then you'd have to first uninstall and then update. You can uninstall drivers from the device manager; and then uninstall from safe mode. Then delete in the INF directory and at last, uninstall in registry.

1.4.4 Experience summary for laptop maintenance

The "Repair assessment" in the chapter 1 includes these 3 items:

a). Basic rules for laptop repair
b). 6 "hard" methods to repair laptop
c). 4 "soft" methods to repair laptop

These are the rules needed repeatedly during the troubleshooting and repair process. Successful repair not only needs care but also knowledge and ability. Following the instructions herein to perform the operations and observations, repeated as necessary, will lead you to make the right decisions.

The 9 failure classes in chapter 2 and the 13 repair flow charts in chapter 3-15, are a summary of my laptop repair experience, and when used together provides the knowledge you will need for a successful repair. For similar failure symptoms, you may need to follow 2 to 3 failure classes and several flow charts to find a solution. During this process, you will be developing the experience and more importantly, self-confidence and patience to become a competent repair technician.

In the chapter2 of 9 failure classes, along with the <<13 repair flow charts>>, we sum up a part of the processes required to repair a laptop, and classify laptop failures. Of course, the failure symptoms listed in each failure class, are a part of many possible failure symptoms the symptoms not included here, might be classified with these, but some cannot. This manual will only provide relevant instructions and thoughts for the failure symptoms included here, but may be classified by using the basic elimination method. Failure symptoms which cannot be classified will be added to this manual as they become know to us.

CHAPTER 2

Introduction to diagnose common laptop failures

2.1   Analysis diagnosis table for common laptop failures

2.1.1   Diagnosis table for failures occurring after power-on (or reset) until the self-test finishes.

This chapter will classify the failures happening during the time interval from the startup of the laptop till shutdown. According to the common failure symptoms, you can find what you need in "Repair flowchart 03, 04, 05, and 06, 08 or 13". Confirm which "Repair flowchart", you'd have to use in Chapter 1. <<1.4.1 Judge and repair the simplest way>> section and Chapter 1 <<1.4.2 >> <<1.4.3>> section (Six "hard" and four "Soft" methods to repair laptop), to find the failure. According to the article failure analysis of "Repair flowchart", replace the defective parts

How useful is this diagnosis tool? The advantage that the analysis diagnosis table has, is that each listed failure is linked with the previous chapter (chapter 1) "The repair method" and subsequent chapter "Repair flowchart". Regardless of whether the software or hardware solution is used, or which component is involved, these three sections always link to each other. The final section is a detailed description and explanation of the repair procedure, which you should read in conjunction with the flowchart.

The failure symptoms listed in each class are just part of a broader range of failures. For the failures not listed here, some may be listed in another chapter, and some may not.

The following table is the failure analysis for incidents happening to a laptop during the period of power-on (or reset) to the finish of self-inspection. For some common laptop failures, we can initially diagnose the most likely location of the failure, and the flowchart to use.

Common failure descriptions	Symptoms or comment (explanation)	Fault location with diagnosis flowchart
Laptop does not start	No response by pressing the power button, indicator light is out, power goes off at start up	Motherboard, power adapter, power switch, power board; Use repair flowchart 03 & 08
No display when power on	Indicator light is on at start up, screen not responding, power fan does not rotate	Motherboard, BIOS, display card, RAM, Inverter / backlight; use repair flow chart 08 & 05
Alarm occurs at start up	No display at start up, and warning beep sounds.	Motherboard, RAM, keyboard, battery; Use repair flow chart 08,04 & 13
Laptop does not work in battery mode	Laptop does not work normally without the external power supply	Motherboard, battery, battery interface board; use repair flow chart 04 & 08
Laptop doesn't work in external power supply mode	Laptop only works in battery mode	Motherboard, power adapter, power interface board; use repair flow chart 03 & 08
Laptop doesn't work in battery mode	Timing start-up or intermittent auto shutdown	Motherboard, battery, thermal part; use repair flow chart 04 & 08
Self test doesn't finish at start up	Self test doesn't complete during starting up, and the machine keeps restarting	Motherboard, thermal part, RAM, CPU, power adapter; use repair flow chart 03 & 08
System freezes during self test	After starting up, error message appears or interface freezes	Motherboard, RAM, CPU, thermal part, power adapter; use repair flowchart 03, 06 & 08
Cannot enter BIOS or BIOS setup cannot be saved	After starting up, system requests password validation, clock is not accurate, or BIOS auto switch setup prompts error	CMOS battery, motherboard validation chip, BIOS Check by component replacement to isolate the failure.
Keyboard failure	Some keys on keyboard is unavailable or completely out of use	Motherboard, keyboard, keyboard interface use repair flowchart 13 & 08

Display problems	Laptop screen is blurred or faint, there are spots or lines	Display card on motherboard, motherboard, RAM, signal cable, power inverter, and display; use repair flowchart 05 & 08
Laptop is noisy	Loud noises, new noises, or strange Sound	Fan, hard disk, power adapter. Check by component replacement to isolate the failure.

2.1.2   Analysis and diagnostic table for laptop start-up and shutdown failures

Start-up failures are the problems that occur during the self-test process and until entering the operating system interface; shutting down system means all processes from clicking the shut down button to the power off state. This chapter lists all relevant failures happening during the process of laptop start-up and shutdown.

According to the common failure symptoms, you can find what you need in "Repair flowchart 03, 05, and 06, 07, 08". Confirm which "Repair flowchart", you'd have to use in Chapter 1. <<1.4.1 Judge and repair the simplest way>> section and Chapter 1 <<1.4.2 >> <<1.4.3>> section (Six "hard" and four "Soft" methods to repair a laptop), to find the failure. According to the article failure analysis of "Repair flowchart", replace the defective parts

How useful is this diagnosis tool? The advantage that the analysis diagnosis table has, is that each listed failure is linked with the previous chapter (chapter 1) "The repair method" and subsequent chapter "Repair flowchart". Regardless of whether the software or hardware solution is used, or which component is involved, these three sections always link to each other. The final section is a detailed description and explanation of the repair procedure, which you should read in conjunction with the flowchart.

The failure symptoms listed in each class are just part of a broader range of failures. For the failures not listed here, some may be listed in another chapter, and some may not.

The following table shows the analysis for failures that happen to laptops during the process of start-up and shutdown. For some common laptop failures, we can initially diagnose the most likely location of the failure, and the flowchart to use.

Common failures description	Symptoms or comment (explanation)	Fault location with diagnosis flowchart
No display at power on	Indicator light is on at start up, display has no response, there's a disc starting sound from hard disk	-Motherboard, display card, signal cable, Inverter / backlight screen; use repair flow chart 08 & 05

System freezes after finishing self-test	System freezes during OS starting (boot) process, the cursor flashes at the top left corner on screen, hard disk isn't recognized	Hard disk, interface board, motherboard; use—repair flow chart 07;
Numeric error prompts at start up	At start up system fails and error 1720 SMART, hard drive detects imminent failure, is displayed on screen.	Hard disk, interface board Advice: remove and reinstall again or replace it to see if problem is solved
Hard disk doesn't boot	After self-inspection is completed, there's abnormal and loud sounds from the hard disk	Hard disk advice: check whether the failure is gone by pulling and plugging the part again or by replacing it.
Cannot enter operating system interface	System auto restarts several times then shuts off, a blue screen error appears	Hard disk, RAM, OS, virus, power adapter, thermal parts, motherboard; use repair flow chart 07,03,06
Computer OS is unstable or system randomly freezes	Registry table sometimes get corrupted without any reason, system prompts user to recover or auto close	Operation system, virus, RAM, hard disk; use repair flow chart 07;
During start-up process, an unnecessary operation is always executed	Scandisk error comes on, often for invalid operation sometimes scan disk cannot continue or repair process, system is quite slow or freezes when scanning	Hard disk, RAM, operating system, virus; use repair flow chart 07;
file error prompts during start up process	Message showed at start up: "C:\WINDOWS\SYSTEM\xxx\xxxx.vxd could not be found" or logon failure, system crash error	Hard disk, RAM, operation system, virus; use repair flow chart 07;
OS is unavailable or error prompts	Message shown at start up "Primary master hard disk fail" or "DISK BOOT FAILURE, INSERT SYSTEM DISK & PRESS ENTER".	Hard disk, motherboard Advice: check whether the failure's gone by pulling and plugging the part back in again or by component replacement

Power goes off at start up	Machine turns off before loading operating system	Hard disk, RAM, thermal parts, power adapter, motherboard; use repair flow chart 07,06,08
Operating system doesn't finish loading	Windows runs extremely slow, disk formatting speed is slow, Window system reinstallation is extremely slow, other information is prompted	Hard disk, motherboard, interface Advice: check whether the failure's gone by pulling and replugging the part again or by component replacement.
Can't enter once started	Windows system only loads in safe mode	Hard disk, RAM, operating system, virus; use repair flow chart 07;
System Fails to shut down normally	System freezes or error is displayed when turning off laptop	Operating system, motherboard, Advice: check whether the failure's gone by pulling and re plugging the part again or by component replacement.

2.1.3. Analysis and diagnosis table for laptop power failures

This chapter will deal with failures relevant to laptop power.

According to the common failure symptoms, you can find what you need in "Repair flowchart 03, 04, 05, and 06, 08 or 11". Confirm which "Repair flowchart", you'd have to use in Chapter 1. <<1.4.1 Judge and repair the simplest way>> section and Chapter 1 <<1.4.2 >> <<1.4.3>> section (Six "hard" and four "Soft" methods to repair laptop), to find the failure. According to the article failure analysis of "Repair flowchart", replace the defective parts

How useful is this diagnosis tool? The advantage that the analysis diagnosis table has, is that each listed failure is linked with the previous chapter (chapter 1) "The repair method" and subsequent chapter "Repair flowchart". Regardless of whether the software or hardware solution is used, or which component is involved, these three sections always link to each other. The final section is a detailed description and explanation of the repair procedure, which you should read in conjunction with the flowchart.

The failure symptoms listed in each class are just part of a broader range of failures. For the failures not listed here, some may be listed in another chapter, and some may not.

The following table shows the analysis for some common laptop power related failures.

Common failures description	Symptoms or comment (explanation)	Fault location with diagnosis flowchart
Laptop doesn't start with power on	No response when clicking power switch button, indicator light is out, black screen	Motherboard, power adapter, power switch, power interface board; use repair flow chart 03; 08;
Laptop doesn't work in battery mode	Laptop doesn't work normally without connecting the external power supply, battery doesn't charge or battery heats up when charging	Motherboard, battery, battery interface board; use repair flow chart 04, 08
Laptop doesn't work with external power supply connected	Laptop only works in battery power supply mode	Power adapter, power interface board, motherboard; use repair flow chart 03, 08
System freezes at start up	Remove battery then the laptop works normally, when installing battery back, system freezes immediately	Battery, battery interface board, motherboard; use repair flow chart 04, 08
Battery shows 100% when charging, but doesn't start the laptop	Battery doesn't last very long after a full charge, system operation interface doesn't load	Battery check by pulling and reseating parts or component replacement
Laptop is unstable or freezes randomly	Laptop continuously freezes when using it. Laptop power adapter overheats	Power adapter, battery, battery interface board, motherboard; use repair flow chart 03,04, 08
Laptop is unstable or system freezes when reading a DVD	System frequently restarts or shuts down when installing software or large application from DVD	Power adapter, RAM use repair flow chart 03,08
The power light at the front of laptop suddenly lights up and then dies out	Power light is on, but sometimes it would suddenly die out, the power cable and the laptop power receptacle feel hot	Power adapter, power joint, DC jack; use repair flow chart 03

Laptop's speakers make noises	very loud crackling sound from speakers system often restarts or auto shuts down	Power adapter, motherboard, Check by component replacement; use repair flow chart 03,08 &, 11
Unusual noise when hard disk is running	When disk is running, occasionally there's a "Click" sound, and system freezes continuously	Hard disk, power adapter, check by pulling and reseating parts or component replacement; use repair flow chart 07,03
Wavy screen on laptop	When battery supplies power, laptop works normally, but when connected to external power supply, screen is wavy.	Power adapter, motherboard; Check by component replacement;
Battery doesn't charge normally	Laptop is always charging, but the battery capacity only stays around at 10%	Power adapter, battery, motherboard, Check by component replacement; use repair flow chart 03,04, 08
Charging state remains at zero	Battery doesn't charge, the charging state always remains at 0, even after installing a new battery, the battery still shows 0	Power adapter, motherboard; use repair flow chart 03, 08
Battery charging state shows 0%, but battery works normally	Battery charging state shows 0%, but holds normal charge.	Operation system, BIOS Check by changing hard disk or reinstall operating system or update BIOS
Battery only charges for 5 minutes	Power adapter appears to work correctly, but soon laptop battery stops charging and makes unusual sounds	Power adapter, battery, BIOS check by pulling and reseating parts or component replacement; use repair flow chart 03, 04, 08
Battery power still shows 50%, but laptop auto shuts down	Battery shows 50% power capacity, but laptop doesn't work and needs external power supply to restart again.	Battery, BIOS, use repair flow chart 04,08

2.1.4 Analysis and diagnostic table for laptop hard disk failures

This chapter will classify failures relevant to the laptop hard disk.

According to the common failure symptoms, you can find what you need in "Repair flowchart 06, 07, 08, 12". Confirm which "Repair flowchart", you'd have to use in Chapter 1. <<1.4.1 Judge and repair the simplest way>> section and Chapter 1 <<1.4.2 >> <<1.4.3>> section

(Six "hard" and four "Soft" methods to repair laptop), to find the failure. According to the article failure analysis of "Repair flowchart", replace the defective parts

How useful is this diagnosis tool? The advantage that the analysis diagnosis table has, is that each listed failure is linked with the previous chapter (chapter 1) "The repair method" and subsequent chapter "Repair flowchart". Regardless of whether the software or hardware solution is used, or which component is involved, these three sections always link to each other. The final section is a detailed description and explanation of the repair procedure, which you should read in conjunction with the flowchart.

The failure symptoms listed in each class are just part of a broader range of failures. For the failures not listed here, some may be listed in another chapter, and some may not.

The next table shows the analysis for some common laptop disk failures, which can be helpful.

Common failures description	Symptoms or comment (explanation)	Fault location with diagnosis flowchart
After finishing self-inspection, a black screen occurs	Hard disk stops just as the laptop starts up, fan works but disk indicator light dies out	Hard disk, DVD-ROM, motherboard, RAM etc. Advise: repair flow chart 06,07,08
System doesn't recognize hard disk	System doesn't recognize hard disk after starting up machine, enter motherboard BIOS and then hard disk is still not found. Disk indicator light sometimes is on and or out	Hard disk, disk interface on motherboard, BIOS, the influence to the disk from other drives; Advise: repair flow chart 07,08
Logical drive volume is lost	BIOS finds hard disk, but screen shows hard disk is lost or cannot partition	Hard disk, disk interface on motherboard, motherboard; Advise: check whether the failure's gone by pulling and plugging the parts or by replacing them; use repair flow chart 07, 08
Hard disk doesn't start	Hard disk doesn't start and there's a prompt message. Sometimes there's a cursor appearing at the top left corner of the screen	Hard disk, disk interface on motherboard Advise: check whether the failure's gone by pulling and plugging parts or by replacing; use repair flow chart 07, 08

Prompt error message	Prompt "Primary master hard disk fail or "DISK BOOT FAILURE, INSERT SYSTEM DISK AND PRESS ENTER".	Hard disk, disk interface on motherboard Advise check whether the failure's gone by pulling and plugging parts or by replacing
Laptop auto restarts, or there's a blue screen error	System runs slowly, laptop frequently restarts within a short period of time, laptop could not work normally, blue screen error	Hard disk, motherboard, RAM, operating system; Advise repair flow chart 07, 08
Error prompts when entering hard disk	Disk capacity is incorrect, disk data has been changed, there's bad track, cannot partition or format	Hard disk, BIOS, operation system; Advise: repair flow chart 07;
Hard disk locks up often	Laptop disk is locked up, and, keyboard and mouse don't respond, you can only press power button to restart system	Hard disk, motherboard, RAM, operating system; Advise repair flow chart 07, 08, 06
Data protection on hard disk	Hard disk cannot be read/written or when read/write, power suddenly goes off and then system auto restarts	Hard disk, motherboard, operation system Advise repair flow chart 07, 08, 06
Error prompted when application is running	System runs extremely slowly, disk error can be found by running scandisk application, system is slow or even freezes when scanning	Hard disk, disk interface on motherboard, RAM; Advise: repair flow chart 07, 08
Windows system reinstallation fails again and again	"DLLfile, xxxx is missing" error prompts, after repairing it, same error message is shown	Hard disk, RAM, motherboard; Advise: check whether the failure's gone by replacement method: use repair flow chart 07, 08

Machine auto shuts down at a set time after starting up	After shutting down automatically, system doesn't start immediately to load OS, and you need to wait a period of time before re starting but after starting up, it will auto shut down at a set time again	Hard disk, RAM, motherboard; Advise: repair flow chart 06,07,08
S.M.A.R.T error prompt	After starting up, 1720—SMART Hard Drive detects imminent failure prompt, or prompts that data should be backed up	Hard disk Advise check whether the failure's gone by replacement method
DVD-ROM is very noisy	DVD-ROM often scrapes discs, DVD-ROM' drawer does not pop up or close, weak disc reading ability and so on.	DVD-ROM Advise check whether the failure's gone by replacement method
System can't inspect DVD-ROM	BIOS finds DVD-ROM, but screen shows DVD-ROM is lost or modified	Operating system, motherboard, influence to DVD-ROM from other drives; Advise repair flow chart 12, 08
DVD-ROM doesn't work normally	System freezes or error is prompted when visiting DVD-ROM, only CD but not DVD can be read or DVD but not CD	Operation system, DVD-ROM, disc; Advise repair flow chart 12;

2.1.5   Analysis and diagnostic table for laptop display failures

This chapter will classify failures relevant to laptop display. According to the common failure symptoms, you can find what you need in "Repair flowchart 05, 07, 08". Confirm which "Repair flowchart", you'd have to use in Chapter 1. <<1.4.1 Judge and repair the simplest way>> section and Chapter 1 <<1.4.2 >> <<1.4.3>> section (Six "hard" and four "Soft" methods to repair laptop), to find the failure. According to the article failure analysis of "Repair flowchart", replace the defective parts

How useful is this diagnosis tool? The advantage that the analysis diagnosis table has, is that each listed failure is linked with the previous chapter (chapter 1) "The repair method" and subsequent chapter "Repair flowchart". Regardless of whether the software or hardware solution is used, or which component is involved, these three sections always link to each other. The final section is a detailed description and explanation of the repair procedure, which you should read in conjunction with the flowchart.

The failure symptoms listed in each class are just part of a broader range of failures. For the failures

The following table is analysis for some common laptop display failures:

Common failures description	Symptoms or comment (explanation)	Fault location with diagnosis flowchart
Black screen occurs after laptop starts	Screen is out, without any letters or image display	Motherboard, BIOS, CPU, display card, RAM, signal cable, screen etc; —Advise, repair flow chart 05,08
There's ripple interruption on laptop display	When in battery supply mode, laptop works normally but when used with external power supply, there's ripple interruption on display	Power adapter, RAM, signal cable, screen etc Advise: check whether the failure's gone by pulling and plugging parts or by replacement method; use—repair flow chart 05,08
Laptop screen is dark	An image can be seen on the display, but very dim, and can only be seen with a flashlight	Signal cable, Inverter, backlight, switch, motherboard; Advise: repair flow chart 05;
Large scale red color appears on laptop screen	The red on the screen sometimes shows for a while, and then turns normal later. But under some circumstances, the red would be on the entire screen without any changes	Inverter, backlight Advise: check whether the failure's gone by replacement method; use repair flow chart 05;
Laptop self-inspection information shows normal but screen blacks out after awhile	Sometimes backlight would flash for a while, but subsequently die out. Under some circumstances, you can hear buzz sound from the bottom of the display	Inverter, backlight, signal cable, screen etc. Advise: check whether the failure's gone by replacement method; use repair flow chart 05;
Blue screen occurs on laptop	Laptop starts normally, but often with some problems. Sometimes within a short period of time, system would restart frequently, and finally a blue screen occurs.	Hard disk, motherboard, RAM, operating system; Advise: repair flow chart 07, 08

Laptop background turns yellow with some grey	Normal background screen reaches maximum performance, should be pure white, but under "Power management" has already increased the brightness to the maximum, screen remains grey	Screen, Inverter, motherboard Advise: check whether the failure's gone by replacement method; use repair flow chart 05, 08
Doodle appears on laptop background screen	Primarily there's dust or flax or something inside screen, and there's water inside the LCD which leaves dirt inside the screen	Screen, LCD or background surface Advise: check whether the failure's gone by replacement method;
Laptop screen shows 4-8 identical windows	Under DOS state, display is abnormal, such as self-inspection information, after entering Windows, it would be divided into 4-8 small system interfaces of the same size	Motherboard, display card, drivers; Advise: check whether the failure's gone by replacement method; use repair flow chart 05, 08
There's one or a few horizontal lines or vertical lines on the screen	Horizontal lines or vertical lines have two colors, black or white, which always show on the screen	Advise: check whether the failure's gone by replacement method;
Screen shows blank	Opposite to black screen failure, the entire screen shows white, no letter, no image displayed	Screen, signal cable, motherboard; Advise: check whether the failure's gone by replacement method; use repair flow chart 05, 08
Abnormal spots shown on screen	Laptop shows blurred screen, letters could not be seen clearly, the spots look like red snowflakes or tiny rain drops	Display card part on motherboard, motherboard, RAM, signal cable, screen; —Advise repair flow chart 05 08
White spots appear on screen	Normal screen background should be of one clear color, but the screen has white spots, different from the surrounding background	Screen, background surface Advise: check whether the failure's gone by replacement method;

Black spots and black threads appear on the screen	Normal background screen should be of one clear color, but the screen background has black spots and black threads, different from the surrounding background	Screen, LCD internal damage Advise: check whether the failure's gone by replacement method;
Screen brightness changes and screen auto flashes	Background screen brightness isn't stable, sometimes light, sometimes not; the variation speed is sometimes fast and sometimes slow. The fastest is just like a flash	Inverter, backlight, signal cable, screen etc. Advise: check whether the failure's gone by replacement method; use repair flow chart 05;
There's one black or white band appearing on screen	Under some circumstances, only top half or bottom half shows on the screen, sometimes only left or right half part displayed	Screen, LCD internal damage; Advise: check whether the failure's gone by replacement method;
Screen brightness scale is very small	Screen brightness almost has no adjustment scale, either the brightness shows the maximum, or minimum, no middle scale	Inverter, motherboard; Advise: generally it is caused because of incompatible inverter, check whether the failure's gone by replacement method

2.1.6 Analysis and diagnostic table for OS and driver installation failures

This following table listed failures occurring and an error appearing when installing software to a laptop. According to the common failure symptoms, you can find what you need in "Repair flowchart 07, 08 and 11". Confirm which "Repair flowchart", you'd have to use in Chapter 1. <<1.4.1 Judge and repair the simplest way>> section and Chapter 1 <<1.4.2 >> <<1.4.3>> section (Six "hard" and four "Soft" methods to repair laptop), to find the failure. According to the article failure analysis of "Repair flowchart", replace the defective parts

How useful is this diagnosis tool? The advantage that the analysis diagnosis table has, is that each listed failure is linked with the previous chapter (chapter 1) "The repair method" and subsequent chapter "Repair flowchart". Regardless of whether the software or hardware solution is used, or which component is involved, these three sections always link to each other. The final section is a detailed description and explanation of the repair procedure, which you should read in conjunction with the flowchart.

The failure symptoms listed in each class are just part of a broader range of failures. For the failures not listed here, some may be listed in another chapter, and some may not.

The following table shows analysis for some common laptop failures happening when installing an operating system and drivers:

Common failures description	Symptoms or comment (explanation)	Fault location with diagnosis flowchart
System freezes when installing operating system.	· When installing operating system (OS), system freezes or · auto shuts down when copying files	-RAM, hard disk, DVD-ROM, DVD disc, motherboard etc. -check by pulling and reseating parts or component replacement; -use repair flow chart 07, 08
After installing OS system, error prompts at restart.	· Just when the OS is installed, the registry table gets corrupted for no reason, and it prompts user to repair	-RAM, hard disk, motherboard—check by pulling and reseating parts or component replacement; use repair flow chart 07, 08
Operating system installation doesn't complete.	· Installer is unstable, · invalid operation error occurs, or · system auto shuts down	-RAM, hard disk, motherboard -check by pulling and reseating parts or component replacement; use repair flow chart 07,08
Windows system cannot be reinstalled, there's a system error prompt.	· When installing an operating system or after system restarts, this message appears: "C:\ WINDOWS\SYSTEM\xxx\ xxxx.vxd could not be found" reinstall Windows, unchangeable.	-RAM, hard disk, motherboard -check by pulling and reseating parts or component replacement; use repair flow chart 07, 08;
Only DOS applications appear, such as self-test information, Windows doesn't appear.	· When system is running Windows, black screen or system frozen symptoms occur.	-Display card driver, display card, motherboard -check by pulling and reseating parts or component replacement; use repair flow chart 08;
Windows system shows up, but DOS self-inspection information doesn't show.	· When System is running the application under DOS state (such as games running in DOS), black screen occurs.	-BIOS, display card, motherboard -Start Windows in safe mode, uninstall display card driver, setup BIOS again, check if the failure's gone; use repair flow chart 08;
Hard disk cannot be formatted normally or there's a prompt saying that the hard disk is in protection state.	· Hard disk might have bad tracks, which disables disk being used normally. · Windows system cannot be reinstalled	-Check the disk with disk test application to see whether there's a bad track or other possible problem -check by pulling and reseating parts or component replacement

Black screen occurs after installing drivers	· Black screen occurs when system enters Windows	-Drivers—under safe mode, uninstall drivers, and then re-install drivers, check whether the failure's gone.
When installing a system, laptop prompts that hard disk cannot be found.	· An HP uses a SATA disk, when reinstalling operating system, if you use OS disc without integrated SATA driver and install directly, then computer cannot find the hard disk.	-Hard disk SATA driver -Insert SATA driver disc when installing system and check whether the failure's gone.
Reinstalling Windows system is very slow, which seems like the system is dead.	· Disk CODE error, · Windows runs extremely slow along with disk formatting, · Windows system reinstallation is extremely slow · and other information is prompted.	-Hard disk, disk interface on motherboard, -Check the disk with disk test application to see whether there's a bad track on hard disk or some other possible failures, -check by pulling and reseating parts or component replacement
Install system with integrated SATA driver, computer still doesn't recognize hard disk.	· Repeat install and hard disk cannot be found in BIOS.	-Hard disk, motherboard -check by pulling and reseating parts or component replacement
DVD-ROM isn't recognized.	· Before complete system installation, system restarts, but the laptop prompts that DVD-ROM can't be found	-Hard disk, DVD-ROM, disk interface, BIOS -check by pulling and reseating parts or component replacement, or formatting disk
Installing display card driver, but only 16 colors appear.	· Laptop only works in low color and low resolution, even after reinstalling display card driver, no changes occurs	-Display card driver, display card, motherboard -under safe mode, uninstall display card driver and install driver again, then check whether the failure's gone; use repair flow chart 08;
Operating system doesn't recognize sound card, but is recognized in BIOS.	· Install sound card driver, but still no change	-Sound card driver, sound card, motherboard -Under safe mode, uninstall sound card driver, reinstall driver again, then check whether the failure's gone; use repair flow chart 11.

When laptop is running, noises are heard from speaker.	· When Windows system is running, there's sound made, such as "buzz" or "rustle" sound.	-Power adapter, sound card, motherboard -check by pulling and reseating parts or component replacement; use repair flow chart 11;
After starting up, multimedia application is running, and very noisy.	· When playing sound/ video file, intermittent or continuous "snapping" sounds can be heard.	-Multimedia software, sound card, motherboard -Under safe mode, uninstall multimedia software, then install another type of player software, check whether the failure's gone; use repair flow chart 11

2.1.7 Analysis and diagnostic table for laptop Internet failures

This chapter would classify relevant failures about laptop Internet. According to the common failure symptoms, you can find what you need in "Repair flowchart 10, 14, and 15". Confirm which "Repair flowchart", you'd have to use in Chapter 1. <<1.4.1 Judge and repair the simplest way>> section and Chapter 1 <<1.4.2 >> <<1.4.3>> section (Six "hard" and four "Soft" methods to repair laptop), to find the failure. According to the article failure analysis of "Repair flowchart", replace the defective parts

How useful is this diagnosis tool? The advantage that the analysis diagnosis table has, is that each listed failure is linked with the previous chapter (chapter 1) "The repair method" and subsequent chapter "Repair flowchart". Regardless of whether the software or hardware solution is used, or which component is involved, these three sections always link to each other. The final section is a detailed description and explanation of the repair procedure, which you should read in conjunction with the flowchart.

The failure symptoms listed in each class are just part of a broader range of failures. For the failures not listed here, some may be listed in another chapter, and some may not.

The table below is the analysis for common laptop Internet failures.

Common failures description	Symptoms or comment (explanation)	Fault location with diagnosis flowchart
Cannot dial, no dialling sound, noise mixed in dialling tone, offline	During the process of Internet online sometimes offline happens automatically	Modem, telephone set, telephone line, terminal station, network card, switch (including HUB, router and so on), network cable power and relevant components; Use repair flowchart 14, 15, 10.

Slow Internet speed, some WebPages could not be opened	The speed when connecting the network is extremely slow, sometimes even a fail to connect.	Modem, telephone set, telephone line, terminal station, network card, switch (Including HUB, router and so on), network cable and relevant components; use repair flowchart 14;15;10
When surfing on the Internet, system down, blue screen error and so on	When connecting network, sometimes screen stops, even system down, system prompts error message.	Network card, motherboard, hard disk, power, system and relevant components; use repair flowchart14;15;10
Mail receiving/ sending failure	When system receives and sends mails, system prompts error message, could not receive and send mails	Network adapter, Modem, system and relevant components; use repair flowchart14;15;10
Invalid network device installation	System prompts abnormal status, could not install	Modem, telephone set, telephone line, terminal station, network card, switch (including HUB, router and so on), network cable, motherboard, hard disk, power and relevant components; use repair flowchart14;15;10
Modem has no response	No response when system connects network, could not access network	Modem, telephone set, telephone line, terminal station, network card, switch (including HUB, router and so on), power and relevant components; use repair flowchart 14;15;10
Hardware could not be found	Network card could not be found in device manager, and the icon of disconnection could not be seen in the taskbar either	Modem, telephone set, telephone line, terminal station, network card, switch (including HUB, router and so on), network cable and relevant components; use repair flowchart 14;15;10
System fails to access the Internet	Not any response after plugging network cable, the connection icon on taskbar has any change either.	Modem, telephone set, telephone line, terminal station, network card, switch (including HUB, router and so on), network cable, power and relevant components; use repair flowchart 14;15;10
Network adapter(network card) settings and computer resources are conflicted	Fail to connect the network, system prompts the information that the network card is not matched with system	Modem, telephone set, telephone line, terminal station, network card, switch (including HUB, router and so on), network cable, motherboard, hard disk, power and relevant components; use repair flowchart 14;15;10

Prompt displays on the screen: "Dialling network could not deal with the specified compatible network protocol in 'server type' settings"	System could not dial to access network	Modem, telephone set, telephone line, terminal station, network card, switch (including HUB, router and so on), network cable, motherboard, hard disk, power, system and relevant components; use repair flowchart 14;15;10
When check "Network neighbourhoods", it would prompt "cannot browse network", the network could not be accessed.	Fail to browse network neighborhoods within the same LAN	Modem, telephone set, telephone line, terminal station, network card, switch (including HUB, router and so on), network cable, system and relevant components; use repair flowchart 14;15;10
Connection failure with the single machine within the LAN	Only the local machine name could be found in "Network neighbourhoods" or "Explorer"	Modem, telephone set, telephone line, terminal station, network card, switch (including HUB, router and so on), network cable, system and relevant components; use repair flowchart 14;15;10
ADSL could not get IP address discontinuously	Sometimes network could be accessed, and sometimes fail to connect	Modem, telephone set, telephone line, terminal station, network card, switch (including HUB, router and so on), network cable, motherboard, hard disk, power and relevant components; use repair flowchart 14;15;10
IE would always test proxy server	When open IE, it would always test proxy server settings, the speed is really slow	Modem, telephone set, telephone line, terminal station, network card, switch (including HUB, router and so on), system and relevant components; use repair flowchart 14;15;10
Could not open webpage secondary links	Open browser, browsing certain webpage, but could not access relevant links	Modem, telephone set, telephone line, terminal station, network card, switch (including HUB, router and so on), system and relevant components; use repair flowchart 14;15;10

2.1.8 Analysis diagnostic table for laptop ports and peripherals failures

This chapter would classify relevant failures about laptop ports and peripherals. According to the common failure symptoms, you can find what you need in "Repair flowchart 13". Confirm which "Repair flowchart", you'd have to use in Chapter 1. <<1.4.1 Judge and repair the simplest way>> section and Chapter 1 <<1.4.2 >> <<1.4.3>> section (Six "hard" and four "Soft" methods to repair laptop), to find the failure. According to the article failure analysis of "Repair flowchart", replace the defective parts

How useful is this diagnosis tool? The advantage that the analysis diagnosis table has, is that each listed failure is linked with the previous chapter (chapter 1) "The repair method" and subsequent chapter "Repair flowchart". Regardless of whether the software or hardware solution is used, or which component is involved, these three sections always link to each other. The final section is a detailed description and explanation of the repair procedure, which you should read in conjunction with the flowchart.

The failure symptoms listed in each class are just part of a broader range of failures. For the failures not listed here, some may be listed in another chapter, and some may not.

The table below is the analysis for common laptop ports and peripheral failures . . .

Common failures description	Symptoms or comment (explanation)	Fault location with diagnosis flowchart
Keyboard fails to work normally, function keys don't work	Keyboard input has no response, I/O input error, key button could not pop up, repeat key-press automatically	Components equipped with relevant port (like motherboard), power, connection cable, BIOS setup, keyboard hardware badness use repair flowchart13
Mouse doesn't work normally	Mouse could not move cursor, no cursor displayed, mouse not working	Components equipped with relevant port (like motherboard), power, connection cable, BIOS setup, mouse hardware badness use repair flowchart 13
Could not print or under certain operation system, print doesn't work	Communication failure between laptop and printer	Components equipped with relevant port (like motherboard), power, connection cable, BIOS setup, printer hardware, connection settings use repair flowchart 13
Serial port communication error	Data transmission error, data missing, serial port device could not be recognized and so on	Components equipped with relevant port (like motherboard), power, connection cable, BIOS setup use repair flowchart 13
USB device could not work normally	USB disk could not work, several USB devices could not work together and so on	Components equipped with relevant port (like motherboard), power, connection cable, BIOS setup use repair flowchart 13
Touchpad failure	Touchpad doesn't work, cursor moves but could not double click, lockup failure	Components equipped with relevant port (like motherboard), power, connection cable, BIOS setup, touchpad hardware badness use repair flowchart 13

External sound box failure	External sound device, no sound, sound output abnormity, noise, sound change, disconnected sound and so on	Components equipped with relevant port (like motherboard), power, connection cable, BIOS setup, relevant hardware, internal speaker, sound control chip use repair flowchart 13
USB interface is invalid, interface damage failure	USB interface doesn't work, fail to connect any peripherals, USB interface power supply chip is easily burnt	Components equipped with relevant port (like motherboard), power, connection cable, BIOS setup, USB motherboard control chip use repair flowchart 13

Please take a look at Figure 2-1; 2-2. 2-3;

Figure 2-1 USB and eSATA ports

Figure 2-2 PCMCIA and Audio ports

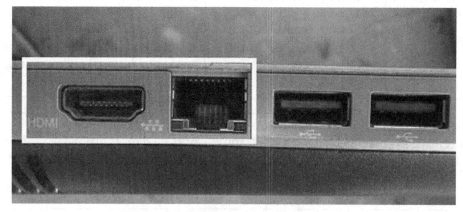

Figure 2-3 HDMI and RJ45 jack Ports

Please take a look Figure 2-4; 2-5.

Figure 2-4 digital media slot and VGA ports

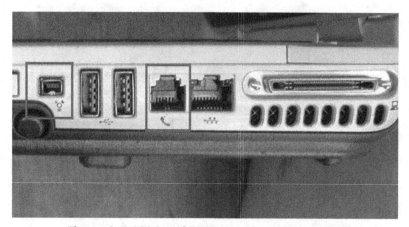

Figure 2-5 1394 and RJ11 (modem) jack ports

2.2   BIOS update and optimization

2.2.1   The main purpose for BIOS update

1)   Get new functions for free

The most direct advantage for a BIOS update is to get new functions without spending extra money. CPU support of a new frequency is an example. On the previous HP Pavilion dv2000/dv6000/dv9000 and Compaq Presario V3000/V6000 series notebook PCs, after updating the BIOS on the motherboard, the fan control algorithm system is updated and improved. While your laptop is running, it will measure the temperature more accurately and control the fan speed at a reasonably low state to prolong the life of the fan while maintaining thermal and capacity limitations. You can now use a larger capacity hard disk and a better startup method. The previously shielded functions can be enabled, and can now recognize other kinds of new hardware.

2)   Solving the BUG in an old version BIOS

The BIOS is also a program, so naturally, there might be an existing BUG. The hardware technology development changes and improves every day, as the market competition intensifies. The time between motherboard manufacturer releases of their products is shorter and shorter and each one includes BIOS improvements you do not have. Bugs existing in your BIOS and corrected in later versions will usually cause unexpected failures. For instance, your system may restart without any reason, frequent system crashes, low system performance, device conflicts, and hardware devices lost without any reason and so on.

After users' feedback to manufacturers, a conscientious manufacturer will release a new BIOS version to revise those known Bugs and to solve these indescribable failures.

2.2.2   Ensure the BIOS version is current with the basic setup of your laptop

BIOS is software integrated into your computer system by default in order to inspect and control the internal hardware system, such as the hard disk, display card, disk and so on. If you want your laptop to have more options and perform better, then it's a good idea to update the BIOS. By updating the BIOS the system you will benefit greatly by updates such as hibernation, standby, sleep etc.

When do you judge whether your laptop needs BIOS updating? First confirm what the current BIOS version is:

1.   System information

Click Start—Run, and then type "winmsd", the system information dialog box will pop up, in the column where the system is outlined; you can see the BIOS version/date. Now you can directly see the BIOS version of your current system. "Vista system information" window provides information for current relevant hardware resources, components and the software environment. If you want to open this system information window, click "Start" and enter "information" to search the field, and then choose "system information" from the list.

2. BIOS version in registry

The registry also includes almost everything and the BIOS version is no exception. You can enter the next address:

HKEY_LOCAL_MACHINE\HARDWAR\EDESCRIPTION\System

Now you can see a few files relevant to the BIOS, including system Bios Date, System Bios Version, video Bios Date, Video Bios Version

Please take a look at Figure 2-6

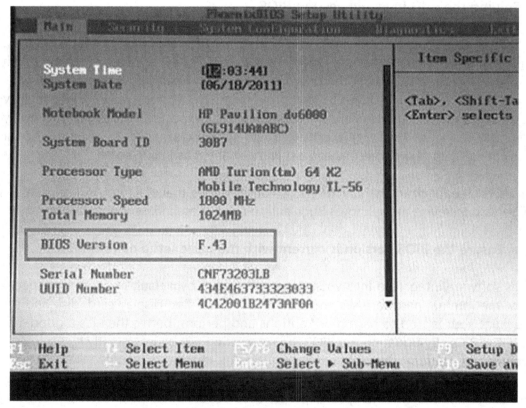

Figure 2-6 BIOS Version

3. Restart system

Another method to check the system BIOS is to simply restart your system and follow these steps:

1.   Press the power button to start the laptop;

2.   When an HP or Compaq logo appears, press F10 key to enter the BIOS Setup;
3   When the main menu shows up, please pay attention to the BIOS version. You'll need the information to ensure whether there's an update available.
4.   To exit the BIOS Setup, press F10, and choose "Yes" then press Enter.

If the BIOS version listed is earlier than the versions listed on the HP website, then it means there's a necessity to update the BIOS. Other brand laptops also have similar functions; just the key is different.

4.   Use third party software

If the methods above did not help you to find the system BIOS version, then you can download a third party software from the Internet, such as Everest. This free application can tell you everything about your hardware and software and of course the BIOS version. All of the above will get you the system BIOS version.

2.2.3   The steps to update BIOS

WinFlash is software used to refresh BIOS in Windows, which is the same as many other Award and Phoenix BIOS refreshers without using a dangerous command line method in DOS. According to your machine model number, find the BIOS updates from HP or other website and download it and click on the installer, which will auto decompress and do the update. New versions support Win2K/XP/Vista system, (usually the name is: WinFlash for HP Notebook System BIOS), besides, it supports refreshing the PnP area of BIOS.

I suggest printing this instruction before starting so you can refer to it.

NOTE: during the update process, I suggest using the AC power adapter and a cable connection to the Internet, to avoid an installation failure caused by either a run down battery and or a bad connection with the wireless Ethernet.

1.   Open the browser, go to the HP or other website to download the software and relevant drivers;
2.   On the driver and software download page, type your model in the search field and then press Enter;
3.   Choose your current operating system (such as XP or Vista) which is installed on your laptop;
4.   On the BIOS part, click WinFlash for an HP laptop system BIOS. The Version should be listed as the one identified in the table above or later.
5.   Click the download button on the webpage, just click to download the BIOS update. Save the file into a convenient folder on your PC;
6.   Double click the file downloaded to start the installation. Follow all directions and restart the laptop once installed. Don't turn off the laptop until the system prompts you to;
7.   First save the BIOS file on your system and rename it (old BIOS), in case your system becomes unstable, and then you can always go back to it . . .

8. To do that first rename the present BIOS file (old bios) and click Save;
9. Saving progress bar appears, click "Backup" to start BIOS backup.
10. After finishing the save, prepare to refresh the BIOS (update BIOS).
11. Choose the BIOS file you prepared to refresh it in advance, double click the downloaded file and start the installation.
12. When the refresh progress bar appears, click "Update" and start refreshing;
13. When the progress bar goes to the end, the refreshing finishes, it will prompt you to click "F1" to restart system or "F10" to exit the refresher application. Generally we choose to restart, press DEL to enter BIOS Setup, except to set "HDD, FDD, DATE . . . .", you should also choose "Load Setup Defaults" to load system preset settings, up until now, you've completed the BIOS update job.

NOTE: during the refresh process, make sure no other applications are running and ensure the computer cannot power off, in case the machine fails to start up. This process is irreversible. You have only one chance. Because the BIOS update has certain dangers, we never suggest refreshing your laptop BIOS, except if you are familiar with BIOS and have an enough manual ability and experience, then you should be ok.

2.3   Rescue a failed BIOS update and BIOS password crack

2.3.1   First aid measures after a BIOS update fails (Software repair)

After refreshing the BIOS, the system doesn't open after restarting. Then it's quite likely that the BIOS update failed. Here we provide two rescue measures:

A.   BootBlock repair of BIOS

During the process of updating the BIOS; if something happens with the laptop (like system crash, power-off); the laptop then will display nothing. Fortunately the BIOS on newer units generally, have a BootBlock section keeping the basic boot codes. During BIOS update process, this part will not be affected. When starting up, the computer will start the application from the bootblock area, if at this moment, the BIOS is perfect, with no damage, it can boot normally. If it finds that the BIOS is damaged, the application in the bootblock area will be executed. So we can use the Bootblock to repair a laptop which was refreshed incorrectly. Generally, it is called a blind refresh. Here's the method below:

B.   This is the general solution for a BIOS update problem for most HP laptops with Phoenix BIOS: here we take an HP DV6000 laptop for an example: please don't use the same BIOS version on HP website if that is what you initially used, if the last time this update caused a problem for your machine, then probably this time it will happen again

1. Find a USB disk larger than 200MB to make a startup disk for a BIOS repair. It needs to be done in Windows XP or a Vista system.

2. **Notice:** when making a startup disc, all data on the U disk will be cleared;
3. Download the BIOS blind refresh tool WINCRIS (you can download it from the FTP server of www.computercare.ca,
4. Use CRISDISK (download BIOS blind refresh tool) to make the BIOS refresh U disk, start the file WINCRIS.EXE in CRISDISK folder, and then it asks you to choose your U disk and click Start to begin making a startup disc for the BIOS repair; Please have a look at Figure 2-7; 2-8.

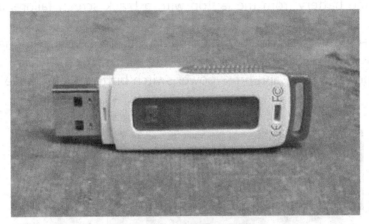

Figure 2-7 USB flash drive

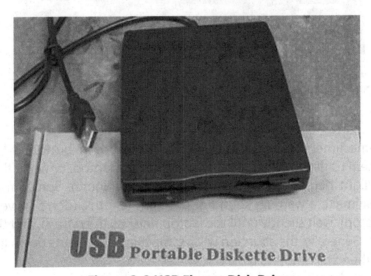

Figure 2-8 USB Floppy Disk Drive

5. Then it asks you to delete the data on the U disk and recover the U disk. Click OK, and then wait for a prompt saying the U disk creation is finished. And finally click OK.
6. Pull out the U disk according to the prompt, and then plug it back again. Check the U disk to verify the three files are included: "MINIDOS.SYS", "PHLASH16.EXE", "bios.wph" files. If the previous two are not there, then you can copy them from the WINCRIS directory. But if there's the file "bios.wph", please delete it. And replace it with the BIOS files you need for the update.

7. Download BIOS version (F3D or later), copy the latest HP BIOS file bios.wph (the bios file name should be changed to BIOS.WPH (capital letters)) to your U disk and replace the files inside. The startup U disk download of the BIOS is now complete.

C. Resume steps:

8. Insert the completed U disk to the USB interface of the laptop you want to repair; remove other USB devices.
9. Remove the battery from the laptop with a black screen failure, and remove the power adapter.
10. Press Fn+B, don't release it (according to different laptop models, it might be Winkey+B or Fn+ESC or Winkey+ESC, Toshiba is Fn+B), while you connect the external power supply, and press power switch button. Please have a look at Figure 2-9.

Figure 2-9 Win+B key

11. At the same time, as you press Win+B and the power button (3 keys), you don't release them until you hear a "De" sound form the laptop, or when the laptop power indicator light begins flashing (20 seconds to 1 minute). Sometimes, a laptop will continually make a warning sound of different lengths, (don't move the other keys on the laptop), wait silently until the laptop finishes the refresh, and then restarts the computer. Generally, the situation will be: machine auto shuts down after making the sound, it then starts normally.
12 If the laptop hasn't started automatically for a long period of time, (5-10 minutes later), then pull out the power adapter to force it to shut down. Then manually restart the laptop.

2.3.2 First aid measures after BIOS update failure (hardware repair)

If your BIOS update fails, you can try the "replacement method" to repair it (the condition is that you must find a scrapped motherboard of the same model as your laptop with the BIOS still working), Here are the correct steps:

First: let the static out, and then open the shell of the laptop, find the BIOS chip on the motherboard and verify that the BIOS chip is soldered on the motherboard. If it is, then you must have a soldering-iron tool and a professional BGA rework system. Sometimes, the BIOS chip is soldered on the jack of the motherboard and we can pull out the BIOS chip from the jack carefully, but because of its special encapsulation form, we need the appropriate chip clip to do it.

Second: use the scrap motherboard of the same model with the BIOS still working. Using the method above, remove the correct BIOS chip from the motherboard. However, you need to pay attention when using the "Replacement method", to whether the BIOS pins are compatible and whether the BIOS chip is from same manufacturer. Some motherboards will not support the BIOS chip you are intending to use.

Third: when changing the BIOS chip fails, the most common causes are:

1) The chip specified voltages or BIOS chip types are different.
2) Components have certain heat limitations and a ROM chip is no exception. When soldering components with pin heat endurance limits; during the soldering process, the aluminum film down-lead inside the chip can be fused or broken causing the chip to fail and therefore be disabled
3) Check the pulled out chip pins carefully, whether they are bent or not and if they are, straighten them, and insert them back to the base or solder them back. Make sure you keep each pin well connected with the motherboard.

2.3.3   BIOS password crack

(1)   Discharge

I often hear my clients talking about this situation: A password was not set in BIOS, but when they start up the computer, it requests a password validation. Some other related problems can develop:

1) A laptop hasn't been used for a long period of time, and when it is used again a password is requested.
2) After updating hardware, such as the hard disk, when restarting the laptop, it requests password validation;
3) After downloading certain software or updating an application, when restarting the laptop, it requests password validation.

Problems like this caused by a password not set in BIOS, can be solved by the "Discharge method". A full "CMOS battery discharge" is required. You must disassemble the laptop main case, and find the button battery on the motherboard. It is called CMOS battery and is used to supply power for the BIOS when the computer is shut down so that the BIOS setup is not lost. Remove the CMOS battery, wait for 5 minutes and then put it back, (sometimes, the battery is soldered onto the motherboard and you need to unsolder to take it off).

However, even after that, if the password problem still is not eliminated; then you can remove the CMOS battery again and wait for about 3 to 5 hours before plugging the CMOS battery in again. Generally, the failure would be gone. If you have the time do the long wait the first time so you don't have to disassemble it twice.

(2) Reset chip program

If your BIOS remains locked up and the discharge method does not crack the password set in BIOS, then you must use the "Reset chip program" to repair it. Most laptops have a BIOS password stored on a special chip on the motherboard; when you set the password in BIOS, at the same time, the password and information about the laptop (service label, owner information, property name, other material) would all be stored on a special NVRAM chip, which would not be lost even after BIOS loses power or resets. On this point, NVRAM chip technology is totally different from RDRAM and SRAM. And that's why NVRAM chip technology is broadly used by laptop manufacturers

Now, of course, its security has also improved greatly. The problem is that when a valid user is locked from his/her laptop, it's really a problem that you can do nothing about. It is said that there's a "master" password which can crack and solve this problem, so, you can enter both the BIOS setup and the operating system. Of course, you can also use the password you have set if you remember it. This service is not that easy to get, so it would be very important to repair the laptop by the "resetting chip" method.

First of all, you must find the right chip. Here let's take Dell ATMEL 518 laptop for an example. Disable the eighth pin for the chip selectively, (of course, for different chips, the choice might be different) to let the computer think that this is a brand new machine and now is being used for the first time. Identify the eighth pin of the chip, heat the soldering line with a soldering iron, and then tilt the eighth pin up gently with a knife, letting the pin gradually disconnect from the motherboard.

Next, check whether the laptop will start up; it might refuse to work. This is normal, because without the chip, you cannot start the laptop. When the chip pin is connected, you can start it, but now you have to enter a password. So now what you have to do is to insert a small screw or metal bended hook (a tool) between the eighth pin and motherboard, letting the chip eighth pin connects to the motherboard temporarily.

Now start the laptop, but immediately when screen shows, take the small screw or metal bended hook off. Then the laptop would enter a special production mode. The computer retests again and sets up hardware, including resetting the chip. After that, it will exit the production mode. After that you solder the chip eighth pin back to the motherboard again.

At this moment, the password in BIOS setup has already been solved by the "reset chip program", but programming is needed if you still want to set a new password.

(3) Change chip

If the laptop BIOS password could not be bypassed or deleted or reset by these methods; we advise you to find a professional company to change the chip and solve the problem, because the operations above might complicate the problem and cause other system errors that you cannot recover from.

A professional company provides the service to change the security chip for laptops. These chips will allow you to solve the laptop's BIOS password problem. Please note; when the chip is changed, and soldered back to system board (using a sirocco soldering tool package), it lets the password stored on the chip take the place of the laptop BIOS security chip, and deletes the original BIOS password. However, if you set a disk lock password again, it would still exist.

2.4   Several approaches to increase laptop running speed

2.4.1   How to increase a computer starting speed?

1)   BIOS optimization setup

Press F10 to enter the BIOS Setup home page, here we take HP Pavilion dv 6000 for an example, choose "System configuration" option, and move the cursor to "Boot option→Boot order". The default value is "USB floppy", "ATAPI ROM Driver", which indicates that when started, the system would read boot information first from the floppy drive (or DVD-ROM). This would increase the machine starting time, and shorten the life of the DVD-ROM. So we choose "Hard drive" to start from the hard disk directly, which would be several seconds faster.

2)   Start the DMA way, increase hard disk speed (the next solution is for an XP example)

The next step is quite essential, right click on "My Computer"—"Property"—"Hardware"— "Device manager", expand "IDE ATA/ATAPI controller", shown as the picture below:

Double click to open the property "Secondary IDE channel", shown as the picture below: Please take a look Figure 2-10;

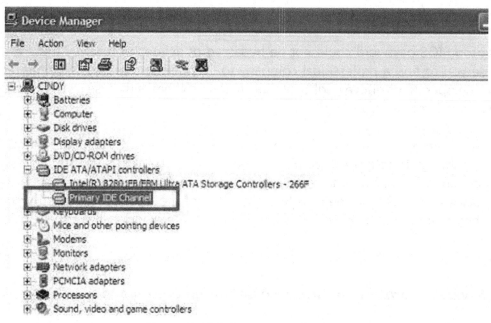

Figure 2-10 Primary IDE Channel

Click the "Advanced Setup" tab, change the "Auto inspection" to "None", change the device 1 and 2 transmission mode to DMA, if available, you can set the device type to "None". Click OK to finish the configuration. Set up the "Primary IDE channel" with the same method. Then the start speed would triple or more. Please take a look Figure 2-11;

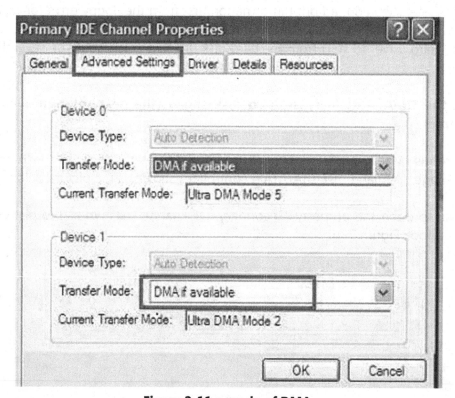

Figure 2-11 a mode of DMA

3) Optimize the "Start" button

A) This is the method: open "Control panel"—"System"—"Advanced setup"—"Startup and resume", then remove two "√" marks in the "System startup" area. You have to keep "Display the time of operation system list" if there are multi-system users. Click "Edit" and ensure the startup item's additional property is /fastdetect, but don't change to nodetect. Why not first add the /noguiboot property.

B) Many users like to try all kinds of software, but would delete them within a short period of time. But mostly, because of various reasons, this software would stay in the "Start" object, so there're too many windows in the startup item, which would influence the starting speed. To solve this problem is quite easy; you can open "Start"—"Run", and on the prompt dialog, enter "msconfig" to the "Open" column, and then click "OK", "System configuration utility" would appear. Click the "Start" label, generally, we could just preserve the ctfmon.exe input method and antivirus software and remove the "√" before the applications that do not need to be loaded in the start-up group. Press "Apply" and "OK". In this way, we would shorten the starting time at least 10 seconds. Please have a look Figure 2-12.

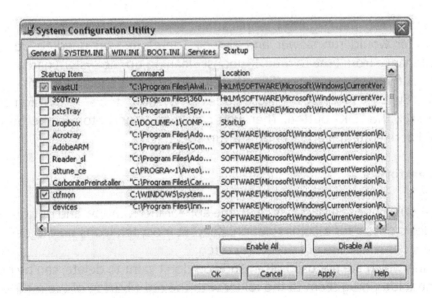

Figure 2-12 Optimization of the "Startup"

4) Clean up and optimize registry

After Windows XP starts, the system would read relevant information in the registry and store it in RAM temporarily. Therefore, it seems quite necessary to clean up and optimize the registry. Open registry (Start—Run—regedit), click "My computer", "Find" in the "Edit" menu, shown in the picture below:

Enter AutoEndTasks, and click "Find the next". Double click the found result and modify the "Value date" as 1, shown in the picture below:

And then under AutoEndTasks, you can find "HungAppTimeout" and "WaitToKillAppTimeout" and set the "Value data" as 2000 or smaller. You can also change the menu delay time, under AutoEndTasks, find MenuShowDelay, the value is in the unit of millisecond, if you want to erase this, set menudelay as 0.

After modifications, click "Edit" menu, open "Find the next" (shortcut is F3), change the found results by the method in the last step. Find WaitToKillServiceTimeout with the method above and set the value the same as HungAppTimeout.

5) Ensure system configuration

Restart the laptop, when the starting finishes, there's a window popping up on the desktop, prompting that the system configuration utility changes, check the small pane, and then click "OK".

2.4.2 How to speed up computer running operations

1) Maintain the system frequently

A)   If there're too many games, applications and old material in system, then your computer would run slower and slower. Therefore, you need to do a complete maintenance from time to time. I suggest cleaning up the system garbage frequently (such as the system garbage files, system registry garbage and so on)

B)   Click "Start"—"Programs"—"Accessories"—"System tools"—"Defragmenter", and then click the "OK" button. Then you can keep your laptop in the best state and would accelerate the application startup speed.

2) Clear desktop

A)   You should choose a classic style for the appearance window and button, and choose Windows classic for a color solution. Keep at most ten icons on the desktop, delete some icons which are not used very often.

B)   The files which are not used often and you don't want to delete, can be put together in one folder; drag them to the folder with the right button of the mouse.

3) Remove "wallpaper", "screensaver" flaring setups

Disable effects in the system property, as an easy and effective way to increase speed. Right click my computer—Properties—Advanced—Performance—Setup—Visual effect, adjust it to the best performance, and then click OK. Right click on the desktop blank area and on the prompted menu, choose "Properties", and on the popup dialog, choose "Background" and "Screen saver" labels separately, set "Wallpaper" and "Screensaver" as none.

4) Enlarge the virtual memory size

If your hard disk is large enough, then please open My computer (right click it)→Properties→Performance settings→Advanced→Virtual memory modification. In the option of virtual memory setting, open "Virtual Memory", select the second item: user sets virtual memory size, point it to a drive not used as much, and set one fixed value for the maximum and minimum values, twice as much as the physical memory. In this way, when virtual memory uses the hard disk, it ignores the difference between big size and small size, but just uses a fixed space as the virtual memory. This will accelerate accessing speed.

5) Accelerate switch time

Start—Run—type regedit and then press Enter to open REGEDIT, find the branch HKEY_LOCAL_MACHINESYSTEMCurrentControlSetControlSession ManagerMemory ManagementPrefetchParameters, on the right side panel, find the primary key EnablePrefetcher, set the default value 3 to 1, then the scrollbar's scrolling time would be reduced.

6) Reduce unnecessary fonts

Fonts occupy too much system resources, it makes it very slow to boot, and it occupies too much disk space. Therefore, we should reduce unnecessary fonts. But if we delete the font file by mistake, then Windows will not work normally. We can use the next method: first open the font folder (such as f:\zk), select all true type fonts, right click them and drag to the folder c:\windows\fonts. On the popup menu, choose "Create shortcut on current position", then you can create the shortcut of font files under font folder. When you need these font files, just insert the font disc thus avoiding memory loading.

7) Release preserved bandwidth

"Start"—"Run", type "gpedit.msc" to open the Group Policy Editor. Find "Computer configuration"—"Administrative templates"—"Network"—"QoS Packet Scheduler", choose the "Limit reservable bandwidth" option on the right side panel. Choose "Property" and open "Limit reservable bandwidth" dialog, choose "Enable", and change the original "20" to "0", then the reservable bandwidth would be released.

CHAPTER 3

Power failure repair

3.1 Laptop power system failure repair

3.1.1 Laptop power system common failures

1) Laptop doesn't start, and the power indicator light is out.
2) Fails to start up when not connected with the ac power adapter, and running on battery
3) Fails to start with the battery, but starts with the ac power adapter.
4) Battery run time is short, even when fully charged.
5) Battery doesn't hold or heats up when charging.
6) When the battery is charging, the laptop suddenly shuts down or froze.
7) When using the laptop, it shuts down suddenly.
8) Laptop power adapter overheats.
9) The laptop sound card is noisy and sometimes there is a "humming" like a bad connection or AC current noise.
10) Laptop goes dead or shuts down when reading a DVD
11) Laptop dies easily or shuts down when running a large application.
12) Although the power light of the laptop is on, it intermittently goes off or flickers, and you notice that the connection of the power cable to the laptop is hot.
13) You notice the hard drive occasionally has an intermittent clicking noise
14) There's a ripple-effect on your display.
15) Laptop often starts up twice or auto shuts down.

3.1.2 Power system failure causes for a laptop

1) The laptop adapter or battery is not properly connected to the laptop.
2) The laptop power control board connection to the motherboard is loose or deteriorated.
3) The laptop adapter overheats or malfunctions causing damage to the internal hardware of the laptop.
4) Battery terminals are corroded.

5) The laptop power board is defective.
6) A laptop motherboard BIOS failure causes the power controller to fail.
7) A short circuit or open circuit occurs on the inside circuitry of the laptop liquid crystal screen, preventing it from working, and causing a black screen.
8) A laptop memory failure, caused by a defective low voltage supply, results in a black-screen.
9) A current-limiting resistor (fuse) blows, and interrupts power.
10) DC voltage output from a power supply is incorrect, noisy, or unstable
11) The power load is marginally high and blows the current-limiting resistor-fuse.
12) The power filter and/or the starting capacitor is defective.

3.1.3 Troubleshooting process for a laptop power system

1. First, check the power adapter connection to the laptop. Place your finger on the rear of the jack and jiggle it slightly to see if the power indicator light is affected. If so, the power jack male or female will need to be changed when the problem becomes intolerable.
2. Check the external power adapter output insulated power cable for cracks. If so, then you should change the power cable or use electrical insulated adhesive tape to repair it.
3. Remove the battery and inspect it for defects. Check the battery and laptop terminals for discoloration, corrosion, or distortion. Check the battery and laptop terminals for spring tension.
4. After inspection, DC voltages should be checked. Using a multi-meter on the DC scale, measure the output voltages of the battery and power adapter. Voltages must be slightly higher than the nameplate specifications. Abnormally low/high adapter voltage indicates a fault that requires adapter replacement. If the adapter is OK, plug the external adapter into the laptop and measure the voltage across the laptop terminals that connect to the battery. These should be slightly higher than the battery nameplate voltage; otherwise there is a problem with the power regulation board connected to the female jack. If you can access these terminals with the battery and adapter installed, measure the voltage with the computer operating. It should never be less than the battery rating and only slightly higher. An abnormally low voltage indicates a serious battery fault and it should be replaced. If these conditions are met, the power supply system is functioning properly.
5. If everything seems OK, then the failure might be on the motherboard. Open the laptop shell and check the connection between the power board and motherboard. (Most power boards are connected to the motherboard). If there is bad connection the simplest fix is to install a new power board.
6. If the connection is OK, replace the power board with a known good one (include DC jack) to see if it solves the problem.
7. If power board is OK, DC jack is OK, then probably the laptop motherboard is defective (start-up circuit failure), you will need to repair or replace the motherboard.

3.1.4   Laptop power adapter use and maintenance

1) Do not press out or abuse the power adapter cable. The insulation is thin and the cable easily shorted.
2) Do not place items on the power cable
3) Do not let the power adapter fall or be impacted, the shell and circuit board is easily damaged.
4) When the laptop is off and unused, disconnect the power adapter from the DC jack.
5) Plug or unplug in the power adapter jack carefully. This connection is a common source of problems and is expensive to repair.
6) Avoid exposure to heat, rain and moisture.
7) Do not touch the power adapter with wet hands or allow liquids to spill on it.
8) Do not use the power adapter from another laptop without insuring it is the different voltage, you can severely damage the laptop otherwise.
9) When travelling to a foreign destination, make sure your adapter is compatible with the local electricity supply and outlets. Enquire about voltage, line frequency, and outlet type before leaving. Obtain a plug adapter if all else is OK, otherwise obtain a compatible power adapter or do not bring your computer.
10) Avoid using the laptop in extreme heat and avoid rapid temperature changes larger than 15C. This has detrimental affects on both the computer and adapter.
11) The stress relief entrance of the DC power cable into the adapter body can be damaged by being abused. Avoid bending it tightly. Damage to your DC power cable usually means adapter replacement.
12) Do not disassemble the power adapter.

3.2   Eliminating laptop power problems and the repair flow chart

3.2.1   The techniques and shortcuts to troubleshoot Laptop Power Problems

If your laptop does not power up at all, or starts but will not boot, you can solve these problems at home without sending them to a repair center. Here are some troubleshooting tips you can use to solve the problem, I may not have covered all situations, but I will update this as some come to mind, however, this is a good start.

1. The laptop is dead, after you plug into AC power. The indicator lights (power light, hard disk light, battery charging light etc . . .) are all out, and when you press Start button, the laptop doesn't respond at all.

   Generally, people judge a power adapter only by its power indicator light, if the power light is on, then it works, but if it's out, then the power adapter is not working. Actually, this is not the case. In my 20 years' repair experience the indicator light whether on or off is not necessarily an indication that the power adapter is faulty. Before coming to this conclusion you need to test it first.

Test the AC power output voltage at the end of the power cable nearest the adapter body with a voltmeter and then at the DC output jack. Optionally, find a good power adapter compatible with the laptop and try it. If either test does not identify an adapter problem, it may be a problem with the jack connection. Check it as explained in previous sections. According to my 20 years experience, the statistical power system failure rate reaches as much as 55%, and mostly comes from the power adapter and battery. Please take a look at Figure 3-1; 3-2.

Figure 3-1

If you have to replace your power adapter, make sure to use a compatible model, the output voltage must match the laptops requirement, and the output current must be the same as the original, or higher, but never lower than this value.

Figure 3-2

2. If your power adapter is deemed to be in good working condition, the issue is probably with the power board and most likely with the female power jack connector on the laptop. Please take a look at Figure 3-3.

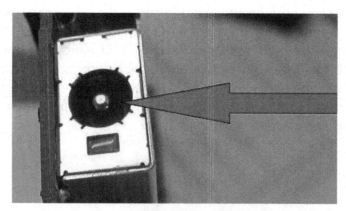

Figure 3-3

Here is an example: I plug the power adapter jack to the laptop, and then press it gently from side to side. I notice that the power indicator light on the front side of the laptop will flicker but the battery charging display light is still off. I removed the battery and try again, I noticed that when I removed the battery and plugged it in again, the laptop started, but as I moved the cord it turned off again. It seems the laptop's power connection jack is loose. If you have this problem, then most likely the issue is either with the power adapter jack or the female side on the laptop.

3. You can verify a jack connection problem with, a fully charged battery if you can find one. Make sure you use the same battery model, the output voltage must match with original battery model, and the output current should be the same too. If the laptop starts normally, then it is quite likely that the problem is with the power adapter or the power jack. If the laptop doesn't start then the issue may be with the power control area on the circuit board.

    According to my 20 years' repair statistic, 35% of power system failures come from the solder connection of the female power connector to the circuit board . . .

4. Repair shortcut for power system failure:

    a) Check the power adapter, or find a good power adapter to test your laptop.
    b) Check the power adapter jack and the power female jack on the circuit board, and ensure they are connected well. Replace either the jack on the adapter or the female jack on the laptop.
    c) Find a fully charged battery to test your laptop, check whether it starts normally. This will definitely narrow you're testing especially if notebook starts up normally, your success rate rises to as much as 90%. To see more details on this aspect, please go to 3.2.4 flowchart

    (Laptop power system failure analysis and repair progress)

3.2.2 55 % power system failures coming from the power adapter and battery

Power adapter:

- The Power adapter is the most important component of a laptop power system. It is generally, comprised of a shell, cables, power transformer, rectifying and filtering circuitry.
- Power adapters are not made to be repaired, and not worth the effort. They eventually will fail for one reason or the other due to component degradation with time and use, or abuse.

Here are a few examples of failure:

- The power adapter indicator light is off when plugged in the wall outlet.
- The power adapter output cable is damaged by pulling on it too often. This can cause insulation damage or bad connections at the jack or adapter body. Eventually the battery discharges and the computer cease to operate. This is a very common failure mode.
- The computer starts up normally with the adapter, but without the battery, the laptop does not start. Some older laptops need a battery to assist starting up, and this is normal, but it can also be a defective adapter problem.
- When the laptop powers on and starts up, you can hear arcing or other strange noises from the adapter, and you can feel obvious overheating when you hold the power adapter. Please take a look at Figure 3-4.

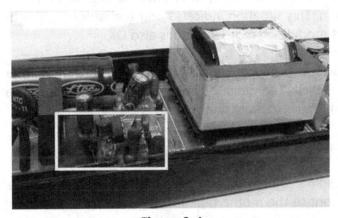

Figure 3-4

- The laptop power adapter sound is too loud, even worse, makes a "Groan" sound, it might start twice and then auto shut down by the internal protective circuits.

Battery:

- The common end-of-life failure of a laptop battery is when it no longer charges properly or has a short discharge time when fully charged. You might be able to restore some life back to the battery by several full charge and discharge cycles, but this has diminishing results and only delays the inevitable. Don't do it too often.
- Battery failure, can be caused by the internal circuit board in the battery, It can sometimes be repaired but is usually not worth it. You might be able to take apart the plastic shell of the battery, and when doing so, be careful not to damage the internal battery or the circuit board. It is a difficult process. Buying a new battery is the best way.

Here're some common battery failure examples:

1. The battery often fails to fully charge, or battery doesn't hold its charge for long.
2. The battery no longer holds its charge no matter how long you charge it.
3. The laptop no longer starts up when using the battery, and even when using the power adapter. If you remove the battery, it starts up normally. You might notice that the battery is a bit lighter when you remove it
4. The battery does not charge, overheats, or becomes discoloured during charging. Even worse, you may also experience a software freeze during charging.

3.2.3　35% Power system failures related to the DC jack on the laptop

The laptop fails to start up when using the power adapter without the battery, but works when the battery is in. This situation indicates that the laptop motherboard is OK, and the power management module on motherboard is also OK.

The problem likely lies with the connection between the power adapter and laptop power jack or the adapter itself. The circuitry between the laptop power jack and the power management module can also be at fault.

Here are some failure examples:

1. The DC Jack solder joint to the motherboard is broken; it becomes loose, and affects the power input to the motherboard. The power light goes on when you press the power adapter jack. Once you let it go, the power light dies suddenly. Please take a look at Figure 3-5.

Figure 3-5

2. The laptop doesn't start (therefore battery doesn't charge), when you pull and plug the power adapter. You find the jack pulls in and out too easily or is loose when plugged in. The jack connection might be hot to the touch

3. The power adapter indicator light is on, when it is plugged in, but the laptop only works for a short time, say 5 minutes to 1 hour, and then it auto shuts down. The adapter light remains on.

4. The laptop charging indicator light is intermittently on/off, the DC Jack turns hot, and the machine suddenly shuts down.

3.2.4 Failure analysis and repair flow chart for a laptop power system

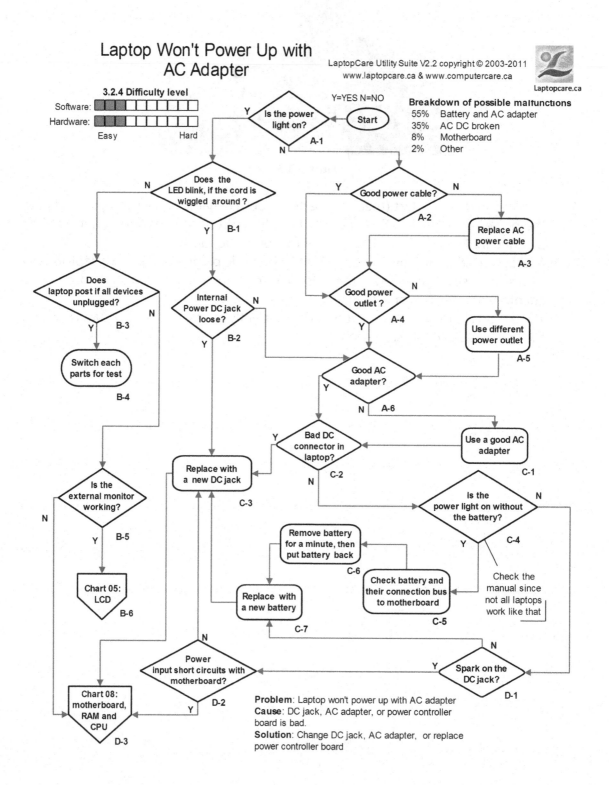

Laptop Won't Power Up with AC Adapter

LaptopCare Utility Suite V2.2 copyright © 2003-2011
www.laptopcare.ca & www.computercare.ca

Laptopcare.ca

3.2.4 Difficulty level

Software: ▆▆▆☐☐☐☐☐☐☐
Hardware: ▆▆▆☐☐☐☐☐☐☐
Easy   Hard

Y=YES N=NO

Breakdown of possible malfunctions
55% Battery and AC adapter
35% AC DC broken
8%   Motherboard
2%   Other

Start

Is the power light on? A-1

Does the LED blink, if the cord is wiggled around? B-1

Good power cable? A-2

Replace AC power cable A-3

Does laptop post if all devices unplugged? B-3

Internal Power DC jack loose? B-2

Good power outlet? A-4

Use different power outlet A-5

Switch each parts for test B-4

Good AC adapter? A-6

Use a good AC adapter C-1

Replace with a new DC jack C-3

Bad DC connector in laptop? C-2

Is the power light on without the battery? C-4

Is the external monitor working? B-5

Remove battery for a minute, then put battery back C-6

Check the manual since not all laptops work like that

Chart 05: LCD B-6

Replace with a new battery C-7

Check battery and their connection bus to motherboard C-5

Power input short circuits with motherboard? D-2

Spark on the DC jack? D-1

Chart 08: motherboard, RAM and CPU D-3

Problem: Laptop won't power up with AC adapter
Cause: DC jack, AC adapter, or power controller board is bad.
Solution: Change DC jack, AC adapter, or replace power controller board

78

This tutorial will help you troubleshoot power up problems with the ac adapter.

1. You plug-in the power adapter, press the power start button and you do not hear normal starting sounds. Indicator LEDs do not light and the fan also does not rotate. The adapter LED in ON.
2. When moving the power adapter cable with the laptop running, it auto powers off or various indicator lights on your laptop flicker. The battery charge light also flashes intermittently.
3. The laptop only works when powered by the battery. The power adapter only holds 1-2 minutes' charging, or in the worst case, the laptop will not start up.

In this article, I will explain how to find the cause of the problem—"power adapter does not start the laptop". Theses clues will work for all brands and models of laptops.

Step: 1

Assessment Procedure.

When you press the power button, and there is no sound or power LED indicates on your laptop, keep in mind that the power switch itself might be defective. You might notice that the power switch does not feel right when you push it; maybe it is binding or pushes in too far. If you sure of it, please to fix this power switch. You need to be satisfied that this is not your problem before proceeding. If it feels right, it is probably OK

Begin with Step A-1 on the flowsheet,

Decision Y. When plugged into a laptop power adapter, is the power light on? If the power light is on, then your problem may be still related to the power adapter or the power cable connected to the laptop. Enter Step: B-1 on the flowsheet to troubleshoot.

Decision N. Adapter plugged in and the laptop power LED is off. Your problem may be with the power cord or the mains power, please enter Step: A-2 to troubleshoot.

When connecting the power adapter and pressing the start button, Pay close attention to your laptop's LCD screen.

1. **Black screen and the laptop power light off.**
    -   If the LCD is dark and the laptop's power indicator light is also out, the problem is not covered by this article,
    -   Use (04) laptop LCD display tutorial guide.
2. **When moving the power adapter cable, the power light flickers**
    -   Follow STEP B-1 N on the flowsheet.
    -   if you haven't moved the power adapter cable or have not touched the jack, and the laptop indicator light still flickers and unstable,
    -   please check another tutorial guide

3. The laptop works only when powered by the battery.
  -    Please check another tutorial guide,

If you have not identified the fault after following the instructions above, you can refer to chapter2 of the <<2.1 common laptop failures to determine>> section called: The 6 Classification Methods, to determine another possible procedure to use. If this does not help, use the principle to troubleshoot the easiest things first and the more complex items after. Follow the tutorials, step by step for any troubleshooting you decide to do.

Step: A-1

Let's take a look two different situations:

Situation 1: The laptop is totally dead

When you plug in the power adapter and press the start button, and there is no response, no start sound, no LED light display, the fan also doesn't rotate. Nothing appears on the screen etc, the laptop does not start. Under these circumstances, your problem might be with the power adapter or power connection cable. Please enter STEP: A-2

Situation 2: There is power but no start up

-Press the start button, the laptop power light is on but laptop doesn't start.

When moving the power adapter cable, the power light and battery charging light on the front of the laptop flickers and is unstable. Please enter STEP: B-1

Go to Step A2 if the power LED on the laptop is off

STEP: A-2: This step is to ensure that your power adapter cable is good.

First make sure that the AC power cable is connected properly and plugged into a working power outlet. Is the power adapter LED on? If not you may have a fault in the power adapter body or something is wrong with the power cables. You can follow section 3.1.3. to perform a complete adapter power check or Proceed to STEP: A-3

STEP: A-3

This step will identify problems with the AC power cable, by trying a new cable or using a confirmed good cable to test the power adapter problem. If your problem is not solved continue to STEP: A-4

STEP: A-4

This step ensures there is power at your wall outlet. Plug in any other AC device (such as a desk lamp) and see if it works. If no, use a different power outlet (STEP A-5) and see if the LED on the power adapter is on. If no, check that outlet. If yes, go to STEP A-6

Note: If you do not have a LED on the power adapter the only way to check if it is working, is to measure the DC voltage on the jack at the end of the DC power cable. Please take a look at Figure 3-6.

Figure 3-6

STEP: A-5

This step is to suppose that the laptop problem is due to a bad internal connection in wall power jack, which disables the supply of power to the laptop. So you should try another wall jack or use a confirmed working wall jack to test the power supply problem. If this step doesn't help, then please continue STEP: A-6

STEP: A-6

The goal of this step is to confirm that your power adapter is good and that the laptop is getting power from the adapter. Many people assume that as long as the power adapter light is on, the adapter is working, and they do not check to make sure it is working. This is a mistake. We've encountered many cases, which prove this point. You need to verify that the adapter is working even though the LED is on or you may do a lot of unnecessary troubleshooting and not solve your problem. I recommend doing the following:

1. Whether the adapter light is on or not, use a multimeter to test it. Measure the DC voltage at the jack on the end of the DC cable. The voltage should be close to the value specified on the adapter nameplate. Generally an HP adapter voltage is between 18.5-19.5V. This will validate whether the output voltage is correct and confirm that the power adapter is working in most cases, but there is an exception. Some power adapters do not have an output without a load on the jack (not plugged

in). When there is no load, the adapter output voltage is 0. In this case do not assume the adapter is defective. You will need a further test. Item 2 below is one possibility.

2. If you don't have a multi-meter or you cannot use a multi-meter or the output voltage was 0, you can use a known good laptop that has the same type of jack, the same voltage, and equal or lower current rating on its adapter as a load. Remove the battery from the laptop and try it with the suspect adapter. If it starts, then the power adapter is good; otherwise, it's an issue with the power adapter, which you should replace or repair.

3. Another method used by technicians is to calculate a resistor ohms and watts and connect it to the jack to provide a load. Then measure the voltage. R=V/I, W=VI.

4. Otherwise proceed to STEP C-1

If you confirmed that the adapter is good, continue with STEP: C-2 or STEP B-1

STEP: B-1

This step checks the connection of the power adapter to the laptop power jack.

Let's take a look at the two different situations Y/N:

Situation 1: laptop power indicator light is on, but it doesn't blink. (N)

When you plug the power adapter and press the power start button, the laptop power light is on, but there is no start-up sound or activity. Pressing of wiggling the jack does not affect the power indicator light, it is on and stable. This means there is no problem with the power adapter jack male/female part. The problem is somewhere else. Go to STEP: B-3

Situation 2: laptop power light unstable but blinking. (Y)

When I plug-in the power adapter, the battery LED goes on and it begins charging. However, when I am not touching the adapter jack, the battery LED is off and it stops charging. The laptop power light flickers or goes off. It indicates that the laptop power adapter jack male/female is defective. If you observe this, go to STEP: B-2

STEP: B-2

This step checks the condition of the power jack input to the laptop.

If you notice that the DC jack connection to the laptop is overheating, and/or power LED instability, you know there is a problem with that connection. It can be caused by a loss of spring tension, or a bad solder joint on the internal end of the jack. First make sure the problem is not somehow caused by the power adapter. You should have already checked that in, STEP: A6 otherwise do so now. If the adapter is OK go to STEP C-3

STEP: B-3 Troubleshooting the laptop fittings

When you plug-in the power adapter and press the power switch button, the laptop begins making sounds, the LED light shows normally, but there's nothing on the screen. The laptop still doesn't start. Disconnect all external accessories. Does the laptop work now? If Y, go to STEP B-4. If N go to STEP B-5

Use an external monitor to test your laptop screen. Connect the external monitor to the VGA video port on the laptop. Check your manual to determine the process to use an external monitor. Press FN and F4 keys on an HP laptop at the same time, to switch the video output mode between the laptop monitor and the external monitor.

If the external monitor displays normally, but the laptop LCD screen still has no output, your problem might be with the LCD screen or video connection cable. Go to STEP: B-6

If the external monitor does not work, the laptop main board or accessories may be the problem, Continue to STEP D-3 Flow Chart 08.

Try reassembling your memory module, probably the memory stick is not plugged in the correct slot, try cleaning the memory stick with an eraser and moving to the other memory slot, or try using another good memory stick to replace the old one. Probably the old one is broken.

If you have two memory modules, you may try removing them one by one, by doing the elimination method, you may find that there's one bad or broken module, you could also try plugging different memory sticks into different slots. If the method doesn't help, then I'm definitely sure it's not a memory issue, so let's move on to the next troubleshooting section.

Try removing the battery, HDD, DVD-ROM and start the machine without these components

If it doesn't start normally, then I guess the issue may be with the fittings that are still on the laptop, so you should continue dismantling the laptop.

I would continue disassembling the machine part by part and then test step by step by restarting after every removal. If it didn't help when you removed the HDD and DVD-ROM, then it would be useless to disconnect the video connection cable.

Remove wireless network card, modem, and disconnect the keyboard connection . . . if you still have no success and the laptop doesn't start. Please enter STEP: B-5

Please pay attention: please make sure the video output cable is connected well between motherboard and monitor. Try reconnecting and resetting the position of the connection cable. If it now works, then please enter STEP: B-4

STEP: B-4, the objective of this step is to identify the failed hardware device.

How do you determine the reason why a laptop will not start? Which hardware device is causing your problem? The simplest way is to strip the laptop down to the minimum components needed for it to operate, and start troubleshooting there.

This method has already been introduced in the first chapter <<1.4.1 Use the simplest method for repair judgment>>, which is the hardware minimum system configuration explained in the B) article. At a minimum, in order to operate, a laptop needs a power adapter, motherboard, and CPU. No other connection or device is needed and we test it by observing that the fan is working and listening for normal sounds. If this test reveals a problem, you know it is in the motherboard or CPU because you have previously checked the adapter, and the power jack input connector condition.

The procedure to be followed is this: remove the wireless network card, modem, screen, keyboard battery, hard drive, DVD/CD drive, PCMCIA card, USB device and Mini PCI interface card. Restart the laptop to check whether the failure symptom disappears. If the failure symptom does disappear, you re-install each item, one at a time, and test each time until the failure re-appears. You now know which device is defective and can repair or replace it.

Important! Each time you work on the laptop, you must first shut down the laptop, pull out the AC adapter, and remove the battery, then start your work.

An optional method is to use parts from another working laptop to test the parts in the defective one. This is a risky process as you might end out with 2 defective laptops.

If in minimum configuration, the failure symptom does not disappear, recheck the power system components as described in previous sections, especially the power jack connection to the motherboard. If this step doesn't help solve the problem, then go to STEP: D-3;

A typical example of the use of the minimum configuration to troubleshoot a laptop is as follows: Your laptop does not respond when the ON switch is pressed. It operates normally in the minimum configuration. I shut down the laptop, and install the wireless network card. I restart the laptop to test, and the laptop starts normally. The wireless card is OK. I shut down the laptop and install the Modem card to test again. This time there is no activity on the screen. The screen is black, after this result; I can conclude that the problem must be in the Modem card.

To verify this conclusion, I re-assemble the laptop without the modem card. If it now operates normally a modem failure is confirmed. Install a new modem card and recheck the laptop to make sure it is still operating normally.

After successful repair of a laptop a full operational check must be performed.

The following checks are recommended:

-Time test

Check the time and date posted on the laptop. Correct it if necessary. Entering the Bios is not necessary.

-Keyboard test

Check that all keys on the keyboard are performing their function. This includes function keys, arrow keys and touchpad. Nothing is excluded.

-DVD-ROM/CD-ROM test

Check that the DVD-ROM/CD-ROM reads and writes normally, and the speed is correct;

-Mouse test

Check that the touchpad and serial mouse functions are OK;

-Fan test

Check that the fan functions properly;

-FIR test

Check that the infrared function (Ir, Sir, Fir) is OK;

-Shortcut buttons test

Check that the shortcut button function is OK;

-Network card test

Connect the high speed internet cable and verify that internet access is achieved or a request for password appears.

-Audio test

Check that the audio interface functions, both input, and output, and the sound decoding chip function is OK;

-LCD display test

Observe that the LCD screen is functioning correctly;

-1349 test

Check that the 1394 interface function is OK by the application matched with 1394 connection cable and host;

Check that the system electrical performance is all right with application;

-External display test

Check that the VGA interface function works properly by connecting an external monitor;

-Hibernation lever test

Check that the hibernation mode is functioning;

-SFT test

Check whether the entire system function is OK or not;

-Modem test

Check that the modem is functioning by connecting the telephone line and dialling your cell phone.

-USB test

Check that the USB interface is functioning by inserting a flash drive.

-PCMCIA test

Check that the PCMCIA interface is functioning;

-SPDIF test

Check the SPDIF infrared output functions of the audio interface;

-S port, AV port test

Check the TV output S port and AV port

Battery test

-Use the battery until the laptop auto shuts down, observe the battery working time.

-Test finishes.

Note: During the minimum configuration troubleshooting process, you may find that no device is defective, and the computer starts up normally. By plugging in and out the various components you likely cleared up a connector problem. Sometimes a bit of luck is needed to reach a satisfactory conclusion

STEP: B-5, the goal of this step is to ensure that all components are well seated.

I have disassembled the computer part by part, and tested them one by one. When complete and I have still not resolved the problem, I remove the motherboard.

In this picture, you can see the final result; a fully disassembled laptop with motherboard removed.

1. Motherboard, just like on most laptops, in this case the graphic card is integrated on the motherboard.
2. CPU thermal flake and thermal fan
3. Confirmed good memory stick
4. Start button control board, used to boot system.
5. Available external power supply.

Please take a look at Figure 3-7

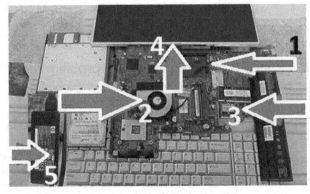

Figure 3-7

However, there is still no video information received by the external monitor, although the system is running, and the thermal fan is rotating but the screen is still black.

Note: If there's still no image on the LCD screen of the laptop, then you should use an external monitor to test your laptop. Connect the external monitor to the VGA video port on the laptop. Press FN and F4 keys on an HP laptop at the same time' to switch the video output mode between the laptop monitor and external monitor. For a Toshiba laptop, the combination is Fn and F5 keys, IBM is Fn and F7, other brands may use different combinations.

If the external monitor displays normally, but the laptop LCD screen still has no output, your problem might be with the LCD screen or video the connection cable. Go to STEP: B-6

If the external monitor remains black after the system started, and the fan is rotating, I am 95% sure there is a motherboard problem. Generally a CPU failure is rare, so the possibility of a motherboard failure is more likely. Go to STEP: D-3

STEP: B-6, Refer to (Chapter 05) laptop LCD display tutorial article

STEP: C-1

This step will finally determine if the problem is with the laptop or the power adapter. Use a confirmed good power adapter of equal voltage and equal or higher current, to test if it is the power supply. Remove the suspect adapter from the laptop, remove the battery, wait for 1 to 2 minutes, and then plug in the good adapter, and restart the laptop.

1. If it starts successfully, under these circumstances, your problem was your power adapter. Replace it with a new/used adapter suited to the laptop. i.e. the same voltage and equal or higher current rating.
2. If replacing the adapter does not solve the problem, the problem may exist in the input power jack or the motherboard. It will most likely be an input power jack problem, either in the jack itself or the connection to the motherboard. Under these circumstances, you would have to disassemble the laptop and replace the input power jack. You may check out this article: http://www.computercare.ca/forum/showthread. php?t=3747

    And Go to STEP: C-2

STEP: C-2, the goal of this step is to determine if the problem resides in the input power jack. Let's take a look at two different situations below:

1. When moving the external power supply, the battery stops charging.

    This laptop has a problem when I move the power adapter or DC cable and observe that the battery LED flickers or goes out. If I position the adapter and cable in a certain way, sometimes it will work as long as I do not move anything. I might notice the jack connection gets hot. This is likely a problem with the input power jack. To further confirm your suspicion, shut down the computer, remove the battery, and restart. If the laptop does not power up, but does so if you move the adapter or cable or it powers up but goes off when you disturb the adapter or cable, your suspicion is confirmed. Go to STEP: C-3

2. The laptop power light is always out. Due to normal wear from plugging in and out, the, DC Jack is the most common component that fails on a laptop. Check the input power jack by unplugging the AC cord, plugging in the DC jack and wiggling it to see if some thing is loose or broken. If the answer is YES, go to STEP: C-3

If the jack feels firm when you plug it in and it does not move when you wiggle the jack, it is not likely a jack problem. Go to STEP: C-4

Step: C-3

This step is to replace the broken DC Jack

STEP: C-3 the target of this step is to change the damaged power jack

Disclaimer: this repair manual is intended for those who have soldering and computer repair experience. We cannot be responsible for work carried out by unqualified individuals.

For this repair, the following is required:

1. Laptop disassembly experience and laptop professional service manuals.
2. Soldering techniques and tools. These have been explained in the manual about changing the power jack provided elsewhere.
3. Inexpensive replacement jacks can be found here:

    http://www.computercare.ca/home.php?cat=250

The content above is only for the technicians who have the relevant experience. Without this you may damage your laptop. If you feel that you are not suitable for this job, then please do not attempt this repair. You should take your laptop to a professional repair shop.

If you decide to fix it up manually by yourself, then start by, disassembling your laptop. Take the motherboard out then read the article <<How to change power jack>>. Here you will find disassembly instructions for some well known laptop brands (http://laptoprepair.ca/category/25.html), such as IBM, Dell, HP, Compaq, Toshiba and Sony. If your laptop brand is not on the list, then you will have to rely on your own skill to disassemble it.

Now the situation of this case is like this: the laptop motherboard power jack is loose, and leads to the problem that the laptop does not start with the power adapter. Carefully resolder the jack pins to the motherboard. Check the solder connections with a multimeter, and if

OK, reassemble and restart the laptop. If the failure still exists you will have to dissemble the laptop again and follow the next steps.

1) Recheck the solder points with a multimeter.
2) Connect the adapter and apply voltage to the motherboard. Measure the output voltage of the jack where it connects to the motherboard. If OK removes the adapter, clean up the dust and check the components one by one, for signs of damage. Assuming no abnormal symptoms are found and the problem still exists continue below.
3) The possibility is a defective jack. It is best to just replace it, but assuming you are not in a position to do that and you need the laptop, you can try this.

   Turn off power switch, and remove the adapter. Use a tiny straight screwdriver to adjust the inside contacts of the jack. Alternately insert the straight screwdriver to both sides of the metal contacts inside of the jack and try to bend them towards the centre a bit. This will tighten up the connection.

4) Attention: when doing this work be gentle. You can push the jack assembly inwards so that the jack cannot properly plug in when the laptop is assembled, and thus you have created more problems for yourself
5) If you have not cleared up the problem at this point, the jack assembly will have to be replaced.

After the power jack has been repaired or changed, and the problem is not fixed, you likely have a motherboard problem.

continue to STEP: D-3

Step: C-4

They are many reasons why a laptop screen does not operate or post.

One is the battery. A battery failure can cause the adapter to self protect and there is no power to the laptop. It may restart if you remove the battery but some laptops can work only with the power adapter and others need both. Refer to your owner's manual for further information.

Situation 1: Laptop may start with the power adapter and the battery removed

After removing the battery, the laptop recovers and the power light shows normal, but it still doesn't start. It is possible that the laptop BIOS is locked in a self-protection state. So the next thing I really recommend and worth a try is:

1. Pull out the AC power.
2. And then press power button continually about 30 to 60 seconds.
3. Reconnect AC power and start the laptop.

If step C-4 doesn't help, please continue STEP: D-1

Situation 2: for laptops that require the battery for start-up. If the power light is not on and the laptop does not start with both the adapter and battery, try removing the battery. If the power light turns on you have a defective battery. Confirm this by reinstalling the battery and observing that the power light is off.

If this happens proceed to STEP: C-5

Situation 3: After removing the battery, the laptop power light doesn't show, and the laptop doesn't start. This indicates there is no DC power reaching the motherboard. The problem exists somewhere between the wall plug and the power connection to the motherboard. We have covered troubleshooting techniques for this in sec.4.

If this doesn't help you locate the problem, please continue STEP: D-1

Step: C-5

A bad connection between the battery and the laptop motherboard may cause the failure to start up the computer. To start with you should always check the battery connection to the motherboard. The pin condition is important as well as the connections to the motherboard.

Batteries all have very thin connector pins. Please check the interior connection pins to ensure none are broken or bent. You can straighten the bended pin with a small screwdriver, but be patient and focused during the process.

If it fails to work after reinstalling the battery, check all connection cables again, check the connector pins on the laptop motherboard, examine them closely, you might not have noticed that some pins are still bent. Ensure the connector pins on the motherboard are working correctly and perfectly.

Fortunately, most new laptops already use different types of improved connectors that are more rugged and dependable, If this step doesn't solve the problem, please continue STEP: C-6

Step: C-6

Connector pins can become oxidised when exposed to a damp environment. Of course the connector pins on the battery are no exception. Generally, when metal pins are not oxidised, they would shine, while oxidised metal pins would be dark or even become black. Make sure the internal connector pins are not discoloured with tobacco tar dust residue on them. You can use a little sharp knife to clear the dust or oxidation. During the process be very careful to make sure there's isn't any bent, misplaced or broken pins. All right, now reinstall the battery and see if the laptop works. If not continue with the next step. STEP: C-7

Step: C-7

Install a new battery identical to the old one. This is because different versions of BIOS have different abilities to recognize a new battery. Generally speaking, old versions of BIOS have limited capability to recognise new batteries. If you use different type of new battery (meaning compatible number); the problem of BIOS versions can cause unexpected situations and increase the difficulty to repair it. Some batteries seem exactly same, but actually they are totally incompatible. Using this kind of new battery will only create more problems.

If you solve the problem by changing new battery, then you should still check whether the new battery installed is not loose, the size is proper, or whether the connector is too tight and might interfere with ongoing operation.

Check the installation of the new battery. It should feel exactly like the old one when being inserted. If not like this, try again to make sure you are doing it properly. After reinstalling the new battery and there is not an error, but the laptop still will not work with the external power supply, continue to STEP: C-3;

Step: D-1

When you plug in the adapter first into the wall outlet, and then plug the jack into the computer you may see a tiny spark. If you plug in the computer first and then plug the adapter into the wall outlet you may also see a spark but that is normal. A spark occurring when you plug the adapter into the laptop can cause damage to the motherboard. This is due to not following the proper procedure, which is plugging into the wall outlet first and next plugging into the laptop. In this case, there will be no spark.

If later you hear "Zizi . . . sizzling or sparking noise when you plug the jack into the computer, then the jack or the input may have been damaged by the sparking. This sound may be almost inaudible but it is serious. There is damage due to a poor connection, and it will only get worse if not repaired. Eventually the motherboard or the adapter may fail.

If yes, then enter **Step: D-2** to continue validation

If not, then enter **Step: C-3** to continue validation

Step: D-2

Physical or electrical damage in the laptop can cause a short circuit, which will over load the power of adapter, and the laptop will not start up. If you plug the adapter into the wall outlet and observe the indicator light on the adapter is on, but when you connect the laptop the light goes out, you likely have a short circuit failure in the laptop. If you try another adapter and see the same thing, you know that there is a short circuit.

We generally use the minimum system method to locate a short circuit failure in the laptop. Remove the battery, hard drive, DVD-ROM/CD-ROM, PCMCIA card, USB devices and Mini-PCI interface card. Restart the laptop to check whether the failure symptom disappears or not. If the short circuit failure is eliminated, then you can use "Rebuilding the system to add and subtract" to judge and locate the failure part. A process of elimination is used. If the short circuit exists in the minimum system, it is in the motherboard or whatever else is left. If not, add hardware one at a time and test until the short circuit appears. The last hardware added is at fault.

If in minimum system, the failure symptom doesn't disappear, then you can troubleshoot the fault further by checking the memory stick, CPU and the power jack on motherboard. Use a multimeter to measure ohms at the power jack. The resistance between the cylindrical metal and inside pin should not be less than 3 ohms. If it is, there is a short circuit which may be caused by distortion of the brass sheet. Normal resistance should be near (adapter voltage/ laptop current).

If there is, then please enter **Step: C-3** to continue validation;

If there is not, then please enter **Step: D-3** to continue validation

Step: D-3

Please check another tutorial article (in chapter 08) concerning the failure analysis for problems like laptop black screen or system was freezing.

3.3 Twenty-three Repair Cases for Laptop Power Failures

3.3.1 HP laptop—10 repair cases that laptop AC power adapter failure

001) HP Pavilion DV6 laptop power adapter cable failure:

Failure symptom:

Laptop screen is completely blank.

When you plug in the power adapter and press the start button, if there is no response with the start up, plus no sound and no LED light on, also there is no rotating fan and the laptop screen is blank.

Touch the on-off power switch carefully, if there is sound but you find that the power indicator light on the adapter is off, and then we conclude that you are not getting power from the power adapter.

Solution:

This failure symptom belongs to the description of flowchart 03 that belongs to this repair sequence:

Start->A-1->A-2->A-3;

Repair summary:

First pull out the power adapter cable, and then plug it back in ensuring the connection is good. Plug the power adapter back into the wall the result is that if, the power adapter indicator light is still off; In this case change it with a new adapter and the problem is solved.

Hint: this issue happens quite often as the power adapter cable sometimes get loose, resulting in the adapter failing to supply power. The solution is to pull out the cable and then plug it back in its original place. But many people think that such a thick cable wouldn't not get loose. Most people will go out and buy a new adapter to solve the problem, which is unnecessary and a total waste of money.

002) Compaq Presario V2000 laptop power failure:

Failure symptom:

The power adapter this client uses has no power indicator light. When you plug the power adapter and power up the laptop, the laptop power light is off, and the laptop screen is blank, so you would suspect it is a power adapter issue. What you should do is see if there another of the same laptop around test the adapter and probably you will find that the power adapter works. Then you send the laptop to the repair store. Strangely, during your testing process, no problem is found.

Solution:

This failure symptom belongs to the description of flow chart 03, which belongs to this repair sequence:

Start->A-1->A-2->A-4->A-5;

Repair summary:

After the technician arrives at the client's office, he unplugs the power cable of the adapter, and plugs it back in to ensure it is well connected. He plugs it back into the wall jack and then found out that the laptop power indicator light is still off, he tries another jack on the wall and the problem is solved.

Hint: The client confirms that the power adapter worked, but neglected to verify the wall jack. If the laptop power adapter has no indicator light, Make sure the wall jack is not the problem by testing it with a working lamp/light.

003)   HP Compaq 8510p Business Notebook power adapter failure:

Failure symptom:

When the adapter is plugged in, the indicator light is on, but when you press the start button, the laptop has no sound or LED light. The laptop screen is also blank. The client claims that the power adapter was purchased not long ago and had no issues with it. The possibility may be a loose power jack on the motherboard that causes a charge failure. The laptop will only last until all of the batteries power has run out.

Solution:

This failure symptom belongs to the description of flow chart 03, which belongs to this repair sequence:

Start->A-1->B->B-0->A-6->C-1;

Repair summary:

Experience tells us that whether the power adapter light is on or not, you should use a voltage meter to test the power adapter in order to confirm whether it is working properly or not. HP power adapter voltage generally is around 18.5~19.5V. You can then validate whether the output voltage is normal or not according to the instruction on the adapter. However, some power adapters have voltage output when they are loading. It is then difficult to judge. So by using a known good adapter to test the issued laptop it may solve the problem from the beginning.

Hint: It is quite important when repairing a laptop to first, test the power adapter to see whether it is working or not. But, be very careful because even though it may seem that an adapter is working because the light is on, it does not necessarily mean there is not an issue with it. I have seen many cases where, when testing an adapter with a tester it has failed. So never assume or avoid testing it, as it may avoid having to continue troubleshooting.

004)   HP dv5t laptop power adapter overheating failure:

Failure symptom:

Laptop power adapter suddenly stops working, but during the past two weeks, when it was running normally it would enter in battery mode without any symptoms. Most times, the battery indicator light is yellow (charging state) which means the power adapter is still working. Yesterday, it auto jumped to battery mode automatically again, and after that, it never returned back to normal state and the power adapter is very warm.

Solution: This failure symptom belongs to the flow chart 03 that belongs to this repair sequence:

Start->A-1->B->B-0->A-6->C-1;

Repair summary:

The failure symptom above indicates that the laptop power adapter has some hardware problems or the charge circuit of the laptop motherboard has some kind of failure. First change with a confirmed working power adapter to test and the problem is solved.

Hint: under some circumstances, the power adapter may not be hot. Because as an electrical power carrier, it is quite normal for the power adapter to be somewhat warm. If testing it with another adapter and it becomes hot, it may be that your adapter is too small or there may be an issue with the power jack on the laptop motherboard.

005) DV9000t laptop power adapter error causes auto shutdown failure:

Failure symptom:

After the laptop system loads the BIOS, the laptop auto shuts down, 5 seconds later;

1. Connect the old battery without the external power supply—the laptop starts and works;
2. Pull out the old battery with the external power supply—the laptop loads Windows and the laptop auto shut downs 10 seconds later:
3. Try shaking the power jack pins of the laptop, feeling the connection, check if it is loose or not and whether there is a broken connection pin on the laptop or adapter.

Solution:

This failure symptom belongs to the description of flow chart 03 that belongs to the repair sequence:

Start->A-1-> B->B-0->A-6->C-1;

Repair summary:

By changing with a good working power adapter, the problem is solved and the laptop is working normally.

Hint: DV9000t laptop power adapter needs at least 70W, but if the adapter is too old, it cannot reach 70W output power, or use several laptop devices at the same time, such as watching a DVD movie and downloading a software package. If there are other external devices consuming power, such as USB fan, then the output power needed should be higher. So a 90W output voltage power adapter is even better.

Generally, HP Pavilion DV SERIES laptop power adapters all use a general standard pin, except for the HP Pavilion DV9000 which is a little different; please check the pin of the adapter carefully, whether it is the same as the pin of the original laptop power adapter. If it is not, check it as carefully as you can, when you plug it to the HP DV9000 laptop motherboard, Verify that the interface LED shows a blue light, and it is stable. If there is no blue light out or the light is unstable, then it means the power adapter cannot be used on a HP Pavilion DV9000 laptop.

006) HP540-259 laptop always makes a sizzle sound and power adapter fails:

Failure symptom:

HP 540-259 laptop makes a sizzle sound right from the beginning when using it. Although the sound is not loud, it can be heard clearly from the power jack. The power adapter begins to heat up around 15 minutes after it has been plugged in and laptop is not running well or auto shuts down.

Solution:

This failure symptom belongs to the description of flow chart 03 that belongs to this repair sequence:

Start->A-1->B->A-6->C-1;

Repair summary:

By starting the issued laptop with a new working power adapter, the problem is solved.

Hint: Generally, a bad connection occurs between the pin and jack. When the pin is inserted into the laptop charge jack, there is a slight short that occurs. And after that, you can hear a sizzling sound around the jack and pin. Although the sound is very low, this is not normal. The cause is a slightly damaged power adapter and it should be changed as it may cause damage or burn the laptop motherboard

007)   HP COMPAQ X6000 laptop power adapter always makes sizzling sound:

Failure symptom:

HP COMPAQ X6000 laptop makes a sizzling sound right after it begins working. The sound is very sharp but not loud, but you can clearly hear it from the power adapter and then it is gone.

Solution:

This failure symptom belongs to the description of flow chart 03 this belongs to the repair sequence:

Start->A-1->B->A-6->C-1;

Repair summary:

By changing to a confirmed good power adapter, the problem is solved.

Hint

1.   Power adapter's function is to act as a transformer + rectifier. It transforms AC 110V/220V through the transformer and turns to DV 18.5V through rectifier. During the process electrical power is consumed. The consumed electrical power turns to heat, that is why power adapters get warm. But it is different if it overheats as, it is an indication there is a problem.
2.   Current power saving technology used in the laptop industry saves power to the most extent on software and hardware basis, which prolongs the battery life. This method includes the situation when CPU is free, it forces the system to enter "Low consumption mode". Laptops switch quite frequently between normal working mode and low consumption mode, which makes the power supply circuitry to form power waves with the same frequency. This way, power supply circuit produces normal high-frequency noise without any worry
3.   After the transformer is powered on, magnetic flux forms. The function of the magnetic flux is to let the contact between the coil of the transformer and the magnetic core to create a very weak sizzle sound (buzz), This is normal. But if the sound gets too loud, then there is an issue with the adapter.

There are many reasons causing such a problem:

➤   power leak from filter capacitor
➤   the core is broken;
➤   short circuit occurs among circles;
➤   other parts are damaged etc.

008)   HP Presario CQ40 laptop auto shutdown failure:

Failure symptom:

- Sometimes laptop auto shuts down without any warning;
- When you vibrate the power adapter at the back of your laptop, power indicator light and charging light begin flashing. Battery does not charge.

Solution:

This failure symptom belongs to the description of flow chart 03 which belongs to this repair sequence:

Start->A-1->B->B-0->B-1->B-2->A-6-C-1;It is oobvious this failure is with the motherboard power jack.

Repair summary:

Enter B-0 link, test the power adapter with a multi-meter, the output voltage is OK, 18.5V;

Enter B-1 link, move the power adapter around, left and right, about 10 times, and power is off 1 time. It seems there is something wrong with the power adapter pins and the laptop internal power jack.

Enter B-2 link; check the soldering point at the bottom of the DC jack with a magnifier, whether there is a tiny crack. Also check the AC power adapter pin carefully, whether there is noticeable trace of burning. Test the laptop motherboard power jack with a multi-meter, finding no problem.

Enter C-1 link; try changing to a new power adapter, to see if the problem is solved.

Hint: this case indicates that power adapter cable is broken inside or the external insulated cover is cracked after being pressed, resulting in not being able to supply power. Therefore, never allow the power cable to be stained with example food, drink, oil or insects, bugs or pets may lick or bite it and end up breaking it; do not let the power cable hang or stretch also avoid dropping it as it may or can damage the internal parts or the connector.

009)   HP dv9744ca laptop does not work normally in battery mode, but fails to start with the power adapter:

Failure symptom:

When using the power adapter to supply, the laptop does not start, but when using it in battery mode it works. However, when plugging the power adapter, the battery begins to charge. And when you remove your hands from the pin the battery stops charging and the laptop indicator light sometimes turns dark and sometimes flashes.

Solution:

This failure symptom belongs to the description of flow chart 03 that belongs to this sequence:

Start->A-1->B->-B-0->A-6->C-2->C-3 or Start-> A-1->B->-B-0->A-6->C-1;

Repair summary:

Enter A-6 link, test the power adapter with a multi-meter, the output voltage is OK, put the power adapter on another laptop, it works well.

Enter C-2 link, the laptop starts with the battery on, which indicates that the laptop motherboard is OK, test the vacant loading state voltage with a multi-meter, and you will find an issue with a loose power jack

Enter C-3-> link, after changing the power jack, the failures gone.

Hint: when failure happens to the laptop, there are usually two accessories that have problems. So you should check the original power jack for any damages or cracks, and then move to the power jack to see if it is loose. If it is, changing your power adapter will definitely not solve your issue so you need to repair the pins and then decide whether to replace the adapter

010) HP HDX18-1058ca laptop does not start up when connected with power adapter:

Failure symptom:

According to the client's recollection, before the laptop got the failure, there was a charging issue problem. The laptop did not start until the battery power ran out. Then when only using the power adapter, the laptop did not start even when changing it with a new one.

Solution:

This failure symptom belongs to the description of flow chart 03, which belongs to the repair sequence:

Start-> A-1->B->-B-0->B-1->B-2->C-3; or Start->A-1->B->-B-0->A-6->C-2->C-3

Repair summary: Previously, if the laptop started with battery is work fine, then it means the laptop motherboard is OK; the power management module on motherboard is all right.

Then the problem should be with the laptop power adapter or the power jack is loose. After changing the power jack and plugging the original power adapter, the situation changes: the power indicator light sometimes turns dark or flashes but once you change the power adapter, the problem is solved.

Hint: this is a typical failure caused by two issues happening at the same time. So after checking the adapter for damages or cracks and replacing the power jack the issue is resolved.

3.3.2 HP laptop—6 repair cases where laptop does not start up with power adapter

011) HP pavilion 6725us laptop power adapter is not recognized and system does not start:

Failure symptom:

Laptop does not recognize the power adapter but after starting the laptop with the battery, the indicator light begins flashing, and the screen lights up once then quickly goes blank. Plug the power adapter, and no matter how you move the adapter cable the laptop gets no power and the laptop is dead.

Solution:

This failure symptom belongs to the description of flow chart 03 that belongs to the repair sequence:

Start->A-1->B->-B-0->A-6->C-2->C-3

Repair summary:

Enter A-6 link, power pin is one of the parts of a laptop which can easily get broken. First, take a look at the power adapter pins, whether it is broken or loose, and then test it on another laptop, finding the result is OK;

Enter C-2 link, according to the repair path, start the issued laptop, and then move the power jack gently with a little screwdriver to find out if the pins are cracked

Enter C-3 link, after changing the power jack, the problem is solved.

Hint: because of the bad distortion of the power adapter pin and jack, working under large current environment, the distorted jack overheats so the soldering point of the motherboard and the jack expands and when the laptop is shut off the components no longer shrinks back properly. With time the repeated expanding and shrinking of the soldering points of the jack end up cracking because of frequent pressure so the solder symptom appears creating a problem with the power adapter not being able to power up the laptop.

012) <u>**HP Pavilion dv3**</u> **no longer charges after 20 minutes and laptop auto switches to battery mode**

Failure symptom:

20 minutes later, laptop stops charging, and no longer starts with the power adapter and the pins heats up quite a bit and laptop also auto shuts off. Changing with a new power adapter does not resolve the issue either.

Solution:

This failure symptom belongs to the description of flow chart 03 that belongs to this sequence:

Start->A-1->B->B-0->A-6->C-1->C-2;

Repair summary:

Power jack heats up, which mean there is a bad connection failure between the laptop power jack and internal jack, changing the power adapter for testing does not change the issue so the indication is that the power jack has formed bad soldering on the motherboard. Solder the power jack again and the problem is solved.

Hint: this is typical with the power jack, especially when working under big current environment, the distorted part of the jack begins to heat up and approximately 20 minutes later, the soldering point of the jack un-solders itself due to expandability and the laptop no longer gets the required power it needs from the power adapter. After shutting down the machine or stopping to use the adapter, the overheating and expand factors disappear. The component begins shrinking to the right position. But when you start up the machine again the symptom re appears over and over again.

013) **HP pavilion dv5000 laptop auto shutdown failure when connected to the external power supply**

Failure symptom:

After the laptop works for over 6 hours non-stop, the power adapter suddenly makes a screeching sound and auto shuts down. After connecting the power adapter for the second time you can still hear the noise and is gradually increasing and the machine auto shuts down again without posting and does not power up in battery mode.

Solution:

This failure symptom belongs to the description of flow chart 03 that belongs to this sequence:

Start->A-1->B->->A-6->C-2->C-4->C-5->C-6->-C-7

Repair summary:

When you press the power switch button the laptop begins making sound and auto shuts down quickly,

Enter A-6 link, test the power adapter with a multi-meter, if the output voltage is normal, plug the power adapter to another laptop, and the problem is resolved;

Enter C-2 link, test the power jack with a multi-meter, and then test the circuitry one by one. The Laptop internal power jack should have no issues.

Enter C-4> link, when we remove the battery the laptop power indicator light shows normal, but when we plug the battery in again, the laptop power light dies out. It seems that the issue is with the laptop battery, so after changing it with a new battery, the failure is gone;

Hint: There are many reasons that can cause the laptop screen not to start, when a short circuit occurs inside the battery, such a failure would happen again. Would the laptop recover after removing the battery? It is not that simple, some laptops can start up with a single power adapter and without the battery in; but some laptops must have a battery to start up. When battery is changed, the laptop recovers normally and the power light displays, but it might fail to start up. The reason is that the laptops BIOS is locked in a self-protection state, so the next jobs below are really worth trying.

1. Pull out the AC power and remove the laptop battery;
2. Press the power button for 30 to 60 seconds and then release;
3. Reconnect the AC power and start the laptop.

014)   HP pavilion dv9644ca laptop LED light shows normally, but the screen is blank

Failure symptom:

HP Pavilion DV9644ca laptop falls off from the table while in use and no longer starts. When I press the power button, all the blue indicator lights are on, but the laptop screen is blank.

Solution:

This failure symptom belongs to the description of flow chart 03 that belongs to the repair sequence:

Start->A-1->B->B-0->B-1->B-3->B-4-> B-5

Repair summary:

Enter B-1 link, test the power adapter with a multi-meter, the output voltage is OK, no matter how much you move the adapter the power remains on. It appears that there is nothing wrong with the power adapter pins or the internal power jack.

Enter B-3 link; test the laptop with an external display. Press the Fn+F4 keys to switch laptop from internal to external display output modes. But blank screen failure still occurs.

Enter B-4 link, disassemble the machine one part at a time, and then test each one by one. Remove wireless network card, modem, cut off keyboard connection . . . , under minimum system, laptop failure disappears.

Enter B-5 link, start by installing the wireless network card onto the laptop and test, finding the laptop starts normally. (Important!) Each and every time you are testing a component shut down the laptop and pull out the adapter and battery and reinstall.

Turn off the laptop, install modem and test again, but there is still no display. Previously, screen display was okay but now I get a blank screen. Through this test, I can conclude that the problem is with the modem.

After changing the modem, press the power switch button, the laptop starts making sounds and works normally.

Hint: Under some circumstances, some accessories may have connection problem and can cause start up issues. But after you finish the entire STEP: B-5, there will be no issues with any connection problems where accessories are concerned so the laptop will work normally.

015)   HP pavilion dv2201ca laptop power and hard disk light are all on, but black screen failure still occurs:

Failure symptom:

After HP Pavilion DV2201ca laptop starts up, power and disk lights are on, you can even hear the disk & DVD rotating, but the laptop screen is still blank.

Solution:

This failure symptom belongs to the description of flow chart 03, that belong to the repair sequence:

Start->A-1->B->B-0->B-1->B-3->B-6

Repair summary:

Enter B-1 link; test the power adapter with a multi-meter, the output voltage is normal, confirm that the power adapter pins and laptop internal power jack have no any problem.

Enter B-3 link, test the laptop with an external monitor, the test result shows it is OK and the screen displays normally;

Enter B-6 link, test with flow chart 05, finding the problem is solved.

Hint: on HP (COMPAQ) laptops, you can use this method by pressing the Fn and F4 key at the same time to switch video output modes until you can see something on external display. Some model laptops would not auto inspect external display. In order to switch to external display, you have to first connect the external display onto the laptop, and then restart it.

Apple PowerBook and Apple iBook, generally, can switch automatically to an external display.

016)   HP Pavilion DV2700 laptop power adapter needs to be changed quite often:

Failure symptom:

Without warning, laptop auto shuts down, the battery does not charge, after changing with a new power adapter everything returns to normal but a few days later the same issue occurs.

Solution:

This failure symptom belongs to the description of flow chart 03 that belongs to the repair sequence:

Start->A-1->B->B-0->B-1->B-2->A-6->C-2->C-4->C-5->C-6->

Repair summary:

Enter A-6 link, test the power adapter with a multi-meter, the output voltage is normal, test the power adapter on another laptop, it works well;

Enter C-2 link test the internal power jack with a multi-meter—no problem is found;

Enter C-4->link, when we remove the battery, there is no change with the laptop, but when we install the battery again, we would hear a slight sizzling sound, the sound is not loud. It seems related with the laptop interface, check the laptop power adapter again carefully, if you find that certain area on the pin turns dark and black, then can we can conclude that there is an irregular spark symptom, which makes the power adapter to load an unstable voltage which creates the failure. After changing the power jack, the failure is gone.

Hint: The solution in this case may be too complicated. You can make it simple by observing the laptops surrounding and environment along with the position, power, connection and other devices along with temperature and humidity, the indicator light and any other sounds with what the normal usage situation is. First check the color of the adapter pin; this will cut a lot of your repair time.

3.3.3   Four repair cases for HP laptop motherboard, DC power jack failures

017)   HP Pavilion DV4-1104TX power failure

Failure symptom:

After connecting the power adapter, when moving the power cable pin the indicator light on laptop dies out or flashes continually.

Solution:

This failure symptom belongs to the description of flow chart 03, according to the repair method; we can conclude it belongs to this sequence:

Start->A-1->B->B-0->B-1->B-2->C-3; the solution is quite easy, just solder the power jack on the motherboard again or just change it:

Repair summary:

1.   Disassemble the power jack off of the motherboard totally by de-soldering it
2.   Clean the remaining solder from the original pins with a knife and then wipe away the new solder flux
3.   Clean the joint part on the motherboard and wipe new soldering flux
4.   Assemble the power jack back to the motherboard and solder it securely.

Hint: if you move the power cable, and the indicator light flashes, there are two possibilities here: one is that the power adapter pin is bad and the other is the power jack would also be bad on the motherboard.

018)   HP ZV5000 does not supply power failure

Failure symptom:

When connecting the power adapter, laptop does not start up normally. It consumes all the power left in the adapter. The battery power amount left in system does not seem to display properly. Sometimes the laptop starts and works with an external power mode but after a period of time, the system suddenly prompts you that the battery only has 5% power left, and other times the laptops screen brightness would auto change.

Solution:

This failure symptom belongs to the flow chart 03 according to the repair method and we can conclude it belongs to this sequence:

Start->A-1->B->B-0->A-6->C-2->C-3;

Repair summary:

Enter A-6 link use a multi-meter to test the power adapter, the output voltage is normal, test the power adapter on another laptop, it is all right;

Enter C-2 link try moving the joint of the pins, if failure disappears or occurs again. The issue is with a bad power jack connection;

Enter C-3->link after changing the power jack, the failure is gone;

Hint: because of a bad connection with the power pins it causes to sometimes charge the battery and other times not and therefore it switches between the external power modes to battery mode. Warning would appear when battery capacity is low. The screen brightness changes because the settings are different under external power mode and battery mode.

019)   HP pavilion DV9600 power jack failure

Failure symptom:

-Shut down the laptop; connect the power adapter to charge. The laptop power charging light shows up normally and it seems that it is fully charging. However in most cases, when the charge is not finished, the indicator light will suddenly die out and the power adapter has not supplied enough power the laptop continually.

- Check the charging state, the power capacity always is less than 85%. When you plug the power adapter in again, the charging light might show up or not. As long as you either shake or press on the power cable, the battery indicator light will always shows up for about 1 second and would disappear again.

- When the laptop shuts down and charges, the battery is always less than 85%. If you start the laptop, the charging light would auto die out within a few seconds, so it means the laptop cannot charge the battery and run at the same time.

Solution:

This failure symptom belongs to the flow chart 03 according to the repair method and we can conclude it belongs to this sequence:

Start->A-1->B->B-0->B-1->B-2->C-3; or Start->A-1->B->B-0->A-6->C-2->C-3;

Repair summary:

Enter B-1 link by moving the connection part of the adapter, the failure might disappear or just appear again; this is usually a typical bad connection failure with the power jack;

Enter A-6 link use a multi-meter to test the power adapter, output voltage is OK, test the adapter on another laptop, it should work normally.

Enter C-3->link this is a bad power circuitry caused by common power jack problem. Disassemble the machine, usually the power jack on the motherboard is broken, but after changing it for a new one, the failure is gone.

Hint: first test the connection between the power adapter joint and the laptop power jack, plug a good power adapter to the suspected laptop to see if there is any problem. If it is normal, the issue is with the power adapter; you can just repair the original power adapter or change it.

020) HP Pavilion DV6500 suddenly powers-off failure

Failure symptom:

When you plug the power adapter, the blue power light on the front panel of the laptop does not show anything. But when you shake, knock or pull on the plug, the power cable again, the power indicator light sometimes displays something. However, when the blue power light shows, the laptop system sometimes does not start.

Solution:

This failure symptom belongs to the flow chart 03 according to the repair method and we can conclude it belongs to this sequence:

Start->A-1->B->B-0->A-6->C-2->C-3;

Repair summary:

Enter A-6 link and use a multi-meter to test the power adapter, the output voltage is normal, test the power adapter on another laptop, it works normally;

Enter C-2 link use a multi-meter to test the power jack, you will usually find that the internal power jack has an issue but after changing it the failure disappears.

Hint: such failure symptoms sometimes would happen on the laptop where the system overheats, or there is a bad connection between the motherboard and some components. The solution is to do an electronic cleaning of the motherboard by tightening the screws to keep the machine compact. A bad connection caused by overheating is random and even auto shutdown.

3.3.4   HP laptop—3 repair cases for power failures caused by other reasons

021)   HP DV2700 laptop gets black screen failure when connecting the external power adapter:

Failure symptom:

DV2700 laptop with Vista system suddenly does not start when connecting external power adapter. When pressing the power button, all blue indicator lights are on, but the laptop does not start up even after 20 to 30 minutes later so you turn it off by force, and then start it up again but all attempts are useless.

Solution:

This failure symptom belongs to the 03 flow chart, according to the repair method, we can conclude it belongs to the sequence: >A-1->B->B-0->B-1->B-3->B-4->D-3

Repair summary: if you press the power switch button, laptop begins making sound, LED light comes on normally, but there is nothing displayed on the screen, enter B-1 link by using a multi-meter to test the power adapter. The result shows that the output voltage is normal, no matter how you move the power adapter; the power will not go off, so it seems there is nothing wrong with the power adapter interface and laptop internal power jack. Now enter B-3 link by using an external display to test the laptop. Press Fn+F4 key at the same time, switch laptop internal/external display output mode. The black screen failure still occurs.

Enter B-4 link and disassemble the machine part by part, and then test. First remove wireless network card, modem and disconnect the keyboard which proves not to make any sense. Under the minimum system, the laptop still shows a black screen failure.

Now enter the D-3 link. Remove the CMOS battery from the motherboard for about 3 to 5 hours. Reconnect with a new CMOS battery, the failure is usually gone.

Hint: CMOS battery is used to store system information, such as time and start-up sequence or system related data. If CMOS battery fails, then system cannot start up or hardware may not be recognized. Therefore, it is really important to check laptop CMOS battery.

You can also try these next steps:

-1)   Remove the battery and pull out external power adapter
-2)   Press the power button for 30 seconds or more
-3)   then reconnect the power adapter and start the laptop.

022)   When connecting the external power supply, HP Pavilion DV6300 laptop does not always start up as it sometimes auto shut down.

Failure symptom:

-When laptop is in a dormant state and you connect the power adapter to charge, the power charge indicator light shows up normally. It seems it can charge fully. However, in most cases, the indicator light suddenly goes off before finishing charging and therefore the power adapter does not supply the laptop continually.

-When the laptop is starting up, it will auto shut down from time to time. When you pull out the power adapter and plug it back into the laptop again, the charge light might display for a few seconds or does not light up at all. When you move the laptop, the charge indicator light auto dies out immediately, so laptop does not charge the battery when running at all.

Solution:

This failure symptom belongs to the description of flow chart 03, according to the repair method with the sequence:

Start->A-1->B->B-0->B-1->B-2->A-6->C-2->C-4->C-5->C-6->

Repair summary:

Enter A-6 by using a multi-meter to test the power adapter, the output voltage is OK. Test the power adapter in another laptop and it works normally;

Enter C-2 by using a multi-meter to test the power jack and finding no problem;

Enter C-4 by removing the battery, the laptop power light display returns to normal, but when we install the battery again, the original problem reappears again. It is quite obvious the issue is with the laptop battery. Use a new battery and replace the original one, if the situation does not change check the laptop carefully again, and usually you will find that the battery release latch to lock the battery is broken. After changing it, the failure disappears.

Hint: this symptom is quite common when the battery release latch fails and it causes issues with the power supply. First of all, disassemble the machine, check the battery release latch on the back cover, whether it is damaged or not. Usually, if the spring is ruptured, just change it, as it will only cause a distortion problem. You can remove it and install it back again. Battery release latch failure would cause an issue with start up or battery charging etc. During the process of disassembling and assembling, pay close attention not to damage the motherboard power circuitry.

023)   HP Compaq Presario V6000 cannot start up with external power adapter

Failure symptom:

Power adapter indicator light is on, but the laptop does not start up both in battery mode and external power supply mode, when there is no light on, system totally freezes.

Solution:

This failure symptom belongs to the description of flowchart 06, according to the repair method; we can ensure the repair path, finding it accords with the sequence:

Start->A-1->B->B-0->B-1->B-2->A-6->C-2->C-4->C-5->C-6->C-3->D-3

Repair summary:

Enter A-6 by using a multi-meter to test the power adapter, the output voltage is OK;

Enter C-2 no matter how you move the power adapter, the power is not off, and there is no problem with the power jack;

Enter C-7-> when you replace the battery with a new one the situation does not change;

Enter D-3->check the laptop carefully, you will find the integrated block of the power control on the motherboard has been broken. After changing it, the failure disappears.

Hint: In most cases the cause is due to overheating of the laptop, which makes the motherboard chip too hot, and being overheated and increasing the load sharply. The integrated block ends up burnt and therefore the failure will occur. After disassembling the laptop, clean the thermal system, and verify closely the soldering of the power dc jack on the motherboard and replace it if it is loose or damaged.

CHAPTER 4

Battery charge failure repair

4.1 Laptop battery could not charge and cause

4.1.1 Laptop battery structure

1) The internal structure of laptop battery is composed of a shell, a working circuitry and a battery assembly.

2) The main part of a laptop battery is the internal battery assembly. Generally, a laptop battery provides 10.8V or 11.1V. A single battery will not satisfy this requirement, so a number of batteries are connected together in a series parallel configuration to provide the required voltage. The laptop battery capability is indicated on the nameplate on the outside of the shell. 3300mAh, 4400mAh is typical and is the capacity of the battery. It indicates the current the battery can provide during a one hour discharge. For example: a 4400mAh lithium battery can provide a discharge of 4400mA for one hour. If the laptop requirement is less than this, the discharge time will be longer than one hour. If a battery is provided with a larger rating, the discharge time will be longer. If the battery rating is lower the discharge will be shorter. The actual discharge time is a function of the laptop load and the battery rating.

3) Charge/Discharge control and protection circuitry, just as its name implies, controls the battery charging/discharging cycles and protects it from malfunctions. During the process of charging the lithium battery, a full charge is detected by a slight drop in voltage. The control circuitry detects this and terminates the charging to prevent overcharging. When discharging, battery voltage remains stable until near the end of the battery capability. At this point there is a drop in voltage that is detected by the control circuitry which then shuts off the discharge to prevent over discharge that can damage the battery or shorten its life.

4.1.2 Structure of laptop power circuitry

1) The laptop power system is the third level key component next to the CPU, motherboard and display. The power system is composed of the power adapter,

battery charging, and power management system, with various internal power supplies, fuses, distribution etc.

2) The power adapter, generally, is composed of a shell, power transformer, and rectifying and filter circuitry. The laptop power adapter shell is not easily opened. The shell is fused shut. It's almost impossible to open it without damage. After opening power adapter shell, it will be difficult to re-assemble it. This is typical of OEM power supplies.

3) The effect of the metal shield layer on it is self-evident. It could keep out the damage to the circuitry from static. The internal components of the power adapter, includes capacitors, resistors, switching diodes, power core chip etc, which all emit heat.

4) Most laptop power adapters are rated about 65 to 70W, the heat produced inside is dissipated through the plastic shell. The surface temperature of the power adapter is still quite high, while the inside of the adapter is almost a standard stove. Generally the AC adapter's maximum normal working temperature is about 70-80 degrees, therefore, when using a laptop, don't pile anything on the adapter that obstructs the cooling, especially flammable material. Ignore this and unpredictable and unnecessary danger may happen.

Watts=Volts x Amps x PF for AC. The PF is near = to 1and can be neglected. Watts DC =VA. The AC input to the adapter might be 120V * 1.5A=180W. In order to provide 70W to the computer, the adapter uses 180W from the wall outlet. The difference 180-70=110W becomes heat in the adapter. This is the same heat that is emitted from a 100W light bulb. This is the reason an adapter becomes hot and must not be covered to obstruct the heat dissipation.

4.1.3 Laptop power startup sequence (principle)

1) MAX1630/1361/1632/1633/1634/1635 series chips are a DC voltage supply switch used to provide DC voltage for movable electrical equipment such as laptops. This kind of chip works in switch working mode by external MOSFET. You can choose a boot sequence of different output voltages, and provide a power ready signal at a proper time. With an external resistance divider circuit, it can produce non 12V voltage flexibly (the so-called secondary feedback feeds back the chip output voltage to the chip, from the mutual inductance coil or a transformer in the peripheral circuitry of the chip).

2) "5V LINEAR" is an interior 5V linearity voltage stabilizer, that is used to provide power for each working module inside the chip when operating. After the chip starts up, the voltage stabilizer will stop at the proper time, and as a replacement, the 5V PWM voltage stabilizer, will supply power. On some motherboards, the voltage is provided by other parts of the circuitry.

3) "12V LINEAR" is 12V linear voltage stabilizer, providing 12V output. "3.3V SMPS" and "5V SMPS" are two PWM voltage stabilizers or switch power, which are used to control four external MOSFET connections and disconnections, ensuring needed DC voltage can be produced. "POWER-UP SEQUENCE" is used to control the start sequence of "3.3V SMPS" and "5V SMPS".

4) "POWER-GOOD" would provide low level at the end point within 3200 clock periods after chip starts up, later it jumps to a higher level and informs relevant circuitry to get ready (such as to inform the power controller on the laptop motherboard), namely, "Power ready signal".

5) The DC power switch connects and cuts off with a high-speed through circuitry control switch, and converts DC to high frequency AC, provided to the transformer that finally forms a group or multi-group voltage that is needed.

4.1.4 Laptop battery usage and maintenance

A) Battery usage

1. The initial charging of the battery, should be continuous for 12 hours, and then charge and discharge it 3 times to completely waken the new battery; Please take a look at Figure 4-1.

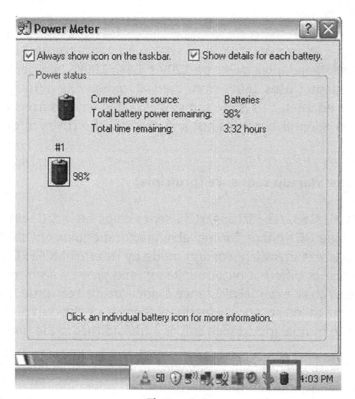

Figure 4-1

2. If you use the external power supply continuously, remove the battery. Charge and discharge the battery periodically.

3. Do not interrupt the charging cycle until fully charged. Don't pull out the power supply when charging. Charging when the computer is off shortens by 30% the time it takes to fully charge. It can also prolong the battery useful life. You should use the laptop 30 minutes after finishing charging.

4. Avoid exposure to humidity and chemical liquid corrosion, and avoid contacting metal with the battery connectors, in case a short circuit happens.

5. Generally, a lithium battery can provide about 800 charge/discharge cycles till end of life. Each cycle will shorten its life. I suggest you use the external power supply as much as possible. Each time you unplug and plug power with the computer in use, and the laptop internal battery is not removed, then the battery useful life will be shortened. This is because unplugging is a discharge cycle, and plugging is a charge cycle.

B)   Battery maintenance

1. You don't have to fully charge each time to store it after discharging completely.
2. Periodically, a full discharge under the control of the protection circuitry, can improve battery performance. However, it will not increase the actual power capacity of the battery.
3. If the battery is not being used, you should store it in a cool environment, to slow down the rate of internal discharge.
4. The battery protection circuitry cannot control the battery internal discharge rate. If the battery is not used for long periods, it will require occasional recharging to insure that the internal discharge does not damage the battery. If left for too long without charging, the battery can be ruined by over discharge due to internal discharge.
5. Remove or turn off unused peripheral equipment. Use the battery management software to select a scheme that best suits your usage habits.
6. Avoid using your laptop in an environment with very high or low temperatures. The safe environmental operating range is above 15°C and below 30°C.
7. Set up the standby time for the screen, hard disk and system hibernation, exit screen savers. You know that the working principle of LCD screen is different from CRT screen, to prolong user life and save more power, please end screen savers.
8. For further instructions on prolonging battery useful life, please see sec. 1.2.1 <<Factors affecting laptop battery life>>

4.2   Eliminating Laptop battery charge issues and repair Flow chart

4.2.1   Repair shortcuts and tips for power adapter and battery problems

Today's laptop adapter power output is around 65-70W. The heat produced inside is conducted through the plastic shell. The temperature of the power adapter surface can get quite hot resulting in a life span of about a year or so. If you ever have the need to change one, I suggest replacing it with one where the wattage is higher then the original one. For example: replace a 65W power adapter with a 90W one and 90W with 120W adapter. The important thing is to make sure that the output voltage is the same, such as 18V, 19V (The information is usually written at the bottom of the laptop as well as on the adapter)

Repair tips for power adapter

1. Current power adapter uses patch components, once a component goes wrong, it is difficult to repair, making the adapter's power increase day by day. In this case, electrical components will experience more problems. If the power adapter's electrical component has a bad connection or the PCB deployment is improper, then failure rate increases. Here a summary of some of the repair processes I have used and hope these tips will help you.

2. When handling the power cable connecting the adapter to the computer, be gentle with it and avoid stressing the connection to the adapter or the jack. The conductors can be easily open circuited. If the external power supply doesn't charge, then you insert the battery and try again. If the machine starts up normally, then the issue may be with the cable or the adapter. Use a multi meter to test the adapter output and check if the power cable is broken. Don't attempt to open the adapter shell at this time. For ordinary users, it's a very difficult task to do unless you are experienced.

3. If there's an issue with the original power adapter and the power indicator light is out, it can be the AC line cable. If you have another cable to try, do so. The AC power cable plugs into the wall outlet and into a socket on the adapter. Don't assume the issue isn't with the AC cable because it is thick and stout. Problems with this cable are quite common. We repair this type of issue 2 to 3 times a month.

4. If you cannot repair nor have time to repair the power adapter, a replacement can be purchased as long as the output voltage and power is similar (0.5V error allowed). Laptops have internal circuitry that regulates and filters the voltage. As previously mentioned, higher power is desirable. No need to worry about small differences in output voltage.

5. Some readers may have concluded that an adapter problem burnt their motherboard. This is really infrequent although it may happen sometimes. During my 15 years' maintenance career, I've only had it happen 4 times, and 3 of those were caused by a "universal" adapter, which uses a switch to adjust output voltage from 15V to 24V. This makes it easy for something to go wrong if the switch gets in the wrong position. This would quite likely damage the mother board.

6. If the adapter shell breaks, electromagnetic radiation can enter the adapter, which will influence the machines stability. If shell breaks, you should fix it as soon as possible. When repairing the power adapter, you should first open the shell and then open the shield layer, and check the solder connections visually. If there is a circuit intermittent problem, it is generally because of a bad connection, and it needs to be soldered again.

7. Check the capacitors, resistors and semi conductors. If a capacitor is bulging or discolored, replace it to avoid having to change it later.

Easy way to repair and renew your laptop battery that doesn't charge

Solution 1:

a. Turn off your laptop, remove the battery, and disconnect the power adapter from the laptop.

    b.   Start the laptop, and press the power button for about 10 seconds duration.

    c.   Now plug the battery back in again

    d.   Connect the power adapter again e. Now start the laptop, check to see if the battery charges and works.

Have a try, hope this helped!

Solution 2:

For most laptop lithium batteries, when they aren't used often or for a long time, an "excess discharge" symptom may be created. The result is that the batteries will no longer charge. You should contact the dealer immediately and have it repaired or replaced. Some parts of batteries can be saved. To prevent the "excess discharge" symptom, remove the battery and place in a cool and dry place when the laptop is not used for a long period of time. It is important to charge and discharge the battery completely at least twice a year when being stored.

Solution 3: Using the Power management software:

Enter device manager, uninstall Microsoft ACPI Compliant Control Method Battery, enter menu option, and then choose "scan hardware change", then it will reinstall device. After installation, your battery will probably be able to continue charging. But if it doesn't, then shut down your laptop and remove the battery, wait about 30 seconds and re-plug your battery, start the laptop. You may need to repeat this step several times. Sometimes refreshing your laptop BIOS may solve your batteries charging issues.

For more details, please check chapter 1.1.4 Updating BIOS, Also chapter 4.2.4. Professional method to repair and resume laptop battery that doesn't charge.

4.2.2 88% of Issues regarding batteries that do not charge comes from the AC Adapter or the battery itself

Reasons that may cause the laptop battery to not charge:

    a.   Laptop power adapter problems;

    b.   Laptop battery failures;

    c.   Laptop motherboard power control chip problems;

    d.   Failures of other circuits on laptop motherboard;

Among these problems, about 88% of them come from the original power adapter and battery:

    1.   Laptop power adapter problem A: laptop works normally only with battery light on and power adapter's power light is on. To ensure whether the power adapter is good

or not, the best way is to test the voltage with a multi-meter. You can also test the laptop with a confirmed good work adapter.

2. Laptop power adapter problem B: laptop doesn't start, when pressing the power switch, but the power light is on, it shuts off shortly thereafter. Probable issue is with the power adapter as it cannot charge the battery. And when battery runs out of power, the laptop shuts off. To test whether the power adapter is good or not, get an identical power adapter to try on the laptop. If everything runs OK, then we know the issue is with the original adapter itself.

3. Problem A: Laptop battery doesn't charge: The simplest method to test the battery is to get an identical working battery and try it. This will quickly provide a solution. If the laptop charges normally with the new battery, then the problem is with the original battery. How to solve the battery problem? For more detailed steps, please go to chapter 4.2.1Shortcuts and tips to repair power adapter and battery failures, or chapter 4.2.4 how to repair and resume laptop battery that doesn't charge.

4. Problem B: Laptop battery still doesn't charge: if the laptop still fails to charge the new battery, then there is another problem. Do not jump to the conclusion it is a motherboard problem. Do you have an original adapter or is it a replacement? A common problem with generic replacements is they just do not work properly for various reasons. Try another original factory's (or OEM) power adapter and your problem just might be solved.

5. Attention: you must from time to time use the battery as your power source because if you don't you will eventually kill it. So you should charge/discharge battery completely at least once a month. If you don't intend on using it often at least make sure it is charged in order to help keep its charge when needed.

6. Other circuit problem on laptop motherboard: Check the power inlet jack on the laptop as it may be worn out and loose or the solder joints holding the jack in place broken. This will give you intermittent power problems and interfere with battery charging. For more details, please check chapter—Eliminating HP Laptop battery charges issues and repair Flow chart.\

4.2.3. 8% power system issues from an incompatible AC adapter and battery

When a laptop power system problem occurs, usually, the laptop fails to start and the indicator light is out. This is likely a power system problem and there are many reasons that may cause power system problems. It is important to work through each failure mode, one at a time, until the fault is located. Among my repair experiences, about 8% of power system failures come from an incompatible power adapter or battery.

Examples of some failures:

1. System instability caused by power supply shortage

Failure symptom: the system becomes unstable when connecting an external USB laptop disk, the laptop cannot read the disc and auto restarts without any reason. You might also notice abnormal heat from the fan vent. The fan may emit abnormal sounds as if running rough.

Resolution: The issue indicates that the power adapter has exceeded its load. The power adapter cannot generate enough energy for the motherboard because the USB disk is overloading it. Replace the AC Adapter and the issue is resolved.

2. **Battery doesn't charge but laptop works**

Failure symptom: The laptop operates normally with either the AC adapter or the battery, but not both. The system becomes unstable when both are operating. In this case the laptop auto restarts and the image freezes. You also feel abnormally high heat coming from the power adapter when using the laptop. The battery charges when the laptop is turned off.

Resolution: This is caused by an aging power adapter that is no longer able to provide enough power to operate the computer and charge the battery simultaneously. Replace the Power adapter with a new one and the problem is resolved.

3. **Laptop doesn't start normally**

Failure symptom: The laptop fails to start up with the battery installed, but when you remove it, the laptop starts without issues.

Resolution: The battery has a short circuit which prevents the power adapter from supplying power. This is a serious problem that can cause damage to the power adapter or the motherboard. Do not try using the battery again; it must be replaced with a new one recommended for your computer. This issue often occurs when a battery meant for a computer of the same brand but slightly different model number is used by mistake.

4.2.4. Professional method to repair and resume laptop battery that doesn't charge.

You might purchase a brand new battery and realize after 2 months usage, that its charge only lasts 20 minutes and getting worse depending on the way it used and charged. But there may be other reasons. Many clients come to me and ask why a brand new battery would be discarded and considered useless after 6 months although it's not being used a lot. It is a known fact that the so-called nickel-hydrogen battery that replaced nickel-cadmium battery is not as good. Knowing this, I want to disassemble this scrapped battery to check whether it's possible to repair it. I know it is designed not to be repaired. When produced, it is sealed completely with special glue. Finally, you would have to pry it open and then it is no longer recyclable or re-usable.

Laptop batteries are not as complex. Just a piece of hard plastic shell with a thermocouple and several batteries inside. All these little batteries provide the voltage needed. The black wire fastened with transparent adhesive tape between two batteries is the thermal couple, which is used to measure the air temperature inside the battery group, but not the surface temperature of it. Maybe the temperature is the reason why batteries fail easily.

The last component inside the battery group is the little circuit board (as picture shown below), there's almost nothing on it, except the line of golden fingers used for the laptop battery slot. Seen from the outside of the battery group, you may easily think there is a precise charging circuit inside. Actually that isn't true. When you open the inside of the battery, you may find that the craft and soldering only belong to common or low-end technology products. When you buy a new laptop battery, your new battery has already depreciated due to shelf life.

The little batteries inside a laptop battery are simply lashed together by soldering little films (as picture shown below). If you want to fix a laptop battery, then you need to replace all of them and solder them together again. Then I ran into this issue. I searched on the web to get a quote for batteries, and the best I price I could find was the SANYO HR-4/3AU, for 4$ each. To assemble a battery of 10.8 V, I would require 9 cells at 1.2V each. This means the cost would be well over 40$.

During my repair practice, I found that not all single battery cells have an issue. Often 1 to 2 of them have gone bad in a battery group. So you just need to change those. That would now bring the cost down.

To fix a laptop battery and minimize the repair cost, try finding some old laptop batteries to cannibalize. Usually they can be purchased at a used Notebook store for less then 20$. Open them and get the good ones from the battery groups. Assemble and connect them up and will you end up with close to new battery. This is better then spending between $75 up to $150 for a new one plus shipping & handling. Remember to carefully read you manual regarding battery usage in order to have a healthy one for as long as possible.

Circuit board

4.2.5   Laptop battery repair—change internal batteries and unlock the EEPROM.

Many name brand laptop batteries have a self-lock function in their design.

They are called a smart battery and software is contained on an EEPROM contained internally that controls the battery operation. Under certain conditions the EEPROM will lock the battery out from further use. When you replace the internal battery core, you also have to reset the EEPROM software or your repaired battery will not work. Hardware and software kits are available to perform this function. Some electronic skills are needed to perform this work. You will need to construct the adapter. It is not that difficult for anyone with electronic experience.

"Smart Battery Workshop" software and adapter is a very useful tool to repair a laptop battery. With this software loaded in your computer and the adapter connected according to the instructions supplied with the software, the job is done. Smart battery software reads the battery interface information through the computer LPT==>adapter. The EEPROM chip records the original aging telegraphic program, this information includes battery lock, full capacity, usage times, date it's made, first date used and so on. "SB-workshop" program will modify the content stored on the EEPROM when the reset is activated, restoring it to its original state. In other words this would clear the usage records stored in the battery, including the full charged capacity, circulation times, and lock, making the battery exactly the same as the original new one.

The repair process is quite simple once you have obtained or constructed the adapter, and doesn't need any special knowledge and skill. You'd just need to connect EEPROM to the adapter with jumper wires, no programming involved; just click the key "Reset" in the software and it is done. As for the rest, you have to assemble the battery and install it back in the laptop.

4.2.6 Analysis and repair—Flow chart for laptop battery that doesn't charge

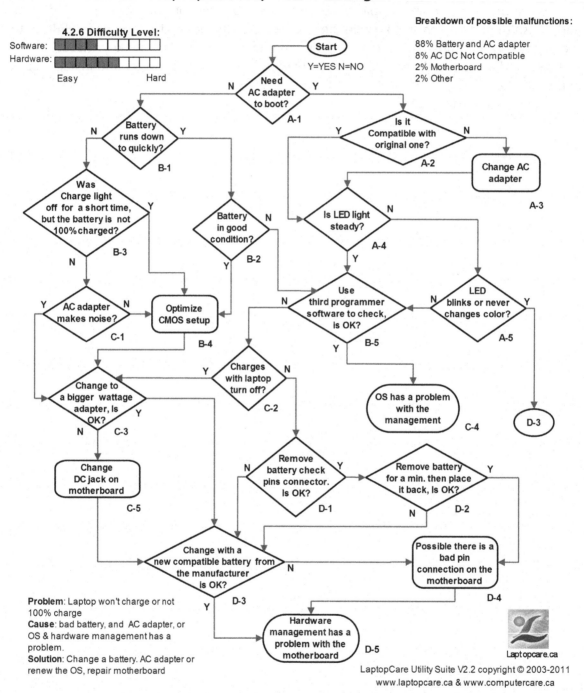

Laptop Battery Won't Charge At All

Problem: Laptop won't charge or not 100% charge
Cause: bad battery, and AC adapter, or OS & hardware management has a problem.
Solution: Change a battery. AC adapter or renew the OS, repair motherboard

This tutorial will help you solve the laptop battery issue.

Symtoms Discussed:

-1) Fail to charge. When connected with the power adapter, the battery does not charge.
-2) The laptop does not work under battery mode, the system turns off when you remove the power adapter.
-3) after charging for a long time, the charge light remains on. The power capacity remains at the same level and not higher after a discharge test.

In this article, I will explain how to find the causes of these failures, and the reasons why the laptop battery fails to charge. The solutions here are not for specific laptops but will work for most brands and models.

Step: 1:

When you plug in the power adapter and press the power button, the system starts. Watch the battery information display at the bottom of the screen carefully, as it will relate to the failure description in this tutorial;

If the battery does not charge when you plug in the power adapter, and also the laptop doesn't boot with the power adapter, certainly the battery will not charge. If this is the case, it is not covered in this article. Please check article 03 in the tutorial.

Step A-1

Start the laptop with matched power adapter plugged

The first thing needed before solving the problem regarding a battery not charging, is to plug-in the power adapter. First make sure that your power adapter is functioning properly. If there is a sign it might be defective, the power adapter must be verified to be good before continuing with anything else.

Generally, the first step is to test the reliability of the power adapter:

1. **Appearance:** check the appearance, there shouldn't be any visible damage. Check that the model, voltage, and current rating is according to the manual. Check the cover for bulges and the pins for oxidation, dirt, oil or paint etc.
2. **Performance:** test the no load output voltage. Check the nameplate load output current, ripple voltage and other functions, which should be within the required range. (The tolerable deviation from specs should be no greater than +/-5%.) The amperage of the new adapter should be exactly the same as the previous one or even higher. If the original adapter was 18.5V, 19V is also acceptable, and if the original adapter was 3.5A, 4.7A is tolerable and better.

3. **Reliability:** Any tests of reliability need to be according to industry standards. There is really no point in carrying these out on a used adapter as they further reduce the life expectancy. Reliability can only be maximised by recommended care of the adapter.

Let's take a look two different situations:

Situation 1: The laptop only starts with the adapter plugged-in.

In this case, your problem may be due to the charging circuit of the battery enter STEP: A-2

Situation 2: The laptop only starts with the battery and not the power adapter

This indicates that the laptop works in battery mode. In that case, your problem might be related to the battery electrical storage function, enter STEP: B-1

STEP: A-2 this section will help ensures that your power adapter is compatible with your laptop.

Now ask yourself is this power adapter compatible with this laptop? No matter what adapter you choose to replace the original one, it must meet or exceed the specifications of the original. If you don't change or purchase the same kind in terms of power and pin size, your notebook will never start or you will never solve the issue. You should always use an original power adapter to troubleshoot a laptop.

Why test with original power adapter?

Many technicians will say: that "theoretically speaking, the original power adapter is comparatively better and practical even when the non-OEM unit meets specifications. During the repair process a non-OEM adapter could in some instances make troubleshooting more difficult. The working principle of the power adapter is as follows: the loaded voltage is divided into two voltages after further filtering and regulation. One is for the laptop, and the other is to charge the battery. The battery charging voltage passes through the charging control circuit to then reach the electrical core of the battery. It can be said that the control circuit is complicated. Simply speaking, it has to pass through at least two conditions in the BIOS software validation process.

If using a non-original adapter, such as a generic one, the marked voltage might be different and therefore the output also might be and will not pass through the BIOS inspection and validation, or will pass the inspection partially and in turn cause some new problems. For instance, the Dell power adapter 19.5V 4.62A (90W) cannot start the HP G60 laptop, although Dell's power adapter parameters are quite close to the HP G60 power adapter. The interfaces are the same, but it will not pass through the circuit inspection and validation. Tolerable ripple and regulator response are factors that can prevent compatibility and are not specified to enable selection of a replacement adapter that is not identical.

This is the difference between the original power and normal power adapters. The original power adapter has no compatibility problems with the laptop and troubleshooting can progress without misleading results caused by an adapter incompatibility.

Now, if your power adapter is not a factory's originally one and you are unable to confirm that your power adapter is working and compatible with your laptop, and then please enter the STEP: A-3

If your power adapter is a factory's originally one, or if you are sure your power adapter is working and compatible with your laptop, then please continue to STEP: A-4

STEP: A-3 this section is to confirm that your laptop power adapter can supply charging function normally.

1. Validate whether the power adapter's output voltage is normal according to the explanation on the adapter. Test the power output with a multi-meter to see whether it's within the specified **V and ensure whether the power adapters Voltage is between 18.5V and 19V;
2. If you have no multi-meter or cannot judge whether the power adapter is good or not simply by a multi-meter, then you can estimate the suspected power adapter with a known good laptop and the method is quite simple: start a known good laptop of the same brand and model with the suspected power adapter. If it starts successfully and the battery charges normally, then it means the power adapter is good. Otherwise, it's probably faulty.

If the process above didn't help solve the problem, then please continue STEP: A-4

If your power adapter is original and is working, then please enter STEP: A-4

STEP: A-4 this section will help ensure whether your issue is with the battery or the battery faucet

Let's first take a look at two different situations:

Situation 1: laptop power charge light is on, but is not blinking

When you plug the power adapter and press the start button, the laptop power charge light is on and stable, which means there's nothing wrong with the battery faucet and laptop internal charge circuit. It's quite likely to be some other issue. If your situation belongs to this kind, please enter STEP: B-5

Situation 2: laptop power charge light is on, but blinks continuously

When you plug the power adapter, the battery begins charging. But the brightness of the laptop power charge light is continually changing and back to bright. It seems relevant with the power adapter or battery. If you have such a problem, please enter STEP: A-5

STEP: A-5 this link is to see whether your problem is connected with the battery

If the laptop power charge's light always blinks or has never changed its display state such as: the power charge's light turns green from yellow, and again turns yellow from green, then we can come to the diagnosis conclusion: you need to change your laptop battery;

However, the bad contact situation between battery and laptop motherboard may also cause charging failure problem. So from the get go, I would always check the battery connection first, recheck the faucet connection between them again, probably this will help you solve the issues.

The HP battery has 6 connector pins, which upon inspection, should shine without dark or black oxidation. Check the connector pins of the battery to ensure there are no particles or dust and oily buildup. You can use a very small sharp knife to clean the oil dust or obstruction and oxidation layer. But during this process, be careful not to damage or scratch the pins. A pencil eraser is often sufficient to clean the pins and will not damage them. Please take a look at Figure 4-2.

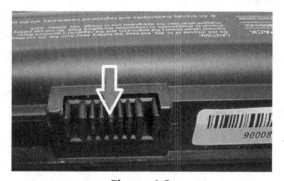

Figure 4.2

Now plug the battery in again, if no error occurs, but the laptop still does not charge from the external power supply, please continue STEP: D-3

If the laptop power charge's light stop blinks, please continue STEP: B-5

STEP: B-1 Determine the reason for a battery fails to charge problem

Let's take a look at four different situations below:

Situation 1: the laptop battery consumes its power too quickly and no matter how many times you recharge the battery, the capacity to keep its charge diminishes. If the battery shows a full charge but after pulling out the AC power adapter, the system begins turning off immediately, the battery is likely defective. If this is the case, the battery should be replaced.

Situation 2: the laptop battery power shows 0% no matter how long it has been charged. The battery remains in a charging state, even charging from the external power supply.

Check the power capacity remaining on the screen display. If you find the battery always shows 0% with no increase, but the laptop starts with the battery, then your problem might be with the inspection software. Go to STEP: B-2;

If the laptop doesn't totally work in battery mode, then your problem could be with the battery. Try replacing with a new. Please enter STEP: B-2;

Situation 3: when you start the laptop in battery mode, the battery state shows "online", but the laptop enters in hibernation mode immediately, and no longer works normally. If you want to use the laptop, you will have to plug-in the adapter. After checking the battery state while charging with the adapter, it is found to be charging, "Plugged in, charging". However, the power stays at one level, around X%, without increasing. If you are faced with this, then please enter STEP: B-2

Situation 4: sometimes the battery will charge normally, but not completely. When starting the laptop in battery mode, the battery charges to a level around xx% capacity and no more. The laptop auto switches to battery mode until the power management software prompts that the power is almost drained, and at this moment, there's only about 7% power left. However, if you take the battery out for a time, and then put it back, it seems to charge normally again. After turning off the laptop, the power adapter does charge the battery. If it is your situation, then please enter STEP: B-3

STEP: B-2 this link verifies that your battery is ok.

How to check whether the battery condition is normal? There is expert software available to do this called—Batterymom. The size of the file to install it is very small, only about 400KB. Batterymom can determine the total time (theory value) that the battery has run, the battery power capacity and the usable time left. After seeing these results, click the "Battery information" in "Information" and you'll get a pretty good idea of the state of the battery.

If you cannot download the software, an alternate method is to use a known working laptop to test the suspected battery. Simply put the suspected battery in a laptop of the same brand and model, if the charging is normal, then it indicates the battery is good; otherwise, it has a problem.

If either the software or an identical laptop is available, then please continue to STEP: B-5

If the software test result shows the battery performance is in good condition, then please enter STEP: B-4

STEP: B-3 this link is to determine whether the failure is from hardware or software

Let's take a look at two different situations below:

Situation 1: generally, the power adapter supplies by priority, which means if the battery and power adapter supplies the laptop at the same time, the laptop will first use the power adapter. After starting the laptop in battery mode if you plug-in the power adapter then the BIOS will auto switch to the power adapter to supply.

However, if your power adapter is several years old and aging, or you use a generic adapter of lower power, the adapter will eventually have no ability to supply the power for charging and starting the laptop at the same time. The BIOS will auto switch to battery power supply mode. If this is your situation, please enter STEP: C-1

Situation 2: When the laptop BIOS determines battery and computer power consumption, the battery charging state is displayed by the OS internal test software. BIOS takes control of the charging process of the battery and will stop the charging power before the battery over charges. This is the control process: when the battery is close to full charge or when discharging, the power left is really low, and then the hardware power manager sends the required signals to BIOS. OS battery test software only reflects the present battery state, *if there are any issues between these 3 links, then a battery charge state error will occur.* If this is your situation, please enter STEP: B-4

STEP: B-4 this link is to ensure the laptop BIOS has no problem

Generally speaking, HP laptop BIOS has no option settings for battery charging. The so-called battery charge settings is to update the BIOS, while there's many advantages to update BIOS, for instance, HP /dv6000/dv9000 and Compaq Presario V3000/V6000 series notebook PCs, the algorithm of fan control system could be updated on motherboard, then you can test the precise temperature. It's also great to solve BUGS in the old BIOS version. Besides, these BUGS often cause some indescribable failures, including the system battery charge failure. If you have already updated your BIOS version, or your laptop BIOS version is new, then please continue STEP: C-3;

STEP: B-5 this link is to ensure the actual capacity of the laptop battery

When the laptop has been used for a period of time, you might feel that the battery usable time is becoming shorter and shorter. Usually this is not because of the normal aging of the battery, but because during the charging and discharging process, the laptop BIOS system makes an incorrect judgment of the batteries power capacity, which means the BIOS inspection doesn't equal with the actual battery power.

To help solve the problem, some manufacturers add a "Battery Calibration" function in BIOS to help users to fill the laptop battery fully; it discharges the battery completely and charges it back again. The purpose of this calibration operation is to restore a battery that has not experienced a full discharge for a long time period.

Unfortunately now HP laptop BIOS software has fewer options. You will have to install third party software to solve battery this calibration problem. BatteryMom is a very nice laptop battery calibration software, and also a nice battery supervision tool for the laptop.

Battery calibration is a deep charge/discharge operation when the present battery capacity is different from the recorded one in the control circuit. It lets the control circuit refresh its record to the actual condition of the battery. This operation shows the real capacity of the battery but does not improve the capacity. The key factor here is the actual capacity of the battery. If the actual capacity is higher than the recorded one in control circuit, the calibration would make the battery capacity seem higher than it is. If the actual capacity is less than the recorded one in the control circuit, then the calibration would make the battery seem lower than it is. Please remember the calibration just gives you a true picture of the batteries capacity and corrects the record is the control circuit. Whether the shown capacity is increased or reduced, is decided by the battery state itself, and not the calibration process.

It is important to know the "Design capacity" and "Full charge capacity" two columns. For a brand new battery, the design capacity should be completely the same as the full charge capacity. If you don't have test software, or find the battery not charging, then please continue STEP: C-2;

After the laptop battery has passed calibration, but the operation system charge state still shows 0%, without an increase, use the battery mode to start the laptop. If the laptop works for a long period of time on battery, then please continue STEP: C-4;

STEP: C-1 this link is to determine whether your adapter has a power shortage problem.

Let's first look at these three different situations:

Generally, we can carry out the steps below to test the reliability of the power adapter:

Situation 1: check the appearance of the power adapter, there should be no damage, the load output voltage and load output current should be in the requested range, according with the ratings on the adapter. The amperage on the adapter must be same as the one marked on the laptop or even higher; (if the laptop rated input current is 6.5A, and you use an adapter rated 3.5A or 4.7A, the power adapter is not acceptable). If this is the situation, please enter STEP: C-3

Situation 2: under normal circumstances, when you are more than 10 inches away from the power adapter, there is no way to hear a sizzling like sound made by the power adapter. If you can hear a tiny and acute sound, then it means the power adapter is of bad quality, or is already overloaded. If this is the case, please enter STEP: C-3

Situation 3: under normal circumstances, 20 minutes to a few hours after the power adapter is on, it starts to feel warm to the touch, but if it becomes hot, then you know it has already reached the overload state. If you are sure that your power adapter is the right one according to the specs of your laptop, you can conclude that it has now reached its life expectancy and you will probably encounter power issues with it. If your situation is this, please enter STEP: C-3;

STEP: C-2 this link is to determine if your adapter has a power shortage problem

For an adapter power shortage problem, there are 3 different representations:

Situation 1: for a slight adapter power shortage, sometimes it shows it is charging and other times not. With external power supply, check the amount of battery power left as displayed on the screen. You will find that the battery power is x% with a slight increase or none at all. After turning the laptop off, the battery charges up again. If your symptom belongs to this situation, please enter STEP: C-3; if battery doesn't charge after turning it off laptop, then please enter STEP: D-1;

Situation 2: Moderate power adapter shortage. The laptop starts singularly with external power mode, but fails to charge the battery. Sometimes the laptop will auto switch to battery mode; after turning off the laptop, the power adapter can charge the battery again.

If your situation belongs to this type, please enter STEP: C-3;

If after turning off the laptop the battery still can't charge, then please enter STEP: D-1;

Situation 3: Severe adapter power shortage. Removing the battery, sometimes will start the laptop and sometimes not. After putting the battery back in again and the laptop doesn't go into external power supply mode or after turning the laptop off, the power adapter still doesn't charge the battery.

If this is your situation, then please enter STEP: D-1;

STEP: C-3 this link helps solve your adapter power shortage problem

Under this circumstance, you have to check your power adapter by measuring the output voltage with a voltage meter. If you can't do that, find a good and more powerful adapter to test your laptop. Then you can eliminate the possibility of power shortage that causes the battery to not charge.

To change to a more powerful adapter ensure that you use a correct model. The output voltage must be equal to the initial adapter, or within the acceptable +/-5% range. For instance, if the original adapter shows 18.5V, then a 19V is acceptable. Output current amperages must be higher than the original adapter, not less than. If the original adapter was 3.5A, a 4.7V power adapter is acceptable.

Let's first look at to 2 different situations here:

1. The original charge situation doesn't change at all. If it's the case, please enter STEP: D-3;
2. Sometimes it charges and sometimes not, this situation never changes, if this is the case, please enter STEP: C-5;

STEP: C-4 this link is to solve the issue that your OS doesn't show correct battery charging status.

Any error or damage with the laptop OS can cause the problem with a screen not displaying the correct battery charging state. For instance, virus infection, hacker software and deletion of files by mistake etc. even though you have already deleted the virus and hacker software, may not solve the problem. Some files may have been corrupted by it and there is no way to recover them, and the laptop still fails to display the correct charging state.

1. If you test the battery with your third party software, then the result will show that the performance is good, but the remaining battery power is 0% when you check it with your OS screen, and the value is not increased;
2. Without using the power adapter, singularly start the laptop that has 0% power left. The result shows that the batteries performance is good. If this is the case, your problem is with the internal supervision software of you OS

Generally, the way to solve the OS failure is to format the hard disk, and reinstall the OS to try and eliminate any software problems that occurred.

STEP: C-5 the purpose of this link is to change the damaged power jack

For a damaged power jack, there are 3 different situations:

Situation 1: the power jack is slightly damaged. Rough handling of the jack can cause damage. The damage is visible with a magnifying glass but probably not with the naked eye. If you look at the bottom of the DC jack carefully with a magnifier, you might see a hair-like crack. It will cause intermittent problems such as a failure to start. You might be able to repair the jack by re-soldering it, or you can solder on a new jack. If the problem is not solved, and you still have charging problems, then please enter STEP: D-3;

Situation 2: The power jack is moderately damaged. Expansion and contraction of the metal parts of the jack due to heating caused by the relatively high currents passing through it, eventually will deteriorate the jack to a point where it does not work. In this case, after repeated expansion and shrinkage, the welding points of the jack may crack. This leads to the laptop no longer charging the battery or switching to battery mode. Generally the one solution is to solder on a new power jack. Please take a look at Figure 4-3.

If the problem is still not solved, and battery still fails to charge, then please enter STEP: D-3;

Figure 4-3

Situation 3 the power jack is severely damaged. Remove the battery, connect the adapter, and laptop starts normally, and often when you remove your hand, the laptop auto powers off and shuts down. Sometimes the laptop may work for a short time. You may hear a sizzling sound from the jack, caused by a spark between the jack and plug and also the jack may overheat very quickly. This is why the laptop occasionally starts with the external power supply mode, and other times not. With this problem, the power adapter cannot charge the battery. The solution for the failure is to install a new power jack, but also check the AC plug of the power adapter to ensure it isn't damaged or burnt.

If the problem is still unsolved, please enter STEP: D-3;

STEP: D-1 this link will ensure the integrity of the connection between the battery and the laptop motherboard

A poor connection between the battery and the motherboard can cause battery charging problems. When the battery doesn't charge, I would immediately check the terminals of the battery as a first step, and recheck the connectors between the battery and the laptop motherboard. That may solve the issue.

If you're sure the connection between the battery and the laptop motherboard is good go to STEP: D-3 ; If you aren't sure of the connection state then please continue STEP: D-2

STEP: D-2 the goal of this link is to ensure there is no problem with the battery connection pins

Generally an HP battery has 6 connector pins. First check the inside of the connector pins to ensure they are not damaged or bent. Then also confirm there is no foreign matter such as lint, dirt, paper, hair or oil dust etc. obstructing the pins. If there is, use a small sharp knife and remove the material, and do not scratch or damage the pins while doing this. If your problem belongs to this situation, please enter STEP: D-4;

If no error occurs, install the battery back in again, if the laptop still doesn't not charge the battery, then please continue STEP: D-3

STEP: D-3 the goal of this link is to change to a new battery

To replace a battery, you must ensure it's the same model; because some BIOS versions have different abilities to recognize the new batteries. Generally speaking, older BIOS versions do not have this ability to recognize other types of new batteries. If the battery has different numbers (compatible numbers), some unimaginable situations can occur. It increases the difficulty to repair, so pay close attention as some batteries may seem like to peas in a pot when in fact they are totally incompatible. Using such a battery would only cause you more trouble.

If the problem is solved by changing the new battery, then you should still check whether the new battery is a little loose or the size is proper or the jack is too tight, to ensure its well plugged in.

Check the installation of the new battery; it should always be first installed into the laptop from the side that doesn't have a slot. Follow the proper instruction. All right, now the new battery is plugged in. There's no error, but the laptop still doesn't charge the battery. Please continue STEP: D-4

STEP: D-4 the goal of this link is to ensure there's nothing wrong with the motherboard connector pin

After changing the battery, if it still doesn't charge, then there is something wrong with the connector pin between the motherboard and the battery. The motherboard doesn't recognize the battery and therefore it is not charging. Check the connector pins for the battery on the motherboard, ensure they are not damaged or bent. Ensure also that there is no foreign matter obstructing the pins. Please take a look at Figure 4-4.

Figure 4-4

Check the connector pin voltages of the battery when connected to the motherboard with a multi-meter. Generally speaking, you should just need to connect 4 cables: power cable, ground cable, SCL and SDA. After connecting these cables, the laptop can communicate with the battery, to charge, discharge or other normal operations. It still needs a set of complicated charge/discharge control circuit functions.

Next are some tests recorded for HP's laptop battery interface voltage, for example let's take the HP Pavilion DV6000, when 432307-001 battery is fully charged without starting the laptop:

Pin 1: ground cable, 0V

Pin 2: +0.3V, battery connection confirm

Pin 3: 0V

Pin 4: +3.3V

Pin 5: +3.3V

Pin 6: +11.4V battery power pin, which connects the battery output and machine, charging and discharging.

So the point is, is to check the batteries 1,2,4,5,6 pins, especially pin 2. Are the voltages correct and reaching the motherboard? If there are no errors after installing the new battery, and the laptop still doesn't charge the battery, and then please continue STEP: D-5

STEP: D-5 this link provides instructions to repair the charging circuit of the laptop battery

It still doesn't charge after installing the new battery, it means there's something wrong with the motherboard charging circuit.

The failure that HP DV600 /DV9000 battery doesn't charge is quite common. You have to start from the batteries interface to solve the problem. First check whether the charge pin has voltage output, the position should be the first pin 6 on the right side. Most HP laptops supply the battery with 18.5V voltage to charge. The multi-meter test result shows the pin has no output voltage.

As the picture shows, this part is the charge circuit of the battery. Let's first take a look at the accessory in the yellow circle. Here's a resistor, capacitor, a diode and a MOSFET. First test the diode, finding there's no voltage at the end, proves that the current was cut off previously. Then next test the 8 pin MOSFET. After testing the pins with a multi-meter, the conclusion comes out quickly. You can Google the chip number and get a list of pin voltages. The control pins of the 8 pin MOSFET have voltage output. In that case, it means the problem is on the diode and MOSFET.

Next focus on the 8 pin MOSFET chip. As it is already tested and there is no current to the diode, probably the 8 pin chip is defective. After testing, and confirmation that the problem is really there, the solution is very simple. Install a new chip.

So why does such a problem occur? It's no big secret. It is caused by improper operations. We all know that during the battery charging process, high voltage is produced each time you pull and plug the battery because high current is interrupted and creates a spark in the interface. It is a bad practice to interrupt the charging process by pulling the laptop power jack. It can cause damage to the battery or the laptop motherboard. Usually, when laptop is running and working, don't randomly pull or plug the battery, as it might cause damage to the charge circuit of the battery and even the power supply circuit, which can burn.

In this machine, generally, the current while charging can damage the resistor at the end of the motherboard power supply circuit, and thus the laptop's 8 pin MOSFET is burnt. Probably it caused the problem with starting up using the external power supply.

Once I repaired a HP Pavilion DV9000 laptop that did not start with the external power supply. The reason was also the 8 pin MOSFET that was broken. After changing the chip, everything returned to normal again. However, the 8 pin MOSFET's position is different. It is on the face of the motherboard, close to the right bottom of the battery interface.

In conclusion, after summarizing this tutorial, here is the analysis result for a failure causing a battery charging issue. Batteries or adapters do age, but there may also be failures with system power, hardware management and even the OS.

Solution: change the battery or power adapter, and update your system hardware functions.

For more details, please refer to the tutorial. Thank you so much!

4.3   Twenty-four repair cases of HP laptop battery charge failures

4.3.1   10 repair cases for the problems caused by HP laptop original battery

024)   HP DV7t laptop would not charge, it always stays around 10%

Failure symptoms:

DV7 laptop would not charge, it always stays around 10%. When plug in an external power supply, the fan rotates very quickly, and I point the mouse to the battery icon on the system tray it shows that the battery would not charge normally . . .

Solution:

This failure symptom obviously belongs to the description of flowchart 04 according to the repair method; confirm the repair path, finding it's accorded with the sequence:

Start->A-1->B-1->B-3->B-4;

Repair summary: HP laptop's CMOS setup has no special inspection function to test the charging of the battery. According to general method, first turn off the laptop, pull out the external power supply, and then remove the battery; after that, press the power button of the laptop for about 15 to 20 seconds; then reconnect the battery and the power supply, usually everything should be all right afterwards. If it still does not work out, then I suggest you try several more times.

Hint: optimize CMOS setup would also be done by software which updates the BIOS. Most times, the failure is that laptop would charge and not be solved by this path; however, you would have to follow the principle "simple first and then complicated". First use the "general method", which is quite an important step to simplify the repair process. Keep this in mind: before pressing the power button, you will have to ensure that all power is out, including removing battery and power adapter.

025) HP nx8220 laptop would not charge, the charging display status tells us it is not charging.

Failure symptoms:

Battery fails to charge, the charging status shows 0. Put the battery on a working laptop of the same model to test, as a result, it still would not charge. So definitely this is a battery problem, but what is not clear is that after installing a new battery, it still fails to charge.

Solution:

This failure symptom obviously belongs to the description of flowchart 04, according to the repair method; confirm the repair path, finding it is accorded with the sequence:

Start->A-1->A-2->A-4->A-5->D-3;

Repair summary: but now the problem is that the new battery would not charge either, would it be the problem of the charging circuit? Let us check the repair work just now:

1) Plug the old battery, connect external power supply—the laptop works, but the battery still will not charge;
2) Plug the old battery without the external power supply—the laptop would not even start;
3) Pull out the old battery, and connect the external power supply—the laptop still will not work;
4) Try jiggling the laptop power joint, still the battery would not charge;

However, if we compare this to our previous work carefully, we found that there is one difference, that would be the second point, plug a new battery without the external power adapter, and then the laptop would start up normally. It seems the problem is here, adjust the repair thought, and confirm the new repair path:

Start->A-1->B-1->B-3->B-4;

1) Turn off the laptop and then remove the battery. Meanwhile, disconnect the power adapter off from the laptop;
2) Start up the laptop, meanwhile, press the power button for about 15 seconds;
3) Right now plug the battery again and connect power adapter again;
4) Start the laptop, check up the battery, it would charge normally again, then the problem is solved.

Hint: actually, most times laptop has more than 2 problems, but most users have not thought of this level. Therefore, usually they deny the previous correct repair method and come to the conclusion incorrectly, finally losing the chance to solve the problem successfully. As a matter of fact, as long as you can take care, then similar problems would be avoided later.

026) HP Pavilion HP DV6226US laptop auto cuts off power and shut down. Battery charging status shows 99%

Failure symptoms:

Laptop has the symptom that it cuts off power and shuts down automatically, in a blink of time; screen and all other display lights on keyboard are off. If you restart it, you will have to plug external power adapter. Check the battery status, it is at the charging status, and the power is kept around 99%;

Solution:

This failure symptom obviously belongs to the description of flowchart 04, according to the repair method; confirm the repair path, finding it's accorded with the sequence:

Start->A-1->A-2->A-4->A-5->D-3;

Repair summary: but now the problem is that the battery is of 99% power, would it be the problem that the adapter power is not enough?

Here is the repair process as below:

1) Plug the old battery, and connect external power supply—the laptop would work;
2) Plug the old battery without external power supply—the laptop starts 2 seconds and then shuts down automatically;
3) Pull out the old battery, and connect the external power supply—the laptop would work too;

Pull out the old battery, observe the slot of the battery carefully, check and compare the battery joint of the laptop, finding everything is all right. Then it would be the problem of the battery or the power circuit. Change big power 90W to 120W adapter and charge for 3 hours, the power still marks 99%. Now change with new battery and start up the laptop, it would work normally again.

Hint: in fact, even you do not start up the laptop, battery would charge as usual. At this moment, even BIOS does not run, usually our laptop has software (such as Battery on) to test the laptop battery, while laptop itself just checks battery, but not test. So for users, usually it would mix these conceptions, because radically speaking, 99% power mark would not prove that the laptop battery has no problem itself.

027) HP Pavilion DV9000 series laptops would not charge, battery charging status shows 4%;

Failure symptoms:

Battery would discharge but fail to charge. When use battery mode to start up laptop, battery status shows "online", but the laptop enters hibernation mode immediately, then you cannot continue using the laptop normally, but if you have to use, then you must plug external power supply. Check up the battery status, whether it is charging or not, "plugged in, charging". Power stays around 4%, no any rise.

Solutions:

This failure symptom obviously belongs to the description of flowchart 04, according to the repair method; confirm the repair path, finding it's accorded with the sequence:

Start->A-1->B-1->B-2->B-4->;

Repair summary:

But this battery power always stays around 4%, would it be the problem of the battery? Here is the repair process:

1) Plug the old battery, connect the external power supply—the laptop would work normally;
2) Plug the old battery without external power supply—the laptop starts for 2 to 4 seconds and then enters hibernation mode;
3) Pull out the old battery and plug on another HP Pavilion DV9000 laptop to test, the result shows the battery charges normally;

Check up the battery slot carefully, check and compare the battery joint of the laptop, finding that everything is OK, and then it would be the problem of the BIOS or the charging circuit. Update BIOS Power Drain Power Management, and then reinstall battery and start the laptop, the failure is gone, the problem is solved then.

Hint: now those BIOS are also an application, then there must be some Bugs in the BIOS, absolutely there is something unsatisfied on BIOS program. While these Bugs would often cause indescribable failures, such as restart without any reason, frequent system down, device confliction and battery charge failure etc. After user feedback and manufacturers find, new version of BIOS would be released in time to revise these known BUGS, finally to solve these problems. However, you would have to pay attention to BIOS update, which has certain damager.

028) HP Pavilion dv2500 laptop would not start up with (AC Adapter) external power supply;

Failure symptoms:

When battery group is plugged on the laptop, laptop would not start up even with external power supply. Pull out the old battery and connect external power supply, the laptop would start normally again;

Solution:

This failure symptom obviously belongs to the description of flowchart 04, according to the repair method; confirm the repair path, finding it's accorded with the sequence:

Start->A-1->A-2->A-4->A-5->D-3;

Repair summary:

1) Plug the old battery, and connect external power supply—the laptop would work
2) Plug the old battery without external power supply—the laptop fails to start up
3) Pull out the old battery, and connect the external power supply—the laptop would work

According to the repair process above, it is not difficult to find that it is the problem of the battery. Pull out the old battery and put on a HP laptop without any problem, and then test it. The result shows that the good laptop also has the same problem. It seems that we can conclude that the problem is the battery. Change a new battery, then the failure disappears;

Hint: Generally, laptop battery would not cause a laptop not to start up because of external power supply. But if the battery inside storage medium is broken, then such a failure would happen when circuit has a little short circuit because of this. When a battery short circuit, power adapter would enable self-protection, stopping the supplying of power or leading to the problem that power is serious out of use. These two situations would make the problem, even worse; it would get the power adapter or motherboard burnt.

029) HP NX7400 laptop battery charging progress is quite slow, after charging full, it would only work for 2 minutes.

Failure symptom:

NC6320 laptop battery charges quite slowly in a sudden, averagely it takes 15 minutes to increase 1% power, while normally it's 2 to 5 minutes to increase 1% power. The laptop power charging indication light is on, but keeping flashing. Besides, it would not charge full.

Solution:

This failure symptom obviously belongs to the description of flowchart 04, according to the repair method; confirm the repair path, finding it is accorded with the sequence:

Start->A-1->A-2->A-4->A-5->D-3;

Repair summary:

Step to A-2 repair flow, check whether HP original power adapter is used or not? This point is quite important to repair the laptop, check carefully, finding that it is really the problem of the HP original power adapter. Step to A-4 repair flow, experience tells us that the biggest possibility is the battery problem. Use a confirmed working battery to test and validate. The result shows that the battery charges and discharges normally, that means the original old battery has some problems, which causes the problem that it fails to charge normally. So this belongs to the problem of battery core aging. Generally, the solution is to change the original battery.

Hint: if the laptop power charging light is always flashing or has not changed the display status, for example: if the power charging light changes from yellow to green, and turns from green to yellow. Then we can come to the conclusion that you need to change your laptop battery;

030) HP 530 laptop shows that the battery charges normally, but it always stops at 0%

Failure symptoms:

HP 530 laptop, equipping with Pentium D (Centrino Duo Core), now the problem is that the battery keeps its charging status, when plug in external power to charge, check up current battery state for displayed on the screen in a longer times, finding that the battery always shows 0%, no any increase. Laptop would not start up with battery mode at all.

Solution:

This failure symptom obviously belongs to the description of flowchart 04, according to the repair method; confirm the repair path, finding it is accorded with the sequence:

Start->A-1->A-2->A-4->A-5->D-3;

Repair summary: generally, this failure is related with laptop battery, DC interface and charging control chip (on the motherboard). Most cases are that the laptop is already old, and we can prove that the problem is the old battery. After changing the old battery, the problem is resolved. Of course, if you do not change battery, then just connect power adapter, laptop would also run normally.

Hint: The times of battery charge and discharge relate to the lifespan of the battery, the more times you charge the battery, you reduce the lifespan of the battery.) If you usually pull and plug the power adapter several times in a day with the laptop battery on, this usually can do a big damage to battery. Since every time you connect to external power adapter is equal to charging the battery once again, naturally the battery would get the battery's lifespan would reduce. Theoretically, although it is, every time it is not that convenient to remove the battery, plus, under the circumstance that there is no battery, if suddenly power goes off, then data would get lost. So we do not suggest users removing battery to use a laptop. However, if client really wants to save the battery, or most time always uses the laptop, besides, in order to avoid the danger of power-off, then you can choose to remove the battery when using the external power adapter. But the most effective way is to change a new laptop battery.

031) COMPAQ PRESARIO A910CA laptop charges to 100%, but it shows that the battery is still charging.

Failure symptoms:

Battery charging already shows 100%, but seems it is still showing charging. Laptop would start with battery mode, but the battery usable time sometimes shows 3 hours, and sometimes just more than 1 hour.

Solution:

This failure symptom obviously belongs to the description of flowchart 04, according to the repair method; confirm the repair path, finding it is accorded with the sequence:

Start->A-1->B-1->B-3-> C-1->C-3->D-3->D-5

Repair summary: battery information is just there as a helping tool; this would let you know the battery performance according to actual battery test. Battery information show is also according to each power consumption conclusion of the laptop. The battery already charges to 100%, but it shows still charging. This is a normal symptom, but if after 10 to 20 minutes, it still shows charging, and then there must be some kind of problems, which means the problem is related with the laptop battery. Generally, protection circuit has some problems; the simplest and fastest solution is to change a new laptop battery.

Of course, when starting the laptop with battery mode, usable time sometimes shows 3 hours, and sometimes more than 1 hour; this is also normal, because battery usable time is changing as the consumption of the laptop, but if after starting the laptop with battery mode, it would only works for 10 to 20 minutes or even less, then it is because the laptop battery is already aging.

Hint: During the charging process of lithium battery, voltage would get down a little when is close to full. Therefore, when control circuit inspects such a situation, it is confirmed the battery is still full charge; protection circuit would work, cutting off power to avoid over charging; when discharging, battery voltage is stable basically. It would drop suddenly only when the rest of the battery power is quite little. When control circuit inspects such a situation, it would confirm the battery power is out of use, and power on to start charging. However, if there is something wrong with the protection circuit, then abnormal symptom would occur.

032) HP pavilion DV2700 laptop charging shows 100%, but after starting the laptop with battery mode, it shuts down 2 minutes later.

Failure symptoms:

Only 10 minutes, laptop finishes charging, it shows 100% power. But when you start the laptop with battery mode, it only runs for 2 minutes. After connecting power adapter and checking again, the rest of the battery power is only 3%. The battery lightens obviously;

Solution:

This failure symptom obviously belongs to the description of flowchart 04, according to the repair method; confirm the repair path, finding it's accorded with the sequence:

Start->A-1->B-1->B-2->B-5->C-2->D-1->D-3;

Repair summary:

1) Plug the old battery without external power supply—the laptop would work normally;
2) Pull out the old battery and connect external power supply—the laptop would work too;

3)   Check the BIOS version, finding it is already been updated to the latest one;
4)   Change with a new adapter with higher power, the failure symptom does not change;
5)   Change with a new original laptop battery, the problem is then solved;

If the charging time is too short or the battery feels light, you can tell the battery is aging, which is the fastest way to judge the state of the laptop battery, because after battery is working for a period of time, it would get "old", the concrete symptom is that the internal resistance becomes bigger; the voltage of the two ends when charging is fast. Then charging control circuit would easily judge that the battery is charged full, of course, the capacitance would drop. As the battery internal resistance is kind of big, voltage drop range is big; also speed is fast when discharging. Aging is a process of vicious circle. When we find that the battery working time is kind of short, you should take some related actions.

Hint: Normally, battery charging time and battery discharging time has a direct ratio relationship. Generally speaking, a laptop battery would work for 3 hours, of which charging time (from 4% to 100%) needs more than 3 hours; similarly, a laptop battery would work for 1 hour, of which the charging time (from 4% to 100%) needs at least 1 hour above; therefore, laptop battery taking 10 minutes to charging to 100%, actually, the usable time would not exceed 10 minutes;

This is because certain section of battery core inside the battery group is lapsed. As the battery core property of every section of battery is impossible to be completely same, so after using for a long time, some with bad quality would start aging, finally damaging the discharging curve of the entire battery (after serial connection). If you are an experienced hardware technician, then you should pay close attention to change aged laptop battery or battery chip in time, inspecting the connection pins inside the battery. And then use the battery after adjustment again.

033)   HP 540 laptop cannot charge, besides, the power would not reach 100% full.

Failure symptom:

HP 540 laptop starts and charges till 70% above, then the charging pauses. Later after discharging the battery, continue charging the battery, but would only charging till 23%.

After shutting down for a period of time (pull out the power adapter), then start up and continue charging, finding that the charge light would flash once about every 10 to 20 seconds, generally, it would keep lightening for 5 to 8 seconds. Turn it off again, wait until the power adapter cools down completely, then connect power adapter, but the green indication light on the adapter has no display directly.

Solution:

This failure symptom obviously belongs to the description of flowchart 04, according to the repair method; confirm the repair path, finding it is accorded with the sequence:

Start->A-1->B-1->B-3->B-4->C-3->-D-3

Repair summary:

Laptop would not charge full, charging indication light is unstable, and then according to the direction of the flowchart, this failure belongs to power adapter or battery badness. When adapter power is not enough or overheating problem occurs, then voltage would be unstable, finally leading to unstable charge, intermittent charging symptom occurs then. General solution for this is to change a new adapter or change a new battery.

Hint: before this, you need to do one test for the laptop BIOS, recovering BIOS to factory settings, excluding the factor the problem is caused by BIOS.

First of all, it is required to turn off the laptop, disconnect AC power adapter, remove the battery, and then press power button for about 30 seconds. By doing this, you can recover laptop system to BIOS factory settings.

Plug AC power adapter to power jack without any problem, and then connect to the laptop.

If the laptop would start and run normally, then plug the battery again, and then run HP Battery Check to continue dealing with the problem.

If the laptop problem still always exists, then it means the AC power adapter or the battery has some problems.

4.3.2   Nine repair cases for HP laptop power adapter or power manager failures

034)   HP 2133 laptop would not charge when starting up

Failure symptoms:

After starting up, the charging light shows yellow, but a few minutes later, it goes out. If you pull out and plug the power plug again, then the light would be on for a second. But before long, it dies out again. Strangely that the second day after shutdown, you will find the battery has already been charged full.

Solution:

This failure symptom obviously belongs to the description of flowchart 04, according to the repair method; confirm the repair path, finding it is accorded with the sequence:

Start->A-1->B-1->B-2->B-5->C-2->C-3

Repair summary:

According to the failure symptoms, we know that the battery is good, also the power adapter works. Just the laptop would not charge when starting up. So observe and check the battery slot, check and compare the battery joint of the laptop, usually you find that everything is all right, then step to C-3 repair flow. Change a new adapter with bigger power, then the failure disappears;

Hint: under some circumstances, power adapter would really turn quite hot; this is because of power aging, battery aging and big increment of power consumption by the laptop. You can try changing a new power adapter of the same model, try plugging it on, whether the status is same as the previous one. If it still power part has some problems.

035) HP Pavilion DV6560US laptop sometimes charges normally and sometimes would not charge completely:

Failure symptoms:

This client often takes his laptop outside with him, he found that sometimes the laptop would charge normally, but sometimes would not completely. When it fails to charge, the laptop would not work normally either. However, 40 minutes later, restart the laptop, and then everything is all right. Under all circumstances, it's nothing about the battery power, the problem above would occur always when power is around 12% to 95%.

Solution:

This failure symptom obviously belongs to the description of flowchart 04, according to the repair method; confirm the repair path, finding it is accorded with the sequence:

Start->A-1->B-1->B-2->B-4->C-3->D-3;

Repair summary: the problem is not solved by updating BIOS, after changing an adapter with higher power, the problem is still unresolved; at last, you change to a new battery, but the problem still persists; could it be the problem of the joint between laptop battery and motherboard? Or there is a bad soldering problem existing on the power jack? But after 40 minutes, restart the laptop, then everything is back normal, how to explain this? Probably the problem is somewhere else.

After careful inquiry, client found that when the laptop fails to charge, it always happens when moving the laptop outdoor to indoor, and besides it all it is in the cold of winter, where the temperature difference between the two places is above 30 degrees, the battery pack is in the temperature difference margin), 40 minutes later, wait until the laptop battery group reaches to room temperature, naturally the problem would be solved.

Hint: it is quite necessary to keep the laptop used under suggested temperature, if you use the laptop under cold and overheated environments; it would accelerate the aging process of the internal components, even worse that system would fail to start up. Therefore, avoid moving the laptop from somewhere cold to warm place suddenly, and starting up the laptop right away. If the temperature difference between two places is 10 degrees, then it might cause dew forming inside the machine, finally damaging the storage medium.

036) after changing power adapter for HP COMPAQ 6910p laptop, finding that the laptop battery would not charge

Failure symptoms:

HP 6910p laptop, equip with Intel Centrino 2 platform, is always been working normally. But one day, when client took the laptop outside, found that the power adapter was lost, then bought a "universal" power adapter in a computer store, as a result, he found that when connected with external power adapter and charged, the percentage of the battery use showing on the screen was always decreasing, which means the laptop battery would not charge.

Solution:

This failure symptom obviously belongs to the description of flowchart 04, according to the repair method; confirm the repair path, finding it's accorded with the sequence:

Start->A-1->A-2->A-3->;

Repair summary: according to the clients' memory, before the original power adapter was lost, the battery would charge normally, which means the failure must be related with the "universal" power adapter, usually, it is because the power adapter is incompatible with the laptop, and the simplest and fastest solution for this is to change a HP power adapter.

Hint:

1. "Universal" power adapter, generally, would be used for most of laptops, but not 100% suitable, HP power test system has no any Hint message for some incompatible power adapters;

2. Generally, "universal" power adapter has few joints, you must pick up the one that matches with the jack properly, besides, check up whether the power is on, is there a contact problem, you must be clear whether there is enough power, because when adapter power is not enough, laptop would auto inspect and not allow system starting up.

037) HP pavilion dv6500 laptop battery charging status shows 0%, but when start up the laptop with battery mode, the battery would be used for about 2 hours

Failure symptoms:

HP pavilion dv6500 laptop battery charging status shows 0%,

Solution:

This failure symptom obviously belongs to the description of flowchart 04, according to the repair method; confirm the repair path, finding it is accorded with the sequence:

Start->A-1->B-1->B-2-> B-5->C-4

Repair summary: this failure obviously is related with laptop battery test software, which indicates that the laptop BIOS or hardware power manager test part has some problems. The simplest and fastest method is to put the battery on HP laptop of the same model and test, now if the battery would charge to 100%, then it means the assumption above is right. The solution is to reinstall the OS and update the BIOS version. Of course, if there is something wrong with the hardware test part of the power manager, then it would not be easy to solve the problem. However, it would not affect the laptop normal work condition.

Hint: battery charging status is displayed after laptop OS internal test software summarizes each power consumption of BIOS. The BIOS masters the power consumption of each components in a laptop, including the control of the charging process of the battery, and cutting off power to prevent overcharge of the battery; the main task of hardware power manager is to ensure that voltage keeps stable basically when battery is in use, meanwhile, when battery charges are close to full or when the remaining battery power capacity of the battery is quite little, it sends different signals to the BIOS; OS battery test software only reflects the battery status at current stage. If any of the three—the BIOS, the hardware power manager and OS battery test software—goes wrong, then battery charging status would not be displayed correctly.

038) HP pavilion DV6700 laptop would not charge, power always shows 40%.

Failure symptoms:

When HP Pavilion DV6700 laptops connect power adapter to charge, check up the dormant power of the battery at the same time, you would find that the battery always shows 40%

value, no any increase. 15 minutes after starting the laptop with battery mode, the remaining battery power capacity of the battery would drop to 39%, then plug external power adapter to charge, finding that the battery always shows 39% value; besides, it does not show that the battery is charging at the moment.

Solution:

This failure symptom obviously belongs to the description of flowchart 04, according to the repair method; confirm the repair path, finding it is accorded with the sequence:

Start->A-1->B-1->B-3->C-1->B-4->C-3->D-3->D-5;

Repair summary: work process:

1) Plug the old battery without external power supply—the laptop usually would start up;
2) Pull out the old battery and connect external power supply—the laptop would work also;
3) Check up the version of the BIOS, finding it is already updated to the latest one;
4) After changing to a new adapter with higher power output, the failure symptom has no change;
5) Replace with a new original laptop battery, the failure symptom has no change either;
6) Put the battery on an HP laptop of the same model to test, the result shows the battery charges to 100%.

The conclusion of the operation process above indicates that your laptop power manager hardware part has something wrong, which would not provide BIOS with the signal that battery needs for charging; or we can say that BIOS would not control power manager to activate the motherboard power system to charge the battery. Here is one temporary method that will solve the problem: if you only plug the power adapter, the laptop would run normally.

Hint: focus on the few points below:

1. Be clear whether the power adapter has enough power and whether it is the original one, because power shortage or faked power adapter would cause the problem that the battery does not charge sometimes.
2. Check the BIOS version, whether it's already updated to the latest one, when there's something wrong with the BIOS, battery charge failure symptom would also happen;
3. Change related power manager's hardware or the entire motherboard, completely solving the problem that the battery would not charge.

039)   HP PRESARIO R4000 SERIES laptop battery stops charging after 5 minutes

Failure symptoms:

According to my clients' memory: the HP Presario R4000 laptop always worked fine, but one day he found the power adapter cable was bitten by a mouse, he then bought a new power adapter from a computer store, as a result, he found that the laptop would work normally after changing the power adapter, but 5 minutes later, the laptop battery would not charge, and make "beeping noises";

Solution:

This failure symptom obviously belongs to the description of flowchart 04, according to the repair method; confirm the repair path, finding it is accorded with the sequence:

Start->A-1->B-1->B-3->C-1->C-3;

Repair summary: according to the client's memory, before changing the original power adapter, the battery would charge well, which indicates the problem is related with the power adapter, generally, it is because the adapter power is too small, which is incompatible with the laptop. The simplest and fastest solution is to change a new power adapter design and made for HP Presario R4000 laptop.

Hint:

1.   HP PRESARIO R4000 SERIES power adapter, generally, 120W would be proper for any laptops, but when you use 90W power adapter, such a problem might occur, namely, due to power shortage, the moment you start using the laptop, battery it would not charge, and when you stop using the laptop, the battery charges normally; as for incompatible power adapters, HP laptop does not show any notice on the screen.
2.   Be clear whether the adapter power is enough or not, whether the battery has enough power, because when system is charging, battery would scrabble for power with other components, like CPU, fan, hard disk and so on. When adapter power is of severe shortage, laptop auto test system would not allow the laptop to start up;

040)   HP Presario R3000 SERIES laptop Battery starts charging after shutting down laptop

Failure symptoms:

When HP PRESARIO R3000 laptop is charging when plug with (AC adapter) external power adapter, checking the rest of power at the same time, we find that the battery shows 80% value, but when you check up the working power mode of the laptop carefully, it is found that the laptop works with the battery, 15 minutes later, the doormat power of the battery would drop to 75%. Pull out power adapter and then plug back in again, finding that the laptop has not switched to external power mode; besides, the battery does not show that it is charging at all. After shutting down for 20 minutes, start it up again, it is found that the battery has already charged to 81%.

Solution:

This failure symptom obviously belongs to the description of flowchart 04, according to the repair method; confirm the repair path, finding it is accorded with the sequence:

Start->A-1->B-1->B-2->B-5->C-2->

Repair summary: work process:

1) Plug the old battery without external power supply—the laptop would start up;
2) Pull out the old battery and connect the external power supply—the laptop would work too;
3) Check up the version of the BIOS, finding it is already updated to the latest one;
4) After shutting down the machine, battery starts charging and it would reach 100%.

The conclusion of the operation process above indicates that your laptop adapter power is critically insufficient, which would not provide the power required by laptop and battery at the same time; the solution for the problem is to change a new original laptop power adapter.

Hint: focus on the few points below:

1. Be clear whether the adapter really has enough power 120W, such as some marked 120W old or bad quality power adapters, actually, they would not reach the marked power, when you use, the failures above would occur;
2. Sometimes when you use non-original power adapter, problem might happen that the laptop would not work with external power supply mode;

041) When HP PRESARIO R4200 SERIES laptop charges, sometimes it works but sometimes not.

Failure symptoms:

HP PRESARIO R4200 laptops sometimes charges normally, but sometimes would not charge completely. When it fails to charge, the laptop would work normally with battery mode, however, sometimes everything becomes OK again. If you use the laptop on the way when you drive a car, then such a situation would happen quite frequently, if you nip the power adapter's plug, then insert into the laptop and hold still, then the problem would be improved within a short period of time.

Solution:

This failure symptom obviously belongs to the description of flowchart 04, according to the repair method; confirm the repair path, finding it's accorded with the sequence:

Start->A-1->B-1->B-2->B-4->C-3->C-5;

Repair summary: work process:

1) Plug the old battery and connect external power supply—the laptop would start up normally

2) plug the old battery without external power supply—the laptop would start up normally;

3) Pull out the old battery and connect external power supply—the laptop would start and work, but sometimes it would not;

4) After changing to an original adapter of 135W power, the problem is still not solved;

5) After updating the BIOS, the problem still exists.

According to the test process above, it is not difficult to find out that it is quite likely the connection between laptop battery and motherboard has something wrong, or there is a bad soldering problem existing on the power jack. After starting the laptop, replace with a new power jack, then the problem disappears;

Hint: When power jack are loose, damage are quite common laptop failures, especially when power adapter is dropped, compacted, dragged, with laptop, the external vibration would also cause damage to the power jack or even breakdown. If you place the laptop on the surface which vibrate for a long time and use, then such a problem would occur if power jack is loose, then it would cause the problem that sometimes laptop would charge normally, but sometimes would not completely charge; besides, it would cause excess current, which would cause overheating in the jack and the adapter, even worse, it would get power adapter or motherboard burnt.

042) HP Compaq V6000 laptop would not start with battery mode, even same with new battery changed

Failure symptoms:

When HP COMPAQ V6000 laptop is plugged with external power supply, check up the dormant power, we find that the battery shows the value 0%, the battery is at charging state, but no any power increased, after changing to battery mode charge, it is found that the laptop would not start up, only work when with external power adapter plugged;

Solution:

This failure symptom obviously belongs to the description of flowchart 04, according to the repair method; confirm the repair path, finding it's accorded with the sequence:

Start->A-1->A-2->A-4->A-5->D-3->D-5;

Repair summary: work process:

1) Plug the old battery without external power supply—the laptop would not start up;
2) Pull out the old battery and connect external power supply—the laptop would work;
3) Check up the version of the BIOS, finding it is already updated to the latest one;
4) After changing to a new adapter of bigger power, the failure symptom has no change;
5) Change with a new original laptop battery, the failure symptom has no change either;
6) Put the battery on a HP laptop of the same model to test, the result shows the battery is in good condition, and it would keep running for about 2 hours.

The conclusion of the operation process above indicates that there is something wrong with the laptop power manager hardware (south bridge chip), so that the BIOS fails to control or monitor the battery. Meanwhile, it would not control the power manager to activate motherboard power system to charge the battery. The way to solve the problem is to only plug power adapter temporarily and use the laptop, the best way is to change the entire motherboard, then the problem would be solved thoroughly;

Hint: focus on the two points below:

1. Be aware whether the adapter has really enough power and whether it is the original one, because power shortage or non-original adapter would cause the symptom of the battery failing to charge sometimes;
2. Pay close attention to whether the original laptop battery or the original battery are 100% compatible, because if it is not the original adapter, or you use a battery incompatible with the laptop, then such a symptom of not charging and no power would occur;

4.3.3   2 repair cases of typical failures caused by HP laptop power manager

43)   HP COMPAQ Presario V5000T laptop battery indication light flashes and it enters hibernation status, would not be awaken up then

Failure symptoms:

Battery indication light flashes and laptop enters hibernation status, and then it auto shuts down and would not start up again.

Solution:

This failure symptom obviously belongs to the description of flowchart 04, according to the repair method; confirm the repair path, finding it's accorded with the sequence:

Start->A-1->A-2->A-4->B-5->C-2->C-3->D-3;

Repair summary:

1)   Remove CMOS battery from the motherboard for about 3 to 5 hours, and let laptop enter hibernation status again, but later still would not wake it up or start up;
2)   Plug back the CMOS battery in, change the adapter with higher power, let the laptop enter hibernation status, but later it would not wake up or start up;
3)   Pull out the old battery, change a new battery—then the failure disappears;

Hint: When the laptop is left unused, it would auto shut down, meanwhile, power/wait indication light dies, the system enters hibernation status, generally, you can exit hibernation status by pressing the power button, but the laptop power is not enough, then under this circumstance it would not exit hibernation status, you need to do something as below:

1)   Shut down the laptop, and then remove battery, meanwhile disconnect the power adapter from the laptop;
2)   Start the laptop, meanwhile, press power button for about 15 seconds to exit hibernation status;
3)   Now plug a charged battery group or plug the power adapter again;

044)   HP PAVILION DV2020US laptop enters hibernation status, but would not wake up.

Failure symptoms:

Battery indication light flashes, and system enters hibernation status, and then it auto shuts down, besides, you cannot start up.

Solution:

This failure symptom obviously belongs to the description of flowchart 04, according to the repair method; confirm the repair path, finding it's accorded with the sequence:

Start->A-1->A-2->A-4->B-5->C-2->C-3->D-3->D-5;

Repair summary:

1) Shut down the laptop, and then remove the battery, meanwhile disconnect the power adapter from the laptop;
2) Start the laptop, meanwhile, press the power button for about 15 seconds and then exit hibernation status;
3) Plug the power adapter again;

However, afterwards, the machine still would not be taken up, remove the CMOS battery from the motherboard for about 3 to 5 hours, then plug CMOS battery again, the failure is gone;

Hint: generally, if system enters hibernation status, you can exit by pressing power button, but under the circumstance if the laptop BIOS would not exit hibernation status, then you need to remove the CMOS battery off from the motherboard, and test the battery voltage, you'd better to change a new CMOS battery, meanwhile, update the BIOS software.

4.3.4 Three repair cases for the failures caused by other reasons happening to HP laptop

045) COMPAQ Evo 610c laptop auto cuts down power and shuts down, battery charging status shows 100%

Failure symptoms:

Laptop has auto shutdown symptom, screen and all other lights on the keyboard would be off in a second. Try restarting it, but it would start up except plugging with external power supply. However, what is baffling is that under all circumstances, battery is at charging status, staying around 100% power.

Solution:

This failure symptom obviously belongs to the description of flowchart 04, according to the repair method; confirm the repair path, finding it's accorded with the sequence:

Start->A-1->A-2->A-4->B-5->C-2->c-3->D-3->D-4

Repair summary:

Now the problem is that the battery stays around 100% power always; would it be a battery problem?

1) Plug the old battery and connect external power supply—the laptop would work;
2) Plug the old battery without external power supply—the laptop would not start up;
3) Pull out the old battery and connect external power supply—the laptop would work too;

Pull out the old battery, observe the battery slot carefully, you could find that one pin is full of putty. Check carefully again and compare the laptop battery connection pins, usually there is a little difference, which is that there is one pin already rusty, clean the putty on the battery slot with a cotton swab dipped in rubbing alcohol, and scrape the rust speckles off the battery connection pins with a knife, until the copper pin shines metal light. Now plug the battery back again, start the laptop again, check whether the battery would work normally again.

Hint: bad contact is one of many common laptop failures, generally, bad contact shows on all kinds of boards, cards, memory sticks, CPUs and motherboard; also bad contact between battery, power cable and motherboard is common, usually as long as you clean up the (Edge Connector) gold plated board with an eraser or solder the joint again, then the problem would be eliminated.

046) **HP Compaq V3700 laptop would not charge; plug the original battery on a HP laptop of the same model to test, it charges normally, and would continue working for about 2 hours.**

Failure symptoms:

Check up the dormant power of the battery when HP COMPAQ V3700 laptop is with external power supply, finding that the battery value showed is continually decreasing. The battery is not at charge status, then change with a known good working power adapter to supply power, it is found that it fails to charge, but after removing the battery, power adapter would not start the laptop.

Solution:

This failure symptom obviously belongs to the description of 04 flowchart, according to the repair method; confirm the repair path, finding it's accorded with the

Start->A-1->A-2->A-4->A-5->D-3->D-5;

Repair summary: work process:

1) Plug the old battery without external power supply—the laptop would start up;
2) Pull out the old battery and connect external power supply—the laptop would not start up;
3) Check up the version of the BIOS, finding it is already updated to the latest one;
4) After changing to a new adapter of bigger power, the failure symptom has no change;
5) Change with a new original laptop battery, the failure symptom has no change either;

The conclusion of the operation above indicates that the laptop power manager hardware part has something wrong, which makes the BIOS failing to manage power adapter for power supplying. Meanwhile, it would not control power manager to activate the motherboard power system to charge the battery. The methods to solve these problems are: changing the entire motherboard, which would solve the problem;

Hint: focus on the next two points:

1. Pay close attention to whether it is the original laptop power adapter, whether it is 100% compatible with the laptop, because power shortage or non-original adapter would cause the failure symptoms that battery does not charge at all and power adapter would not start the laptop.
2. Be aware whether the power interface on the motherboard is damaged or not solder well or distorted. Whether the power adapter really has enough voltage and whether the current reaches the motherboard, otherwise, such symptoms would happen where the battery does not charge and power adapter would not start up the laptop;

047)   HP Pavilion dv9000 laptop battery would not charge

Failure symptoms:

Battery conditions is good, but would not start up the laptop with battery mode; put the original battery on same model HP laptop, then it would start up and would continue working about 3 hours.

Solution:

This failure symptom obviously belongs to the description of flowchart 04, according to the repair method; confirm the repair path, finding it's accorded with the sequence:

Start->A-1->A-2->A-4->A-5->D-3->D-5;

Repair summary: work process:

1) Plug the old battery and connect external Ac Adapter—the laptop would work;
2) plug the old battery without external AC Adapter—the laptop would not start up;
3) unplug the old battery and connect external AC Adapter—the laptop would work too;

Enter repair flow step D-5, try solving the problem from the battery interface. First of all, check the charging pins, whether there is a voltage output, measure with multimeter, and the result shows that the pin has no voltage output.

It seems the problem is on the battery charging circuit, as the picture shows, (the backside of the motherboard), first take a look at the part in yellow circle, here is one diode and a MOSFET, first measure diode, finding that one end has no voltage, which proves that the current is truncated before through the diode. Then test the MOSFET, the result would be out quickly, the control pin of the MOSFET has voltage, which indicates the problem exists at the place of diodes and MOSFET.

It seems that it is quite likely that the chip is damaged. And after the test, the result shows that the problem is right here as expected. The solution is quite simple, change the chip then.

Hint: when laptop is working, if you pull out the charging battery from laptop and then plug in battery back to continue charging again, high voltage would be formed, even usually there will be sparks at the interface end. At, this moment, it is quite easy to get the laptop motherboard and battery damaged.

If you unplug the battery and replace it back quite frequently, such a problem would always make the battery not charge. Besides, the quality of the components motherboard use is also quite essential problem. Generally speaking, big current during charging momentarily would damage the diodes at the end of motherboard power supply circuit and the MOSFET (chip with 8 pins) of the control terminal. So, if you do need to pull out and plug in a battery to a laptop, it would be better to do so when the machine is turned off.

CHAPTER 5

LCD failure repair

5.1   Laptop LCD common failures—Screen black, dark or red repair

5.1.1 Laptop LCD failures and causes

There are two kinds of primary failures for the Laptop LCD:

Faults and defects of the screen itself are mainly caused by mismanaging and carelessness

1.   The main symptoms of screen problems are: "dead pixels" or "color spots".

Dead pixels: pixel spots appearing on the screen are always non-luminous pixels; generally, they are caused during the production process and rarely occur as a result of regular usage and cannot usually be fixed.

Color spots: are coloured pixel spots permanently on the screen. They are the same as dead pixels or bad spots, and cannot be repaired. The main symptoms due to improper operation are: "White speckles", "Black screen" or unstable screen.

2.   **White speckles** are generally caused by impacting or pressure put on the screen. If the damage is excessive it usually can't be fixed.

Black Screen: usually means the screen is either broken, the LCD cable is off, or the inverter is finished, or some other issues with the notebook.

3.   **Unstable Display:** usually means there's a problem with the cable connection being loose, or the back light is burnt or a failure with the Inverter.

Laptop LCD common failure symptoms:

a)   Screen not lit
b)   Color stripes occur on screen;

c)   Screen darkens
d)   Screen turns yellow;
e)   Screen turns red;
f)   Screen flashes;
g)   Screen shows white.

5.1.2   LCD imaging system and backlighting system

Principle of liquid crystal imaging

Liquid crystal is a state of matter that has properties between those of a conventional liquid and those of a solid crystal. It has liquid flow patterns and solid optical properties. When affected by voltage, liquid crystal can change its physical property and deform. At that moment, the light passing through it in an angle would change and form colors.

There's a backlight behind a liquid crystal screen. The lamp-house first passes the first polarized layer and then reaches onto the liquid crystal. When the light passes through crystal, color and lustre changes occur. The lights reflect from the liquid crystal then passes through a color-filter and then the second polarizer. As the two polarizer's polarize in 90 degrees, plus, the variation of voltage and some other devices, it creates a liquid crystal display and therefore forms the colors we want.

LCD backlight system

CCFL is a gas-discharging lamp, which has a strong flashing frequency that follows the sinusoidal periodic alternating frequency of 60Hz used to provide AC voltage. The irradiancy luminous flux changes periodically. Generally, a home fluorescent daylight lamp connected to single-phase AC circuit, reaches about 55% of maximum light intensity, while because of a Tungsten filament's thermal inertia, an incandescent lamp's light fluctuation is only about 5% to 13%.

LED Screen

An LED Screen is like a television, but with one fundamental difference that instead of the picture being beamed from a cathode ray tube, so, its long life, high stability. Each pixel is made up of a cluster of tiny LEDs; each cluster on an LED screen has a red, green and blue LED, which light up accordingly to create the correct colour.

5.1.3   Laptop Inverter converter and signal controlling

The backlight inverter takes low voltage power and then steps-up to high frequency and high voltage power (a few hundred or thousand volts) to light the lamp on an LCD panel. It is a power converter device, which heats up easily, is very fragile and therefore fails easily.

In fact, the backlight inverter board is a switching power supply, except in relation to the ordinary switching power supply that supplies DC; it is a DC to AC converter. It takes low voltage power from DC on the motherboard (generally more than 12V or 5V) through a switch into a high-frequency alternating current chopper, and then raises the voltage by a high-frequency transformer to reach the voltage illuminating the lamp.

The backlight inverter's power and signal comes from the motherboard. Cables interconnect with the motherboard: power V+, power ground G, switch signal S, lightness signal F (some don't have one).

When the laptop starts, power goes on, and then the switch signal S starts the switch surge circuit. The chopper begins working, and the transformer raises voltage to illuminate the lamp. These components (surge circuit, switch pipe and transformer) are on the high-voltage board and can fail or be damaged easily:

5.1.4   Laptop LCD usage and maintenance

1.   During daily usage, avoid operating under direct sunlight as much as possible
2.   Clean the screen daily
3.   The best way to protect the screen is to use it in ambient room lighting
4.   Remember to shut down the screen when not in use
5.   Don't touch the screen with fingers, as time passes, a dead spot will appear on the screen;
6.   When the laptop is not being used for a short period, temporarily shut down the power of the LCD by using the function key on the keyboard;
7.   Never close the upper LCD cover forcefully or place anything between the keyboard and the display;
8.   Never touch the surface of the screen with your finger nails or anything sharp that can scratch the screen;
9.   The LCD screen easily gets dusty, so you may need to brush away dust with a dry soft brush. It is all that's needed to keep the screen clean. If it does get dirty, only use cleaners that are specifically designed for the LCD.
10. When transporting and carrying your laptop, ensure no pressure is applied to the screen or upper cover as the screen. You can damage the screen, case, or cables.

Maintenance and repair

1.   The LCD surface attracts dust because of static. It can be easily be cleaned with a soft wet cloth by gently wiping the dust off the LCD.
2.   Always Use the appropriate cleaner which can be purchased at any electronic store.
3.   Keep your working environment clean and dry and avoid spills. According to the working principle of the laptop LCD, it's quite obvious that it has a critical requirement for low humidity. It is important to make sure the laptop is used in a dry environment.
4.   Pay attention to your working habits such as drinking liquids near your notebook.
5.   Avoid unnecessary vibration. The notebook LCD screen is composed of multi-layer reflectors boards, reflective plates, filter plates, and protection films, and these

materials are very fragile and can easily be damaged. The shock can be severe enough to damage it to the point of no repair.

6. Clean the LCD periodically

5.2 Eliminate laptop display failures and flow chart

5.2.1 Shortcut tips for troubleshooting LCD display failures

A) Simple visual observation

Open the back cover of your laptop, using common sense, Visually inspect the inside of the machine for abnormal symptoms such as broken, loose, discoloration, distortion or burnt hardware. Power off and power on the laptop and see if there's a peculiar smell or abnormal sound. If there's nothing displayed on the screen, then I suggest you plug it to an external LCD screen to determine whether it's the screen, video cable or something else. When you are observing and troubleshooting it is very important to pay attention to details as this is what will give you a pretty good clue of what the issue is. For instance, the screen is totally dark. Issues like this are tough to deal with. For these problems above, you need to verify that the external LCD works. If it works, then the problem is with the internal screen or the video circuit. But if it doesn't, then the problem might not be with the LCD screen. In this case, the failure possibilities are greatly narrowed, and it will be a little easier to find the problem. Now that we've narrowed the issue, we can now come up with some conclusions.

1. Disconnection failure
2. Get burnt by short circuit
3. Overheating by short circuit
4. Bad connection failures
5. Other failures

B) Failure symptoms

When it comes to display failures the first thing that comes to mind is the main circuit as it plays a really important role in the repair process. If you know a lot about laptops, you will know that checking settings may resolve the issue quickly

1. Try function key "Fn" + brightness key to change the brightness of LCD screen;
2. With the external LCD screen, set the computer BIOS or "Power management" to the highest of the screens brightness;
3. Make sure the display switch is at the show state; or disconnect the cable between the motherboard and the display switch, and leave it at a non-sleep state;

C) Replacement method

Just as the name implies, replacement means to replace suspected components with good ones. If the failure disappears because of this, then your suspicion was correct. If not then there may be more than one issue and you must continue your troubleshooting. If you are going to use the replacement method check all components of the display such as the LCD backlight, LCD data cable and high-voltage inverter as these are harder to judge.

When using replacement parts ensure they are in working order.

1. When replacing or changing a backlight, test it to ensure that it is good. Don't disassemble it randomly.
2. Don't hurry to buy and replace the high-voltage inverter you suspect, first you should examine the pin 1 grounding voltage (generally +12V).
3. Don't rush out to buy and replace the suspected LCD data cable, first check whether it's disconnected or shorting by slowly twisting the data cable. To make a more detailed judgement, please refer to chapter 5.1 Laptop LCD Screen Dark or Red when the power light is on.

D)   Measuring Voltage method

Voltage measurement is one of the most used methods to judge display failures. It gives you a good indication of where the failure exists by checking the voltage at points in the circuits where the normal voltage is known No or abnormal voltage indicates the location of the failure. This method is used most in the troubleshooting process. Some voltages are constant and some will be varying. This requires two methods of measurement: static DC voltage measurement and dynamic voltage measurement.

Generally, I use static DC voltage measurement to troubleshoot screen failure. Use alligator clips and a multimeter and connect the common on ground on the bottom board. Touch the positive probe on the high-voltage inverter pin 1 (test point). One hand is used to measure, and the other hand is free for assistance as needed.

The static working voltage of pin 1 point is +12V. If the static working voltage is 0V, or actual tested voltage is quite small, then you know there's a problem in that circuit. For a more detailed procedure, please refer to chapter 5.1 Laptop LCD Screen Dark or Red when power light on.

E)   Resistance measurement method

Resistance measurement is another of the important methods to repairing a monitor. With the multimeter's ohm function, we can measure the resistance at suspect points on a board or components to identify short circuits, grounds, incorrect values, or lack of continuity. The resistance to ground for each pin of a chip or component in a circuit can be measured and compared to expected results to identify the failure. You must always be aware that there can be parallel circuits at the point you are measuring that will change the resistance value.

There are two kinds of Resistance measurement; in-circuit resistance measurement and isolation resistance measurement. With in-circuit measurement, parallel circuits must be considered. It is a circuit rather than a component measurement. The isolation method requires that the device be unsoldered or otherwise isolated from the circuit in order to obtain an exact reading without parallel circuits. Generally, it is used to measure the high-voltage inverter and the LCD data cable:

1. Short circuit failure
2. Resistance change problem
3. Open circuit failure

F) Open and short circuit method

An open circuit occurs when there is a physical break anywhere in the circuit or indeed within an individual component forming part of the circuit. Due to this physical break, no current is able to flow, thereby either failing to reach the load or return through the battery.

A short circuit, meanwhile, occurs when a component or the wiring is damaged, for example, as a result of the insulation chaffing and exposing the copper, the electrical current in the circuit finds a new parallel path back to the battery. Typically, the wiring short will occur when exposed wire(s) are able to touch each other. . Observe relevant voltage, current, resistance and other measurement data, by which you can analyze and determine the problem.

Common short circuit methods and applied test are shown as below:

If you directly connect 2 points with a wire you can cause problems or failures leading to an incorrect conclusion. Don't do this unless you know exactly what you are doing. Use a capacitor, or resistor to connect the two ends of the relevant circuit.

G) Vibrating Method

This is one of the most effective methods to check software problems caused by intermittent bad connections such as cold or broken solder joints. While observing the performance of your laptop, and knocking or pressing on various components, connectors, and circuit boards with the insulated handle of your screwdriver, you might make the problem happen and thus know which component is at fault. Try flexing a circuit board slightly by pulling or pressing it. Slowly twist and flex interconnecting wires. Flex a suspect LCD slightly. Use of these techniques can lead you to the source of your problem be it poor soldering, improper connector seating, crack on a PCB, and many other poor connections.

H) Heating and cooling method

When there is a temperature related problem, failure may happen during a few minutes after starting up, or it can be due to varying ambient temperature conditions. Generally, this failure is caused by temperature stability of certain components inside the machine. For this situation, you can use the cooling and heating method to identify the problem. Cooling is used for suspected components where the temperature rise is noticeably abnormal. The failure can be affected when the component is touched and cooled slightly. A good method is to hold an alcohol soaked tampon against the shell of the suspected component to let it cool down.

I)   Circuit modification method

If you have determined there is a motherboard problem, such as a failure to supply +12V static working voltage to pin 1 of high-voltage inverter, it is possible that a circuit modification will solve it. You might add a diode to connect the +12V to pin#1. for instance. This may get the inverter working properly assuming there is no other problem

J)   Combination method

You might have saved a used inverter that is partially failed. If the good functions match the bad ones in the installed inverter you can combine the 2 units to make one functioning unit. Effectively you use two or more high-voltage inverters, whose partial functions are broken, as one inverter with complete functionality by taking full advantages of their working components.

K)   Integration method

Some failures of an LCD monitor are impossible to diagnose when the motherboard has no +12V static working voltage output. Using simultaneous checking methods can help to eliminate some complex failures. Integration of more than one troubleshooting procedure is a necessary method to use to find and repair hardware and software failures.

5.2.2   90% Dark screen and red screen failures from inverter board and backlight.

There are four possible reasons that can cause a dark screen: 90% due to the high-voltage inverter and backlight

A)   Broken backlight: these are some of the causes.

1)   The laptop fell on to the ground causing serious damage to the lamp
2)   There's something (foreign body) between the hinges and LCD screen resulting in the Backlight being crushed when the cover was folded.
3)   The back cover of the laptop is pressed or pushed too hard

B)   inverter unable to supply enough power to backlight

1)   As the chip ages or is burnt by the transformer device, there's no voltage output
2)   Output power from motherboard is insufficient.

C) Inverter connection cable is broken,

1) There are two cables connected to the high-voltage inverter and backlight. The connection cable can break off after many closings/openings of the LCD screen so the inverter cannot supply power to the backlight.

2) Due to a short circuit or chip aging, the motherboard +12V power supply outputs low voltage or even no voltage. The pin 1 of the inverter no longer gets the +12V needed and therefore no longer produces high voltage to light the backlight, thus causing the dark screen.

This rarely happens because most motherboards have a circuit voltage protection device

Generally there are a few reasons causing the red screen problem:

90% of them are mostly due to the bad condition of the inverter board and backlight;

➢ Chromatic aberration failure may happen when the backlight is old; however, the actual symptom of the red color can be due to the fact that the entire screen is affected by grounding. For this problem, you just need to replace the backlight;

➢ A bad connection between the motherboard/ inverter and the connection cable causes a blurred screen and chromatic aberration failures. When the machine is off, pull the supply cable, and check the pins carefully to see whether they are bent or istorted, or whether the supply cable is broken.

➢ If just one part of the screen, especially the corner of screen, has the chromatic aberration problem, generally, it is caused by interference from a strong magnetic field. At this time, look for a strong magnetic device near the laptop, like a sound box, or a high powered transformer and place these devices away from the laptop

➢ Test the LCD screen by the replacement method. If the color cast is still the same after replacing the LCD, then the problem has to come from the motherboard or the integrated block by the inverter which could be broken, or some capacitors on the motherboard are gone bad. When encounter this situation, replace the inverter and test it. The Four points above are the solutions to the primary problem causing red screen and color cast. It shows that backlight aging is a most common cause!

5.2.3 6% dark screen or "chaotic" screen failures come from the switch and cable of the LCD screen

A less common reason for dark screen failures is the monitor switch and cable. When the switch and cable are stretched or impacted by external force, the failure can easily occur.

This would directly lead to a dark screen; however, it's less probable unless you accidentally drop the laptop.

Chaotic laptop screen failure can also be quite common. Chaotic screen means that there are irregular stripes or shapes appearing on the LCD screen.

There are many reasons for this, and these can cause differing symptoms, with several different solutions. Text may behave with distorted characters, and graphics would also be erratic or distorted. Horizontal strips may occur because of internal or external interferences. Even worse, the system screen of death symptom may follow. Generally, the chaotic screen is caused because of a broken cable.

1. Move the cable around, if the screen becomes "chaotic" you know the cable is faulty and should be replaced.
2. The problem may also happen if the graphic card chip is faulty or there's bad soldering. It's quite rare that the LCD itself is defective.
3. Improper monitor setting may also cause the problem, reset resolution and reinstall the latest driver.

5.2.4   Dead pixel failure of the laptop LCD screen

LCD dead pixel is also called "Point absence",

What causes a Dead Pixel?

Occasionally the individual transistors responsible for carrying current to a pixel will either short out or remain open resulting in what is called a dead pixel.

A "lit" pixel is one that appears as one of several randomly placed white, red, blue or green pixel elements on a dark background, or you may have a "missing" pixel which shows up as a black dot on a light colored background.

The most annoying thing for an LCD is a dead pixel. Once there's a dead pixel, no matter how the display is shown the dead pixel will always appear as one color.

The "Dead pixel" is not repairable; you'd just have to replace the entire screen to solve the problem. There are two kinds of pixels: dark dead pixel is a black point which would never work no matter what the content is showing on the screen. And the most annoying part is that it would be a "high-light point" and noticeable every time you start the laptop. So far, crystal liquid technologies still aren't able to overcome this shortcoming.

How to inspect dead pixel?

It's quite easy to inspect for dead pixels, you'd just need to adjust the LCD brightness and contrast to the maximum (showing whitening the image) or to the minimum (showing dark black image). You may find that there's highlight or dark spot existing on screen. A pixel is a light spot. Each light spot has an independent transistor to control its current strength. If the transistor of that pixel is faulty then that spot would never shine again. This is the highlight or dark spot mentioned above, and is called by the nickname "Dead pixel". You should differentiate between "Highlight" and "Dead pixel". If there's no highlight, it could still mean there is a dead pixel.

Use the laptop correctly to avoid the formation of a dead pixel

Dead Pixels can occur over time as the LCD is used. So, in daily use, never poke the screen, wipe the screen with caustic liquid, and don't place a heavy object on the laptop. When wiping the screen use a damp cloth as dry as possible as the LCD screen is fairly fragile.

If you notice a dead pixel try massaging the screen gently with your finger on a cloth around the area as it may bring it back to life, although there is no guarantee, it does sometimes work.

5.2.5 "Chaotic" screen failure of a laptop LCD and maintenance

A Laptop Character disorder screen is a common failure, and there are many reasons for it. Different reasons have different failure symptoms and solutions.

It behaves as disordered characters and messy pictures!

1. The thermal performance of the main display chip can be affected and can cause the disordered character screen symptom.

Solution:

Improving the thermal performance of the display card.

2. The running speed of the display video card RAM is too low, and the driver is malfunctioning. When the display cache speed is too slow, it doesn't match with the speed of the machine, and this is what may cause the symptom.

Solution:

Replace the display cache with a higher speed, or lower the speed of the machine or upgrade the display card driver.

3. Display video card memory is bad

When the display video card memory is bad, at start up, a disordered character screen and disordered characters will occur.

Solution: You have to replace the display card.

Note: some display cards are integrated on the motherboard, you would then have to change the display card chip too.

4.   Signal cable connection is bad

A bad connection between the motherboard/high-voltage inverter and the display signal cable can also cause the problem. When the machine is off, unplug the signal cable and plug it back again, check whether the pins are bended or distorted. Replace it with a good signal cable and have a try!

5.2.6   Analysis and repair Flowcharts for the failure of a laptop LCD. Screen black, dark or red

Laptop LCD Screen Black, Dark Or Red When Powered On

LaptopCare Utility Suite V2.2 copyright © 2003-2011
www.laptopcare.ca & www.computercare.ca

Laptopcare.ca

Problem: Screen black,dark or red
Cause: Power Surge, Voltage instability and instant contact power interruption
Solution: Change backlight, invert, LCD, cable, Switch or motherboard

Backlight inverter hardware: **5.2.6   Difficulty level:**

Other hardware:

Easy   Hard

Breakdown of possible malfunctions:

90%	Inverter and backlight
6%	Display Switch and Cable
2%	Motherboard and LCD
2%	Other

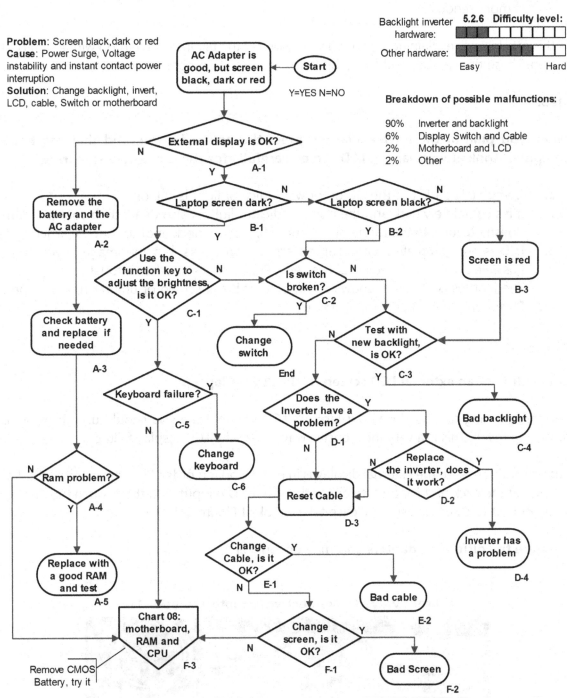

1. Complete darkness, no way to see anything on the laptop screen, but the laptop power indicator light is still on.
2. It's not entirely black. The screen still works, but the image is very dim.
3. Dim images appear on the laptop LCD with some red background color. When the failure is slight, the red background only holds for few seconds, but when the red background is consistent to the point that you cannot read anything then the issue is more serious.

In this article, I will explain how to find the reason for the failure—the laptop with a dim LCD screen. These tips can be used for all brand or models of notebook computers.

Step: 1

When you plug in the power adapter, press the power button, and then start the computer. Look at your laptop LCD screen carefully for these possible scenarios:

1. Completely dark, but the laptop power indicator light is still on.
2. If it's completely dark and the power indicator light is also dead, then your problem doesn't belong to the range of this tutorial. Please check another tutorial article:
3. LCD is not completely dark. Laptop screen still works, but the image is very dim. Possible cause is a defective LCD screen. Please check another tutorial article . . .
4. The laptops LCD screen shows a red, blue or blank screen or uninterrupted stripes. Please check another tutorial article

Step: A-1

Connection of an external LCD screen to check your laptop

If there's nothing displayed on your laptop's LCD screen, then you should use an external display to test it. This is a very inexpensive way to test the LCD display failure.

But be careful; ensure the external display is in good working order. Plug the external display adapter at the back of the laptop to either the VGA or DVI input, and then switch the display video output to external display. Please take a look at Figure 5-1; 5-2.

Here are the different adapters you may encounter:

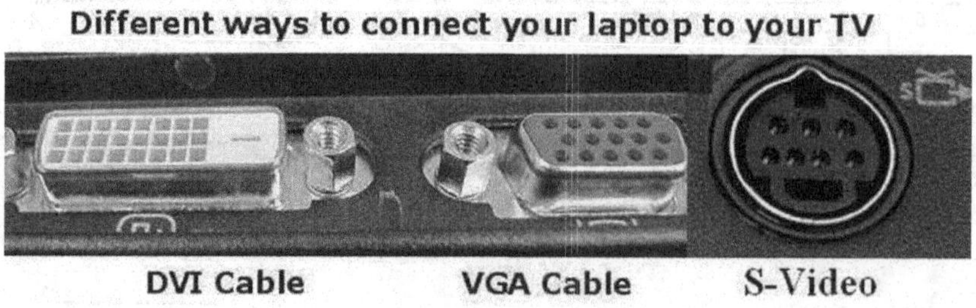

Different ways to connect your laptop to your TV

| DVI Cable | VGA Cable | S-Video |

Figure 5-1

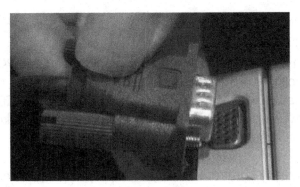

Figure 5-2

There are several ways depending on the make of your laptop, to switch it to external display

The "Fn" key is mainly located on the lower-left corner of the keyboard, usually between the CTRL key and ALT. Key, If you are unable to find the switch for your specific model, try searching the function keys in your user manual or you can get the information on the laptops website.

Here are a few of the examples for some of the laptops

HP (COMPAQ) laptops, pressing Fn+F4 combination keys will switch video.

IBM = Fn+F7;

Toshiba = Fn+F5

Acer varies with the model, either = Fn+F5, Fn+F3, Fn+F8,

Sony, Fn + F7

Dell = Fn+F8,

For Macs it will usually auto detect the external monitor

For some other brands of laptops, in order to switch to the external display, you must plug in the external monitor before starting the laptop so it can auto detects it.

Now if the external display is working properly, but the internal LCD screen doesn't show anything, your problem may be with the internal LCD screen or the internal connection of the video cable. Please enter STEP: B-1

If the external display and the internal LCD screen has no display, then most likely your problem is with the LCD screen and or the internal connection of the video cable

Go to STEP: A-2

STEP: A-2

There are many reasons that may cause a laptop black screen. No POST, nothing showing on the screen but you can hear the sound of the hard drive, and the indicator light will not turn on, or you hear the DVD-ROM rotating and trying to read the CD. If there is a CD disk in there and it still won't start it is likely that the laptops OS has locked itself in protection mode. I recommend you keep trying.

All right, I see you've already confirmed that your laptop has a problem with a black screen even when connected to an external LCD screen.

Follow these steps:

1. Unplug the AC power supply;
2. Remove the battery
3. Hold down the power button (press) power button for 30 to 60 seconds, and then release;
4. Reconnect AC power supply and start the laptop.

We have found that when following these steps it resets the notebook back to normal. Of course, if the symptoms happen over and over again, then it indicates that your laptop has some other issues, and needs further testing and analysis.

If the laptop screen returns to normal after following these steps, congratulation you've succeeded in fixing the laptop. If this step is not any help, please continue to STEP: A-3

STEP: A-3

1. Unplug the AC power supply;
2. Remove the battery
3. Hold down the power button (press) power button for 60 seconds, and then release;
4. Put the battery back in the laptop
5. Reconnect AC power supply and start the laptop.

After following the steps above and still having problem continue to STEP: A-4

STEP: A-4

If step A-3 didn't help, I would try changing the Ram Memory. Most laptops do not come with an independent graphic card like some PC's. Most are integrated on the motherboard; therefore, the video ram is shared with the system. So if you have a bad Ram memory, the system will not start, and the video will not work. Most cases are caused by bad memory, which will most likely cause the laptop not to start or you'll get a blue screen and not POST. If bad memory is suspected it is the easiest part to replace. That is the importance of going through every step before replacing the LCD screen.

The Ram is in most cases situated at the bottom of the laptop, you just need to remove one or two screws from the bottom of the laptop board. On some laptops they are located under the keyboard.

Check the user manual or visit the websites. At this point remove both sticks

Why do this? Because sometimes a loose stick can also cause a blank screen. Please take a look at Figure 5-3.

Figure 5-3

Re-insert 1 stick and start the notebook to test the ram, place it in the A slot then the B slot respectively, then do the same with the other stick, then with both sticks until you get a picture on the screen.

Why do this? Because sometimes the Ram is not compatible with the laptop or the Ram is damaged.

By doing this, we can confirm that the issues may be with the Memory stick or the Ram slot.

If your laptop only has one RAM module, then you just need to borrow a compatible RAM from another laptop and ensure you use the same type of memory i.e.: pc133, pc400, Pc800 etc.

Important! Each time you follow these steps; you must unplug the AC adapter and remove the battery first.

If step A-4 doesn't work, please continue to STEP: A-5

STEP: A-5

1. shutdown the Laptop and unplug the power adapter if it is connected, finally, disconnect the power source and remove the laptop battery.
2. Remove the ram memory cover under the laptop. Note: the ram memory on some older laptops may be located under the keyboard, if unsure, look through the Service

Manual of your laptop. Once you have found the cover, remove it using a small screwdriver and set it aside.

3. Remove the old memory by pushing the two metal clips away from the ram and remove them once they lift from the socket. Look at the kind of memory you have for replacement. There are many kinds of memory out there such as Kingson PC 100,133, PC4200 SODIM, DDR, DDR2, and DD3;

4. Find the same type of RAM and install the new memory, Align the new memory chip into the correct slot at a 45-degree angle. Push down on the RAM until it clicks in place.

5. Put the RAM cover back and put the proper screws in place.

6. Start the laptop and ensure that the RAM is being recognized by the laptop's bios. If nothing happens (black screen or message), the RAM is not compatible with that laptop.

STEP: B-1

B-1, B-2, B-3 are the observations you made with your laptop display, the descriptions of the 3 independent failures, whichever one fits your laptop failure

B-1 enter STEP C-1, B-2 enter STEP: C-2 and B-3l enter STEP: C-3

STEP: C-1

90% of LCD problems are caused by the backlight lamp or an inverter failure. In both cases, the screen would become very dark and the image on the screen turns very weak, which is what people usually call "Dark screen". It is also important to check the other 10% as it is the easiest part to replace after you have fixed the other 90%.

As we all know, there is a function key that can be used to change the brightness of the LCD screen, but if some laptops the "Fn" key fails to work, and the LCD screen is not bright enough and you might not be aware of this problem. That is why it is important to troubleshoot everything beforehand before coming to the conclusion that it might be the Inverter or backlight

If you suspect that the "FN" key is faulty, the first place you should go is the "Power Management" and increases the screen brightness. If you cannot get there you can always go into the BIOS

How do you do this (will depend on the brands and models of your notebook computer),

If you are able to add the brightness to the screen, this will indicate that the problem is the software of your computer or the laptop keyboard, in this order, please go to STEP: C-5,

If the step C-1 doesn't help at all, please continue to STEP: C-2

STEP: C-2

If there's still no image on the LCD display screen, then you should test the display switch. It turns off the screen when it is closed and the laptop not powered down. This is a safety feature that protects the screen from failure. It is important to locate it and ensure it is working.

The display switch is usually located on the top left corner on the laptop keyboard, but some are on the top right corner. Some may not be visible. It is a small button that is pressed when the screen is closed and spring returns when the screen is open. What this does is when the switch is OPEN; the screen is an ON state; if the computer is closed while on, it turns off the display. Some might call the display switch a sleep switch. If you cannot find the display switch, please consult the user manual or search on the Internet.

I've observed many times that when the sleep switch is closed, as if the lid was down, but it is still up, the screen is in Black mode, or less often in Dark mode.

In the cases I have dealt with, it indicated to me that the display switch was broken as if the switch was closed, and causing the screen to be in Black mode or Dark mode. It rarely happens but is still possible.

HP DV2000 V3000 Switch Module 417087-001 50.4F606.001 are known to have faulty switches and most people neglect this point, and judge it to be the motherboard as the main problem.

The next step I am going to do:

Open my laptop, find the display switch terminals, and break the connection to separate the display switch from the motherboard. This is equal to the sleep switch being OPEN, and enabling the screen display.

There are 2 situations that can happen after this:

1. The screen is still in Black mode or Dark mode, which means the problem, has nothing to do with the switch. If this is the case, you should test the LCD display further, and please enter STEP: C-3
2. If the display returns to normal, when I start up the laptop, there's only one conclusion: we have a failed Display Switch. If this is the case, then replace it with a new display switch circuit board. This replacement job is quite easy. please enter STEP: End

STEP: C-3

OK, after the test steps above, now I doubt the backlight has a problem, actually the backlight failure is very similar to the problem of inverter failure. They both cause screen display failure. Under these two circumstances, the screen would be very dark and the image on the display becomes very faint. So you can hardly see the image without a strong light.

In most cases, I use a known good backlight to test the laptop. Why? Because the backlight is inexpensive and common. One backlight could work with many different inverters (about 99%). It almost could be a tool used to test laptops. This is a good method which cost the least amount of money and does most of the job.

Some beginners are always anxious to just buy a new LCD screen in the hope that it resolves all the problems. This method is not the best choice, because it may not be the problem. There is no return on LCD screen, and they can be very expensive depending on the make and model. What if the problem wasn't with the screen or the backlight? Quite an expensive proposition as you are now back to square one.

Even if you doubt it's the Inverter that failed, I still suggest you use a reliable method to test it. Don't use a known good inverter to replace the old one to check if it's faulty, but instead connect it to a known working backlight. If the good light doesn't work, then you may consider buying a new inverter and try replacing it. This method could save you time and money. While inverters are not often interchangeable between different laptops, it's not an ideal test tool, so be cautious when buying an inverter.

And here's what I am going to do:

1. I will pull out the LCD screen connection cable from the inverter on the right side. You see, the pin I pull out is used to connect to LCD screen backlight.
2. I will connect my plug-in, the known good backlight, to the inverter of the laptop, then you may see the picture below. Please take a look at Figure 5-4.

Figure 5-4

Results I expect:

1. If my test backlight lights up, I know the backlight inside the screen has failed, and the problem has nothing to do with the inverter. If you face this situation, change the backlight or the LCD display. Tip: the length of backlight directly affects the job. The replaced backlight's length must be the same original length! (It's really a tough job to replace a backlight!), and you will enter STEP: C-4.
2. If my test backlight does not work, when I start the laptop, we can conclude we have a failed Inverter. If this is the case, you need to replace the Inverter circuit board, an easy task . . . Please take a look Step: D-1.

3. Important: if you decide to buy a new backlight for testing, you must ensure the connector on the inverter matches with the light. Usually, the backlight purchased does not include the cable connection. If you plan to use the backlight as a test device, then you should find a backlight with a cable connection.

We sell inexpensive backlight cables.

There're two different types of backlight connections as can be seen in the photo below.

Picture 1 (Big) the wire connection bases are not in the same plane.

Picture 2 (Small) Most LCD backlights have the small one. Please take a look at Figure 5-5.

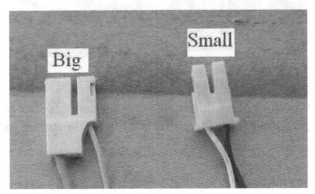

Figure 5-5

STEP: C-4

If my test backlight lights up, then the backlight in the screen has failed. If this is the case, you would replace the backlight (of course this is not an easy job).

You could check out the previous posts about the installation for a laptop backlight.

However, you could fix this broken backlight problem by replacing the entire LCD screen, although it costs more money, it saves a lot of trouble, assuming you are completely competent for the simple installation job.

Check out my previous posts about how to install a laptop LCD screen.

STEP: C-5

Set up the computer in "Power management", and increase the lightness of the screen with the highest efficiency or you could add screen lightness in the BIOS. If you do add the lightness, then I would assume the problem is on the software or the keyboard. For common laptops, generally there're 2 to 4 screws locking the keyboard, not including the plastic lock on the border of the keyboard. Generally there's a screw on the bottom cover of the laptop and under certain circumstances, screws are also distributed on the upper cover.

For keyboards where there's a constrictive screw on the bottom, you can locate the screws on the bottom cover according to the orientation the keyboard. Remove the screws, pry the keyboard gently, and then hold up the keyboard lightly at about 30 degrees. You will see a flat cable connecting to the motherboard from the keyboard. Please take a look at Figure 5-6.

Figure 5-6

Notice: many people would neglect this point: the flat cable is locked by a plastic buckle, if you don't unlock it and drag it by force, the connector, keyboard, and the motherboard might be broken.

Actually it's quite easy to unlock it: use a flat screwdriver, gently uplift the both sides of the cable lock within 1 millimeter.

After unlocking it, the cable lock's orientation cable function abates. Now gently remove the flat cable, and the keyboard will free itself from the laptop.

STEP: C-6

I look for the keyboard I need from two aspects:

1. To replace a keyboard, you should first check up the position of the front keys, which should basically match with each key of the original keyboard with exactly the same size. Of course, this is not the most important thing for you to do.
2. the most important thing is that you should find out the part number on the back side of the original keyboard. Find out the number of the part you need, all keyboards have a part number paper pasted on the back, such as HP dv2000's part number is Model No: K061130B1—P/N: 90.4F507.S0U—HP Spare: 417068-031

Check out my previous posts about how to find the right keyboard.

STEP: D-1

After the tests above, if the test backlight is still out, then it's quite likely that we have a failed inverter, which is located at the bottom part of the LCD display. Most laptop inverters connect on both sides

The left side connects to the cable of the LCD display, while the right side of the inverter connects to the backlight inside the LCD display, see picture below.

To make sure that inverter board is getting power from the motherboard (via the LCD cable); you could test it with a multi-meter. In this tutorial, the pin "+" Lead of the multi-meter is used to connect to the pin 1 of the inverter, while the "-" Lead pin connects to the ground. Now the multi-meter displays 19.4V DC, so pin 1 of the inverter is getting power from the motherboard. Please take a look at Figure 5-7.

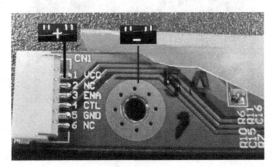

Figure 5-7

Warning! During the process of testing the inverter, if you cause a short circuit on the inverter contacts unintentionally, you may damage the inverter or even the motherboard. This is not for Novices this should be tested by a professional

If it is the case, you could replace the inverter circuit board, which is comparatively easy. Go to STEP: D-2

Check up my previous posts about how to install laptop inverter.

If now the multi-meter doesn't show DC voltage or just shows 3V to 5V DC, it indicates that the 1 pin of the inverter is not receiving voltage from the motherboard or the voltage is too low.

In this case, your problem might not be the inverter.

If it is the case, you should test the LCD screen cable further, enter STEP: D-3

STEP: D-2

Next thing I am going to do before I replace the inverter is in STEP: D-3, you may be surprised

1. To remove the old LCD inverter, you must learn how to disassemble your laptop screen first. You don't need any special tools to do this. With only a few magnetic screwdrivers of different sizes, you can open the front cover of a laptop. First remove the screws from all four corners around the screen. Generally, a laptop has 6 screws,

4 are on the upper part of the LCD, while the other two are at bottom part. All these screws are concealed under the rubber button around the edge of the screen, just as shown below: Please take a look at Figure 5-8.

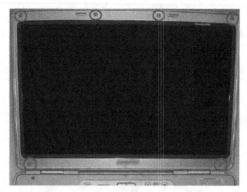

Figure 5-8

2. Remember the screw position on both sides of the display, as the screws are of different sizes, Ensure you do not miss any screw, as when you try opening it, you might damage the laptop. After confirming that all screws are removed, pry along the LCD front cover with a screwdriver slowly until the entire front cover is removed. You will often find that the laptop inverter circuit board is installed under the display. Some few brands' and models of inverter circuit boards are installed on the right part of the display. Please take a look at Figure 5-9.

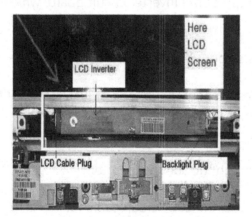

Figure 5-9

3. Generally the laptop's inverter has two different pin sockets: one is a two-line pin connecting to the LCD screen from the right side of the inverter. High voltage AC output lightens the fluorescence inside the LCD screen. The other side is a multi-line pin (4-8Pins) connector connecting to the main circuit board from the left side of the inverter to receive current and voltage signals. Sometimes you may find the inverter is locked by a little screw, so you have to remove the screw first, and then remove the

2-line cable pin and multi-line cable pin from the inverter. By doing this, the inverter is removed without any damage.

4.   Finally, I used a known good inverter to test the laptop.

If the screen lights up and the display are normal, then the inverter was faulty and you managed to fix it. Please continue to STEP: D-4; If the step D-2 doesn't work, then please go to STEP: D-3

STEP: D-3

There is also a possibility that you would get a black or dark screen if the video cable isn't connected properly with the inverter board. Your first step would be to check the connection state of the video cable, re-connect the video cable between the LCD screen and the inverter board and that may solve the issue.

1)   If after re-connecting it the issue isn't resolved; check all cable connections again starting with the video cable and the connector of the LCD display as it may have not been installed probably, lay it flat and reconnect it, also on some older displays the connector pins are extremely thin and may be damaged or bent. Use a very little screwdriver and be careful when straightening the pins. Be patient and take your time.

2)   For newer models the connectors do not have pins therefore reconnect all cables together, and if this again does not solve the problem, take a close look at the video cable where there is adhesive tape around the cable, remove it gently and turn the laptop on. Move the cable and keep an eye on the screen, if there is a distortion or some flickering of an image then you know the problem is with the cable.

If during this process you feel the cable is getting hot, shut off the power immediately to not cause a short circuit Replace the cable by a certified technician STEP: E-1

Warning! If you chose to do it yourself, do it at your own risk as you may damage the Inverter, LCD screen or motherboard.

STEP: D-4

When looking for an Inverter there is two important things to look for

1.   Look at both connectors, the 2 wire cable plug and the multi-line cable plug must be a perfect match even though they may seem the same, verify the part number; for example:

COMPAQ nx7400LCD inverter board, whose part number is Model NO: 76V0A YNV-10

Take a look at my previous posts regarding Troubleshoot for Laptop LCD screen (Bad inverter)

STEP: E-1

Attention! All power, including AC adapter and battery must be removed before removing the LCD video cable or you'll damage your laptop.

Generally, there are three kinds of laptop video cable pin plugs, the top is flat, single-row, multi-line cable to connect to the LCD display, the bottom end line is: double-row, double-line plugs (4-8 Pins) cable that connects to the inverter; and the other end is: multi-row, multi-line plugs cable that connects to the main circuit board.

Follow these steps before replacing the video cable:

1. Ensure the top end of the video cable is connected to the LCD display in order to take out the old video cable, so you will know how to disassemble and remove the entire LCD display.

    As for the details, you could check up my previous posts about how to replace a laptop LCD Screen.

2. In order to remove the old video cable you must first know how to disassemble your laptop and unplug the inverter. For details see my previous post on how to replace a laptop inverter.
3. In order to remove the other end of the video cable from the bottom where it connects to the motherboard, you must know how to remove the keyboard and the indicator cover of the laptop. For more info you can view the user manual or you can go to the laptop's website.

Generally the LCD cable is plugged into a socket on the main board, underneath the indicate cover.

There are no screws to secure this indicator cover. It is all secured by a clipping system.

Once the cover is removed, unclip the connection

In some laptops the video cable is set through the bottom of the hinge and connects to the motherboard of the laptop, so you have to remove the hinge cover. Most laptop hinge covers have no screws. If there are screws on your laptop, then all these screws must be removed before removing the covers.

The LCD cable is easily recognized underneath the indicator cover. There is no standard when it comes to the LCD screen.

Sometimes, you may find that the bottom of the video cable is locked by a very little screw, so you must remove it first, and then remove the multi-line plug cable from the motherboard. Proceed with caution to ensure you do not damage the video cable.

Sometimes, the video cable is taped on the cover with adhesive, if this is the case carefully remove the tape and then disconnect it from the Motherboard. Now that you have the video cable you must find the part number for the specific video cable you will need and replace it. Continue to STEP: E-2,

If step E-1 doesn't help, please continue to STEP: F-1

STEP: E-2

Video cables are very specific to the make and model. It is all based on the LCD screen. You must ensure that the part number is the same as the original one.

You could check up my previous posts for details about how to replace a laptop screen cable.

STEP: F-1

If after the previous steps above the issue has not been resolved, I would now replace it with a new or refurbished LCD screen. The issue is probably with the internal circuit in the screen

Remove the frame gently by using a small screw driver after all the screws have been removed. Locate the LCD screen's cable, and remove any tape holding the screen until it's free. And then unplug the cable cords.

The Part number will be located at the back of the LCD screen, Make sure you have an LCD screen that matches your original LCD part number, or that it's compatible with your laptop.

Plug in the new LCD screen, do not pinch any wires or pull as you press the LCD screen back into place. Turn the power on to see whether it works. If all is good, install it ensuring you do not twist the wires and screw the cover back on. please continue to STEP: F-2

If the new LCD screen still doesn't work, remove the battery and adapter and the screws and the framework. Double-Check your connections and reset it, if it still doesn't work,

Go to STEP: F-3

STEP: F-2

Your problem is probably LCD screen related. Please refer to the flowchart 05 (chapter 05)

Change a screen to your laptop

STEP: F-3

Before go to "repair analysis tutorial article flowchart 08", please follow these steps.

If you pass of the STEP: A-2, you should remember. Black screen doesn't stop the laptop from starting, and it's quite likely that the laptop BIOS was locked in a state of self-protection and has not been unlocked.

IF STEP: A-2 did not solve the problem.

Follow these steps

1. Unplug the AC power adapter, disassemble and open the laptop, take out the motherboard.
2. Unsolder to separate the CMOS battery connected with the motherboard with an electric soldering iron.
3. 10 minutes later, re-connect power and start up the laptop, if it fails, go to step 4;
4. After 12 hours, re-connect power and start the laptop.

We've had several cases that showed that the laptop locked itself in protection mode and that solved the problem and the laptop restored itself to normal.

If STEP: F-3 didn't solve the problem, then you'd have to replace the motherboard of the laptop!

You may also be interested in . . . More helpful articles

In this case, if you have got through STEP: D-1, you will no doubt remember.

If the inverter's pin 1 doesn't receive the power from the motherboard or doesn't have enough power (3V-5V), then what should my next step be

OK, I see that you've already confirmed that your laptop has a dark screen, and it displays normally by connecting to an external LCD screen,

IF STEP: D-3 did not solve the problem.

Follow these steps:

1. Unplug the AC power adapter, disassemble and open the laptop, remove the inverter.
2. Cut off inverter pin 1 cable with a knife to ensure that the existing connection to the motherboard is disconnected and isolated, and separate the pin 1 of the inverter to enable a solder connection.
3. Solder a flexible wire to the inverter pin 1.

Find a +12 V source on the motherboard and solder the other end of the wire to it.

I spent quite a few years' work to get to know this solution. I hope you are able to find a 12V source and complete this job, but the truth is, it's not always this easy because depending on the laptop or models, they are all different.

Keep in mind that, some voltage sources on a laptop may read 12V, but will rise to 14 to 19V after charging. Make sure you do not use that source. Some voltage sources are higher than 12V, but it does not fluctuate. These you can use by connecting a zener or a series of diodes to lower the voltage to the correct level.

A diode will bring the voltage down by 0.65v, so if you need the voltage down by 2v put in 3 or If you need it down to 1.3v put in 2 etc. After completing the connection, check it with your multimeter.

Please don't try this repair unless you are really a skilled computer hardware or electronic technician.

If STEP: F-3 didn't help, the only solution left is to use an external LCD display as if it were a desktop PC.

5.3 Thirty-eight repair cases of HP laptop screen failures

5.3.1 9 repair cases of screen failure caused by the inverter of an HP laptop

048) HP G50-211CA dark screen /black screen failures

Failure symptom:

At the beginning, the laptop starts normally, but after a while, the screen begins to darken. But you can still see something on the screen. Sometimes the backlight is on for awhile but the screen gradually darkens.

Solution:

This failure symptom belongs to the description of flowchart 05 that belong to sequence:

Start->A-1->B-1->C-1->C-2->C-3->D-1->D-2->D-4;

Repair Summary:

1. Disconnect the LCD screen from the inverter on the right side that means the plug is pulled out and is connected to the LCD screen backlight

2. Connect a good known backlight to the inverter on the laptop, and then you will be able to see the pictures below. Pay close attention, when testing backlight, they are usually shorter than the screen, and to tell you the truth, the length of the backlight will not affect your test, the goal is the same.
3. Our test result shows that the known good backlight does not light, which means the problem is not with the screen. It seems like the issue is with the inverter board;
4. finally, remove the inverter and replace it and then the problem is gone.

Hint: The Inverter is responsible for supplying power to the LCD lamp, converting DC low voltage power to high frequency and high voltage power and finally to lighten the lamp. It is an ever changing part whose frequency often changes but easily overheats. So it is only normal for it to break easily.

049)   HP CQ40-612tr screen darkens

Failure symptom:

A few minutes after the laptop starts, the screen begins darkening and you can hardly read the contents displayed on screen clearly.

Solution:

This failure symptom belongs to the description of flowchart 05 that belong to sequence:

Start->A-1->B-1->C-1->C-2->C-3->D-1->D-2->D-4;

Repair Summary:

According to the flow chart tutorial, 90% of this failure is caused by either the backlight or the inverter failure. First pull out the power adapter, remove the battery. In order to see the backlight and inverter plate, you need to remove the LCD frame too. During the disassembling process, do not use anything sharp so as not to damage the laptop screen. Under the screen you will find the inverter plate beside the connected video cable at the left and backlight on the right side; rotate the position, pull out the connection cables at both ends and you will find the high voltage package on inverter shows obvious burn traces. Test the connecting ends of the backlight with a multi-meter, finding there is no voltage there, which proves that the current is no longer passing through the high voltage winding package. Because it is hard to find an exact inverter, we only have to replace the high voltage winding package to fix the inverter for the failure to be gone.

An Inverter has no power supply for the lamp (motherboard has 3 to 4 voltage groups to supply the inverter, and after the chip transformation, the inverter supplies power to the lamp, so aging chip getting high current ends up burning, therefore there is no output power) according to the flow chart, changing to a new inverter, the problem is solved.

Hint:

If the inverter of the display screen works in a high temperature and voltage for a long time, it will easily age and burn. This common failure is caused because the power connection cable gets de-soldered, loose, or burnt in high voltage package. Because some inverters are hard to find it would be a nice idea to repair the inverter by changing the high voltage package, which can be found from a discarded inverter. Generally speaking, as long as the connector pins have the same shape or close to it.

050)   HP COMPAQ 6820S makes strange noises, and then screen failure occurs

Failure symptom:

After the laptop starts for a while, you can hear the sizzling like sound from the inverter, after that, the screen light becomes unstable, flashing a lot and then darkens to the point where you would hardly read the content on screen.

Solution:

This failure symptom belongs to the flow chart 05 flow char that belongs this sequence:

Start->A-1->B-1->C-1->C-2->C-3->D-1->D-2->D-4;

Repair Summary:

As the inverter makes a sizzling like noise and the screen turns dark, we can assumes it is the inverter. Disassemble the LCD frame, remove the connection cable of backlight on the right side, check the appearance of the cable carefully, finding that there is an obvious sign of spark on the connection cable. After replacing with a new inverter and changing the backlight connection cable, the failure is solved.

Hint: Usually, there are two possibilities that an inverter makes a sizzling like noise: one is the quality of the inverter; the other is due to a severe overload. So after disassembling the LCD frame, you should check the appearance of the connection cable, but especially check the connection cable of the backlight. There are two border angles around the LCD frame, whether the color changes by turning yellow or black also you should notice whether there is an overheating symptom, if there is, you should change the backlight connection cable after changing the inverter. Otherwise, the new inverter will burn in no time.

051)   HP Pavilion DV6215CA—water enters screen and suddenly screen darkens

Failure symptom:

When the client was using his laptop he accidentally spilled water over the screen, although he took the proper measure to wipe it off, he begins to have issues with his screen. Although the power light is displayed, and starting sound is heard, the screen remains black. If you check carefully again, you can clearly see the system LOGO interface in the background, which means the system starts normally.

Solution:

This failure symptom belongs to the description of flowchart 05 that belongs to this sequence: Start->A-1->B-1->C-1->C-2->C-3->D-1->D-2->D-4;

Repair Summary:

As water was accidentally spilled on the screen, it turns black; depending on the position or direction of the water, we can focus on the inverter. Disassemble the LCD frame, remove the connection cable of the backlight on the right side, check the appearance of the inverter carefully, finding it is humid in different areas of the connection cables. Blow the inverter and parts dry, and then wipe the sign of spark again. Afterwards, install it back into the laptop and the failure is solved.

Hint:

When water is spilled on the laptop or it becomes damp, the most effective method to use is to: blot up the water on the surface of the key-plate with an absorbent cloth as fast as possible and then wipe with a clean dry cloth, cleaning up the remainder of the spill on the inverter. Try disassembling the inverter and blow dry with cold air. Never blow with a hairdryer, as it can cause damage to the parts caused by high temperature due to the fact that the parts have plastic and are also tiny.

052)   HP PRESARIO V2000 CTO sometimes has dark screen failure

Failure symptom:

According to my client's representation, his laptop randomly gets dark screen failure when starting up. At start up all seems normal but after a couple of hours the dark screen failure appears. If he shuts the laptop for a bit it returns to normal only to go blank again but you can see the windows OS in the background.

Solution:

This failure symptom belongs to the description of flowchart 05, that belong to this sequence:

Start->A-1->B-1->C-1->C-2->C-3->D-1->D-2->D-4;

Repair Summary:

Because the dark screen failure symptom is random, it makes it difficult to diagnose the repair procedure. But According to the failure symptom combined with the flow chart tutorial of this chapter, the initial judgment is that there is a problem with the end connection cable of the backlight. The soldering joint is not soldered tightly, therefore after a period of time; it heats up and causes the problem. Connect a good known backlight to the inverter of the laptop and test it, but after 1 to 2 hours, dark screen failure still occurs. However, we find something that when we test the output voltage of inverter, there is no high voltage output from the connection cable end of the backlight. There is something wrong with the inverter when it supplies the power to the lamp. Removing the inverter and replacing it resolves the issue.

Hint:

1. Because an inverter works under high temperature and voltage environment for a repeated amount of time it expands and shrinks when cooling down so some soldering points end up with cracks in them. So when the laptop is cool it works normally but when it gets hot the issue occurs and the inverter can no longer supply power to the backlight normally.
2. Because the inverter works in high temperature and voltage for a repeated amount of time, the inverter chip also ages or burn out. Some chips will stop working when temperature gets too high, and return to normal working state when temperature drops. That is why the screen works when you first start but not after being on for a while.

053) HP PRESARIO C7000 dark screen failure when starting up

Failure symptom:

When laptop starts and runs, we can hardly see the contents displayed on the screen as the LCD display is dark. Check the screen carefully, but it is unclear we would see some letters.

Solution:

This failure symptom belongs to the description of flowchart 05 that belong to sequence:

Start->A-1->B-1->C-1->C-2->C-3->D-1->D-2->D-4;

Repair Summary:

According to my client's recalling, the dark screen failure symptom that happened to his laptop is kind of special. When the laptop starts, everything is all right, but after a short period of time, the dark screen failure occurs. However, when he pressed the inner part of the laptop screen with his fingers where the inverter is located the screen returned to normal state for a while. This worked every time he did that but eventually it stopped working and screen returned to its dark screen failure.

According to the failure symptom, combined with the flow chart tutorial of this chapter, initial judgment is that the connection end of the high voltage is faulty. Remove the frame of the LCD, check the inverter (AS0231721C1), finding there is a black coat on the protective insulated resistor. Remove and replace it with a new one and the failures gone.

Hint:

Because the motherboard provides 12V power to the inverter, then the protective insulated resistor, the power is loaded onto the inverter chip. The insulated resistor is also a fuse, when the load is too big it will create a short circuit and because of over-current protection, it will destroy itself to protect the chip. Even if there' is still any partial voltage passing through the insulated resistor, the supplied power has no way to reach the required power in order to light up the liquid crystal display, so the screen is dark.

054)   HP PAVILION DV9740US 5 minutes and LCD turns dark

Failure symptom:

After laptop starts up, characters are displayed on screen, but only for 3 to 5 minutes and backlight disappears. Seems there is nothing displayed on the screen, but if you check the screen carefully, you can faintly see something. Vista system though starts normally.

Solution:

This failure symptom belongs to the description of flowchart 05 that belongs to sequence:

Start->A-1->B-1->C-1->C-2->C-3->D-1->D-2->D-4;

Repair Summary:

Pull out the LCD connection cable from the right side of the inverter, this plug is what connects to the backlight of the display. Connect a known good backlight to the laptop inverter and test, finding the known good backlight does not light. 5 seconds later, the LCD turns blank, which means it has nothing to do with the display. The issue is more likely to be with the inverter; remove the inverter and replace with a new one, and the failure disappears.

Hint:

When the laptop has been used for a certain period of time, the screen would turn dark, sometimes slightly but sometimes severe, that is caused primarily because the quality of the inverter chip is going down or the high voltage package on the plate has a short circuit problem that cannot supply power to the LCD normally.

055)   HP PAVILION DV6470US intermittently lights up just like lightning and then dark screen failure occurs

Failure symptom:

Laptop starts up, and during the using process, screen lights up just like a lightning and then turns dark and blinks with no display.

Solution:

This failure symptom belongs to the description of flowchart 05 that belongs to sequence:

Start->A-1->B-1->C-1->C-2->C-3->D-1->D-2->D-4;

Repair Summary:

According to the failure symptom, combined with the flow chart tutorial of this chapter, initial judgment is that there is an issue with the power supply end of the inverter. Remove the LCD frame, when testing the inverter (AS0231720D2), no surface problem is found. However, during the voltage measure process, we find that the voltage is not stable, which belongs typically with issues with the inverter power supply. So during the usage process, the laptop would light up and turn dark from time to time. After replacing the inverter, the problem is gone.

Hint:

The power and signal of the inverter comes from the motherboard, generally there is several cables connected to the motherboard such as: power V+, power ground G, switch signal S, brightness signal F (some do not have). When the laptop starts, the power supply and switch signal S will start the switch surge circuit. If there is a bad connection in the power supply circuit of the laptop inverter, internal striking happens, then the switch surge circuit will work intermittently and of course the transformer will supply power intermittently. That is why the failure symptom (sometimes light sometimes dark) happens.

056)   HP PAVILION DV1220US dark screen failure

Failure symptom:

When the laptop starts up, we adjust the brightness of the display to the highest, then the display will show normally, but randomly dark screen failure will happen. When you turn the brightness a little lower, the screen would turn dark immediately.

Solution:

This failure symptom belongs to the description of flowchart 05 that belongs to sequence:

Start->A-1->B-1->C-1->C-2->C-3->D-1->D-2->D-4;

Repair Summary:

According to the failure symptom, initial judgment is that the problem is with the end of the connection cable of the backlight. Connect a good backlight to the laptop inverter and test it, finding the same dark screen failure occurs. However, we find that the inverters output voltage and the surge circuit switch stops working. Replace the inverter and the problem is gone.

Hint:

As the quality of the inverter chip is going down and when the laptop has been used for a certain period, dark screen failure will happen. However, in most cases, the problem is caused because the repair technician uses an incorrect inverter as replacement. Check the model of the inverter carefully, and ensure it is the same model as the original one. If it is not, have it replaced.

5.3.2   6 repair cases of dark screen failure caused by the HP laptop backlight

057)   HP Compaq PRESARIO CQ60-119TX dark screen and flashing screen failures

Failure symptom:

After the laptop has been used for a couple of years, you may start having issues with the display. When the laptop screen begins turning red and subsequently it turns normal. The symptom has been happening for a period of time and finally the screen is always red. Now the screen often flashes.

Solution:

This failure symptom belongs to the description of flowchart 05 that belongs to sequence:

Start->A-1->B-1->B-2->B-3->C-3;

Repair Summary

Combined with the flow chart of this chapter, it is typical with an aging backlight. Generally speaking, an aging lamp will make the screen to have a reddish flash. If the lamp breaks, then the screen will go black. As with the aging life of the laptop the LCD is limited, it is inevitable that backlight would age also; changing the lamp will solve the problem.

Hint:

If just a certain part of the screen changes color, especially the edge of the screen it is generally caused because of a strong magnetic interference. At this point, we can check whether it is the case by looking around the laptop for a magnetic device such as a sound box, transformer etc. If that is the case move the device away from the area.

058) HP PAVILION DV6-1230CA dark screen failure

Failure symptom:

Dark screen failure occurs just when laptop starts up. Every time you start the laptop, we can see the HP Logo, but the lamp does not seem to light up. The laptop does enter the system normally.

Solution:

This failure symptom belongs to the description of flowchart 05 that belongs to this sequence:

Start->A-1->B-1->C-1->C-2->C-3->C-4;or   Start->A-1->B-1->C-1->C-2->C-3->D-1->D-2->D-4;

Repair Summary

Combined with the flow chart tutorial of this chapter, 90% of the problem is caused by either the backlight or inverter failures. First pull out the power adapter; remove the battery and LCD frame too. Connect a good well known backlight to the inverter of the laptop and test it. The result shows the external lamp is lit normally, which indicates that there is nothing wrong with the inverter. The issue is caused due to a broken lamp so therefore replace it and the failure is solved.

Hint:

In most cases, testing the laptop with a good backlight is the way to go, because backlight issues are easy to solve, most backlights are generic and can be matched with many different types of inverter. Success rate is almost 99%, and it is very cheap to do the job.

059)   HP PRESARIO CQ45-139TX dark screen failure

Failure symptom:

The letters or pictures displayed on screen are very dim and the entire screen is dark.

Solution:

This failure symptom belongs to the description of flowchart 05 that belongs to this sequence:

Start->A-1->B-1->C-1->C-2->C-3->C-4;or   Start->A-1->B-1->C-1->C-2->C-3->D-1->D-2->D-4;

Repair Summary

According to the description of the flow chart, making a judgment regarding the laptop failure, generally speaking, there are two possibilities: one is the circuit voltage increase of the inverter is damaged; the other is the lamp or the connection cable is broken; test result will show that the circuit voltage increase is normal, after disassembling the screen you find the connection cable has aged and has some damage to it. After changing the cable, the problem is solved.

Hint:

When you disassemble the lamp, pay attention as you must first be clear about the entire screen structure regarding screws or bolts holding it. After disassembling the bolts around the screen, make sure you know where each bolts go, because each bolt of each position on the screen is different from each other. If you assemble the wrong size by mistake, you can break the liquid crystal plate of the screen. The lamp for the screen is at the bottom. After moving the adhesive plaster at the side remove the frame of the screen gently, at this moment, we can see the liquid crystal plate, reflector plate, condenser plate folded together. The external frame covers the lamp. At this moment, we can take the lamp out carefully.

060) HP PRESARIO CQ40-415AU laptop dark screen failure

Failure symptom:

Laptop works normally, but there is nothing on the screen. If you change the angle and look carefully, you can see the interface faintly.

Solution:

This failure symptom belongs to the description of flowchart 05 that belongs to this sequence:

Start->A-1->B-1->C-1->C-2->C-3->C-4;or   Start->A-1->B-1->C-1->C-2->C-3->D-1->D-2->D-4;

Repair Summary

According to the client's story, before the laptop had an issue, there was a coin stuck at the joint of the hinge and screen. At that time, it was very hard to fold the cover, when he opened the cover again he removed the coin and that is when the dark screen began because the high voltage connection cable had broken or the backlight cracked. There are 2 cables connected between high voltage inverter and backlight, if there is something stuck at the joint of the hinge and screen, and then when you fold the cover, the backlight is pressed severely and the LCD connection cable may break, high voltage can no longer be supplied to the backlight. After changing the new connection cable, the failure is solved.

Hint:

Before changing the backlight, you can do some simple checks, such as observing the main circuits directly, which plays a really important role in the process of repairing display problems. There are many areas where failures can occur so it is a good idea not to disassemble the soldering parts too quickly.

061) HP PRESARIO CQ35-217TX dark screen failure

Failure symptom:

Laptop starts and works normally, but the interface on screen becomes extremely dark. Even with a strong light we can hardly see the desktop.

Solution:

This failure symptom belongs to the description of flowchart 05 that belongs to this sequence:

Start->A-1->B-1->C-1->C-2->C-3->C-4;or   Start->A-1->B-1->C-1->C-2->C-3->D-1->D-2->D-4;

Repair Summary

According to my client's memory, the laptop screen was changed 5 months ago, now he is not clear why he is getting the dark screen failure; according to his understanding, the screen was refurbished and should not have this issue. The screen problem was caused by some other accessories.

Remove the LCD frame, connect a known good backlight to the inverter of the laptop, test result shows the external lamp lights up normally, which means the problem is caused by a broken lamp. After disassembling the screen we find it is cracked. After changing the lamp, the problem is solved.

Hint:

Generally, there are a few main reasons that cause backlight lamp to break

1) laptop is dropped on the floor and impacted severely
2) There is something stuck at the joint of the hinge and screen, causing a break when closing
3) laptop rear end cover is heavily obstructed or impacted severely.

062)   HP Pavilion dv6000 black screen failure

Failure symptom:

Laptop screen is black, no light on

Solution:

This failure symptom belongs to the description of flowchart 05 flow that belongs to this sequence:

Start->A-1->B-1->B-2->C-2->C-3->C-4;

Repair Summary

A failure like this seems to usually occur with the HP Pavilion dv6000 laptop. Most cases, the problem is with the integrated display card on the motherboard; but this time, the situation is different, when we switch the internal display to the external display of the laptop, the result shows that everything is okay. So it means there is nothing wrong with motherboard. It seems that the black screen failure is related with the high inverter and backlight; connecting a working backlight to the inverter, then the external lamp is lit which indicates the problem is caused because of a broken lamp. After disassembling the screen, you find the original lamp is dark and old. After changing the backlight, the failure is gone.

Hint:

An aging lamp or short circuit will make the screen dark or blank. If there is something wrong with the backlight, the simplest method is to change the entire screen, which also includes changing the backlight. It is quite common that one end of the lamp turns black, but a short circuit symptom is quite rare. Generally, the reason one end of the lamp turns black is because the lamp has been used for a long time or the laptop was dropped (normally, a lamps life is around 3 to 5 years), but short circuit may be caused because the lamp connection cable is broken or the metal shell has a short circuit.

5.3.3   5 repair cases of dark screen failure caused by the HP laptop display cable

063)   HP PAVILION DV2716 CA dark screen failure

Failure symptom:

Dark screen symptom occurs after starting up laptop outdoor with a strong sun shining, unclear we would see the interface displayed on the LCD.

Solution:

This failure symptom belongs to the description of flowchart 05 that belongs to this sequence:

Start->A-1->B-1->C-1->C-2->C-3->D-1->D-3->E-1->E-2;

Repair Summary

There is just a black screen showing after the laptop comes out of hibernation, but once connected to the external PC display, the computer can enter the Windows system normally. According to the flowchart tutorial, connect a known good backlight to the inverter of the laptop and test it, finding that the good backlight also does not light up. Continue by using a multi-meter to test the interface to see whether the power supply is normal. It turns out that the voltage at the motherboard connection is normal, but the other side has no voltage. The screen cable seems like the culprit. It is one of the most common failures because of closing and opening of the screen in the life of a laptop. Disassemble the screen cable, and then test both ends, finding there are 3 cables already broken. After changing the screen cable, the failure is gone.

Hint:

Generally speaking, there are 3 to 4 groups of connection cables between high voltage inverter and motherboard, as the laptop is folded away and opened, the wires are continuously bent. Long-term opening and closing to the LCD would also mangle and break the screen cable being pressed; then the high voltage inverter ends no longer get voltage or control signal and fails to supply power

064)   HP PAVILION DV6646 US dark screen failure

Failure symptom:

Laptop screen is in dark state, system enters normally but there is no light.

Solution:

This failure symptom belongs to the description of flowchart 05 that belongs to this sequence:

Start->A-1->B-1->C-1->C-2->C-3->D-1->D-3->E-1->E-2;

Repair Summary:

After testing, you find the external display is normal, disassemble the laptop, replace the original display with a known good LCD for testing, after starting up, the screen is still dark, which means the problem is not caused by backlight lamp. At this moment, test with a multi-meter, and you find there is no voltage input at the input end of the inverter! This dark screen failure should be caused by the inverter because it does not supply power to the lamp normally. Check again carefully, and exclude the problem of the inverter, finally test the screen cable, and you will find the connection joint of the cable between the screen and the motherboard has obvious abrasion. Change it and test again start the notebook and everything is back to normal

Hint:

After careful observation, I figure out that this laptop had been repaired before, because I noticed there is a piece of plastic fragment stuck between the screen cable and the rotating shell. Now that we have found the reason for the broken cable, as the fragment would often be driven when you rotate the screen. An impossible thing did happen, so you should be careful and cautious about each inspection step of the job.

065)   HP PAVILION DV5029 US sometimes gets blank screen failure

Failure symptom:

Dark screen failure happens randomly when start up laptop. Generally, laptop should be all right the moment just starting up, but when turn the screen to a certain angle, dark screen failure would occur. However, after changing to another angle, it would work again. When dark screen occurs, with external light irradiation, Windows system would be hardly seen.

Solution:

This failure symptom belongs to the description of flowchart 05 that belongs to this sequence:

Start->A-1->B-1->C-1->C-2->C-3->D-1->D-3->E-1->E-2;

Repair Summary

According to the failure symptom, combined with the flowchart tutorial of this chapter, initial judgment is with the screen cable. When removing LCD frame and testing the screen cable, we find a black joint on a separated connection cable. It seems the problem is with this cable. Continue by using a multi-meter to test, after confirming, cut off both ends of the cable, change it with a new cable and solder it on and the failure disappears.

Hint:

The simplest way is to change the entire screen cable, and we would avoid having to solder but sometimes we cannot find or bother to get a new one and this method will do just as good of a job. Generally a broken cable is quite common but impossible to fix if the cable is broken. If you twist the screen cable with your hands and you feel it heats up, pay close attention, and cut off the power immediately, turn off the computer, because it is an indication that there' is a "short circuit" happening to the screen cable, you need to check further and repair;

Warning! With this type of repair, you might damage the inverter or even motherboard and LCD screen. Beware! Do it at your own risk.

066)   HP PAVILION DV2510 TX—screen flashes randomly or blurry screen at starts up

Failure symptom:

Screen flashes randomly when laptop starts up, the interface is not stable, and sometimes screen is blurry.

Solution:

This failure symptom belongs to the description of flowchart 05 that belongs to this sequence:

Start->A-1->B-1->C-1->C-2->C-3->D-1->D-3->E-1->E-2;

Repair Summary

According to the failure symptom, combined with the flowchart tutorial of this chapter, initial judgment is a problem with the screen, screen cable or motherboard. First connect an external display and test it and you find the external display is normal, and then the failure range would be reduced to either the LCD or the screen cable problem. Start the laptop, twist the video cable with your fingers gently, and observe whether there is any change to the screen. At a certain moment, clear interface is displayed, which means there's an "open circuit" symptom in the screen cable. Change it and the failure disappears.

Hint:

Such symptoms like blurry screen or flashing screen failures happen irregularly, or the failure would disappear after clapping and pressing the surface of screen, that is the result caused by a bad contact between the LCD signal cable and interface. We just need to plug the related interface tightly, and the problem can be eliminated. If after restarting the laptop, it still does not work, then please check all the connection cables again and inspect carefully. Probably during the process of assembling the screen, it's possible that it is not completely connected, and that the connection between the screen cable and LCD display is still off, so all video cables must be assembled correctly.

067)   HP COMPAQ NX6330 laptop blurry screen and distortion failure

Failure symptom:

After starting the laptop, the interface is quite unstable, accompanied with distortion symptom on the screen. After pressing the surface of the screen, sometimes, the failure disappears.

Solution:

This failure symptom belongs to the description of flowchart 05 that belongs to this sequence:

Start->A-1->B-1->C-1->C-2->C-3->D-1->D-3->E-1->E-2;

Repair Summary

According to the failure symptom, combined with the flowchart tutorial of this chapter, testing with an external display you find it displays normally. Now you should uncover the adhesive tape carefully, check the status of the video cable, and no issues there either and you now focus on the video cable. Everything is all right. So you reconnect the cable, but nothing helps the issue. You then check all the connection cables, and this time we find that the connection between the video cable and LCD screen head is stained near the connection pin cable. Because the adhesive tape acts as a good insulation and the contact between video cable and LCD screen interface is extremely good. Remove the fixed adhesive tape, clean the connection pins on the video cable and install back you will find the failure will disappear.

Hint:

Generally, laptop video cable has three different pins: the upper is a flat cable pin of single row with multi-head, which is connected to the liquid crystal display. The underside is double rows with multi-head (4-8 pins) cable pin connected to the inverter; another end is Multi-row and multi-head cable pins connected to the main motherboard.

5.3.4 Five repair cases of dark or blank screen failures caused by the HP laptop RAM, motherboard or switch components

068) HP PAVILION DV2000 TX dark screen failure

Failure symptom:

Laptop screen is blank and lights off.

Solution:

This failure symptom belongs to the description of flowchart 05 that belongs to this sequence:

Start->A-1->B-1->B-2->C-2

Repair Summary:

Such blank screen failure seems to be typical for the HP Pavilion dv2000. But when I change from internal to external display, everything is OK. It means the problem has nothing to do with the motherboard. According to the flowchart tutorial, check the link C-2, you will find the switch is already broken. The switch code name is: 417087-001; it does not start or turn off normally. After disassembling the switch, you find the internal part is in pieces. After changing the switch, the failure is solved.

Hint:

Most laptop display switches have two pins, the "SENSOR" usually located at the top left corner of the keyboard or for some at the top right corner. The effect of the sensor is that when the switch is OPEN, screen is on display status; if the computer is closed while on it' will turn it off. So some call it a "Sleep switch". If you cannot find the display switch, please try using this user manual or search the Web.

069)   HP PRESARIO V3000 CTO dark screen failure

Failure symptom:

Laptop screen is on black status mode and no lights.

Solution:

This failure symptom belongs to the description of flowchart 05 that belongs to this sequence:

Start->A-1->B-1->C-1->C-2

Repair Summary:

According to the flowchart tutorial, when checking the link A-1, it's found that when the laptop connects to the external display, everything is OK; when checking link C-2, it is found that the display switch is broken, the code of the switch is: 50.4F606.001; however, there is no way to find out except to disassemble the switch, connect (solder) as permanent "OPEN" status with lead, namely, the screen is on display status, the problem is solved. However, such a way will not allow when folding the screen down entering sleep mode. In order to enter sleep mode you will need to click power management control with mouse.

Hint:

When the laptop is closed while running, the sleep switch folds and therefore most screens would have a black status, with time the switch ends up breaking from repeated folding and that is the main reason why the failure occurs.

070)   HP 510 laptop black screen failure

Failure symptom:

Laptop screen shows black status, nothing appears.

Solution:

This failure symptom belongs to the description of flowchart 05 that belongs to this sequence:

Start->A-1->A-2->A-3->A-4->A-5

Repair Summary:

When you change laptop from internal to external display, screen remains black. That means the problem is probably with the internal display. According to the flowchart tutorial, when you check the link A-4, you find the memory may be bad. Put this memory in another laptop and the machines does not start. After changing the memory the failure is gone.

Hint:

Most laptops have no independent display card, namely, display card is integrated on the motherboard. Video memory is almost always shared with the system. Therefore, if there is a problem with the memory, system and display will not start up. If your laptop has two memory modules, then you can test each of them individually in case only one of them has a problem saving you a bit of money

071)   HP PAVILION DV9010 US dark screen failure

Failure symptom:

Laptop screen is in dark mode but system is available and the light is really dark.

Solution:

This failure symptom belongs to the description of flowchart 05 that belongs to this sequence:

Start->A-1->B-1->C-1->C-2->C-3->D-1->D-2->D-4; Start->A-1->B-1->C-1->C-5->C-6

Repair Summary:

Test finds the external display is all right. Disassemble the laptop; replace the original screen with a known good one, start the laptop, but the screen is still dark, it then indicates that the failure is not caused by the backlight lamp. At this moment, test with a multi-meter, finding the input voltage of high voltage plate is normal, which means the high voltage plate is OK. However, in case of a diagnosis error, remove the high voltage plate anyways and replace with a new one, but the failure remains. So rethink the issue by going to flowchart: Start->A-1->B-1->C-1->C-5->C-6, specifically link C-1. With the combination "Fn+F5", laptop does not switch to sleep mode, so is the dark screen failure caused because the "F7" and "F8" keys do not work? Change the keyboard and test, and you will find the failure is solved.

Hint:

Combination keys would change the brightness of the LCD screen, but all of a sudden the, "Fn" or "F8" key does not work, you have no idea as the screen is at its brightest so you cannot tell whether it is a keyboard issue or something else. The reason is that the keyboard loses the adjustment function, so during the repair process, the C-2 link is key to the repair.

072)   HP PAVILION DV6919 CA dark screen failure

Failure symptom:

Dark screen failure occurs from start up and you cannot see content on screen clearly.

Solution:

This failure symptom belongs to the description of flowchart 05 that belongs to this sequence:

Start->A-1->B-1->C-1->C-2->C-3->D-1->D-3->E-1->F-1->F-3;

Repair Summary:

External display is working, disassemble the laptop, and connect a good backlight to the high voltage plate of the laptop, after starting the laptop, the backlight is still off, it then indicates that the problem is not caused by it. Test with a multi-meter, finding the input port of the high voltage plate has no voltage, which means the problem happens before the high voltage plate. For the sake of it and security reasons replace the high voltage plate, but the failure does not disappear, so now change the screen cable but the issue remains. Now it seems the problem is with the input port on the motherboard which has no voltage with the high voltage plate and screen cable so pull out the connection between the screen cable and the motherboard and test the motherboard pin voltage directly with a multi-meter, the voltage is 0V. Now you know the issue is on the motherboard, switch the connection cable of the input port of the high voltage plate to the interface, start up and test it, and the failure is solved.

Hint:

I have spent a few years working on this solution, hoping to find an interface having +12V to the ground, but the situation is not always the same, motherboards of different model of laptops will have different +12V interfaces and solutions.

Please keep this in mind: some voltage points are higher than 12V, but would not float. So we can continue using this method of diode voltage down protection. Diode will bring the voltage down by 0.65v, so if you need the voltage down by 2v put in 3(Diode), if you need it down by 1.3v put in 2(Diode) etc.

If you are a beginner at repairing laptops, do not try this repair method, unless you do not care if you end up scrapping the laptop.

5.3.5   11 repair cases of HP laptop screen failure caused by other reasons

073)   HP PRESARIO C500 CTO displays white speckle/yellow speckle

Failure symptom:

There is a white speckle on liquid crystal display, it is of a thin white color dot under white background, thin blue dot under pure blue color background etc, but you do not see anything under black color. There is only a speckle. Sometimes, when you repair the laptop, you will find that there are one or two yellow speckles on the LCD.

Solution:

According to the repair method of flowchart 05, when you switch the laptop internal display to the external display, you find there is no white speckle/yellow speckle failure. So you can confirm the problem is with the laptop screen.

Repair summary:

Usually, a white speckle is caused because the reflecting layer inside the laptop screen has a problem. The most common situation is that a partial liquid crystal is pressed or collided, which leads to white speckles; yellow speckle is caused by traces of water that has entered the screen. Both situations calls for changing the backlight board, or you would have to change the entire display!

It is not an easy task to change the backlight board; generally, you first loosen the metal frame from the screen. There are a lot of locks besides the screen. You can unlock them with a small screwdriver. When all locks are removed, you should be able to separate the screen into three independent parts: metal frame, liquid crystal display and "backlight board". If there is dust inside the display, do not use your fingers to touch the surface of the liquid crystal display or backlight board, such operation will directly ruin the screen. After disassembling the screen, separate the LCD from the serial circuit board and off the "backlight board" carefully.

Find a similar screen layer, generally, from a broken LCD, remove the backlight board fibre layer from the broken screen, and then move the white backlight board inside along with the connection layer to the your display. After changing it the problem is solved.

Warning: when disassembling, it is quite easy to break the LCD, even by accident if you make little mistakes. Your display might end up being useless, it is very expensive to replace, caution, and so before you decide to repair it yourself do it at your own risk and expense.

Hint:

If white speckle has just appeared, then check the screens upper cover, and check whether it is distorted or there is a bump mark on the surface of the screen. Sometimes if the keyboard was changed and not installed properly and the screws at the bottom are not the right size or the keyboard is not exact as the original it may when closing the lid, rub against the screen and it may cause speckles. Besides, when you buy a second hand laptop or refurbished you have no idea how it was used or transported and therefore the issue might have been happening for a while and then speckles start appearing.

074)   HP PAVILION DV6120US a straight vertical light thread is seen on display

Failure symptom:

Suddenly there is a straight vertical light appearing on the laptop screen, located on the right side of the desktop icons. It suddenly appeared for no reason and disappeared but this time it remained. However, you cannot see that light thread under pure white or pure white background and the display screen is wavy.

Solution:

According to the repair method of flowchart 05, when you switch the laptop from the internal to external display there is no vertical light thread failure. So the screen is confirmed as the problem.

Repair summary:

It is very obvious if a horizontal or vertical light thread appears on the LCD that we shake the LCD back and forth and notice the thread twinkling. Next when I press the right side around the frame of the LCD the light thread disappears, which means the screen is faulty and due to a loose cable. After changing the LCD, the failure is gone.

Hint:

A Light thread means there is one or several pixels appearing on the screen. The light thread on the display of the screen is either vertical or horizontal; the position is fixed and unchangeable. The color of the light thread will not change in most cases as it is either white or black; in a few cases it will be red and yellow. Generally there are two kinds of cables in the laptop: one is the cable from the screen to the display card, the other is the cable from screen control circuit to the TFT panel. These two kinds of cables all play the role of transferring display contents. The difference is that the cables from the screen to the display card transfers the display signal to the entire screen, after reaching the control circuit, these signals are converted to the content of each pixel displayed and then sends it to the TFT panel. If there is any issue on any of the cables the display will have a problem.

075)   HP PRESARIO CQ50-100CA screen turns yellow and grey

Failure symptom:

The laptop has been used for about a year, now the screen turns yellow. You open a webpage, and notice the display looks like it turns yellow and grey. Sometimes the screen flashes constantly.

Solution:

According to the repair method of flowchart 05, when the laptop switches from internal to external display, you find the symptom disappears. So the problem must be with the laptop screen or a power shortage from the high voltage plate.

Repair summary:

95% of these failures are caused because the screen LED is aging. However, the screen turns grey, the brightness is not high, and it is extremely unlikely the problem is caused because of a power shortage of the high voltage plate. Usually, I will replace the high voltage plate to test it, and confirm whether the voltage is within a normal range with a multi-meter. After this, you can then decide whether to change the backlight or the entire display.

However, the client would put off the aging process of the LCD by the method below:

1.   Lower the screen brightness as much as you possibly can. When the laptop works, set 2~3 grid of brightness for the screen; when not in use, shut down the screen, or put it in standby for a period of time, OS will automatically turn off the display.
2.   Avoid sun exposure as direct exposure to sunshine is a killer for a screen. So you should avoid using it in this condition as much as possible.

Hint:

1.   Screen turns yellow, which means the LCD has been used for a period of time, especially when you adjust the brightness to the maximum, the aging LED will shine a little yellow light. If the latter one causes the problem, just change the LED; but if the previous one, then there is no way to solve. You will have to change the entire display.
2.   Power shortage problem of the high voltage plate is related to the power supply of the motherboard. Test the voltage of the backlight with a multi-meter, not only the 12V power voltage, there should be 3.3V~5V switch voltage and 0~5V backlight adjustment voltage. The switch voltage of the backlight is the most important, if

there is no voltage or very low voltage, you will then have to check the CPU output voltage and the status of the audio. Pay close attention whether there is a short circuit symptom there and if so, change the components.

076)   HP Pavilion zd7360us laptop's white screen failure

Failure symptom:

Laptop screen is white with no picture appearing.

Solution:

According to the repair method of flowchart 05, when the laptop switches from the internal to the external display, you find everything is all right. So it is most likely a laptop screen issue or a loose cable in the display.

Repair summary:

When you convert the laptop from internal to the external display, it shows normally, which means the problem is most likely with the internal display. White screen symptoms means that the backlight board works, so you first check whether there is bad contact in the connection cable where the signal converts from the motherboard to the screen. After replacing the connection cable, the failure still exists, so now change the display and test, everything returns to normal after starting it. The failure is fixed!

Hint:

When a white screen appears it is usually an indication there is something wrong with the power circuit of the liquid crystal display or a loose connection cable between the screen and the motherboard. There are a few cases, where the motherboard cannot supply power. If a white screen occurs at start-up or after self-inspection, the problem is that the power supply circuit of the display has no voltage. However, at this point the backlight is already on, but it seems totally blank when the white screen failure occurs.

077)   HP Compaq R3000 white screen failure

Failure symptom:

Laptop screen is white and no picture is appearing.

Solution:

According to the repair method of flowchart 05, when you switch the laptop from internal to external display and find everything is all right.

Repair summary:

When you convert the laptop to the external display, everything is normal, which indicates the problem must be with the internal display. First of all, check the connection cable where the signal transfers from the motherboard to the screen. Test the joint position power supply with a multi-meter, finding the voltage of motherboard joint is normal, but the other end has no voltage! So the problem seems to be a cracked screen cable. After disassembling the screen connection cable and changing the failure disappears.

Hint:

Screen shows white, from time to time; it is because the motherboard cannot supply power. Disconnect the screen cable from the motherboard, and directly test the end voltage of the motherboard with a multi-meter. If the voltage is too low or 0V, then the problem is the motherboard. Find another joint having the same voltage to the ground, and then switch the connection cable of the screen to this joint.

In actual repair process, we often deal with two kinds of power supply methods of display: one is the motherboard which supplies all kinds of work voltages for display

The other is the motherboard that only provides one voltage; all other kinds of voltages are transferred and provided by the display integrated circuit board. Generally, there are 4 kinds of working voltages that an LCD needs. When you repair the display, primarily check 10V, -6V two groups of voltages.

078)   HP PAVILION HDX9010TX laptop's display brightness is not symmetrical

Failure symptom:

After laptop starts up, half the screen is lit and the other half is dark. It shows normal when you switch to the external display.

Solution:

According to the repair method of flowchart 05, the problem is with the laptop screen. And here is the repair path:

Start->A-1->B-1->C-1->C-2->C-3->C-4;

Repair summary:

There are two kinds of fault phenomenon. For earlier—generation laptops and those small-size monitors, they have a single-tube structure. If the tube is broken, the screen displays dimly under the sunshine. Sometimes, the brightness of a picture is not symmetrical, according to the flowchart; such failure symptom is caused because the laptop LCD backlight lamp is not good. Changing the backlight and the failure disappears.

Hint:

If multi-lamp is broken, then the picture shown would not be symmetrical on bright. For instance, the upper is a little dim, so the upper lamp is broken. Touching the screen lamp position with hands, and generally, you can compare the heat difference. Normal display lamps temperatures are the same. But because most new style displays have high voltage balance protection circuit, so if one lamp is broken, then symmetrical brightness is not the same, but the monitor will not start or you may get a totally black screen at start up. So make a decision according to concrete display circuits.

079) HP PAVILION DV6919CA half the screen is normal, and the other half is black or white

Failure symptom:

Suddenly there is a horizontal thread on laptop screen, at the top and bottom from the middle. The top half screen works normally, characters would be seen, but the bottom half is black with no display, you would occasionally see something but it disappears immediately.

Solution:

According to the repair method of flowchart 05, when you switch from internal to external display, you find there is not any top or bottom separated parts on screen. So you can be confident the issue is with the laptop internal display.

Repair summary:

When the screen shows two parts—the upper is normal and the down is a black screen or blurred screen—In this case, If I twist the LCD screen back and forth and found the bottom part becomes normal, then, when I remove my hands from the LCD, the bottom half part returns to black or blurred screen, which exactly indicates the problem is the LCD. Usually this is caused because the cable inside the LCD is loose, after changing to a new LCD, the failure is gone.

Hint:

Few reasons that half of the screen works:

1. The failure symptom is not fixed on one performance, for some machines, normal display part might appear at the top half, left half or even right of the screen. Normal display is not always equal or symmetrical to the size it displays;

2. The section of some machines that do not display normally might be in the form of a black or white screen status and in a few cases color strips or flashing light threads;
3. Some machines, at start up only displays half the screen and sometimes even in the BIOS interface, and the issue remains the same after entering Windows system.

080) HP PAVILION ZE5385US red snowflake like drizzle blurry screen

Failure symptom:

At start-up there is a red snowflake like drizzle falling on laptop screen, and even the brand icon is covered around by red snowflakes, and the issue remains when entering the Windows system.

Solution:

According to the repair method of flowchart 05, when the laptop internal display switches from the internal to the external display, you find the snowflake like drizzle disappears. So we now know the issue is with the laptop internal display.

Start->A-1->B-1->C-1->C-2->C-3->D-1->D-3->E-1->F-1->F-3;

Repair summary:

Disassemble the laptop, test with a multi-meter, finding the input voltage of the high voltage plate is OK, enter repair link D-1, replace with a new high voltage plate, but the failure still exists, so enter repair link E-1, change the screen cable again, but the failure is still the same; it seems the red snowflake screen issue must be with the high voltage plate and screen cable. Enter repair link F-1, connect a good known display to the laptop and start it up, but the red snowflake screen returns, which means the failure is not caused by the display. Obviously, the problem is on the motherboard, the video signal has a severe interference. After changing the motherboard, everything returns normal again and the failure is fixed

Hint:

If the external display shows normally while the internal display has problems, then in most cases, such a failure is associated with the motherboard, but there is also exceptions and in this case is the explanation. The case is very much similar to the blurry screen symptom because of overheating. But the failure is caused by the laptop overheating and usually, would also show on the external display. But in this case, the external display showed, which indicated the problem should have been on the circuit between the display cards to the internal display, but mostly the reason was with the shielding or filtering circuit. Usually, it is caused because certain resistance goes bad or few capacitors dry rot.

081)   HP COMPAQ V3776 snowflake screen failure

Failure symptom:

The laptop LCD definition is not good enough; it looks grey under white background, just like frosted glass, not white and bright, but glazed. And under grey picture background it twinkles; when you browse pictures with lots of colors only a parts of the picture has snowflake symptom.

Solution:

According to the repair method of flowchart 05, when you switch from internal to external display, you find there are no grey display or snowflake symptoms. So it is estimated the issue is with the laptop internal display.

Repair summary:

After disassembling the laptop, you find that it uses SAMSUNG LTN141w1-L04 LCD, connect a new LCD of the same make and model to the laptop, start it up, but the snowflakes still appear. However, if you watch the screen from the just right angle, you may feel nothing's wrong, but from a different angle, especially under pure color background, you can see there is white spots standing out. The bigger the oblique angle is, the more severe the snowflake problem is. When you lean to a 30 degrees angle and watch the pure color background screen, it is full of snowflakes all over the screen. According to the previous experience, I guess this entire batch might have a problem, so use the other compatible brand products to replace it. After changing a LP141WX3 (TL) (B2) LCD, the failure disappears.

Hint:

What is so-called a "snowflake screen" is caused by 6 bit grey-scale modulation technology. It would be said that all 6 bit screens have such a problem to a certain extent; this is the boundary of technology, which is also an imperfect and immature representation of TFT-LCD display technique on 6 bit grey-scale modulation.

Early TFT-LCD had no such problem, because they did not use any grey-scale modulation technology. So there is no such "snowflake screen" problem that existed. Of course, there are not many grey-scale levels, so the picture level is bad.

082)   HP PAVILION TX2500 dark screen failure

Failure symptom:

Dark screen appears at start up; you cannot even see what is displayed on the screen.

Solution:

According to the repair method of flowchart 05, when you switch from the internal to the external display, finding everything is all right. So the problem is with the laptop internal display.

Start->A-1->B-1->C-1->C-2->C-3->D-1->D-3->E-1->F-1->F-3;

Repair summary:

External display is all right, then disassemble the laptop, connect a known good backlight to the laptop high voltage plate, but the backlight is still out at start up, which indicates the problem is not caused by the backlight lamp. Test with a multi-meter, finding the input end +12V voltage of the high voltage plate is normal. After changing the high voltage plate and a new screen cable, the problem still exists; it seems there is no problem transferring high voltage to backlight, it is unrelated with the high voltage plate or screen cable. Pull out the connection between the screen cable and motherboard, test the end voltage of the motherboard directly with a multi-meter, finding the boot signal sent from the motherboard (display card) is very low, the voltage is 1.8V, but normal working voltage should be between 3.3V to 5V. Seem the problem is on the motherboard, after changing the motherboard and then test, everything is OK. The failure is fixed!

Hint:

I spent a lot of time on this problem, hoping not to change the motherboard and to find a solution for it. But the situation is not that easy to do. HP laptops of different models have different high voltage plates. Fortunately, other model HP laptops (15") of the same production period have the high voltage plate with the same interface. After testing, it works all right, but it is a real pity that the size of the high voltage plate is too big and does not fit inside the client's machine. However, it does give me a thought: 1.8V switch signal S still can start some circuit surge switch, so I want to solve the problem by changing the high voltage plate.

Here is the method to change high voltage plate:

1. Test the power supply voltage at the client's machine's high voltage power supply place.
2. Find the brightness signal cable on client's machine's high voltage plate. Adjust brightness switch (FN+"F7"), to ensure it's at its brightness.
3. Find the boot signal. Generally it will be either over or under the brightness signal cable; the voltage is 3.3/5V. Here in the case is 1.8V;
4. Find an OEM high voltage plate similar to the client's high voltage plate machine, the size should be proper enough to put exactly the same original place;
5. Find the power cable and ground cable and change it for high voltage plate, and connect it to the external adjustable power supply;

6.   Touch the left cables with 1.8V battery, the cables with the lit lamp is the boot signal cable; the other is the brightness adjustment cable.
7.   Solder the power supply cable and the ground cable on the clients' machine high voltage plate one by one with the replacement one, power on and test.

Please remember: the sixth usually uses 3.3V battery to touch the rest cables, the one lit lamp is the boot signal cable, but because of the particularity of this case, we would only use 1.8V.

083)   HP laptop screen shows 180 degrees upside down

Failure symptom:

Unconsciously, certain keys have been pressed on the laptop, and now the information displayed on the laptop is upside down.

Solution:

This is the visual regression function of display card driver, many different brands of laptops all have such a function—this screen reversion function. We can use hot-key functions to make the display return normal. Such as:

[Ctrl]+[Alt]+[↓] combination: rotates the screen 180 degrees (upside down)

[Ctrl]+[Alt]+[↑] combination: Makes screen to return normal visual angle;

[Ctrl]+[Alt]+[←] combination: rotates the screen 90 degrees (sideways);

[Ctrl]+[Alt]+[→] combination: rotates the screen back to normal.

5.3.6   2 repair cases of special screen failures caused by HP laptop motherboard

084)   When HP DV2501TX laptop starts, there are 6 windows of the same size appearing on screen.

Failure symptom:

Random screen twinkle occurs when laptop starts up, the interface is not stable, accompanying with flashing symptom. And 6 windows of the same size appear on the screen.

Solution:

This failure symptom belongs to the description of flowchart 05 that belongs to this sequence:

Start->A-1->B-1->C-1->C-2->C-3->D-1->D-3->E-1->F-1->F-3;

Repair summary:

According to the failure symptom, combined with the flowchart tutorial of this chapter, initial judgement is caused by the display card or driver. First, connect an external display and test, finding the external display also has the same issue, so the failure possibility range is reduced, as it excludes the internal display failure. It is proved that the initial judgement is correct; so now uninstall the display card driver, and then reinstall the driver with the latest version, start the laptop, and observe any changes on the screen; but the results remain the same, which indicates the integrated display card on the motherboard is faulty, change the motherboard, and the failure disappears.

Hint:

This case is quite similar to the one caused by an incorrect driver, or the user adjusts the screen resolution too high, consequently, multi-windows appears on the screen. Is it the internal display that is faulty? This is also a concern for repair technicians. Without an external display you can use this method for diagnostic purposes: start the laptop, enter BIOS page, if the failure symptom disappears, then the failure point might be with the screen setup. If multi-window symptom still occurs, then it's with the internal display.

085)   HP COMPAQ Presario V3030CA laptop occasionally has image distortion failure on screen.

Failure symptom:

Occasionally the interface becomes unstable and is accompanied by distortion symptoms at start up. And few minutes later, the failure auto disappears.

Solution:

This failure symptom belongs to the description of flowchart 05 that belongs to this sequence:

Start->A-1->B-1->C-1->C-2->C-3->D-1->D-3->E-1->F-1->F-3;

Repair summary:

According to the failure symptom, combined with the flowchart tutorial of this chapter, test with an external display, finding the result is normal. Uncover the stationary rubberized fabric, check the state of the video cable, finding no obvious repair or break on the video cable; test the high voltage plate with a multi-meter, finding the voltage of the input end is normal, then enter repair link D-1, change with a new high voltage plate, but the failure does not disappear, so you then enter repair link E-1, now change the screen cable, the failure still exists; it seems the interface distortion problem is with the high voltage plate and screen cable. Enter repair link F-1; connect a known good display to the laptop, start it up, the interface distortion symptom still appears, which indicates the problem is not caused by the display. Apparently, the problem is on the motherboard, the video signal gets interfered, so after changing the motherboard, everything returns to normal and the failure is fixed

Hint:

External display works normally, but the internal display is not, in most cases, such a failure is caused by the motherboard. However, there is an exception. This case is quite similar to the flashing screen symptom caused by a bad contact between the laptop LCD signal cable and interface, so you would have to check it closely and carefully:

1) Tighten the interface to the screen cable again; in case you did not do it right and it might save you some money by not having to change the motherboard which would be costly

2) In this case, the external display shows normally, which means the problem should be with the display circuit card to the internal display. This would be the reason that the video signal gets interfered, usually, some resistance metamorphoses, which causes the voltage to become unstable.

CHAPTER 6

Overheating failure repair

6.1 Laptop overheating failures and causes

6.1.1 Laptop temperature and fan controlling

How to change CPU fan temperature at start up

For the HP laptop, you can enter the BIOS interface the moment you press "F10" at start up. (And F2 for an old model). The HP BIOS interface is quite simple consisting of four sections. Main, Security, Diagnostics and System Configuration. In file, the user can check the basic hardware information of the laptop, such as product serial numbers, processor specification, and memory size and so on.

In BIOS, you can setup your system CPU to either maximum or minimum temperature.

However, because they come from different laptop motherboard manufacturers, the configurations are different. HP laptop motherboards all have a temperature control chip, as a result, they all have the ability to start and turn off the fan automatically. However, these types of machines have no such function to setup or modify the fan start temperature.

1. What is the normal working temperature CPU?

This question is hard to explain or answer. Depending on the motherboard, temperature testing is different, even on some same brands or models, because of where the CPU and temperature probe is located on the motherboard; the testing of the temperature is different. Generally speaking in my experience the temperature should range approximately 30-35 degrees for the CPU with the normal working temperature meaning the surrounding ambient temperature around your laptop at 25 degrees, (the environment temperature around the laptop, not indoor or outdoor temperature).

If you add the maximum 35 degree temperature with the environmental temperature, then you know the allowed CPU temperature is 60 degrees. By analogy, no matter how you use your laptop, don't let the CPU temperature exceed surrounding ambient temperature more than 35 degrees; and the lower the temperature is, the better it is. Now I want to add this: you don't have to trust the testing software to much, as long as the working temperature remains within limits. If the fan keeps working at high speed and the CPU temperature rises slowly, then you should keep an eye on it.

2.   How to control CPU temperature?

A rise in temperature is caused when the CPU heats more than the heat sink and fan can cool. Once heat is generated it should be equal to the heat emission, the temperature then will no longer rise. Generally, there is 4 cables on the laptop fan; power cable +12V, grounding cable GND, signal cable Sensor which is used to send fan rotation information to BIOS and finally a control line.

The control line uses PWM (Pulse Width Modulation) to control the fan. This is smart temperature control; The BIOS would auto adjust the voltage according to the CPU temperature in order to control the fan rotation speed.

3.   How to find out if a laptop has an overheating problem?

Overheating is a very common problem for laptops. When the CPU or graphic card chip is overheating, the laptop will probably freeze up or shut down, and even worse the CPU and motherboard may burn resulting in a pretty much useless laptop.

Most overheating problems are caused by accumulated dust piling up on the cooling fan and heat sink. This stops the air from flowing and prevents the heat dissipation from cooling the CPU or display card chip. When dust accumulates with time, the fan's ability to remove the heat diminishes drastically. Early overheating detection would be noticed if you run into these situations when you are using the laptop for a period of 4 to 5 hours. It can freeze the software or automatically shut down the laptop. If you don't pay attention to this, the laptop life expectancy is reduced, and the accessories around the CPU would become quite hot. At that moment, the laptop working temperature is reaching a critical point and you can damage it or several situations such as a blue or black screen of death may occur.

If you want more detailed information, such as how to detect the laptop overheating problem, please check the post I wrote on: How to detect the overheating problem?

4.   How to solve fan speed and noise problems?

Low fan speed may cause an overheating problem, and continual rotation at high speed can cause a loud noise, which can affect your work. So how to solve the inconsistency between fan speed and noise? I recommend that you use a CPU temperature control software with which you can easily solve this issue

SpeedFan Software

SpeedFan is an old computer cooling software tool with small and powerful functions. It can control the rise in temperature of the CPU effectively; it can also monitor the CPU usage rate and power consumption. It can be applied to all CPU products, and is an excellent optimization tool that can protect your CPU.

SpeedFan monitors temperatures from several sources. By configuring SpeedFan correctly, you could change its system temperature and fan speed. Try choosing minimum and maximum rotation speed parameters manually, (use human checkbox of all variables), to ensure the fan noise you want by choosing from a dropdown menu. By choosing the right configuration, you can reduce the noise by 90%. With experience and practice you will eventually get it exactly the way you want

Notice: when the temperature reaches the warning line, the application should set the fan speed as 100—the highest fan speed.

6.1.2 Common CPU fan failures for laptops

a) The fan stops rotating, resulting in a high CPU temperature rise and, frequent crashes. The automatic protection will reduce the frequency, slow down the laptop and finally will automatically shut it down if the temperature becomes too high.

b) A noisy sound when the fan is running and sometimes a grinding noise sounding like "Da, da".

c) The Fan is always running at maximum speed, and making noise. You can hardly feel any air coming out of the exhaust section where the fan is, and it is very hot indicating the CPU is not cooling.

d) The CPU temperature is very high and the CPU cooling fan is still running at a very low speed, not rotating smoothly, and getting worse. This is resulting in a user interface screen freeze and the laptop restarting.

e) When the laptop starts up, the fan speed is kind of slow and noisy and then becomes normal again.

f) Sometimes the fan rotation speed is fast and sometimes it's slow, it alternates continually. It might rotate a few seconds and stops or when the temperature rises it no longer runs smoothly

g) A blue warning screen frequently occurs on the laptop, and freezes the laptop immediately.

6.1.3 Common hard disk and CPU failures after overheating

a) Fail to start up, no display; the fan rotates for a few seconds and stops, and the hard disk light extinguishes.

b) The laptop is always very hot; sometimes it will automatically shutdown;

c) The laptop auto shuts down periodically after starting up (like the BIOS settings for power management). After shutting down automatically, it will not start immediately;

you need to wait a period of time to start it up again. However, after it starts, it still will auto shut down from time to time.

d) The system runs slow, and the laptop restarts in a very short period of time, resulting in the computer not working normally.

e) Blue screen or black screen occurs when the laptop boots up;

f) When using the laptop, it deadlocks frequently, the keyboard and mouse does not respond. You are only able to press the power button to shutdown and restart it;

g) Software test reports that the CPU working temperature is too high, and the CPU occupation/usage rate is too high;

h) The BIOS doesn't recognize the hard disk, (note: not the OS doesn't detect the hard disk)

i) The hard disk doesn't read/write or power suddenly goes off when it's reading/writing and then the laptop auto restarts;

j) The hard disk temperature is too high and the self-test fails, so Windows cannot start normally;

k) Bad sectors occur in the hard disk, leading to the hard disk not working properly;

l) The hard disk cannot be properly formatted, and not able to reinstall Windows;

m) A message appears "SMART" failure or a prompt to backup data occurs;

n) You are able to enter the Windows system, but errors occur repeatedly when applications run. Scanning of the disk fails and often slows down and stagnates or even freezes.

o) The system runs extremely slow, disk errors can be found with disk scanner application.

6.1.4 Solutions for a laptop overheating failure.

1. A bad connection between the CPU and motherboard

Failure symptom: after powering up the machine, it still doesn't boot, only the power light is on and the unit is non responsive. The fan stops rotating after a few turns, and still the same occurs after restarting the laptop.

Failure reason: The client often carries his laptop with him outside and uses it in a bad climate. The laptop was accidentally bumped or dropped not long ago and now each time the laptop temperature rises, it becomes unstable. This is where the issue may lie.

Solution: cut off the power and then shutdown the laptop, uninstall the CPU chip, and observe whether any pins are discoloured or bent. If yes, then gently straighten the pin with pliers. After that, clean the CPU pins and other slots with an alcohol dipped tampon. Blow it dry and then plug the CPU back into the socket. Check the cooling grease (soft-pad) and the heat sink. If there's nothing wrong; reinstall them in the laptop. Then hopefully the system will return to normal and the monitor displays again.

Conclusion: After the laptop hits high temperature or overheats, these problems often occur and you may not realise that the laptop has had an accidental impact. If a black screen happens to the monitor, then first check for a bad connection between the CPU and motherboard. This is an important step which will simplify the repair process.

2.   Heat sink (cooling pipe adapter) failure

Failure symptom: the laptop starts, the display is working, but you can't enter the operating system or auto shut off

Failure reason: because the system is able to start, it's doubtful there is loose hardware causing a bad connection. Open the main case, pull and plug the hardware inside again and then restart the machine. If the problem still exists continue troubleshooting. After taking a second look you find that the cooling grease (soft-pad) on the CPU is dry, so we can suspect that the CPU is overheating. Possibly there is something wrong with the thermal compound on the CPU heat sink. You find that one end close to the CPU is quite hot, while the other end away from CPU is cold. This is where the problem is.

Originally there's fibre and liquid thermal medium (mostly water) inside the cooling piece (tube), and the inside tube is vacuum sealed; one end is close to the CPU while the other end is away from CPU. Basically it is a reverse heat pump or refrigerator. This is the working principle: under vacuum state, the liquid thermal medium boiling point is very low, if one end of the tube is heated; the medium vaporizes, and brings the heat to the other end where it is cooled by the fan and then circulates back to the original place. It repeats this process over and over again, thus drawing the heat away. So the temperature difference between the refrigeration parts (tube's) closest to the CPU and the one furthest shouldn't be that much, and should work effectively for a long period. Over time or various reasons, the vacuum is reduced sufficiently to cause the liquid thermal medium to vaporize and lose effectiveness. That is when problems begin. Please take a look at Figure 6-1.

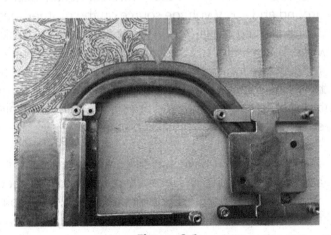

Figure 6-1

Solution: remove the heat sink (cooling pipe adapter), change it, add new compound, and then assemble the machine. Start the machine, and the failure is gone!

Conclusion: if the laptop has an independent graphic card, then similar problems like this can happen. Users cannot tell if the display card has overheated. The first step would be to check the refrigeration piece on the display card and the cooling grease (soft-pad), ensuring the display card chip cooling is in a good state, which helps to simplify the repair process.

3.   CPU fan doesn't work

Failure symptom: during operation, the system is unstable; restarting frequently and freezing.

Failure reason: the client never turns off the laptop, and the machine runs 24 hours a day allowing it to enter Suspend power saving mode. Now, the laptop has become unstable, restarting and freezing frequently. It seems the issue is CPU overheating. As a matter of fact, when the system enters Suspend power saving mode, the BIOS will automatically slow down the fan speed and even completely stop it. This may be beneficial to save power and extend the fan's life; however, today's technology has developed very fast, and the CPU frequencies are much higher, even when it's in Suspend mode. The heat generated can no longer be handled by a heat sink alone and when the fan stops, the CPU will become very hot. Many people may come across this situation: when the laptop switches from suspend mode to normal, Windows OS freezes and the blue screen occurs. These are the errors you will get when the CPU is overheated. Even worse, because of overheating, the CPU can burn out. Today's manufacturers have made many improvements and by updating the BIOS you can prevent this from happening.

Solution: check the CPU heat sink and fan to see that the CPU fan power cable is well connected. Blow on the fan to rotate it, and verify that it is rotating easily. If it isn't remove the old fan, replace it, and restart to check it. If the fan doesn't work, the problem is with the fan's control system. Proceed by pulling out the 4 wire connector between the fan and the motherboard. Find a ground and +12V voltage source on the motherboard. Solder the black cable (grounding end) and the red cable (+12V voltage end) to the points located, and do not use the other 2 wires. That eliminates the failure with the fan running at constant high speed. Of course, if you hear the loud noise when fan rotates at high speed, you can add a resistance between the +12V voltage and the fan red power cable to lower the fan speed and noise; the advantages of this repair method are simple and convenient. The downfall is there is only one speed and it cannot be adjusted by the Bios.

Conclusion: usually a laptop does not have such a complex problem, and users would not normally have to engage in soldering work. Normally you would just need to change the fan and refresh the cooling grease (soft-pad). You don't necessarily have to replace the fan, but just clear away the dust, and keep the intake clear and free for good ventilation to solve the issue. The entire repair process is quite easy.

4.   The blue screen failure occurs when laptop starts up.

Failure symptom: the system runs slowly and the laptop does not work normally. A blue screen occurs during operation, and occasionally, the keyboard and mouse are unresponsive.

All you can do is shut the laptop down with the power button. Touch the machine body with your hands, you will find it's really hot.

Failure reason: the client doesn't use the laptop very much and when he/she does, it is in a dusty environment like a construction site. The laptop ventilation is impaired and it overheats.

Generally, a laptop's primary thermal cooling method is cold-wind technology, to cool the graphic card, power and CPU thermal fan etc. The combination of fan + cooling pipe adapter + cooling plate is most often used.

It is well known to all that there is cooling vents at the bottom of laptop. The vent is either an intake or an exhaust and is critical to laptop cooling. Dust or obstructions can block the cooling system of a laptop and easily cause degradation or catastrophic failure of the laptop. Please take a look at Figure 6-2.

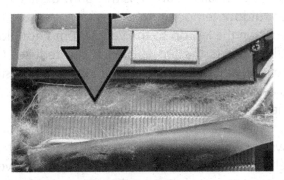

Figure 6-2

Solution: power down, open the laptop, and clean the internal parts of the laptop completely; especially the fan, thermal tube, thermal plate and thermal intake. To improve the thermal effect, wipe silicon gel between thermal plate and CPU, then reinstall it. Check the CPU's working temperature and RAM to make sure they are OK. Restart the computer again, and if the blue screen still occurs, the problem is still unsolved. You need to realize that there probably are 2 problems on this laptop. It must be an integrative failure, and not a simple problem. Something else is wrong. First of all, suspect the operating system software. Restart the laptop from a recovery disc and keep it running for an hour. There is no blue screen failure, no machine lock, and the keyboard and mouse both work. So it seems that the overheating problem has already been solved. The blue screen problem has quite likely been caused by the operation system. Back up the data on an external hard disk, format the internal disk, and then reinstall the operation system. Unexpectedly, if after the machine restarts, the blue screen still occur, the hard disc is defective, must be replaced, and then the problem is solved completely!

Conclusion: Often there are 2 problems existing on the laptop at the same time. It is not the failure that is scary, but that most users would not realize there are two problems. Usually they would deny the early correct repair method and as a result they lose the opportunity to solve the problem successfully.

In fact, taking good care of the laptop will avoid these problems. In case one does not, you have learned these methods to deal with it.

6.2 Eliminate laptop overheating problems and associated repair flow chart.

6.2.1 Repair shortcuts for symptoms such as system crashes due to overheating or auto shutdown

A) Tips to prevent a laptop overheating problem

1. While using a laptop if you find the system freezes or auto shutdown pay attention to it.
2. Avoid using the laptop for a long period of time in a high temperature situation, the high temperature area I'm talking about is the "surrounding area" around the laptop" not the indoor or outdoor temperature.
3. Make sure you position the laptop so the ventilation is not blocked or restricted. Any restriction of airflow affects the fan efficiency and reduces CPU cooling. You must ensure the laptop is on a hard flat surface, and not on a soft surface such as your lap, bed etc, which is a very common cause of thermal problems. A laptop should not sit on your lap as the name implies.
4. Check the "fan", because a fan is one of the most important components of the laptop cooling system. When the temperature rises to a certain level, the laptop will auto protect itself and auto shutdown. If the problem is severe, then it might burn the circuitry. Regular cleaning of dust on the laptop and from ventilation openings is highly recommended to help avoid overheating failure.
5. Accelerated thermal condition: if the temperature gets very high during use, save your files and shut down, Try working in a different environment. If the problem above persists, purchase a USB notebook ventilator to improve your ventilation.
6. Your BIOS can be too old or the software is corrupted causing a loss or impairment of temperature control. Update the BIOS to the latest version to prevent laptop overheating.

B) Simple hardware considerations to repair and solve a laptop auto shutdown problem.

1. The power adapter can be bad or of poor quality, with insufficient power or corrupted DC voltage. Replace the power adapter with a better quality and more powerful power adapter. If it resolves the issue then you know it was with the adapter.
2. Check the memory, as you are aware if the memory is bad, poor quality or of different brands, and frequency etc, the laptop will either auto shut down or not start at all. You should test the memory with Memtest86+ and make the necessary adjustment.
3. Dust is also another factor causing auto shutdown problems. Dust between the CPU radiator and the CPU, or too much dust on the radiator after the CPU fan has been working and not cleaned for a long period of time; are common causes of problems.

If there is too much accumulated heat, the computer will auto restart. Remove the dust regularly.

4. Check the CPU fan rotation and the CPU temperature. When overheating is caused by an aging fan with bad rotation or low speed, overheating will occur. If cleaning doesn't help, replace the CPU fan.

5. A hard knock on the laptop could cause the laptop heat sink or the radiator fastening clip to come loose and totally disable the CPU or video chip cooling. This would initiate an auto protection restart during the working process. You need to refasten the clip which will solve your problem if no damage was done.

6. Check whether the cooling Liquid thermal conductivity inside the heat pipe cooling system is dry or not, if it is dry it will cause overheating. In that case, install a new heat pipe cooling system and while doing this check the silicone compound on the bottom part of CPU heat sink, if it's also dry, clean up the silicon compound on the CPU and the CPU heat sink, and recoat with a fresh application of silicon compound.

7. Hard disk overheating or a bad track may also cause auto shutdown. Here's a simple method to help you quickly judge whether the auto shutdown is caused by hardware (hard disk) or software. You take the original hard disk out of the laptop, and replace it with a new one. After that, format the disk and re-install the Windows system. If the auto shutdown failure disappears, then it means the problem is with software. But if the problem still exists, then basically it would be the hardware problem.

C) Simple methods to repair and eliminate laptop auto shutdown problems (Software)

Virus issues:

The shock wave virus and some Trojans could cause the problem, Use the latest antivirus software to scan and kill them. Generally, it they are present it will find them. When you surf on the Internet, your computer might be invaded maliciously by someone, and some Trojans might be planted in your laptop. In this case, someone remotely could control everything on your computer from the remote place. This may explain why your system restarts. Some Trojans are quite difficult to erase, you are best to re-install the operating system altogether.

System files issues:

For different reasons, when a system file is lost or corrupted, and the necessary files needed to run the system no longer exists, a problem is created. It can cause a failure during startup/ boot, or after successful booting a system restart. Reinstall the operation system.

Application software issues:

If an auto shutdown happens when the computer is running an application, then the problem might be caused by the application. Generally, uninstalling the application software should resolve the issue. For such a situation, we could also open the "Enable" option and check if there is an executable file that you are not familiar with, or other timed working application.

Shield it and then restart the machine and verify. You can also directly enter "msconfig" command from "start", "Run" to choose start-up options.

Large game software issues:

It's also possible that playing a large game application may cause a CPU overheating problem. If the CPU fan speed does not increase soon enough, the laptop would auto shut down. If it is the game software which often causes the auto shutdown failure, then please uninstall and reinstall it.

BIOS auto wake-up functions

You might enable the auto wake-up functions: network wake-up, USB wake-up, remote wake-up and disk wake-up etc. The computer would restart when auto wake-up happens, generally, in BIOS, you could enable or disable this function.

6.2.2   55% of overheating problems are caused by the fan or CPU radiator

1.   Why does the fan and heatsink overheating failures hold the largest failure percentage most of the time? It is because they are the main devices keeping the notebook cool, and these with time, get dirty, are covered with dust or age, and rotate slower or stop functioning. Laptop designers incorporated fan control in the BIOS in order to save power and reduce noise while still adequately cooling the unit. The fan starts running at a specific CPU temperature and the speed varies according to ongoing temperature fluctuations. If dust enters the shaft slip ring assembly of the fan, then the speed will be slowed down from what is required, even worse, the CPU high temperature can distort the structure of the fan, completely destroying the thermal function of the fan and finally catastrophic failure of the laptop.

2.   Fan control hardware failure or old BIOS (with bugs) can be a cause. Generally, a maintenance guy will change the fan on the laptop, thinking that the fan doesn't work. Then he realizes that the problem is on the motherboard and is caused by a fan controller failure or BIOS bug. Generally there's no obvious rule for system freezing symptoms, mostly it happens when the CPU activity is quite high. In order to troubleshoot, you should first check the CPU fan power cable integrity. Is it connected properly and not damaged in any way? Blow with your mouth to move the fan, if it rotates easily and coasts to a stop, then there's likely no problem with the fan. Next power on and start the computer, check if the CPU fan is working normally. If the fan doesn't rotate, then remove it, check it, and finally update the BIOS to solve the problem. If the problem isn't solved in this way, then you can conclude that the fan control hardware has failed. Please refer to the method of example 3 in <<6.1.3 Solutions for common failures after laptop overheats>>.

3.   Thermal grease problem between the heat pipe cooling system and the chipset, which causes CPU overheating auto protection to activate.

The Computer would suddenly turn off or freeze. One of the reasons is that the thermal grease between the heatsink and the chipset has dried up, and the CPU temperature is far too high and activates the auto self-protection. Here's the procedure that will fix the problem:

Depending on who you talk too there is a definite debate on what is the ideal internal temperature of your laptop. My conclusion is that you should check whether the thermal grease is dry or not and if so, replace it with a high quality thermal grease. Make certain that the heat pipe cooling system is installed correctly, and then you can ensure your laptop CPU will be operating within the specified temperature range.

4. Another reason causing CPU overheating and auto self-protection is a bad heat pipe cooling system

The heat pipe cooling system is one of the accessories with a long life expectancy in a laptop. Eventually there's always an end to it like all working parts so check the cooling liquid inside the heat pipe cooling system, it's quite important. If the cooling liquid dries or abates, the laptop will overheat. How do we make a judgment whether the heat pipe cooling system is good? Actually, the process is very simple: originally the heat pipe cooling system is loaded with liquid thermal conductive medium; the boiling point in vacuum state is quite low. If one sector of the pipe is heated, then the medium would vaporize and bring the heat to the other end, and then be cooled by the fan and reflow to the original place. Normally, you can touch the two ends of the heat pipe cooling system with your hands, and you cannot feel a difference in temperature. When you find that the end close to CPU is quite hot, while the one away from CPU is quite cool, it indicates that the liquid thermal conductivity of the medium inside the heat pipe cooling system has already vaporized or abated. Then it is time to change to a new heat pipe cooling system.

5. As much as 55% of overheating problems come from either the fan or CPU heatsink. In other words, with the procedures above, your success rate to repair a laptop overheating problem have already reached above 50%.

6.2.3 25% overheating problems coming from video module and GPU on motherboard

Some laptop overheating problems are caused by the display card module (or GPU) issues on the motherboard, The HP Pavilion dv2000/dv6000/dv9000, have approximately 85% of the above issues.

1. Display card thermal silica grease is dry or degraded.

Causes:

a. One reason for this kind of failure is that the display card thermal grease is of bad quality and there's too much dust on the surface. When the display card chip works for an extended period of time, it can overheat. If you allow the thermal paste to work at a high temperature for a long time, it will age with time and lose its thermal function. You can delay the problem temporarily by refreshing the BIOS and changing the fan functions. But as stated above it is temporary and not a solution

b.   If the gibbous block (uneven surface) on the heat-sink barely touches the graphic card, the distortion of the thermal silica grease can cause a bad thermal connection between the heat sink and the display card chip. Then we know there's something wrong with the thermal function that causes the GPU temperature to heat up. This can create a blurred screen, black screen or frequent system crashes.

2.   GPU high temperature category or BGA sealing-off

a.   If a display card chip works too long and overheats, then the motherboard expands and distorts, after a while the connection is no longer happening and even the soldering points can desoldering and the laptop shuts down. You then get a black screen or the laptop restarts.

Generally, we can use heat to solve the sealing-off problem: the principle is that we heat different parts of the motherboard with a heat gun to create a manual oven, which might help to repair the sealed, off point. This method is occasionally successful.

b.   At the beginning when engineers designed the GPU thermal system, it used the general thermal technical standard; Even the original thermal design on the dv6000/dv9000 machines should accord with the most common thermal resistance design and be able to pass through the test successfully.

c.   As for the problem regarding the attached heat-sink and thermal silica grease that are of bad quality, it will unfortunately burn the GPU chip. Generally you can change the GPU to solve that problem. The BGA sealing (a manufacturing technique requiring special equipment) adopts BGA circumfluence sealing technology, which is of two types: infrared heating stove and sirocco convection heating stove. However, common computer stores cannot take on this repair task, so your only option is to change the independent display card or the motherboard.

6.2.4   12% of overheating problems coming from hard disk

A less common cause of laptop overheating issues comes from the hard disk, such as:

System crashes caused by disk chip overheating

During the process of using a computer, the system suddenly dies or a blue screen occurs or there's no response when pressing keys. The system prompts you that it has failed when the blue screen appears. After restarting the computer, the monitor doesn't display or there's just a flashing cursor and sometimes it just restarts. If the issue isn't bad, shut it off and wait a few minutes, then it might recover again. Touch the shell of the hard disk with your hand

and you will find the temperature is quite high. For such failure symptoms, we can conclude that it is due to the disk circuitry. Please take a look at Figure 6-3.

Figure 6-3

It is normal that the hard disk gets warm because of the speed of which the internal parts rotate, and since there is no direct cooling on it, the temperature rises. As it gets worse the system starts crashing and when the system restarts, the BIOS cannot recognize the disk any more. Shut off the power and wait for several hours. If it still can't be recognized by the BIOS; take the disk out and smell it closely. If it smells like burnt plastic that is different from a heat smell, you can conclude that the disk is burnt due to high temperature.

You can take some effective cooling measures to avoid this issue by buying a USB cooling pad and placing it underneath the laptop. You can also clean the thermal intake and keep ventilation clear inside the laptop.

6.2.5   Repair emphasis for laptop overheating failures

Laptop heat primarily comes from the CPU, the display card chip, the hard disk, the motherboard chip group, and also the north bridge, south bridge, power circuit with the integrated display card chip. Among these devices, the CPU is the biggest heat source; about 1/3 of the heat comes from it. Overheating issues with these components often is fatal. Occasionally the display card and the south bridge are soldered badly and therefore lead to eventual serious damage to them.

Some motherboards with the AMD CPU platform overheat frequently and cause the CPU seal of the base to loosen which cannot be fixed. There are some repairs that can be fixed to deal with overheating:

1.   The fan is one of the most important components affecting the CPU radiating and cooling. As the CPU heats, it directly influences the bottom silicon compound on the CPU thermal conductivity copper, so its important to pay attention to these points:

   a.   If the bottom thermal silicon glue is dried, reapply it

    b.   Dust is also one of the factors causing overheating. When the fan works for an extended period of time, dust can accumulate which may impede radiating. Cleaning it is very effective

    c.   When fan ages, it stops rotating or the speed is lowered causing overheating. Use third party software to keep track of the fan speed and when necessary replace the fan.

2.   Silicone grease thermal compound is the traditional method of conducting heat through the surfaces of the CPU and GPU to the heat sinks. It first transfers the heat the CPU and GPU generates to the thermal aluminum block, which then disperses the heat from the thermal aluminum block by blowing it away with the fan.

    a.   Notice if the heat sink fins are coated with dust and dirt, clear it and it will improve the cooling;

    b.   Notice whether the laptop heat sink is loose, or the fastening clip is off. Refasten it and it will solve your problem.

    c.   When installing the keyboard the bottom of the keyboard will touch the motherboard and it will conduct the heat produced by the CPU.

    d.   The keyboard structure has 4 holes underneath and the heat can be expelled through the buttons. When hot air is expelled from these button holes, cold air will flow into it. Pay attention to these keyboard holes by making sure they are not obstructed. Sometimes food or liquid is spilled on the keyboard so ensure it is always cleared up in time.

3.   Apart from the heat sink and the thermal fan, the laptop's cooling should also include the thermal pipe.

Here's the working principle: one end of the radiating pipe is close to the CPU, while the other end is away from it but closer to the fan; for the part near the CPU, the liquid heats up and then evaporates and migrates to the other end of the thermal pipe where the liquid is cooled and reflowed back to the CPU where it evaporates again.

You also need to check if the cooling oil inside the thermal pipe is dried. If it is, it will cause overheating, and you need to change the thermal pipe;

6.2.6 Failure analysis and repair flowchart due to high temperature or overheating causing auto shutdown

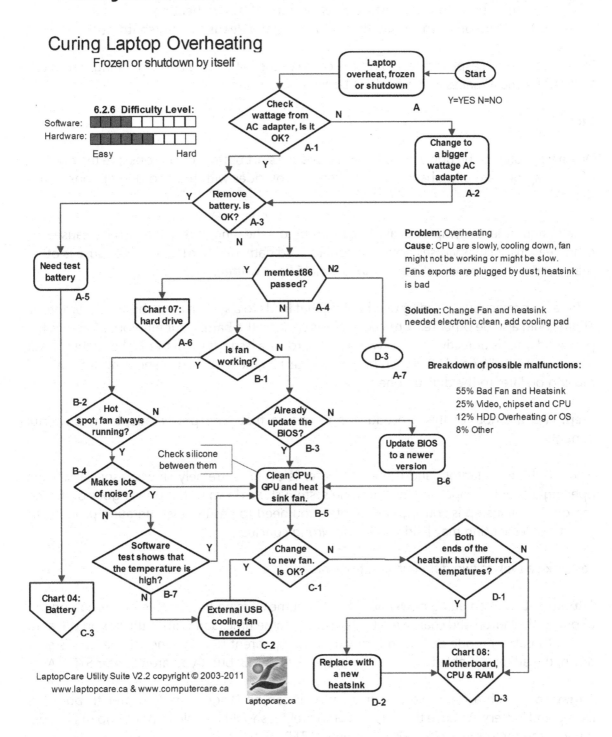

Curing Laptop Overheating
Frozen or shutdown by itself

6.2.6 **Difficulty Level:**

Software:
Hardware:

Easy   Hard

Start

Laptop overheat, frozen or shutdown

Y=YES N=NO

A

Check wattage from AC adapter, Is it OK? **A-1**

Change to a bigger wattage AC adapter **A-2**

Remove battery. is OK? **A-3**

Need test battery **A-5**

memtest86 passed? **A-4**

Chart 07: hard drive **A-6**

Is fan working? **B-1**

D-3 **A-7**

Hot spot, fan always running? **B-2**

Already update the BIOS? **B-3**

Update BIOS to a newer version **B-6**

Check silicone between them

Clean CPU, GPU and heat sink fan. **B-5**

Makes lots of noise? **B-4**

Software test shows that the temperature is high? **B-7**

Change to new fan. Is OK? **C-1**

Both ends of the heatsink have different tempatures? **D-1**

Chart 04: Battery **C-3**

External USB cooling fan needed **C-2**

Replace with a new heatsink **D-2**

Chart 08: Motherboard, CPU & RAM **D-3**

Problem: Overheating
Cause: CPU are slowly, cooling down, fan might not be working or might be slow. Fans exports are plugged by dust, heatsink is bad

Solution: Change Fan and heatsink needed electronic clean, add cooling pad

Breakdown of possible malfunctions:

55% Bad Fan and Heatsink
25% Video, chipset and CPU
12% HDD Overheating or OS
8% Other

This tutorial will help you solve the problem:

1. System shutdown and interface freezing caused by overheating
2. CPU auto protection caused by overheating, that leads to auto shutdown

In this article, I will explain how to find the cause of the failure due to overheating, which can be used for most makes and models of laptops.

Step: 1

When you connect the power adapter and press the start button, please observe the reaction of your laptop carefully, observe which scenario coincides with the two descriptions in this tutorial:

-The system freezes symptom can be caused by overheating, but it can also be caused by other reasons such as viruses, software conflict, and damaged hard disk. If the cause is other than overheating you can check the 07 tutorial I have written.

-CPU auto protection caused by overheating that leads to a system auto shutdown symptom. There could also be other reasons causing this such as: the battery running out of power, the power adapter is defective or a software and hardware issue. If the latter is the problem visit my Tutorial 03,04,07 and 08 Remember always start by the easy troubleshooting Tutorial and moving on later to the difficult ones

Step: A-1 the goal of this procedure is to ensure that your power adapter is powerful enough

After starting the laptop, and if the computer is acting extremely slowly, especially when opening a couple of applications, then the system shuts down or the power goes off for no reason. The first step is your power adapter: you need to ensure it is operating properly as your troubleshooting may lead you to the wrong conclusion.

Let's take a look at two different situations here:

Situation 1: with an aging power adapter sometimes it is no longer able or strong enough to power the laptop and charge the battery at the same time. Sometimes the laptop will auto switch to battery mode or just shut down for no apparent reason. Once the laptop is shut down, the adapter is able to charge the battery enter A-3; but if you aren't enter STEP: A-2;

Situation 2: with a really old power adapter, it can no longer supply power to both the laptop and battery. Remove the battery completely. It should be able to power up the laptop. If this is the case enter STEP: A-3; if not enter STEP: A-2;

Step: A-2 the purpose of this next exercise is to test the suspected laptop with a power adapter that is powerful enough and in good condition

Generally to test the reliability of the power adapter, you can also carry out these next few steps:

1. **Appearance:** check the appearance, there should be no physical damage, oxidation on the connector pin, corruption, dirt, oil, and paint etc

2. **Performance:** Test the loaded output voltages, current; ripple voltage, and performance within the specified range. When the laptop is running at full load, the required source voltage is a little higher. When laptop goes into sleep mode, the power load is lower, and the adapter must have the regulating ability to control the voltage. You may think that using a 65W adapter as opposed to 75W may not make a difference because it has powered it up, but if you take into consideration that you have a DVD-Rom, a CPU, a fan rotating at full speed, and a battery being charged, you will find the laptop will auto shut down in no time or freeze. Change to a new higher wattage adapter and measure the amperage of it which should be higher than the original unit. For instance, the original adapter is rated 18.5V, and you measure 19V, it is acceptable. If the original adapter is rated 3.5A, and you measure 4.7A it is also acceptable.

Step: A-3 the goal of this section is to ensure the connection between the battery and the laptop motherboard is good.

Some cases indicate that the connection between the battery and the laptop motherboard is not good. The system crashes, the interface freezes or the system auto shuts down. When these failures happen, I would always check the connection of the battery first, I would then verify the connector between the battery and the laptop motherboard. Remove the battery, and only using the external power supply to start the laptop; check whether the failure disappears. If the situation is unchanged, then continue to STEP: A-4; if the laptop works normally with no errors, then continue to STEP: A-5;

Step: A-4 the goal of this procedure is to determine the failure mode and the properties of the laptop

Let's first look at these 4 situations:

Situation 1: put a bootable DOS Memtest86 software disc into your CD-ROM/DVD-ROM and start by checking the RAM cards. If the laptop auto restarts, auto shuts down, freezes or has any other failures during the boot process, it indicates the problem is with the hardware or may be with the connection state between accessories, like the RAM, motherboard, and CPU/GPU temperature; please enter STEP: B-1;

Situation 2: the memory is tested by DOS Memtest86 software, (generally speaking, it takes 20 to 60 minutes), and the laptop is in normal status, but as time passes it auto restarts, auto shutdowns, system freezes or it feels really hot when you touch the bottom of the laptop. If this is the situation, then your problem might be with both software and hardware. Follow the repair principle "First the hardware and then software", enter STEP: B-1, after finishing the repair process, if the failure still exists, then please enter STEP: A-6; Please take a look Figure 6-4.

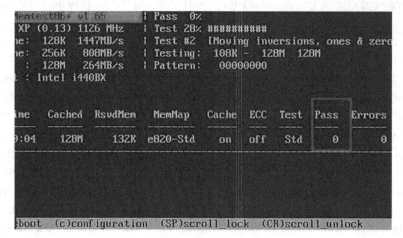

Figure 6-4

Situation 3: the RAM card is tested by DOS Memtest86 software, no matter how much time is added to the test, the laptop always remains in normal status, and it doesn't feel hot on the bottom of the laptop, CPU, and the exhaust port. If this is the situation, then your problem might be connected with software, or the hard disk, please enter STEP: A-6;

Situation 4: the RAM card didn't pass the test by DOS Memtest86 software, error prompt occurs, or blue screen, system freezes symptoms occur, in all, the failure symptoms may happen singularly, or 2 or 3 failure Symptoms appearing together. If this is the case, then your problem may be with software and hardware, please follow the repair principle "First hardware and then software", enter STEP: A-7.

After finishing the repair process and the failure still occurs, then enter STEP: A-6;

Step: A-5 the goal of this procedure is to ensure that your battery doesn't have an issue

There are cases when the connection between the battery and the motherboard isn't good. Check whether it feels too loose when installing the battery, whether the size is right, whether the fit is too tight and can't be inserted properly into position or has to be pried out? Some batteries may seem to be OK when in fact they are completely incompatible and will cause failure when using them.

If you cannot conclude that the battery is OK, then you can put the suspected battery in another laptop that is the same brand and same model and test it. If it charges normally, then the battery is OK, otherwise, it's bad. This step requires changing to a new battery in order to continue validating your laptop, for more detail and a complete solution, please enter STEP: C-4.

Step: A-6

Check the repair analysis tutorial article (Chapter 07) regarding the laptop is not loading Windows or there is repeat restarting and blue screen failure.

Step: A-7

Check the repair analysis tutorial article (08) regarding laptop black screen or interface freezing failure.

Step: B-1 the goal of this exercise is to verify whether the laptop fan works normally.

One of the important causes for high temperature and overheating failure is a fan problem, such as an aging fan or not rotating or the speed of rotation is not fast enough. After the laptop has been working for a period of time, some factors like the static attraction of dust that accumulates on the surface of the fan and sticks to it has developed. The dust then migrates into the bearings of the fan which eventually slows it down. If the CPU temperature continues to rise, then the laptop overheating symptom occurs, and even the fan shape will change slightly and lose some of its ability to move the air.

How to make sure the fan is working normally? Here are 3 distinctive methods:

1) Install third party software, test the rotation speed of the CPU fan; and also check the CPU temperature and core temperature. This will tell you whether the fan is performing its cooling function properly or not.
2) Listen to whether the fan is working or not. At first it may not be running but eventually you should hear it kicking in and probably increasing in speed too.
3) Verify that heat is being expelled from the exhaust port. When the laptop fan is not working, there should be no hot air coming out from the exhaust port and when fan rotates slowly, there will not be much heat being exhausted. When the laptop is getting hot, the fan will rotate at high speed and you should feel a lot of heat exhausting from the port.

Next are some common laptop CPU fan failure symptoms:

a. The CPU temperature is already very high, but the fan isn't running and the computer is processing slowly. At times it even shuts down. If this is your situation, please enter STEP: B-3; if it is not, then please enter STEP: B-2;
b. The fan suddenly makes a loud noise when turning on. If this is the situation, then enter STEP: B-4;
c. The fan always runs at a high speed and is noisy. When you feel the fan exhaust with your hand, you notice very little heat is dissipated and it is very hot, which means so is the CPU, then enter STEP: B-5;
d. The CPU temperature is very high, but the laptop CPU cooling fan still runs very slow and not very smooth. At worst system freezes and the laptop auto restarts. If this is the situation, enter STEP: B-3;

e. The fan speed isn't slow at the beginning but the sound is very loud and after a period of time, it returns to normal. If this is the situation, enter STEP: B-4;

f. The fan is either fast at times or slow at other times. It sometimes even rotates a few times and then stops even at full speed; the rotation isn't as smooth as it should be. If this is the situation, enter STEP: B-5;

Step: B-2 the goal of this exercise is to ensure that the fan works at start-up.

To avoid noise and to save power, designers didn't plan for the fan to rotate all the time, but when CPU reaches a certain temperature, then the fan will start. This increases the difficulty in determining whether the fan works or not. Designers also considered this in advance, so at start-up, the fan will rotate for a few seconds (up to ten), so that it would help users or technicians check whether the CPU system fan works all right. If the fan doesn't rotate at start up, then you should first check whether the CPU fan power cable is well connected. Move the fan by blowing with your mouth, if it rotates smoothly, then the fan doesn't have a big problem. If this is the situation, enter STEP: B-3. If the fan only works for a few seconds and up to ten seconds, then please enter STEP: B-4;

Over a period of time dust builds up on the laptop fan, which may cause difficulty for the fan to rotate freely. For this kind of problem, clean it up. If this is the situation enter STEP: B-5;

Step: B-3 the goal of this setup is to ensure the current BIOS version of your laptop

The biggest advantage of a BIOS update is that you can get many new functions without paying. For instance, after updating the HP Pavilion dv2000/dv6000/dv9000 laptops, the algorithm system controlling the fan is updated and it can now measure the temperature precisely, prolonging the life of the fan to its maximum.

If you decide to update the BIOS of the motherboard, you first have to confirm the current BIOS version of the laptop, so follow the next steps:

1. Press the power button to start the laptop.
2. When HP or Compaq logo appears, press F10 to enter BIOS Setup.
3. When the main menu appears, check the BIOS version. You need the information to ensure whether there's an update available.
4. Exit BIOS setup, press F10 and choose Yes, then press Enter.

Check your laptop BIOS version, whether it's listed as one of the latest or earlier ones. If the BIOS version listed is earlier than the versions listed on HP website, this means there's a necessity to update it. Other brands of laptops also have a similar function, but use different keys. This step is to rectify and improve the fan control system by updating the BIOS.

If your laptop BIOS version is the latest or you don't plan to update it, then enter Step: B-5;

If you plan to update the BIOS, then enter Step: B-6

Here the BIOS update software packet is designed and aimed for motherboard overheating, and these BIOS files include the enhancement of the anti-overheating functions for the motherboard, and protection measures are added for the CPU and other hardware overheating problems.

Step: B-4 The goal of this setup is to ensure whether the noisy laptop fan is failing.

Laptop fans are different from desktop computers. Generally, a desktop computer fans rotates at a high speed right from start up; however, laptop fans are an exception, meaning that only when the temperature reaches the scheduled BIOS limitation will it start running, also, as the temperature of CPU rises, the fan speed will also accelerate, and as the temperature of CPU drops, the fan speed will slow down until the temperature drops below the critical point, and then will stop.

Computer noises are mainly caused by the fan; usually there are three types of fan noises; rotation, shaking, and collision noise.

1. **Rotation noise** is usually caused by bearing wear or lack of lubrication. The solution is to drop some oil on the fan bearing. It's not the best solution it's really a temporary measure.
2. **Shaking noise** is usually caused because fan blades are not balanced, the blades on axis are loose and the bearing gap is too big. The main reason for the noise is because the blades of the fan are out of position. The barycentre (centre of mass) of the new fan blades is on the axis, which is more stable therefore the noise is less. Dust and dirt attaching to the blades causes the weight of each blade to differ and causes them to be "out of balance". As the fan ages the bearings degrade gradually, loosening symptoms appear, and the blades start vibrating. The simplest solution for such a failure is to clean the dust and dirt on the fan, clean each blade and the center position of the rotating axis with a clean cotton swab and alcohol or use one of the air sprays available at most pc stores. If this fails replace the fan itself.
3. **Collision noise** is usually caused by dust entering the fan bearing, which slows down the fan rotation, and may not function even when CPU temperature is high. At this moment, we will find the distorted blades are hitting the frame of the fan continually during the running process and making a loud noise. Such kinds of failures are difficult to repair. You need to remove the blades, hang the leaves with a string by passing it through the little hole in the middle of the blades, and then heat and repair with a heat gun. After repairing, if the leaves are static at plane position, it means the repair was successful. Then add oil to the fan bearing, which has a cushion impact for vibration. Of course, it would be better if you can buy a new fan and change it, because a heated repaired fan might not work for long.

If the laptop fan is free of noise, then continue to STEP: B-7. If it's still noisy go to STEP: B-5;

Step: B-5 the goal of this exercise is to clean the laptop thermal system

No doubt, high temperature and overheating occupy a large portion of issues caused by thermal system problems. This step is meant to clean up the thermal system, especially cleaning the fan and, intake, port.

Let's take a look at 4 different situations:

Situation 1: The fan is the most important part in controlling the temperature, because it does age, it can stop rotating or the rotating speed isn't as fast as it should be. This will cause overheating, so keeping it clean by removing any dust, which is very important. Please take a look at Figure 6-5.

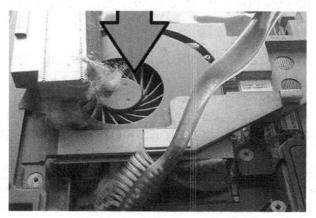

Figure 6-5

1. Prepare necessary tools, such as small screwdriver, forceps and so on;
2. Remove the adapter and battery, and then ground the static;
3. Find the position of the fan installed on the bottom part of the laptop, generally it's around the exhaust port. You will see a board covering, now remove the board, and you'll be able to see the CPU heat sink module. Usually, the HP laptop fan is combined together with the thermal sink.
4. Tweak the screw holding the heat sink. Use a magnetic screw driver where possible.
5. Take the heat sink off of the CPU assembly carefully and pull the fan cable connector from the motherboard.
6. After removing the heat sink, you may find that there's floccules (dust and lint) blocking or heavy dust stuck in the thermal hole, you need to clean that up and then check the blades of the fan carefully, probably there's a heavy layer of dust covering the surface and needs to be cleaned.
7. Tweak the screw fixing the fan and remove both the fan and heat sink, then wipe the blades with cotton and alcohol. Once dried, put a drop of machine oil on the fan bearing part.
8. Brush the thermal assembly with a toothbrush dipped in alcohol, and then blow dust out with compressed air.
9. Add thermal compound to the CPU
10. Assemble all parts back according to the opposite sequence, and then it's done!

If the failure situation hasn't changed at all then enter STEP: C-1;

Situation 2: The fan controller fails and after installing a new fan in the laptop, the fan still doesn't work, so the problem must be on the motherboard. You should first check whether the CPU fan power cable is well connected, and then power on the laptop. The moment it starts up, you may see that the fan rotates a few seconds normally, if the fan doesn't rotate, then you should remove the fan and check it. If the problem is still not solved, then please refer to the method in example 3 from the article <<6.1.4 Common failure treatment when laptop is overheated>>

Situation 3: the thermal silicon grease between the thermal tube and the chip is aging, which sometimes may cause the laptop to turn off or shut down suddenly. One of the reasons is that the thermal function of the silicon grease between the heat sink and chip is going bad, and the CPU/GPU temperature is too high; therefore the laptop will start self-protecting. If the chip works in an overheated environment for a long time, the thermal silicon grease will age, distort and dry quickly, thus causing a bad connection with the heatsink and finally restricting heat conduction through it. Replace the thermal silicon grease on the bottom with one of high quality in order to keep the laptop at low temperature. If this step doesn't change the failure situation, then enter STEP: C-1;

Situation 4: the thermal assembly of the laptop is loose, because it was either bumped or a collision occurred. The fastening clip of the heat sink has fallen, which will cause the CPU/GPU chip to not radiate heat thus, causing auto restarts or system shutdowns due to overheating. Reattach the clip to solve the bad radiating failure caused by the loose hardware. If this step doesn't fix the failure situation, then enter STEP: C-1;

Step: B-6 the goal of this procedure is to upgrade and update the laptop BIOS

1. During this operation, I suggest using the AC power adapter and a cable to connect to the internet modem. If in battery mode, the system may shut down during the process and the download and installation will fail.
2. As a BIOS update does have a certain danger, I never suggest updating your laptop BIOS in a hurry, except if you are familiar with BIOS and have enough ability and experience.

If you intend to update the BIOS, please refer to method in <<2.2.3 the steps to upgrade BIOS>>. If you have already updated BIOS or don't plan to update it, then enter Step: B-5;

Step: B-7 The goal of this exercise is to install a third party software to inspect the CPU, disk temperature and fan speed.

Here's the working principle to adjust the CPU fan rotation speed:

First of all, use the "Temperature inspection system" on the motherboard to inspect the CPU temperature when it gets to a certain level. The CPU fan will start rotating and should increase in speed as the temperature rises, but if it doesn't, this is why downloading software such as Speedfan is useful as it has the function to adjust the fan rotation speed (including manual adjustment and auto adjustment), and it also enables us to know the overall trend of the CPU temperature, disk temperature and fan speed directly by the continual changing curve. The user could set the first critical temperature manually and it will adjust CPU temperature accordingly. HP laptop fans have two kinds: 3-pin and 4-pin, these two kinds of fans have a different way of adjusting and controlling temperature. Basically the working principles are the same.

If the test result indicates that the temperature of the laptop motherboard chip stays basically stable around 50 to 60 degrees, then please continue STEP: C-2; but if the temperature of the motherboard chip reaches around 70 to 80 degrees, continue STEP: B-5;

Next is a group of technical parameters for laptop temperature and fan rotation. As for concrete parameters, according to different machines, there may be a slight change.

When connected with an external power supply:

1. **The FAN START Temp;** when the heat sensor displays that the temperature reaches 34 to 40 degrees, then the BIOS will start the fan to rotate at low speed.
2. **The FAN START PWM VALUE;** the fan starts pulse-width modulation to the initial value of the timing method, when heat sensor shows the temperature around 40°C to 60°C degrees. The fan will work under the timing status according to the comparative proportion of the temperature range, until it reaches back to the normal operating mode which is the function of the fan to keep the temperature at a respectable level of operation.
3. **FAN Limit Temp 69°C;** that is when the fan is working at its full speed in order to bring back the temperature to normal state.
4. When temperature rises to 70°**C** ~75°**C**, the fan will keep rotating at the highest speed and the BIOS would lower the CPU clock speed by 25%;
5. When the heat sensor displays that the temperature rises to 75~ 79°**C**, the BIOS would lower the CPU clock speed further;
6. **Shutdown Temperature;** the computer auto system protection will operate, when the heat sensor shows the temperature at 80°**C**, the laptop will auto shut down to protect the hardware from damage. Please take a look at Figure 6-6.

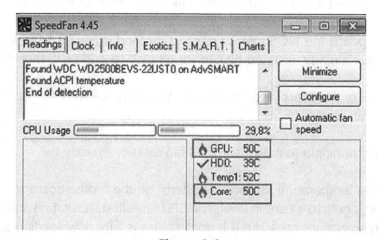

Figure 6-6

The main difference when using the battery as opposed to using the external power supply is the heat sensor shows the temperature reaches 70°C, the BIOS will lower the CPU clock speed by 25%; when the heat sensor shows the temperature reaches 75, the BIOS will lower the CPU clock speed by 50%. When the temperature rises to 75°C, the BIOS will lower the CPU clock speed by 75%; and when the temperature rises to 80°C degrees, the system will auto shut down.

Step: C-1 The target of this setup is to change the CPU fan

Detailed steps to changing a laptop fan:

Before replacing the fan, turn off the laptop, cut off external power supply and remove the main battery along with all extended batteries. Find your laptop model on the web, and download the manual. According to the manual instructions, disassemble the laptop by removing all screws from the bottom of the machine. Some are for the keyboard so ensure you gather all the screws together and classify them so you know exactly where they go when re-assembling. Overturn the laptop and first remove the keyboard. For the exact way of doing this refer to the article <<Failure repair for laptop touchpad, keyboard and USB ports>>

To disassemble the old fan, you need to remove a few other parts such as the metal plate under the keyboard which may require removing more screws until the fan is fully exposed and can be removed.

Some fans on many HP laptops are integrated with the heatsink and required them both to be replaced. For instance, HP DV9000/HP DV6000 laptops place the heat sink beside the fan; it extends to the upper part of the CPU/GPU, and another 4 to 6 screws need to be removed. Many beginners neglect this point, so it's important to unscrew them simultaneously in order to not damage the CPU. After removing the screws, pull out the fan power cable from the motherboard power jack, then the fan can be removed completely. Install the new one just as you removed the old one that reverse operation, then put screw it back in place and re-install the notebook parts as it was before.

Step: C-2 The goal of the procedure is to add an external USB fan

Although the laptop has an adequate internal thermal cooling system, in hot summer days, some machines may still end up burning out the motherboard and CPU because of the extreme ambient heat. It's important to add an external cooling base.

Now there are not many laptop thermal products on the market, generally, you can find: a laptop fan thermal base, laptop liquid thermal base and so on. A professional laptop thermal base is inexpensive, anywhere around 10 to 20 dollars. It is placed under the laptop and hooks up to the USB interface; it usually comes with 2 fans on the base. It will help to dissipate the heat from the bottom of the notebook and keep it a little cooler.

Professional laptop liquid thermal base products can be expensive, around 100 dollars because the special refrigerant inside can quickly absorb the heat from the bottom and dissipate the heat quickly in a short time. Please take a look at Figure 6-7.

Figure 6-7

If a laptop has some issues, it can cost you a bit of money but buying a USB powered fan may save you a few dollars.

STEP: C-3

Your problem is quite likely due to the laptop battery power supply, please first check the tutorial article about failure analysis and repair flow when the laptop battery doesn't charge. Please refer to the flowchart 04 (in chapter 04)

Step: D-1 the target of this exercise is to verify if the laptop thermal tube has an issue

The thermal tube is one of the accessories in a laptop which has a long life, but it can sometimes lose its' efficiency once the cooling liquid inside the thermal tube becomes dry or null. Generally, the cooling liquid at one end of the thermal tube absorbs the heat coming from the CPU /GPU and then vaporized at the other end cooled by the fan then flows back, making every place of the thermal tube cool. How to check the thermal tube? It's quite simple: when you find the end of thermal tube close to the CPU to be quite hot, while the other side away from CPU is cool, then it means the liquid thermal medium is done and it's time to change to a new thermal tube.

If the laptop thermal tube has no temperature difference, then go to STEP: D-3; if the temperature difference of the ends are quite different, then go to STEP: D-2'

Step: D-2 the goal of this exercise is to change the heat sink

The steps to change a heat sink are quite similar to changing laptop fan, refer to the method of

<< Step: C-1 to add an external USB fan >> in this chapter.

However, pay attention: many HP laptop fans are integrated with the heat sink, so you'd have to also change the fan. For instance: HP DV9000/HP DV6000 and most HP products have different fans and heat sinks, because of different CPU's (such as Intel/AMD) and depending which country they're from.

There are cases where the thermal connection between the heat sink and the CPU has become impaired and resulted in damage to the CPU or the motherboard. It is important to check the integrity of the heat sink and make sure it is not loose. Ensure any replacement heatsink is exact because many beginners will make that mistake and find it to be completely incompatible.

Check the heat sink beside the fan carefully, one branch just extends to the upper part of the GPU, where there's one or two screws fixed on the motherboard, after fixing the screws tightly, many people will not have checked the thermal connection between the heat sink and the GPU. Don't do that. If you use the original heat sink, you will find the thermal copper piece, thermal silicon grease, and the GPU chip are connected tightly, with no gap; however, when you use an incompatible heat sink, you may find the copper piece of the heat sink, thermal silicon grease and GPU chip are not connected tightly enough. There might even be a gap which is very bad. If there is a gap or the contact area to the GPU chip is only 1/2 or 1/3 of the original full area, you have a major problem. Using such a heat sink for more then 1 to 2 weeks and sometimes less then 2 to 3 hours will burn the motherboard or GPU chip. You need to pay close attention to ensure that everything is exactly correct.

When buying a new heat sink, you must compare it to the original one repeatedly, especially the side with the copper protruding (the side connecting GPU/CPU). The copper protruding side must have three identical points to the original heat sink, namely, same position, same size and area, same height and the copper protruding side position is the same. The area can be a little bigger than the original one; the height could be a little higher than the original one but the opposite is not acceptable. If the copper protruding side is too small or too thin (the thickness is not enough), then the thermal silicon grease may have a bad connection with the display card chip, and it will create an increase in temperature that is too high for the GPU. You will notice immediately that you have a blurry screen, a black screen or even an auto shutdown, and at worst burn your GPU or motherboard.

After finishing the repair process in this step, and if there's still no change to the failure, enter STEP: D-3;

Step: D-3

Please check the failure analysis tutorial article (in chapter 08) regarding a laptop black screen or system freeze up.

As the description above, a summary for the tutorial, laptop overheating failure follows:

Cause: The CPU and thermal system performance may slow down, the fan might not work or the performance slows down. Thermal silicon grease is aging, the heat sink radiating abates, and too much dust on the fan and in the intake/exhaust ports, has affected heat dissipation.

Solution: change the fan or thermal system accessories, clean up the dust on the thermal system as for details, please read the tutorial. Thank you!

6.3 Twenty-two repair cases of laptop overheating failures

6.3.1 7 repair cases of system freezes or auto shutdown failure caused by HP laptop fan issue

086)   HP PAVILION DV2770TX auto shutdown failure

Failure symptom:

The laptop always auto shuts down even after being used for a short period of time and lately not long after it starts up. Laptop heats up fast especially around the keyboard and when you feel the fan intake with your hands, you find not a lot of air exhausts from the grills and then it shuts down. When you restart it, it shuts down again a few minutes later.

Solution:

This failure symptom belongs to the description of flow chart 06 that belongs to sequence:

Start->A-1->A-3->A-4->B-1->B-2->B-3->B-5

Repair summary:

Seen from the failure symptom and combined with the flow chart, put a pure bootable DOS Memtest86 software disc into the DVD-ROM/CD-ROM to start, test the memory stick. The laptop is in normal status, 35 minutes later, memory stick passes the test of the software, but not long after the laptop auto shuts down. Touch the bottom of the laptop, feeling it to be really hot; it seems the problem is with hardware; disassemble the laptop, remove the screws from the bottom of the machine gradually. Then remove the motherboard cover and you will see the fan exposed completely now, and you will notice a lot of dust piled up on the fan so follow the repair flowchart 06 of step B-2;

Now start the laptop power supply, and you notice it only runs for under 10 seconds which you remember the client saying he had just updated his BIOS. Obviously it has nothing to do with the old BIOS version, because of the dust piled up in the fan, it stopped it from rotating, which causes the CPU to overheat and reach the power-off protection point and system shuts down. Therefore, check the CPU fan, finding the motherboard does supply power to it normally. Remove the thermal parcel of the heat sink, finding there is a thick layer of fluff blocking it, which needs to be cleared up completely. Remove the screws that keep the fan in place, remove the fan along with the heat sink and wipe clean the leaves of the fan with cotton dipped in alcohol. Brush the thermal parcel with a toothbrush dipped in alcohol and then re-assembles the parts back together and the failure disappears.

Hint:

As fan stops rotating, then CPU overheats and reaches the temperature point to auto shut down, which is a quite common overheating failure. Therefore, it is quite important to judge whether fan is working or not. There is a simple way—listen to the sound, you can judge whether the fan is rotating or not. When laptop just starts up, I will press my ear close to the fan position at the bottom part of the laptop, if there a fan rotating sound would be heard, or you can feel that the air is steamed out from the exhaust hold at the bottom part of the machine, then it means the fan works.

087)   HP 510 laptop auto shutdown failure

Failure symptom:

Laptop auto turns off after an hour working, the salver is obviously heated, and CPU fan becomes noisy at high speed.

Solution:

This failure symptom belongs to the description flow chart 06 that belongs to sequence:

Start->A-1->A-3->A-4->B-1->B-2->B-4->B-5

Repair summary:

It is obvious from the symptom that the CPU has overheating issues, because fan cannot radiate heat effectively, which is accumulated into the machine which in turn overheats and shuts down. Follow the repair flowchart 06 to step B-5;

This step will show you how to clean the laptop thermal system, and cleaning the dust is the main point of this exercise

Prepare tools needed, such as small screwdriver, snippets. Pull out all power connections and batteries, and then release the static it carries.

1.   Remove all the screws one at a time from the bottom of the laptop and mark them for reference purposes when you re-install them. Afterwards, remove the motherboard cover and the fan is now exposed, on this particular model the fan is separated from heat sink. Remove the screws holding the fan and remove fan. Wipe and clean the leaves with cotton dipped in alcohol. And then inject a drop of machine oil into the fan bearing.

2. Clean the dust from the outlet position and finally re assemble the fan and the failure is gone.

Hint:

The Fan is the most important part in controlling the temperature, so you should not only clean the dust on the surface of the fan, but also add an external USB fan to cool down the laptop. Once I asked my client I had served, asking whether it made a difference to the laptops life by using an external USB fan to cool down laptop or not. The client, who did not use an external USB fan, generally had overheating issues occur between 15 months to 18 months later after the new laptop was bought. However, while the ones who used an external USB fan, the laptop overheating failure would only occur 40 months later from the time they had bought their laptop. The impact for the USB fan to the laptop life is self-evident.

088)   HP Pavilion DV2621tx Automatic shutdown

Failure symptom:

The moment the laptop starts up, the fan makes especially noisy sound when running, mixing with rubbing collision sound. 20 minutes later, laptop auto shuts down, and when it starts again, it quickly shuts down without allowing the OS to load completely.

Solution:

This failure symptom belongs to the description flow chart 06 that belongs to sequence:

Start->A-1->A-3->A-4->B-1->B-2->B-4->B-5->C-1

Repair summary:

Harsh noise from the fan comes when the CPU temperature is high and the speed of the fan is running at high speed and the fan blades are rubbing against the frame of the unit. In this example the fan is connected to the heat sink. Disassemble the laptop until you can see the heat sink and remove it noticing the blades are distorted. You try and order the part but it is out of stock which puts a halt to your repair. Then we check the fan and heat sink carefully, and realize that although they are integrated together, fan is fixed on the heat sink by three screws, so the fan itself can be changed by itself. After comparing the removed fan repeatedly, you find the fan of a COMPAQ V3000 is similar to the one you have 450096-001. So purchase it and replace your old one and the sequence disappear.

Hint:

Changing a fan is one of the problems that a repair technician often faces, as most HP fans are integrated with the heat sink, so it can be very expensive, and, it is often out of stock, which makes the repair work difficult.

After observing many HP fans and heat sinks carefully, even though they are integrated together, the fan is fixed on the heat sink by several screws. I always remove the fan first and I take a look at other Hp models and will end up finding a similar fan or one of the same sizes. Sometimes the screws may not align properly so I would drill new holes and assemble the fan and insert it in the fan box and glue it on. This is an easy and convenient and inexpensive way to cut repair cost.

089)   HP COMPAQ NX7400 Centrino Duo laptop auto shutdown failure

Failure symptom:

Laptop starts normally, but no fan rotating sound. 30 minutes later, CPU temperature is very high, and fan never goes on. I would touch the fan intake with hands to feel for wind or heat from the thermal holes but system becomes quite slow, and turns off automatically.

Solution:

This failure symptom belongs to the description flowchart 06, which belongs to sequence:

Start->A-1->A-3->A-4->B-1->B-3->B-5->C-1

Repair summary:

It is obvious from the failure symptom that the laptop has overheating issues. As fan stops rotating, the CPU's heat is not expelled normally, so the system starts overheating protection and the laptop auto shuts down. First pull the CPU fan blades gently counter-clockwise with a small screwdriver and you find it difficult to rotate. Clean the fan completely with alcohol, getting rid of the dust all over it, and then add a drop of machine oil to the fan bearing. Next start and test but fan still does not work, so replace it with a new one and the failure are gone.

Hint:

Laptops need periodically to be cleaned for thermal reasons; otherwise, after a while, dust enters the bearing core of the fan and causes the fans rotation speed to slow down raising the CPU temperature continuously, and in turn raise the fans temperature also. When it gets too high the fan structure will change and finally the fan loses the ability to rotate.

090)   HP COMPAQ F700 auto shutdown failure occurs during start up

Failure symptom:

Laptop always auto shuts down, at first it starts normally but after awhile it shuts off automatically. After several auto shutdowns, it no longer starts and every time you attempt to start it, it shuts off

Solution:

This failure symptom belongs to the description flowchart 06, which belongs to sequence:

Start->A-1->A-3->A-4->B-1->B-3->B-5->C-1->C-2

Repair summary:

We can conclude from the failure symptom described that the system has suffered a severe overheating problem. First clean the CPU thermal module completely as dust creates invalidation with the thermal module. Start the machine and test again, you will find the CPU fan stops rotating. Obviously, this is the main reason. When the fan stops rotating, it directly creates the issue regarding the release of the heat from the CPU because it has nowhere to spread it to, and therefore the system goes into overheating protection mode and cuts the power supply. After changing the fan, it will basically work all right. But in hot summer days, when the surrounding temperature is around 32 to 37 degrees, the machine will only be able to work at the most 2 to 2 ½ hrs so the best bet is to add a USB cooling fan underneath it and your problem should be solved

Hint:

Installing third party software to test the temperatures of CPU and hard disk and the fan speed. Update fan control system, prolong fan using life. When settle temperature arrives 35 to 60 degrees, fan enters the status according to the proportion timing within the temperature range and rotates; according to the comparative proportion of the temperature increase or decrease, laptop would auto adjust the speed of the fan to spread heat?

091)   HP PAVILION DV6810US auto shutdown failure

Failure symptom:

Laptop frequently shuts down automatically, after testing; the CPU kernel temperature is too high, the part of the laptop bottom corresponding with the position of CPU is very hot. Start the laptop again, the power indication light is on for 1 to 2 seconds, and then machine auto shuts down.

Solution:

This failure symptom belongs to the description flow chart 06, which belongs to sequence:

Start->A-1->A-3->A-4->B-1->B-3->B-5->C-1->D-1->D-3

Repair summary:

The temperature of the CPU core is very high, which means the CPU fan and thermal system are not playing a good role with the thermal radiating. Test the CPU fan and thermal system, and you will find the fan blades are severely distorted. The plastic shell covering on the bearing core has changed color and there is obvious burn traces, the fan has completely stopped functioning. Enter repair flowchart 06 of step B-5; change the fan and continue validation, finding that even the new fan does not work. Either.

Enter repair flowchart 06 of step D-1, considering that this model's fan is integrated with the heat sink, and has to be changed together, so the key thing to consider is the fans power supply from the motherboard. Pull out the 4 power jack cables between the fan and the motherboard; test pins 3 and 4 of the fan interface on the motherboard with a multi-meter, the pin 3 is the joint of the fan's black cable end and the motherboard joint end (grounding end), and the pin 4 is the joint of the fan's red cable and the motherboard joint end (+12V voltage end), finding the pin 3 is disconnected from the grounding end of the motherboard, making the black cable end of the fan separated from the jack. Find the grounding end from another port on the motherboard and solder the fan's black cable end here and the failure is solved.

Hint:

Because there is a certain danger to solder the motherboard, I do not suggest it unless you are quite familiar with soldering and have a certain manual ability and experience. Most times, laptops do not have such existing complex problem so it is rare you have to do soldering work.

If you do need to do soldering work, please first refer to the method mentioned in example 3 of the article <<6.1.4 Common failure treatments for laptop overheating problem>>

092)   HP PRESARIO V3020US auto shutdown failure

Failure symptom:

Laptop keeps shutting down and when re starting still turns off automatically. Sometimes fan stops rotating.

Solution:

This failure symptom belongs to the description flow chart 06 that belongs to sequence:

Start->A-1->A-3->A-4->B-1->B-2->B-4->B-5 and Start->A-1->A-3->A-4->B-1->B-2->B-3

Repair summary:

Enter repair flowchart 06 of step A-4, put Memtest86 software disc into the CD-ROM/DVD-ROM to start, this way it will eliminate the possibility the issue is caused by the memory stick; disassemble the laptop, and you will find there is a lot of accumulation of dust on the fan, It is now obvious why the system is auto shutting down because the CPU overheats and reaches the power-off protection temperature point. Clean the CPU fan completely, and then test the laptop CPU thermal system. During the test, the laptop usually works well but after exceeding 6 hours of running time it will occasionally auto shutdown. It is difficult to come to a Hint but from the failure symptom, we can conclude that the auto shutdown symptom is still caused because of CPU overheating and auto power-off protection.

Adjust the repair thoughts: Start->A-1->A-3->A-4->B-1->B-2->B-3

Check the CPU thermal system further again, confirming that the fan control system is not good. Fan start has some delay and lags. After updating the laptop BIOS, the failure disappears.

Hint:

CPU heats up a lot during the normal work process; therefore, it is quite important to keep good ventilation going. If CPU overheats, it will affect the laptop overall stability and reliability. So pay close attention and clean the CPU thermal system periodically, to avoid overheating problem again. It is not a bad idea to purchase an external USB fan to cool down the laptop, which will definitely stop overheating problem from happening again.

6.3.2 3 repair cases for the auto shutdown failure caused by bad CPU heat sink of HP laptop

093) Compaq Presario CQ50 Auto shuts down at starts up, cannot enter system

Failure symptom:

Laptop starts when you press the start button, but a few minutes later, system turns off. It lasts around 10 to 25 minutes, there is no way it is an overheating symptom on salver or keyboard.

Solution:

This failure symptom belongs to the description of flowchart 06 that belongs to sequence:

Start->A-1->A-3->A-4->B-1->B-2->B-4->B-7->B-5->C-1->D-1->D-2

Repair summary:

Use step process A-4, as the laptop working time is too short; there is not enough time for Memtest86 software to test the memory. Test the suspected memory stick on other known good laptop, finding the memory stick works well. Then we can eliminate the failure possibility of the memory; after disassembling the laptop, you find there is lots of dust piled on the fan, then enter repair step B-7.

The software testing result shows that after the laptop motherboard chip works for 7 minutes, the temperature reaches as high as 70°C and quickly rising to 85°C, soon after the machine auto shuts down; we can know from the failure symptom that it is still an overheating problem, which is related with the CPU. Next disassemble the laptop, test the CPU thermal system, clean the thermal system, add new thermal silica gel between thermal module and CPU, and reassemble the thermal system. Start it up and the issue is a little better and laptop works in normal mode for about 20 to 25 minutes. After checking the temperature of the CPU, hard disk and the fan rotation speed, it is found that the motherboard chip temperature still reaches above 85°C within a short time.

The problem is still with overheating. Strangely, the fan (486636-001) speed is within the normal range, so why is the CPU temperature not dropping? Would the problem be with the CPU itself? Enter repair step D-1, it feels quite hot close to the CPU of the thermal tube, but the other end (away from CPU end) feels very cool. So it seems that the liquid heat conduct medium inside the thermal tube is almost dry, which can no longer help the thermal radiating of the CPU. After changing the heat sink, the failure is gone.

Hint:

It is quite rare that the CPU thermal module/heat sink have issues but most repair technicians overlook the thermal module of the laptop, and then conclude the issue is with the motherboard and therefore miss the chance of properly diagnosing the real issue. So when you cannot check the reasons for system auto shutdown problem, always check the temperature of the CPU, hard disk and fan speed carefully. If the CPU temperature is very high and the fan rotation speed is normal, then do not forget to check the thermal tube, as it is quite likely that the heat sink does not work, which causes the auto shutdown failure.

094)   HP PAVILION DV9730US auto shutdown problem

Failure symptom:

One or two minutes after start up the laptop auto shuts down right away, even after removing the hard disk, it shuts down automatically.

Solution:

This failure symptom belongs to the description flow chart 06 that belongs to sequence:

Start->A-1->A-3->A-4->B-1->B-2->B-4->B-5->C-1->D-1

Repair summary:

First of all, make sure the auto shutdown failure is not caused by a memory stick problem, and then continue following the flowchart 06 to eliminate the problem. Because the laptop normal working time is especially short, you cannot test the temperature of the CPU, hard disk and fan rotation speed with software. So the first process with overheating issues is the usual method of cleaning the CPU radiator, cleaning up the dust inside and out and then applying new thermal silica gel and then testing whether the failure has been eliminated. After starting up, the situation is better but the laptop works for about 5 minutes and then it auto shuts down again.

After careful analysis, the biggest possibility for such a failure is bad thermal with the CPU and it causes auto shutdown protection. Primarily there are two reasons First possibility: The fan stops rotating, or severe dust accumulation and failed CPU silica gel. But all these, generally, would not make the laptop shut down after 1 or 2 minutes. Second possibility: the heat sink/module of the CPU is broken or there is a bad connection with it. After checking the CPU heat sink carefully, you find one of the four screws used to fix the heat sink has thread problem. A corner of the heat sink is not pressed tight with the CPU, so namely, the heat sink does not connect properly to the CPU. Once you change the screw the problem is solved.

Hint:

Because of bumping and collision, the laptop thermal parcel might get loose, or the clips falls so the CPU/GPU chip cannot radiate. All these would make the machine auto restart or auto shut down within one or two minutes during working process. You can change or fix the heat sink again to solve this kind of radiating problem.

095)   HP PAVILION DV6751US grey screen and system freezes failures caused by overheating

Failure symptom:

30 to 40 minutes after laptop runs, system freezes, and restarts again, and the thermal sound is quite loud.

Solution:

This failure symptom belongs to the description flow chart 06 that belongs to sequence:

Start->A-1->A-3->A-4->B-1->B-2->B-4->B-7->B-5->C-1->D-1

Repair summary:

According to clients' memory, 20 or so days ago, the laptops fan and heat sink was changed, so there must be another reason causing such system failure. First analyze the symptom; the thermal sound is quite loud, which indicates the thermal fan is running at high speed, but obviously the fan has not played a related cooling down action, system still continues to go down. Enter repair step B-7, test the temperature of GPU, hard disk and fan rotation speed with software carefully, finding after a short period of time, the laptop GPU chip's temperature reaches above 85°C. So we are sure it belongs to an overheating GPU problem and what is strange is the fan and heat sink was replaced so why is the GPU temperature not dropping down?

Enter repair step D-1, check the heat sink (451860-001) beside the fan, there is a branch extending to the upper place of GPU, check the area of the connection between the heat sink and GPU, finding the copper block of the thermal parcel is badly connected with the thermal silica gel and GPU chip, which does not play a real thermal part for the GPU. Compare the heat sink with the original one repeatedly; especially the side with the copper block close to the GPU which seem a little different than the original one. 20 days ago, fan and heat sink were changed so it looks like the new one is incompatible with the motherboard. After changing the new heat sink (451860-001), the failure is gone!

Hint:

Prepare the thermal parcel for change, the copper blocks outstanding side must be exactly the same as the 3 original heat sink and namely in the same position, same area, same thickness and height;

Some thermal parcels may look exactly same when in actual fact they are completely incompatible with the motherboard. Many beginners would neglect this point, and think as long as the screws line up with the holes of the motherboard all is good which is a big mistake that happens and they still have no idea about the reason.

6.3.3 Seven repair cases of system freezes or auto shutdown failures caused by GPU/CPU overheating problem

096) HP DV2726 system crash failure after starting up

Failure symptom:

20 minutes after start up system freezes and then it auto shuts down within seconds.

Solution:

This failure symptom belongs to the description flow chart 06 that belong to sequence:

Start->A-1->A-3->A-4->B-1->B-2->B-4->B-7->B-5

Repair summary:

Enter repair step B-7, software test result shows that after 20 minutes of running time motherboard chip temperature reaches as high as 70°C, and quickly rushing to 80°C, and not long after it auto shuts down; Disassemble the laptop, finding there is a lot of dust piled up on fan, which indicates it is an overheating problem with the CPU. Next, clean the CPU thermal system and put some new thermal silica gel between the thermal module and CPU, and re-install the thermal system. Restart the laptop and failure is gone!

Hint:

The reason for changing the CPU thermal silica gel is that it has gotten old and is no longer doing what it is meant too which is to help protect the CPU from overheating, you should also clean the heat sink extreme carefully, also pay close attention not to touch the CPU elec-conductive copper pole. and do not wipe thermal silica gel on the conductive copper pole and spot as it will affect the thermal performance.

097) HP Compaq Presario CQ60 system freezes failure

Failure symptom:

30 minutes after system has been running it freezes. Test the display card temperature, if it reaches 83°C, there is an overheating issue.

Solution:

This failure symptom belongs to the description of flowchart 06 that belongs to sequence:

Start->A-1->A-3->A-4->B-1->B-2->B-4->B-7->B-5

Repair summary:

According to the failure symptom, combined with the flowchart, eliminate the problem one by one. First check the adapter then the battery for overheating issue. Secondly check whether there is something wrong with the thermal module, many times it can lose its function which will cause direct overheating followed by system crashes, or auto shut downs. If system crashes still occurs, then continue checking whether the display card has overheating failure. It shows a temperature of 83°C, which means it is overheating.

Enter repair step B-5, according to my experience, most of the causes regarding thermal performance is due to bad silica gel between the heat sink (489126-001) and the GPU chip, because of that the GPU's temperature becomes too high. Because of years of usage the high temperature of the chip ages the silica gel and ends up drying and in turn creates bad contact with the heat sink resulting in bad thermal function. After changing the thermal silica gel cushion with one of high quality, start the machine and test again, the failure disappears.

Hint:

As important process structure for characters and pictures, the stability and reliability of the display card will directly affect the working performance of the laptop. But in practical application, because the graphic process chip of the display card uses a tiny thermal cushion, with time it gets distorted and loosens or the fan breaks and stops working, all these would make the display card process chip to overheat creating a blurry screen or system freeze up.

098)   HP Tablet TX2500 auto shutdown failure

Failure symptom:

Stripe interference occurs on laptop screen, sometimes lasting for quite a while, system would die or black screen symptom would occur.

Solution:

This failure symptom belongs to the description flow chart 06 that belongs to this sequence:

Start->A-1->A-3->A-4->B-1->B-2->B-4->B-7->B-5->C-1->D-1->D-3

Repair summary:

First of all, make sure the stripe interference, system crash or black screen symptoms are not caused by the memory stick. And then follow the repair flow chart of step B-7 to eliminate the failure; however, the laptop only works for a short time, and there is no way to test the temperature of CPU/GPU with software therefore follow the process dealing with overheating problem by cleaning up the fan with alcohol completely, erasing all dust on it. Next, start and test it but the problem remains. Go to repair flowchart 06 of step B-5, and change the thermal silica gel between the thermal module and CPU/GPU, reinstall the thermal system. After changing to a new fan and heat sink (441143-001) and trying again, the situation slightly improved, but not solved. As the core temperature of the display card chip is really high, the heat sink is not close enough to the GPU, so get a penny or a dime and polish both sides and put it on the copper side of the heat sink, and paste thermal silica cushion. Afterwards, hold down on the GPU chip, the core temperature of the display card lowers and the failure disappears.

Hint:

Put a coin between heat sink and thermal silica cushion to increase heat radiating, but be extremely careful and ensure the coin does not touch the GPU elec-conductive copper poles and spots. You should separate these conductive copper poles and spots with thin adhesive tape. Now only expose the core plane of the GPU, making the thermal cushion pressed on tightly and ensuring there will be no short circuit between the coin and elec-conductive copper poles and spots and this will eliminate the possibility that the motherboard burns out.

099)   HP PRESARIO F500 starts up normally then auto shuts down failure occurs

Failure symptom:

Laptop starts, power indicator light is on, but 5 seconds later, system auto shuts down.

Solution:

This failure symptom belongs to the description flow chart 06 that belongs to this sequence:

Start->A-1->A-3->A-4->B-1->B-2->B-4->B-7->B-5->C-1->D-1->D-2->D-3

Repair summary:

First make sure there is no problem with the memory stick, and continue following the method of flowchart 06 to eliminate the failure; Because the laptop only works for a very short time, follow the overheating failure process by cleaning the dust on the CPU heat sink and changing to a new thermal silica cushion, start the machine and test, finding the failure remains. Enter repair step D-3, use minimum system method to inspect the laptop by removing the battery, wireless network card, network card, Modem, card reader, hard disk and so on. If the laptop still does not start, and there is no change there can only be two main sources for the failure: one is a CPU issue; the second is the motherboard. After changing the CPU the failure is solved.

Hint:

Minimum system method: The primary reason for this is to judge whether the system will work under the most basic software and hardware environment. If it cannot then we only have a couple of things left to verify as we removed most of them and the laptop is at its basic state. For more concrete operation refer to the method in the second chapter (minimum system judgment) of <<1.4.2 6 "Hard" methods to repair laptop>> to solve the problem.

100)   HP PAVILION DV9720US auto shutdown failure

Failure symptom:

One or two minutes after the laptop starts, it auto shuts down, and does not even finish self-inspection.

Solution:

This failure symptom belongs to the description flow chart 06 that belongs to this sequence:

Start->A-1->A-3->A-4->A-7

Repair summary:

According to clients' memory, before the failure occurred, everything was all right with the laptop, until it was dropped by accident. First make sure the auto shutdown failure is not caused because the memory stick is loose, then go to the flow chart 06 to eliminate the problem and enter repair step B-5, considering it is quite likely that the fact it was dropped it might have caused the heat sink to loosen which will make the CPU/GPU chip to fail to radiate and in turn cause the machine to auto shut down after a couple of minutes. The general method is to remove the heat sink, clean the thermal silica cushion, and install the heat sink back again making sure the CPU is well connected with the heat sink, start the machine but the auto shutdown failure still occurs.

After careful analysis, the biggest possibility of the failure is that there is a bad connection with the CPU and makes the system to send the power-off protection signal by mistake namely because the motherboard is not connected tightly with the CPU causing the shut down. The second reason is that after the laptop was dropped a short circuit happened to a certain area, the motherboard is burnt; after removing the CPU, and cleaning it up the failure disappears.

Hint:

Because of bumps and collisions, the laptop CPU might have slipped off, then CPU/GPU might fail to radiate and system sends power-off protection signal by mistake, which behaves as an auto restart or auto shutdown within minutes after start up. So removing or reinstalling the CPU may solve this kind of bad connection issue.

101) HP PAVILION DV6622CA auto shutdown failure for no reason

Failure symptom:

After laptop starts, no running software, then laptop shuts down suddenly. System has no obvious overheating symptom.

Solution:

This failure symptom belongs to the description flow chart 06 that belongs to this sequence:

Start->A-1->A-3->A-4->B-1->B-2->B-4->B-7->B-5

Repair summary:

You can put a pure bootable DOS Memtest86 software disc into the DVD-ROM/CD-ROM to start, and inspect the memory, before the inspection is completed the laptop auto shuts down, which indicates the laptop failure might be related with the connection status between accessories and the temperatures of RAM, motherboard, CPU/GPU;

First make sure there is no memory problem, and then continue following the method flow chart 06 to eliminate the problem then enter repair step B-5, follow the overheating process method by removing the CPU heat sink and thermal silica cushion, finding there is full of silica mud of poor quality wiped all over the CPU elec-conductive copper poles. It seems that the laptop had been repaired by a rookie once, otherwise, how would there be such a mess? Clean the CPU completely with alcohol, removing all bad silica mud and change the thermal silica cushion, and test the laptop, the failure disappears.

Hint:

If there's full of silica mud of poor quality over the CPU elec-conductive copper poles, the thermal performance isn't good; this stops the CPU heat to the CPU thermal parcel to move perfectly. To the opposite, it would make the heat transfer speed slower; as the temperature of certain parts of the CPU is too high, directly affecting the accuracy of the inspected system temperature. The temperature inspection fails or the error is too big, causing the CPU to send the wrong signal and make the system to think that CPU is extremely hot and needs to power-off. This is a manual failure, which should be avoided as much as possible.

102)   HP COMPAQ NX7000 always auto shutting down

Failure symptom:

15 minutes later after laptop enters system, it shuts down. Start the laptop again, but 2 minutes later, system freezes again. After testing, the laptop has no obvious overheating symptom.

Solution:

This failure symptom belongs to the description flow chart 06 that belongs to this sequence

Start->A-1->A-3->A-4->B-1->B-2->B-4->B-7->B-5->C-1->D-1->D-3

Repair summary:

Enter repair step B-7, software test result shows that after laptop works for 7 minutes, GPU chip basically reaches 70°C, and quickly reaches 85°C, before long, system freezes; known from the test result, the failure is still a GPU overheating problem. Disassemble the laptop, check the GPU thermal system, wipe new thermal silica gel between the thermal module and GPU, and put back the thermal system. After starting up, situation has improved. The laptop works normally for about 20 to 25 minutes and issue returns. Finally, after changing the 64 MB ATI display card (336970-001), the failure disappears.

Hint:

It is known from the failure symptom that GPU overheating symptom should be the root reason directly causing system to freeze. As the laptop has no obvious overheating symptom, it means the laptop CPU thermal performance should be good. Open the laptop, you will find that the CPU thermal module is separated from the GPU heat sink. Because of this the CPU fan is not that effective to cool down the display card GPU.

This type of machine has a design bug, which often has system freeze ups, black screen or auto shutdown failures. Most cases, GPU has an issue in itself, which needs to be replaced. Therefore, it is quite necessary to add an USB fan. The heat at the bottom of the laptop would be spread around by the fan, which will avoid from accumulating and causing the laptop to overheat and end up burning the display card.

6.3.4   Five repair cases for system freeze ups and auto shutdown failures caused by HP laptop hard disk and other accessories

103)   after HP G61-409CA starts up, system freezes failure happens only after system loads

Failure symptom:

System gets down not long after laptop starts up, and there's no way to enter system. Restart the computer and BIOS cannot inspect hard disk;

Solution:

This failure symptom belongs to the description of flowchart 06 that belong to this sequence:

Start->A-1->A-3->A-4->A-6

Repair summary:

According to the method of flowchart 06, Step: A-4, put a pure bootable DOS Memtest86 software disc into DVD-ROM/CD-ROM to start, memory inspection starts, it runs for 1 hour and 20 minutes (3 inspections in all), after passing all software inspections, laptop remains in normal status, no restart, auto shutdown or system freeze symptoms. Meanwhile, touching the CPU and intake positions at the bottom part of the laptop and it isn't very hot. So the problem should be related with software or hard disk. Check all parts one by one, finding the disk has a severe overheating problem, it feels really hot to the touch. Remove the hard disk; smell the hard disk and it smells like burnt plastic, which is very different from the normal plastic smell of a hard disk.

It seems that the hard disk is burnt because of high temperature which causes system freezes. Test the hard disk with software, and ensure that the hard disk is not good. After changing the hard disk and re installing the operating system, the failure disappears.

Hint:

Generally speaking, a lot of heat is generated from the high rotating speed of a hard disk and heat can exceed over 57 degrees, and sometimes indescribable system freezes symptom would occur. HP laptops have no special cooling down measures for hard disk, so it relies on natural radiating. Because system thermal performance is not enough, hard drives can heat up. In order to help with system radiating I suggest cooling it down by using an external USB fan which will help to radiate heat from the bottom of the laptop effectively.

104)   HP PRESARIO V5310US auto shutdown failure

Failure symptom:

After laptop works 1 to 2 hours, auto shutdown symptom happen indescribably, you restart the computer but display does not show or there is only a cursor flashing. But, when you touch the hard disk shell you notice the temperature is really high.

Solution:

This failure symptom belongs to the description of flowchart 06 that belongs to this sequence:

Start->A-1->A-3->A-4->A-6

Repair summary:

According to the auto shutdown symptom, and the upper salver over the disk heats, probably the problem is related with the laptop disk overheating. Follow the method of flowchart 06, Step: A-4, check the memory stick, finding that through the test and after inspecting the disk with software, it is confirmed that the disk is good. Seems the overheating disk directly causes system auto shutdown failure. Add an external USB radiator to cool down the bottom of the laptop which will in some control the disk temperature within a low range, and then the failure's gone!

Hint:

Generally speaking, laptop disk overheating is because of the machines design. Some laptops' internal design is quite rough, there's no heat insulation layer between the hard disk and the motherboards surface, which allows the heat to directly spread to the hard disk. Or the main thermal channel is blocked, and then heat with flow back to the disk. Besides, a bad connection between hard disk and motherboard would also cause system freezes or auto shutdown failure. You'd have to clean the dust on the hard disk slot, ensuring the outlet hole of the cover to extract the heat which would be beneficial for air circulation. You can also cushion up the laptop, by keeping enough space for the disk to the desktop and radiate it well from the bottom. But there's something wrong with the new hard disk and it needs to be changed in time. Make sure the disk temperature is controlled and avoid it from overheating and the problem is solved.

105)   HP PAVILION DV9920US system auto shutdown failure

Failure symptom:

When laptop connects to the external power adapter only, it auto shuts down a minute later. After pulling out adapter and plugging it back to the laptop, it still shuts down automatically.

Solution:

This failure symptom belongs to the description flow chart 06 that belongs to this sequence:

Start->A-1->A-2

Repair summary:

Known from the failure symptom that the problem might be with the power adapter, after testing further, this adapter is of 70W, which is also the minimum watt requirement for an HP DV9000 laptop If the power adapter is too old, it will be far from 70W output power, so the laptop will not start; if the laptop has overheating symptoms, then it will not supply normal power for the laptop. After changing the power adapter to a 90W, the failure disappears.

Hint:

No matter if the power adapter light is on or not, you should always use a voltage meter to test whether the output voltage is between the standard 18.5V to 19.5V. Because the power indication light is on, it only indicates that the power adapter is getting power from the jack in the wall, but it does not represent that the adapter is working normally. Many people would neglect this point and make an extreme low-grade mistake! Finally miss on the success of the diagnosis

106)   HP PRESARIO F761US system crash failure

Failure symptom:

During the normal working process when laptop runs on the power adapter the system freezes symptom occurs from time to time. After changing to a 90W power adapter, nothing changes.

Solution:

This failure symptom belongs to the description flow chart 06 that belongs to this sequence

Start->A-1->A-3->A-5->-C-3

Repair summary:

As system crash symptom only happens when you use the power adapter, after changing to a 90W power adapter, the situation remains the same, so enter repair step A-3, when you move to the battery mode, laptop resumes normally and finishes to loading the system. But when you plug the adapter on again, system freezes again or even powers off. It seems the problem of the laptop is with the battery. After changing to a new battery, the problem disappears.

Hint:

There are many reasons causing laptop screen to fail to start. Slight short circuit or battery overheating inside battery would make this symptom to happen. Generally after removing the battery, laptop would recover normally; but sometimes the situation is not that simple, some laptops would only use the power adapter without the need of a battery while other laptops need the battery to start it

107)   HP PRESARIO CQ40-425TX system auto shutdown failure

Failure symptom:

One minute after laptop starts, it auto shuts down. You restart it again, blue screen occurs, and then system freezes.

Solution:

This failure symptom belongs to the description flow chart06 that belongs to this sequence:

Start->A-1->A-2->A-4->A-7 and Start->A-1->A-2->A-4->A-6

Repair summary:

According to the method of flowchart 06, Step: A-4, put a pure bootable DOS Memtest86 software disc into the DVD-ROM/CD-ROM to start, test the memory stick, as a result, during the test process, it still auto shuts down. So you can conclude the problem is related with hardware; first check the memory stick further, change memory to repair, as the most common reason is that after a memory stick fails, laptop will not light or start therefore, remove both memory sticks, and test them individually by inserting one at a time in slot A or B. Test each one in each slot; 4 tests for two memory sticks, for auto shutdown symptom or blue screen failure. If you get a failure does it mean both memory stick are bad? To solve this doubt, remove one memory stick from a known normal laptop, and then put it in the suspected laptop and test it, finding out it is still down. So now there may be another problem with the laptops, many rookies have not considered this point, which can make the repair more complicated.

Now continue following the method of flow chart06 to eliminate the problems; check the memory stick again, finding that no matter how much time increases, the laptop always stays normal state. The temperature of the CPU and intake positions feels normal. So it seems that the second problem might be related with software or hard disk. After further inspection, it is found that the hard disk cannot be formatted normally, there is no way to reinstall the operating system; besides, there is a severe overheating issue and cannot work normally with several bad sectors in hard drive. After changing it the failure disappears.

Hint:

Memory does not pass the software test and has error prompt, blue screen or system freezes failures. Basically we are sure the problem is related with hardware; probably failure symptom would happen singularly and 2 to 3 failure symptoms would occur at the same time. If this is the situation, then your computer might have more than two existing problems and are probably related with software and hardware. Follow the repair principle "first hardware and then software" to finish the repair process. If failure still occurs, then please enter the method of flow chart 06 to eliminate the failure again.

CHAPTER 7

OS load failure, loop restart and blue screen repair

7.1 Causes for the failures that Windows could not be load or system repeats restarting and blue screen

7.1.1 Common laptop memory failures

1) When the Windows system runs, it's found that memory capacity and performance has diminished drastically.
2) Windows system often goes to safe mode.
3) Applications are unstable, invalid operations often occurs, or the system auto shuts down.
4) REGEDIT often gets corrupted without any reason, and it prompts user to resume.
5) System auto restarts several times at start up, or a blue screen occurs.
6) Application won't install because of incompatibility between the memory and motherboard
7) Windows fails to be loaded and auto turns off.
8) No display at start up and you can hear beeps.
9) No display at start up and no warning signs.
10) Memory short circuit prevents the machine from power on and starts up.
11) When the memory rams are of different speeds and are installed, the BIOS doesn't recognize the capacity correctly.
12) The computer is unstable and intermittently freezes.
13) The laptop no longer starts up normally, and there's no way to reinstall Windows. Ann invalid operation error occurs when trying to configure the system.
14) A prompt "Out of Memory", or there's many errors relevant with the system memory when certain software is running.
15) At start up, it shows the information as below: "Memory ERROR"
16) In Windows system, when you run some applications under DOS (like some game software in DOS), various symptoms would occur, like black screen, blurred screen, and system freezes etc.

17) At start up, the system will show information like: "C:\WINDOWS\SYSTEM\xxx\ xxxx.vxd could not be found" and cannot be changed even after a fresh install of Windows.

7.1.2 Laptop hard disk failure and possible causes

1. Common laptop disk failures

a) The disk does not start for some apparent reason and sometimes the cursor flashes on the top left corner of the screen;

b) The disk isn't found when the system starts up, even after entering motherboard BIOS.

c) During the startup self-inspection process, information is shown on the screen that the disk is lost or there is no partition.

d) The disk doesn't start; you get a prompts "Primary master hard disk fail".

e) The disk doesn't start; it prompts "DISK BOOT FAILURE, INSERT SYSTEM DISK AND PRESS ENTER".

f) When reinstalling it takes forever to format the disk and the installation is extremely slow, it also prompts for some other information.

g) There's a possibility the interior of the hard disk is damaged or has failed, which forces the system to re start several times or a blue screen would occur.

h) There's damage inside the disk, and it prompts the error "DLLfile, xxxx is missing", and an error would prompt even after repairing the area.

i) There's damage inside the disk, and it fails to reinstall the Windows system, or a system auto restart occurs.

j) When the machine starts and self-inspects, the disk makes beep sounds, and the system will not boot from the disk.

2. Causes for disk failure

1) The disk data cable or the power cable is not properly connected or there's a loose connection elsewhere.

2) The disk partition is lost

3) The disk is infected by viruses or gets a logic lock.

4) The disk has a bad track.

5) The disk interface circuit is faulty.

6) The disk magnet head or another component is broken.

7) Disk power interface failure.

8) Principle disk axis motor, locator card, and some other components have failed.

7.1.3   Laptop disk failure diagnosis and repair method

General steps to deal with disk failures

When it comes to a disk failure, you should first relax and analyze the problem. If it's a physical problem and there's no important data on the disk, then your best bet is to replace it with a new one or return it for repair at your dealer if it's still under warranty.

If there's important data on disk that you have to recover then you'll need to deal with it or find an experienced professional repair man or friend as it involves dealing with internal hardware parts.

A physical disk problem involves bottom level hardware (such as disk parcel, control circuitry board and so on), if you make an attempt to take it apart and repair it, you might cause severe damage to the disk.

Here I'll introduce a soft disk problem repair method, you can try by yourself. But be careful, I want to point out that all these methods here are based on the preconception that no data needs to be recovered and you are just looking to repair the disk. If you want to recover the data on the disk, then the repair method might be different. Please go and have a look at my previous post "basic skills of data recovery"

https://www.computercare.ca/forum/showthread.php?t=190&keep_https=yes

You can refer to the relevant contents on this site about data recovery. All in all here is a general overview on how to eliminate soft disk problems.

Common failure 1: system doesn't recognize hard disk

The system doesn't start from the hard disk, even fails to enter drive C when booting from a CD, and there's no way to find out the existence of the hard disk with the CMOS auto inspection function. Mostly the problem occurs in the linkage or IDE/SATA port. It's less likely to be a hard disk problem. We can pull and plug the disk again or try changing the IDE/SATA port linker. Soon you will find where the problem is.

a. This issue mostly happens when a high capacity disk is used with an old motherboard. If the new plugged-in disk isn't accepted, start from the CD and then you'll be able to enter drive C, the reason is that the primary disk device is vacant while the backup disk device installs the OS, for instance: HP DV9000 laptop has two disk devices, you then have to be clear of the principal and subordinate relationship.

b. The disk isn't recognized with the auto inspection function of CMOS, and the system doesn't recognize the disk. The main reason for this problem is because the data on the primary boot sector of the disk is corrupted, as the primary boot mark of the disk or partition label is lost. The main culprit of the failure is a virus, which covers the primary boot sector with incorrect data. The easy method for this is to repartition. I use FDISK.com a lot; generally, this method can help revive your disk. However, because of repartition and format, it's basically impossible to preserve the data inside.

Common failure 2: the hard disk cannot read/write or cannot be identified

Generally, this problem is caused because of a CMOS setup failure. The correctness of the disk type in CMOS affects how the disk is directly used. Different CMOS versions have some small differences when inspecting a hard disk; sometimes the system fails to start, and sometimes it is successful, but a read/write error will occur. For instance, if the disk type in CMOS is less then the actual disk capacity, then the latter sector on the disk might not be read/write; if it's in a multi-partition state, then some partitions may get lost. There's still one more important failure mode: if you store data on one laptop, and then put the disk on another laptop, because of different versions of CMOS, there might be a disk read/write error. As the mapping relationship has changed, then there's no way to read the original correct disk position. You can reformat the disk and install the operating system and applications to solve the problem.

Common failure 3: system doesn't start

The failure is usually caused by four reasons listed below:

1. Primary boot program has failed;
2. "Invalid Partition Table";
3. Hard Disk Partition Table-Error!!!
4. DOS boot file is broken.

    a. The primary boot program has failed and the partition valid bit is corrupted—generally we can use FDISK/MBR to override it.
    b. A corrupted partition table will cause the system to not recognize a partition and take it as an undistributed partition disk. As a result, some software might fail to work but you can still use fdisk/mbr to rebuild the partition table.

There's another simple way—change the issued hard disks into an USB external disk, and then find a computer with Windows 2000 system. Then plug the damaged disk into it, start it up, and allow Windows 2000 to scan the new plugged hard disk. Because Windows 2000 disk scanner CHKDSK has a great ability to repair issues with hard disks for all kinds of reasons, so after scanning finishes, basically, the hard disk has been repaired too.

    c. Among these, DOS boot file damage is the easiest, after booting from the start-up disc, transmit a boot file to the system.

Common failure 4: hard disk capacity doesn't match the marked value size

Generally speaking, after formatting, the disk capacity shows less then the marked size, but the disparity should never exceed 20%. If the disparity is really great, then you should enter BIOS at start up to verify it. If there is a large difference in size in the BIOS to the marked value, then it means that your motherboard doesn't support a large capacity disk or you just used format software incorrectly. At this point, you can try downloading the latest BIOS version and refresh or just reformat the disk to solve the problem. For instance: HP Compaq NC6000 has a 160GB hard disk and it only finds 100GB when tested in WinXP. Remove the hard disk, and then put it in another laptop, format it and then install it back in the HP Compaq nc6000 laptop, reinstall OS and test it again, and the capacity should show correctly.

Additionally, if the partition table is corrupted, then there will be a "partition mapping" failure, and a partition like active partition will appear. Similarly, it includes file structure, content and partition capacity. Suppose you've changed the partition content in any area, there must be an embodiment somewhere else, just like a mapping shadow. Once I got a problem with a 15G hard disk that became 20G (mapping 5G drive C). This problem is quite awkward, although the problem doesn't affect usage, it is harder to repair, such as when you use NORTON DISKDOCTOR and PQMAGIC, you will find that they will turn a blind eye to the total partition capacity and actual disk size, and the problem still hangs there. Actually, you want to solve the problem? "GHOST" could help resume the partition table.

With GHOST software, we can easily and quickly format the partition. First, find a small disk; say 10GB would be the best. Then connect it onto your machine, partition the disk and format it in (FAT32). Remember not to store any files on this disk. Restart the computer with the DOS boot disc, run GHOST, and choose the menu "Local—Disk—To image", make this partition into a GHO image file. As there's no file on this disk, so the image file formed will be quite small, you can store the file GHOST.EXE together with this image file on a boot floppy disk. Next time when you want to partition or format the disk, you can start the machine with this floppy disk. Run GHOST, choose "Local—Disk—From Image", and then choose the image file on the floppy disk, choose the target disk, and then on the window "Destination Drive Details", adjust the capacity for each partition manually in the "New size" text. You can also leave it as is and press the "OK" button and then "Yes", after a few moments the issue is resolved.

Common failure 5: cannot boot the system correctly no matter what device is used

This is due to a manual setup or an invalid operation (such as bad compression by mistake) or a virus infection or some kind of "Disk dead lock" failure to the hard disk. Disk dead lock means that a virus has changed the primary boot partition record, causing the first logical disk of the extended partition to point to itself. During the process the laptop boots and loads the operating system, after the first logical disk is found, it then checks the next logical disk, in this case, the laptop gets into a loop state, and cannot start the operating system normally. Once the disk dead lock occurs, this is the failure symptom: as long as the disk is installed onto the laptop, you cannot start the operation system from a disk or floppy disk normally. Even if you set the issued disk as a slave IDE device, similarly, it would still cause the problem, and the machine won't boot from hard disk or floppy disk normally. The exterior symptom of this disk failure seems even worse than the actual physical disk, but the actual truth is, it's just a pure software problem.

An easy method to unlock the "Logical lock": is to remove the laptop disk and put it on a desktop computer to unlock it. As DM software doesn't' rely on the motherboard BIOS to recognize the disk, even if the disk is set as "NONE" in motherboard BIOS, DM will recognize the hard disk, partition and format it, thus we can use DM to help unlock a disk.

First of all, copy DM to a system disc, connect the locked disk and then start the machine. Press "Del" to enter the BIOS setup. Set all IDE interfaces as "NONE", save the settings and then exit. Restart the system with a floppy disk so the system could start with "lock". At this moment, it's just as if the system has no hard disk. Start it and then run the DM application, you will find that DM will recognize the hard disk. Choose the disk, partition and format it.

Common failure 6: bad sectors occur in the hard disk, the OS auto restarts repeatedly

When you use the Windows system disk scanner application SCANDISK, the system will prompt that the hard disk may have bad sectors, and then a "B" would be marked on the box . . . .

Actually, most of these bad sectors are logical ones and are repairable. So there's no need to have it sent for repair, but what can be done if this occurs?

Once we use "SCANDISK", if it prompts you that there's a bad sector, the first thing we should use is a self-inspection application of each brand of disk again to finish a complete scanning. What's worth it to mention is that you should not choose quick scan, because it could only find out about 90% of the problems. Rest assure that it's worth the time for a full scan.

If the tested result is "Repair succeeded", then we can be sure it's a logical bad sector; but suppose it's not, then use the repartition method to test it, and reformat the disk under DOS again. Generally, this method will help revive your hard disk. But if we still find bad sectors on this disk, then there's no need to repair it. Just replace it with a new one!

7.1.4 General laptop hard drive failures

Start-up failure:

When we use a laptop, it's quite likely that we may encounter a non startup issue. There are many reasons that may cause a system startup failure, and most of them are related to the hard disk. Generally, when a disk failure occurs, BIOS will prompt you with a message. Due to different motherboard manufacturers or different versions of BIOS, the messages given may be a little different, but basically they are largely identical with some minor differences.

During the starting period, there's a System BIOS error message on the black screen "Imminent Hard Disk Failure".

1. **Hard disk controller failure,** this is one of the most common error messages. When this situation occurs, you should check the connector of the data cable, is it loose, or and is it connected properly? Is the disk parameter setting set correctly?

    1720-disk failure imminent; if the disk drive finds that the failure is going to happen or it will stop rotating, then probably an error will appear. The error would show letters as below:

    1720—SMART Hard Drive detects imminent failure. Your hard disk drive is detecting an imminent failure. To ensure no data loss; backup the contents and replace this hard disk. Attribute Failed: #10

    Before continuing to run the procedure, backup the data first, even though the laptop may continue to start Windows after the message is displayed, I still suggest that you make a backup of the personal data on your computer: Copy the data onto a network drive, CD, DVD or USB storage devices.

    After backing up your data, please use one of these methods to eliminate the failure.

Step 1: test disk drive

Execute the next step and use the HP Hard Drive Self Test to inspect the disk drive:

1. Plug the AC power adapter into the laptop;
2. Press the power button for about 5 seconds to turn off the computer;
3. Press the power button to start the laptop. When the laptop screen first posts information, hit F10;
4. After the BIOS Setup Utility appears, use → key to choose "Tools" menu;
5. Choose "Hard Drive Self Test"
6. Press the Enter key to start testing.

    ➢ The Hard Drive Self Test will display "Estimated test time". Press the Enter key and then execute Quick test, Comprehensive test, and SMART test.
    ➢ If any test fails, you should replace the disk drive.
    ➢ If all tests are successful, then it indicates that the disk drive is not faulty. Generally, the disk is not faulty once it has passed through the HP Hard Drive Self Test and should not be replaced, as it's OK to use it.
    ➢ Many computer problems are connected with a soft failure of the disk drive. The HP Hard Drive Self Test will repair the soft failure of the disk drive, but not report the failures. After testing is finished, make sure to restart the computer to ensure that the test has solved your computer problem.

Step 2: carry out this repair if the method above didn't eliminate the failure; contact your local repair center to arrange maintenance.

2. **Data error.** When this situation occurs, probably the system data reads from the disk with some unrepeatable error or there's a bad sector on the disk. At this time, you can try starting the Scandisk application and scan to rectify the logical error on the sector.

3. **No boot sector on the hard disk drive.** For this situation, probably the boot sector on the hard disk is faulty; generally, this is because the system boot sector is already infected by viruses. If you use Win XP system, then you can recover the primary boot sector by the FIXMBR command.

4. **Bad track failure:** A bad Physical disk track is also a common disk failure. A logical bad track is a hard disk failure that occurs in the daily life of laptop usage. Actually, it is due to the (ECC) on the disk track that is not matched with the data on the tracks or the server information. The main reason for such failure, generally, is because of some invalid operations, or it's just that the magnetism mediums of the sectors become unstable. In fact, because of vibration, scratch or some other "hard" reasons, the magnetism mediums on some sectors lose their magnetic memory function. Generally, it's kind of troublesome to repair such damage. You're better off to replace the disk drive.

7.1.5 The laptop prompts the failure that no disk is found when installing the Operating system Software problem

The HP laptop cannot install the Windows XP system? The reason why this problem is put forward is because most people get this problem when installing Windows XP. The HP laptop cannot find the hard disk when installing the Windows XP system. Actually the answer is that HP laptop can install the XP system but some models may have incompatible drivers. You will need to find the drivers and install the SATA disk driver.

Here we take an HP DV2621TX laptop for example. When installing the Windows XP Operating system, it prompts that the disk is not found. The current HP laptops all have a SATA hard disk so when reinstalling the OS, if you directly install it without the integrated SATA driver, the computer might be unable to find the hard disk.

Solution: first initialize BIOS and then set up the system configuration—disable the SATA native support property, and then install it.

Start up and press F10 to enter BIOS and find the SATA setup, disable SATA.

For HP dv6000 series and dv9000 series laptops, press F10 at start up to enter BIOS and find Virtual Technology, and disabled it.

Once this is completed, you can install the system normally. If the installation disc already has an integrated SATA disk driver, then you don't need to download the SATA driver.

Here's how to install the disk SATA driver:

Download the HP laptop SATA driver for your computer, and save it to a floppy disc. Afterwards, connect the USB floppy drive to the laptop. Use the XP installation disc to start installing the XP system. During the installation process, press F6 to load the SATA driver. Then there will be a prompt asking you to choose. Press S and then Enter. However, this method needs an external floppy drive.

Secondly, there's an installation disc with the integrated SATA drive off-the-peg on the Internet, choose the system with the SATA driver, download it and then install.

Hardware problem

Sometimes when we start the machine, we may get a prompt "DISK BOOT FAILURE, INSERT SYSTEM DISK AND PRESS ENTER", and the disk cannot be read even in BIOS. There are many reasons for such a failure. We can remedy this case by.

Cause 1: the hard disk connection to the motherboard is loose, oxidized or open.

Solution: remove the disk and try re-installing it. Try removing the disk cable connector and then plug it back, or replace the disk cable;

Cause 2: some motherboards disable the SATA interface by default, so when loading the default BIOS settings, we may encounter that the SATA disk could not be found.

Solution: Update BIOS or enter BIOS and enable the SATA interface. As different motherboards have different configuration methods, please refer to the motherboard manual before modifying it.

Cause 3: some HP laptops (like dv9000) have 2 hard disk devices, which have a "Master" and "Secondary". If the "Master" disk drive is vacant, and the system is installed on the "Secondary" disk drive, BIOS cannot inspect the hard disk.

Solution: install the Operating system back to the "Master" disk drive.

Cause 4: if you use the laptop under heavy a heated environment for a long period of time, the components on the hard disk might get damaged because of overheating.

Solution: connect an external USB fan to cool down the laptop hard disk. Position the fan closest to the laptop hard disk. If the hard disk is already damaged by overheating, then you'll need to replace it promptly.

7.2 Repair flow chart to eliminate failures such as windows not loading, auto restart and blue screen error.

7.2.1 Repair shortcuts for failures such as Windows not loading, machine restarting, and blue screen error.

The laptop doesn't load Windows or restarts repeatedly

A) General easy replacement

Windows doesn't load or auto restarts repeatedly and a blue screen error appears. Any of these failures can be a real headache for a technician during the repair process. The occurrences of these failures are caused by either certain hardware problems, or software issues, or a combination of both. In all, Windows 7 / Vista/XP blue screen failures can be a combination of very complex causes which cannot all be explained in this article, but we will focus on hardware incompatibility of drivers, software issues, and viruses. I will provide some general solutions for you. When it comes to repeated restarts or blue screen failures, you should first check these solutions to eliminate them. Get prepared to solve more than 2 problems at once; usually we'll start with software then the hardware failure:

This is a simple and convenient method:

1) Go to the back cover of the laptop and feel the air flow of the intake with your hand. Observe if there's an accumulation of dust blocking the intake, and then open the back cover of the laptop, take a look at the fan, look for dust built up or whether the fan may have signs of aging or rotation issues. Power on and check it again to ensure there is no noise and the rotation is good and fast. If the fan doesn't rotate properly or is slow, there may be overheating problems, which can cause the system to turn off automatically to protect itself. Refer to overheating issues in chapter 6.

2) After confirming that the failure is not due to overheating, the next step and easiest solution is to remove all original hard disks. Install a good working hard disk and then reinstall the operation system again. Verify that the Operating system can be completely installed successfully and working. If the OS installed is now working properly, it then indicates that it was software or the hard disc, but if the failure symptom still exists after changing the hard disks, then I believe it has nothing to do with software. In this case, the possible failure range has been shortened greatly. You can now easily find the issue by eliminating parts one at a time. The problem comes from the hardware (excluding original hard disks);

B) Check the laptop memory

65% failures of Windows startup issues come from either the original hard disk or the laptop memory. If you are unsuccessful in installing the OS as explained above, then of course the problem comes from hardware. Then the possibility of it being the laptop memory issue increases. You can use software to test the memory or replace the memory RAM cards, but it's best to use the method by elimination. This way we can quickly locate where the issue is.

Next are some detailed methods:

(1) Try Memtest86 to check the memory, the accuracy rate could reach 99.6%

Memtest86 is a test application based on Linux core. It is open-source software, the test accuracy is very high, and some memory recessive problems can also be inspected.

Although the accuracy of Memtest86 test memory would not reach 100%, compared to some common test software, it can inspect more accurate memory values, because Memtest86 doesn't need an operating system. It is designed to start from a floppy drive or disc and no matter what system the computer installs; it can be used to test the memory in any way. All that it means is that it could test accurately in any system platform such as Linux, UNIX, and Windows etc.

Another advantage of Memtest86 is the E820 technology, which makes Memtest86 like the BIOS menus to display all usage situations of memory resources. How do you use Memtest86 software to test the laptop memory? Click the link below for a more detailed description:

http://www.computercare.ca/forum/showthread.php?t=236

(2) Use the memory replacement repair method to find the faulty memory;

Many cases indicate that the most common reason for startup issues such as blue screen, repeated restart or beeping at start up, is that the memory has failed. The memory is the easiest part to inspect and replace on a laptop. So you can do this and if there are two modules in the laptop, then you don't have to buy a new RAM module to test it. You can first remove the two memory cards. (For most models, you first need to remove one to two bolts at the bottom of the laptop) and then install one memory card at a time and test. Install one memory card to slot A and B2 once, and there are 4 tests in all for both memory cards. If you need a memory module from another laptop to test your laptop, ensure that they are the same type of module

Important! When testing the memory step by step remember to pull out the AC adapter and remove the battery.

(C) Check up laptop hard disk

If disk replacement helped to finish the OS installation successfully, then the problem comes from software or the original hard disk. Just as its name implies, if you doubt whether the problem is from software, then back up your personal material and reinstall Windows. If the failure is gone, then your doubt is correct, otherwise, the hard disk itself is the issue; however, if 2 failures exist at the same time, then you should continue to investigate further. Test the hard drive of the laptop with the HP Hard Drive Self Test, usually the test result is accurate, but not 100%. So it's still easier to test with another had disk. Please take a look at Figure 7-1.

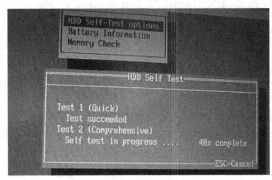

Figure 7-1

(1) Auto restart and blue screen failures caused by software

Sometimes viruses might cause a Windows blue screen and crash like some shock wave and surge wave viruses. Spyware may cause a blue screen too. One of the most common methods is to use antivirus software and anti-spyware to scan the disk. Put the laptop disk into an external hard drive box with a USB interface to make it into a USB movable disk. Then connect it to a normal working PC through an external USB port, and then scan and check twice with some spyware or adware removal tools. As for the problems of virus damage, we can use the latest antivirus software to kill viruses; as for Spyware damage issues, generally we can eliminate them with an anti-spyware. This method is quite effective to repair laptops and is widely used.

1) New driver and new service

If you have just installed a new driver for a certain hardware, or just installed some software, (Such as antivirus software, CPU cooling software, firewall etc.) which adds a complication to system service and a blue screen error occurs when restarting or running, then it is typically a software problem, and can be removed under safe mode.

2) Timing software or plan task software

For example, if you set "Restart" or load some work applications in the "Plan taskbar", when the time arrives, the computer will start again. This is the so-called auto-start failure. For this situation, we can use "Startup" and check whether there are some unfamiliar executive files or other timing applications. Shield them and then restart to check this. Of course, we can directly type "Msconfig" command to "Run" dialog to choose startup items.

3) System file damage

When a system file is corrupted, for instance, the basic files are corrupted when the system runs, then the system cannot finish initialization and is forced to restart. For such a failure, as you cannot enter normal desktop, you would just have to recover or reinstall Windows.

4) Trojan invasion

Of course, there's also another possibility that when surfing on Internet, your computer is invaded maliciously and Trojans or downloaded. Then the other side could control everything on your computer from a remote place, of course, including allowing your computer to restart. For some Trojans, those are difficult to eliminate it much easier just to reinstall your operating system.

(2) Auto start and blue screen error caused by hardware

1) New hardware

If there were no issues prior to installing the software and all of a sudden you get start up issues or a blue screen then you are sure it's a software problem. If it occurs after installing hardware, then it would be a typical hardware problem. You should check if the new hardware is plugged in properly.

A problem neglected by many people usually may cause some inexplicable failures. For instance, before installing the wireless network card, memory stick, hard disk and DVD-ROM, you should first confirm that the hardware itself has no problem, pull it out and plug back in again. Meanwhile, you should check if the hardware is compatible from the manufacturer website and whether the hardware installed is compatible with the motherboard.

2) If there's no restart or blue screen error after installing the hardware, then after installing the new driver a problem is detected, then it's a typical combination problem of software and hardware. When faced with this situation, we should check if the hardware driver installed is incorrect, please enter "My Computer"—"Control Panel"—"System"—"Device manager", check the laptop, whether there's some hardware installed incorrectly or there's a conflict. Remove the driver under Windows safe mode and then download the correct driver, try reinstalling different versions of drivers. If the blue screen still occurs after changing drivers, then probably there's an incompatibility issue between the hardware and the laptop motherboard or the hardware driver and the operating system, which might belong to a software combination problem. Refer to the hardware compatibility type on the Microsoft website; check whether the hardware is compatible with the operating system. If your hardware is not in the list, then you should go to the hardware manufacturer website.

3)   Defective DC power cable, power adapter jack or a bad connection causes restart.

A problem with the DC power plug on the cable or the laptop can easily cause an issue when the soldering points are oxidized or broken with use. Additionally, if the pin of the power adapter is degraded, then it would cause a bad connection with the laptop DC jack and a large resistance would be produced. After prolonged use, the jack connection might loosen due to heat, which activates the power protection output because the power adapter is short of power. When the DC output is stopped, the load drops right away, and then the DC power output starts again. At this moment, the computer will restart and the power indicator light will keep flashing.

Solution: replace the power adapter with one of higher power and better quality and change the DC jack input on the laptop.

(4)   Hard disk problem

During the regular usage of the laptop, if you move it briskly or it is manipulated from one area to the other and you aren't careful when it is still running, it can impact the hard drive. It is constantly rotating at high speed and may cause damage to the internal software and hardware, causing bad tracks and sectors, or making the machine start slowly and fail to load windows. Meanwhile, during the working process, probably sudden restart or blue screen error will happen. If this is the situation, then you can use some special tools to eliminate the problems or if seriously damaged, then you can only replace the hard disk.

(5)   Adjust the hard disk cache

When the system partition capacity is very small, probably the virtual memory value of the machine is very low. This situation would cause a blue screen error. When problems like this occur, we should release space on the disk or let the system auto set up virtual memory to settle the problem down. The easiest way is to delete the temp files on system partition (generally drive C) and keep the system space around 5%, in other words, 100GB disk needs 5GB space left. If the files on drive C cannot be deleted, then we can enter "My Computer"—"Control Panel"—"System"—"Advance", "Configure Performance" option. Find the "Virtual Memory" option, set "Customized Size" as "System Management Size" for the drive page file. In this case, the blue screen issue is due to the fact that there is a shortage of system drive and very low cache.

(6)   Update laptop BIOS

If we get the blue screen error during the process of using a laptop, such as the motherboard BIOS does not support hard disks of large capacity, then we could update BIOS to solve the problem.

7.2.2   65% of repeated restart and blue screen error comes from hard disk and memory

Most of laptop repeated restart failures are due to hard disk and RAM memory.

1. During the process of using a laptop, suddenly, the machine restarts repeatedly, a blue screen error occurs, and there's no any response by pressing any key. Occasionally, it will restart, but fails to finish loading Windows. Touch the disk and heated parts on the laptop, and if you find that the temperature is normal. (If there was no overheating symptom that occurred before), then you can eliminate the possibility of startup protection because of overheating. If there's no way to repair the installation with a Windows disc, then this kind of failure, mostly, is connected to hard disk and memory issues;

2. As much as 65% of blue screen errors and repeated restart failures are due to aging hardware such as the hard disk which can over time end up with bad tracks and sectors, and also RAM memory modules can be used or of bad quality; therefore, failures would easily happen when the machine is running. We can use the HP Hard Drive Self Test to test the disk drive of the laptop. It is the most common failure that the disk self test would uncover, generally, the main solution for it is to repair the disk or directly replace it.

3. A blue screen error will also happen if the memory RAM card is loose. You should first remove the RAM card and then plug it into the slot again; if it is because of the quality of the memory chip itself, then a similar failure would appear. The only solution is to change to a new RAM card. However, pay close attention when updating RAM memory, if you mix memories of different specifications or the memory card is incompatible with the motherboard, then the failures will also happen.

4. It is very rare to get the blue screen due to other hardware issues other then the hard disk or memory; knowing this, 65% of your repair troubleshooting have been solved

7.2.3   25% of repeated restart failures and blue screen errors are from motherboard overheating and viruses.

25% of the time these issues are from motherboard overheating and viruses problems:

The GPU chip and CPU produce a lot of heat when the notebook is operating, so it's quite important to keep them cool, and ensure they have good ventilation. The laptop cooling affects laptop stability, if the thermal cooling is not good enough and the machine works for a long period of time. It will then probably cause problems;

Most people might think that there's no problem with software updates, but in fact, during the update process, shared components will also update, and in turn may not be compatible with some applications, will not support the components updated, and finally all kinds of problems may occur. Occasionally, when downloading the software, there might be viruses attached to them that can modify your system when updating, and that can cause blue screens and restart issues. If you encounter this problem, restart and go into safe mode to remove or disable them, and then clean the virus with a virus scan.

Attacks by unknown Trojans or viruses, is the reality today on the Internet, especially on some BBS sites. You may expose your IP, so "Hackers" can attack you with their software. Restarts are caused by computer viruses, such as the typical "three waves" virus causing large damages to global computers, especially "shock wave", outbreaks that will prompt you that the system will auto start in 60 seconds. As for the restart failures caused by viruses, we can scan and kill them with the latest antivirus software. Also some Trojans are not that easy to get rid of. Here we suggest reinstalling the operation system and setting up security options to hide your computer IP.

7.2.4   5% of repeated restart failures and blue screen errors are caused by Windows itself

There are a small percentage of system failures, caused by Windows. For example:

1)   Windows important files have become corrupted or missing;
2)   Windows registry table is corrupted and it causes incorrect file pointing;
3)   Windows system files are damaged, and initialization could not finish when the system starts;
4)   DirectX problems as below:

   (a)   DirectX version is too old or to recent;
   (b)   A game is incompatible with it or not supported;
   (c)   Assistant important files are missing;
   (d)   The Graphic card doesn't support it.

For these failures, repair with the Windows installation disc, or reinstall the OS system and you may need to upgrade hardware where possible.

7.2.5 Failure symptoms and repair flow chart when the laptop is unable to load Windows, includes repeat starts and blue screen.

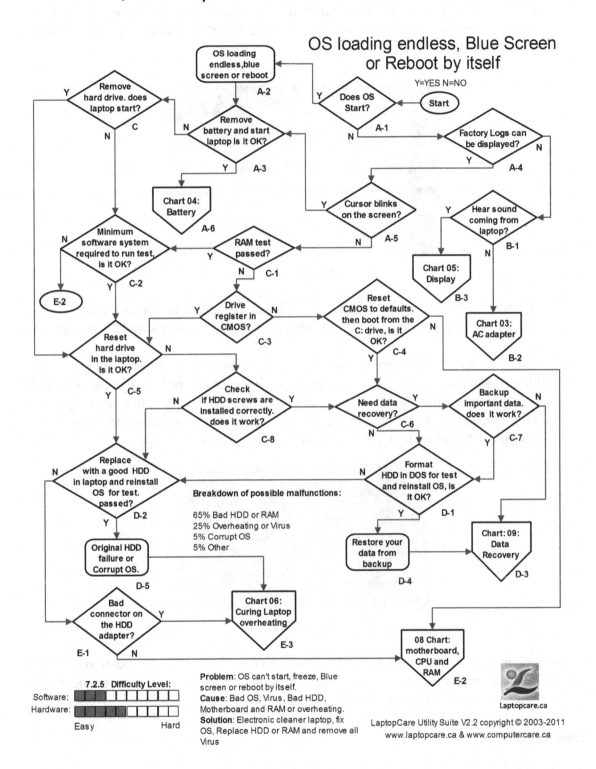

OS loading endless, Blue Screen or Reboot by itself

Y=YES N=NO

Breakdown of possible malfunctions:

65% Bad HDD or RAM
25% Overheating or Virus
5% Corrupt OS
5% Other

7.2.5 Difficulty Level:

Software:
Hardware:

Easy — Hard

Problem: OS can't start, freeze, Blue screen or reboot by itself.
Cause: Bad OS, Virus, Bad HDD, Motherboard and RAM or overheating.
Solution: Electronic cleaner laptop, fix OS, Replace HDD or RAM and remove all Virus

LaptopCare Utility Suite V2.2 copyright © 2003-2011
www.laptopcare.ca & www.computercare.ca

This tutorial will help you solve the problem

1. When you plug-in the power adapter, press the start button, the laptop starts, but doesn't load Windows and there's no error prompt except the cursor is flashing. Please take a look at Figure 7-2.

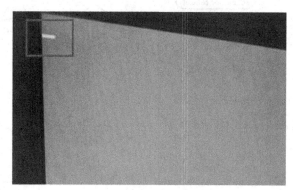

Figure 7-2

2. Windows appears at start up but doesn't finish loading or Windows loading endless, freezes, or it shuts down automatically, and restarts automatically over and over again.
3. After the laptop starts up and works, Windows begins loading. But before long, a blue screen occurs, there's an error prompt, or the blue screen doesn't appear, but it prompts that some files are missing and you need to reinstall the operating system. After reinstalling the operating system, the error prompt remains the same and the OS cannot be reinstalled. Please take a look at Figure 7-3.

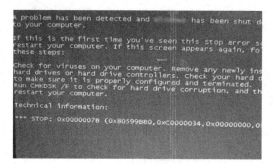

Figure 7-3

In this article, I will explain how to find the failure cause for a failure to load Windows or repeated failed starts, Windows freezes or a blue screen error occurs. This is generic and can be adapted to many brands and models.

Step: 1

You should first ensure that your power adapter is in good working condition. If something is wrong with it, it will affect the reliability and accuracy of your troubleshooting process.

When you plug-in the power adapter, start the laptop, watch your laptop reaction carefully. It should not have one of the 3 independent problems below.

1- After starting up, the power adapter light is on, but the machine doesn't start, the system configuration cannot be loaded, and the screen is totally black, no logo appears, and the cursor is not flashing. If this is the case it doesn't belong to the problems covered by this tutorial, check another tutorial article: such as 04, 05 or 08 tutorials.

2- Windows appears after the laptop starts up, but takes forever to load or takes over 10 minutes and then Windows freezes. Occasionally it might automatically start. Probably this is caused by the motherboard overheating or for some other problem and it's quite likely that this situation might not be covered in the range of this tutorial. Take a look at tutorial (06).

3- After the laptop starts running and finishes loading, a prompt appears on Windows that some files are missing, and there is no blue screen failure happening. This situation is not covered here and is an application or software problem covered elsewhere.

If you cannot determine your laptop failure cause, then you can refer to the chapter <<2.1 Common judgment for laptop failures>>, which has 6 sections to help you define the problem. If it still doesn't work, then you can follow the principle of "easy first and difficult next", adopting these tutorials one by one, and then taking it step by step.

Step: A-1 the target of this setup is to ensure whether your laptop can finish self-inspection

Let's take a look at 3 different situations below:

Situation 1: the laptop has no display at all

When you plug-in the power adapter and press the start button, the laptop makes a starting sound, the LED light is on, but the screen has no Windows loading display, even the manufacturer logo doesn't appear, and the screen is blank. If this is the case, then your problem is not part of this tutorial, please check repair flowchart: 03 or 05 tutorials.

Situation 2: The power adapter is good, the manufacturer logo appears normally, but self-inspection is extremely slow, and after a period of time you don't see the system loading picture. Occasionally there may be a cursor flashing on the top left side of the screen. With this scenario, the first step is to check your hard disk interface, whether it's loose or not; you would have to confirm whether your hard disk is connected properly to the motherboard. If you are sure of this situation, then enter STEP: A-4;

Situation 3: if after pressing the start button, the laptop power indicator light starts, the manufacturer logo appears and just when self-inspection finishes, the system speed becomes extremely slow, no longer loads, and freezes for a long time. After it shuts down automatically, it restarts. This repeats over and over again. The worst scenario is a blue screen error appearing. So as long as you can confirm one of these situations enter STEP: A-2.

Step: A-2 the goal of this procedure is to verify that the system freezes, and blue screen or restart symptoms happen when the laptop loads the system?

Error prompt, blue screen, Window freezing, auto shutdown, are issues we all encounter at one time or another. Some of these failures come from software; but a majority of them come from hardware. These last few years, because of the improvement and quality of the operating system and the security defence of the advanced features of antivirus software, these kinds of failures caused by software have decreased dramatically. In turn these failures have increased dramatically with hardware problems, and have become more complicated which can lead to software issues. Therefore, first make sure the hardware is good, and then check the software. If you believe this is the case enter Step: A-3: If the laptop has been used for a period of time, or alternately every 10 minutes and A Windows freezing symptom appears, or the machine starts up automatically, then it IS NOT COVERED BY the range of this tutorial, please check tutorial article 06.

STEP: A-3 the goal of this setup is to ensure the laptop starts normally under external power supply mode?

We have many cases indicating that because of battery issues, Windows does not load. Just because the battery is new does not eliminate it as a problem. Sometimes you will notice that the battery is dead within a month. Probably before you bought this battery, it was stored in a warehouse for more than 6 months or even a year and it has deteriorated due to self discharge. Even if it was never used this can happen. If the battery is not new; it is more likely to be suspect. Additionally, laptop BIOS can also cause some incompatibility symptoms with certain batteries. To check this, remove the battery and only use the power adapter to start the laptop. If it starts normally you have confirmed a battery problem. This test method is necessary, but if it doesn't help, then also use a new power adapter to make sure the adapter is not the problem. If the problem is solved, continue using STEP: A-6 to test your battery, if it's unsolved, continue STEP: C-3

STEP: A-4 the goal of this procedure is to determine the types and properties of the issues with your laptop.

Let's take a look at the two different situations below:

Situation 1: plug-in the power adapter, press the start button, then watch your laptop screen carefully to see if the manufacturer logo appears even briefly. As long as logo appears, it means the laptop screen is working properly. Under this circumstance, please enter STEP: A-5

Situation 2: press the start button and you notice that no manufacturer logo appears. Observe your laptop screen closely under a strong shining light, check the screen from a side angle carefully to see if the picture is very dim, and hold your ears close to the laptop to check if the fan and disk rotation sounds can be heard. And enter: STEP: B-1

STEP: A-5 the goal of this setup is to verify the hardware issued with the laptop

The laptop starts, the manufacturer logo appears, then it transitions to a blank screen indicating the laptop can't boot the operating system. There is no information on the screen and the white cursor flashes at the top left corner of the screen. We have many cases that can cause this:

1. The condition of a RAM memory card is bad and stops the laptop from loading Windows.
2. The hard drive boot application is corrupted or missing and reads the wrong message and therefore can't create a disk table or parameter table, which finally leads the system to freeze. For example, a virus destroys the files of the boot application.

If you find your laptop has a similar symptom, then probably the hardware has an issue. Please continue STEP: C-1, if it doesn't help continue to STEP: A-3.

Step: A-6

It indicates the problem is related to your battery; please check tutorial flowchart 04 (in chapter 04) regarding analysis and repair flow chart for a failure from the battery not being able to charge.

STEP: B-1 the goal of this setup is to choose a new repair flow chart

Let's look at two different situations below:

Situation 1: the laptop power indicator light is on, but it doesn't blink.

When you plug-in the power adapter and press the start button, the laptop power indicator light is on and laptop starts. Get close to the laptop and listen to determine if the fan and the disk is rotating. No matter which key is pushed at start up, you cannot see the manufacturer logo or system loading interface, which means the laptop, has some hardware problems. If it belongs to this situation, then enter STEP: B-3

Situation 2: the laptop power light is on or out.

Press the start button, and determine if the laptop power indicator light is on or out, either way, and the laptop has no starting sound from the disk or fan rotation. All devices that should make sound seem very quiet. It seems the problem might be with the power management and the motherboard. For these kinds of problems, first check the external power adapter with a multi meter to see if there's enough incoming voltage power, over voltage or low voltage which will all cause a condition that would make the machine auto shut down. If there's no problem observed above, then first focus the repair job in STEP: B-2

STEP: B-2 The goal of this setup is to choose repair flow chart 03

Your problem might be relevant to power, please check flowchart 03 (in chapter 03) tutorial article regarding laptop power failure analysis and repair flow.

STEP: B-3 The goal of this setup is to choose repair flow chart 05

Most often, when a laptop has a black screen failure after start up, the panel indicator light will be on, and the fan rotates normally, but sometimes there's speaker warning sound. Then follow the methods below.

The most important symptom is the warning you get from the speaker and that will help you determine the cause of the failure. Observe the on/off situation of the laptop when the failure happens. Try reinstalling your RAM memory module as it may not be seated properly. Try cleaning the RAM memory with an eraser or try moving the RAM card to the other slot. If all of these are not a problem, then your problem is quite likely with the LCD screen. Please check tutorial article 05 (in chapter 05) about laptop LCD failure analysis and repair flow.

STEP: C The goal of this setup is to find the reason why the failure occurs

The reasons why a laptop freezes, restarts and has a blue screen failure are quite complex, and sometimes you might see that a machine has more than one failure symptom. This chapter repair flowchart shows that the disk and memory occupy 65% of the failure rate and laptop overheating. Viruses and operating system issues occupy 30% of the failure occurrence rate, so both software and hardware might lead to this kind of failure, and at times both combined.

It's quite important to judge whether the laptop failure is caused by either software or hardware. To do this refer to the minimum system judgment method

<<1.4.2 Basic laptop repair methods>>

How do you determine what's causing the laptop failure? The key is that you need to confirm when the failure occurs, does it happen before or during the loading process. If you aren't sure then remove the hard disk from the laptop, and put a pure bootable DOS software CD into the CD-ROM/DVD-ROM. Next start the machine and test it. If the failure disappears, it indicates that the failure is with the hard disk and the installed operating system, so go to STEP: C-5, if the failure still occurs, then the failure range would be from overheating, memory stick or other hardware; please continue STEP: C-2

STEP: C-1 the goal of this setup is to confirm the failure is not related to laptop memory

1. I recommend you use Memtest86 software to test the memory as the accuracy is as high as 99.7%-99.9% and will confirm if there is a potential problem with the RAM memory card. Memtest86 is an application based on Linux kernel, supporting a 64-bit CPU, and is also an independent application needing, no any operating system required. The installation and usage of it are a little different from other memory test software. You have to create a bootable CD with Windows or Linux. On the homepage of Memtest86, there's an ISO file for the software, you can directly burn it into a CD, which can be tested with DVD-ROM/CD-ROM at start up.

2. Check whether the problem disappears if you pull the RAM memory card and re-insert it; before pulling and plugging it, you should first clean the dust and clear the (Edge Connector) gold plated board, including the slot too; pay attention when installing it to see whether it inserts smoothly. Not sticking, loose or the jack is too tight which can make it hard to insert it. Please take a look at Figure 7-4.

Figure 7-4

3. For some HP laptops, when the DIMM A doesn't have a plugged memory card, but there's one in the DIMM B slot, there may not be anything displayed or the laptop may auto restart. This problem is caused because this model's integrated display card requires the graphic memory to be a shared physical memory, while the designed physical memory is from the memory card plugged in DIMM A. So when there's no memory stick plugged in DIMM A, a problem would occur.

If the steps above doesn't help or you don't have Memtest86 memory test software to help you test the memory or you do have it, but failure still occurs then enter STEP: C-2, if you are sure that there's nothing wrong with your memory then enter STEP :C-3,

STEP: C-2 the goal of this setup is to run at minimum system with software to eliminate the laptop issue.

1. The Minimum system software is composed of the power adapter, motherboard, CPU, memory, display card, LCD display, keyboard and DVD-ROM/CD-ROM. All other hardware should be removed, such as the network card, hard disk and so on.

Use a pure bootable DOS disc (such as: Memtest86 memory test software) or other professional Windows system disc (notice: not system installation disc), put it into laptop DVD-ROM/CD-ROM and start. It is mainly used to analyze and judge whether the system can finish normal start up and is running well.

2. If you cannot ensure 100% that the memory is good, then you are better to change to a known working memory card to validate the test; however, you have to make sure of the technical index of the original memory, such as DDR1, DDR2, and you have to find out the running speed of these memory types. Make sure the memory you are changing is compatible with your laptop 100%, and it should work normally. Afterwards, install it in the computer and then test and validate.

3. It is more convenient when you have two memory modules. Likely one of the memory modules is defective; you can try to eliminate the problem by removing all the memory cards, and then try putting one memory card into the other memory slot and test it. Then you can do the same with the other. If the method of memory card exchange cannot help, then I'm quite sure the problem is with the memory.

4. Through pulling and plugging the CPU, check whether the failure disappears or not. Before pulling and plugging in the CPU, first clean and change the thermal silica gel. Most cases of a bad contact between the CPU and motherboard will cause a problem. When installing a CPU, pay attention to whether it had been too loose or the jack is too tight. Sometimes, some pins may be a little bent which would prevent the CPU from inserting in the right position. Under this circumstance, fix the bent pin and reinstall the CPU; and then press the chip down gently, don't push too hard to avoid damaging it. Make sure it is oriented the right way.

5. When a laptop overheats, the RAM (cache) easily gets damaged, and puts up a blue screen error, auto shutdown or system freeze. Usually at start up, when the laptop finishes the self-inspection, the hard disk should start the operating system. You should therefore test the CPU on another laptop motherboard, which will give a good indication of the problem of the cache. If you are sure it's defective, you should consider changing the CPU. However it's very rare that the CPU causes this problem, the rate of such an issue is 1 in a thousand. Please take a look at Figure 7-5.

Figure 7-5

6. When the laptop overheats, the GPU cache would also get easily damaged, and it behaves as a blue screen, black screen, disordered codes, blurry screen or interface freezing problems; therefore, this step requests changing the display card (except if

it's integrated) to validate the test. If the steps above don't help, then your problem is likely to be with the motherboard, please enter STEP: E-2, if the problem is solved, or there's no problem found at all, then your problem may still be relevant with the hard disk, continue STEP: C-5

STEP: C-3 the goal of this setup is to confirm that CMOS can recognize the hard drive

The System doesn't recognize your hard disk, such failures are quite common, namely, the operating system doesn't start from the hard disk and there's no way to enter drive C. The CMOS auto inspection function also fails to find the existence of the hard disk. Fortunately, now the CMOS has the function to recognize the type of hard disk automatically, and will automatically inspect it. When the disk type and capacity are incompatible with the motherboard, then the system might fail to start, sometimes it will, but a read/write error will occur, or a blue screen failure will appear:

1. For instance, the disk recognized the capacity in CMOS but less than the actual disk capacity, namely, the total capacity of the used disk is bigger than the maximum capacity that the CMOS sees. The backside sectors of the hard disk cannot read/write if it's partitioned, then some partitions may be lost.

2. Another important failure cause is that some hard disks have been used on another brand of laptop with the installed operating system data of the former laptop, and then it was installed into another laptop and used. If you haven't formatted the hard disk, then you'll get a "read/write error". As CMOS can recognize the hard disk correctly, it directly influences the normal use of the disk, after using it in another laptop. The change in CMOS might lead the data position of the original disk to not be available. Finally the laptop cannot load Windows or repeat the system start up and blue screen failure occurs.

STEP: C-4 the goal of this procedure is to confirm that the issue is with the CMOS of the motherboard.

1. The CMOS auto inspection function failure when it doesn't find the hard disk is usually due to the hard disk or the IDE (SATA) port connected to the adapter. A CMOS failure is quite rare; so we should use the elimination method. Remove the laptop hard disk, pull and plug the hard disk connection adapter, or change the IDE (SATA) disk port. You will quickly find the failure. Replace it with a new hard disk and test, but pay attention that the disk is installed on the motherboard through a connecting adapter. There are one to two screws tightly locking the disk interface, which you should remove. Be careful when disassembling, otherwise you can break the connector pins and that would cause a disaster.

2. If the CMOS still doesn't recognize the hard disk, then the common reason is that the disk capacity is incompatible with the maximum CMOS capacity, and therefore the result is it cannot be inspected. If the capacity of the new plugged hard disk is

the same as the original one, then it's quite likely there's something wrong with the CMOS, which needs to be discharged and repaired.

3. Is the new disk recognized and the displayed parameters correct? Is the disk size equal to its actual value and the capacity after formatting correct?

Attention: generally the marked capacity takes 1000 as a unit label, while in BIOS a formatted capacity is shown in the unit of 1024, there's 3% to 5% difference between them. After formatting the capacity is less then the one displayed in BIOS.

4. The CMOS battery is used to store system information, such as the time, the boot sequence and other relevant system data. If the CMOS battery voltage is too low or disabled, then the system will not start, hardware will not be recognized, that sort of thing. Therefore, it's obviously important to check the laptop CMOS battery. Remove it for about 5 minutes and then plug-in a new CMOS battery. Before starting this, you will need to remove the main battery and pull out the external power adapter. When complete, press the power button for 30 seconds then connect the power adapter on its own, then start the laptop. Set the first boot device as the hard disk in the BIOS.

If the steps above didn't help you and the CMOS still doesn't recognize the existence of the hard disk, then your problem is quite likely to be with the motherboard. Enter STEP: E-2; if the problem is solved and the CMOS recognizes the new disk parameters correctly, then the failure might have been with the original disk. Please continue to STEP: C-6

STEP: C-5 The goal of this setup is to confirm the failure is not with the laptop hard disk or the disk connection adapter.

1. **After removing the disk, you need to look, smell and touch it;**

    a. **Look:** whether the element component on the disk circuit board is distorted, turns color broke or incomplete;
    b. **Smell:** take the disk out and see if it smells like burnt plastic rather then what a normal hard disk would smell;
    c. **Touch:** touch the disk circuit board and feel to see if it seems to have been overheated or really hot. If so we now know it has failed.

2. **Check the disk connection adapter;**

    a. Check the adapter that connects to the hard disk, whether it's connected properly or not.
    b. Whether the disk connection adapter is broken or cracked or not, if so think of replacing the disk adapter;
    c. Whether the disk connection adapter jack has some bended or broken pins or not; other then observation we can change a disk connection adapter to check it;
    d. The connection between the disk adapter and the hard disk should not be loose or out of position.

3. **Check the connection between the disk adapter and the motherboard:**

   a.   The Connection between disk adapter and motherboard should not be too loose or out of position;

   b.   Whether there's a break or crack trace on the motherboard disk interface or not. We can check the motherboard closely with a magnifying glass.

   c.   After powering on, check whether the disk drive rotation sound is normal, there should not be abnormal sounds or loud noise;

   d.   After powering on, check whether the machine disk light flashes normally or not, it should not be either out or always on.

   e.   Listen to for an abnormal sound at start up from the disk. If the disk has an abnormal sound or is noisy, replace it.

4. **This is the diagnosis method for the problem that the operation system will not start up**

   First check at start up, whether there's an abnormal sound or none at all from the hard disk, then check to see if there's something wrong with the disk connection adapter, only then you can conclude that the issue is with the disk.

Observe through the displayed contents: pay close attention to the error contents and the positions of the blue screen when the system freezes to ensure which part has the issue.

   a.   When the operating system is starting, if the system goes down, a blue screen occurs, or it just auto restarts, then it means the disk partition table and main boot record are OK, so we can eliminate that as a failure factor. Next continue the method of STEP: D-2 to diagnose further.

   b.   If the self-inspection passes, and just before the operating system starts, it goes down and you get a either a white cursor flashing or a system auto restart, then you should first check if there's something wrong with the connection between the disk and motherboard, and then consider whether the hard disk has issues Next continue the method of STEP: C-8 to diagnose further.

STEP: C-6 The goal of this setup is to confirm whether your data (file) needs backup.

To a certain extent, the most important part of a laptop is the hard disk, because it carries all kinds of data. For such disks, the value cannot be valued in money. Almost every user has important personal data stored in their personal computer. There might be digital pictures, trade invoices, technical material, emails and personal files and contacts.

Digital pictures are very valuable. Digital cameras are very popular, so many users take hundreds of pictures of family members, special occasions and then simply store them on their personal computer. Young parents tend to take many pictures of their kids as they grow up and also store them on their computer. If there was ever something that happens to their computer or had disk, all data would be lost along with all other information stored in it. You can imagine the devastation it would cause.

If you have an independent backup for your important data, then continue to STEP: D-1; If your data hasn't been backed up yet, then continue to STEP: C-7;

STEP: C-7 The goal of this procedure is to confirm that the backup of the data (file) is completed.

a.   Decide what to backup

It's up to each individual to decide what needs to be backed up. Anything that cannot be replaced such as pictures, important files, favourite web sites, contacts etc. Make a list of the important information that is irreplaceable. This list will help to make sure all necessary files are backed up and also provide you a reference list when searching for them. Next are some file suggestions to backup:

* Personal documents and letters;
* Digital pictures;
* Bank records or financial information;
* Music and videos;
* Emails and contact names, your mail address book (Microsoft Outlook)
* Software you bought or the one downloaded from Internet;
* Bookmarks of Internet browser.

b.   Find the storage position for the files

To back up files successfully, you'll need to spend some time searching where on your hard drive they are located. By default settings, most applications save files to the folder "My Documents"; but some users sometimes change the path to another area which makes backing up take longer then it should. Most backup utility tools allow you to choose the backup file type or folder. When you execute a backup for the first time, you may need to backup twice; one is for some specified types and the other is for specified folders.

Note:

In Win XP system, the default position of users file is C:\Documents and Settings\<user name>\My Documents.

In Vista, the default position of user's files is: C:\Users\<user name> \Documents

To search files and ensure which folders are included in the file for backup, please finish the next tasks:

1.   Click "Start"—"My Computer", open Windows explorer, and then choose "Local disk (C:\)"drive;
2.   Choose "File"—"Search", open the "Search result" window;

Enter the file extension of common file type to the field "All or partial field name", and then click "Search".

3. For instance: keyed text *.doc, *.xls, *.txt, *.pst, then you can search Word documents, excel tables, plain text file and the mails in Outlook. Separate the file name by comma and blank;

4. After searching finishes, choose "View"—"Detail information", then you can check the file name and full path;

5. Check the list; decide which files to save and the storage position.

If you have finished backing up the important data, go to method STEP: D-1 to repair. If some of your data cannot be backed up, such as:

1) folders that cannot be opened,
2) D drive and folders are locked and so on, and then please continue STEP: D-3

STEP: C-8 The goal of this procedure is to confirm that the connection between the disk and motherboard is in good condition

1. This will check the contact problem between hard disk and motherboard. The method to follow is to pull out the disk connection adapter, and check whether there's dust inside the connector, or any other obstructions. If there is, then use a brush or air compressor to clean it up. Sometimes dried up liquids should be cleaned up with a needle to remove them.

2. Most HP laptops have 1 to 3 screws that attach the hard disk to the motherboard. When repairing a laptop, you need to check whether these screws are well in place and are tight enough. This is a potential cause of failures.

3. Pull out and plug-in the hard disk, and then check whether the failure disappears. The power on/off process is the most fragile time for a hard disk. At this moment, the rotation speed of the disk bearing is not stable, and if there's some vibration, a bad track easily forms. Therefore, I suggest waiting for about 10 seconds after shutting down the machine to allow the disc rotation to stop before moving the laptop.

4. Power on and test the hard disk, notice the vibration from the hard disk. If there is a lot of vibration it may be due to bad tracks or the magnetic head is damaged. So be extremely careful when removing and transporting the hard disk.

STEP: D-1 The goal of this setup is to confirm whether the original hard disk works or not.

The Hard disk is one of the most indispensable components; It is also very fragile and as you use it, as time goes by, you will start getting issues that will begin appearing such as: the read/write speed will be slower, Windows will prompt "cannot read or write to the file", blue or black screen errors. Always back up your data on a regular basis because once errors begin to happen you may end up losing it if the hard disk decides to fail. Don't assume you can repair a hard disk because you will run into bigger issues.

The test and repair methods below are carried out without considering data backup, if you have very important data to backup, do so and try again or directly go to STEP: D-2 to repair the laptop. You can later go to situation 3 of STEP: D-5, there is detail information on how to diagnose and repair the software on the hard disk.

3 steps to test hard disk:

The first step: format the hard disk with a DOS 7.1 version, there are two functions for this:

1. Repair all problems caused by software, such as: corrupted disk partition, infected by viruses or logical lockup and so on.
2. Check the disk interface for bad physical tracks or sectors.

The second step: format the disk with a WIN XP/WIN 7 disc, there are two functions for this:

1. Repair issues caused by software, such as: missing NTLDR, and disk fails to start
2. Validate the original disk to verify if there is anything wrong.

The third step: Inspecting disk performance, if the two methods above still didn't eliminate the failure, then use the manufacturer's "Test Utility" software to inspect the disk completely.

The point of the first step is to first enter into DOS but not the command prompt in Windows. Download DOS 7.1 software and then make a boot disk, but because nowadays most notebook no longer have a floppy disk, it needs to be on either a USB flash drive or on a CD/DVD. Once done, insert it and then type format c: If the hard disk finishes formatting successfully, then the issues below caused by software will also be solved:

a. Disk cannot read/write;
b. Primary boot application is corrupted;
c. Disk capacity doesn't equal with the marked value;
d. Disk gets infected by viruses, hacker software or gets logical lock;
e. The system auto restarts several times when booting up.
f. During the self-inspection process, the screen displays the disk is lost or not partitioned;
g. The system auto restarts several times, then a blue screen occurs;
h. The system often enters safe mode automatically;
i. Error prompts "DLL file xxxx is missing"
j. The disk partition is corrupted;
k. Logical bad sectors occur on the hard disk;
l. The system is unstable, and invalid errors often occur;
m. The registry often gets corrupted for no reason, and the system prompts the user to recover it;
n. The Computer has no display, or goes down randomly.

However, according to my years of experience, during the formatting process and or partitioning hard disk, the life of the disk is coming to its end and it is time to replace it.

1. During the formatting or partitioning process of the disk, the screen shows it's lost or can't be partitioned.
2. The hard disk doesn't format, the screen prompts "hard disk fail" and other information;
3. When doing self-inspection, the disk makes a "crackling sound" and the disk doesn't boot;
4. The disk formatting speed is extremely slow, and once formatted is completed, the screen prompts: xxxMB bad sectors.

Pay attention: The bad disk sector mentioned here means a physical bad sector, which is totally different from the logical bad sector mentioned previously. A logical bad sector doesn't affect much on the disk; it is generally caused by a wrong operation, viruses, and so on (such as accidental shutdown, power-off). The disk parcel and the disk body have no issues, to repair it, we only need to either format or use software tools.

A physical bad sector is caused by a damaged disk track, which cannot be repaired with any software or formatting. In fact, because of vibration, scratches and some other "hard reasons", the magnetic medium of some sectors has lost the ability for magnetic memory. Once there's a physical bad sector, it means the quality of the disk has diminished.

The point of the second operation: is when you install WinXP or Vista (Win 7), under Windows; you must format the disk again (initialization operation) and then the structure of the logical disk would be recreated, finally activating the partitions on the disk. Repair all disk boot failures caused by software, and then the NTLDR file missing problems. If no similar failures re-occur, it indicates that the laptop has been fixed. Please continue to method of STEP:-D-1 to continue. If you can't reinstall the operating system or the failure still exists after reinstalling the operating system, then continue to step three;

The point of the third step: first you would have to confirm the disk brand you use, and then use the manufacturers released software to test the disk. For instance, if you use a Seagate disk, then use the "Seagate test utility" software to inspect the disk; if you use a Western Digital disk, then please use a Western Digital manufacturer released software; there are several versions of inspection software so choose the correct version for the correct disk

Pay attention: this step is primarily for the inspection of the disk performance, usually, it is to test whether there's something wrong with the CODE. When the disk code has an error; the failure symptom would be that Windows runs really slow, the disk formatting speed is slow, and even the installation speed of the Windows system is so slow that you can't even finish the installation. After finishing the inspection of the disk performance, if there's a confirmed hardware issue with the disk, then continue to STEP:C-2 to repair it. If there's no issues with the disk, then continue to STEP: D-2 but if it's useless return to STEP:C-2, under minimum system and test the remaining hardware to see if there's something wrong;

Step: D-2 The goal of this procedure is to confirm an issue is with the original hard disk.

The best method to keep data: don't have the attitude of trying to fix the software of the original disk, but instead choose another good working one and install it on the laptop, then reinstall the operating system to validate it;

If you decide to replace it with a new disk, then follow these next rules:

1) the interface of the new hard disk must accord with the interface of the original hard disk, namely, if the original disk is an IDE interface, then the new one should be an IDE.
2) The capacity of the new disk should be better or close to the original one. It's not a good idea to use an oversized one when testing as BIOS may not recognize it, and if it's too big, it will cause yet another issue.

"Step: D-2" the goal of this step is to confirm whether the failure comes from the original hard disk or the software of the original disk.

It's better to do the testing with a new one, but you must ensure that the operating installation disc and DVD-ROM/CD-ROM are 100% free of issues; otherwise, it will be hard to make the right decision. During the operating system installation process or after finishing the installation, if the problem still exists, continue to method of STEP: E-1, or you will have to return to STEP: C-2 (After changing the disk, test whether there is something wrong with other hardware under the minimum system mode): if the system runs normally after installation, please continue to STEP: D-5.

STEP: D-3 If you cannot back up your data, then please go to the tutorial article 09 (in chapter 09) "laptop folder lock-up failure and hacking analysis".

STEP: D-4 The goal of this procedure is to confirm that the data (files) you need have already been recovered from backup.

According to our years of working experience, pay attention to the problems below, which will help you prevent any data loss.

1. **Recovery from the backup data disk to the laptop;** it needs to be scanned twice to recover data, one to scan for virus, and one to scan for anti-spyware. Many cases of data loss are caused by both of these. If your data is very important, then don't forget to use antivirus software which will lower the threat of viruses to a minimum. If you do not, viruses will return the same problem and you will lose your data.
2. **Use the "Copy-Paste" method instead of the "Cut-Paste"** to recover data, so that if an error occurs you still have a copy and can be recopied

3. When pasting data, we don't advocate using the method "Paste-Cover" to recover it, because some of the operating system files may be damaged and copied to the new installed operating system and fail to start the laptop.

4. Generally speaking, "My Documents", "Desktop", "Favourites", "Pictures" and "Music" folders are very important and have no operating system files. If your disk has a partition D, I suggest making a backup of these data files on drive D, including Outlook, Outlook Express and any other important files, that should also be put on a non-system partition, as the failure rate on system partitions is much higher then on others.

5. After the system crashes, if you do a backup for data like pictures, it usually will include the operating system along with any spyware or viruses. When recovering data, first recover the entire picture to data, and then put it into another hard disk and partition it. After checking and confirming what you did, copy the original data into drive C.

6. If you decide to use the "Picture-data" method to recover the backup file, then you must be clear about a few conceptions regarding the source disk, target disk, partition and the entire hard disk. Be cautious when operating, because even a computer expert can make some careless mistakes.

7. If you decide to partition your hard disk, then first finish this job before installing the operating system and recovering the data. Be cautious about PQ/DM (partition software), although some of the functions of this software are useful, they are a very dangerous tool. Once errors occur the data will be lost. Avoid using them as much as possible.

8. During the laptop repair process and recovery of data, pay attention when the disk is reading. Do not jar the laptop and there should be no undue vibration, otherwise, bad sectors might happen to the disk, which can cause a loss of data. Even when the disk is not reading, you should always avoid accidental shutdowns or, power-off. During the process pull and plug the USB interface and move or disassemble the disk, you must be very careful to follow the rules to avoid loss of data.

If all data is recovered without any issues, you have succeeded in repairing the computer. If the recovery fails, such as a locked folder or something else refer to the step of Step: D-3

Step: D-5 The goal of this procedure is to analyze and confirm the reason why the original disk has failed and various solutions to use.

Through the repair flow process above, we clearly indicated the hard disk and the software on the original hard disk was the problem. Here are 3 situations.

Situation 1:

From the repair flowchart path A-3->C->C-5->D-2-> to Step: D-5, there's apparently no back up data or disk formatting procedures. So if you need "data backup", you can refer to the operation methods of STEP: C-6 or STEP: C-7: to confirm that the data (files) needed are backed up.

If you need to format the disk, you can refer to method STEP: D-1: and verify if original disk can be reused, of course, if you have "Data backup" and don't want to format disk, then you can use the method of situation 3, and try repairing the operating system.

Situation 2:

From repair flowchart path C-4->C-6->D-1->D-2-> to Step: D-5, if the disk is already formatted go to STEP: D-1, Once, you've identified the problem, then you need to analyse it carefully, if one of the situations below happens to your laptop, then it's quite likely that your laptop has overheating issues, which has overheated the disk and created a failure. For instance:

1. The BIOS doesn't always see the hard disk, and after shutting down and letting it sit for a while, it works again.
2. The circuit board of the hard disk smells burnt which is different from usual normal plastic smell.
3. 20 minutes after starting up, the hard disk circuit feels really hot to the touch.
4. After changing to a new disk, and after a few hours of operation, the system freezes up and the symptoms start re appearing again.

    HP laptops are known not to have any special cooling apparatus for the hard disk but basically it relies solely on natural radiating. To compensate for this we suggest using a USB laptop cooling fan that can be placed underneath the laptop.

Situation 3:

From repair flowchart path C-4->C-6->C-7->D-1->D-2-> to Step: D-5, non DOS disk formatting procedure, first test the hard disk to see if there's no errors with the disk itself, then consider repairing the system software.

Generally speaking, HP laptops have a self disk inspection tool software in the system BIOS, although the accuracy of the tool isn't 100%, it's easy, convenient and safer especially for users unfamiliar with these types of software.

Here are the steps for the operation:

1. Press the power button to start the laptop;
2. When the HP or Compaq logo appears, press the F10 key to enter BIOS Setup;
3. When a main menu appears, pay attention to the BIOS version and find the option "HDD self-test options" or "Primary Hard Disk self test"
4. Choose the tool "software" and press Enter.

Disk scanning begins, the program uses the option "Full disk inspection", once scanning is completed, the results are shown on the screen, telling users the status of the disk. This is the simplest disk inspection method for beginners to use, but this is not a guarantee and there may still be issues. If the disk passes the inspection, then you can now consider repairing the system software:

The first step: first start the laptop in Safe Mode, check whether it starts, if it doesn't, then it's probably infected by a virus, system files are lost, the operating system is corrupted or there is an incompatible driver.

The second step: if it does start in safe mode, run your antivirus software. If there's a virus, then it probably caused the failure. After removing the virus, you need to restart the laptop; if it still fails, then think back whether you've installed new software before the failure occurred, such as an updated display card driver or new antivirus software. If this is the case you need to restart the laptop in Safe mode, undo the change, and restart it to see if you solved it. If the failure still exists, then you need to follow the fourth step below: and install the drivers one by one, restarting after each install.

The third step: if the laptop doesn't start in safe mode, then you need to remove the disk, and put it into a USB box, making it into an external USB hard disk. Then plug into a working laptop or desktop. Run updated antivirus software, and scan and kill any viruses. Remove the hard disk and re-install it in the laptop and restart to validate it. If the failure still exists, then follow the fourth step below.

The fourth step: to reinstall the operating system, some laptops have a "system recovery" function. For the purpose of this exercise we'll use an HP laptop. At start up, press the (F11) key. During the installation process, if a system crash, blue screen, restart or something happens, then maybe there's a hardware problem. Change the hard disk and return to STEP: C-2, After the system recovery is completed and the laptop works normally, the cause was a damaged operating system.

Conclusion of chapter: if your case belongs to <<Situation 1 or 2, please continue to the method of STEP: E-3

Step: E-1 The goal of this procedure is to analyze reasons why the disk doesn't work and implement solutions.

Situation 1: if we start from the repair flowchart path A-3 or A-4->C-5->D-2-> and then continue to Step: E-1, then the job has already been done, that is, the testing of the hard disk and the interface adapter is complete. What you now need to pay attention to is the second inspection method, if you don't use the "Replacement" method to test the disk interface adapter, you'll need to reconfirm it. If the problem isn't resolved follow situation 3 to deal with it.

Situation 2: if we start from the repair flowchart path C-4->D-1->D-2-> and continue to Step: E-1, then you'll need to make an analysis carefully and if you haven't done the failure confirmation process that Step: C-5 requires, then follow all 4 methods of Step: C-5. If the problem is still unsolved, then follow the situation 3 to deal with the problem.

Situation 3: if (situation 1 and 2) didn't help to explain why or resolve the hard disk problem, then try entering the BIOS process. If BIOS recognizes the hard disk, then it's kind of easy to solve the problem, the worse situation is that BIOS displays a "haven't installed" prompt. The result indicates that the problem is much more severe than what we considered. No matter what the situation is, it's time to shut down the computer, pull out the plug and disassemble the computer shell. Now check the power jack for the power adapter connection on the motherboard, to verify if it's OK and the disk connections, to ensure they are not off and the solder connections are solid. Since you are there, solder every joint again but be careful not to bend or solder two pins together to avoid a short circuit. Same goes for the solder points on the board, don't solder them together. According to the knowledge and experience already mastered, make a sound judgment. For the technology you are unfamiliar with or have no idea at all, consult someone with experience before adventuring into unknown areas as you can do some serious damage to you expensive laptop.

If the problem is still unsolved, remove the DVD drive, and then install the operation system with a USB external disk. Please check the post I have written previously << Install 64-bit Windows 7 from a USB disk >> (http://laptoprepair.ca/news/12117.html)

This method also works for the IDE interfaces on the motherboard. If you succeeded in installing the operating system with a USB disk, then you can try installing the removed DVD driver back to the laptop again, if the same problem appears again, then it's quite likely the laptop motherboard has some functional failures, which leads to a conflict between the DVD driver and the hard disk. Of course, chances are there's no issues with the DVD drive.

Conclusion of this chapter: if <<Situation 3>> solved your problem, then it's quite likely that laptop overheating caused the failure. To solve this problem, please continue to STEP: E-3. If <<Situation 3>> doesn't help solve your problem, then the problem is with the hard disk; so continue to Step: E-2; check the laptop motherboard failure tutorial for the processor to get further assistance.

STEP: E-2 the goal of this setup is to ensure that you choose repair flow chart 08. Your problem might be relevant with the motherboard and CPU, please check chapter 08 "failure concerning a laptop black screen or interface freezing".

Step: E-3 the goal of this procedure is to choose repair flowchart 06

Your problem might be caused by laptop overheating, therefore check the repair tutorial failure article (in chapter 06) regarding "curing laptop overheating" for help.

In summary to conclude this tutorial concerning laptop unable to load Windows or system repeat starting up, or blue screen failures; the possible reasons are system failure, virus infection, motherboard or memory failures, and laptop overheating.

Solution: clear up your laptop system, format the hard disk, or change the hard disk for one that is working, and recover your data. As for details, please refer to this tutorial. Thank you so much!

7.3 Twenty-eight repair cases for HP laptop repeated auto start and blue screen failures

7.3.1 Five repair cases of HP laptops for the repeated auto start and blue screen failures caused by viruses and Trojans

108) HP CQ61-306TX laptop repeatedly restarts after entering system

Failure symptom:

It enters system normally, but after installing application software, I restart the laptop and the antivirus software scans, but before entering the system, the hard disk light goes out, and then the system restarts over and over again, but after re-installing system the issue still remains.

Solution:

This failure symptom belongs to the description of flow chart 07 that belongs to sequence Start->A-1->A-2->A-3->C->C-5->C-8->C-6->D-1

Repair summary:

Step to repair C: remove the disk from laptop, put a pure bootable DOS software disc into the DVD-ROM/CD-ROM, then start the machine to test. The test result shows that the failure has disappeared. This indicates that the failure must be with the original hard disk and the operating system on it. To repair this issue use flow chart C-5, unplug and plug the HDD adapter again connect the hard disk back to the laptop. As a result of the above, the failure still remains. Thus, we exclude the bad connection failure between the hard drive disk and the motherboard, and we confirm the previous assumption further. If the customer does not which to keep their original data, then move to step D-1: First format the hard disk with DOS 7.1 version, then after format the hard disk with WIN XP/WIN 7 disc. Then reinstall the operating system, then start the machine and test again, this time the failures would have disappeared.

Hint:

Systems sometimes can be infected with viruses and even hacker software resulting in issues where the system goes into a loop and repeatedly restarts. Re installing the operating system isn't enough we need to format it with DOS to completely remove the viruses and then reinstalling a fresh copy of your operating system.

109)   HP dv4-1428TX blue screen failure

Failure symptom:

When laptop finishes self-inspection and begins loading operating system you get the "blue screen" failure, and there is no way to recover the system.

Solution:

This failure symptom belongs to the description of flow chart 07 and belongs to sequence: Start->A-1->A-2->A-3->C->C-5->C-8->C-6->D-1

Repair summary:

We know from the failure symptom that blue screen failure occurs when the system starts up, there are many reasons for this, they are software, and hardware problems. Here we solve the problem by process of elimination and exclude the possibility that there's a bad connection with the ram memory, hard disk, network card or just a quality issue. All these may affect the system from starting normally and leads to blue screen failure. First of all, remove the hard disk from the laptop; put in a pure bootable DOS Memtest86 software disc into the DVD-ROM/CD-ROM, start machine and test. The blue screen failures disappears; after excluding the possibility of hardware failure) hardware (RAM and so on) so now on to repairing the system software because we cannot recover it. It is either damaged or there is a virus and because the client did not request a back up of the data we can format and just reinstall the operating system.

Hint:

Some of the issues listed here such as: registry errors, shortage of virtual memory, dynamic link library file (. dll) is missing, resource is consumed and therefore can lead to situations where of driver error or application error occurs. Besides, hardware conflicts and hardware quality problem usually will spread to the system kernel level. Under these circumstances, the laptop will pause and stop the system from running, and thus enable the function named "KeBugCheck" to check all processes interrupted. Compare it to the preset stop code and parameters, and at that time, the screen will turn blue and display an error message and a failure prompt. We call it the scary "blue screen" of death.

When blue screen failure occurs, the culprit software or hardware will force and shut down the laptop abruptly and if it is repeated too many times, this can make the system become more and more unstable. You need to pay close attention to the error message and resolve it as soon as possible.

110) HP ELITEBOOK 8730W laptop shuts down after starting up

Failure symptom:

After self-checking, laptop begins loading the operating system, the laptop shutdown.

Solution:

This failure symptom belongs to the description of flow chart 07 that belongs to sequence:

Start->A-1->A-2->A-3->C->C-5->C-8->C-6->C-7->D-1->D-4

Repair summary:

When we analyze the failure symptom and combined it with step C of the flowchart, Remove the hard disk from the laptop, put a pure bootable DOS Memtest86 software disc into the DVD-ROM/CD-ROM and start the test. Laptop works normally, an hour later the laptop is still working with no freezes. For this problem, we can eliminate the possibility that overheating and hardware caused this issue; Now go to repair flowchart 06 of step C-7; according to the the request of the customer, finish backing up the data and then carry out step D-1: after formatting the disk with DOS, and installing operating system. The problem is solved.

Hint:

To copy the back-up data into the laptop, you need to scan the recovery data twice: one is to scan for virus, the other is to scan for anti-hacker applications; many cases of data loss are caused because of viruses and Spyware. If your data is quite important, always use antivirus software to lower the threat of viruses. Otherwise viruses will come back and then the same issue will happen again and you may lose all your data.

111) HP dv3-2228tx—blue screen failure occurs when system is running

Failure symptom:

Blue screen suddenly occurs when laptop is running; you do a forced shutdown, afterwards you restart the system, the blue screen failure will appear again.

Solution:

This failure symptom belongs to the description of flow chart 07 that belongs to sequence:
Start->A-1->A-2->A-3->C->C-5->D-2->D-5

Repair summary:

Software and hardware problems may cause blue screen failure. So you need to first confirm whether the blue screen is caused by hardware or software. First remove the disk from the laptop, and put a pure bootable DOS Memtest86 software disc into DVD-ROM/CD-ROM, next start the machine and do a memory test. An hour later, the memory module test finishes and there's nothing wrong but the "Blue screen" error remains telling us that the problem is not hardware related, Enter repair flowchart 06 of step D-5; follow the method of situation 3, try repairing the operating system. First test the hard disk, here is the operation method to follow:

1. Press the power button to start the laptop;
2. When the HP or Compaq logo appears, press F10 to enter BIOS Setup;
3. When the main menu appears, pay close attention to the BIOS version and find the option "Hard disk security test";
4. Choose the tool software and then press Enter.

An Entire disk scanning begins, after the scanning finishes; it shows the disk status is normal. Start the laptop in safe mode, and it succeeds in loading and ran successfully. Next run antivirus software, you probably find the operating system has viruses. It seems the virus causes the blue screen failure. After removing the virus and restarting the laptop in normal mode the failure disappears.

Hint:

If after removing the virus, the laptop does not start normally, then I suggest checking whether the most recent driver updates are installed, then remove or disable any recently added application or driver, in order to eliminate the system incompatibility problems. Secondly, I suggest trying starting the system with "The last known configuration", and check whether it can recover. If it doesn't work out, it means the system normal boot sequence was damaged by the viruses. The best solution is to format the entire disk and reinstall the operating system again.

112)   HP ProBook 5310m laptop's blue screen failure

Failure symptom:

Laptop just finishes loading, then the blue screen failure occurs and there is usually a prompt on the screen: "system has unknown error, please press any key to continue" The system restarts. But after restarting, you are unable to into the system.

Solution:

This failure symptom belongs to the description of flow chart 07 that belongs to sequence:

Start->A-1->A-4->A-5->C-1->C-3->C-4->C-6->C-7->D-1->D-2->D-5

Repair summary:

Go to repair flowchart 06 of step C-1, put a pure bootable DOS Memtest86 software disc into DVD-ROM/CD-ROM, and start the machine to do a memory test. 50 minutes later, the memory memory module is ok, so we can eliminate the possibility that it is related to hardware and overheating problem; now we turn our attention to the Software. Go to repair flowchart 06 of step C-7, first make a backup of all your necessary data, and then enter flowchart 06 of D-5, follow the method of situation 3, try repairing the operation system. First test the disk, and nothing is found. Then scan the software and system to kill the viruses; next start the laptop in safe mode, and it succeeds in loading. The thing to consider is there might be an incompatible issue with the system, so uninstall and disable recently added or updated driver and software, restart in normal mode and test and the failure disappears.

Hint:

We suggest using antivirus software to kill viruses but also pay close attention to some Trojans and spyware, which can also cause blue screen failures. Therefore, you are better off scanning and checking with related special tool. However if possible back up your data when using some of these tools as they can cause data to be lost.

7.3.2 10 repair cases about system going down caused by HP laptop disk, repeated auto restart and blue screen failure.

113) HP Compaq 2230s laptop suddenly shuts down when running

Failure symptom:

When the laptop is running, the system suddenly goes down; it does not shut down normally. If you force it to shut down, it will usually occur several times a day. After restarting, it will resume normally but before long the system crash failure re appears again.

Solution:

This failure symptom belongs to the description of flow chart 07 that belongs to sequence:

Start->A-1->A-2->A-3->C->C-5->C-8->D-2->D-5

Repair summary:

Enter the Step C, remove the hard disk from the laptop, put a pure bootable DOS Memtest86 software disc into DVD-ROM/CD-ROM to start and test. The laptop will usually work normally, an hour later; the laptop is still running well, with no crashes. It means that the failure must be related to the original hard disk and the operation system in on the disk. Enter repair flow step C-8; considering the disk interface has many pins connected with the motherboard, the system might freeze if any of these gets loose or have a bad contact. By removing and plugging the disk again, check whether the failure disappears. As a result, if it remains an issue, go to repair flow chart D-2, Replace with a good working hard disk and inspect, then reinstall the operating system, and test the machine again. After running for a period of time, the failures disappear.

Step to repair flowchart D-5, according to the method of situation 1, try making a backup of your data, and then reformat the disk with the DOS 7.1 version. The result shows that there are many bad tracks on the disk; this proves that the disk failure caused the problem. Replace the hard disk it and the issue is resolved.

Hint:

The bad track of HDD mentioned above means physical bad track, which is totally different from the logical disk bad track mentioned previously; logical bad track is caused because users operate by mistake or system gets damaged by viruses and some other reasons(such as accidental shutdown and power-off). Generally, this could be recovered by some tool software or reformatting the disk.

However, physical disk bad track means the hard disk has physical damages to the disk tracks, which could not be repaired by software or some advanced formatting, actually, this is caused because the magnetic medium of the sector losses magnetic memory capacity.

114)   HP Pavilion dv7000 laptop passes self-checking, but freezes, crashes, before starting operation system

Failure symptom:

Laptop starts and passes through self-checking, then it freezes, and then crashes). The white cursor flashes on the top left corner of the screen.

Solution:

This failure symptom belongs to the description of flowchart 07, according to the repair method; we can ensure the repair path, finding it meets the sequence:

This failure symptom belongs to the description of flow chart 07 that belongs to sequence

Start->A-1->A-4->A-5->A-3->C->C-5->D-2->D-5

Repair summary:

Enter repair step A-3, remove the battery from the laptop, and then restart the laptop, the failure symptom has no change, go to repair flow step C, remove the hard disk from the laptop, meanwhile, put a bootable pure DOS Memtest86 software disc into DVD-ROM/CD-ROM to start and test, 50 minutes later, the laptop still works normally, without any system crashes, then it means that the failure comes is from the removed hard disk or the operation system on the disk; Enter repair flow Step C-5, put the disk back into the laptop and follow the Situation 1, remove and plug the disk, check whether the failure disappears. Afterwards, follow the Situation 2, after powering on, listen to the rotation sound of the disk drive, usually you will find there is an abnormal sounds after the disk starts, which means that the disk has problems itself. So go to repair flowchart step D-5 to prove the accuracy of the assumption further. Use a specialized software or DOS 7.1 to test and format the HDD, finally the screen prompts ". . . hard disk fails . . ." and some information; after changing a disk with normal functions, the problem is solved.

Hint:

After replacing the hard disk, if system crash failure still occurs, then check the motherboard and disk interface slot, whether there's something wrong. If there's an interface problem, then the system will not recognize the disk and then a system crash failure will occur. Sometimes, the system failure is caused by the hard disk but this isn't always the case because a hard disk has been running for a period of time and due to the many components in a disk it will accumulate more and more if you do not deal with them in time, the speed and performance will drop and system will become unstable, and finally system crash failure will occur.

115) HP pavilion dv2000 laptop finishes self-inspection, then black screen failure occurs

Failure symptom:

The laptop starts and enters self-checking mode normally, but every time it finishes inspecting the memory, it seems to freeze automatically, then black screen appears and fails to load the operating system.

Solution:

This failure symptom belongs to the description of flow chart 07 that belongs to sequence:

Start->A-1->A-4->A-5->C-1->C-3->C-5->D-2->D-5

Repair summary:

Enter repair flow Chart C-1, put a pure bootable DOS Memtest86 software disc into DVD-ROM/CD-ROM and start the test. The laptop works normally for after 45 minutes later without any black screen failures or system freeze ups. It means the problem comes from the software or the original hard disk;

Step to repair flow C-5, put the disk back into the laptop, remove and plug the disk interface adapter again, finding the failure symptom hasn't changed, follow step flow D-5, test the disk with special software tool, finding the disk is infected with hacker software and there's a logical lock.

Remove the disk from the laptop and put it into a desktop computer to unlock. Usually, I use DM software (disk management) to unlock disk. As DM software doesn't rely on motherboard BIOS to recognize disk, so it can easily recognize the disk, do some partitioning and formatting operations. At last, format the disk with the DOS 7.1 version software, next reinstall a clean operating system and the problem is solved. This case indicates that the software on the disk caused the system freezes failure.

Hint:

If the disk can be reformatted successfully, then the failure caused by software can be repaired favourably, for example:

1) Computer has no display or freezes up randomly;
2) Disk gets infected by viruses, hacker software or gets a logical lock;
3) During the start up self-checking process, screen shows that disk is lost or isn't partitioned;
4) After system auto restarts several times, blue screen failure sometimes occurs;
5) System often enters safe mode automatically;
6) Disk partition is broken;
7) Disk has logical bad tracks;
8) Disk cannot read/write;
9) System runs unstably, invalid error often occurs;

116) HPCOMPAQ nc6220 laptop has blue screen failure when starting

Failure symptom:

The laptop has blue screen error when starting, prompting message: disk error.

Solution:

This failure symptom belongs to the description of flowchart 07 that belongs to sequence:

Start->A-1->A-2->A-3->C->C-5->D-2->D-5

Repair summary:

Considering the failure symptom and combining with the flowchart Chart C of this chapter, remove the disk from the laptop, put a pure bootable DOS Memtest86 software disc into DVD-ROM/CD-ROM and test, An 1 hour later, after testing the memory, no issue is found, and no blue screen failure occurs. According to this situation, we know that the failure must be with the removed disk and the software in the disk; Use the steps of flowchart 07 of step C-5 to repair; to prove the previous assumption, put the disk back in the laptop, remove and plug the disk interface adapter and you'll find the failure hasn't changed.

Use flowchart 07 of step C-5, test the disk with the special software tool, finding the disk usage rate reaches as high as 99.5%, (only 300MB free space), but under normal circumstance, 5% to 10% free space should be preserved to keep operating system to run normally. The solution is to update the hard disk and clone the original operating system to a bigger disk, restart the laptop and test, and the problem is solved. This case indicates that there is too much software installed on the disk, leading to memory shortage and causing the system to multitask causing operational error and finally getting a blue screen failure.

Hint:

Virtual memory is a special solution for system resource shortage in Windows; generally, it requests the primary boot disk space to be 2 or 3 times more than the physical memory. To take full advantage of the limited space of the hard disk, some users use their disks to their full capacity and neglecting the critical requirements of the operating system, which causes virtual memory and system operation error due to shortage of space.

Generally, if you keep an eye out, there is a file named "pagefile.sys" in the root directory of drive C, which is an application file providing virtual memory for the system. Generally, this file is set 1.5 times as much as the systems physical memory, however, the size of this file also depends on the free space of the disk, most people will find that for different machines, even the files with the same name pagefile.sys have different sizes of pages and it can be changed. You can even delete the virtual memory option, but when the operating system uses and runs this file, it does need your disk space and can therefore make Windows extremely unstable, and even breaks down.

117) HP COMPAQ nc8230 laptop prompts "xxxx.DLL file is missing" when starting up, and cannot load operating system

Failure symptom:

After the laptop starts up, error prompts: "xxxx.DLL file is missing", after copying the same file from a normal machine and putting into the laptop to repair the same error message prompts again.

Solution:

This failure symptom belongs to the description of flowchart 07 that belongs to sequence:

Start->A-1->A-4->A-5->C-1->C-3->C-5->D-2->D-5

Repair summary:

Considering the failure symptom and combining the repair flowchart 07 of step C-1 of this chapter, put a pure bootable DOS Memtest86 software disc into DVD-ROM/CD-ROM to start and test, 55 minutes later, the memory module passes the inspection, but no other problem is found or prompts. Concluding from this is that the failure cannot be related to the memory and other hardware; Use flowchart 07 of step C-5; put the disk back into the laptop, remove and plug the disk interface adapter again, finding the failure hasn't changed; step to repair flowchart 07 of step D-2, test it with other known good hard disk, and after reformatting the disk with DOS, reinstall the operating system again, finding there's no error prompt appearing again. It seems that the source of the failure is software or the original disk itself. Step to repair flowchart 07 of step D-5, follow the method of situation 1, try making a backup of the data, and then format the disk with DOS 7.1 version software, the test result shows that the disk itself has many bad tracks, proving the failure is caused because of disk issue. After replacing the disk, the problem is solved.

Hint:

After bad tracks happen to disk, system might fail to start normally. Therefore, error prompt or blue screen failure might occur, then it won't work even if you reinstall or try repairing the operating system. Even the process of reinstallation cannot finish, every time after restarting, same error prompt will appear; this is because the disk has physical bad track and is a hardware problem, but not a software one. You need to change the hard disk to solve the problem.

However, other than the disk failure, maybe the motherboard and memory may also cause the same failure symptom. So you'd have to follow the flowchart and check carefully, to avoid making the wrong assumption.

118)   HP Elitebook 6930P laptop cannot start up, and cursor flashes at the top left of the screen.

Failure symptom:

Hard disk doesn't start and no error message is showing but sometimes the cursor flashes at left of the screen;

Solution:

This failure symptom belongs to the description of flow chart 07 that belongs to sequence:

Start->A-1->A-4->A-5->A-3->C->C-5

Repair summary:

Considering the failure symptom and combining the repair flowchart step C of this chapter, remove the disk from the laptop, put a bootable pure DOS Memtest86 software disc into DVD-ROM/CD-ROM and test, 53 minutes later, the memory module passes the test, no problem is found, the laptop has no failure other than the cursor flashing on the screen. From this we know that the source of the failure comes from the original hard disk or the software in the disk; step to repair flowchart of step C-5: to prove previous assumption; put the disk back into the laptop, by removing and plugging disk interface adapter again, finding the failure symptom disappears. Finally, it is found that the bad contact between disk interface adapter and motherboard caused the problem.

Hint:

Another important failure reason is that some hard disks worked on other brands of the laptops, and have installed operating system data, and then continued using it in another brand of the laptop. If you haven't reformatted the disk, then probably the disk doesn't start and there's no prompt message. Besides, a cursor will flash at the top left corner of the screen; as CMOS doesn't recognize the hard disk correctly, which directly affects the normal usage of the disk. So, when you replace the laptop disk, CMOS cannot access the data position of the recently installed disk. Finally the laptop doesn't load Windows or keeps restarting with a blue screen failure. The best solution is to format the disk.

119) after HP Pavilion DV2621TX laptop starts, system cannot find hard disk, computer keeps searching for network adapter to restart

Failure symptom:

After starting the laptop, the laptop tries starting from the network adapter, but ends in failure and keeps restarting continually. Try reinstalling operation system, but screen prompts that hard disk is not found.

Solution:

This failure symptom belongs to the description of flow chart 07 that belongs to sequence:

Start->A-1->A-4->A-5->C-1->C-3->C-4->C-6->D-1->D-2

Repair summary:

Considering the failure symptom and combining the repair flowchart 07 of step C-1 of this chapter, put a pure bootable DOS Memtest86 software disc into DVD-ROM/CD-ROM to start and test, 49 minutes later, memory module passes the test with no issues found and without any error prompts. From this we know that the failure has nothing to do with the memory or other hardware; step to repair flowchart 07 of step C-3; enter the motherboard BIOS and find disk information, we find the disk isn't recognized by the auto inspection function in CMOS. Disassemble the laptop disk, remove and plug the disk connection adapter, and then put it back to the laptop and test. The failure symptom has not changed; it seems the problem has nothing to do with the disk port; after changing the disk to test, the situation changes immediately, the auto supervision function in CMOS finds all the information of the disk. This case indicates that the original disk caused the failure.

Hint:

1. If the disk existence could be found by the auto supervision function in CMOS, but system doesn't recognize the disk, then the primary cause for such a failure, usually, is because the data on the disks main boot sector is damaged, or the partition mark is missing. The main culprit for this kind of failure, is a virus, which writes) the main boot sector with wrong data. The most common method is to use FDISK.com software, which can revive your disk, but you'd have to repartition and format, the data there could hardly be preserved.

2. Take HP dv2621 TX for an example, if it prompts that disk can't be found when installing XP system, this is because all HP laptops use SATA disk, so when reinstalling the operating system you have to use system disc with integrated SATA drive to install directly so the solution is: initialize BIOS and set up System Configuration—SATA Native Support, set the property as Disabled, in order to install. If it doesn't work, press F10 at start up, enter BIOS to find SATA Setup, set the SATA as Disabled. If this doesn't help, then download the SATA driver and install. Make a SATA drive floppy disc, and use an external floppy drive to help during the system installation process, press F6 during window installation to load SATA driver. This method requires an external floppy drive.

120) HP dv6628US laptop starts but disk doesn't, there's no cursor flashing on the screen

Failure symptom:

Cannot load Windows; the OS installation process is extremely slow.

Solution:

This failure symptom belongs to the description of flow chart 07 that belongs to the sequence:

Start->A-1->A-4->A-5->C-1->C-3->C-5->C-8->C-6->D-1->D-2->D-5

Repair summary:

First confirm that the failure has nothing to do with overheating, according to the flowchart 07 of step C-1 of this chapter, put a pure bootable DOS Memtest86 software disc into DVD-ROM/CD-ROM to start and test, An hour later, memory module passes the test, there's no error prompt happening to the laptop. From this we know that the original failure is within software range or original disk hardware. Step to repair flowchart 07 of step C-3; enter motherboard BIOS and find the disk information, as a result, it finds the disk. Follow the method of flow C-5, disassemble the disk from the laptop, remove and plug the disk connection adapter, and then put it back in the laptop and test, the failure symptom remains.

According to the method of flow D-1, format disk with DOS, as a result, (100GB disk takes about 6 hours to finish formatting), but there's no bad track found on the hard disk. And the speed to reinstall Windows system is extremely slow (take about 4 hours to finish installing Windows XP system), use **HP Hard Drive Self Test** to inspect the disk drive of the laptop, no problem is found. But the laptop issue does exist, strangely, when processing flowchart 07of step C-1 the laptop boots and reads disc in (DOS), the speed is OK. Reconsidering flowchart 07 of step D-2, uninstall the original disk, and install another known good disk onto the laptop and reinstall the operating system, the failure disappears.

Hint:

Test the laptop disk drive with HP Hard Drive Self Test software, usually, the result is accurate, but not 100%; for the failures like this kind which can be difficult to repair, you can find a solution by the failure analysis and repair of this flowchart 07. Test the disk with replacement method, namely, change disk and test again, it's still the best additional repair method. If the disk replacement method quickly finishes the installation, then it means the problem is with the original disk, and not the HP Disk Drive Self Test.

121)   Disk doesn't start after HP Compaq V5000 laptop starts up; there's prompt "Hard Disk Partition Table—Error!"

Failure symptom:

After system starts and shows the HP logo, error prompt appears. You can't start from the disk.

Solution:

This failure symptom belongs to the description of flow chart 07 that belongs to sequence:

Start-> Start->A-1->A-4->A-5->C-1->C-3->C-5->D-2->D-5

Repair summary:

From the failure symptoms: system keeps restarting, cannot boot up from disk and so on, combined with the flowchart tutorial, we can summarize the solution: first change hard disk to test, the result shows the problem is solved, which indicates the problem is caused because of a disk issue.

Hint:

During the usage process we will at some point run into this kind of situation. There are many kinds and causes of system boot failure, and many of them are because of hard disk. Generally, when disk failure occurs, BIOS will give us some prompt information. Different motherboards or different versions of BIOS have different ways of given us the information.

a.   Prompt "Primary master hard disk fail";
b.   Prompt "Imminent Hard Disk Failure";
c.   1720—SMART Hard Drive detects imminent failure. Your hard disk drive is detecting an imminent failure. To ensure no data loss, backup contents and replace this hard disk. Attribute Failed: #10

122)   HP Pavilion ze5500 laptop cannot load Windows after staring up, prompting "DISK BOOT FAILURE . . ."

Failure symptom:

After system starts up and finishes self-inspection, system prompts an error "hard disk start fails, cannot load Windows"

Solution:

This failure symptom belongs to the description of flow chart 07 that belongs to sequence:

Start-> Start->A-1->A-4->A-5->C-1->C-3->C-5->D-2->D-5

Repair summary:

From the failure symptoms: system keeps restarting, cannot boot up from disk and so on, combined with the flowchart tutorial, we can come up with the solution that first change hard disk to validate (test), the result shows the problem is not eliminated, same error prompt appears on the screen, follow the method of flow C-5, disassemble the laptop disk, check the connection between hard disk and motherboard, and clear the dust or impurities of flocculent dust in the slot with a brush or compressed air. Finally it is found that one pin on the hard disk is loose, after soldering it, the failure disappears.

Hint:

Most HP laptops have 1 to 3 screws that fix the hard disk up on motherboard. When repairing the laptop, check these screws first to ensure they are all tight, because disk interface has many pins connected with the motherboard, if a pin gets loose or there's a bad connection, it's likely that the system may not recognize the hard disk intermittently. There are cases indicating that the cause for these failures above is due to the fact that they are not tight enough.

Under some circumstances, if you cannot ensure whether there's a problem with the disk, then you can uninstall the disk, put it into another machine and test. Check whether the system recognizes the disk, and then decide whether to reformat it or not. When disk gets infected by viruses, such as Trojan it will damage the system boot sequence, at this moment, you're better off to just format the entire disk, which could finally eliminate the viruses completely.

7.3.3 Six repair cases for HP laptop memory (RAM) issue causing restart, system crash or blue screen failure

123) HP Presario CQ50 laptop suddenly freezes when running

Failure symptom:

When browsing WebPages on the laptop, system crash failure occurs. There's no response by pressing any key, machine cannot turn off normally, and you'd only have to exit by force. The situation becomes worse and worse, after restarting, sometimes it could recover normal, but most cases, it will freeze again immediately.

Solution:

This failure symptom belongs to the description of flowchart 07, according to the repair method; we can ensure the repair path, finding it accords with the sequence:

This failure symptom belongs to the description of flowchart 07 that belongs to sequence

Start->A-1->A-2->A-3->C->C-2->C-5->

Repair summary:

Step to repair flowchart 07 of C, remove the hard disk from the laptop, put a bootable pure DOS Memtest86 software disc into DVD-ROM/CD-ROM to start and test, the laptop could work normally, 30 minutes later, system reports that some problem is found with RAM, which indicates the failure must be related with the memory; step to repair flowchart 07 of step C-2; eliminate the laptop failure by running under minimum system like power adapter, motherboard, CPU, RAM, display card (except the one with integrated display card)/LCD monitor, keyboard and DVD-ROM/CD-ROM. All other hardware should be removed, such as network card, hard disk and so on.

Considering there are two memory modules in the laptop, probably one of the memory modules is broken. Here we use the elimination method, remove allmemory modules, and then try putting one memory module to different slots and testing, (still pass through the test by Memtest86 software) finding there's one memory module broken. After replacing it and starting the machine, the test shows normal, then step to repair flowchart 07 of step C-5, install all originally removed hardware back to the laptop, and install the hard disk as it was, then restart the laptop again, after running for a period of time, no any system failure any more. It proves the memory defects causes the laptop failure, after replacing it, the problem is resolved.

Hint:

There are many reasons causing the laptop system to shut down, Memory failure can cause such fault phenomenon. So whether the laptop could resume normal after removing the issued memory? The situation is not that simple, some laptops probably have more than two problems, such as overheating or viruses and so on. Usually, same failure symptom will also occur: system freezes or blue screen. Most cases, the laptop technician hasn't thought about this point, therefore, usually, they will dismiss the previous correct repair method, discarding the correct assumption already made. So after replacing memory, if some failure symptom still occurs, then you should follow the repair flowchart 07 to step to D-2, D-5, continue repairing and seize every opportunity to solve the problem.

124)   COMPAQ Presario R4000 laptop blue screen failure after starting up

Failure symptom:

After the laptop starts up, it restarts several times automatically, or blue screen failure occurs.

Solution:

This failure symptom belongs to the description of 07 flow chart, according to the repair method; we can ensure the repair path, finding it accords with the sequence:

This failure symptom belongs to the description of flow chart 07 that belongs to sequence

Start->A-1->A-2->A-3->C->C-2->C-5->D-2->D-5

Repair summary:

From the failure symptom, combining the step C of this flowchart 07, remove the hard disk from the laptop, and put a bootable pure DOS Memtest86 software disc into DVD-ROM/CD-ROM to start and test, 45 minutes later, system reports that memory problem is found,(notice: this is the test result when putting two memory modules together) which means the problem must be related with the memory; step to repair flowchart 07 of step C-2; eliminate the laptop failure by minimum system. with elimination method, remove the two memory modules, and then first install only one memory module to the laptop and test, separately on A, B slot, test once by Memtest86 software, strangely, none of the two modules is defective, the repair job gets into a difficult position, however, check the two memory modules carefully, suddenly finding that one external frequency speed is PC333, while the other one is PC266. So it's estimated the operation error made because of incompatibility of the memory modules. Therefore, we assumed that it was the incompatibility of the memory modules that caused the operation error. Replace the PC266 with a new memory module of PC333, meanwhile, recover hard disk and start the laptop again. Next, something unexpected happens, blue screen failure still occurs! Could it be the previous assumption is wrong? The repair job seems to be difficult, however, review the entire repair process carefully again, no wrong process is found, according to the repair flowchart 07, step to step C again, test the memory, (test the two memory modules together), 45 minutes later, system reports that there's nothing wrong with the memory, it seems that the laptop has more than two problems at least, displaying the same failure symptom—blue screen.

Step to repair flow D-2, replace with a known good hard disk to test, next reinstall operation system, start the machine and test again, finding that no blue screen failure is found during the running process. According to the method of the situation 1 of repair flow D-5, try making a backup of the data, the result shows that when testing hard disk it is infected with a virus, proving that the second failure is caused by the software. Scan and remove the virus in the backup data, and then format the disk with the software of DOS 7.1 version software, after reinstalling the operation system, the problem is resolved.

Hint:

The operation error caused by incompatibility of memories or memory damage here primarily means the error prompt appears before Windows loading finishes after system starts. The main reason causing such a failure is because the memory modules are damaged, similarly, the memory modules may cause incompatibility failure. So you should pay close attention to the consistency of the default memory operation frequency. Most cases, after adding memory, operation system might get broken, at that moment, even you remove the added memory stick (memory module) again, the operation system would not recover.

125) HP COMPAQ nc6230 laptop's application runs unstably, often entering safe mode or shutting down automatically

Failure symptom:

When the laptop starts, system will auto shut down randomly, the computer runs unstably, often entering safe mode automatically. After repairing and reinstalling operation system, the failure has no change.

Solution:

This failure symptom belongs to the description of 07 flow chart, according to the repair method; we can ensure the repair path, finding it accords with the sequence:

This failure symptom belongs to the description of flow chart 07 that belongs to sequence

Start->A-1->A-2->A-3->C->C-2->C-5->D-2->D-5

Repair summary:

From the failure symptom, combining the step C of this flowchart 07, remove the hard disk from the laptop, and put a bootable pure DOS Memtest86 software disc into DVD-ROM/ CD-ROM to start and test, 48 minutes later, system reports that memory problem is found, which means the problem must be related with the memory; step to repair flow C-2; eliminate the problem by running minimum system with the software. Remove two memory modules in all, and then try testing one memory module in a different slots, still pass the test of Memtest86) finding that the memory module B is broken. After replacing with a new one, start the machine and test again, confirming that the random auto shutdown failure is gone. But the problem that it often auto enters safe mode still exists. Considering the reason of memory, there are a lot of cases that lead to operation system breakdown. So continue following the repair flowchart 07.

According to the method of the situation 1 of repair flow D-5, try making a backup of data, and then format the hard disk with DOS 7.1 version software, next reinstall the operation system; start the machine and test again, finding that after running for a period of time, no any problem is found, the failure symptom that operation system auto enters safe mode has already been resolved!

Hint:

If it's truly the problem of the quality of the memory, then the problem could be solved by replacing the memory module. Except in the quality problem of the memory, sometimes, the memory module is loose, bad solder May also cause the similar failure symptom. After replacing the memory module, if the problem still not resolved, then you'd only have to solve the problem by recovering the registry or updating system.

126) **after HP pavilion DV2781TX laptop starts, system prompts: "C:\WINDOWS\ SYSTEM\xxx\xxxx.vxd could not be found" and then freezes.**

Failure symptom:

When system starts, error prompt always displays: "\xxxx.vxd could not be found" and then system freezing failure occurs. Even when you start in normal mode, or reinstall operation system, the situation would not be changed at all.

Solution:

This failure symptom belongs to the description of 07 flowcharts, according to the repair method; we can ensure the repair path, finding it accords with the sequence:

This failure symptom belongs to the description of flow chart 07 that belongs to sequence

Start->A-1->A-2->A-3->C->C-2->

Repair summary:

From the failure symptom, combining the step C of this flowchart 07, remove the hard disk from the laptop, and put a bootable pure DOS Memtest86 software disc into DVD-ROM/ CD-ROM to start and test, 39 minutes later, system reports that memory problem is found, which means the problem must be related to the memory; step to repair flow C-2; remove two memory modules in all, and then first install one to the laptop and test, separately installing to slot A and, B and test once for each, After testing with by Memtest86 software, it is found that when test the two memory modules at slot A, they all pass; but when testing on slot B, you get a problem, it seems the problem is caused because the motherboard memory slot B is damaged. To confirm the correctness of the assumption, only install memory in slot A, start the machine and test, there's no system file missing or system crash failure prompt on screen again, so the problem is resolved.

Hint:

1) After the laptop starts, error prompts when Windows loading still hasn't been finished, such as xxx file is missing, sometimes such a failure might be caused by hardware problem, it could also be probably a software issue. But if after the laptop finishes loading, the error prompts on the screen: xxx file is missing, usually, it is a problem caused by certain software.

2) The case like memory slot defects of the laptop motherboard is not that common, usually you should pay attention when installing:

    a). Whether memory module is too loose or the jack is too tight, which makes it not being in at correct position or extruded;

    b). before plugging the memory module back, you should clean dust and clear the (Edge Connector) gold plated board, including the slot too;

c). Check whether the failure disappears by removes and installs the module again.

127) after HP dv9700US laptop starts, it runs unstably or it will restart randomly.

Failure symptom:

When large applications (such as game software) run in system, blue screen or restart symptom will occur.

Solution:

This failure symptom belongs to the description of 07 flowcharts, according to the repair method; we can ensure the repair path, finding it accords with the sequence:

This failure symptom belongs to the description of flow chart 07 that belongs to sequence

Start->A-1->A-2->A-3->C->C-2->C-5->C-8->C-6->D-1->D-2->D-5

Repair summary:

First confirm the failure is not related with overheating, according to the flowchart 07of step C-1, put a bootable pure DOS Memtest86 software disc into DVD-ROM/CD-ROM to start and test, An hour later, the memory passes the test, the laptop has no any error prompt either, concluding from these, the original failure should be within the software or on the original hard disk. Step to repair flow C-5; remove the hard disk of the laptop, remove and plug the disk connection adapter, and then put it back to the laptop and test, the failure symptom has no change.

Step to repair flow D-1, format the disk with DOS, finding no bad track on the hard disk, after reinstalling the operation system, it's still normal, but when running game software, the restart failure still occurs. Step to repair flow D-2, remove all hard disks, and then install another known good hard disk to the laptop, next reinstall operation system, and then run the game software, same failure symptom still happens. The repair gets difficult.

However, after observing the laptop carefully, a strange symptom draws my attention: if it does not run large application software, the laptop will rarely get this problem, considering it needs huge memory support when running large application, would it be the problem with memory? Remove the two memory modules, and then change to a new memory module with the same brand, model and technical standard to meet the high demands for memory by the application, maintaining a stable operation environment. Next start the machine and test again, the failure disappears.

Hint:

As one of the three most important accessories of a computer, memory takes charge of many tasks like temporary data access. During the working process, some problems are inevitable, some memory modules might have nothing wrong when use in low speed status, but once switch to high speed running status, some subtle abnormal phenomenon happening to the memories will lead to operation failure.

When testing the laptop memory with Memtest86 software, usually, the result is accurate, but not 100%; just like the memory of this type, usually it works normally, but error happens when running in high speed. In that case, it would be quite difficult for Memtest86 software to test the problem; of course, we can remedy and solve with the prompt method of this flowchart 07. Test the memory with replacement method. You know that replacement method is always one of the best. If the memory replacement could quickly solve the problem successfully, then it means the problem comes from the original memory itself, but without considering the memory test result by Memtest86 software.

128) After HP Compaq Presario V3414TX laptop starts, blue screen occurs or system auto shuts down the moment manufacturer logo just appears.

Failure symptom:

After the laptop starts, power light is on, sometimes screen has no display, and there's beeps warning; sometimes the laptop would auto shut down the moment manufacturer logo just appears, but without any beeping warning.

Solution:

This failure symptom belongs to the description of 07 flowchart, according to the repair method; we can ensure the repair path, finding it accords with the sequence:

This failure symptom belongs to the description of flow chart 07 that belongs to sequence Start->A-1->A-4->A-5->C-1->C-2->

Repair summary:

As the laptop normal working time is especially short, there's no way to test the memory with software, then the repair flow should go directly to Step C-2, test the laptop with minimum system, remove battery, wireless network card, network card, Modem, card reader, hard disk and so on, remove the two memory modules, and then first install one memory module to the laptop and test, separately on slot A, B and once for each, finding that operation system would work normally only when a memory module is tested on slot A, but error prompts when test on slot B, however, the other memory module becomes defective when put in the Slot A and Slot B to test. It seems the problem comes from one memory module and memory slot B, to confirm the assumption further, check the methods below:

a) Do electrical cleaning on the memory slot B, finding there is large flocculent dust stuck in the slot, besides, it's very sticky. Get rid of them with a needle and then clean with air compression.

b) Clean the (Edge Connector) gold plated board to another memory module, next test it on the laptop again, the failure is solved then.

Hint:

1. You'd better to test whether the laptop could work normally with minimum system method, finally to shorten the range of the issued accessory to the minimum; usually the minimum system minimum methodology should coordinate with cleanness method, which could locate the issued part correctly. As for detail operation, please refer to the method of second chapter (minimum system judgment) in <<1.4.2 6 "Hard" methods to repair the laptop>>.
2. Usually we clean the (Edge Connector) gold plated board with an eraser, and check up whether there's damage trace to the memory slot, after processing, if the problem still exists, then it means the memory has already been broken, at this moment; you'd only have to change a new one. Please note: the technical data standards of the changed memory must be same as the original ones.

7.3.4 Three repair cases of repeated restart and blue screen failure caused by laptop hard driver

129) HP CQ40-612TX laptop continual restart failure after starting up

Failure symptom:

After CQ40-612TX laptop starts up, it restarts continually, cannot enter system normally, either cannot start up/shut down normally. Your only option is to force shut down to terminate the continual restart.

Solution:

This failure symptom belongs to the description of flow chart 07 that belongs to sequence:

Start->A-1->A-2->A-3->C->C-5->D-2

Repair summary:

For this type of continual auto start failure, which belongs to typical system failure, the suggested solution is to reinstall the operating system. Because system files are damaged, system starts and cannot finish initialization therefore it forces the computer to restart. However, the customer said that the the reason this failure is happened is because of a network card driver he updated. Start the laptop in safe mode check all drivers and software, and then uninstall the recently added drivers. By doing this, we can eliminate the system incompatible problem from happening again.

Start the laptop in normal mode but the result is still a failure, and the laptop still restarts. It's likely that the boot configure file has an issue, so try "The last known working configuration" Finally we succeed in recovering back to normal status without the blue screen failure. The repair is done!

Hint:

If you cannot start the computer from safe mode, then you need to remove the hard disk and put it into a USB box, making it an external USB movable disk and then insert the external USB hard disk to a working computer. Next run the antivirus software to scan and remove any virus. When finished, insert the hard disk back in the laptop, and then start the computer in safe mode to test. If the failure still occurs, then you need to reinstall the operating system. Afterwards, install each driver one at a time and restart the computer after every install to test.

130)   HP Pavilion dv4000 laptop blue screen failure

Failure symptom:

During the working process of the laptop, blue screen failure occurs.

Solution:

This failure symptom belongs to the description of flow chart 07 that belongs to sequence:

Start->A-1->A-2->A-3->C->C-5->D-2

Repair summary:

Blue screen failures occur due to either hardware, software or sometimes both, usually, I will put a pure bootable DOS Memtest86 software disc into the DVD-ROM/CD-ROM to start and test to analyze whether the blue screen failure comes from hardware or software. However, as customer said that the cause of this failure happened after he updated the sound card driver. So boot the laptop in safe mode. Check the recently installed or updated drivers, and uninstall all of them to eliminate system incompatibility problems. Next start the laptop back in normal mode and the laptop works. However, there's no sound, considering it's quite likely that the boot configuration file has an issue, so recover the system to the last known good configuration without blue screen failure. But the speakers still has no sound!

According to the method of situation 1 of flowchart D-5, back up your data, and then format the hard disk with DOS 7.1 version software, next reinstall the operating system; start the machine to test, as a result, the Internet is running and sound is back. The failure occurred because the system files were damaged and it cause the sound issue.

Hint:

If your XP system has installed SP3, then your sound card driver also needs to be updated. Probably you still not aware that many sound card drivers are not made for SP3. So many people think the sound card on motherboard work better but in reality the result always show a failure. To solve this problem, read my post I wrote in detail.

http://www.computercare.ca/forum/showthread.php?t=1852

131)   HP dv3-2121tx laptop's restart failure after blue screen appears

Failure symptom:

Laptop starts, but getting Internet issues, the screen turns blue and the network browser function is disabled. System function can only be recovered after restarting. But the screen will turn blue and system will restart once you get on the Internet; after recovering and reinstalling the operating system, the failure still occurs.

Solution:

This failure symptom belongs to the description of flow chart 07 that belongs to the sequence:

Start->A-1->A-2->A-3->C->C-5->D-2->D-5

Repair summary:

Network unavailable failure is quite common, but after getting the Internet, blue screen or auto restart failure is not a common occurrence. Let's still start repairing from step C, remove the hard disk from the laptop, put a pure bootable DOS Memtest86 software disc into DVD-ROM/CD-ROM to start and test, 55 minutes later, system reports there's nothing wrong with the memory. Uninstall the wireless network card of the laptop, and then wipe and clean the (Edge Connector) gold plated board with an eraser, and then checks the network card slot, for damage. Reinstall the wireless network card back, start the machine and test, to find that the failure still remains. Uninstall the wireless network card driver and reinstall with the new driver, start and test, but same issue remains; the laptop wireless network card switch is disabled, but the direction light of the wireless network card is still on and flashing.

Install a good working wireless network card and then test. The failure also remains so according to the method of the situation 1 of repair flowchart D-5, back up your data, and then format the disk with DOS 7.1 version software, and reinstall the operating system; start and test the machine again, finding everything is now working and no re starts or blue screen issues occur. This failure is caused because the laptop system files have been damaged by hacker applications, which stops the system from starting normally.

Hint:

After getting attacked by "Hackers" through the network, such a failure will happen, because your IP address was found accidentally by them and you've been attacked by some software, under this circumstance, the best defence is to install a recovery software on your own machine. When you go to those sites (such as BBS) you are easily exposed so after you logon, set up security by hiding your IP address.

7.3.5 Four repair cases of repeated restart and blue screen failures caused by other reasons for HP laptop

132) Compaq Presario R3320US laptop gets blue screen failure and down after starting up

Failure symptom:

Blue screen failure appears and system goes down after the laptop starts.

Solution:

This failure symptom belongs to the description of flow chart 07 that belongs to sequence:

Start->A-1->A-2->A-3->C->E-2

Repair summary:

Repair from step C, remove hard disk from the laptop, and then put a pure bootable DOS Memtest86 software disc into the DVD-ROM/CD-ROM to start, it's primarily used to analyze and find out whether the system can finish running the normal start-up. 8 minutes later, system reports there's an issue with the memory which mean the memory may be bad.

Step to repair flowchart C-2; eliminate the laptop failure with minimum system. Remove disc, network card and hard disk etc. Remove all the memory and clean the (Edge Connector) gold plated board of the memory, put onememory module in opposite slot and test, (start DOS software with U disk), failure remains, remove memory, and plug the other memory module and test again, failure remains. Replace memory modules in the laptop, start and test again but failure also remains.

Because the Memtest86 software is not only used to test memory, it also tests motherboard and cache of CPU (catch ram), so there may be an issue with the motherboard or CPU high cache. Go to step flowchart E-2, try putting a good known CPU in the laptop and then test again, now the issue is gone and the problem is solved.

Clean the (Edge Connector) gold plated board of the memory stick with an eraser, put a memory stick to different slots and test, (boot DOS test software from U disk), finding the failure result hasn't changed, after removing the memory and plugging in another memory it still hasn't changed.

Hint:

When the laptop has overheated, CPU cache RAM can easily get damaged which finally leads to the system running error and resulting in a blue screen failure message or the laptop restarts. Usually, after the laptop starts and enters the self-checking option, the hard disk enters the operating system and then your settings are set and you're ready to use your laptop. Therefore, if you encounter this issue, put your CPU on another laptop motherboard and test, which will help identifying if the problem is with the high speed cache (catch ram). If you are sure it's broken, consider changing the CPU. However, the rate of CPU failure of this kind is quite low, about one in a thousand failure rate.

133) HP Presario V3703TX laptop's blue screen and interface freezing failure after starting up

Failure symptom:

After the laptop starts up, blue screen failure or distorted characters on screen and interface freezing failures occur

Solution:

This failure symptom belongs to the description of flow chart 07 that belongs to sequence:

Start->A-1->A-2->A-3->C->E-2

Repair summary:

Use Step C, remove hard disk from the laptop, and then start the laptop with Memtest86 software, and then use it to analyze and judge whether the system works normally; 20 minutes later, system reports there's something wrong with the memory.

Use Step C-2; to eliminate the laptop failure with minimum system running software. Remove the disc, network card and so on. And then use replacement method by putting a known good memory module in the laptop, start it and test, (boot DOS test software with U disk), the failure still exists.

Use Step E-2; now that the memory module isn't the cause. The issue under minimum system must be with the motherboard and CPU, as the display card cannot be changed because it's integrated. Try putting a working CPU in the laptop and test it finding the failure still exists. After changing the motherboard, the failure disappears.

Hint:

1) Sometimes hardware isn't plugged properly, hardware is incompatible with motherboard, then a blue screen failure or system crash failure will occur. Probable cause can be due to conflicts with PCI IP and system.

2) When the laptop overheats, GPU cache can easily get damaged and shows up in the form of blue screen, black screen, distorted characters, blurry screen or system freeze ups, therefore, this step requires changing the display card (expect the ones that are integrated) to test and verify.

134) HP CQ41-206TX laptop gets blue screen failure after system failure

Failure symptom:

A while after the laptop has started the system will shut down or blue screen will occur and you are no longer able to enter system, CD/DVD ROM has abnormal noise.

Solution:

This failure symptom belongs to the description flow chart 07 that belongs to sequence:

Start->A-1->A-2->A-3->C->E-2

Repair summary:

Knowing from the failure symptom that system freezes at start up, according to the flowchart, the action to take is to replace hardware for testing. Because from the failure symptom the CD/DVD ROM has abnormal sounds so probably the DVD-ROM/CD-ROM is in the unloading state, leading to system crashes and therefore cannot enter system. So the first step is to use repair flowchart E-2, disassemble the laptop and remove the DVD-ROM/CD-ROM, check the motherboard interface, whether there's a broken pin failure, after confirming it's all right, put the DVD-ROM/CD-ROM back in the laptop, lock it and then start it up, system starts normally with no failure.

Hint:

1) When DVD-ROM/CD-ROM is accessing data, blue screen or system crash occurs because of mistaken operation after starting. This situation doesn't affect system from running, as long as it's not put into the DVD-ROM/CD-ROM, or press ESC to solve the problem easily.

2) Sometimes failures like system shut down or blue screen errors occur because system hasn't succeeded in loading hardware, but it's not for sure, you cannot boot DOS software to test the laptop with disc. This brings a lot of issues to repair flowchart C.

by this time, you can remove the hard disk, the DVD-ROM/CD ROM from the laptop and start DOS software with USB flash disk.

135) HP PAVILION DV6670CA laptop cannot load system after starting up, it keeps restarting

Failure symptom:

After starting the laptop, computer will try starting from the network adapter, finally resulting in a failure in the end.

Solution:

This failure symptom belongs to the description of flow chart 07, which belongs to sequence:

Start->A-1->A-4->A-5->C-1->C-3->C-4->C-6->D-1->D-2

Repair summary:

Use repair flow C-1, put a pure bootable DOS Memtest86 software disc into the DVD-ROM/CD-ROM to start and test, 43 minutes' later, memory module passes the test and no issues is found with it.

Use repair flow C-3; enter BIOS at start up, as a result, the auto inspection function in CMOS doesn't see the existence of the hard disk. Disassemble the hard disk from the laptop, remove and plug disk connection adapter, and then put it back in the laptop and test again, the failure symptom doesn't change. Even after replacing the disk. CMOS still doesn't see the hard disk; it seems the failure is not related with the disk ports. But there must be something wrong with the motherboard, first remove the main battery and pull out the external power adapter, and remove the CMOS battery for about 10 minutes or more, then reconnect a new CMOS battery and test the machine again, the failure disappears.

Hint:

CMOS battery is used to store system information, such as time and boot sequence or kind of system data. If a CMOS battery is dead or the Voltage is to low, then the system may not start or you may have a black screen. The hardware will not be recognized and problems will happen. Therefore, it's quite important to check the laptop CMOS battery. After changing CMOS battery, don't install the main battery and power adapter until you first press the power button for about 30 seconds, and then singularly connect the power adapter to start the laptop, and set the first boot device as hard disk.

CHAPTER 8

Black screens or frozen screen repair

8.1 Reasons why the laptop screen will not light up at start up or the laptop freezes

8.1.1 Common failures of a laptop motherboard

- Press the laptop switch and no response results, the indicator light is out, the laptop doesn't start.
- Press the laptop switch and the indicator light turns on, but there is no display on the screen;
- The laptop display card driver is lost and displayed colors are abnormal, there's only 16 colors;
- The laptop screen is blurred, difficult to see writing clearly or there are abnormal spots and patterns
- When the laptop starts up, there's number error prompting, and no way to enter the system;

a) The laptop doesn't recognize the DVD-ROM or the hard drive;
b) The laptop doesn't recognize the floppy drive, serial ports, paralleled ports, USB ports and so on;
c) The laptop doesn't recognize the touch pad and the keyboard;
d) The laptop doesn't recognize the network card, wireless network card or the Modem etc.
e) The laptop often freezes, powers off or auto restarts from time to time;
f) The laptop battery doesn't charge;
g) The laptop doesn't work in battery mode, but works with the external power supply;
h) The laptop works in battery mode, but doesn't work with the external power supply;
i) The laptop turns off from time to time;
j) The laptop software freezes occasionally;

k) The laptop will not install the operation system;

l) The laptop password is lost, and you can no longer enter the system;

m) A File is lost when the laptop starts up, it can't be fixed, and the system is unavailable.

The next table shows the analysis for these common laptop failures. We will initially diagnose the main parts of the issues of the laptop. It has certain practicality.

Common failures description	Symptoms or comment (explanation)	Fault location or parts
Laptop doesn't start	There's no response by pressing power switch, the indicator light is out	Motherboard, power supply, power switch, power board
No display with power on	Indicator light is on after starting up the machine, but the display doesn't respond	Motherboard, BIOS, CPU, display card, RAM, signal cable
Error prompts when machine starts up	After starting the machine, unable to enter system	Motherboard, BIOS, hard disk
Doesn't work in battery mode	Laptop doesn't work normally without external power supply	Motherboard, battery, battery interface board
Doesn't work with external power supply	Laptop only works in battery mode	Motherboard, power adapter, power interface board
Cannot fix or install operation system	Operating system installation and maintenance doesn't complete	Motherboard, hard disk, RAM, CPU, DVD-ROM, System disc, thermal part
Lost password or forgotten	At start up, system asks for password validation	Motherboard validation chip, BIOS
Battery doesn't charge	Charge with external power supply, but the battery shows nothing	Motherboard, battery, power adapter, battery/power interface board
Abnormal color display	Display card driver is lost repeatedly, generally only 16 colors displayed	Display card part of motherboard, driver
Blurred writing or abnormal spots	Laptop display is blurry, writing is blurry and there's no abnormal spots or red snowflake like	Display card part of motherboard, RAM, signal cable, driver

Hard drive isn't recognized	Hard drive isn't recognized in BIOS	Motherboard, BIOS, hard disk, interface board
DVD-ROM isn't recognized	DVD-ROM isn't recognized in BIOS	Motherboard, BIOS, DVD-ROM, interface
External device isn't recognized	ie: USB, PC card, Modem etc.	Motherboard, peripheral devices, interface, BIOS, interface board
Keyboard fails	Some keys fail or the entire keyboard	Motherboard, keyboard, interface
Power goes off at start up	Timed start-up or auto shutdown from time to time	Motherboard, power adapter, CPU, power interface board
System freezes when machine starts up	After start up, system doesn't enter or some applications don't execute at a certain time	Motherboard, operation system, RAM, CPU, thermal parts
System no longer starts after initial start up	System doesn't start normally	Motherboard, hard disk, operation system, RAM, CPU, interface board

8.1.2 Common display card failure symptoms and cause analysis

Failure 1: no display and 2 consecutive beeps when the machine starts up.

This kind of failure is usually caused by bad connections between the display card and the motherboard or the motherboard slot. For motherboards with an integrated display card, if the display memory is the main memory of the system, then you need to check the position of the RAM memory card. There should always be a memory card in the first slot, don't leave it empty. If there is no display failure because of the RAM memory card, after start up, generally, there's a beep. If the indicator lights of all status adjustments on the display keeps flashing at the same time with the black screen, then it means the display card connection to the motherboard is OK, and probably there's something wrong with the chip. Under these circumstances, there may not be any beep; most HP DV6000 /DV900 black screen failures belong to the latter situation.

Failure 2: a black screen occurs when starting the machine

Generally, there are a few reasons for such a failure:

1. The display card connection to the motherboard is defective, or the display card has failed. Check the display card connections or just replace it with a new card to solve the problem. In most cases, display cards are integrated on the motherboard. Distortion caused by overheating or a bad connection cannot be seen with the

human eye. The card may look normal but there can be a bad internal connection, which can cause many indescribable failures.

2. For most recent display cards, that are integrated on the motherboard, you would have to remove the damaged display memory with a BGA process and replace it with the exact same type to repair it. Of course, to change the chip, you will need the right soldering technology and good luck (finding the same display chip). Replacing the motherboard sometimes is simpler.

Failure 3: Blurry display screen and characters not clear

1) This failure is generally caused by a bad connection inside the display memory or chip, but the problem also might occur when there's signal interference. When the problem is only slightly evident, a blurry screen and characters would occur with low resolution settings, and the failure disappears when the monitor is set to a high resolution. When the problem is more severe, whether the monitor is set to high or low resolution, there will always be red snowflake like dots visible. The only solution is to change to a new display chip using the BGA process to repair the system, or change the entire motherboard.

2) Driver problems can also cause similar failures because of LCD incompatibility or the display card doesn't support high resolution. When the blurry screen occurs, you can switch the Windows start mode to safe mode, then enter display setup, click "Apply" to choose 16 colors state, and then click the "OK" button. Restart, the Windows XP system in normal mode, and delete the display card driver. Restart the computer which should install the driver correctly.

Failure 4: System crash

Such failures usually happen when the motherboard overheats and stops the display card from working normally; namely, there's something wrong with the GPU. When the problem is less severe, you can add an external USB fan or clean the circuitry of the motherboard, and change the thermal gel on the CPU and GPU. That may solve a less severe system failure, but when the problem is more severe, whether you change the thermal gel or not, the system will continue to crash, and you have no choice but to change the display chip with the BGA process or change the entire motherboard.

Failure 5: Display card driver is lost and color is displayed abnormally

When the d display card driver is loaded but after running for a period of time, the driver is lost. If you reinstall the display card driver, it will again be lost automatically. Such failure, generally, is caused by a defective display card or a very high working temperature which causes an unstable system. This problem will cause the display card driver to be lost creating the colors displayed to be abnormal. The solution is to replace the display memory chip or change the entire motherboard.

Failure 6: the character and interface display is incomplete

For this, you can try solving the problem according to the blurry screen solution above, but be careful because if you change it with an incompatible LCD screen, you will get the same issue. If you can see the interface clearly, delete the display card driver, restart the computer, and load the display card driver, then it will be OK again.

Failure 7: abnormal spots or patterns occasionally appear on the screen,

1) This failure generally is due to the display memory of the display card or the display card is overheating, or there is a bad connection to the motherboard. You need to clean the GPU chip surface, change the thermal gel for the GPU or change the entire motherboard.

2) Check the LCD cable and its motherboard slot, and verify the connection between LCD cable and LCD screen to see if it's loose or not connected properly. Generally speaking, you can disconnect the cable from LCD screen and motherboard slot, and then reconnect it. When necessary, you can try replacing it with a new one.

8.1.3 Diagnostic methods to use when the laptop freezes or fails to light up during start up.

1. At Start up, the screen doesn't light up or turns black soon after. After checking the screen carefully or moving the viewing angle and watching from the side; the Windows start-up interface can be seen, and the desktop is there. Sometimes, after a while, screen lights up again. This situation is caused by a failure of the high voltage board (INVERTER) located on the bottom of the screen or a screen backlight failure. Please refer to the method of the chapter 5 to solve it;

2. The screen doesn't light up when the machine starts up. It doesn't matter what you do, it's useless, and there's probably something wrong with the motherboard, or other software or hardware problems. Please use the next discussed method to solve the problem.

A) A laptop will not light up if the motherboard's BIOS have issues

Almost all manufacturers will release new BIOS versions on the Internet for customers to refresh their laptops in order to gain new functions and help to rectify a BIOS BUG. Occasionally when you refresh the BIOS, the system will freeze or will return to the desktop when certain applications are running. There are also many cases where people use the latest BIOS from the laptop manufacturer and damage the laptop so it no longer starts up! There are more unexpected soft problems relevant with a BIOS update. For instance, after refreshing the BIOS it seems normal when executing most tasks in Windows, but there may be some driver errors, like a PHOTOSHOP error.

Suggestion:

If your laptop works normally, then don't "update" BIOS, because all BIOS versions have different adaptabilities (compatibilities) for computer motherboards and power supplies. If your laptop is working smoothly, do not make any BIOS changes; those so-called new functions after refreshing, are mostly just useless. Only new functions supporting the CPU can be considered as worth while if they improve the performance of the cooling system. You can then update the BIOS. Otherwise, it's really risky to update BIOS if there is no important reason to do so.

B) The laptop won't light up if there's something wrong with the CPU

In a laptop, the rate of CPU failure is not that big, however, failures caused by the CPU are not as easy to deal with as general ones. A blank screen or system freeze may occur as a result of a CPU problem. It' really difficult to see the prompts on the screen, and even when the user is really experienced; it's still hard to eliminate the problem. Therefore, if you encounter these CPU problems, send it to a professional repair center to have it inspected and repaired. However in most cases these kinds of problems are not caused by CPU hardware damage and we can use other methods to eliminate the problem.

After starting up, if there's no display on screen, then we should first check whether the connection between the CPU and the motherboard slot is OK, not loose or a bad connection. In most cases, the bad connection is caused by a slight distortion of the motherboard and cannot be seen by the naked eye. If one side of the CPU is high, and another side is low, we can eliminate the problem easily but in some machines the CPU may look as if it's properly installed, but in fact it isn't and caused the failure. Generally speaking, you can remove the CPU from the motherboard, and then re-install it to correct the problem. When necessary, you can try changing it with a new one. This method should totally solve and eliminate big problems like a bad connection between the CPU and motherboard slot.

C) A laptop doesn't light up if the display kernel section is either faulty or control functions are lost.

Nowadays motherboards provide many advanced power management functions, such as power saving, sleep, and standby etc. Some drivers may have conflicts with power functions of the motherboard, and therefore cause a blurry or blank screen when the laptop re-enters the Windows system.

1. Suggestion 1: when the display is abnormal, pay attention to the CMOS battery, if the setting has been changed, then you need to adjust it to the factory default value. If the problem still occurs, then you can try disabling the factory default values such as the power saving, sleeping, standby and so on. Additionally, because the AMD CPU consumes a lot of power, some poor quality batteries cannot generate enough power and may also cause some undesirable failures. You can check this by elimination and replacement methods.

2. Suggestion 2: when the display is abnormal, enter Windows in safe mode, and then delete the display card driver and restart the computer in normal startup mode. Usually after Windows finishes starting, the new driver will be installed automatically. This often works well for black screen failures caused by a driver.

3. If suggestions 1 and 2 doesn't solve the problem, the indicator lights on the laptop will keep flashing. But the screen will remain black and the issue is probably with the display chip. Under this circumstance, you can only send it to a professional repair center for repair. Most HP DV6000/DV9000 laptop black screen failures come from the display chip.

D) The laptop doesn't light up if there's a RAM issue

This symptom sometimes happens on an integrated display card, of where the display memory is the main memory. To start with, we must check the position of the RAM memory card. There should always be a memory card plugged in the first memory slot; if the first memory slot is unoccupied, then there might be a black screen problem. If there's a memory card plugged in the first memory slot, then probably the memory card is not plugged in properly or has failed. When this occurs in HP/COMPAQ laptops, there won't be any warning sound, so you should check whether the memory card is in tight enough; and clean the oxide on the golden fingers of the memory card; or replace it with a known working one.

E) The laptop doesn't light up and there may be an issue with the laptop video cable output circuit.

The most common failure symptoms are: no self-test interface, abnormal spots, speckles, patterns and black screen. What you need to concentrate on is the elimination of the possibility that the problem is with the monitor or its signal output data cable, so you don't waste time on something else irrelevant.

Connect an external LCD screen to the VGA or DVI video port of the laptop, and then switch the video output from the display of the laptop to the external display. This is the procedure:

For an HP (COMPAQ) laptop, you can press Fn +F4 keys simultaneously to switch to video output mode. Sometimes, in order to operate successfully, you will have to first connect an external display onto your laptop, and then restart the laptop, then the external display will be recognized by the laptop;

1. If the external display works well, but the LCD screen of the laptop has no picture or there're some abnormal spots or speckles, the problem might be related to the LCD screen or the video connection cable;

2. If you run into the issue that there is no display in either the LCD screen of the laptop or the external one, or there are abnormal spots or speckles displayed, then the issue may be with the screen itself, or with the video connection cable. Testing the laptop with an external display is quite important as it may eliminate one of the issues.

8.1.4 Some common errors after a laptop start up, and their causes

Symptom analysis for 20 active error prompts for laptop failures

When starting a laptop, if the system finds a problem, it will prompt an active error. These are some of the error messages you may encounter:

1.   —Bad CMOS Battery:

   The CMOS battery on the motherboard is dead or nearly dead;

2.   System CMOS checksum bad—default configuration used

   a),   CMOS battery is dead or nearly dead;
   b),   the system CMOS has already been corrupted or a modification is incorrect;
   c),   the motherboard is damaged.

3.   Non-System Disk or disk error replace or strike any key when ready, means there is no system boot disc, or the computer doesn't recognize the existence of the hard disk;

4.   Failure Fixed Disk 0, explanation:

   a),   the connection between hard disk and motherboard is loose;
   b),   the hard disk is damaged,
   c),   the motherboard is damaged.

5.   PXE-E61: Media Test Failure:

   a)   The laptop has been set to enable using a network card server from a remote place, but the start. Procedure could not find the start path on the network device.
   b)   Disk failure, the laptop could not inspect it; try the next available device to start, such as a network card.

6.   A Disc Read Error Occurred, use Ctrl+Alt+Del to restart.

   a),   probably the MBR (main boot record) of the hard disk is corrupted,
   b),   there's a problem with the disk drive itself.

7.   "SMART failure predicted on hard disc Warning: Immediately back up data and replace your hard disc drive. A failure may be imminent. Press F1 to continue.

   -      the 0 track of hard disk or the part that controls reading/and writing is dying;

8. Missing operating system

    a), start-up file is lost or damaged,
    b), computer viruses,
    c), boot record is already damaged;
    d), disk failure or the disk has already been deleted.

9. NTLDR is Missing, Press any key to restart

    a), the computer starts from a non-starting source, such as non-start CD disc and U disk;
    b), the hard disk hasn't been reformatted after replacement;
    c), the connection between the hard disk and the motherboard is loose or the boot sector/main boot record MBR is damaged;

10. Checking file system on c: one of your disks needs to be checked for consistency

    a) The computer wasn't turned off correctly, which forces the system to check for consistency
    b) There's something wrong with the disk drive, or the 0 track of the disk is damaged
    c) A bad sector or track occurs on the disk;

11. Error loading operating system; <Windows root>\system32\XXX.dll;

    a), the computer operating system is infected by one or more viruses;
    b), the hard disk has bad sectors or bad tracks;
    c), a RAM memory card is damaged;

12. HDD name: \Documents and Settings\user (name) is not accessible, Access is Denied;

    a), after reinstalling a Windows XP system, the folder created previously could not be read;
    b) involves an external hard disk and U disk, but the internal OS on the hard disk comes from another machine;
    c), Problem with the security identifier ID that doesn't match with the folder to open it;

13. No permission to read the contents after a fresh install of Windows XP, although it's the same name and password, but there is no right to read original created files;

    a), the file might be locked or the second user of the machine uses password protection for this, you might have no authority to open the text file;

b), if you haven't joined a domain, and would like to check the security option card, check setup,

View, change or delete parts of the article and file special authority.

14. Write protects error writing drive C:

a), repeated reinstallation of Windows system causes the security identifier ID to not match and no edit authority (the domain might be locked to edit),
b), there's an internal virus protection, and the protection time of the domain comes exactly from the startup scanning of the software;
c), several tools have been used repeatedly, such as compression, decompression, modify or delete large files (like movie files), and files with special characters, you haven't done a low format to hard disk to let it return to factory state;
d), BIOS (bug) error, restart the computer and it will return to normal;
e), code error of disk drive, hardware problem of disk.

15. Keyboard Error, explanation:

a), keyboard connection error or the keyboard is faulty;
b), the keyboard management chip on the motherboard is faulty;

16. Keyboard Controller Failed,

a), the keyboard has short circuit damage;
b), the keyboard management chip on the motherboard is faulty;

17. -Memory Error / Memory Parity Error—System crash,

a), the DRAM, SIMM or the accessory memory card on the motherboard is broken;
b), the Cache Memory controller on the motherboard is broken or there's a driver running error;
c), the Video Memory on the motherboard or the Memory on the accessory display card is broken or
d), there's a driver running error;

18. Memory Size Change /. Memory Size Mismatch,

a), the RAM memory card capacity is incompatible with the previous one
b), there's partial damage on the motherboard memory card or the accessory memory card;

19. DVD drive not reading discs—"no disc in drive" error message

  a), DVD disc is severely damaged or OS is unable to read the type of DVD
  b), DVD-ROM drive is damaged or the laser head is aging
  c), the disc drive is not properly connected to the motherboard;
  d), the motherboard is damaged.

20. Real Time Clock Error:

  a) The computer is infected with Spyware, which causes problems with the system clock;
  b) Hardware device parameters don't match when inserting PCMCIA USB card, hardware conflict causes problem to system clock;
  c) motherboard setup CMOS (bug).

8.1.5 Another black screen failure symptom: the power indicator light is out partially or completely

This kind of failure not only includes the failure caused by the display device or component, but also by some components that may no longer be good, and leads to abnormal symptoms to the display. That is why we should observe the symptoms carefully before passing judgment.

1. Possible failure symptoms:

  1) No display at start up, laptop doesn't always power up.
  2) No way to wake it up after hibernation;

1.1) Possible parts involved

  Display screen, display card and their settings; motherboard, memory, power and other relevant parts.

  Troubleshooting sequence

1.2) Power checkup:

  A. Whether mains voltage is around 110V±10%. 60Hz and stable;
  B. Test the power adapter and battery with the replacement method;

1.3) Connection checkup:

  A. Power and battery connectors;
  B. Is the power adapter connected to the main voltage correctly and is the power indicator LED correct (whether it's lit and coloured);

C.   Whether the power connection of the power adapter or the power connection to the motherboard is loose or not;

1.4) Memory checkup:

A.   Whether the RAM memory card is plugged properly by re-seating it, and use an eraser or alcohol to wipe the golden fingers as they may be dirty;
B.   Test whether there's a short circuit or temperature rise on the RAM memory card.

1.5) Display card check and other checkups

A.   Whether the independent display card is plugged in properly or not. You can check it by plugging it in again, and wipe the interface part of the display card with alcohol as it may be dirty
B.   After pulling out DVD-ROM, hard disk, battery and other accessories, verify the power on the main computer, to see if it is self test are normal
C.   Pull out the network card, wireless, modem and other accessories, then test the laptop.

Motherboard checkup:

i.   Whether the components on the motherboard are distorted, discoloured or the temperature rises fast;
ii.   Whether the driver of the display card is matched with the laptop and whether the version is proper.
iii. Try discharging the permanent DC on the motherboard (remove the BIOS battery on motherboard, 5 minutes later, put it back again), then you have cleared the BIOS setup.

1.6) Failure judgment points

A.   Power adapter or battery failures

After pressing the laptop start button, if you encounter a black screen and the power light along with all other indicator lights are out, generally, the cause will be with the power adapter, the battery itself, the power connector or motherboard management chip failures. For these types of failures verify each in the order mentioned above.

1.7) The laptop power indicator light is on, but screen remains black, also the laptop doesn't come out of hibernation mode even after pressing the power button; follow these steps:

A.   Turn off the laptop, and then remove the battery, also disconnect the power adapter from the laptop;
B.   Start the laptop, press power button for about 15 seconds to let the laptop exit hibernation state;

C.   Plug-in a fully charged battery or connect the power adapter.

However, if after doing the above you still having issues; remove CMOS battery from the motherboard for about 3 to 5 hours, and then put the CMOS battery in again and the problem should be solved, Of course make sure the CMOS battery is a good one. If not replace it and update the BIOS software as necessary. Please take a look at Figure 8-1.

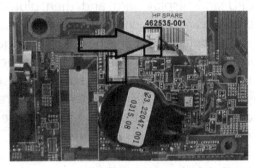

Figure 8-1

8.2   Repair flow chart to eliminate black screen or frozen system failure

8.2.1   Repair shortcuts for laptop black screen & system freeze ups.

General solution for black screen failure at startup.

1.   Check the power supply, power adapter and power connector

   a)   Check the laptop power adapter indicator light, if it's not lit, then the problem is with the ac adapter or the AC input to the adapter. You can try another power outlet or check it with meter or appliance and if the problem is still unsolved, then check the AC input cable of the power adapter. Make sure to pull the power input wire out and plug it in again. Check the voltage of the plug at the adapter end of the AC cable. If there is no voltage, repair or, replace it. After these verifications, if the indicator light is still off, consider changing the adapter with a good replacement one.

   b)   If the power adapter indicator light is on, check whether the power connection of the laptop with the DC power output cable is good. If the connector or the power output wire is damaged or cracked, then you should change it.

   c)   Check the motherboard power input connector, if it looks OK, then pull out the connector and plug it in again. If that does not clear up the problem, press the power switch, and move the power wire gently to see if that turns on the power LED or causes it to flicker, because of a bad connection where the wires enter the connector or the solder connections of the connector to the board.

   d)   Use a replacement adapter to see whether it will start the laptop or not, then you can judge if the issue is with the original power adapter. Pay special attention to whether the adapter connects correctly or not, some power adapters have a voltage adjustment switch. Make sure it is set correctly before using the adapter.

2. "Minimum system method" remove the RAM memory card, clean it with a soft bristle brush or an eraser. However, you can also use a blower or a cold hair spray. Most of the times failures are caused by dust build up.

   a) Remove the CPU and display card and then plug them in again (if it's an independent display card), and check whether the machine starts. Meanwhile, you could use the replacement method: install a good CPU, RAM memory card and display card, one at a time and test between each install; you can then judge where the problem is. You should pay close attention to ensure the replacement is compatible, especially when you upgrade the CPU. First ensure that the motherboard supports it and that a black screen failure does not occur because of a mistake.

   b) Remove the battery, wireless network card, network card, modem, card reader, hard disk, and DVD-ROM etc. In all, if under minimum system, the machine still doesn't start, and the CPU, display card and memory card are all proven good, then you can conclude that it's the motherboard. As for the repair and test method for the motherboard, check another article.

General solution for system freeze up

System freezing errors or problems is an annoying thing. Most system freezing symptoms are interface freezes, "blue screen", system doesn't start, image "blocks" without any response, mouse doesn't move, no keyboard input, and abnormal interruption when the software runs. Despite all the reasons that may cause a system freeze up, it all boils down to either software or hardware.

The most popular method to deal with system freeze up, is first with the software and then with the hardware. First consider the application software and then the hardware failures. This operation is mainly with the application installation setup, and installation of some drivers. Usually such measures are mostly ineffective and wastes a lot of time. In fact, it's quite easy to quickly figure out the reason for a system interface freeze. By using the method below, you can quickly find out the reason within a few minutes on whether the problem comes from software or hardware or from both together.

Repair judgment shortcut.

A. Put a DOS startup disc into the DVD-ROM/CD-ROM, after the laptop succeeds starting up, Press any key on the keyboard to do the typewriter test, if no system failure occurs, then it means it has nothing to do with laptop hardware. At this moment, the key reason for the failure in the operating system or applications is viruses, hacker software, and drivers relevant with the hardware.

B. After the laptop finishes and DOS start up, tap any key and if a system freeze occurs, it means there's something wrong with the laptop hardware. Now the failure judgment process is: the minimum system test method, BIOS, battery, power adapter, and RAM memory card, display card, CPU, motherboard and the operating temperature of the hardware.

Sometimes, software-hardware problems may happen together, and cause system freezes. After solving the hardware failure, (no system freezes happens in DOS system), the failure still occurs in the Windows operating system. Therefore, we need to continue repair of the laptop following the method for software failures.

28 reasons for system freezes

Every person who uses a laptop will eventually meet dead system problems, Next are some common system freeze situations for reference:

System frozen failure caused by hardware

Situation 1: (CMOS battery invalidation) ensure correct BIOS setup and the CMOS battery voltage is not too low, when the CMOS battery is dead or the voltage is too low, a laptop black screen or system freeze up occurs.

Situation 2: (Power adapter not giving out enough power) the power adapter output quality is poor or is severely deficient, resulting in a system freeze up. Poor quality power adapters can cause large voltage swings when supplying power, resulting in motherboard power current variations that are either too high or too low and can even cause damage to the laptop. So it's very important to ensure that the power adapter supplies the correct power;

Situation 3: (laptop battery is bad or of poor quality) the motherboard power battery is bad or of poor quality, or maybe the battery has internal short circuit heating symptoms, and this will stop the power adapter from supplying power normally. Even worse, it can damage your power adapter. So remove the battery, ensure the power adapter works by itself, which is an essential step to test a laptop;

Situation 4: (plug-and-play device fails) devices such as the printer, burning software, scanner, U disk and many other peripherals can fail, but plug-and-play technology will enable the system to start, and when testing these devices, the system goes into a loop and finally the system freezes.

Situation 5: (inadequate cooling) clean up the case intake periodically. The heat produced by the monitor, DC power connection CPU, and GPU when they work, are quite large, so it's very important to keep it dustless to allow good airflow. If there's too much dust, the laptop's temperature will rise causing a system freeze up failure. GPU/CPU thermal connections to some important areas, which matters for the laptop for stability, can become a "disaster area" for overheating problems with HP laptops.

Situation 6 (Improper movement) if during the transportation process of the laptop the machine is shaken abruptly causing the internal components to come loose which in turn will cause a bad connection or system freeze failure. So check the connections of the laptop components if this happens. Avoid acute vibration as much as possible when moving the laptop and ensure to shut it down prior to doing so.

Situation 7: (RAM memory card issue) this is mainly caused because the memory card is loose, bad soldering or memory chip quality problems. Eliminate possible memory connection problems first. If you hear a long solo "beeping" sound at start up (most HP laptops do not have this symptom), the problem might be solved by changing to a new memory card.

Situation 8: (Disk issue) bad tracks or sectors are caused by hard disc aging or improper operation. The system freezes easily when the machine runs. You can use some professional tool software to eliminate these problems, but when it's damaged you should just change the disk.

Situation 9: (Dust killer) such problems can occur when the DVD-ROM laser head is aging or there's too much dust on the laser head. When the DVD-ROM laser head sticks due to too much dust, a read/write error will occur. Even worse, system freezes will happen.

Situation 10: (CPU over-clocking) over-clocking can make CPU work more efficiently, but it may also cause the system instability. Originally, the CPU speed is accessing data from the memory faster than the speed of data exchange between the memory and the hard disk. Over-clocking tweaks this situation. Laptops working in abnormal frequency and high temperature for a long period of time may cause system restarts or system freezes but it can also in a worse scenario, burn your display card or motherboard.

Situation 11: (hardware resource conflict) invalid errors occur because of conflicts between the internal sound card and the external PCMCIA (USB) or settings of the internal display card. Interruption of other devices, DMA or conflicts appearing on a port may cause system freezes or cause minor abnormal drivers and system crashes. As for situations where you get an invalid driver error, we can use anti-install to uninstall the old drivers, and then upgrade to the latest version and restart the computer.

Situation 12: (device mismatch) hardware device parameters are not compatible, the, main frequency is not matched, such as: After plugging PCMCIA USB card, a hardware conflict error appears, which causes a system clock frequency problem. So the systems stability is compromised and it ends up crashing frequently.

Situation 13: (Incompatible Software and hardware) 64-bit software and some special software won't work or install on some laptops; if you try installing them, you may receive errors like system crashes or blue screen. Software and hardware conflicts can be caused if drivers are not matched with the hardware on the laptop, like the sound card, wireless network card and the display card. As for system freezes with blue screen, most have to do with compatibility issues.

Situation 14: (minimum memory capacity) computer hardware configuration is too low, the memory speed doesn't match or there isn't enough memory, the machine running speed is too slow, all these will cause a system freeze up. If such problem occurs, then you should add as much memory as possible. The memory size should not be less than 0.5~1% of disk capacity.

System freeze up caused by software

Situation 1: (Virus infection) viruses will cause a system crash. Viruses will cause the computer to work inefficiently, and cause the system to freeze up. Keep on scanning viruses carefully. Don't use an unknown disc or floppy disk, and first use antivirus software to scan the attachment in emails before opening it, and always ensure you have the latest virus updates

Situation 2: (Improper CMOS setup) this failure symptom is quite common, for instance, improper settings of a disk parameter, mode, and fan will cause the system to freeze up or the laptop doesn't't start up normally.

Situation 3: (Incorrect shutdown) the computer is turned off prematurely. Power is cut off before an application exits normally, and causes system files to be lost or corrupted;

Situation 4: (BIOS update failure) the system freezes after updating the BIOS: an error occurs when refreshing the BIOS. The solution is to "tap randomly without seeing anything", generally, after the BIOS gets corrupted, there's a "root area" preserved for emergency, which supports USB floppy drive startup. If the USB floppy drive is still responsive, then try a general DOS command to recover, (although there's no display on screen at this moment), the laptop can still execute commands. Make a floppy disc which can auto refresh the BIOS, letting the laptop auto execute the file Autoexec.bat established on the startup disc, and the content of the file is a BIOS program for the same model laptop.

Situation 5: (very little hard disk space left) if there's very little space left on the disk or there's too many fragments; While some applications need a large amount of memory to run, the laptop needs virtual memory to supply it. The system will take unoccupied parts on the disk as virtual memory to satisfy the requirement of the laptop; when the space left on the disk is not enough, the system freezes up

Situation 6: (Shortage of resources) system crashes caused by shortage of resources: too many applications are started at once, occupying a large amount of system resource and if there isn't enough system resource, the system freezes; so avoid running several tasks at once to solve this issue. It's important to only run some programs such as the disk cleaning utility or the anti virus software by itself.

Situation 7: (Shared file is deleted) anti-installer or Windows internal install/uninstall is not used, but you directly delete the application folder. Some files might be shared with other applications, and once these shared files are deleted, other applications cannot use them, and then a system failure can happen. Another case is when you install a new application, there's file cover prompt, if you choose the operation to preserve the file or cover file incorrectly, conflicts between software will occur and the performance becomes unstable with system freeze failures and a blue screen.

Situation 8: (Registry information and main boot records are deleted by mistake) system registry information and main boot records are changed incorrectly, then file initialization is corrupted. Windows needs to access the main boot record file to start up, so the registry file is especially important. As long as there's a slight error there, the system cannot start up or shut down when running; so when changing the disk main boot record, always save the original record first, in case the modification fails and you can not recover it back to the original boot records. For system files or important files, you're better off to use a hidden property, (hide them), then there is no way you can delete them because of incorrect operation, and cause system failure.

Situation 9: (Drive Bug) if you often update the drivers for your hardware, and you don't know exactly about the latest drivers, there may be bugs with them. These latest drivers might cause damage to your system, causing a system crash. Remember: the latest one is not always the best one.

Situation 10: (Incompatibility between software) it's normal when you run certain applications at the same time that system freezes happen; the reason causing such a failure probably is that there's a conflict between the applications causing system crashes because there is not compatibility, with 64 bit and 32 bit software at the same time.

Situation 11: (Hidden Trojan software) the system freezes after starting certain applications or the running speed is extraordinarily slow. The mouse and keyboard have no response at all. Usually there's Trojan software hiding in the application, even occupying 100% CPU resources. Often the only way to get by it is by using the Ctrl+Alt+Del combination to end the task. Then you should clear up the hidden Trojan software with your anti-virus application before continuing.

Situation 12: (Conflict between applications and the operation system) the screensaver causes a system crash. During the process when using Windows, there's no system freezes, which means that some applications run normally in the Windows platform, but when the screensaver starts, the system freezes without any reason. This symptom might be caused because of a conflict between the screensaver and the operation system or the screensaver has a bug.

Situation 13: (system freezes when shutting down) a system crash happens when exiting the operating system, which means the failure occurs when Windows returns back to the DOS state. If Windows doesn't turn off completely, then the data on the disk buffer is written onto disk, it then creates a loop; the only way to end this is to cut off the power and restart the system. The reason for this problem might be the way the operating system is setup or some drivers are setup improperly. Generally, when Windows exits or turns back to the DOS state, all running drivers are stopped, and these drivers would do a writing-back operation according to the situation of the time. If the drivers are set up improperly, they cannot find the devices, so they just keep searching for the devices and cause the system freeze up symptom.

Situation 14: (Fan start temperature is set too high) the fan driver is set improperly and the fan start temperature is set too high. Under these circumstances the hardware produces a large amount of heat that cannot radiate in time, so the issue occurs. Generally, we can solve the problem by resetting the fan starting temperature in the BIOS. Most HP laptops' BIOS have no such function so you must rely on updating the BIOS version or installing a third party fan driver to solve the problem.

8.2.2   88% Black screen failures or system freezes from motherboard and video card issues

Most black screen and freeze problems are caused by motherboard or display card problems.

Generally, we would first consider that the motherboard has failed except for some obvious symptoms like the onboard cable that is either distorted or broken, or parts on the motherboard that are burnt. The motherboard is distorted because of mechanical pressure or a short circuit on the motherboard. As for the motherboard problem, only after confirming that all accessories on the motherboard are OK, can we conclude that it is damaged. Occasionally you may find that certain components on the motherboard overheat quickly and you can feel it to the touch. It indicates a serious problem with that component. 88% of HP Pavilion laptop failures causing a black screen or image freeze up come from the motherboard or video card. Please take a look at Figure 8-2.

Figure 8-2

Use the minimum system method to determine if it's a motherboard problem. Remove the laptop battery, wireless network card, Modem, card reader, hard disk, DVD-ROM and other accessories, then test the laptop. At this moment, there is only the motherboard, CPU, and RAM memory, (if there is an independent display card, please don't remove it) and then power it on to see if the machine self-inspection is normal.

Under minimum system, if self-inspection doesn't work, then it indicates that the problem is on the remaining accessories. The next step is to put the accessories like the independent display card, CPU, RAM on a good laptop, (to test the independent display card, you must use the same model and manufacturer), and then judge where the problem is. You can also use the replacement method: plug a known good CPU and RAM on the laptop motherboard, and test them. If your CPU and RAM all work on another laptop, then you know the motherboard or display card is faulty. If you follow the next method, you will within a few minutes solve your laptop black screen problem. Try discharging your CMOS battery on the motherboard (remove the BIOS battery on the motherboard, 5 minutes later, put it back again). If you still cannot wake your laptop, remove the CMOS battery off from the motherboard for 3 to 5 hours, and then plug the battery on again; if the problem is still unsolved, then you should consider changing your motherboard.

If the computer works all right under minimum system, then it indicates the problem is caused by one of the removed accessories. The next step is to plug the accessories one by one back into the motherboard. You need to restart the computer each time until you find the faulty accessory. Replace it with a confirmed working one and restart the computer, if black screen or system freeze symptom is eliminated, you've resolved the problem. But if the black screen or system freeze still exists, then the original accessory must be incompatible with the motherboard, or there's a problem on the motherboard. Most people might think that when you get a black screen or system freeze there must be something wrong with one or two accessories, however, occasionally, I find that when laptop self-inspection is all right under minimum system, and when I plug the accessories like battery, wireless network card, network card, Modem, card reader, disk and DVD-ROM/CD-ROM one by one to the laptop motherboard, nothing is found. This is because the internal parts are loose and a bad connection probably caused the black screen or system freeze up. During the test process, I always clean the accessories to ensure there is no dust built up.

8.2.3   5% Black screen failures or system freezes due to memory problems.

Most laptops do not have an independent display card, namely, the display card is integrated on the motherboard. Video memory almost always is shared with system memory. If the problem is with the RAM, then the laptop screen will not light up or Windows will not start. That's what we call a black screen or system freeze up.

The likely reason causing memory failures is the RAM memory is loose or the quality is poor. We can eliminate this problem by either cleaning the contacts with an eraser, and checking if there is dust in the slot, or just simply replacing it with a known working one.

If the laptop has two RAM memory card modules, usually I will remove both memory sticks, and test each one individually, but ensure you restart every time. Try plugging each memory card into slot A leaving B empty, then A & B, so 4 tests for 2 memory cards, until there's something showing up.

Why do you do this? Some memory slots may not work in the laptop. If a good memory stick is actually installed in a bad slot, then an incorrect judgment would be caused. This will prevent you from needing to buy new memory.

If the laptop only has one memory stick module, usually I would use a compatible memory stick from another laptop. Of course, you have to ensure they are the same type such as

DDR1, DDR2, SD, and the correct speed, to confirm that the memory is 100% compatible with the original laptop, (the memory must be exactly the same as the one existing inside the computer), At last, install it in the laptop and test. (Caution! Each time you do this, first pull out the AC adapter and remove the battery)

System freeze up failure due to memory quality, comparatively, is hard to distinguish. Sometimes the failure happens randomly. For instance, the screen freezes or the machine auto turns off when playing games or editing a picture. This is caused because there are probably faulty components inside the memory stick; or the faulty chips array at the end of the 2.0 GB memory stick. Usually when using the laptop, the RAM memory stays at a non-full-loading state and the faulty unit of the memory is not in use. When the laptop runs a big game application or you are editing a large picture, the memory card will become fully loaded. The previously unused memory resource will now be used. Usually we can use Memtest86 software to test the memory card and identify the hidden problems in the memory.

Memtest86 is memory test freeware software and the test accuracy is very high, although it's not 100% accurate. It's among the best available and it doesn't need support from any operating system because the software memory test starts before the operating system begins loading in memory. This means you can do a comparatively accurate test if you have Windows, Linux or the UNIX system.

Memtest86's other advantage is that it uses E820 technology, which enables it to list out all occupation situations of memory resources like the BIOS list. You mark all valid unused memory resources and the power supply list (ACPI).

8.2.4   2% black screen failures that come from a CPU error

There's a slight chance that a CPU problem might cause a system black screen symptom. It is due to CPU over frequency increasing the working frequency of the CPU. This probably would also cause the performance to be unstable. Of course the solution for this is quite simple, namely, enter the BIOS to enable the over frequency software to adjust the CPU to normal frequency. Most newer model laptops have already used frequency locking technology; so generally speaking, such a symptom would not ever happen.

CPU off-welding could also cause this kind of failure: it is common mostly on super thin models, and the typical failure symptom is a blue screen, system restart or system freeze occurring when you move the machine or type quickly. To judge whether it's the problem of the CPU, usually you can use the exchange method. Install a normal CPU of the same model to test the suspected laptop, if there's no black screen or system crash, generally, we can assume it's a CPU problem.

Some users like placing laptop on their legs or a soft sofa, which interferes with the laptop cooling, making the CPU overheat and finally causing the system frozen symptom. If there's no severe damage that has occurred, generally, it could help solve the system freezing problem by installing an external USB fan.

8.2.5   HP DV9000/6000/2000 laptop motherboard failure maintenance

The first step of learning to repair a motherboard

1) First of all, you need a little digital electronics theory, get to know the motherboard function, what the components do, as well as structure, features, performance parameters and so on;
2) Prepare some common tools used to repair a motherboard, including multimeter, soldering iron, hot-air gun, wire nipper, screwdrivers and some discarded old motherboards of HP DV6000/DV9000 series.
3) Take the reins of the performance and usages of these common tools used to repair a motherboard;
4) Master the marks, parameters and corresponding physical shape of each part on motherboard;
5) Master the functions, measurements (like capacitance, resistance, chip, diodes, audion etc) of each part on motherboard;

The second step of learning to repair motherboard

1) Master the components of each circuit on the motherboard so that you can find the basic components on each circuit and be familiar with the circuitry features;
2) Master the important circuit modules of the HP motherboard, and be proficient in the principle of physical circuitry on the motherboard;
3) Be proficient in applying Internet resources, according to the model of the chipset, find out the main performance and parameters;
4) Master the boot working principle of the motherboard, be familiar with the composing and functions of the circuits, and be able to find out the installed components on the motherboard according to the failure diagnosis flow and repair technique;
5) Master the working principle of some common CMOS circuits, be familiar with its circuitry and function on the HP motherboard, and learn the basic failure measurements for CMOS circuits;
6) Master the working principles of the power supply circuitry used on the board, be familiar with its composing and function on HP motherboard, and learn the basic failure measurement methods of power supply circuitry;
7) Master the composing and function of time clock circuitry, get to know the working principle, and learn the diagnosis flow for basic failures of time clock circuitry;
8) Master the composing and function of reset circuitry, get to know the working principle, and learn the diagnostic flow for basic failures of reset circuitry;
9) Master the composition and function of keyboard/mouse interface circuitry, get to know the working principle, and learn the diagnostic flow for basic failures of keyboard/mouse interface circuitry;
10) Master the composition and function of serial port/and parallel port circuitry, get to know the working principle, and learn the diagnostic flow for basic failures of serial port/parallel port circuitry;

11) Master the composition and function of USB interface circuitry, get to know the working principle, and learn the diagnostic flow for basic failures of USB interface circuitry;

12) Master the composition and function of BIOS software, get to know the working principle, and learn the BIOS setup for updates/upgrades for basic input/output application;

The third step of learning to repair motherboard

1) Master the circuitry rule of each circuit on some common motherboards, the parameter of key measurement points on some common chipset circuitries, and then you can accurately find out the failure cause quickly when repairing;

2) Summarize the circuitry features of HP motherboards, find out the parameters of key measurement points on the HP motherboard, and accumulate abundant repair experience by repairing a large amount of issued motherboards;

3) Master different structures of some common HP motherboards and repair methods, summarize the failure diagnosis flow for some common failures:

A) North Bridge chip's off-welding (soldering issues), short circuit and surrounding capacitance and resistance problem;

B) Power control chip is burnt, or short circuited and surrounding capacitance and resistance problems;

C) South Bridge chip's off-welding, short circuit and surrounding capacitance and resistance problems;

I.   HP Pavilion DV2000 laptop's display failure

Failure symptom:

The screen is out when the machine starts up, but the indication light is flashing;

Repair abstract:

Disassemble the motherboard; test it at the RAM memory slot with a digital oscilloscope, as a result, the display card could not be recognized. This is an independent laptop display card, so first of all, check the display memory; observe and test carefully the display card chip and surrounding components, finding no obvious damage, features like cracks, color change, poor solder joints, short circuits, and so on. Next connect the power adapter, start the laptop, and meanwhile, touch each main chip on the display card with your fingers. If you find that the chip temperatures are not rising quickly, it means its unlikely that the display memory is faulty. Measure the connection cable from the North Bridge to the display card with a digital multimeter, If the resistance value shows open circuit, its likely the solder joints of the data cable for the North Bridge could be the problem,;

Solution:

Remove the display card, and then measure it correspondingly. If it is found that any BGA joint has resistance, which means a poor solder joint, but not striking out or a short circuit. Reinstall the display card chipset, and after that, assemble the display card and then re-measure resistance. If the result shows OK, the problem is solved! As repair experience shows that the motherboard display card's soldering is the common fault for these kinds of laptop motherboards.

II   HP Pavilion DV9000 laptop's motherboard fails to work

Failure symptom:

Screen is not on when machine starts up, and the indication light is also out.

Solution:

It fails to power on when you try starting, the standby current is only 0.02A, and there's not any response after pressing the start button. Analyzing the failure cause: I estimate there are three possibilities for this kind of failure situation: one is a motherboard problem; the second is power supply damage; and the third is the switch or switch circuitry issues.

1) Try the power adapter in another laptop to test it, the result shows everything is all right;
2) So the switch is now suspected to be the problem. When I disassemble the motherboard and test it, I found that the switch or the switch circuitry has nothing wrong;
3) I check the motherboard carefully, I find that the North Bridge has been re-soldered previously, and also the power supply chipset and FET (Field Effect Transistor) are changed. But strangely, when the motherboard is out from the shell, it does start up, and the screen is on too. I put the motherboard into the shell again, but when tested again, it fails to power on. In order to solve this problem, I should only have to disassemble the motherboard from the shell, and test it while disassembling; when I disassemble the display card's heat sink, and suddenly the machine starts again. Till now, finally the problem is found out: the insulating paper under the display card's heat sink is not added! The function of the insulating paper is to isolate the copper heat sink, avoiding the heat sink directly contacting conducting parts on the motherboard, which would cause a short circuit. The problem is this, with the absence of insulating paper between the heat sink and the device has caused a short circuit. After pressing the start button, as the motherboard power management system has a current short circuit protection function, the power supply would be cut off automatically.

Therefore, add insulating paper between the motherboard and the heat sink, then start the machine again. The failure disappears. Thus it can be seen that during the laptop assembling process, even a little mistake would cause very big problem. A small problem if the laptop just fails to start up, but a severe problem if the power supply has been damaged. So you should be very cautious during the repair process.

III HP DV6000 laptop fails to start up

Failure symptom:

The laptop fails to start up, even with either the power adapter or battery or both.

Solution:

After initial inspection, it is found that there's much dust inside the machine, even worse, there's a heavy layer of black dirt on the fan. It's quite likely that the laptop had overheating problems before, which has caused component damage or a bad contact. Test the CPU voltage with a multimeter, if you find that the value is much lower than the normal specified range, try changing the CPU, if the voltage still has not normalised, it indicates that the failure has nothing to do with the CPU itself but probably there's something wrong with the control circuitry interfacing with it;

As the South Bridge chip takes charge of the communication between I/O bus, such as PCI Bus, USB, LAN, ATA, SATA, audio controller, keyboard controller, real-time clock controller, advanced power management and so on, and when there's something wrong with the advanced power management, first of all, you should consider whether it's a problem of the South Bridge chip or the connected circuitry with the South Bridge chip;

Locate the power supply resistor of PQ25 (MOSFET), and test it, finding the voltage is normal, proves the current supplied from the power adapter has already passed through it. Next test the 8 pin MOSFET, finding the transistor has input/output voltage, which means the problem is probably on the South Bridge. Next continue:

a)   Check the South Bridge to see whether there's a vibration;
b)   Check up the RSMRST voltage of the South Bridge to see whether it's within normal range;
c)   Check up whether there's bad soldering or connections between the power key to the South Bridge or the I/O transistor. After confirming that the South Bridge chip has problems, change it, start the machine and test again. The failure disappears!

Please pay attention: all this repair work needs to be carried out with the power cut off, namely, remove the laptop main battery and disconnect the power adapter. For more detailed cases, please refer to the article of this chapter < <8.3 28 repair cases for HP laptop black screen or system freezing failure> >

8.2.6 Failure analysis and repair flow for laptop black screen and system freezing symptom

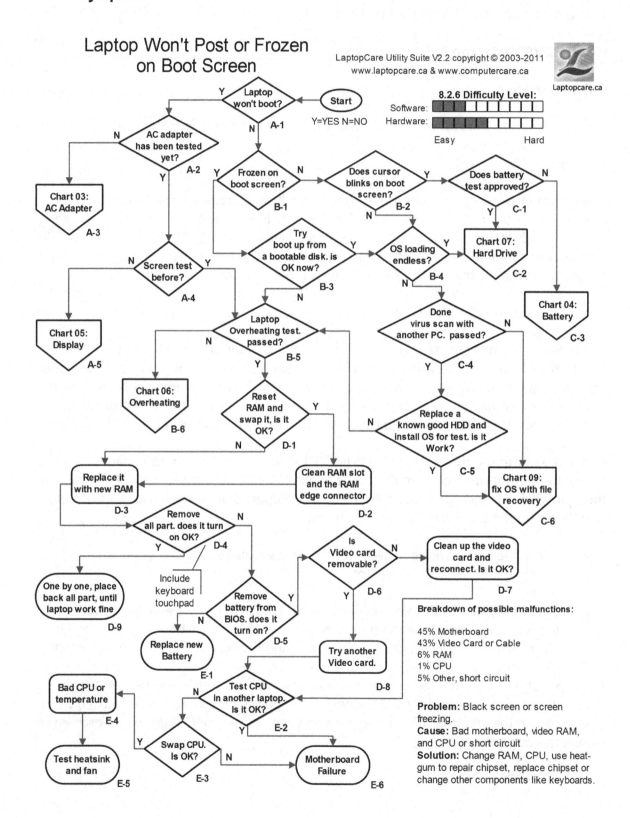

This book will help you solve the following laptop problems:

1. When you plug the power adapter in, press the start button, the laptop power indicator light is on, but there's no response (unable to start), and the screen has no display, just black. Please take a look at Figure 8-3.

Figure 8-3

2. During the Windows loading process it freezes, or the characters are very blurry to see, or there are abnormal spots or patterns; Please take a look at Figure 8-4.

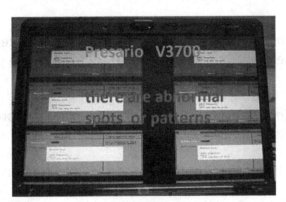

Figure 8-4

3. The laptop display card driver is lost or corrupt and the displayed color is abnormal, usually there are only 16 colors, after installing the new driver, it gets lost or corrupt again when you restart and after reinstalling the operating system, the situation remains the same.

In this chapter (or section), I will explain how to find the cause(s) for—laptop black screen or system freeze. The examples here apply to the most commonly used laptop makes and models.

Step: 1

You need to make sure that power adapter is working properly; otherwise, it will affect the reliability and accuracy of diagnosis and elimination of the problem(s).

When you connect the power adapter and press the power button to start, pay close attention to how your laptop reacts, the symptoms should fall into one of the three unrelated categories:

a)   The laptop power light is on after the power button is pressed, but POSTING will not start or complete. The screen is totally black with or without a cursor flashing on the upper left corner. This problem is not covered in this Chapter. Please refer to the Chapter 07.

b)   Windows appears after the laptop starts, but the Windows loading process does not complete, or the system freezes, or the system restarts repeatedly. Please note: this symptom may also be caused by motherboard overheating or possibly other causes. If it's other causes, it is not covered in this Chapter. Please refer to Chapter 06 or 07.

c)   After the laptop starts, it appears to be working and the Windows loading process completes, then the white screen appears, or it turns yellow and grey, or there are white or yellowish spots on the screen. The problem remains the same even after OS re-installation. In this case please read Chapter 05 first.

If you are uncertain about the cause of the problem, please refer to the chapter **<<2.1 Common laptop failure diagnoses>>,** there are six methods in determining failure causes.

If it still doesn't work, you may follow the "easy first and difficult later" approach, using the methods outlined in the chapters one by one and try to solve the problem one step at a time.

There should be sufficient help from the flowchart to solve the problems that meet the descriptions of the common laptop motherboard problems.

Step: A-1 the goal of this step is to confirm whether your laptop can start

The cause for laptop freeze is quite easy to find, but to find the cause of a laptop black screen is not that easy, the three most common causes for black screens are laptop power system failure, self-test failure, and the black screen after the self-test completed. Next we will check the symptoms and the causes.

4 different situations:

Situation 1:

After pressing the start button, the laptop power light is on; the manufacturer logo appears and the self-test runs though without issues. Next, after the OS loading process started it keeps going for an unusually long period of time, or freezes at certain points during the process. If you can identify one of two situations, then proceed to STEP: B-1

Situation 2: After you plug in the power adapter into a power outlet and pressed the laptop power button, there is no light on the power adapter (if so equipped), no power light and no beep sound on the laptop. If that is the situation you are facing, the black screen is more than likely caused by power system failure, and please proceed to the repair flowchart 03

Situation 3:

Your power adapter is confirmed in good working order and the laptop power light is on after the power button is pressed. But there is no manufacturer's logo on screen and the fan spins only for about a second or two. In normal situations the fan would spin for at least several seconds or up to about 15 seconds, which sometimes is accompanied with flashing light(s). If this description matches your situation, please proceed to STEP: A-2

Situation 4:

Everything appears working fine, such as the power light is on, the fan spins OK, the self-test passed, and the sound of the hard disk rotating and the CD/DVD-ROM drive initiation light is on, except there is no display of the manufacturer logo on screen. If that is what you see on your system, it may indicate a problem with your LCD display. Please proceed to STEP: A-2 and STEP: A-4 to check laptop LCD display.

Step: A-2 the goal of this step is to verify the power adapter's working condition

1) Check the output voltage value with a multi-meter to see if it is within the specifications indicated on the adapter. An HP power adapter's output voltage usually is between 18.5-19.5V;

2) The power adapter's light is on or off but that does not necessarily represent its working condition. Without the help of a multi-meter you cannot be definitively certain about the adapter condition, either good or bad. You can use the Method 3 to verify the adapter's working condition. In any cases where you suspect the culprit is the power adapter, try it on a different laptop.

3) The easiest way to determine the condition of an adapter is to find a working laptop of the same model, remove the battery pack from the second laptop, use your adapter to start the second laptop and run it for some time. If the laptop works fine, the adapter is fine.

STEP: A-3 the goal of the step is to direct you to the Flowchart 03 (or Chapter 03)

If not sure how to determine an AC adapter's working condition, please read chapter 03 and the flowchart in the chapter.

Step: A-4 the goal of this step is to verify whether the LCD display is in working order

After the power button is pressed, the laptop power light is on you can hear the sound of a spinning fan and hard drive, but there is no manufacturer's logo and no sign of loading the OS. If this resembles your situation you should connect an external LCD to the laptop to isolate the problem.

This is what you need to do but you need to be careful. For HP (COMPAQ) laptops, press Fn and F4 simultaneously to switch between the laptop display and an external monitor until you can see the normal image on the external monitor. For some models, you have to connect to the external monitor before you start the laptop to make the switch work. Please take a look at Figure 8-5.

Figure 8-5

If the external monitor works fine but the laptop LCD screen doesn't show any picture, the black screen problem is likely caused by the LCD screen or the internal video connection circuitry. Please refer to STEP: A-5

If both the external monitor and the laptop LCD display have no pictures, the black screen problem may not have much to do with either the LCD display or the internal video connection circuitry. Please proceed to STEP: B-5

STEP: A-5 is to direct you to the flowchart 05 (in chapter 05)

Your problem is probably LCD screen related. Please refer to the flowchart 05 (or chapter 05)

Step: B-1

The goal of this step is to identify whether the system freeze happens during the OS loading process

Many people experience laptop freeze. Most of such freezes are caused by software problems, while a freeze caused by hardware problems still counts for not so small a percentage. The freeze caused by hardware problems is much more difficult to diagnose in laptops because laptops are not like desktops where you can use the method of process of elimination (minimum system components) to isolate hardware problems.

There is also another more complex situation where the hardware may initially cause the problem which in turn causes a software problem. Therefore hardware should always be tested first, and then test the software. Please refer to STEP: B-3

There is another situation where after laptop started, but it failed to boot the OS. There is nothing being displayed on the screen except a cursor flashing on the top left corner of the screen, or the system simply freezes. Please refer to STEP: B-2

STEP: B-2 the goal of this step is to identify the type of problem

When the laptop power is on, the manufacturer logo appears, there is a black screen with a cursor at the upper left corner, either flashing or not. This symptom indicates the problem may relate to:

1)   The quality of the RAM memory;
2)   The hard disk controller is damaged or corrupted data is read;

If your laptop has this symptom, the problem is likely related to these hardware components. Please check STEP: C-1. If it doesn't help, check STEP: B-4

STEP: B-3

The goal of this step is to verify that the problem is not hardware-related

The programs used to test laptop can be a Windows PE system disc (not Windows Installation disc) to check if there is any problem with booting and running, or our DOS System Utilities CD-ROM which includes Memtest86 (for memory test). We often use Memtest86 to test memory and CPU L1/L2 caches. One of the functions of this utility is that it can perform testing hours or days on end. If the laptop freezes for whatever reason, the information on how long this utility has been running and how the laptop dies may help us make a better diagnosis.

If during the period of testing, there is a visual error message from the testing utility or a display freeze, it means the problem is likely hardware related. You need to check: points of connections, RAM memory, motherboard, temperature of the CPU and GPU etc. You may go to STEP B-5 for diagnosing overheating problems. If there is nothing wrong during the period of testing (i.e. no system freeze etc.) the problem may be related to the OS, hard drive and hardware drivers. If that is the case, please refer to STEP: B-4.

STEP: B-4 The goal of this step is to distinguish the source of the problem between the OS and hard drive

These are the steps to follow:

1.   Press the power button to start the laptop;
2.   When a HP or COMPAQ logo appears, press F10 to enter the BIOS Setup;

3. When the main menu displays, find the entry "HDD self-test options" or "Primary Hard Disk self test" in the BIOS. Note that different BIOS versions may have the entry in different locations;
4. Choose this tool, and press Enter.

It starts a hard disk surface scanning. When it finishes scanning, there will be a message displayed about the scanning result. This is the simplest method of testing a hard drive, but it won't guarantee the hard drive does not have other problems, even if the hard drive passes the test.

If the hard disk passes the test, we can now consider repairing the system software:

1) First try to start the laptop in safe mode. If it can run in safe mode then the following are likely to be the cause of the problem: hardware driver(s), OS related issues or virus infection.
2) If it can run in safe mode, run an antivirus program or other security programs.

   a) Scan and clean the user's machine with an antivirus program;
   b) Check to see if the user's machine has installed two or more antivirus programs or firewall programs. If so, suggest to user that it's more stable to install only one antivirus program and one firewall program;
   c) Check if it has Trojan infection. Scan and clean the system with the latest anti-Trojan program. Also suggest installing a firewall and the latest security patches for OS.
   d) If the problem still remains after having scanned and cleaned the system and restarted it, recall if a software program was upgraded or updated or installed before the problem was noticed. If so, that program should be uninstalled. Also, Windows System Restore can be tried. If the problem still remains, try the Flowchart 07, please refer to STEP: C-2.

3) If the laptop can not run in safe mode, the diagnosis will be a bit more complicated. In this case, please proceed to STEP: C-4;
4) Reinstall the OS. For HP laptops, pressing F11 gives you the option of "System Recovery" to recover the system to its original state. If during the recovery process an error message, blue screen or request to restart or auto restart appear, proceed to shut down the system and press the power button to restart (it may happen several times). If it still doesn't solve the problem, it may still be a hardware problem. Try replacing hard drive and go to STEP: C-2;

Step: B-5 the goal of this step is to identify if laptop has overheating problem

If a laptop overheats, these symptoms will appear:

1. The system or interface will freeze

2. The system will shut down automatically caused by the CPU's self-protection mechanism.

One important cause for laptop overheating is fan related issues. For example, dirty fans, aging and deformed fan parts caused by excessive heat are the common causes for slower fan speed. If heat keeps rising, it may eventually cause the fan to stop completely.

There are three methods to determine if the fan is working properly:

1) Install a third party utility to test the fan speed;
2) Listen to the sound. It should be quiet if the fan is not spinning;
3) Feel the airflow and its temperature near the heat emission outlet when the fan is spinning. Fan speed is proportional to the heat, so the higher the heat temperature, the faster the fan spins.

If:

A) Your laptop base is quite hot and there's no hot air coming out of the heat emission outlet. Or
B) The fan is spinning at high speed, but the CPU temperature is still gradually rising. In this case the fan is probably too old or too dirty to function properly. If that's the case check the flowchart 07 and go to STEP C-2.

STEP: B-6 the target of this step is to confirm to choose repair flowchart 06

Your problem might be related to laptop overheating, please first check tutorial article (in Chapter 06) about curing laptop overheating failure analysis

STEP: C-1 the goal of this step is to confirm that your laptop has no battery issue

As my repair experience shows, the connection state between the battery and laptop motherboard, if there is a bad contact, will cause system freeze ups or black screen. So when the laptop doesn't start, I will always first check the connection status of the battery, and check the connector condition between the battery and the laptop motherboard again. A HP battery, usually, has 6 connector pins, please check the inside of the connector pins, ensuring there's no damage or none are bent, and there should be no hair or dust attached to the surface.

Here you should especially pay attention, some batteries, although they may seem the same, can be completely incompatible. If a customer uses the battery by mistake, then he'll run into to some major trouble. So check the battery model carefully, ensuring the battery is completely compatible with the laptop. If the testing is all right and the battery has no compatible issues then please enter STEP: C-2; if the test result is wrong and the battery is overheating then please enter STEP: C-3

STEP: C-2 the goal of this step is to confirm choosing repair flow 07

Your problem is quite likely to be relevant with the laptop hard disk; please first check tutorial article (in chapter 07), regarding the failures; laptop cannot load Windows, or repeatedly restarting and blue screen failure.

STEP: C-3 the goal of this step is to confirm repair flowchart 04

Your problem is quite likely due to the laptop battery power supply, please first check the tutorial article (in chapter 04), about failure analysis and repair flow when the laptop battery doesn't charge.

STEP: C-4 the goal of this step is to analyze and confirm whether the operating system has been infected by viruses.

If a laptop cannot start from the safe mode, then we need to uninstall the hard disk and put it into an USB box, making it into an external USB movable disk, and then plug the external USB disk into a running laptop, next execute the antivirus software to scan viruses, checking whether there's Trojan; with the latest anti-spyware. After finishing, we need to put the hard disk back into the laptop and then restart it and validate. If the failure still exists, then you should consider backing up your important data such as pictures, documents, favourites web pages etc. then please continue to STEP: C-6;

If you already have the independent backup for the important data, then please recover your operating system method to fix it; if after recovering, the failure still isn't eliminated, then initialize the hard disk, and then reinstall operation system (clear up the disk partition completely first), please use method of STEP: C-5 to diagnose.

STEP: C-5 the goal of this step is to confirm that the problem is relevant with the original hard disk

If you decide to use a new hard disk to replace the original one, then you need to pay attention to the next 2 points:

1)   The interface of your new hard disk must be the same as the original disk, if the original matched hard disk is the IDE interface, use IDE, but if it's SATA use SATA
2)   The capacity of the new disk should be close to the original one, it is inadvisable to use one whose capacity is too large, avoiding the issue that the BIOS may not be able to recognize a disk of larger capacity, finally leading to some other problems.

This (C-5) step is to confirm that the failure comes from the original hard disk, it is best to test it with a new one and make sure the operating system installation disc and DVD-ROM/ CD-ROM are 100% OK. During the installation process of the operating system you may receive either an error message prompt, blue screen or system freeze. Try restarting the laptop several times.

Check whether this works; if not, then you should consider that there's a hardware issue and continue to the following method of STEP: B-5.

If after changing the hard disk or reinstalling the operating system, it runs normally, and there's isn't more failures, then you need to recover your data from the old hard disk as per method of STEP: C-6 to carry on.

STEP: C-6 the goal of this step is to confirm the repair flow 09

Your problem is relevant with data backup and data recovery, so please check another tutorial article (in chapter 09) regarding failure and solution for the symptom that the laptop folder is locked up.

STEP: D-1 the goal of this step is to confirm the failure is not due to the laptop memory.

1) If your laptop has two memory modules, then it will be easier, because it's most likely that one of the memory modules is defective, leading to a black screen failure or system freeze symptom. You can proceed by the elimination method, remove both RAMS, and install one of them in slot A and then in slot B and restart the laptop each time so you'll have a total of 4 tests. If after the test the issue remains then the problem isn't with the memory.

2) For some HP laptops, when RAM card isn't plugged in DIMM A, but is in DIMM B, there will be no display at start up or it will auto restart. The integrated display card of this type of machine requires shared physical memory; however, the physical memory required by design is taken from the memory plugged on DIMM A. When there's no memory stick plugged in DIMM A, a black screen failure will occur.

3) If the steps above didn't help or solve your problem, you'll want to investigate the memory further, please enter STEP: D-2, if you think there's an issue with your memory, then enter STEP: D-3, this step requires you to change the memory with a known working one and test.

STEP: D-2 the goal of this step is to test the RAM memory by using software.

1) Pull and plug in the memory again, check whether the failure disappears; before plugging it in again, you should first clean the (Edge Connector) gold plated board of any dust or dirt and also the slot. When re-installing the memory pay attention to whether the RAM memory card is loose, or the connector is too tight and will not enable you to insert it in the right position.

Please take a look at Figure 8-6

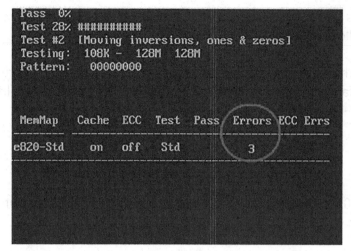

Figure 8-6

2) If this step above doesn't help, I suggest you using Memtest86 memory test software, which can be booted from a disc as it does not require an operating system and will enable you to see at this point whether the system starts and runs normally. If you cannot test or verify the memory, then please enter STEP: D-3;

STEP: D-3 the goal of this step is to confirm the problem by replacing the memory stick

If you cannot ensure that your memory stick is 100% good, then you're better off to replace it with a known good one to validate the test; however, ensure the RAM memory is compatible with your laptop and is an identical type to the original such as; DDR, DDR2, DDR3, and the running speed of it is correct, such as 667mhz, 333mhz etc.

Memory incompatibility or memory damage can cause an operating error, for instance, if the external frequency speed is PC333, and you install a PC266, you know an error will occur, and the primary cause for this kind of failure is due to the different chip groups on the memory cards creating an incompatibility problem. In most cases, this combination will cause damage to the operating system and even if you change to the compatible memory card, the system cannot recover and the only solution is to reinstall the OS.

STEP: D-4 the target of this step is to eliminate a laptop failure using the minimum system

According to this requirement, run the system in minimum mode by removing the network card, hard disk, keyboard, battery and any other removable hardware parts. You need the power adapter, motherboard, CPU, RAM memory card, display card, LCD monitor and DVD-ROM/CD-ROM. I suggest using an external keyboard, because the integrated one may cause a black screen failure if there's an issue. Afterwards, test with the pure bootable system disc, (such as Memtest86 memory software) or other professional Windows PE system disc to start, analyze and confirm whether the laptop works normally.

A) If the laptop succeeds to start from CD-ROM/DVD-ROM and passes through the software test without errors, in other words, the laptop black screen or interface freezing symptom disappears, then it indicates that the original failure is caused by one of the removed accessories, the hard disk or the operating system on the disk. Please check with the two separate methods below:

1) (Hardware loose) a black screen or interface freezing symptom is caused by overheating or the connector slot is loose, which leads to the abnormal error. Before accessory re-installation, first remove any dust and clean the (Edge Connector) gold plated board, including the slot. When installing pay attention whether the accessory is loose or the jack slot is too tight and stops it from being plugged in right. After installation of the accessories, if the same failure symptom occurs, then you can conclude that the accessory is faulty or the slot has issues. To confirm this further find a known good and working accessory, install and test it. If it works normally, then the original one is faulty. But if it doesn't work then the issue is with the slot on the motherboard.

2) (Hard disk failure) the interface freezing symptom is primarily caused because the hard disk is aging or isn't used properly, causing bad track and bad sectors. When such a machine is running and unexpected goes down, your issue is probably the hard disk so I would check tutorial repair flow (07) on how to eliminate failure with a professional software tool. If it's badly damaged, replace it.

B) If a black screen or freezing interface failure still exists or the laptop doesn't start up from the DVD-ROM/CD-ROM, or it starts but freezes again, or the software memory test doesn't pass, then the original failure is with the working hardware. Please check the different situations below:

1) Black screen

a) A black screen failure is probably caused because the display or its signal output data cable has an issue, so we need to eliminate this possibility first, so we don't diagnose it wrong. The test method is to connect an external display to the laptop. For a more detailed explanation go to Tutorial (05) regarding the repair flowchart for laptop LCD failures.

b) Quick or abrupt vibration during the transportation of the laptop will sometimes loosen the internal parts, leading to a bad contact, such as the CPU/display card and it will cause a black screen or system failure. You need to pull and plug the CPU/display card (except an internal display card) to check whether the failure disappears.; before re-installing, clear any dust off, recheck the connection between the laptop CPU/display card and the laptop motherboard and it probably will solve your problem. In general the CPU/display card will have many pins; check to ensure there's none broken, short circuited or bent. You can use a very tiny screwdriver to straighten the bent pins. However, during this process, great patience and attention is needed.

c)   When the laptop is overheated, the CPU catch ram can easily get damaged and the symptom is auto shutdown, freezing interface or black screen failure; therefore, test the CPU on another laptop, or install a known good CPU to the laptop and test it again, this will give you a better indication if it's faulty, and if it is, then replace it but the chance of it being faulty is about one in a thousand.

d)   When the laptop has overheated, the display card cache can also burn easily, the symptom can be a blue screen, black screen, blurry screen or freezing interface failures. You should test the display card on another laptop, or just install a known good display card into the defective laptop, this will help you better judge if it's faulty, if the display card is integrated onboard, then the problem is with the motherboard, please enter STEP: D-5, for an independent display card, then follow the solution in STEP: D-8;

e)   This symptom mostly happens on an integrated display card. The integrated display card shares the main memory. Since a distorted motherboard can cause a bad contact in the RAM memory slot for the card or even short it, you won't likely be able to distinguish it visually. Even though everything looks fine the damage is already done and when you install the memory card into the slot, a black screen or system down failure will occur. Here's the solution: install one memory stick in slot A and then B, and test once for each slot, this will confirm if there's a problem with the memory slot. If the memory card works in slot A, but a black screen failure occurs when plugged on slot B, it indicates that slot B has a circuit problem, and other situations can be deduced logically. (Pay attention: there is one situation that is excluded, the integrated display card of some laptop models requires sharing the main memory, which must be plugged in DIMM A; if not black screen failure will occur). If you encounter a problem when a card is in slot B only, this might be the reason.

f)   If there's too much dust inside the machine, and the heat sink vacuum is low or the thermal gel is dried and abated, this will also cause system shutdowns or black screen failures. The laptop CPU and display card creates a large amount of heat when working, so it's quite important to maintain good ventilation. If the laptop CPU, display card chip is overheated, then colors and pictures on the display will distort, or even a short on the motherboard may occur.

g)   The stability and reliability of the display card can directly influence the computers working performance. In practical application, if the heat sink washer that isolates the display card is too small or distorted and loosens because of aging or dust build up, and the liquid thermal medium is dry, it can make the display card chip overheat and finally cause a blurry screen, system shut down, or even a black screen failure. If this is the case, then the problem is most likely due to overheating. Please check tutorial article (06) regarding repair flow for system shutdown or auto shutdown failure caused by laptop overheating, or you can directly follow the method of STEP: D-5.

h) If the laptop black screen failure still isn't solved, then try removing the keyboard and using an external one, as the internal keyboard or touchpad can also cause a black screen failure under some circumstances.

2) If system down failure doesn't disappear

a) If it fails to boot from the DVD-ROM/CD-ROM, or after succeeding to start up, the system interface freezes, then please check these situations below:

1) The computer was shaken abruptly by mistake and caused the CPU/ display card/ the connection between memory and motherboard to come loose, finally leading to a bad contact and system shutdown. You need to pull and plug the parts such as the display card again (also including the CPU and RAM memory), to see if the failure disappears.

2) If there's too much dust inside the machine, if the DVD-ROM/ CD-ROM laser head is also dusty you'll get read/write errors, the laptop won't start up, or also lead to system down failures. You need to clean the laser head of the DVD-ROM/CD-ROM with an anti-static cloth, or install a known good DVD-ROM to the suspected laptop and try it.

3) If the silica gel thermal washer is too small or has dried up and is loose, it stops the heat from the heat sink close to CPU/north bridge chip from dissipating effectively. Also for some reason, the vacuum rate of the heat sink is too low and the liquid thermal conductivity medium vaporizes or abates and as a result, it looses its cooling effect. You can check another tutorial article (06) repair flow, and follow the repair method.

4) The fan control system fails or the BIOS version is old (with Bugs) causing the temperature to be out of control. This system freeze symptom usually has no obvious rule to follow, it mostly happens when the CPU loading is too high. Please refer to the method of example 3 in the article <<6.1.3 Common failure solutions after laptop overheats>>

5) The laptop once had overheating issues, and the CPU catch RAM was damaged, which causes a system freeze failure. Please test the CPU on another laptop, or install a known good CPU into the suspected laptop to test.

6) If the laptop still overheats, and the motherboard stability and reliability is still bad, or the display card cache is already damaged, it can lead to a system freeze failure. If this is the case, then your problem is complex, please enter STEP: D-5.

b) If you succeed to boot up from a DVD-ROM/CD-ROM, but the memory test with software still doesn't pass, follow these steps:

1) The laptop once had an overheating problem, the catch RAM is already damaged, which leads to a system freeze failure. Please put the memory in another laptop and test, or install a known good memory into the failed laptop, and come to a conclusion. When it comes to an incompatibility problem, check the specification and standard of the RAM memory, such as: whether they are from the same factory, same spec, and same capacity and of the same batch of memory modules. Confirm whether they can be used together.

2) The laptop once had an overheating problem; the motherboard is distorted, which caused a bad contact in the RAM memory slot, finally leading to system freezing. Here's the solution: install one RAM card separately in slot A and B and test each one individually, to confirm if there's something wrong with the memory slot.

3) Now the laptop still overheats, the motherboard is unstable so it's important to know the actual repair operation process, check tutorial article (06) regarding the repair flowchart for system freezes or auto shutdown failure caused by laptop overheating, or just directly follow method of STEP: D-5.

c) You succeed in booting from the DVD-ROM/CD-ROM, and there's no problem, but the machine freezes after connecting the hard disk.

For this situation, please refer to the article <<8.2.6 Failure analysis and repair flow for laptop black screen or interface freezing symptom>>; solve the problem with the method of example A from STEP: D-4. If you need to follow a more detailed troubleshooting process, please check tutorial article (07) regarding Failure analysis and repair flowchart for the symptoms that the laptop doesn't load Windows or there's repeated restarts and blue screen failures. Please follow the methods of disk check up and data backup.

STEP: D-5 The goal of this step is to confirm that the failure isn't with the laptop motherboard

If the CMOS battery voltage is too low or nil, then chances are the system won't start, or a black screen or other malfunction will occur. Therefore, it is very important to check the CMOS battery of the laptop. Remove the CMOS battery from the motherboard for about 5 minutes, and plug in a new one, but before doing this, you have to remove the main battery and pull out the external power adapter too. Once you change the CMOS battery, don't install the main battery or power adapter just yet. Press the power button for 30 seconds and then only connect the power adapter to start the laptop to remove the sleep mode from the auto sleep status. If the problem is handled, please continue to STEP: E-1, if the problem isn't solved, then continue to STEP: D-6.

STEP: D-6 The goal of this step is to confirm that the failure isn't with the laptop display card (chip)

A display card is one of the most important accessories in a laptop; there are two types; an integrated display card and an independent one. The latter one has many kinds of interfaces, almost one interface for one model. These are the main failure symptoms for display cards: there's a warning sound when starting; no self-inspection interface shown; and self-inspection doesn't pass; abnormal spots, speckles, patterns appear on the screen; and black screen and blue screen failures occur. What you need to pay attention to is to first eliminate the failure possibility on the display screen itself, and its data interface cable. For the right method to test the display and its data cable output, check also tutorial article (05) regarding the repair flow for laptop LCD failures.

If you want to confirm whether there's something wrong with the display card, you will need to open the shell of the laptop to check further. After confirming the display card is integrated on the motherboard, please enter STEP: D-7, if you are sure it's an integrated independent display card, then try the next few situations to judge and process:

1)   Bad contact, dust, oxidation on "pins" and so on.

For this situation, in most cases, there will be a warning sound prompt at start up, you open the main case, pull and plug the display card; clear up any dust or "rusted speckles"; observe the "interface" contacts of the display card for black discolouration. The metal will oxidize with air, so make sure to clean it as well as the slot it plugs into. The card and slot all have many tiny pins; please check for broken pins, short circuit or any bent pins. You should also check for loose installed parts or whether the slot is too tight and would prevent hardware from being properly inserted. Use a small knife and a cotton stick with alcohol, to re align pins and clean up "rust speckles", and generally speaking, the problem should be solved.

2)   Be sure to check the thermal condition of the display card

There can be problems after the laptop starts and runs for a long period of time. As with the CPU, the display card chip will produce a large amount of heat when working, and the cooling system has to be functioning at peak efficiency. If there's too much dust inside the machine, the vacuum rate of the heat sink lowers or the cooling oil dries and cracks, then the laptop will overheat. A fan also ages, can stop rotating or the speed isn't fast enough. This will overheat the display card and affect its stability. Here's the solution for it: ensure the heat sink is installed correctly, and replace the thermal silica gel with a high quality product to control the temperature of the laptop properly. Following these solutions will eliminate a large part of the display card failures.

If the method above didn't help you, then your problem may be within this range so enter STEP: D-8.

STEP: D-7 the goal of this step is to confirm that the failure is due to the laptop display card (chip)

The failure rate for display card in a laptop is quite large and is primarily caused by overheating. It isn't easy to deal with these problems as compared to other general failures. The laptop might display a black or blurry screen or a total system failure, with no prompt on the screen for reference. Users or even experts cannot eliminate the failure. If there's something wrong with the display card itself, you should send it to a professional repair center for testing and repair. However in most cases, black screen failures happening to a laptop is not that serious, because we can eliminate it in different ways.

Next is the concrete operation method for reference purposes. After confirming there's an issue with the display card, we can make a judgment using these few clues:

1) **If it's a black screen failure, due to auto shutdown, and the power auto turns off, then the key of your failure might not be with the display card, go to STEP: D-4, which checks the laptop failure using the minimum system method, the points are as below:**

   a) Check the power supply, the DC power could be noisy or inadequate due to aging and no longer satisfies the power requirement for the laptop and its accessories. Replace it with a more powerful one and of high quality.
   b) Use the elimination method; check the memory, CPU, display card, heat sink, and thermal silica grease etc.
   c) The problem may be with CMOS, remove the CMOS battery for 5 minutes from the motherboard, and plug in a new CMOS battery. The goal is to let the BIOS recover the default settings, eliminating any laptop auto shutdown failure. If this job was already completed from STEP: D-4, then omit this job.

2) **If it's a black screen failure, and power starts and ends normally and there's no abnormal symptom with the indication light:**

   a) First of all, check the display card memory, observe if something looks wrong with the display card chip, and then observe the external components with a magnifying glass carefully, for traces of bad soldering or damage (like cracks, discolouration, soldering off, short circuit and so on). Power on and test again, touch the main chips on the motherboard with your fingers, (except CPU/north bridge chip), within 20 seconds, there should be no chip in which the temperature will rise so quickly as to burn your finger. Testing in this way can eliminate the possibility or assure you that there's definitely a problem on the motherboard.
   b) If the display card chip is working for a long period under overheating conditions, then the motherboard will expand and distort, and eventually cause open or bad solder connections, finally leading to the black screen or system failure that we often see. Generally, I use the "heat gun" method to solve soldering and bad welding problems: heat different parts of the motherboard with a heat gun to simulate the overheating conditions; finally try repairing the soldering points that appear defective. This method is quite successful. Please take a look at Figure 8-7.

Figure 8-7

c) If the "heat gun" method and fixing the soldering points of the display card chip doesn't work, then unfortunately, the display card chip may be burnt which is the cause of a complete black screen failure to the laptop. Usually, we will solve this problem by replacing it with a new chip. BGA circumfluence soldering technology is one of the most common technologies, of which there are two types: the infrared calefaction stove and the sirocco convection calefaction stove. However, a computer retail store repair facility cannot normally assume this kind of repair; they are only able to change to a new independent display card or motherboard.

d) If the "heat gun" method fixed the suspect soldering points on the display card chip, then you should also determine the reason for the soldering defects. One typical reason for such a failure is the display card thermal silica grease which could be dry, poor quality, or there is too much dust on the surface, therefore restricting the heat radiating. You should change the thermal silica grease to solve the problem and change the fan algorithm by updating the BIOS, delaying this problem from happening again. If you want to solve the problem completely, then please use the method below. Please take a look at Figure 8-8.

Figure 8-8

e) The second reason is a design flaw of some HP models, as the small protruded base on the heat sink that's connected to the display card is not low enough; the radiator is not pressed tightly enough to the chip, which makes the temperature of the display card heat up. Finally a black screen failure occurs to the laptop and the system often shuts down. Use either a penny or a dime and shine both sides and then put it on one side of the radiator where the copper protruded base is. Apply thermal silica grease to it and press it on the north bridge chip. This will improve the cooling down of the core temperature of the display card and the failure is eliminated. You should be extremely cautious doing this, pay attention that the coin doesn't touch any live bare electric conductive poles and spots of the north bridge. Insulate these electric conductive poles and spots with thin adhesive tape. Just expose the core plane of the chip, ensuring there will be no short circuit happening to the electric conductive poles and spots.

f) Sometimes a CPU thermal module is combined with the radiator of the north bridge chip, when installing this kind of radiator, pay attention to not touch the CPU electric conductive poles and spots as much as possible and do not wipe silica gel on the surface of electric conductive poles and spots, it can affect the thermal performance by slowing down the fan speed when transferring heat; even particle temperatures on the CPU will be higher, causing a temperature test failure and a wrong signal sent, causing power to cut off for protection.

g) Sometimes the CPU thermal module is separated from the radiator of the north bridge chip. With this system, CPU fan cooling down performance is less effective for the north bridge chip. This is a design flaw and cannot be solved by the method above. You need to add an external USB fan to spread the heat produced from the laptop base to the surrounding space. In this way, you can avoid a large amount of heat building up at the bottom of the laptop and avoid internal overheating that can burn the display card.

STEP: D-8 the goal of this step is to confirm that a new independent display card is required to replace the old one

a) There are many kinds of independent display cards, almost one type of interface for each laptop model. Some laptop display cards might have two kinds of memory of different sizes available, but most laptops only use a specific display card with no other choices. You need to understand that some display cards look exactly the same including the interface when in actual fact they are completely incompatible. If you test the laptop with the wrong display card; it can cause you major problems.

b) If you decide to replace your display card, then follow the next rules,

c) The accessory number of your new display card must be the same as the previous display card. The memory size should also be the same as the original one or larger.

d) Independent display card chips can also be repaired by the "heat gun" method; generally, it's quite effective in finding abnormal spots, blurry spots and some other situations. What you need to pay attention to is that after repairing and polishing both sides of a penny; follow the method of the "e" step mentioned in STEP: D-7.

STEP: D-9 the goal of this step is to confirm the issued accessories are OK

If a black screen or interface freezing failure disappears; obviously, the failure must be relevant with the removed accessories, or the hard disk and the operating system on the hard disk. Based on the minimum system, add one component at a time to the system, and then start the laptop to check the failure symptom and see if it disappears or if something has changed, we can then conclude and locate the failure.

Note: each time you plug an accessory back, you need to restart the computer. Each time you add another component, ensure the laptop is turned off and the battery is removed. When re-installing accessories and testing, if a black screen or system freeze failure occurs, we can conclude that the problem is with that accessory. Usually, we should always use the matched accessory method so we can then locate the proper position accurately, and determine if it's the accessory or the slot on the (motherboard)

Under some circumstances, due to connection problems of some accessories, the laptop will get a black screen failure or the system will freeze. The result is that when you recover and install all accessories, you find the laptop is working normally, without any issues occurring.

STEP: E-1 the goal of this step is to confirm that the failure isn't due to the laptop CMOS battery

Laptop design is completely different from a desktop computer. Desktop computers will give users a direct prompt when the CMOS battery voltage is too low or done, or will leave a message showing xxx error. With laptops it's different, the system might fail to start up, or a black screen kind of problem will occur; so it seems quite important to check the CMOS battery.

Before recovering and installing a CMOS battery, you must use a multimeter to test the voltage of the battery, ensuring the voltage is 3V. If the voltage isn't right then change the battery. Before doing this, you need to remove the main battery and pull out the external power adapter. Press the power button for about 30 seconds, and then re-install the main battery and power adapter thus recovering the CMOS back to factory settings. This is quite a simple operation.

STEP: E-2 the goal of this step is to confirm the failure isn't caused by the laptop CPU.

CPU failure takes a minimal role in most laptop problems, but checking the CPU is a task that should not be neglected. Here's is an example: One technician checked an HP machine and concluded that the problem was with the motherboard; but later, an experienced engineer checked the same machine and concluded that the issue was the CPU. The Technician insisted that he had replaced the CPU and that he tested it and it didn't work so that is how he came to the conclusion that the motherboard was faulty.

The engineer did the same but it worked for him and that's why he concluded it was the CPU. So why is that? After long reflection, the conclusion was that he used an incompatible CPU with that motherboard. In other words, Both CPUs were good and so was the motherboard but one CPU was incompatible, and it did not work.

Experienced repair technicians know, that if you take an AMD CPU for example, they may be of the same manufacturer, but the production sites, models, specs, high cache rams, batches and other parameters will all affect the compatibility if used between the CPU and motherboard.

1) Check whether the new installed CPU has the same parameters with the original one, along with the production site, model, spec, catch ram size, which would be better if it came from the same batch, but if it doesn't, you'll need to confirm if it can work with this type of motherboard.

2) When replacing the CPU and testing, first use CPU loading, check whether the power supply voltage of the motherboard is within the allowable range, under normal voltage input. Then you can replace the CPU. If exceeding the range, directly change the motherboard. As for the CPU allowable voltage value, information data can be found on the internet. When necessary, contact the supplier on whether there's any other prompt.

STEP: E-3 the goal of this step is to confirm if the failure is due to the laptop CPU

CPU failure is uncommon when it comes to laptop problems, but an incompatibility situation between the CPU and motherboard is quite common, so install a suspected CPU into a working identical laptop and test to see if it's working. If it isn't don't conclude that the issue is with the CPU or motherboard just yet, check the parameters carefully, like the CPU production site, model, spec, catch ram and batch to ensure there isn't an issue combining it with that motherboard. If it doesn't pass, then install a good CPU that is known to be compatible with the suspected laptop and try it to help conclude whether it is the CPU or not. So if it is replace it.

STEP: E-4 The goal of this step is to determine what the issue is

Install a good working CPU and test, as a result, the laptop works normally, which is good news, but don't hurry to close shop as now you have to determine what created the issue and why the CPU failed. Will the new CPU installation fail again because the original fault still exists? It's very important to find out the cause of failure.

Follow the next four situations, carefully:

Situation 1: Overheating is caused because either the fan is aging, stops rotating or the speed is slow, and in turn will burn the CPU. Solution: please refer to the method of Step: B-5 in chapter <<6.2.6 failure analysis and repair flow for system freezes or auto shutdown due to overheating>>

Situation 2: If the fan controller fails, the fan will not work even if you replace the fan. Therefore the laptop CPU will overheat and burn. Solution: Refer to the method of example 3 in chapter <<6.1.4 Common failure solutions for laptop overheating problem>>

Situation 3: the thermal silica grease between the heat sink tube and CPU is aging, which will sometimes cause the laptop to shut down or freeze suddenly; it can even burn the CPU. It's a good idea to carefully check the bottom part of the heatsink from time to time to see if the thermal silica gel is dried and replace it with one of high quality.

Situation 4: the laptop heat sink is loose, or the radiator fastening clip has detached, the cooling oil inside heat sink tube is dried or abated. Any of these will cause laptop overheating, and finally the CPU/GPU fails to dissipate the heat sufficiently leading to catastrophic failure. You can reinstall and fasten the heat sink to solve a bad radiating problem.

STEP: E-5 The goal of this step is to confirm whether the failure is due to the heat sink tube

How do you check up the heat sink tube? Do you need a professional device or test techniques? Actually, nothing is required; the operation process is quite simple; just touch the heat sink with your fingers. In fact, the inside part of the heat sink tube is all liquid thermal medium, under vacuum pressure, the boiling point is quite low, if one end of the tube is hot,(usually the end close to the CPU), the medium inside will evaporate. As the media always flows from high temperature to low, heat will be brought to the other end, where the thermal tube connects with the fan. Then the vaporized medium condenses and flows back to the original place after it's been cooled by the fan. When the heat sink tube is working normally, the temperature at both ends of it will feel the same. If the temperature at the end of the heat sink tube close to the CPU is really hot and the one away from the CPU is cool, then it means the liquid thermal medium inside the heat sink tube has evaporated away or has lost its effectiveness. Replace the heat sink tube.

STEP: E-6 the goal of this step is to confirm whether the failure is caused by the motherboard.

Which part of the motherboard needs to be repaired?

Before repairing the motherboard, you must first understand how many primary parts there are on a laptop motherboard.

These are the power hardware control part, Chip group and BIOS, Motherboard chip group: usually defined as north bridge chip and south bridge chip as data will transfer between north and south bridges at all times. Other important components are RTC (real time clock controller), all kinds of interfaces on motherboard, USB, KBC (keyboard controller), integrated sound card, integrated RAID card, integrated network card and so on, which are all controlled by the north bridge chip.

It's quite important for everyone learning computer repair to get to know the structure of a motherboard, because this is the important repair points.

How to eliminate motherboard failure?

When the motherboard has failures, there are many bad symptoms, and we need the computer repair technician to observe carefully in order to confirm the problem. If you decide to fix the motherboard yourself, you need to first understand the types of causes of motherboard failures. The simplest way is to start by checking the power indicator light, by pressing the power button, and see if the indicator light is turned on. Usually if the light stays off, the cause is always connected with the power adapter, power plug, jack or the power control chip on the motherboard.

Please follow the next steps:

1) Check the power adapter

A. Whether or not it's distorted, color changed, a peculiar smell around the power plug and shell;
B. Whether or not the power cable wire is exposed, bended or otherwise has abnormal symptoms;
C. After powering on, notice whether the power adapter has a peculiar smell, or the temperature is abnormal.
D. After powering on, test the DC output voltage with a voltage meter, the result should be between 18.5V and 19.5V. Move the power adapter cable to verify if there is any power cut off, output voltage fluctuates repeatedly or drops to 0. If the answer is yes, then you need to change the power adapter.

2) Check the motherboard power-on situation:

A. Is the DC power jack firmly inserted into the laptop? It should not be loose. Check the female jack solder connections to the motherboard. They should not be loose, or any pin unsoldered or broken.
B. Check the jack voltage on the motherboard, it should be between the ranges 18.5 to 19.5V. Move the power plug cable gently and check the voltages at both ends of the jack to see whether they will fluctuate or drop to 0. If the answer is yes, then you need to replace the power jack on the motherboard;
C. Check whether the power switch turns on or off normally, the sound should be clear, and no beeps or bad contact symptoms;
D. Check that the cable of the power switch connecting to the motherboard is not broken or shorted.

3) Check the internal connections on the motherboard:

A. Check that there's no foreign object stuck on the motherboard (like a small screw), which might have caused a short circuit; or the resistors and capacitors of various accessories haven't changed color, carbonized or shorted out.
B. Generally the HP battery jack has 6 connector pins. Check to see if there's a broken or bent pin, and it connects firmly and properly. Make sure the battery is not loose

or the jack too tight when installing the battery, it can stop the battery from being in the right position. Check for bulges on the outside case of the battery and make sure there's no hair or dust in the connector slot. Please take a look at Figure 8-9.

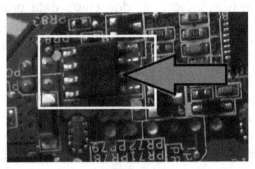

Figure 8-9

C.   Change chips: first find the key chip, which is the hardware power controller. Here we take an HP DV6000 /9000 laptop as an example: the right upper side of the battery jack, on the side corner of the motherboard (as picture shows: sometimes on the back side of the motherboard), there is an 8 pin chip which is the power controller. First check the 8 pins carefully, and then heat the soldered joint with the soldering iron, next turn the pin up slightly with a blade, under the function of the iron heating and turning-up force, the chip pins will gradually begin to deviate the solder on the motherboard, until it's removed. (All these jobs should be carried out with power off and remove the battery and power adapter), as for concrete operation, please refer to the article <<8.2.5 Motherboard failure maintenance for HP DV9000/6000/2000 laptop>>

4)   How to recognize a non motherboard black screen failure?

If power works normally, then the next step is solving the video issue. There may be many reasons for video issues. How to eliminate a non motherboard black screen failure? Actually it's quite simple:

First of all, find an external LCD screen, connect it to the laptop. This is an essential check-up step. Some laptop models need you to connect the external display first, and then restart to ensure the external display will work. If the test result of the external displays shows normal but the LCD screen has no picture, then in this case, your problem is quite likely to be with the motherboard.

How to eliminate a black screen failure relevant with the motherboard?

North Bridge is the most important component of all motherboard chip groups. It has a leading role, and is also named Host Bridge. North Bridge is in charge of connecting with the CPU, control memory and so on. The location of it on the motherboard is usually close to the CPU. We consider the communication between the North Bridge and the processor to be the closest and the goal is to shorten the data transfer distance to improve communication performance.

Now the HP laptop's North Bridge is mostly part of the integrated chip group, which integrates the display core (GPU). North Bridge chip's data processing function is quite large and generates considerable heat. So the North Bridge chips on HP motherboards now include a heat sink. Most cases the heat sink and fan is shared with the CPU.

95% of black screen failures happen to HP DV9000/6000/2000 laptops because the temperature of the North Bridge is too high, and causes the solder to detach (the North Bridge chip uses Lead-free soldering, so when temperature is too high, the solder easily detaches itself). To solve this kind of problem, you need a blow soldering gun at around 400 degrees, remove the motherboard from the laptop, heat the surroundings of the North Bridge chip which creates a oven like solder condition, then repair the solder on the North Bridge chip. This practice proves to be very effective. As for a complete operation, refer to article <8.2.5 Motherboard failure maintenance for HP DV9000/6000/2000>

How to eliminate other failures relevant with the motherboard?

The South Bridge is an important component of the motherboard chip group, compared to the North Bridge, but its data processing activity isn't as large. Usually there is no heat sink and it isn't connected directly to the processor, but is in some other way.

The South Bridge chip is in charge of communication in the I/O BUS, for devices such as PCI BUS, USB, LAN, ATA, SATA, audio controller, keyboard controller, and real clock controller, advanced power management and so on. Generally speaking, all these are somewhat stable comparatively. South Bridge chips of different groups may be the same and integrates more functions, like network card, RAID, IEEE1934, even WI-FI wireless network and so on.

If the functions of these parts go wrong, then you first need to check these accessories and designated drivers. You could also use a good known accessory to replace the issued one. For example, a known working keyboard cannot work normally on HP motherboard if the keyboard data cable slot has a problem so we then need to consider the South Bridge chip at this moment.

In all, we can conclude that the failure analysis and repair flow for laptop black screen failure or system interface freezing are possible symptoms from the CPU, integrated display card, motherboard or memory problem.

Solution: replace the CPU with a normal functioning one and use the "hot gun" method to repair the points of solder on the North Bridge chip and the motherboard. As for detail on how to, refer to this tutorial, thank you so much!

8.3.1 Nine repair cases for black screen failures caused by HP laptop display card

136) HP Pavilion DV9720US laptop black screen failure

Failure symptoms:

When you press the start button, the LED light is on, but no manufacturer logo appears on the screen. Once power is on, the fan rotates for a few seconds and several indication lights keep flashing—then you get a black screen failure.

Solution:

This failure symptom belongs to the flowchart 08 that belongs to the sequence:

Start->A-1->A-2->A-4->B-5->D-1->D-3->D-4->D-5->D-6->D-7

Repair summary:

Step to repair flow D-3, remove and install the memory module, clean the (Edge Connector) gold plated board, including its slots. Check whether the failure disappears; replace the memory stick (of the same spec and same capacity) into the laptop, restart and test. The failure still remains

Go to step flow D-4: Use the minimum system method of elimination by removing Disc, network card, hard disk and so on. Restart laptop, you will find that the black screen failure remains, try replacing the CPU and re test. The problem still remains.

Go to step flow D-7. It seems the problem is coming from the display card chip. Because the laptop has been working under overheating condition for a long period, the motherboard bends because of heat expansion and the resistance increases and ends up causing bad connection. Finally North Bridge chip solder points becomes unsolder, which explains the black screen or system shut down symptoms that we see. Once we pin pointed where the problem is, it's easier to repair the issue. Disassemble the laptop motherboard, heat different parts around the North Bridge chip with a blowing soldering gun at about 400 degrees. As for the distance between the blowing soldering gun and the North Bridge chip depends on the experience you have. But the "hot gun" method is been quite successful to solving the unsoldering problem. Start the machine and test again, finding the issue is gone.

Hint:

Now HP North Bridge chips are mostly an integrated chip group, which integrates display core (GPU). Because the North Bridge chip's data process quantity is quite large, it heats up quite easily. The North Bridge chip on an HP motherboard shares the heat sink with the CPU.

137)   HP PAVILION DV6625US laptop black screen failure

Failure symptoms:

When you Press the start button, the LED light is on, manufacturer logo appears on the screen, but 2 seconds' later, black screen failure occurs. Several indication lights keep flashing.

Solution:

This failure symptom belongs to flowchart 07 that belongs to the sequence:

Start->A-1->B-1->B-3->B-5->D-1->D-3->D-4->D-5->D-6->D-7

Repair summary:

Go to step flow D-4: Use the minimum method of elimination system. By Removing the network card, hard disk, keyboard, battery and so on. Keep the power adapter, motherboard, CPU, memory, DVD-ROM/CD-ROM etc; and then use a bootable system disc to test and analyze. Finding the problem is not solved yet. 2 to 3 seconds' later, the black screen failure reoccurs again. So basically the source of the problem is coming from the hardware;

Go to step flow D-7, considering the display card has been working in overheating mode, its stability and reliability becomes reduce and the system will shut down or black screen failure will occur. The key here is to check the heat sink' quality of vacuum degree, liquid thermal conductor and ventilation condition. If there's too much dust found inside the machine, the fan speed will not work properly and heat sink for the display card chip will age, distort bend, and loosen. So the issue here seems that the problem is with an overheated display card. Here's the solution: clean the surface of the North Bridge chip, change the thermal silica grease with one of high quality, and clean the fan, heat sink and intake to a controlled low temperature standard. Afterwards, start the machine and test, the failure disappears.

Hint:

Such kind of failure, generally, happens when the motherboard overheats so the display card cannot work normally; because there's something wrong with the GPU. When the problem is not serious, you can add an external USB fan, or clean the circuit of the motherboard once, or change the old thermal silica gel and the failure will disappear but when the overheating issue is extreme it no longer matters anymore and you'll continue getting the failure. Here's the solution: So best bet is to use BGA repair system in order to change a North Bridge chip or just change the entire motherboard . . .

138) HP dv6-1001tx laptop black screen failure while in use

Failure symptoms:

When the laptop was started up 2 weeks ago, the laptop displays a blurry screen and the writing was also blurry on the screen when resolution was very low. But the failure disappears when the resolution is high; now it has become blurry in both resolution mode and the interface freezes.

Solution:

This failure symptom belongs to the description of flowchart 07 that belongs to sequence:

Start->A-1->B-1->B-3->B-5->D-1->D-3->D-4->D-5->D-6->D-7-

Repair summary:

Go to step repair flow D-4: Use the minimum method of elimination method. By Removing the network card, hard disk, keyboard, battery and so on. Use bootable pure system disc to test and analyze. As a result, the issues aren't yet solved, the laptop doesn't successfully boot up from DVD-ROM/CD-ROM, or the interface will freeze and does not boot up. So this means the failure must be with the current working hardware;

Go to step repair flow D-7, Supply heat to repair the North Bridge chip with a blowing soldering gun at around 400 degrees. Disassemble the laptop motherboard; heat each parts around the North Bridge chip for about 6 minutes, change the thermal silica grease of high quality and install the heat sink and fan. But this time the "Hot gun" method is not successful solving the North Bridge chip problem. Few hours after machine starts up, the black screen occurs again.

Heat the North Bridge chip with blowing solder gun again, and polish both sides of a one penny coin, then put it on the side of the heat sink with copper protruding platform, then paste thermal silica grease on it, after that, press it onto the North Bridge chip, lowering down the core temperature of the display card, then the failure is eliminated; start and test the machine again and the issue is resolved.

Hint:

1) Laptop CPU and display card chip create a lot of heat when in operation; therefore, it's quite important to have a good ventilation. If laptop CPU and display card chip overheat, then the color and image can distort and even shorten the life of the motherboard.
2) Polish a penny coin smoothly, then paste it with thermal silica grease cushion, then press it onto the North Bridge chip which will be quite an effective thermal method.

139)   HP EliteBook 2530P laptop black screen failure

Failure symptoms:

The user once dropped the laptop to the ground by accident, which after that created a black screen failure. There was no display on the screen, but indication light was still on.

Solution:

This failure symptom belongs to the description of flowchart 07 that belongs to sequence:

Start->A-1->A-2->A-4->B-5->D-1->D-3->D-4->D-5->D-6->D-7

Repair summary:

Press the start button, laptop power light is on; listen carefully to see if you can hear the fan and disk rotating, also see if the manufacturer logo appears, if not go to repair flow A-4; connect to an external LCD screen to check the laptop, finding you r still getting the black screen. Therefore, it's obvious that the laptop black screen failure has nothing to do with the screen and video connection cable;

Go to repair flow D-4; Use the minimum method of elimination. By Removing the network card, hard disk, keyboard, battery and so on. Afterwards, start the machine and test, you find that the failure situation hasn't changed. Considering the fact the laptop was once dropped it probably damaged the internal components and they may have become loose inside the machine. Finally CPU/display card with a bad connection will lead to black screen or system freeze up failure. So remove and install CPU/display card/memory (except if display card is integrated) again, start the laptop, and the failure disappears.

Hint:

If self-checking under minimum system is all right, then the problem would be with the accessories removed. Next step is to plug each accessory back in order like motherboard battery, wireless network, network card, Modem, card reader, hard disk, DVD-ROM/CD-ROM back onto the laptop motherboard and then test one at a time by restarting the laptop.

If you've plugged an accessory into the laptop motherboard and system shut down you need to replace that part and restart; besides, generally the CPU/display card have many pins, check both to make sure there's no broken pin, short circuit or any bended pin.

140) HP PAVILION DV2812TX laptop black screen failure

Failure symptoms:

Start the laptop, LED light is on, but there's no display on the screen. 15 to 20 minutes later, suddenly, the display becomes bright, and everything displays normally.

Solution:

This failure symptom belongs to the description of flowchart 07 that belongs to sequence:

Start->A-1->A-2->A-4->B-5->D-1->D-3->D-4->D-5->D-6->D-7

Repair summary:

We know from the failure symptom that after a certain time, the black screen failure will occur. It seems that a component isn't connected right or there is a bad connection and when the temperature rises, the failure points connect normally;

Go to step flow D-4; Use the minimum method of elimination. Remove network card, hard disk, keyboard, battery and so on. Next start the machine and test, the situation hasn't changed. Remove and install CPU/ display card/memory (Except for the integrated display card), the failure situation hasn't changed. So we can conclude that the issue is with the motherboard; and that it's likely due to a bad the loose contact of the North Bridge chip. When motherboard expands due to heat the failure points will connect again and the laptop returns to normal again;

Go to step flow D-7, disassemble the motherboard from the laptop. Heat the different parts surrounding North Bridge chip with a blowing soldering gun at about 400 degrees. Repair the position of desoldering on North Bridge chip, start the machine and test. The issue is resolved.

Hint:

When the failure occurs, the motherboard presents several kinds of symptoms which computer repair technicians need to observe and confirm carefully. First you have to know the different reasons or causes of motherboard damage. For instance, after pressing the power button several times, the power light turns on. Usually the failure is with the power switch, power data cable and power control chip. And usually, it will have nothing to do with the North Bridge.

141)   HP Pavilion DV6718CA laptop black screen failure

Failure symptoms:

Start the laptop, LED light is on, everything displays all right. But 10 minutes' later, the display turns black, after turning it off and restarting it the screen still will not light up.

Solution:

This failure symptom belongs to the description of flow char 07 that belongs to sequence:

Start->A-1->A-2->A-4->B-5->D-1->D-3->D-4->D-5->D-6->D-7

Repair summary:

Go to repair flowchart D-4; use the minimum methodology to exclude other possible causes of the failure. Remove network card, hard disk, keyboard, battery and so on. Next start the machine and test with no result. Remove and install CPU/display card/memory (except for the integrated display card), with no changes either. So the failure range can be isolated within the motherboard; according to my experience, these few HP models have a common failure which is the black screen failure. Generally, within 1 to 2 years, most machines will have encounter this kind of problem. If the user is a game player, then the problem will occur earlier. Because usually when the GPU is working, the temperature of the chip can reach 79 degrees. When playing games, the temperature will reach even higher. So GPU chip solder joint will loosen and this is the primary reason for the problem.

Go to repair flowchart D-7, disassemble the laptop motherboard, heat the different parts surrounding the North Bridge chip with a blowing soldering gun at about 400 degrees to repair the soldering points which has become unsoldered off from the North Bridge chip. Start the machine and test again, the result shows the issue is gone.

Hint:

The material used to connect the GPU to the motherboard has a different flexibility rate compared to those used for other parts and therefore it also expands differently. So every time the GPU goes through the cold-hot alternation, it will somehow loosen. That is why the repair method of blowing soldering gun will succeed temporarily because with time it will reproduce enough heat to loosen it again and you'll need to repeat this step again.

142)   HP PAVILION DV2781TX laptop black screen failure

Failure symptoms:

Screen flashes randomly when laptop starts up, four windows of the same size appear. And few minutes' later, black screen repeat itself again.

Solution:

This failure symptom belongs to the description of flow char 07 that belongs to the sequence:

Start->A-1->B-1->B-3->B-5->D-1->D-3->D-4->D-5->D-6->D-7->E-2->E-6

Repair summary:

This case is quite similar to the failure caused due to wrong drive (software) installed in the laptop. Or the user set the screen resolution too high, and then a multi-window symptom occurs. Is it possible that the issue is with the integrated display? This is what worries the repair technician.

Go to step repair flow A-4, first connect an external display, testing result shows that the external display also has the same problem.

Go to step to repair flow D-4; put a pure bootable DOS software disc into the DVD-ROM/CD-ROM to start and test. Observe whether there's any change on the screen; if there isn't then the problem is not with the operating system, but with the display card chip on the motherboard.

Go to step to repair flow D-7, repair GPU chip with blowing soldering gun, the result failed; Go to step to repair flow E-2, repair the display card on BGA rework station: remove the BGA with lead-free BGA rework station. And then draw the pin of the chip flat with tin belt, next re-ball the BGA. And then install BGA back. This repair process is kind of complex, which is affected by temperature control, the balance of the plate and the working attitude when repairing.

In all, repair project BGA technology has a high requirement. After finishing BGA, BIOS version af.39 update is required for the HP Pavilion dv2000 and Presario v3000 laptops. However use BIOS version F.3D update for HP Pavilion dv6000/dv9000 and Presario v6000 series. Increase the fan rotation speed by force. The effect is good, the performance is stable, and will usually stabilize for about a year.

Hint:

If you do not have the pure DOS software boot disc, you can use this other method of recognition: boot laptop, enter BIOS page, if the failure disappears, then it means the problem might be with the screen setup, if the failure symptom still occurs, then we can say that it's not the internal display, but instead with the connected display card chip on the motherboard;

Solder the display card again, or replace it and then try not to play large network games again and pay Hint: to CPU fan dust.

143)   PAVILION DV9823US laptop black screen failure

Failure symptoms:

Laptop starts but the interface is unstable, accompanying with distortion symptom. Several minutes later, system goes down. After restarting the laptop, it freezes frequently.

Solution:

This failure symptom belongs to the description of flowchart 07 that belongs to sequence:

Start->A-1->B-1->B-3->B-5->D-1->D-3->D-4->D-5->D-6->D-7->E-2->E-6

Repair summary:

Go to step to repair flow A-4; eliminate the possibility caused due to the internal display; Go to step to repair flow D-4; use the minimum methodology to exclude other possible causes of the failure, as the result, the situation doesn't change. After removing and installing the CPU/display card/memory (except for an integrated display card), the failure remains. Put a bootable software disc into the DVD-ROM/CD-ROM to start and test but still no change, which means the problem must be related to the onboard display card

Go to step to repair flow D-7, repair the GPU chip with blowing solder gun. As a result, it also fails; Go to step to repair flow E-2, change the display card chip. The display card in the laptop is soldered on the motherboard, while the desktop computer has an independent display card. So this job should be left to a professional repair technician (a lead-free BGA rework station). After changing the display card and refreshing the BIOS. Start the machine and test again, the result shows the issue is gone.

Hint:

It's not a simple thing to replace a display card from a laptop; it recommended that it's done by a professional repair technician. Generally users can take the laptop to an after-service store to repair and solve. Laptop display cards rarely in it have problems. But in most cases the issue is due to a badly soldered or power short circuit, which disables the display card function. For a more in depth method: please refer to article <8.2.5 HP DV9000/6000/2000 laptop repair for motherboard failure >

144)   HP hp520 laptop black screen failure

Failure symptoms:

Once the laptop starts, black screen failure always occurs. And no way to recover. The display card has been soldered once, CPU has also been changed.

Solution:

This failure symptom belongs to the description of flowchart 07 that belongs to sequence:

Start->A-1->A-2->A-4->B-5->D-1->D-3->D-4->D-5->D-6->D-7->E-2->E-6

Repair summary:

Go to step to repair flow D-3, remove and install memory again, clean (Edge Connector) gold plated board, including the slot. As a result, the failure remains.

Go to step to repair flow D-4; Use the minimum method of elimination system mode. Remove disc, network card, hard disk and so on. Connect an external LCD screen to check the laptop and restart then check whether the black screen failure still exists. Before trying to change the CPU and voltage test has already been done to it, you find there's only 0.9V, which is not the normal value. After changing the CPU you find the voltage is still 0.9V, just as the previous one. Then you know there's something wrong with the control circuit;

Go to step to repair flow D-7, as the display chip has already been soldered, there should be nothing wrong with the North Bridge chip soldering point. Test the voltage of the display card, 3V value is the normal range.

Go to step to repair flow E-6, repair the motherboard. In regards to the CPU voltage of 0.9V that doesn't come up, there are two possibilities:

1) South Bridge chip;
2) BIOS problem.

According to the client's description, the laptop got this problem when being used. So it's quite less likely to be BIOS problem. So the point is to check the South Bridge; heat up the soldering points of the parts surrounding the MAX8770 power chip with a blowing soldering gun at about 400 degrees. And then pull and turn the chip gently up with a nipper, lifting the MAX8770 chip's soldering pin gradually off from the motherboard with the help of a blowing soldering gun's heat and then pulling upward with the nipper, until the chip is removed. According to the opposite procedure, recover and solder a good MAX8770 chip back to the motherboard, start the machine and test again. The result shows the failure is gone!

Hint:

1) South Bridge chip takes charge of the communication between I/O Bus, such as PCI Bus, USB, ATA, SATA, audio controller, keyboard controller, real-time clock controller, advanced power management and so on. So when advanced power management has an issue, then you should consider the South Bridge chip as the culprit, which needs the PG collection from CPU power supply. When it's confirmed that all parts supply power normally, then start the latter NB CPU reset, which is what we often say: first supply power, then clock, and then reset.

2) MAX 8770 chip key pin has the definition like this: 8PIN TON adapter input voltage; 11PIN REF; 19PIN /25PIN VCC/VDD; 38PIN SHND main switch pin 3.3V.

8.3.2 Three repair cases regarding failure caused due to HP laptop bad memory or memory slot

145) HP Pavilion dv5000 laptop black screen failure when starting up

Failure symptom:

Laptop has black screen failure when pressing the start button, fan, hard disk, DVD-ROM/ CD-ROM d rotates normally, but the disk light doesn't flash, there's no voltage output at USB port.

Solution:

This failure symptom belongs to the description of flowchart 08 that belongs to this sequence:

Start->A-1->A-2->A-4->B-5-> D-1->D-3 . . . .

Repair summary:

Go to step to repair flow A-4; connect an external LCD screen to check laptop, the result is still a black screen. Therefore, it's obvious that the laptop black screen has nothing to do with the screen problem.

Go to step to repair flow D-3, remove and install memory stick again, clean the (Edge Connector) gold plated board, including the slot. Test but the failure remains, you go to the manual and realize there's another memory stick hidden under the keyboard. That memory may be bad and it may be the cause for the black screen failure so remove it also and now install one memory in slot A and then B and test once more. You should have a total of 4 tests in all with 4 restarts. As a result, there's only memory B, when you insert to slot A and B, the failure disappears! However, when you plug memory stick A to slot A and B to test, it shows black screen. Obviously the memory stick A is defective.

Hint:

For HP laptops, when you don't plug a memory stick in DIMM A but there is one in DIMM B there will be no display after starting up or it will auto restart. The problem is because the machine's integrated display card needs to use the shared physical memory from the plugged memory in DIMM A, so if none is there then you'll get a black screen failure.

146)   HP ProBook 4411s laptop black screen failure

Failure symptom:

Black screen failure occurs when starting up, LED light is on, but there's no manufacturer logo appearing on the screen.

Solution:

This failure symptom belongs to the description of flowchart 08 that belongs to this sequence:

Start->A-1->A-2->A-4->B-5-> D-1->D-3 . . . .

Repair summary:

Go to step to repair flow A-4; connect an external LCD screen to check the laptop. If the result is still a black screen, then the problem must be with the laptop screen itself; according to my client's memory, after updating the laptop memory, black screen failure occurred.

Go to step to repair flow D-3, remove all memory sticks, and then try installing one memory separately in slot A and B and test. Test the other memory stick in the same fashion. Finally the result is when used separately whether in slot A or B it works normally. But when you plug both in the black screen failure would occurs; check both memory and you'll find that the two memory sticks have different memory frequencies and parameters and therefore causes an incompatibility problem which results in a black screen failure. Ensure that when replacing your memory that they are of the same frequency and same parameters as the current one to update. Then start the machine and the failure disappears.

Hint:

When updating laptop memory, check if the memory sticks are of different brands and make sure that their frequencies are the same. For instance, one is a PC4200, while the other is a PC6400 so you know it will be incompatible if used together and the main reason for this is the chip groups are different. Sometimes such kind of combination can cause damage to the operating system and even not be able to recover it and the only way to fix this is to reinstall the OS.

147).   HP ProBook 5310m black screen failure

Failure symptom:

The laptop always ran well, but a few days ago, suddenly a black screen failure occurred, after system started up, CPU fan rotated normally, which seems like when the North Bridge chip solder came loose.

Solution:

This failure symptom belongs to the description of flowchart 08 that belongs to this sequence:

Start->A-1->A-2->A-4->B-5-> D-1->D-3 . . .

Repair summary:

Go to step to repair flow A-4; connect an external LCD screen to check the laptop, as a result, screen remains black. So the problem isn't with the internal screen.

Go to step to repair flow D-3, remove and install the memory stick, clean the (Edge Connector) gold plated board, including the slot. Check if the failure is gone, if not remove all memory sticks, and install each one separately and test by restarting each time. As a result, when you install them individually they work in slot B but not in Slot A so it means that the memory slot of the motherboard caused the issue so replace memory stick with one of high capacity and insert it in the slot B only and the failure will disappear.

Hint:

Because of high rotation speed, the airflow created by the CPU fan brings a lot of dust and is continually blowing on the memory stick and slot. Because the memory stick and slot have many connection points and very little space it ends up accumulating dust and as time goes by it can cause a short circuit to the memory stick and slot connection points. So it's a good idea to clean and remove dust from you laptop.

8.3.3 4 Repair cases for black screen or system freezing failure caused by of HP laptop CPU/BIOS;

148) HP Compaq CQ511 laptop black screen failure

Failure symptom:

Laptop starts, initially fan rotates normally, but there's no on screen display.

Solution:

This failure symptom belongs to the description of flowchart 08 that belongs to this sequence:

Start->A-1->A-2->A-4->B-5->D-1->D-3->D-4-> . . . .

Repair summary:

Go to step to repair flow A-4; first of all, connect an external monitor to test the laptop, but you get the same black screen failure. Therefore, the black screen failure isn't caused by the screen.

Go to step to repair flow D-3, remove and install the memory stick again, clean the (Edge Connector) gold plated board, including the slot. Check whether the failure disappears; plug a new memory stick and test, but the failure remains

Go to step to repair flow D-4; use the minimum methodology to exclude other possible causes of the failure. Remove DVD-ROM/CD-ROM, network card, hard disk and so on. Restart the laptop, as a result, the black screen failure remains. Try putting a good CPU in the laptop, then start the machine and test again. The black screen failure disappears and it enters the system normally. It seems that the CPU caused the black screen failure.

Hint:

When laptop overheats the CPU cache ram can be easily damaged, and it behaves as auto shutdown and black screen failure; whereas the laptop CPU and display card chip are the components that heat the most, so it's important to change the thermal cushion and keep good ventilation on time before disaster strikes.

149)   COMPAQ PRESARIO V3705TX laptop black screen failure

Failure symptom:

Press the start button, the power light is on, and you can hear the fan and disk rotation, but there's no display on the screen;

Solution:

This failure symptom belongs to the description of flowchart 08 that belongs to this sequence:

Start->A-1->A-2->A-4->B-5->D-1->D-3->D-4->D-5->E-1 . . . .

Repair summary:

Go to step to repair flow D-3, remove and install memory again, clean the (Edge Connector) gold plated board, including the slot. Check whether the failure disappears; plug a good normal memory stick to the laptop and test, but the failure remains

Go to step to repair flow D-4; use the minimum methodology to exclude other possible causes of the failure. As a result, the black screen failure hasn't changed, try plugging a good CPU into the laptop, restart the machine and test again but the black screen failure still exists.

Go to step to repair flow D-5; pull out the CMOS battery and the motherboard connection cable, (some HP laptop CMOS battery is soldered on motherboard, which requires an electric iron to separate it from the motherboard connection cable), remove it for 5 minutes and replace it with a new one, start the machine and test again. Finally the black screen failure disappears;

Hint:

If CMOS battery voltage is low or done, the system probably wills not start up, or a black screen. Before taking such action, remove the main battery and pull out the external power adapter; after replacing the CMOS battery, press the power button for 30 seconds and then re-install the main battery. Afterwards, separately connect the laptop adapter to start the laptop to release the laptop from hibernation mode.

150) HP ProBook 4710S laptop keeps shutting down automatically after starting up, and black screen failure occurs.

Failure symptom:

According to my client's description, the laptop had been repaired at some other store before, but few weeks later, black screen failure happened again, and it shuts down from time to time. There's no display on the screen, but the indication light still on.

Solution:

This failure symptom belongs to the description of flowchart 08 that belongs to this sequence:

Start->A-1->A-2->A-4->B-5->D-1->D-3->D-4-> . . . .

Repair summary:

First of all, eliminate any possibility that the laptop black screen problem is related with the internal screen; and then remove and install a new memory and test but the failure remains.

Go to step to repair flow D-4; use the minimum methodology to exclude other possible causes of the failure. The black screen failure still remains. Try removing and installing the CPU again, and checking the connection status between the CPU and the laptop motherboard, and test again. As a result, the failure disappears. But after 20 minutes, the laptop auto shuts down. Touch both sides of the heat sink, finding that the side close to CPU is very hot, while the other side is still cool, which indicates that there's an issue with the heat sink, (normally, the medium inside heat sink tube will vaporize and reflow, taking the heat from one end to the other so as the heat is spread equally, so it's obvious that this failure was neglected when client had brought it for repair.

The heat sink doesn't work after awhile due to high temperature and resulting it from drying out and becoming loose, which causes black screen failure and auto shutdown; the solution is to change the radiating pipe. Restart the laptop afterwards and the failure is gone.

Hint:

Thermal silica gel is practically all gone, dried and loose, so the heat sink temperature closest to the CPU/North Bridge chip doesn't spread effectively. Because of certain reason, the heat sink vacuum rate is too low that even the liquid thermal medium vaporizes and finally loses the thermal effect. You can check repair flow tutorial article 06, and follow the method directly to repair.

151)   HP EliteBook 8530p, 8530w laptop black screen failure

Failure symptom:

After laptop starts up, system freezes frequently and black screen failure occurs, fan is also very noisy.

Solution:

This failure symptom belongs to the description of flowchart 08 that belong to this sequence:

Start->A-1->A-2->A-4->B-5->D-1->D-3->D-4->D-5->D-6->D-8 . . . .

Repair summary:

Go to step to repair flow A-4; connect an external LCD screen to check the laptop, but the black screen remains, so the issue isn't with it the screen.

Go to step to repair flow D-3, remove and install the memory and test, but the result is the same; so the screen problem isn't with the memory;

Go to step to repair flow D-4; use the minimum methodology to exclude other possible causes of the failure, remove network card, hard disk, keyboard, battery and so on. Next start the machine to test, the situation remains. The black screen failure isn't with the hardware either; considering that maybe the CPU/display card may have a bad connection which can cause black screen or system shut down remove the CPU/display card, and restart the laptop again. But the failure still exists.

Considering that system shut down frequently and the fan rotation is quite loud, which indicates that the system has an overheating problem. Therefore, the fan's working frequency increases and it's quite likely that the system overheats therefore the display card also overheats creating the system to freeze.

Go to step to repair flow D-6; this laptop uses an independent display card, the accessory number is: 502338-001 PULL, the display memory is 512 MB. Open the main case, remove and install the display card again, and clear up any dust or "rust" speckles; observe whether the "faucet" of the display card is dark. And ensure the slot is also clean. When installing the display card, pay attention hint: to whether it's loose, too tight that it makes it hard to position it. Start the laptop again, but unfortunately, the situation remains.

Go to step to repair flow D-8; change the display card and restart the machine and test. The black screen failure disappears.

Hint:

1) There are many kinds of independent display cards, almost one interface for every model. Failure symptoms related with display card are: alarm sound (not all notebooks) at start up; no self-checking interface, self-checking fails to pass; there're abnormal spots, blurry speckles, patterns on screen; black screen and blue screen.
2) Most laptops only use one specific onboard display card. You must really pay Hint: to display cards as they may seem similar, the interfaces may also seem the same, but in fact, they are completely different and incompatible. If you test the laptop with this kind of display card it could create a bigger trouble.
3) For independent display cards, we can also use the "Hot gun" method to repair the chip. Usually, it's quite effective for abnormal spots, blurry speckles. You'll also notice that after fixing it up, you need to polish both sides of a penny coin and according to the method e of the STEP: D-7, put it on the side of the heat sink with copper block, and paste thermal silica gel cushion there.

8.3.4 Five repair cases for black screen failures caused by HP laptop motherboard power problem

152) HP Pavilion dv6100 Series laptop black screen failure

Failure symptom:

When forcing a shut down of the laptop, it no longer starts up again. When pressing the power button there's no response that is when the black screen failure occurs.

Solution:

This failure symptom belongs to the description of flow chart 08 that belongs to this sequence:

Start->A-1->A-2->A-4->B-5->D-1->D-3->D-4->D-5->D-6->D-7->E-2->E-6 . . . .

Repair summary:

Go to step to repair flow D-4, use the minimum methodology to exclude other possible causes of the failure, as a result, the failure situation remains. Test the motherboard with a new memory stick and a new CPU, the failure situation still remains which means that the problem must be related to the power on the motherboard;

Actually, for HP DV6000 /DV9000 laptop, such kind of failure symptom is quite common. We would have to start the troubleshooting from the power adapter interface to solve the problem. First check the 4 pins in the power interface, whether there's voltage input, red line is positive, black line is ground, most HP laptop power adapters supply 18.5V-19V. Test with multi-meter, and the result shows that the ground voltage for red line is normal.

As the picture shows, this part is the power control circuit, (434723-001), let's first check the part in the yellow circle. Here's a resistor, capacitor and one PQ25 (MOSFET); first test the resistor, finding that the end has voltage, which proves the current supplied from the power adapter passed through. So next step is to test the MOSFET with 8 pins, after testing the pins with a multi-meter, you'll find that the input pin of the 8 pins MOSFET has voltage input. This means the problem comes from the delete MOSFET or the circuit right after.

The next step is to determine if the MOSFET has any voltage output. It seems that it's quite likely the chip is damaged. Solution is quite simple, change the chip. Restart the machine and test, the black screen failure usually disappears.

Attention, change the chip with the same function chip as the same model one is always difficult to find. This is true providing you use a chip that does the same function, it'll work.

Hint:

First find the key chip, which is the hardware power controller. Here we take HP DV6000/9000 laptop for an example: on the right bottom corner of the battery jack, (as picture shows: sometimes it's at the back or side of the motherboard), there's a chip with 8 pins, which is the battery controller chip. First identify the 8 pins of the chip carefully, and then heat the solder thread with soldering iron. Next turn the pin up slightly with knife. With the help of the soldering iron's heating and upward force, until the chip gets separated from the motherboard gradually, until it's totally removed. (All this work has to be carried out without the power supply and the battery removed), as for concrete operation, please refer to the article <<8.2.5 HP DV9000/6000/2000 laptop motherboard failure maintenance>>;

153)   HP Pavilion DV9700 Series laptop black screen failure

Failure symptom:

After laptop starts up, lights are on, but 3 seconds' later, they die. The LED light of the power adapter gives out normal green light. But there's no response when pressing the start button. Black screen failure happens.

Solution:

This failure symptom description of flow chart 08 belongs to this sequence:

Start->A-1->A-2->A-4->B-5->D-1->D-3->D-4->D-5->D-6->D-7->E-2->E-6 . . . .

Repair summary:

Go to step to repair flow D-4; eliminate laptop failure in minimum system mode, as a result, the failure hasn't changed. Test the motherboard by replacing the memory stick and CPU resulting in no change;

Go to step to repair flow E-6; in fact, this failure rarely occurs with an HP DV6000 /DV9000. So we should start from the power adapter's interface to solve the issue. Test the voltage input of 4 pins with a multi-meter. As the result shows, the red ground voltage is normal value is around (?) for HP DV6000 /DV9000;

As the picture shows, this part is the power control circuit, (444002-001), let's first check the part with the yellow circle. Here's a resistor, capacitor and one PQ1 (MOSFET); first test the resistor, finding that the end has voltage, which proves the current, has already been cut off before. Seems the current will not pass though the 8-pin-MOSFET, so then test the MOSFET pins with a multi-meter, as expected, the input voltage is 0.

The Next part you need to test is the resistor, because previously power adapter's interface (4 pins) input voltage tested normal. After current passes through the resistor, the output voltage is 0V. There's input voltage but no output. The resistor itself is a problem too! Change with a fusible resistor of the same function, restart the machine and test. The black screen failure disappears.

Hint:

Why thus these problems happen? Actually there's no secret to it as it's caused by an improper user operation. Every time when you unplug or plug the battery during its charging process, it will produce very high voltage and even spark around the power interface.) And at that moment, damage is quite likely to occur to the battery or laptop motherboard. Usually, when laptop is started and running, don't remove and install the power adapter randomly same as the battery, which will cause severe damage to the charging circuit or even burn the power supply.

154)   HP G50 /G60 laptop black screen failure

Failure symptom:

According to my client's memory, he once had a message prompt saying that the battery power status is quite low, and before long a black screen symptom happened. Press the start button, the light is on and then goes out immediately with no more response.

Solution:

This failure symptom description of flow chart 08 belongs to this sequence:

Start->A-1->A-2->A-4->B-5->D-1->D-3->D-4->D-5->D-6->D-7->E-2->E-6 . . . .

Repair summary:

Go to step to repair flow D-4; use the minimum methodology to exclude other possible causes of the failure, test with a new power adapter, finding the result remains. Test the motherboard with a new battery, as a result, the laptop works normally but doesn't charge, which indicates the problem must be related to the power supply on the motherboard;

Go to step to repair flow E-6; start from the power adapter's interface. Test the voltage output of 6 pins with a multi-meter, the result shows that the voltage is normal; next test the resistor, finding the end has voltage, which proves there's current from the power adapter that passes through. After testing the 8 pin MOSFET with a multi-meter, it is found that the input pin of the MOSFET has input voltage. Next is to check the diode. And the result indicates that the end has no voltage, which proves the current has already been cut off before. In this case, it means the problem already exists on the diode and the MOSFET.

Check the diode; namely, removing one end of the soldered diode off from the motherboard, then test the resistor on the positive and negative ends of the diode. The test result shows that the resistor value is infinite. It seems then that the diode inside is burnt. Replace the diode with another with the same function, restart the laptop and test again. Battery shows it's charging, and the power volume table is rising, which means the battery is able to charge and black screen failure disappears.

Hint:

When there's something wrong with the power supply, the system motherboard doesn't receive power and the battery will run out of juice and finally a black screen failure occurs. But such kind of failure sometimes will seem as if there is a battery charge failure and even changing it will not solve the issue, even when you replace the battery, the failure will remain and you should instead concentrate on the battery charging circuit on the motherboard. Solution is basically the same as the one mentioned above:

1) Test the battery charge/discharge circuit to ensure the control signal is correct, if charging control chip has input voltage but no output, and then you should consider the issue to be with the charging control chip!

2) Then the MOSFET or capacitor is damaged.

155) HP 530 laptop black screen failure

Failure symptom:

Black screen symptom with no response from pressing start button.

Solution:

This failure symptom belongs to description flow chart 08 that belongs to this sequence:

Start->A-1->A-2->A-4->B-5->D-1->D-3->D-4->D-5->D-6->D-7->E-2->E-6 . . .

Repair summary:

Go to step to repair flow D-4; use the minimum methodology to exclude other possible causes of the failure, test with a new power adapter, finding the result remains. Then test the motherboard with a new memory stick and CPU, the failure also remains, which indicates the problem must be related with the power supply on the motherboard;

Go to step to repair flow E-6; start from the power adapter's interface. Test the voltage output with a multi-meter, the result shows the voltage is normal; next test the resistor, finding the voltage is OK, which proves the current from the power adapter has already passed through. After testing the 8 pins MOSFET, it is found that the output voltage of the MOSFET is abnormal. Then check carefully, finding the MOSFET D-class and S-class resistor values are too low, after changing it, restart the machine and test again, the failure still remains.

Therefore, check the South Bridge, the main power supply chipsets, the output MAX8770 power supply chip and the 38PIN SHND main switch pin is of 3.3 V/OFF, no voltage. Testing the surrounding circuit has no short circuit either. Take one end of the resistor for power supply off the motherboard soldering and go upwards, check whether it is a short circuit or not. As a result, it is found that the short circuit comes form the MAX8770 chip. Then remove the chip. Solder a good MAX8770 chip back to the motherboard, restart and test again and the failure disappears.

Hint:

When there's a problem happening to the power supply, first check the power adapter to see whether there's voltage output, such as:

1) Check the fusible resistor to confirm whether it's broken;
2) Then check the power supply chip which provides 12V, 5V and 3.3V, whether there's reference voltage and standby voltage of 5V.
3) Check whether the battery charger supplies power;
4) Whether the CPU power supply circuit is normal, the voltage should be 3.3V;
5) Whether the high-low driver of the MOSFET has power? Whether the voltage passes and arrives at the to power management chip;
6) Whether the filter capacitor is of standard voltage and whether it is defective or not;

156) HP Compaq V6000 laptop black screen failure

Failure symptom:

Laptop starts up normally, but black screen failure occurs and the indication light is on.

Solution:

This failure symptom belongs to flow char 08 that belongs to this sequence:

Start->A-1->A-2->A-4->B-5->D-1->D-3->D-4->D-5->D-6->D-7->E-2->E-6 . . . .

Repair summary:

Go to step to repair flow D-4; use the minimum methodology to exclude other possible causes of the failure, as a result, the failure situation hasn't changed, remove the memory stick and CPU, and reinstall it into a good working motherboard and test. The result shows they work normally, which indicate the problem must be with the original motherboard;

Go to step to repair flow E-6; start from the interface of the power adapter. Test the voltage output with a multi-meter, which shows as normal; next test the resistor and it works normally.

At last, somewhere at the backboard (the front piece of the North Bridge), there's a broken Transistor. After changing it, start the machine and test again, the failure still exists. There's no way out, change all capacitors and resistors for connection, after that, change the MOSFET all together, in case certain components are broken, which may leads to other accessory being broken; now the North Bridge chip's temperature begins going back to normal. But in a moment, it heats quickly, and then the transistor is broken again so the problem is with the North Bridge replace it restart and the failure disappears.

Hint:

When there's something wrong with power supply, you must find out the true reason. You cannot just replace it and assume that is the issue. Actually, for this motherboard, at first we thought that the Transistor was broken, but why? The key is because there a short circuit inside the North Bridge. So even if you change with a good Transistor, the capacitor and resistor will still have this issue. The reason is quite simple, the loading (North Bridge) has something wrong!

8.3.5   7 repair cases of black screen failure caused by some HP accessories such as sound card, DVD and so on.

157)   HP CQ40-612TX laptop system freeze failure

Failure symptom:

Open device manager, finding there's a yellow exclamation mark beside sound device, after reinstalling sound card driver, laptop fails to turn off. You force shut down and now the laptop freezes and black screen failure occurs.

Solution:

This failure symptom belongs to flow chart 08 that belongs to sequence:

Start->A-1->B-1->B-3->B-4->C-4->C-5->C-6 . . . .

Repair summary:

Go to step to repair flowchart 08 of step B-3, put a pure bootable DOS Memtest86 software disc into

DVD-ROM/CD-ROM to start the laptop and then test. Analyze whether the failure comes from hardware or software, as a result, the laptop works normally in DOS;

Go to step to repair flow C-4, according to what my client said, the cause of this failure is because the sound card driver has just been updated. So start the laptop in safe mode, check the latest installed or updated drivers, and then uninstall it to eliminate any system incompatibility problems. Next start the laptop in normal mode, and this time, it successfully starts up, no system freezes or black screen failure. But there is still no sound from the speakers!

According to the method of repair flow C-5, change the hard disk with one known to not have issues and re install the operating system and the sound card driver, and then restart the machine and test again, and the issue is solved so now go to flow c6 to restore the backed up data.

Hint:

1) If it fails to boot from safe mode, then you need to remove the hard disk, and put it into a USB box, making into an external USB hard disk. And then plug the external USB hard disk to another working machine and run antivirus software to scan and kill viruses on the disk. Once finished, reinstall the hard disk back into the laptop.

2) Start the laptop in normal mode, if it fails, then you can try restarting the laptop by pressing the F8 key so a boot menu appears. Choose to start system by "with the last known good configuration". Check whether system can restore back to the last normal status without failure.

158) HP Pavilion dv4000 laptop's black screen failure

Failure symptom:

Black screen failure suddenly occurs when laptop is running normally, the indicator light is on, even after restarting the laptop, CPU fan is still running, but black screen failure still appears.

Solution:

This failure symptom belongs to flow chart 08 that belongs to this sequence:

Start->A-1->A-2->A-4->B-5->D-1->D-3->D-4->D-9 . . . .

Repair summary:

Go to step to repair flowchart 08 of step A-4: first connect an external monitor to test the laptop, finding that the external monitor also has the black screen failure, so we know the issue isn't with the screen

Go to step to repair flow D-3; remove and install) the modern module again, clean the gold plated board (bottom edge of pins), including the slot. Restart the laptop, the failure still exists; plug another good known working memory stick to the laptop and test, but the issue remains.

Go to step to repair flow D-4; use the minimum methodology to exclude other possible causes of the failure. Remove disc, network card, hard disk and so on. Then restart the laptop, finding the black screen failure disappears. Obviously the failure must be related with the accessories just removed, hard disk and the operating system on the disk. So now based on the minimum system mode, add each removed part back in individually and restart the laptop every time to see whether the failure symptom disappears or happens again. When you put the network card (Modem 384623-001) back into the motherboard and you restart the machine the black screen failure occurs again. Obviously the black screen failure is caused because of the network card. So replace it.

Hint:

Every time when plugging an accessory back to the motherboard and test, you need to restart the laptop every time, for every operation, power must be cut off first, by pulling out the AC adapter and removing the battery. When a certain accessory is plugged back into the motherboard, and black screen or system crash happens, then we can conclude that the problem must be related with this accessory. Usually we need to use the replacement method and then we can judge whether it's the accessory or the accessory slot on the motherboard.

159)   COMPAQ Presario F700 laptop system freeze and black screen failure

Failure symptom:

Start the laptop, manufacturer logo appears and then system freezes. Laptop cannot boot the operation system, even there's no any information on screen, and sometimes what you can see is only black screen.

Solution:

This failure symptom belongs to flow chart 08 that belongs to this sequence

Start->A-1->B-1->B-3->B-5->D-1->D-3->D-4->D-9 . . . .

Start->A-1->B-1->B-2-> C-1 . . .

Repair summary:

Go to step to repair flowchart 08 of step D-3; plug a known good working memory stick to the laptop and test, the failure doesn't change;

Go to step to repair flow D-4, use the minimum methodology to exclude other possible causes of the failure. Remove the battery, network card, hard disk and so on. Put a pure bootable DOS software disc into the DVD-ROM/CD-ROM and start to test. The laptop works in normal mode for over an hour without any system freeze up failure. Obviously the failure is with the removed accessories and operating system on the disk. Now based on minimum system mode, each time you add a part back into the system, restart it and test whether the failure disappears or remains the same. When you restore all accessories, it is found that the laptop now works normally with no issues. It seems that some of the failures were caused by badly connected accessories.

Sometimes, it might be too early to be celebrating because once you plug the battery the system suddenly freezes. So now the issue is due to the battery. I now take a quicker method for the repair by checking the battery and power adapter before using the minimum methodology to exclude other possible causes of the failure method, which will save me a lot of time.

Hint:

1) The connection status between the battery and laptop motherboard is quite important especially if there is bad contact which will create system freeze up and black screen failure. So when laptop doesn't start, you should singularly use the power adapter to start the laptop to ensure it's not the battery that causes system freeze up black screen failure.

2) Some batteries seem exactly same, but are totally incompatible with each other. If client uses such battery by mistake, it can create a lot of problems. So you should check the battery model type carefully, ensuring the battery is completely compatible with the laptop.

160) HP CQ40-506AU laptop black screen failure

Failure symptom:

After starting the laptop, all lights die out and no response when pressing the start button and black screen failure occurs.

Solution:

This failure symptom belongs to flow chart 08 that belongs to this sequence:

Start->A-1->A-2->A-4->B-5->D-1->D-3->D-4->D-9 . . . .

Repair summary:

Go to step to repair flowchart 08 of step D-3; put a good known working memory stick in the laptop and test but the issue remains;

Go to step to repair flow D-4; use the minimum methodology to exclude other possible causes of the failure, namely, remove the battery, network card, hard disk and so on, and then test the laptop. As a result, black screen still exists. Maybe the laptop was shaken or moved abruptly causing the internal parts inside the machine to come loose and therefore bad connection finally leads to failure. So we should eliminate the failure by removing and installing CPU/ display card (except the one with integrated display card); before removing and installing, first clear any dust built up, and then check the connection between the CPU/ display card and the motherboard; after the test is completed the failure disappears.

However, when reinstalling the keyboard, and starting the machine to test, you get a black screen immediately therefore we know there's a short in the keyboard that causes the problem;

Hint:

Minimum system means running the laptop in the most basic hardware and software environment in order to better judge the issue. In minimum system environment, judge and locate the failure, then add hardware and replace the suspected parts and test.

You must pay attention that in this method; we only use the power adapter, motherboard, CPU and memory and only use the external monitor and carry out the repair work.

161) COMPAQ Presario V3700 laptop black screen failure

Failure symptom:

After reinstalling the display card driver, black screen failure happens to the laptop.

Solution:

This failure symptom belongs to flow chart 08 that belongs to this sequence:

Start->A-1->B-1->B-3->B-4->C-4->C-5->C-6 . . . .

Repair summary:

Go to step to repair flowchart 08 of step B-3, put a pure bootable DOS disc into the DVD-ROM/CD-ROM to start. Analyze whether the failure comes from hardware or software. As a result, the laptop works normally in DOS, obviously the problem is with a driver;

Go to step to repair flow C-4, start the laptop in safe mode, and it starts up. Check the latest installed or updated drivers, and uninstall them all to eliminate system incompatible problems. Next start the laptop in normal mode. And the result is still a failure, besides, machine restarts automatically. After forcing a shut down by force and restarting by pressing the F8 key to enable boot menu, choose to start the system with "The last known good configuration", as a result, it restores it without failure.

Hint:

For general display card, it's not always good to update it to the latest driver. Generally, new versions have patches that repair and optimize the new display card, but if to update the old display card with the latest version driver, you'll get many incompatible problems, such as black screen, blue screen and so on.

162) HP G50-215CA laptop system freeze failure

Failure symptom:

After laptop starts up, manufacturer logo appears, but the laptop doesn't boot up in the operating system therefore system freeze failure occurs.

Solution:

This failure symptom belongs to flowchart 08 that belongs to this sequence:

Start->A-1->B-1->B-3->B-5->D-1->D-3->D-4->D-9 . . . .

Repair summary:

Go to step to repair flowchart 08 of step D-3, remove and install memory stick (memory module) again, clean the (Edge Connector) gold plated board, including the slot. Restart the laptop, but the failure remains;

Go to step to repair flow D-4; use the minimum methodology to exclude other possible causes of the failure. Remove the battery, network card, hard disk and so on. Put a pure bootable DOS software disc into the DVD-ROM/CD-ROM to start, finally it fails to start up. Occasionally, it starts up, but the interface freezes along with the system, which means the original failure must be with the working hardware.

Remove and install the CPU to eliminate the failure; first clean any dust, and then check the connection between the CPU and motherboard; as a result, system freeze failure still appears. Remove the memory stick and CPU, and then install another known good working motherboard and test. As a result, they work which means the problem must be related with the original motherboard or DVD-ROM/CD-ROM. Remove the DVD-ROM/CD-ROM, then restart the laptop, press F10 to enter BIOS Setup, go to BOOT ORDER, set the first boot as USB Diskette on key/USB hard Disk, and then connect a bootable USB movable hard disk with no failure. Restart and failure disappears.

Clean the original DVD-ROM/CD-ROM again, remove and install, and then connect them as usual. But failure still exists; change the DVD-ROM, and the failure disappears. Now it's confirmed that the circuit problem inside the DVD-ROM caused the system freeze failure.

Hint:

1) When you find an issue with the DVD-ROM/CD-ROM, system will continually inspect it, and then goes into a loop. If you use it for too long the failure may occur in the form of freeze up or black screen.

2) Machine is very dusty and laser heads are dirty which will create read/write errors and eventually will fail to start the disc, which will also cause system freezes. The solution for this is: clean the laser head gently, or install another working DVD-ROM/CD-ROM.

163) COMPAQ Presario V2000 laptop black screen failure

Failure symptom:

Press start button, LED light is on, and manufacturer logo appears on the screen. But after laptop boots in the operating system, several indication lights keep flashing and black screen occurs.

Solution:

This failure symptom belongs to flow chart 08 that belongs to this sequence:

Start->A-1->B-1->B-3->B-5->D-1->D-3->D-4->D-9 . . . .

Repair summary:

Go to step to flowchart 08 of step A-4, laptop has black screen failure along with an external monitor So the failure isn't caused by the monitor.

Go to step to repair flow D-3, install a known working memory stick into the laptop and test, the failure hasn't changed;

Go to step to repair flow D-4; use the minimum methodology to exclude other possible causes of the failure. Remove battery, network card, hard disk and so on. Put a pure bootable DOS software disc in the DVD-ROM/CD-ROM to start. And test result shows that the laptop works normally in DOS, which indicates the problem is with a removed accessory, hard disk and operating system.

Now that the system is in minimum mode, add one part at a time and then restart the laptop. Observe whether the failure disappears or if any changes occur, connect the hard disk back into the motherboard, and then restart the laptop and test again, but the black screen failure appears.

Next clean the hard disk interface, eliminate any pins that are cracked, bent or loose. Remove and install hard disk and then connect normally. The result shows the failure still exists. After changing to a new hard disk the failure disappears.

Hint:

Before reinstalling accessories, clean any dust and clear interfaces, including the slots. When installing, you should pay attention that the accessory isn't loose and jack isn't too tight, so that it isn't plugged wrong or interfering. After restoring installation, if the same failure symptom happens again, then you can conclude there an issue with the slot. And the method to confirm further is: find a known working accessory to install and test again, if it works normally, it means the original accessory was faulty but if the issue remains then you are guaranteed it's the slot on the motherboard.

CHAPTER 9

Solutions to inaccessible drive or folder

9.1   After reinstalling Windows, drive D and folders are locked up and could not be opened

9.1.1   After reinstalling Windows, drive D or the folders are locked up and cannot be opened

a)   After reinstalling Windows, double-click drive D—could not open it up

b)   At the beginning, only drive D could not be opened, later drive C could not be opened either. If double clicking doesn't work, right click, and choose the application to open, then scan the system and entire disc for viruses, but it still doesn't work.

c)   After reinstalling OS system, drive D could not be opened, and you get a message that the "Drive D is not formatted"; -After reinstalling OS system, the "My Computer", and "My Documents" could not be opened, and the information and files on drive D could not be opened either;

d)   After reinstalling OS system, the laptop restarts repeatedly, and drive D could not be opened, prompts that the plug-in could not be recovered;

e)   After reinstalling OS system, the icon of drive D becomes grey and could not be opened; either the shortcut could not start.

f)   After reinstalling OS system, double clicking the files of folders, you get a message "Windows cannot access the specified device, path or file. You might have no proper permissions to access this item".

g)   After reinstalling OS system, folder could not be opened in windows explorer or "My computer"; even double clicking could not open the folder, but go straight to I.E (internet explorer) search interface.

h)   After reinstalling OS system, When you open a folder on any drive, the "Find" dialog box would appear, but after right clicking the folder and choose "Open", then you able to access the folder.

i)   After reinstalling OS system, original EFS encrypted folder could not be opened;

j)   After reinstalling OS system, one cannot open "Add/Remove programs";

k) After reinstalling OS system, LAN could not be opened;

l) After reinstalling OS system, REGEDIT could not be opened;

m) After reinstalling OS system, Favourites could not be opened;

n) After reinstalling OS system, Temp folder could not be opened;

o) After reinstalling OS system, Although Windows opens, you still cannot open the "Search" function;

p) After reinstalling system, the Group Policy could not be started.

The following table is the analysis for some common laptop failures; we can initially diagnose the main part of the laptop failure by some common symptoms, which have certain utility.

Common failure	Symptom	Main issue parts
Drive D could not be opened	Double clicking could not open it, right click and choose "Open"	Software issue, the file Autorun.inf has some problems
Drive D could not be opened	You get a message that it's not formatted	1) User permissions; 2) Virus
"My Computer" and "My Documents" could not be opened	After starting up the laptop, data files could not be opened, even though the permissions is correct, you get the message : " Access Is Denied"	1) User permissions; 2) The file has been encrypted
System folders could not be opened	Partial folders become "0"KB, which could not be opened, copied or deleted	User's security ID has been changed, which is not consistent with the security ID of the owner. Being able to open the folder.
Error prompts when clicking explorer	Double clicking could not open the folder but takes you straight to I.E (internet explorer) search interface	1) REGEDIT has been modified; 2) The "Advanced" option settings of the "Folder" have also changed.
EFS encrypted folder could not be opened	Error message "access is denied" might be displayed or request to enter protection password or confirmation password	The file could be opened only when you import the backup certificate
Double click the folder, "Find" dialog appears	Whenever you open a folder on any drive, the "Find" dialog would always appear	1) Virus; 2) REGEDIT has be modified; 3) the "Advanced" option settings of the" Folder" has also been modified

Cannot open "Add/ Delete programs"	Sometimes there is a display that the certain file has a problem or something wrong, but in most cases, there's no message	The cause is that "Add/Delete programs" dialog cannot be open or the dynamical link library file's registration has failed, you will just need to register these files again
LAN is unavailable	Browser could not access the Network neighbourhood or only could see default network situation	1) Computer share settings 2) "Microsoft network file" is enabled;3) IP Configuration is in use; 4) Firewall settings is disabled; 5)Access permissions settings; 6)Network connection is wrong.
REGEDIT could not start	When executing these command, you get a message : "REGEDIT edit is already disabled by the administrator"	REGEDIT tool has been locked
Favourites could not be opened	After clicking the "Favourites", left side shows no item, The "Add to Favourites" and "Clean up Favourites", are not responding	1) REGEDIT has been modified; 2) the "Desktop.ini" file in "Favourites" has been modified by Trojan.
Windows cannot start the "Search" function	Sometimes it will show that certain file DLL is missing	1) Virus and Trojan has damage the file; 2) REGEDIT has been changed
Group policy could not be started	Sometimes you will receive an error message or sometimes a few or several error messages	1) Trojan causes, or registry has been modified; 2) the "Advanced" label option settings in" System property "is corrupted; 3) Group policy files are broken.
*.exe file could not start	When executing this command, sometimes you get a message that certain DLL file has an error	*.exe file has been modified or changed the opening method by Trojan or virus

9.1.2 After reinstalling Windows, folder is locked and cannot be opened; failure and cause analysis;

1. Failure symptoms:

- After reinstalling system, double clicking drive D would not open, Display or asked to choose a program to open this file, but the type of application to start does not work, and it's useless even scanning the system and entire disk for viruses.
- After reinstalling system, drive D could not be opened, you get a message Drive D is not formatted.

Cause analysis:

A). In most cases, it's because of viruses, which made consistent modification to change the opening method by Trojan or virus, even if you remove the viruses, you still cannot recover the damage system files. Then you need a manual way to repair and recover the software, usually, the problem is on the Autorun.inf file;

B) If after scanning system and the entire disk to remove the viruses, double clicking drive D still would not open, then you get a message that the hard drive is not formatted, this is because:

1) After reinstalling system, there is a user permissions problem, you need to remove useless user names, add current user name and then change the permissions.
2) When reinstalling system, drive D is deleted accidentally or file partition table is damaged, if you don't want to recover data, then just format with FAT or NTFS.
3) If you need to recover data, first of all, you need a software tool to repair the partition, and then rescue the data with data recovery software, such as "Easy-Recovery"
4) One point to pay attention to is, before recovery, you don't format drive D, and don't write any data onto it!

2. Failure symptom:—After reinstalling system, "My Computer", "My Documents" could not be opened, and the files on drive D could not be opened either;

Cause analysis:

Now most user's computers are using NTFS file system, therefore, all files or folder would be limited by ACL. ACL function is to specify which users or system processes are granted access to objects, as well as what operations are allowed on given objects or SSID.

A) Although after reinstalling system, similarly, we still need "CARE" account and password to access it, at this moment, the relevant SID to "CARE" account is already different from the previous one. So after reinstalling system, "CARE" account cannot access backup folder.

B) The original backup folder might be encrypted;

3. **Failure symptom: double click system folder, you get a message that "Windows could not access specified device, path or file or that no proper permissions to access this item", partial folders then becomes "0" KB, which could not be opened, copied or deleted.**

Cause analysis:

There are many reasons why this happens: primarily because the user's security ID has already be changed, which is not longer consistent with the security ID of the folder, so, the owner which could not be opened.

4. **Failure symptom: error message when you click explorer, double clicking could not open folder but take you straight to the search interface.**

Cause analysis:

Generally, the registry has been modified by virus, even if you remove the viruses, you cannot restore the damages done to the system files.

5. **Failure symptom: EFS encrypted folder could not be opened, probably you will get the error message "Access is denied" or requested to enter protection password or confirm password.**

Cause analysis:

After EFS encryption, you must back up the certificate. Otherwise, when some special situations come up, the encrypted folders could not be opened.

6. **Failure symptom: When you double click a folder, the "Find" dialog box will appear, no matter which file is open in the folder on any drive, "Find" dialog box would always appear.**

Cause analysis:

1) Generally because the registry has been changed due to viruses, so we are better off using antivirus program to scan and remove the virus from the entire disk;
2) Virus has already damaged the registry file.

7. **Failure symptom: "Add/Delete programs" could not be opened, it would display a message that certain file has an error, but in most cases, there's no error message, but after clicking, the system automatically logs off.**

Cause analysis:

The reason that "Add/Delete programs" could not start probably is because the dynamic link library file registration is missing, so we'd just need to re-register these files again.

8. **Failure symptom: registry cannot start, when you run regedit command or double click to execute a registry file (*.reg) command, system would give you a message : "REGEDIT edit has been disabled by administrator".**

Cause analysis:

It looks like that the user account you log on to doesn't have the registry edit permissions for the current Windows system. Actually, it's not that easy, the failure occur because malicious software or Trojan has disabled the REGEDIT edit permissions.

9. **Failure symptom: Favorites cannot open, after clicking Favorites, the right side is blank, and cannot operate. Then when you click on "Add to Favorites" or "Clean up Favorites", there's no response at all!**

Failure causes:

1) Some malicious websites would normally modify the Favorites or change the file "Desktop.ini" under the path "C:\Windows\Favorites"
2) The contents in "Favorites" is not deleted, but "Favorites" is modified, for instance, "Favorites" is changed to "Favorites2" and so on.

10. **Failure symptom: Windows cannot open "Search" function; sometimes it shows that certain DLL file is lost.**

Cause analysis:

There are two causes for such failures: one is file damage, second is the DLL file registration has failed

11. Failure symptom: group policy could not be opened: when trying to open Windows management console and security policy (such as local security policy, group policy or domain security policy) in Windows XP Professional system, the console could not be opened, or sometimes, you might get some error messages.

Cause analysis:

1) Causes are Trojan and the registry is modified, which then need to be recovered manually;
2) The "Advanced" label option settings is changed in "System property"; which needs you to click "Environment variables" button on the tab "Advanced" to recover it manually;
3) Group policy system file is damaged; for instance, group policy cannot find the file framedyn.dll, then you might get this error.

12. Failure symptom: *.exe file cannot be opened, when executing this command, sometimes it would get a message that certain file DLL has an error;

Cause analysis:

1) *. exe open method has been modified by Trojan or virus, then you need to recover it back manually or with other software;
2) When removing viruses, pay attention not to delete the registry items, i.e. Some *.exe files, because they are infected by virus, but if you delete all, then it would bring even bigger trouble for repairing.

9.1.3 After reinstalling Windows, drive D is locked and cause analysis

Failure symptom:

After reinstalling system, drive D is locked and access is refused.

Cause analysis:

1) Some people always think that after reinstalling operation system, damage is made to drive D, this doesn't make any sense. If there's something wrong with the disk, in most cases, system would prompt that there's something wrong with the disk or this drive D is not formatted, Even the drive D volume would not be displayed at all; generally, open the "Disk management" option in the window by right clicking "My computer" icon, then click manage", you can check the status of drive D to see, whether it's OK. If it's basically the same with the total capacity of the file, then it is not the failure of the physical disk or logical circuit, you also get a message "access denied" which also proves this point.

2) The access permissions for the default "Everyone" group on drive D is related to disk security.

In explorer, right click on drive D and choose "Properties" to open "Local disk (D:) then in the Property dialog box, then choose "Security" tab, you can see that there is an unknown user with a question mark on the window, this should be the "Administrator" user of the original operation system. This user could access drive D in the original system, but after installing new system, the original user ID could not be recognized by current OS system. And current user group has no full control permission on drive D, which would not be allowed to access by system.

9.1.4 The solution for the failure that Windows system "cannot open" drive D and folders

1. Failure symptom: Windows system "cannot open" drive D and folders

Solution:

1) Reset local disk D security option tab

   In windows XP "Safe Mode", go to "My computer", right click on drive D, choose "Properties" to open "Local disk (D :) Property" dialog, choose "Security" option tab, and then click the "Add" button on dialog, open "Select users or group" dialog box, the window displays all user group names of local machine. Find "Administrators" user group, click "Add" button, and add administrators group to the list at the box of the window.

2) Modify the permissions of local disk D

   Click "OK" button, return to the dialog "Local disk (D) Properties", then you can see the administrators user group has already been added to the access permissions list of local disk D, choose "Full control"—"Allow" checkbox on "Permissions" window, granting the administrators group all the permissions for drive D. choose the unknown user with interrogation mark, and click "Delete" button. Then the unknown user would be deleted from the permissions list of disk D. And then click "OK" button, save the settings, then you can visit drive D.

3) Something is wrong with the file Autorun.inf

   After removing the property, delete it, and then search the file pointing to the file autorun.inf in registry, after finding it, you delete the entire "shell subprojects", then can open drive D again.

2. **Failure symptom:—after reinstalling system, "My computer" and "My documents" cannot be opened.**

Solution:

A) Actually the solution is quite simple, grant "New user" account access permissions again on the "Security" label tab for file backup.
B) The original backup folder might be encrypted, which needs backup certificate imported into, then we can open the document.

3. **Failure symptom: double click system folder, but system prompts: "Windows cannot access specified device, path or file or just show that there's no proper permissions accessing this subject", partial folders become "0" KB, which could not be opened, copied or deleted either.**

Solution:

If previously the folder has not been encrypted, then you can "right click" on the folders which could not be opened, go to properties—security—advanced—owner, then choose current user name, please confirm the access permissions again.

4. **Failure symptom: error prompts when clicking browser because double clicking cannot open folder but enter search interface.**

Solution:

1) Enter registry HKEY_CLASSES_ROOTD irectoryshell, and then delete "find";
2) Click the "Advanced" option tab "New" in "Folders", then type "OpenNew" to the "Operate", and then set up, next enter "Explorer%1" to the "Application used to execute operation", set "OpenNew" as default settings.

5. **Failure symptom: EFS encrypted folder could not be opened, you might see the error message "Access is denied" or it requests you to enter protection password and confirmation password.**

Solution:

To prevent that encrypted folder not be opened after reinstalling system, we can back up and import key through the method below:

Click "Start—Run", enter "certmgr.msc", press Enter to open certificate manager. Expand "Certificate/Individual/certificate", click the right key on the certificate named as the user name on the right side of the window, and choose "Export" in "All tasks" to open certificate export wizard. Click "Next" and then choose "Yes, export the key", and click "Next", choose default export file format, and then click "Next", enter protection password and confirmation password, click "Next" and specify the file name, at last click "Finish" and done.

Then after reinstalling system, right click the exported key file, choose "Install PFX" and then you can import the key step by step. After finishing importing, then you can successfully open EFS encrypted folder. If you don't back up certificate, then after reinstalling system, the folder encrypted could not be opened ever again.

6. **Failure symptom: double click a folder, and "Find" dialog appears, namely, no matter which folder to open on any drive, "Find" dialog would prompt**

Solution:

In "My Computer", no matter which folder to open on any drive, "Find" dialog would always prompt, but click the right key on the folder and then choose "Open", it would enter control panel, double click "Folder options", and click "File type" label, and find "Folder" in the list "Registered file type" and select it, click "Advanced" button, on the prompted "Edit file type" dialog, if there's only "Find" item, then click "Add" button under "Operation", enter "Open" to the operation on the dialog "New operation", and enter "C:\Windows\Explorer.exe" to the option "Application used to execute operation".

And then click "OK", choose the created "Open", and click "Set as default value" button; if there's already "Open", then directly choose it and set it as default value.

7. **Failure symptom: If "Add/Delete programs" cannot be opened, probably it would prompt that certain file has an error, but in most cases, there's no any prompt, after you click it, immediately the system would auto log off.**

Solution:

Enter the following commands in the "Start—Run" dialog, and take turns to click OK on the prompted window.

regsvr32 Appwiz.cpl
regsvr32 Jscript.dll
regsvr32 Mshtml.dll
regsvr32 Msi.dll
regsvr32 Mshtmled.dll
regsvr32 "c:\Program Files\Common Files\System\Ado\Msado15.dll"
regsvr32 "c:\Program Files\Common Files\System\Ole DB\Oledb32.dll"

8. **Failure symptom: On condition that REGEDIT cannot start, when you run regedit command or double click to execute a registry file *.reg command, system would prompt a dialog "REGEDIT is already disabled by administrator".**

Solution:

There's a simple way to get the REGEDIT edit permissions: use Windows Group Policy Object Editor—gpedit.msc, then you can easily solve this problem. Besides, Group Policy Editor could also realize some functions which could only be done by modifying registry.

9. **Failure symptom: Favorites could not be opened, after clicking Favorites, the left side shows blank, there's no way to do anything. Click "Add to Favorites" and "Clean up Favorites", and there's no any response!**

Solution:

1) You'd just need to delete the file "Desktop.ini" under the directory "C:\Windows\Favorites".
2) If there's no way to open the folder "C:\Windows\Favorites" at all, just go to DOS to delete (First you have to use "attrib -r -s -h", then you can delete it)
3) The contents in "Favorites" are not deleted, but just changed the name, such as "Favorites2", you just need to set the path of system default "Favorites" as specified directory, such as "C:\Windows\Favorites2", and recover normal "REGEDIT".

10. **Failure symptom: Windows cannot open "Search" function, or the computer cannot search files, or probably it would display that certain file DLL is missing.**

There are three solutions:

1) Open the folder "C:\Windows\inf", and find the file "srchasst.inf", right click on it and on the prompt menu, choose "Install", according to system prompt, insert the installation disc, wait until installation finishes, check whether it could run "Search" function, if still not working, go to the next step;
2) Run REGEDIT, locate to the branch "HKEY_CURRENT_ USER\Software\Microsoft\Windows\ CurrentVersion\Explorer\CabinetState", create a new character string "Use Search Asst", set the value as "NO".
3) Open "Notepad", and type the following contents, and save it as .BAT file, then execute it.

```
cd /d "%SystemRoot%\System32"
regsvr32 /u /s msxml3.dll
regsvr32 /s msxml3.dll exit
```

11. Failure symptom: Group policy could not start, besides, you might receive error messages.

There are 6 solutions:

6 solutions for the problem that group policy could not start.

Solution 1:

1) Click "Start" menu;
2) Click "Run".
3) Keyed "regedit" (excluding the quotation marks);
4) Locate to the branches in registry:

   HKEY_CURRENT_USERSoftwarePoliciesMicrosoftMmc{8FC0B734-A0E1-11D1-A7D3-0000F87571E3}Restrict_Run and

   HKEY_CURRENT_USERSoftwarePoliciesMicrosoftMMC{0F6B957E-509E-11D1-A7CC-0000F87571E3}Restrict_Run

   Set the value as 0.

5) After finishing the modification, restart the computer.

Solution 2:

1) Click "Start" menu;
2) Click "Run";
3) Keyed "regedit" (exclude the quotation marks);
4) Locate to the registry branch

   HKEY_CLASSES_ROOTCLSID{8FC0B734-A0E1-11D1-A7D3-0000F87571E3} InProcServer32, of which change the "Default" as

   "%SystemRoot%System32GPEdit.dll".

5) After finishing the modification, restart the computer.

Solution 3:

Check environment variant:

a. Click "Start" menu;
b. Click "Control Panel";
c. In "Control Panel", open "System";

d. Click "Advanced" label in "System Property" window;
e. On "Advanced" tab, click "Environment variant" button;
f. Change the environment variant value named Path in the text "System variant" of "Environment variant" to "%Systemroot%System32;%Systemroot%;%Systemroot%system32WBEM";

Solution 4:

Run regsvr32 filemgmt.dll

a. Click "Start" menu;
b. Click "Run";
c. Type "regsvr32 filemgmt.dll" (excluding the quotation marks)

Solution 5:

If group policy could not find framedyn.dll, such an error would probably happen. If using install script, you make sure the script is under the directory %windir%system32wbem in system path. By default settings, %windir%system32wbem is already in system path. Therefore, if you don't use install script, you would not get this problem ever. Or you can try copying the file Framedyn.dll from the directory "Windowssystem32wbem" to the directory "Windowssystem32"!

Solution 6:

Restart the server system, during the start process, continually press F8 function key until system boot menu appears. And then execute the command "Safe mode with command line prompt", and switch server system to command prompt situation;

Next under the command prompt, directly execute the character string command "mmc.exe", on the prompt system console, click "File" menu, and then click "Add/Delete management unit" option from the prompted dropdown menu. And then click the "independent" label on the following window, and then on the displayed tab page, click "Add" button;

Then take turns to click "Group Policy", "Add", "Finish", "Close", "OK" buttons, thus we can successfully add a new group policy console.

12. **Failure symptom: EXE file could not be executed, when executing this command, sometimes, that certain file DLL has an error would prompt;**

Solution:

Suggest using AVG/Avast antivirus software to scan the entire disk and kill remove the viruses; make sure that your system is clean without any virus.

Besides, you'd better to update everyday, and define as auto scanning disk.

1) First change regedit.exe as regedit.com or regedit.scr.

   Run regedit.com, find the key "hkey_classes_root\exefile\shell\Open\command", and set the default value as %1 %*, then restart the computer, and change regedit.com back to regedit.exe.

2) Save the contents below as exefile.reg, double click it to import into registry; or on conditon of the pure DOS, run regedit exefile.reg to import into registry. (Notice: leaving a blank row behind regedit4)

   regedit4
   [hkey_classes_root\exefile\shell\Open\command]
@=\%1\ %*

3) (For Win XP/Vista):

   (1) Change cmd.exe to cmd.com or cmd.scr;
   (2) Run cmd.com;
   (3) Run the following two commands: ftype exefile=%1 %*assoc.exe=exefile
   (4) Change cmd.com back to cmd.exe.

9.1.5 Another type of failure symptom that Windows system "could not open . . ."

(1) LAN is unavailable, as for detailed operation method, please refer to <<14.2.5 Laptop cable LAN failure analysis and repair flow>>;
(2) IE could not open webpage, as for detailed operation method, please refer to <<10.3 failure repair that HP laptop cannot get to Internet >>;
(3) IE could not open a new window, as for detailed operation method, please refer to <<10.3 failure repair that HP laptop cannot get to Internet >>;
(4) IE cannot open search page, as for detailed operation method, please refer to <<10.3 failure repair that HP laptop cannot get to Internet >>;

CHM (Compiled Help *File for Microsoft*) file cannot be opened, as for detailed operation method, please refer to <<9.3 after reinstalling Windows, 23 repair cases of HP laptop failures that folder is locked up and failed to access "cannot be opened."> >;

(5) TXT file cannot be opened, as for detailed operation method, please refer to <<9.3 after reinstalling Windows, 23 repair cases of HP laptop failures that folder is locked up and failed to access "cannot be open."> >:
(6) Shortcut cannot be opened, as for detailed operation method, please refer to <<9.3 after reinstalling Windows, 23 repair cases of HP laptop failures that folder is locked up and failed to access "cannot be open."> >:

(7) "Tablet" application cannot start, as for detailed operation method, please refer to <<9.3 after reinstalling Windows, 23 repair cases of HP laptop failures that folder is locked up and failed to access "cannot be open.">>:

(8) Second level link cannot be opened, as for detailed operation method, please refer to <<9.3 after reinstalling Windows, 23 repair cases of HP laptop failures that folder is locked up and failed to access "cannot be open.">>

9.2 Repair flowchart to eliminate failures such as driver D and folders "could not open" after reinstalling OS

9.2.1 Shortcuts—Crack the locked folders with Windows' own functions

Introduction to some methods to rescue data

1) Make laptop disk into a movable disk

a) Restart the laptop after cooling it down

As the design problem of laptop, hard disk is close to the motherboard, without heat insulation layer designed for it. When the main thermal channel is blocked, heat would spread directly onto hard disk, which makes the disk to overheat. Generally, what happens is that the system folder could not be opened, when the heat is over 57 degree, at this temperature there will be some system crashes or failures. As a suggestion, you can cool down system by virtue of external device, such as external notebook cooler. Then you can back up the documents. Besides, the bad contact between hard disk and motherboard would also cause system shutdown or auto shutdown failure; you should clean up the dust in the slots of the hard disk;

b) Make laptop disk into a removable disk:

Take out the laptop hard disk, and put it into an external removable disk box, to make it into an external USB removable disk, or so-called portable disk, namely, put a laptop hard disk into a USB disk box. The disk box could convert the disk IDE/SATA interface to USB interface. And then connect USB cable to another computer. Next start the desktop computer power, then connect the USB disk data cable. If USB 2.0 interface could not be recognized, then you can try USB 1.1 interface. Please take a look at Figure 9-1.

Figure 9-1

c)   Use one power cable with double USB interfaces

Don't use USB interface extension cable to connect, due to increase in the consumption of the power, making portable disk function abnormally. You should connect USB portable disk to the backside USB interface of the computer, and connect the cable to the two USB interfaces. Meanwhile, connect it to the two USB interfaces, then test.

d)   Use XP system in safe mode

Under Windows XP safe mode, enter USB portable disk, open the files on USB portable disk, read XP/Vista/Win7 files. As safe mode is the minimum operating system environment without loading any driver, it could easily eliminate problems conveniently and repair the errors. Please take a look at Figure 9-2.

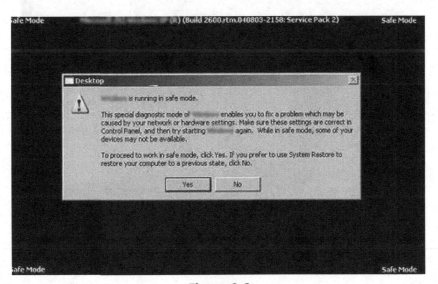

Figure 9-2

e) Use antivirus software

After succeeding in starting from safe mode, next run antivirus software to scan and remove virus. Check whether the USB portable disk has Trojan or virus. You can find Trojan with the latest version of Anti-spyware. After finishing this, back up the important data, such as digital photos, trade invoice and technical materials.

After the methods above, if system still could not recognize the USB device, then you are better off changing to another computer to try again, or even consider using different operating systems. For instance, you can first try Win XP system, and then Win7. As for specific ways, you can refer to the chapter 9, the section <<9.2.6 Laptop folder lockup failure and crack solution>>, there's the way to deal with.

2) Connect a laptop disk onto desktop computer directly

a) Use desktop SATA power cable interface directly

Here take SATA laptop disk for example, plug desktop SATA power cable interface directly into the 2.5 inch SATA laptop disk to test, which is quite simple, quick and safe way, because it does not matter whether it is a desktop hard disk or laptop disk, the power cable interfaces are all the same. Just the two disks have different voltage requirements. Desktop disk needs yellow wire (12V) and red wire (5V), and also black wire (0V); while laptop disk only uses red wire (5V) and black wire (0V). It doesn't need +12V power, so you can directly use desktop power cable interface, because when manufacturer designs circuit, laptop disk 12V power circuit is already disconnected; Please take a look at Figure 9-3.

Figure 9-3

b) Use specific IDE adapter

Vintage IDE laptop disk could be connected to PC desktop machine with IDE converter, usually convert to 3.5" standard PC IDE (40pins) interface with 2.5" mini IDE (44pins) interface. You will have to set the laptop hard drive as a Master or Slave depending on your Desktop configuration.

Attention: It's important to properly connect both ends of the adapter to ensure functionality and prevent the possibility of shorts. On the IDE interface end, the red wire on the ribbon represents pin 1. On the HDD, pin 1 should be labelled by the drive's manufacturer. If the IDE adapter is plugged oppositely, then there's the danger of burnt the disk. Please take a look at Figure 9-4.

Figure 9-4

c) Make sure laptop disk has no hardware problem

If IDE converter and data connection are correct, but on the desktop of PC desktop machine, related icon for disk could not be found in "My Computer", then here's the solution:

1) Remove data cable from the laptop disk and change with another power cable interface, and then listen for any noise from the laptop disk, check whether you could hear the disk rotation sound. If there's no rotation sound, it means the disk itself has a problem, then data rescue is much more difficult. You'd better to seek some professional company; after connecting data cable, if you still could not hear disk rotation sound, it means errors remain in data cable connection or in data cable issue itself.

2) Laptop disk rotation sound is normal, but there's no icon seen in device manager and disk manager, then please put the disk back into the laptop, then execute the following steps:

   a. Press the power button to start the laptop;
   b. When HP or Compaq logo appears, press F10 key to enter BIOS;

    c.   When main menu displays, pay attention to BIOS version and find "HOD self-test options" or "Primary Hard Disk self test" option;

    d.   Choose the tool software, and then press Enter.

Disk entire scanning starts, when scanning finishes, there will be result shown on the screen, telling users that the disk could be used or not. Above is the simplest disk test method, which could ensure the disk has no problem at all.

3)   If device manager and disk manager could find the disk, while disk related icon could not be found in desktop "My Computer", then it's quite possible that the user installs a third party kind of firewall software in system or changes some settings, which disables other device from working. This needs to be done in OS safe mode. If you changed some settings, then it could be changed back after entering safe mode. If the problem is caused by installing other software, then you can solve the problem by uninstalling the software under safe mode. Make sure the laptop disk could be recognized again.

After processing according to the method above, if you still could not back up the data, then you'd better to try with the third method, as for detailed operation, please refer to the process way in chapter 9 section <<9.2.6 Laptop folder lockup failure and crack solution>>.

3)   Make sure "Administrators" user has the "Full control" permission of the laptop disk

Sometimes the reason why data backup fails is because "Administrators" user has no authority to get "Full control" of the laptop disk, which needs further confirmation. First, shut down PC desktop, then press power button to start, press F8 to choose "Safe mode", to load XP system, make sure to logon system with "Administrator" account;

Choose laptop disk from "My Computer", right click "Laptop disk (X:) property" pops up, then choose "Property" option, make sure property dialog has no "Security" label page; if there is, then please refer to the operation way in STEP: D-1 in chapter 9, Section <<9.2.6, Laptop folder lockup failure and crack solution>>, until user has "Full control" of the laptop disk. Such a method is helpful for the locked files:

a)   Folder is "denied to access" or displays there are no proper authority to access this project;

b)   The "Hidden" option in Folder Property has a question mark besides it which is grey, unavailable;

c)   Partial folders become "0" KB, which could not be opened or copied;

d)   Error occurs during the process of file copy, showing that it could not be copied.

As for detailed operation method, please refer to the process way in chapter 9, Section <<9.2.6, Laptop folder lockup failure and crack solution>>.

4) Seek professional software tools or the help of professional company

After processing according to the method mentioned above, if you still fail to back up data, under this circumstance, mostly, the disk has physical bad tracks, including the failure symptoms discussed below, you can use the method of STEP: B-5 in chapter 9, Section 9.2.6, seeking the help of using Media Tools Pro data recovery software or asking professional company to help solve the problem.

Common failure A: system doesn't recognize hard disk. Put a laptop disk onto another desktop computer to test, as a result, the auto supervision function in CMOS could not find the existence of the disk even.

Common failure B: with the auto supervision function in CMOS, disk existence could be found, but system could not recognize hard disk, or disk could not read/write.

Common failure C: double clicking the disk volume, you get a message: "Not formatted, whether to format or not", and disk format turns to RAW.

Common failure D: disk has bad tracks, and the entire disk is broken-down.

Common failure E: disk is encrypted or changed, which makes BIOS and operating system fail in recognizing hard disk.

Common failure F: disk hardware problem, such as while carrying out self-inspection when starting up, disk has "Cracking sound; besides, disk would not be boot

9.2.2 Solution for the problem that "Add /Delete programs" could not be opened and run

Press Start—Run—then enter "cmd—sfc /scannow" to scan all protected system files and replace the incorrect version with correct Microsoft version.

If there's no display, it's generally because the page "Add or delete programs" is hidden, which is probably due to the cause that registry's relevant key value has been changed by someone or some software. The reason why "Add/delete programs" could not be opened probably is that the dynamic link library registration is invalid, it would be OK if only these files were registered again.

Solution: In "Start—Run", enter the command below, and then take turns to confirm in the following popup windows: 9.2.2 Solution for the problem that "Add /Delete programs" could not be opened and run

Press Start—Run—then enter "cmd—sfc /scannow" to scan all protected system files and replace the incorrect version with correct Microsoft version.

If there's no display, it's generally because the page "Add or delete programs" is hidden, which is probably due to the cause that registry's relevant key value is changed by someone or some software. The reason why "Add/delete programs" could not be opened probably is that the dynamic link library registration is invalid, it would be OK if only these files were registered again.

Solution: In "Start—Run", enter the command below, and then take turns to confirm in the following popup windows: Please take a look at Figure 9-5.

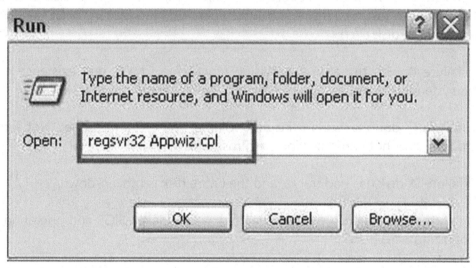

Figure 9-5

regsvr32 Appwiz.cpl
regsvr32 Jscript.dll
regsvr32 Mshtml.dll
regsvr32 Msi.dll
regsvr32 Mshtmled.dll
regsvr32 "c:\Program Files\Common Files\System\Ado\Msado15.dll"
regsvr32 "c:\Program Files\Common Files\System\Ole DB\Oledb32.dll"

Registry three components again

regsvr32 mshtml.dll
regsvr32 shdocvw.dll—
i regsvr32 shell32.dll—i

Thus, you can use "Add/delete programs" component again.

9.2.3 Solution for the problem that "REGEDIT" could not be opened and run

What to do with the locked Registry tool "REGEDIT"?

Solution:

You can solve the problem with Windows XP system's Group Policy, here's the concrete steps as follows:

1. Click "Start—Run" (Win+R shortcut key), enter "gpedit.msc" and press Enter, open "Group Policy";
2. Take turns to expand "User configuration—Administrative templates—System", double click "Prevent access to registry editing tools" on the right side pane as the following picture: Please take a look at Figure 9-6.

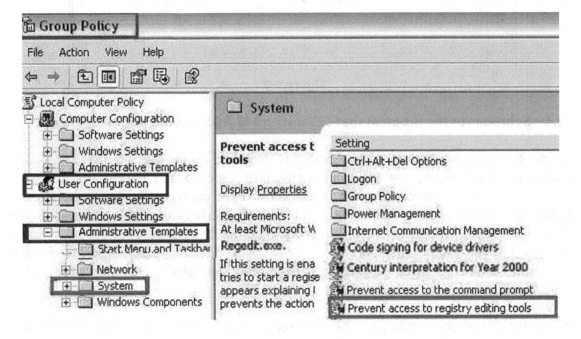

Figure 9-6

3. On the popup window, choose "Disabled", click "OK" then exit "Group Policy" (see the picture below), then you can unlock the registry. Please take a look at Figure 9-7.

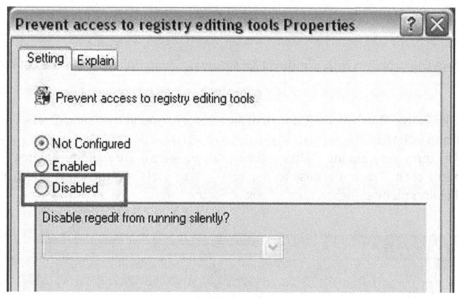

Figure 9-7

9.2.4 Solution for the problem that EFS encrypted folder could not be opened

In order to avoid the situation that encrypted folder could not be opened after reinstalling system, you can execute the following method to back up and import the key: click "Start"—"Run", and enter "certmgr.msc", press Enter key to open certificate manger. Expand "Certificates"—"Personal"—"Certificate", right click the certificate with the name of user name on the right side pane, in "All tasks", choose "Export" to open certificate export wizard. Click "Next" then choose "Yes, export the key", click "Next", choose default export file format, then click "Next", enter the password, click "Next" and then specify file name, at last, click "Finish".

After reinstalling system, right click the exported private key file, choose "Install PFX", then you can import private key step by step. After finishing the import, you can successfully open the EFS encrypted folder. Please take a look at Figure 9-8.

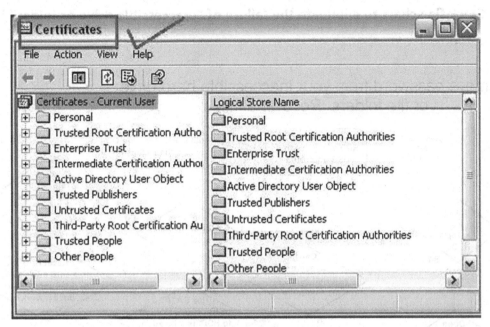

Figure 9-8

Under the circumstance of no backing up the private key, it's almost impossible to decrypt EFS, although there are a lot of popular ways on Internet to do this, it's simply not possible or feasible. Because some EFS use public key certificate to encrypt files; besides, every user has a unique SID (Security Identifier). For the first time to encrypt a folder, system would automatically assign or generate a private key for the user according to the encrypted SID; besides, it would store public key and private key separately. Before reinstalling system, if you haven't backed up current private key, which means no matter how, it's impossible to form the previous user private key, while file decryption not only needs public key, but also password. Therefore, there's no way to open the previous EFS encrypted folder at all.

9.2.5 Crack flowchart to eliminate the failure of "inaccessible drive or folder" issue

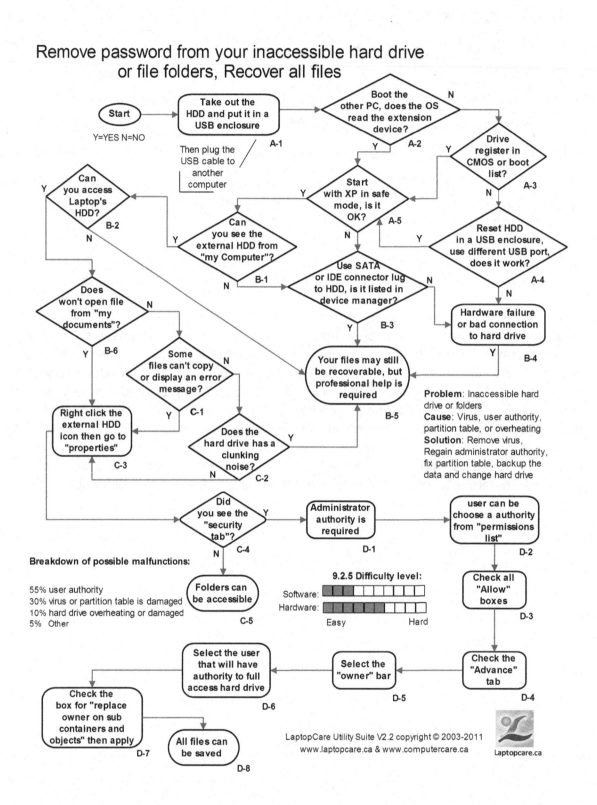

Remove password from your inaccessible hard drive or file folders, Recover all files

Breakdown of possible malfunctions:

55% user authority
30% virus or partition table is damaged
10% hard drive overheating or damaged
5% Other

Problem: Inaccessible hard drive or folders
Cause: Virus, user authority, partition table, or overheating
Solution: Remove virus, Regain administrator authority, fix partition table, backup the data and change hard drive

9.2.5 Difficulty level:

Software:
Hardware:

Easy   Hard

LaptopCare Utility Suite V2.2 copyright © 2003-2011
www.laptopcare.ca & www.computercare.ca

Laptopcare.ca

This tutorial will help you solve this problem with laptop:

1. "My Computer" and "My Documents" would not be opened: you double click the system folder, a message shows "Windows cannot access specified device, path or file, or it shows there's no proper permissions to access this project", and partial folders become "0" KB, which could not be opened, copied or deleted. Please take a look at Figure 9-9.

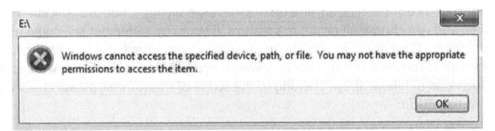

Figure 9-9

2. Drive D could not be opened by double clicking, or it showing which application to choose or open, It is useless even to scan the entire disk and remove the viruses. After reinstalling the operating system, drive D still could not be opened, you get a message that it's not formatted; please take a look at Figure 9-10.

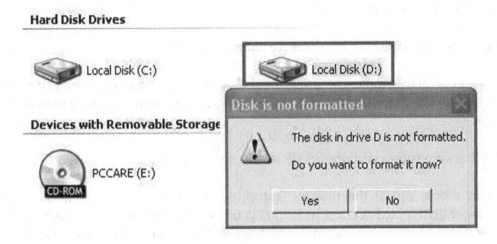

Figure 9-10

3. After reinstalling operating system, the icon of drive D becomes grey out and could not be opened, even the shortcut would not start.

In this article, I will explain how to find out the cause of failure: laptop folder could not be opened, but the error message prompt is not directed against certain special brands or models, it should fit most laptops.

Step: 1

Plug the power adapter into the laptop; press the power button to start the machine, enter system and then check carefully, it should fit the several Independent failure descriptions of this tutorial:

1) Folder could not be opened. Please notice: there are many reasons causing these symptoms that system folder could not be opened normally. For instance, a file would not start by double clicking, and there's message saying "Choose application to open file", and you choose all program software in your computer, but still could not open the folder. This situation is mostly because your computer has no correct software or the useful software in computer is already damaged, which would not work anymore. Such kind of failure doesn't belong to the scope of this tutorial, please check another tutorial article.

2) File could not be recovered. Please notice: if your laptop has the failure symptom that file could not be recovered, then it's probably because your file has been encrypted once before, for example, EFS encrypted folder could not be opened, probably you will see "Access is denied" error message or requesting to enter protection password and confirm password. After EFS encryption, if you haven't backed up certificate, then this situation doesn't belong to the scope of this tutorial, please check another tutorial article. If you haven't done EFS encryption, then under this circumstance, this tutorial could help you a lot.

Step A-1 the goal of this setup is to remove laptop's hard disk

First of all, you need to remove the laptop hard disk and put it to an external disk enclosure turning it into an external USB hard disk, then connect it to another running computer with a USB cable.

Generally, there are three positions for HP laptop disk to stay:

1) Hard disk is put at the base of laptop, namely, the backside, some laptops use independent hard disk cover, as long as you open the hard disk cover, you can remove the disk, while for some laptops, you have to disassemble the entire base (however, this should be quite rare).
2) Hard disk is at the side of laptop, there are few screws to remove fix these, After removing the screws, you can take the hard disk out.
3) Hard disk is at both sides of the touchpad of laptop. Generally, the shell of laptop touchpad is separated from keyboard. As long as you remove the screws on the shell connected the touchpad from the base, you can see the hard disk.

However, here are a few points you have to pay attention to:

A) Even if you remove all screws from the laptop, there's still a clip between the laptop cover and the shell, which would always be clipped together so you'd have to see it clearly and then pry it up slowly. Make sure the direction is correct, don't pry from the opposite direction;

B)   Some hard disks are installed onto the motherboard with a connecting adapter. There is one or two bolts beside the hard disk interface, being locked tightly, which you need to remove. Pay close attention to that when disassembling the disk, don't break the pin for the connecting adapter, or if it's damaged, the entire disk or the entire laptop would probably be scrapped;

C)   Make sure of the sequence when disassembling the shell, after getting the data on hard disk, please restore the hard disk to the original condition according to the opposite disassembling sequence; And then please enter Step: A-2

Step: A-2 the goal of this procedure is to make laptop hard disk to a disk enclosure disk

The so-called disk enclosure disk is used to install a laptop disk into a disk box, the disk box could convert disk IDE/SATA interface into USB interface.

Until now, development of disk enclosure disk box has already gone through a few years, from the earliest parallel disk enclosure disk box till current most widely used USB2.0 +IEEE 1394 interface disk; from the beginning drawer disk box till current more convenient external disk enclosure disk box. We can tell that as the continual development of technology advances, more convenience is brought to customers;

So far on the market, there are two main types of disk enclosures: one is the 2.5 inch disk box supporting laptop (also dividing into thin disk and thick disk); another is the disk box supporting the common 3.5 inch disk.

● **Interface of disk enclosure disk box**

So far there are two mainstream types of interfaces of 2.5 inch disk enclosure: USB, IEEE1394.

USB 2.0+IEEE1394=COMBO

Disk enclosure disk box of USB interface is the mainstream product so far, the biggest advantage is the convenience, supporting hot swappable and plug-and-play in Windows Me/2000/XP, this would work normally without installing driver. According to different standards, USB interface has two standards: 1.1 and 2.0. The biggest difference between them is the transmission speed. USB1.1 interface only has 12Mbps transmission speed, while USB2.0 interface's speed is as high as 480Mbps.

IEEE1394 is also called "Live wire", the data transmission speed of this interface, theoretically, could reach 400Mbps. However, as IEEE1394 interface is not so popular on nowadays motherboards, usually, it needs an expensive special IEEE1394 interface card to work. So this choice makes the cost higher, besides, it's not universal for different computers, which is not proper for most common users. But for some customers using their laptops for things such as drawing, animation and design work, "Live wire" interface is really needed to help them with data transmission on MAC machines and most common PC.

- **Power of disk enclosure disk box**

As for the power of disk enclosure disk box, this point is mainly dead against the guys who choose disk enclosure disk box of USB interface. As the biggest power supply current of USB interface is 500mA, and under some circumstances, this could not reach the requirement of some 2.5 inch disks. If the disk is working under the current lower than rating value for a long period of time, then it easily become damaged the representation is that the disk often losses data, formatting could not be finished with error message showing; While formatting, the task could not be done and errors occur.

Especially, it would not work on a particular laptop, In this case, you'd better to choose a disk enclosure box that could use external power supply or just buy a USB-PS2 interface (or double USB pin) to take the place of the original one. If you use the old-style laptop disk, you should also pay close attention to this problem, for the initial model laptops' disks use power usually a little higher, of which some power supply current can even reach 700 mA-1200mA.

- **Material that the hard disk box is made of**

The material that the hard disk box is made of is often overlooked by most people in their choice. Here, the material I mention means the material the box is made of, but not the appearance design of the disk enclosure disk box, such as colorful shell and some other aspects. So far, disk rotation speed is faster and faster, which also brings heat radiating problem. if the heat radiating ability of the disk box you choose is not good enough, it would have an influence on the disk's stable running.

On the market, cheap disk enclosure box usually uses plastic shell, of which the heat effect is quite bad. Probably within a short period of time, it might be OK to use, no big problem, but if you are doing data transmission for a long time, then probably the data transmission might stop and get damaged, system might crash down and some other problems would happen.

Therefore, you'd better to use aluminum or aluminum-magnesium alloy as the shell material. There prices are a little higher for some of these products, but better radiating measure would make your disk working more stably.

If after USB enclosure disk is connected to a laptop, the system did not prompt you for a message like "USB device is found", the solution would become more complex, please continue to enter STEP: A-3;

If after USB enclosure disk connects to laptop, system shows the error message "USB device is found", then you need to observe whether the icon corresponding to the USB device appears in system, and then double click on the USB device to check whether it could be opened or not. If there's a yellow exclamation mark beside the USB device, or it shows unknown device, then please continue to STEP: A-5;

If it's available to enter USB enclosure disk, then check up whether the important data could be backed up or not, (such as digital pictures, trade invoice, technical material, mails and some hard-won messages), after double clicking the folder, probably you might see some error message like "Access is denied", then please continue to enter STEP: A-5;

Step A-3 the goal of this procedure is to confirm whether the newly-made disk enclosure disk could be recognized by other computers

1) Remove enclosure hard disk and connect it to disk box. First, you have to consider the position of the disk jumper setup on the primary disk, which refers to old-style IDE hard disk, for the laptop IDE and SATA disk nowadays, you don't have to consider this problem, usually, you connect disk enclosure disk to desktop computer by, first, starting desktop computer power, and when it's working normally, you connect disk USB data cable. If system shows that USB2.0 interface could not be recognized, you can try USB1.1 interface.

2) Suggest connecting disk enclosure disk onto the backside of the motherboard USB interface of the desktop computer, when you connect the disk enclosure disk on the front USB interface, usually, you use extension cable to connect from the USB connector on the motherboard to the front side of the computer shell, so to increase the power consumption, prevent the disk from working normally, system could not inspect the device with correct name or just only inspect the enclosure disk box device, naturally, there's no way to choose to install drivers. Probably device could not be recognized. You should connect USB data transmission cable to the backside USB interface on the computer, meanwhile, use an assistant power cable of twisted USB interface, connecting to two USB interfaces on computer and then test.

3) After connecting USB disk enclosure disk to computer, if system doesn't display the error message "USB device is found", then it is quite possible that interruption number for the USB interface hasn't been assigned in BIOS, which disables system to recognize normally and manage USB device. Restart the computer and enter BIOS Setup window, set the item "Assign IRQ For USB" as "Enabled" in "PNP/PCI CONFIGURATION", or just set the item "USB function For DOS" as "Enabled", then system could distribute valid interruption address for USB interface.

4) After connecting disk enclosure disk, computer has no response. According to normal operation, if after you connect USB disk, computer doesn't show the disk enclosure disk. You have to restart the computer, and press Del key when it's starting to enter CMOS Setup. Set "USB Control" as "Enabled" in "CHIPSET FEATURES SETUP" or "INTEGRATED PERIPHERALS", save and then restart the computer. Due to different computer BIOS versions, for concrete setups, please refer to your motherboard manual accompanied with your computer.

After trying the methods above, if USB disk enclosure disk to computer being connected, system still doesn't give you the message "USB device is found", then please continue to STEP: A-4; if after connecting USB disk enclosure disk to computer, system shows the message "USB device is found", but there're still some other problems, such as showing that it's unknown device or could not be opened, then please continue to STEP: A-5;

Step A-4 The goal of this procedure is to confirm whether the new made disk enclosure disk has any hardware problem

1) After going through the methods above, if system still could not recognize USB device, you'd better to change to another computer and try again, even you can consider using different operating system, such as first trying Windows XP, and then trying Win7 again;

2) Supposing you get this problem on nForce motherboard, and there's no way to change to another computer to try, you can try first installing the latest special USB2.0 driver and patch for nForce, then the latest motherboard patch and then the operation system patch;

3) If you use Win2003 operation system, after connecting disk enclosure disk, drive volume could not be found. At this moment, you can specify drive volume manually. First of all, make sure the device assembly is right, and then right click on "My Computer", on the "Computer Management" window, choose "Disk management". At the right bottom corner on the window, there should be "Disk 0", "Disk 1" (or more). The "Disk 1" (should be the actual disk enclosure disk), the long strip shape blocks at the back side show your disk enclosure disk partition situation and each partition situation. But none partition have a volume. You could only add "Drive volume" separately. On the corresponding partition strip, right click and the dropdown menu appears, choose the item "Change drive volume and path" in the menu. After specifying the drive volume according to the prompt on screen, then it's done.

4) After going through the methods above, when connect USB disk enclosure disk to computer being connected, if system still could not find USB device, you should consider a possible hardware problem. Please change to another known good USB disk enclosure disk box, and then continue testing;

5) After processing the methods above, if system shows the message "USB device is found", but there are some other problems, then please go to STEP: A-5; After connecting USB disk enclosure disk to computer, if it still could not be recognized, then you should consider changing to another known working hard disk, namely, you should install it to a disk box and continue testing, determining whether the problem is on the original laptop disk or your computer setting. After changing hard disk, if everything is OK, then I'm sure the problem must be on the original laptop disk, besides, the problem is now quite serious, It is likely beyond what you can handle at this point, And for data recovery, you need the help of a professional data recovery company; after changing hard disk, if the failure symptom has no change, So the problem would be your computer settings and test methods related. (Please double-check all the settings of the computer, best way is to change to another computer and do test job again)

Step A-5: the goal of this setup is to test Mobile HDD (USB enclosure disk) under windows XP safe mode

Regular computer users would not feel strange about OS XP safe mode, which is a special mode used to repair operation system mistakes, with a minimum system environment without loading any driver. If you start computer from safe mode, then it would facilitate user to eliminate problems and repair mistakes.

Enter safe mode in Windows XP environment:

1. After computer starts and BIOS loading finishes, quickly press F8 key, and on the prompt Windows XP advanced option menu, choose "Safe mode";
2. If it's a multi-system boot-up, when you choose Windows XP to start and press Enter key, you should quickly press F8 (you'd better operate with two hands) and on the prompt advanced option menu, choose "Safe mode".

   a) Repairing the failure of a system that, you could not find USB device

   First, try restarting the computer and switch to safe mode to start. Check if the system recognizes USB device? If yes, then it's a system failure caused by registry problem, such a method is quite effective, because when Windows starts in safe mode, it could automatically repair registry problems.

   b) Recover system settings

   Some users installed a third party firewall software in system or modified some settings, thus external USB device is disabled, so you also need to enter safe mode to solve this problem. If some settings are modified, after entering safe mode, you can change it back. If you install some software, you can uninstall it under safe mode.

After the methods above, when connect USB disk enclosure disk to computer again, if system still could not find the USB device, then please go to STEP: B-3; if after connecting USB disk enclosure disk to computer, system could find USB device, then please continue to STEP: B-1.

Step B-1; The goal of this setup is to confirm there's an icon corresponding to the hard disk in "My computer"

1) **Computer could find USB disk enclosure disk,** but in "My computer", there's no icon corresponding to the hard drive: here's the solution for this problem:

   a) Adjust system resources applied with USB device, making every USB device not to interrupt each other. Pull out all USB device interfaces, only keeping mouse, keyboard and enclosure disk;
   b) Open "Device management" and see whether there's any yellow exclamation mark there? If there is yellow exclamation mark it means the disk enclosure disk needs a driver to be installed (although some manufacturers declare that

XP system doesn't need installing driver, it seems not 100% correct, generally speaking, you need to upgrade XP to SP2).

c) If there's still a yellow exclamation mark, it still means there's some system conflict, (if there's none, sometimes still there is conflict, just system doesn't show), then you can try changing to another USB interface;

2) **If the methods above doesn't work,** then click "Start", find "My Computer", and then right click to open the menu, then click "Manage" to open the window "Computer Management (Local)", find "Disk Management" in the menu, double click "Disk Management" and then check all disk 0-X, and look whether there's one disk enclosure disk there? Probably it's also in the list of "unknown devices", if it is the case, here's a solution provided:

a) Power shortage causes the problem, then use the backside USB interface on the computer, another way is to use twisted USB interface cable instead of one USB cable, then insert the two USB ports of the computer to test. What you need to pay attention to is that you have to make sure the disk enclosure disk has enough power supply, otherwise, probably the disk might be damaged because of power shortage;

b) Excluding the reasons above, it's also likely that USB interface type doesn't match, which disables disk enclosure disk from working normally. For instance, USB interface has two standards 1.1 and 2.0, as there are a lot of disk technologies, the connection cable requested to connect computer and disk enclosure disk must support related standard. Otherwise, this device has no way to be installed correctly. Experiment shows that some disk enclosure disks connected to the interface of USB 2.0 standard could not be recognized correctly by system; while in USB1.1 standard interface, it could work normally; besides, there are some situations exactly opposite, after high-speed disk enclosure device (hard disk) is plugged into low-speed hub, the disk enclosure disk of USB2.0 standard could not be recognized correctly. You need to change the connection cable to USB2.0 standard to solve this problem.

c) After using the methods above, if system still could not recognize USB disk enclosure disk, then you'd better to change to another computer to try, even you could consider installing a USB 1.1 PCI card Connect it to USB disk enclosure disk, and I've used such a method to solve many difficulties and problems;

3) **Double click "Disk Management" and then check disk manager**, if there's no disk enclosure disk there, this situation could be handled in the following manner:

a) Plug USB pin to the USB interface of the computer, and place your ears close to the disk enclosure disk box to see whether disk rotation sound could be heard, if there's no rotation sound, it means the disk has no power or there's something wrong with the disk enclosure disk box itself;

b) Change to another known good USB disk enclosure disk box, and place your ears close to the disk enclosure disk box, check whether there's disk rotation sound. If still no rotation sound, then it means the disk itself has some problems, in this case it's quite difficult to recover the data. You'd to seek help from professional data Recovery Company;

c) If disk enclosure disk's rotation sound is normal, but there's no icon in device management or disk manager, in most cases, it's because the disk is encrypted. This encryption disables laptop BIOS and operation system to recognize the disk, so it's difficult to rescue the data, generally, you'd better to ask help from professional data recovery company;

After trying the methods above, if there's icon corresponding to the disk in "My Computer", and it's available to enter, please go to STEP: B-2; if there's still no related icon appeared, or there is an icon shown but no way to open it, please go onto STEP: B-3.

Step B-2; the goal of this procedure is to confirm that mouse could open the icon corresponding to the disk. Take a look at Figure 9-11.

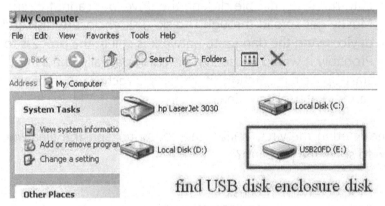

Figure 9-11

1) **If you double click X drive with your mouse to show "Unformatted, whether to format?"** the X represents the USB disk enclosure disk, such as drive D, E . . .), generally it is caused because of disk error. Sometimes, we also suggest checking the disk connection to see whether there's a bad contact, or there's no requirements to use screws to fix up the hard disk, (use screws to fix up the hard disk is not required by the manufacturers of the provisions) which causes loose connection between hard disk and USB disk enclosure disk box, then such a failure would also occur—the icon corresponding to the disk could not be opened. If after confirming the problem with disk connection, the failure still occurs, probably it's the precursor that the disk would be damaged soon, then please go to STEP: B-5.

2) **Drive X could not be opened by double clicking; it requests to show choice of application**

a) Maybe mobile USB hard disk infected with viruses, you can check out all hidden files on drive D and protected system files to observe whether there're rose.exe and autorun.inf files, or autorun.inf and pagefile.com files, or command.com and autorun.inf files. If there are some, your laptop is infected with viruses . . .

and the file Autorun.inf is the virus, so you should first erase the property and then delete. As for specific method, go to the registry and find the file autorun. inf, after finding it, delete the sub item shell, then you can open drive D. Click "Start"—"Run" with your mouse, type "regedit" and press "Ctrl+F" combination key, Find dialog would appear. On the dialog box, type "autorun.inf" and press Enter, then you can see the sub item shell;

b) Disconnect the network, go into safe mode, open "Windows Task Manager", then end the suspicious processes. right click to open drive D (remember never double click to open it), afterwards, delete those two files, then it's OK. You should also be very careful not let drive C get infected by viruses.

Generally, here are the main symptoms of Rose viruses below:

1. A large amount of CPU resource is occupied in system;
2. Two files rose.exe and autorun.inf are created on every partition, it shows auto run when double clicking the drive, but cannot open it;
3. Mostly get spread through U disk, disk enclosure disk and other storage devices. And the danger to network is still in the process to find out;
4. Probably it would cause system crash partially, the symptom is that after start-up self inspection, it restarts directly and repeats restarting, you cannot enter system finally;

c) After deleting the virus, restart the computer and the files would form again. How to solve the problem?

1. First, end ROSE process;
2. Enter registry, find ROSE.EXE, and then delete it;
3. Delete the files AUTORUN.INI and ROSE.EXE under each drive. Check the path C:\WINDOWS\SYSTEM32, if there are the files too, delete them, too.
4. Restart the computer and then it's OK.

d) If the methods above could not solve the problem, then follow the next steps:

1. Back up all files or move somewhere else;
2. Format the drive D;
3. Recover files;
4. OK, done.

If file backup or move fails, then please continue to enter STEP: B-6;

3) **When you double click drive X, the system shows:** "Windows could not access specified device, path, file or shows there's no proper authorization to access this project".

   a) The cause for the failure is that your system disk uses NTFS partition format, besides, there is some administrative permissions, or probably the Admin user account is disabled;

   Solution: check the property of X disk, go to "Security" option and then click "Add", choose one administrator account, click "OK". And then logon with this administrator's account. Afterwards, go to the Control Panel—Folder options, display all files, besides, remove option hide the extension of known file.

   a. Search cmd.exe, and rename as cmd.com or cmd.scr;
   b. Run cmd.com;
   c. Run the next two commands: ftype exefile="%1" %* assoc.exe=exefile
   d. Change cmd.com back to cmd.exe.

   If you still cannot access drive X, then please go to STEP: B-5;

Step B-3: The goal of this setup is to connect one laptop hard disk to a desktop to test without using a USB.

Put laptop disk into an external disk enclosure disk box, turning it into an external USB disk, and then connect the USB cable, then connect to another working computer. This kind of method is quite simple and convenient, but in practical application, there are still two faults as we will show below:

Compared to internal hard disk (it means the hard disk is connected with the motherboard directly), USB external disk enclosure disk has lower speed on data transmission, especially in the case where there are large data sizes, which would waste some time. This is the point that every technician should always take into account;

On data rescue aspect, USB external disk enclosure disk's success rate is always less than internal disk (it means the disk connects to the motherboard directly), so technician would rather like to use internal disk to do the job on data rescue aspect;

1) **Now the question is can laptop disk directly connect to desktop machine?** If yes, how do you connect it? How do we manage safe connection? Let's take SATA laptop disk for an example, what we care about mostly is that whether desktop SATA power could directly plug to a 2.5 inch SATA laptop disk. Would the laptop disk be burnt out?

(I understand that what everyone is worried about is that the desktop power supply voltage can be matched to laptop hard disk?), no matter whether desktop hard disk or laptop hard disk are, their power cable interface are all the same, just the two kinds of disk need different voltages. Desktop hard disk needs yellow cable (12V) and red cable (5V), connected to ground (0V) with black cable; while the laptop hard disk only uses red cable (5V) and black cable connecting to ground (0V).

Generally, there are 15 pins on SATA power cable; actually there are only five groups, each three cables are connected together (this could carry large current, and could use hot swap status), the colors of these five cables are orange, black, red, black and yellow;

The meanings of the SATA power cables' colors are as follows (15 pins)

> Yellow: +12V
> Red: +5V
> Black: ground cable (GND)
> Orange: +3.3V

SATA disk or DVD-ROM/CD-ROM power requirement:

2.5 inch laptop disk doesn't need +12V power, no need for yellow cable to supply power; generally +3.3V power supply is not needed either, not to connect orange cable, generally, it would work normally, but rarely some individual ATA device has the situation that could not recognize.

Therefore: many technicians convert IDE power cable to SATA power cable, they all just connect 12 pins (missing the orange cable). This is because that the IDE power plug has no +3.3V output; new PC power all uses power plug with 5 cables (orange, black, red, black, yellow); it could be plugged into a laptop disk directly and used, as when manufacturer designs the laptop disk PCB, 12V power supply cable has already been cut.

2) **Prepare SATA data cable,** here you should pay attention to the SATA technology, which has two kinds, I and II, their speeds are 150MB/S and 300MB/S. If your motherboard supports SATA II disk, it would be better; but if it does not, and your disk is of SATA II, then you need to do something to the disk jumper, you'd have to let SATA II disk work in SATA I mode by force, if you don't do anything to the jumper, then some motherboards might not recognize SATA II disk. And the concrete operation is to find one jumper cap, and then shorten connection of the two pins far away from power and data cable ends on the laptop disk's 4 pin jumper, and then it's done.

3) **Theoretically,** (The total amount of times of plugging and unplugging for internal SATA data cable is 50 times only!) So you should do as less hot swap action as you could, of course, if it's damaged, then just buy a new data cable. When plugging hot swap disk, you should first install data cable and then plug power cable, and it's exactly opposite when disassemble. If power cable and data cable are too crowded then the hard disk is difficult to be plugged in, then you can first cut off a little plastic

coating of the power cable and data cable, and then plug the hard disk. Or you can buy connected plug to use, which is also a good method.

4) **Not every PC supports hot swap disk;** check to make sure that your PC motherboard support AHCI, BIOS setup center must have AHCI. The operating on system (XP) must also have the AHCI driver.

5) **IF you cannot find SATA power cable**, you can use two cables and change to USB interface to get power. Anything else is unnecessary, because the black cables coming out from power are all parallel connected together. While the black cables on hard disk, except No 11, others are all parallel connected, (generally, No 11 black cable is used for disk LED indication light), in this way, it is easy to change the power cable, only use (456) black cable and + (789) red cable, if you worry about the current size of USB 500MA, you can use two USB interfaces parallel connected to supply power.

6) **Old-style IDE laptop disk could use IDE converter to connect to PC desktop**, generally, we convert 2.5" mini IDE(40pins) interface to 3.5" standard PC IDE (40pins) interface, when plugging to laptop disk, pay attention to the direction of the interface, never plug in reverse, otherwise, the disk will be burnt.

7) **Start-up and check, after powering on**, place your ear close to the disk to hear the sound, if there's abnormal sound, or you can hardly hear the disk rotation sound, you should check whether the disk SATA power cable has some problems, and then decide whether the disk itself has some problems;

8) **After trying the solution above**, if system still could not recognize the laptop disk, you'd better to change a SATA data cable to connect the laptop disk, even you should consider changing a computer and try. I've used such process to solve many issues; however, if after changing the data cable and replacing another PC, you still could not open or fail to recognize the laptop disk, please go STEP: B-4;

Step B-4; The goal of this procedure is to confirm whether the failure has something to do with the laptop disk

1) **After removing the disk**, you need to first take a look, secondly to listen, third, to smell and fourth, to test.

   a) Look: whether the components on disk PCB has some deformation, discoloration and crack, or damage symptoms;

   b) Whether disk (SATA) connection joint has some damage or cracks. You can determine this by observing, or you could also check it up closely with a magnifier;

   c) After powering on, whether the disk indication light flashes normally, there should be no out or always lighted symptom;

2) **Listen:**

   a) After powering on, you need to check whether the disk drive's rotation sound is normal; there should be no abnormal sound or loud noise. Otherwise, this indicates there's something wrong with the disk;

b) Listen whether there's abnormal sound when the system starts. If disk has abnormal sound or loud noise, it means the disk has some problems;

3) Smell:

Remove the disk, smell it a little, check whether there is a burnt plastic smell, which would be quite different from the plastic smell usually on disk. If there is, then it means there's something wrong with the disk;

4) Test:

The following are the questions often being asked: how to test whether there's bad track on disk? What software to use? After starting up, just test directly?

a) Generally speaking, HP laptop has the tool software for testing hard disk, usually, we can find it in system BIOS. The tool software's accuracy rate could not reach 100% although, for most users, it's kind of proper to choose the tool software with the machine itself, which also saves much trouble! Especially for the users who know little about tool software; it would be much safer than to choose other disk test tool software.

As for operation method, please follow the next steps:

1) Press power button to start the laptop;
2) When HP or Compaq logo appears, press F10 key to enter BIOS Setup;
3) When main menu appears, pay attention to the BIOS version and look for the option "Hard Disk self test";
4) Choose the tool software, and then press Enter.

Disk full scanning begins, the procedure uses the option "Disk full test", when the scanning finishes, there will be result shown on screen, telling users whether this disk could be used or not, the above is the easiest disk test method, which is kind of proper for computer beginners to use, but I cannot guarantee the disk is totally problem free.

b) So far disk is still the important place for data storage, of which importance is well known by all. Sometimes, laptop motherboard has a problem or the test software in BIOS has some errors. Then you'd have to use disk test software.

In order to protect user data and allows users the convenient to use the hard drive to reduce hard disk failure and also test disk when failure occurs, each disk manufacturer should release its own disk test software according to their own disk, and here're the operation points as follows:

1) First you need to confirm what brand of disk you use, then please use the software released by this manufacturer to test the disk, for instance, if you use Seagate disk,

then please use "Seagate test utility" software to test the disk; if you use Western Digital disk, then please use Western Digital released software; there are many versions of test software, please choose the right version, matching with the disk which you are using.

2) These applications are matched with the disk of its own brand, so don't be mixed in using, for instance, if you want to test the IBM disk, you should choose DFT disk test software, but not other software; if you mix them, system would not allow carrying out the test job.

3) Most part of these applications are DOS command line utility, so I recommend users using floppy disk to start system, and then run related hard disk test utility from floppy disk, if it's carried out in Windows graphic interface, some utilities are not allowed.

4) These test software might have disk low level format procedure, so you'd have to use them before you figure it out, otherwise, probably your data would be lost for good.

5) When scanning finishes, there's related result shown on screen, telling users current situation of the disk, it suggests whether to continue using or not to use. Generally there will be few situations as follows;

   a) There is bad sector on disk;
   b) Hard disk has already been damaged due to vibration;
   c) Hard disk will be deteriorate, and collapse;
   d) Hard disk could work normally, don't need to be returned to repair or change it.

6) According to the test results to determine what type of help you need If the laptop disk test fails or the result shown on screen says that the disk could not be continued to use, for such case, please go to STEP: B-5;

Step B-5; The goal of this setup is to use professional software tool, or seek help from professional company

If you are not familiar with computer, or you have no experience with data recovery at all, I suggest you seek some help from a local professional company, for technicians with experience, data recovery is just an easy job, if you make some wrong steps, then probably your data would be damaged permanently, you would never be able to correct the mistake you've made, here I will introduce the data recovery method for disk "hard" failures, but I need to point out especially that I cannot guarantee you would not make any mistake during your operation process, except you only want to get some experience, but do not care about the missing of data, then you can try it yourself, but you'd have to take sole responsibility for it!

Some suggestions before you try doing data recovery:

1. Don't use any auto data recovery tool or OS repair tool;
2. Don't use any application/utility to access (change) issued media with any method. for instance, reinstall operation system or use one-key system recovery;

3. Don't try downloading any software free of charge or trial software to change the content of the main boot sector on disk, or try recovering partition table to recover the data on disk;
4. Don't open disk or open any device like this kind of physical medium with any method, just try repairing it by yourself.
5. Pack your hard disk with antistatic envelope.

Common failure A: system could not recognize hard disk

Connect the disk of one laptop to another desktop computer to test; finding that the auto inspection function in CMOS could not detect the hard disk presence either, the symptom is listed below:

a) After starting up, system could not find hard disk, enter motherboard BIOS and hard disk is still unable to be recognized, probably the disk control circuit motherboard is damaged
b) During the self test process, the screen shows that the disk is lost or cannot be partitioned, probably there's some fault with the disk control circuit;
c) Disk could not start, which shows the information "Primary master hard disk fail", then probably there's something wrong with the disk power interface;
d) Screen shows error message "Hard Disk Controller Failure".

When such kind of situation appears, you should check up the connection plug of the data cable, and see whether it's too loose, whether the connection is off, after checking these possibilities, then try replacing the control circuit board of the laptop disk, that is what we usually called the motherboard on the hard disk. If you decide to use a new control circuit board to replace it, you'd have to follow the next rules:

1) Use professional tool to remove the control circuit board of the disk, but don't open the, shell of the hard disk in any way or try to debugging the spindle in the hard disk. control the motor and some other kind of device's physical medium, otherwise, an Irreversibly loss would be caused.
2) New disk control circuit board must be of the same function like previous control circuit board's, namely, same disk manufacturer, same disk size, same disk model, same disk production place and same disk batch number, and it would be better be produced in the same month of the same year;
3) New disk control circuit board must have the same shape like previous control circuit board's, namely, the size; the original parts, the positions of the original parts and the chip model should all be same;
4) After the above, if you succeed to implement the data recovery, although laptop might start Windows, still we suggest you back up all personal data on the computer immediately: copy the data to the network drive, CD, DVD or USB storage device. Because the repaired disk would have data loss failure again at any time.

Common failure B: Disk existence is found by using the auto test function in CMOS, but system could not recognize the disk, or the disk could not read or write

Basically there are four reasons causing such a kind of failure:

1.   Main boot sector's utility is damaged;
2.   Partition table "Invalid Partition Table" is damaged
3.   Hard disk Partition table-Error!!!
4.   Disk main boot sector's data is damaged.

A.   Damaged reasons and feasible analysis for the recovery

Partition table failure, in data damage, is probably the worst disaster breakage except physic damage. As for its reason, there are nothing more than few kinds as follows

1)   Personal wrong operation that partitions deletion, which causes the problem. As long as there is no other action done, the data lost could be recovered completely;
2)   Problem is caused because of installing multi-system wizard software or applying third party partition tool software. There's possibility of recovering the data.
3)   Disk is infected by viruses or the logical block is locked; data could be partially or completely recovered.
4)   Problem is caused by partitioning disk with Ghost clone, the data could only be partially recovered or could not be recovered at all (Guys who use Ghost should pay attention to this).

The existence of the problem above would cause the failure, such as that the system could not recognize the partition, then the system would treat the disk as one "naked partition" that has never been partitioned before, therefore, most software would fail to work;

B.   Solution

EasyRecovery is professional software of one data Recovery Company, which of course has very professional style. EasyRecovery supports many file system formats, like FAT, NTFS. Besides, there is a Novell version. For partition damage and disk accidental formatting, EasyRecovery could recover this files safely, what you need to do is to connect the disk with damaged data to another computer, just recover as much as you like. However, EasyRecovery's effect to the bad track span for hard disk is not that good, sometimes; it would be blocked by the bad track on hard disk, which could not carry out the next data recovery step.

Common failure C: Double click drive, system shows "Unformatted, whether to format", then disk format turns to RAW.

Solution 4: with EasyRecovery software, here's the solution:

1.   Use EasyRecovery Pro 6.04 version, choose data recovery Advanced Recovery (use advanced option, customized data recovery function);
2.   Choose the drive already changed to RAW format, click the advanced option below;

3. In the file system scanning, choose "NTFS" format for file system, click Advanced scan, choose the "Advanced option" at the right bottom corner, set cluster size and data starting position as 0 both;
4. Click partition setup, use MFT way (Be very carefully); and then click OK;
5. Click Next step to start scanning file system, Maybe you have to wait for a very long time, which need patience. After finishing, you will find there's one NTFS drive. Then click to find the drive and begin scanning;
6. After scanning finishes, you would find that all files have been found, and then click to recover, choose one available drive to store your recovered files
7. At last, for the hard disk with formatting problem, just copy the recovery files back.

Common failure D: Bad track occurs on disk, the entire disk breaks down

Physical disk's bad track is quite common disk failure, but if bad track is exactly on the disk main boot sector, data recovery would become quite difficult, system might fail to recognize the disk or it could not be opened by double click. System shows that disk hasn't been formatted or there's mouse freezing symptom.

C: Solution:

Media Tools Pro is a software from another professional data recovery company, which has the professional style in the lead, besides, it uses quite advanced reverse-clone/cycle-clone technology.

Reverse-Clone / Cycle-Clone

Reverse-Clone is the process of cloning from the end of your media to the beginning of it. When your media is severely failing mechanically, "Reverse-Cloning" is often your last chance to extract raw data from it, without having to take it into a clean room. This unique technology, coupled with Cycle-Clone and Cycle-Image, surpasses any cloning or imaging technology available. It has quite good span effect to the bad tracks on disk.

Common failure E: Disk is encrypted or transformed

At this moment, never use FDISK /MBR, SYS to deal with it, otherwise, data would never be found back, you must crack the encryption algorithm reversely, or find the important moved sector. For those viruses encrypting the data on disk, when to clean them out, you must choose reliable antivirus software which could recover encrypted data.

Common failure F: Disk hardware problem

a) When starting and doing self test, disk makes "cracking . . ." sound, besides, hard disk would not booted up;
b) Disk magnetic head and some control components are damaged. After powering on, the disk principal axis motor could not rotate normally (no normal principal axis rotating sound);

c)   Disk principal axis motor, location card and some other parts are damaged. You can hear the internal sound when it vibrates

If the problems above occur, it belongs to physical data recovery range, which needs high professional tool being completely compatible with disk drive, high clean room and environment and precise equipment and accessories. So only data rescue center could provide you such services, I suggest you go to local professional Data Recovery Company for help.

Step B-6; the goal of this procedure is to confirm the folder is "denied to access" and the simple solution for the problem

A)   If certain folder could not be opened by double clicking, but there's no error prompt, then you can use the method below:

B)   click My Computer—Tools—Folder options—File type, find the folder that could not be opened and choose "Folder", click the "Advanced", and on the dialog box "Edit file type", click "Create", fill "open" to the operation (this you could enter whatever you want, if there's already "open" content and pointing to other unknown .exe file, then probably it points Trojan, then choose "Edit"), and fill "explorer.exe" to the application used to execute the operation, and then click OK. Afterwards, return back to the window "Edit file type", choose "open", set it as default value, then click OK. Now open the partition or the folder again, check whether it has been returned to normal.

C)   Sometimes, when we want to open one folder, especially the folder in "Documents and Settings", system would give the dialog "The folder is denied to access", what do we do then?

To solve this problem, you must disable "Simple file share", and then get ownership of the folder:

1.   Disable "Simple file share";

   a).   Click "Start", and then click "My Computer";
   b).   In "Tools" menu, click "Folder options", and then click "View" option tab;
   c).   Under "Advanced settings", click to remove the selection of the checkbox "Use simple file share (Recommended)", and then click "OK".

2.   Right click the folder you want to get its ownership, and then click "Properties";

3.   Click "Security" option tab, and then click "OK" button on "Security" message box (if it appears);

4.   Click "Advanced", then click "Owner" option tab;

5.   In the "Name" list, click your user name, if you logon as the administrator, then please click "Administrator" or click "Administrator group".

If you hope to get the ownership of the content of the folder, click to select the checkbox "Replace the sub container and the owner of the object".

6. Click "OK" button.

You might receive the error message shown as below; the "Folder" is the name of the folder which you want to get the ownership:

You do not have permission to read the contents of directory Folder. Do you want to replace the directory permissions with permissions granting you Full Control? All permissions will be replaced if you press Yes.

7. Click "Yes".

8. Click "OK", and then apply the permissions and security settings for the folder and its content you hope.

Now open the partition or the folder and check up whether it is back to normal?

D) After the methods above, if system still fails to open the folder, then please go to STEP C-3

Step C-1: The goal of this setup is to confirm the problem that some files could not be backed up

A) Most people, sometimes, would have such a problem: when copying file or folder from USB disk enclosure disk or U disk, there is an error message: the copy is denied, please ensure the disk is not full or not write protected, besides, the file is not in use. All my customers told me that they had confirmed that there's enough disk space, and the file is not in use. So what's the problem? How do we solve this problem?

Problem analysis:

1) First, check whether the share setting is correct. After checking current logon user has the [read/write] permissions to the shared directory. Generally, it should be permissions problem, you can try logging in with administrator permissions, and then copy again;

2) Check the permissions of the directory again whether it's "readable, writable and inheritable", after confirming that, every directory all has the read/write permissions. You can try changing with administrator permissions until you can copy it;

3) After expanding the directory, check one level after another, if there are too many directory levels, then check whether the path has exceeded 260 characters. If yes, it means as the file path is too deep, there's no way to copy.

Solution:

a) the situation that file could not be copied shown up above, belongs to the limitation of Windows system: file name and file directory name could not exceed 260 characters, otherwise, some situations like the root directory or upper directory would appear and could not be copied.

b) If you want to copy such directory or folder, you can rename it with simple name, and then try copying again. Or only copy the subdirectory with over long name, and then copy the root directory.

If the problem still could not be solved, then you can use the method of STEP: B-5 in this chapter, to solve the problem by EasyRecovery data recovery software.

B) Partial folders become 0 KB, which could not be opened, copied or deleted. How do you solve the problem?

—Solution:

1) Typical one is the permissions problem, you can click "My Computer—Tools—Folder options—View", clear the selection of the checkbox "Use easy file share (recommended)", and then click "OK".

2) Right click the folder that could not be opened, properties—security—advanced—owner, choose current user name, and then choose the checkbox "Replace owner on sub-containers and objects", and click "OK".

3) In the warning shown up later, choose "Yes" to continue.

If the problem still could not be solved, or cannot open, or copy files, then for this situation, please continue to STEP: C-3;

C) Partial files on disk enclosure disk could not be copied; some part of pictures also could not be opened, so that it leads to system crash finally! If after removing the disk enclosure disk, the computer could return to normal, but it displays that the data was copied before is missing.

1) Partial folders under the directory could be copied, and error that "partial folders or files could not be copied appears", therefore, we can tell it would not be the problem of the share setting. There is some rare possibility that there's permissions problem of the directory, but it's also possible, so we need to check;

2) For many computers, after plugging disk enclosure disk, it would auto play music, and when auto play music, antivirus software would also work together. After finding viruses, antivirus software would auto kill virus, which would damage the file on the disk enclosure disk or get file lost, or failure that file could not be copied would appear. Then you'd have to go to taskbar (manager) to find the application player process, and click to end the process. Then terminate the process working. Try whether you can copy the file or not again.

3) There's virus on disk enclosure disk, for the security of the data, exit your antivirus software or firewall stuffs, because probably they are doing the job stopping copying the files to your disk enclosure, After confirming the data recovery, then scan and remove virus.

4) There's one point that you should pay more attention to! That is, if there's certain file on USB device is used by other application—the file being used might could not be copied, you need to close relevant application then start the file copy.

5) The file protected by system could not be copied; computer would not give any prompt or message either;

6) There's physical bad track on disk, generally when Windows system disk scanning application like SCANDISK scans, the system would prompt that there might be bad track on hard disk. In fact, these bad tracks mostly are logical bad tracks, which could be repaired. But if it's physical bad track, then generally there's no way to repair. If the file is exactly on the bad track, then there's no way to copy. Generally, computer would not give any prompt or message;

7) If after trying the methods 1, 2, 3, 4 above, the system still could not copy file, then please go to STEP: C-3; if there's physical bad track on disk, then could not open or copy file, then you can use the method of STEP: B-5 in this chapter, with Media Tools Pro data recovery software, we can solve the problem.

Step C-2; The goal of this setup is to confirm the disk rotation speed is normal

1) Put laptop disk to an USB disk enclosure disk box (USB 2.0 Hard Drive Enclosure), and then power on, place your ear close to the disk enclosure disk box to hear the rotation sound of the disk axis motor, normally, the rotation should be symmetrical and continuous, with low noise, but there should be no intermittent noise, If it belongs to this situation, some files could not be opened or copied, then please go to STEP: C-3;

2) After powering on, listen to the rotation sound of the disk axis mother, if the rotation sound is symmetrical and continuous, but with very loud noise; or occasionally there's interval noise, namely, abnormal noise, then it belong to this situation that some files could not be opened or copied, then please go to STEP: B-5;

Step C-3; The goal of this procedure is to confirm whether there is "Security" label in the disk enclosure disk property

With "Administrators" user account, it is found that there is no way to enter the backup file on the disk enclosure disk. Why there's access problem?

Reason analysis: most computer disks use NTFS file system, therefore, all files or folder would get ACL (Access Control Limitation). Although the systems on drive C and disk enclosure disk all use "Administrators" account to visit the files in Windows, here you should pay attention that each access account is to one unique SID (Security Identifier), and the function of ACL is to judge whether the account could access certain file with SID.

Even the same hard disk, after reinstalling system, still using "Administrators" account to access. But at this moment, the SID to the relevant "Administrators" account is already different from the one of last time. Therefore, "Administrators" account could not access the disk enclosure disk backup folder.

Actually it's quite easy to solve the problem of access deny, in the "Security" label of the backup folder on disk enclosure, and restore "Administrators" account the access permissions.

First, press power button to start the computer, then press F8 to choose "Safe mode" to load XP system. And then logon system with "Administrator" account, open "My computer", choose your disk enclosure disk, right click on it, at this moment, "Disk enclosure disk (X:) Properties" would prompt, (Here the drive symbol is arranged according to the disk partition in operation system and the DVD-ROM/CD-ROM partition), then choose "Properties" option, switch to "Security" tab on the prompted property dialog, at this moment, you would find one item "Unknown account" (Figure 9-13) in the column "Group or user name", this is because when current "Administrators" account reads disk enclosure disk, SID value changes. So system could not recognize the account, which leads to the problem that current "Administrators" account is refused to access. Of course, you don't need to know or confirm which the "Unknown account" is or what the change on SID value is. What you need to do is quite simple: as long as there's "Security" tab page on the property dialog, then please continue to STEP: C-4; if there's no "Security" tab page on property dialog, then please continue to STEP: C-5; please take a look at Figure 9-12.

Figure 9-12

Step C-4; The goal of this setup is to confirm whether current "Administrators" user has the permissions "Full control" on the disk enclosure disk?

If on the property dialog, there's "Security" tab page, it means the "Administrators" user doesn't have "Full control" on the disk enclosure disk. How to get "Full control"? Please go to STEP: D-1; if on the property dialog, there's no "Security" tab page, it means the "Administrators" user has already has the "Full Control" over the disk enclosure disk, then it could not open some files or copy files, then please go to STEP: C-5;

STEP: C-5: the goal of this procedure is to confirm that "Administrators" user has the "Full Control" over the disk enclosure disk, but could not copy some files.

Sometimes you think that "Administrators" user has "Full Control" permissions over disk enclosure disk, but in fact, it's not true like this. You need to check up further, first of all, shut down the laptop, and then press power button to start the laptop. Press F8 to choose "Safe mode" to load XP system. Make sure to use "Administrators" account to logon system, choose the disk enclosure disk from "My Computer", right click "Disk enclosure disk (X:) Properties", and choose "Properties" option, confirm whether there's "Security" tab page on the property dialog, if there is, please continue to STEP: D-1 and operate, until user has "Full Control" permissions over disk enclosure disk. If there's no "Security" tab page on the property dialog, but there's no way to copy some files out from the disk enclosure disk, for this situation, mostly because there's physical bad track. You can use the method mentioned of STEP: B-5 in this chapter. The problem could be solved with Media Tools Pro data recovery software.

Steps D-1, D-2, D-3: The goal of this procedure is to confirm the permissions that

"Administrators" user needs

Click the "Security" button on the dialog, then "Security setup" dialog would prompt, showing the owner of the item currently (as picture 2 shows), including the unknown account you see. Now you can make permissions choice for "Administrators" user with "Full Control" over disk enclosure disk.

Under "permissions for Administrators":

> Full control
> Modify
> Read & Execute
> List folder contents
> Read

Ensure that the checkboxes "Allow" at the right side all have "√", then you have the full control permissions for the disk enclosure disk, at last, please continue to STEP: D-4; Please take a look at Figure 9-13.

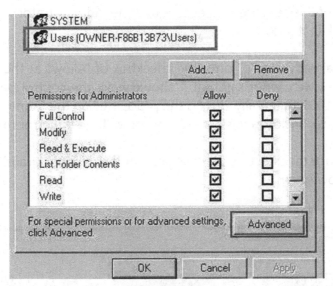

Figure 9-13

Steps D-4, D-5, D-6: The goal of this procedure is to confirm that the user granted with the permissions is "Administrators" user

Click the "Advanced" button on the dialog (as picture 3 shows), then "Advanced security settings" dialog would prompt, showing the owner of the item currently, "Administrators" user, but there's a lot of user names in this group, which is easy to make some mistakes; continue clicking the "Owner" option card on the dialog above, then Current owner of this item (Owner—F86B13B73\Administrator) would appear. and change the owner to the user Administrator now, which would 100% not to make any mistake about the user and ensure the user to grant the permissions

Choose the checkbox below, add "√" to select the checkbox "Replace owner on sub-containers and objects" down there (as picture 6 shows), and then click "Apply" button. You will see the process to get all authorities of all files and folders on disk enclosure disk. Please take a look at Figure 9-14.

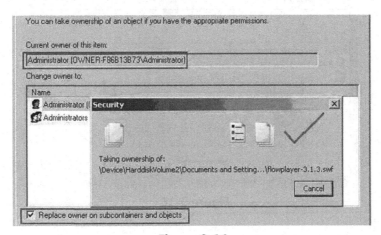

Figure 9-14

Step D-7: The goal of this purpose is to ensure that the "administrator" obtain ownership of the mobile hard disk is "full control"

Although we have already put "√" onto the checkbox of "Allow" at the right side for "Full Control" permissions, we cannot say that it should have the control permissions over the disk enclosure disk 100%, generally, during the process when the "Administrators" user gets the permissions of disk enclosure disk, probably you will get the error message as follows.

Do you want to replace the directory permissions with permissions granting you full control? (As Figure 9-15 below shows)

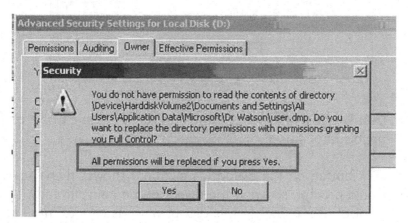

Figure 9-15

Please choose "Yes", make sure the permissions for the disk enclosure disk is "Full Control", but not a part of it, if we choose "No", then probably the entire "Ownership transfer" process would fail (as picture 8 shows), We have to redo starting from STEP: C-3; Please take a look at Figure 9-16.

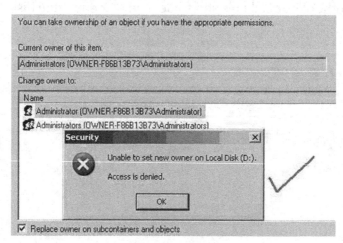

Figure 9-16

Step D-8; The goal of this procedure is to ensure that all files on disk enclosure disk could be "copied completely"

The solution here is to logon with administrator identity, and then change the access permissions for these files or folders, enabling current user to control them completely.

Then, the original specific folders on the disk enclosure disk could be accessed by current user. If you still gets the problem that file or folder could not be opened, then try changing the Read Only property, or change "Valid permissions" on the dialog. For some individual files still could not be opened, you can try changing the permissions singly.

The main reason for the problem is that those files or folders are denied access because when installing operation system, the disk enclosure disk sets access permissions or encrypt the files or folders.

But sometimes there is an error message such as "Cannot copy msoe: Access is denied, you make sure the disk is not full or write-protected and that the file is not currently in use" (as Figure 9-17 shows)

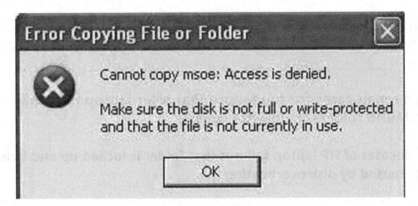

Figure 9-17

If you are sure that current file or folder is not in use, then when such a message appears, mostly it's related to permissions. Please check from STEP: C-3, make sure that the ownership of the disk enclosure disk "Administrators" user is "Full Control", but not just a part of it.

This method works for Win XP and Vista/Win 7 at all.

By the way, there's another problem, if you are sure that current file or folder is not in use correctly, it's not just enough to check whether it's displayed on screen, as when disk enclosure disk works, there's one additional "Cache" conception than U disk, which would produce second-transfer feint, in fact, file is changed to be cache transfer at background, that is, when you see the transfer is done, in fact, the file is still transferring. At this moment, you cannot disconnect USB device, if you disconnect by force, you will find that the file is not copied completely, that's why Windows would not allow deleting safely, this is also because system always judges that transfer is not finished yet by mistake. So this could be manual judgment whether it stops rotating, as the transition approach, if the green light on disk enclosure disk is always on, but not flashing, then generally, you can directly pull it out.

Advice: Never pull out disk enclosure disk even when the disk is not stopped yet (with power on), which easily damage the disk enclosure disk. but most customers complained that it's still running even after deleting the disk enclosure disk safely; in fact, the USB interface of disk enclosure disk not only transfer data, meanwhile, it would supply power for the system also. It's just a software operation to remove the disk enclosure disk, which only tells you that the data transfer mode is finished; you can pull out the USB cable safely. But to stop power supply, you'd have to pull out the USB cable by yourself. And the reason why disk light is on and running is because the USB cable is still providing power. Now it's safe to pull out the USB cable, there won't be any damage to disk. If you don't pull out the USB cable, then the disk enclosure disk would run as much time as the computer does.

In Conclusion, after summarizing the tutorial, it is the failure that laptop could not open some folders;

Cause: system gets infected with viruses or the disk itself is not stable, there's bad sector, "Administrators" user has no ownership and so on.

Solution: reset hard disk, remove unchain the locked folders and then back up all data, as for details, please refer to the tutorial. Thank you so much!

9.3 Eleven repair cases for the failure that after laptop reinstalls OS, the drive D and folders "could not open"

9.3.1 2 repair cases of HP laptop failures that folder is locked up and failed to access caused by disk overheating

164) HP ProBook 6440b laptop folder could not be opened

Failure symptom:

One hour later after laptop starts, you double click certain folder, but fail to open it.

Solution:

This failure obviously belongs to the description of flowchart 09, According to the repair method; confirm the repair path to find whether it's accorded with the sequence:

Start->A-1->A-2->A-5->B-1->B-2->B-6->C-1->C-2->

Repair summary:

According to the flowchart tutorial, the first thing to do is to remove the laptop hard disk, and put it into a USB movable disk box, and then connect it to another computer, and start the computer to check whether the USB device is recognized in system, to find whether that operating system could recognize the hard disk normally, and that there's no problem to back up the files. It seems that the cause that folder could not be opened is because of the laptop overheating failure. Then, clean up the disk slots, and after recovering the hard disk, restart the computer, it works normally again. If the problem repeats again and again, it suggests replacing the disk to solve the problem finally.

Hint:

Because of the laptop design problem, disk is close to the motherboard without heat dissipation and insulation layer designed, when the main thermal channel is blocked, heat would be spread directly onto disk, which makes the disk overheated. Generally, system folders could not be opened, you can cool down the laptop system with external devices, such as external USB cooler fan.

165) Compaq Presario V6000 laptop could not open folders

Failure symptom:

10 minutes later after laptop works, no matter to open the folder on any drive, it's inaccessible, system prompts that no relevant path could be found.

Solution:

This failure obviously belongs to the description of flowchart 09, According to the repair method; confirm the repair path to find whether it's accorded with the sequence:

Start->A-1->A-2->A-5->B-1->B-2->B-6->C-1->C-2->

Repair summary:

According to the flowchart tutorial, remove the laptop disk, use external USB disk box to connect other computer to validate, check whether it could display normally. Operating system OS prompts that movable device is found, but could not display normally. Restart and enter the safe mode, continue checking up the disk, finding that there's overheating symptom only after running a few period of time. Apparently, the disk has hardware bad symptom, which would easily lead to overheating situation, finally making the system unstable, and the folder could not be opened. After several times' shutdown to cool down the disk and several times' file duplication, data back is finished. Change a new disk, reinstall operating system, then the failure disappears.

Hint:

This cause of failure is because of disk issue itself, but the Main reason is the disk overheating. So you need to provide some overheat protection for the laptop, like for instance, cleaning up the laptop thermal system.

9.3.2 Two repair cases of HP laptop failure that folder could not be opened, caused by software conflict or virus infection

166) HP dv4-1030us laptop folder is locked up and could not be opened

Failure symptom:

After reinstalling operating system, enter "My computer" to open certain folder, but it fails; even double click, there will be a search prompt text appeared.

Solution:

This failure obviously belongs to the description of flowchart 09, according to the repair method; confirm the repair path, finding it's accorded with the sequence:

Start->A-1->A-2->A-5->B-1->B-2->B-6->C-1->C-2->C-3->C-4->C-5

Repair summary:

According to the flowchart tutorial, first, remove the laptop hard disk, use USB disk box to connect it to another computer. The USB device could be recognized, then restart system to enter safe mode, under safe mode, enter the disk, try double clicking folder, but still fail to open it. However, screen shows the prompt "Virus is found". Then, click to scan the entire disk, make sure to exit. After deleting viruses afterwards, try double clicking the folder; make sure it could enter normally. Obviously, this is because the system is infected with virus, which makes file configuration error, and breaking down normal system functions. After confirming that all viruses are cleaned, then put the disk back to the laptop and test, the failure is eliminated then.

Hint:

In this failure case, as system is infected with viruses, which makes system dysfunction. Accordingly, scan the entire disk to kill viruses, but you need to be careful to operate, because sometimes after deleting the files infected virus, failure would happen that laptop would fail to start up.

167)   HP Dv5-1000us laptop folder could not be opened

Failure symptom:

Laptop suddenly fails to open system folders, system prompts "0x7E2824A5" instruction referenced memory "0x00000000", and the memory could not be "READ".

Solution:

This failure obviously belongs to the description of flowchart 09, a According to the repair method; confirm the repair path find whether it's accorded with the sequence:

Start->A-1->A-2->A-5->B-1->B-2->B-6->C-1->C-2->C-3->C-4->C-5

Repair summary:

According to the flowchart tutorial, first, remove the laptop hard disk, use external USB disk box to connect to another computer. Restart the desktop computer to enter safe mode, test and check the laptop disk, as a result, the disk could be recognized normally. Then it's estimated that the failure cause might be virus, and then start system security scanning for the entire laptop disk. As a result, after running the antivirus software, no virus is found. Considering probably there's confliction between antivirus software and system, install the disk to the laptop again and uninstall the antivirus software. After finishing this, try double clicking the folder, it could be opened normally. Meanwhile, works could be backup as well, then the failure is solved.

Hint:

This case of failure is caused by the confliction between antivirus software and system software, which leads to system prompt instruction memory error. But there are some other reasons as the following, which might cause the same failure:

1.   When laptop overheats, CPU temperature is over high, and thermal fan doesn't work or always runs at a very low speed;
2.   The memory just added is incompatible with laptop or with other memories. Or there's quality problem with the memory or the memory is not plugged well, you can replace memory or change a slot to plug again.

9.3.3 Four repair cases of the failures that folder is locked up or drive D could not be opened after reinstalling operating system OS

168) HP Dv2910us laptop could not copy folders

Failure symptom:

After system recovery, when copy files or folders, there's an error prompt"; Copying is denied, please make sure the disk is not full or not written protected, and the file is not in use". By confirming, the disk space is big enough, and the file is not in use.

Solution:

This failure obviously belongs to the description of flowchart 09, according to the repair method; confirm the repair path finding whether it's accorded with the sequence:

Start->A-1->A-2->A-5->B-1->B-2->B-6->C-3->C-4->D-1->D-2->D-3->D-4->D-5->D-6->D-7->D-8

Repair summary:

According to the flowchart tutorial, after removing the disk, connect to another computer, after entering safe mode:

1) First, check the correctness of the share settings, by checking up: current logon user is of administrator permissions, which has [Read/Write] permissions to the shared directories. You can try copy again;
2) Check whether the permissions of the directory is [readable, writeable and inherited again, by confirming, every directory has a permissions to read / write. If without that, then you can change with administrator's authorization, until you could copy; at last, click Apply, confirm and save. Recover to the original system, thus the failure is solved.

Hint:

a) The file duplication failure appeared above belongs to the limitation of Windows system; if there are a lot of directory levels; then check whether the path is already over 260 characters. If that is so, then it means the file path is too deep that you could not copy;
b) If to copy such kind of directories or folders over 260 characters out, you can rename as simple name, then try copying again.

169)   HP Dv6830us laptop drive D is locked up

Failure symptom:

After reinstalling system, drive D is locked up and denied to access.

Solution:

This failure obviously belongs to the description of flowchart 09, according to the repair method; confirm the repair path finding whether it's accorded with the sequence:

Start->A-1->A-2->A-5->B-1->B-2->B-6->C-3->C-4->D-1->D-2->D-3->D-4->D-5->D-6->D-7->D-8

Repair summary:

As drive D default "Everyone" group access permissions is relevant with disk security, so according to the flowchart tutorial, disassemble the hard disk, connect to another computer with USB interface, then enter safe mode to configure the disk. Under safe mode, right click drive D and choose "Properties", open "Local disk (D :)" property dialog, choose "Security" option card, then you can see there's an unknown user with an interrogation mark in the window, which should be "Administrator" user in system.

The user could access drive D in original system, because after installing new system, the original user could not be recognized by current system any more, so not allowed by current system to access. Click to enter and choose allow enter user permissions, and then click Apply and confirm, then exit safely. Put the disk back to the original system, then drive D could be accessed normally again, the failure is eliminated.

Hint:

For the sake of data security, stop your antivirus software and firewall kind of things, because probably they stop the file duplication stuffs to your movable disk. After confirming the data recovery, then scan and kill virus.

170)   HP Dv2270us laptop could not open folder

Failure symptom:

After a system recovery, partial folders become "0" KB; you cannot open, copy or delete it.

Solution:

This failure obviously belongs to the description of flowchart 09, according to the repair method; confirm the repair path, finding whether it's accorded with the sequence:

Start->A-1->A-2->A-5->B-1->B-2->B-6->C-3->C-4->D-1->D-2->D-3->D-4->D-5->D-6->D-7->D-8

Repair summary:

It is one of the most common failure symptoms that could not access folder because of folder property change, so connect the issued disk as a portable device onto other computer, then enter safe mode to recover the original property, which is a quite common solution.

According to the flowchart tutorial, remove the disk, connect to another computer with USB, then enter safe mode, on the "Security" tab of the movable disk backup folder, regranted of "Administrators" account access permissions again.

By testing, finding now it's available to enter the disk, right click "the folder could not open", Properties—Security—Advanced—Owner, choose current user name, choose the checkbox "Replace owner on sub containers and objects" down there, and then click "OK".

Hint:

1) Even a same disk, after reinstalling system, similarly, access with "Administrators" account, but this time the relevant SID of "Administrators" account is different from the previous one. Therefore, such a situation would happen that "Administrators" account could not access movable disk backup folder.
2) If USB device has the file used by other application, which means the file being in use could not be copied, you need to close relevant application, then you can copy the file.

171)   HP Compaq nc6220 laptop folder is locked up and could not be opened

Failure symptom:

After reinstalling system for the laptop, enter "My computer", there's no way to open certain folder even, besides, immediately system would auto log off.

Solution:

This failure obviously belongs to the description of flowchart 09, according to the repair method; confirm the repair path, finding whether it's accorded with the sequence:

Start->A-1->A-2->A-5->B-1->B-2->B-6->C-3->C-4->D-1->D-2->D-3->D-4->D-5->D-6->D-7->D-8

Repair summary:

According to the flowchart tutorial, first, remove the disk, use USB disk box to connect to another computer. The USB device could be recognized, then restart the desktop and enter operating system's safe mode, under safe mode, enter the disk, try double clicking the folder, still fail to open. Right click the folder, then enter "Options", you can see "Security" tab, choose the user needed to enter, hook all allowed options, then choose all permitted users, next click "Replace owner user", then click Apply, confirm and exit. Afterwards, try double clicking the folder, it's accessible, so the failure is eliminated.

Hint:

Don't leave the power open when disk is still rotating; pull out movable disk, then it's easily to get the movable disk damaged, you would also lose the transferred data already.

If it is system protected file, then it could not be copied. Besides, computer would not give any prompt or message either.

9.3.4 Three repair cases of HP laptop failure of data backup caused by hard disk hardware problems

172) HP Pavilion Dv6 laptop could not open folder

Failure symptom:

After starting system once, suddenly laptop could not access folders.

Solution:

This failure obviously belongs to the description of flowchart 09, according to the repair method; confirm the repair path, to find whether it's accorded with the sequence:

Start->A-1->A-2->A-3->A-4->B-4;

Repair summary:

According to the flowchart tutorial, remove the disk, use external USB disk box to connect to other computer to validate. In this instance the disk could be displayed normally in other computer system, even in Property, we can see the occupied space of the disk. However, when we try opening the disk volume; it could not display the content it's supposed to show. Considering probably the hard disk has hardware failure, then remove the laptop disk again, observe it carefully, we find the data cable interface and SATA power cable interface have a water trace and rust, which is probably caused by humidity. Then clean up with alcohol, after confirming there's no problem, and then we connect the disk directly with desktop machine's SATA power cable and data cable. After entering the disk, we could back up the data normally again, so the failure is eliminated.

Hint:

The power cable interfaces for desktop machine's SATA disk and laptop SATA disk are the same. The difference between the of them is that the required voltages are different; desktop disk needs yellow wire (12V) and red wire (5V), and also a black wire (0V); while laptop disk only uses red wire (5V) and black wire (0V), which does not need +12V power; however, you don't need to worry about the laptop hard disk getting burnt or not, because when manufacturers designs the circuit, they already disconnect the laptop disk 12V power circuit.

173)   HP Compaq nc6120 laptop could not open folder

Failure symptom:

After resetting hard disk once, laptop could not enter system drive and all folders.

Solution:

This failure obviously belongs to the description of flowchart 09, according to the repair method; confirm the repair path, to find whether it's accorded with the sequence:

Start->A-1->A-2->A-3->A-4->B-4;

Repair summary:

According to the flowchart tutorial, first, remove the disk use an external USB disk box to connect to other computer to validate. Then try starting the system under safe mode, after entering the drive volume and the folders inside are not found. Place your ears close to the laptop disk, you will find that the disk rotation sound is normal. Then change the connection interface, use IDE converter to connect to PC desktop, namely, convert to 3.5" standard PC IDE (40pins) interface with 2.5" mini IDE (44pins) interface. As a result, during the operation process, it is found that some of disk pins are bent which makes it quite difficult to plug the IDE converter. First repair the bent pin of on the disk, then connect to desktop machine, after starting operating system, we now can back up the disk data normally again, then the failure is eliminated.

As for detailed operating method, please refer to the process in Section 9.2.6 Chapter 9 << Laptop folder lockup failure and crack solution>>

Hint:

Laptop disk rotation sound is OK, but the icon could not be seen in the device manager and disk manager, then you can put the disk back in the laptop, and then execute the following steps:

a.   Press the power button to start the laptop;
b.   When HP or Compaq logo appears, press F10 key to enter BIOS setup page;
c.   When the main menu displays, pay attention to the BIOS version and find "HOD self-test options" or "Primary Hard Disk self test" option;
d.   Choose the tool software, and then press Enter.

Disk entire scanning starts, when the scanning finishes, there will be relate result shown on the screen, telling user whether the disk could be used continually or not. The above is the simplest disk measurement method, but it could not guarantee that there is NOT any problem in disk.

174)   HP Pavilion Dv7 laptop Hard disk could not open

Failure symptom:

After laptop starts system once, suddenly it fails to load the operating system.

Solution:

This failure obviously belongs to the description of flowchart 09, according to the repair method; confirm the repair path, finding whether it's accorded with the sequence:

Start->A-1->A-2->A-3->A-4->B-4;

Repair summary:

According to the flowchart tutorial, remove the disk out, use external USB disk box to connect to other computer to validate. In this instance the disk could be displayed normally in other computer system. After trying opening this volume, there's nothing should have been displayed there. Considering probably the disk has hardware adverse failure, then remove the laptop disk again, directly plug desktop SATA power cable and data cable, but the disk volume still could not be displayed. In the light of my experience, remove the issued disk circuit board, then find one normally-operating disk from the same manufacturer, and to a same model and same technical standard. And remove the circuit board, install onto the issued hard disk, then connect to desktop computer again. As a result, it now work normally. The failure is eliminated.

Hint:

If you are not familiar with computer, or you have no data recovery experience at all, we suggest you find some local professional company for help. Data recovery, for the technicians with experience, is not an easy job either. If you do something wrong, it's quite possible to get your data to be permanently. damaged. You will never be able to correct the mistakes you've made. Here the "hard" disk failure data recovery method introduced could not guarantee that you would not make any mistake during the operating process, except you want to get some experience, but do not care too much about whether data would be lost or not. Then you can try to do it yourself, but remember to take your own risk.

CHAPTER 10

Wireless network card, Bluetooth and Router failure repair

10.1 Causes for laptop wireless Internet, include Bluetooth and router failures

10.1.1 Common symptoms for laptop wireless Internet, Bluetooth and router failures

a) The internal wireless network communicates normally, (able to communicate with wireless router normally), but does not communicate with the Ethernet when connected with the wireless router;

b) The wireless network often goes offline;

c) The wireless client does not receive a signal;

d) The wireless client receives a signal normally, but still does not access the wireless network;

e) When the network environment changes, it does not access normally;

f) All settings are correct, but will not access the wireless network;

g) The laptop cannot use the wireless to access a family network to achieve Internet sharing;

h) Other computers within the wireless network cannot be seen;

i) The laptop wireless Internet speed is very slow;

j) The wireless client receives a signal, but cannot browse web pages;

k) In the device manager, the wireless network card or the Bluetooth adapter cannot be inspected;

l) In the operating system, the wireless network card or the Bluetooth adapter icon cannot be found;

m) The wireless network card (or the Bluetooth adapter) could not be recognized in the OS (Device Manager or taskbar), but the wireless network card indication is red;

n) The Bluetooth adapter light is on, but cannot communicate with other Bluetooth devices or cannot find other Bluetooth devices;

Please refer to the first chapter of this article <<10.1.2 Laptop wireless network card and Bluetooth Internet failure and cause analysis>>

10.1.2 Laptop (wireless) Internet access failure and cause analysis

a) The wireless network communicates normally, but will not communicate with the Ethernet connected with a wireless router.

Possible causes for this failure:

(1) LAN port connection failure;
(2) IP address setting error;
(3) Possibly the network administrator installs MAC address filtering to the wireless AP, only allowing specified MAC address to access the wireless network, but refusing an unauthorized user, in this case, to ensure the security of the wireless network.

b) Wireless network often goes offline

When using the wireless at home or in some public networks, occasionally it goes offline without any premonition. This is a quite common network problem. Next, this article will discuss what the problem is, and tell you how to solve it.

(1) Wi-Fi wireless electrical interference

The wireless problem can originate from many kinds of electrical products, like wireless phone, Bluetooth earphone, micro oven or even electrical garage door or another wireless router in the neighborhood etc. All these might disturb the normal function of the Wi-Fi wireless signal.

(2) The coverage of Wi-Fi network is insufficient.

Even without other interference devices, probably it is because the radiation coverage of the Wi-Fi network itself is not enough, leading to an unstable wireless network. As you know, Wi-Fi network connections are closely dependant on the distance between the terminal and the AP.

(3) Link to an incorrect Wi-Fi network

If within the wireless network environment you are using now, there is another Wi-Fi network with the same network name, then you might link to the wrong network and affect your normal Internet access. For this situation, usually there's the symptom of signal interference between each network or the radiation coverage of your network is not sufficient enough to overcome the signal of the other network. If you are connected to another network and it is off; you have no signal and no access to the Internet.

(4)   Incompatible software

If from the beginning your laptop does not connect to the wireless network, then it's quite likely that your computer has incompatible software, which includes operation system patches, operation system service components, or other software affecting your system network. If the network driver is not updated in time; it can also affect the operation of all kinds of functions of Wi-Fi hardware.

(5)   Router (access) loading is too heavy

According to my few years of computer repair experience, overloading of router access points can affect the speed and quality of the wireless Internet. These are the main reasons causing overloading to the router: online games, BT download, or too many other computers connected to the network and various other situations causing high traffic through the router. We can say that when a large batch of data is transferring, generally the router may go offline temporarily. Additionally, if the temperature of the router is too high, then probably it would also go offline frequently.

(6)   The settings of wireless AP might be incorrect

When mix using IEEE802.11b and IEEE802.11g, you must set the wireless AP to MIXED mode. When you use this mode, then you can have IEEE802.11b and IEEE802.11g even though these two modes are incompatible. Otherwise, frequent offline failures would also happen.

c)   Wireless client does not receive a signal

After constructing a wireless LAN, it is found that the client cannot receive a wireless AP signal.

Here are some possible causes for the problem:

(1)   The wireless network card is too far from the wireless AP or the wireless router, exceeding the coverage of the wireless network. When the wireless signal reaches the wireless network card, it's too weak, and makes the wireless client hard to connect.

(2)   The wireless AP or wireless router is not powered on or not working normally, and prevents the wireless client from connecting.

(3)   When the wireless client is too far away from wireless AP, we would often use directional antenna technology to enhance the transmission of the wireless signal, if there's problem with the angle of the oriented antenna, and then the wireless client might not connect normally.

(4)   If the wireless client hasn't set the network IP address correctly, then you cannot communicate with the wireless AP.

(5) The wireless network card may not be on the correct frequency (an AD HOC channel), then the receivable frequency segment is different from the channel launch frequency segment the wireless router uses;

d) The wireless client does not receive a signal normally, and fails to access a wireless network

Here are the possible causes for the failure:

(1) The wireless AP or wireless router's IP address is already distributed. When the wireless client is set to get the IP address automatically, then it might fail to access the wireless network because there's no available IP address.

(2) The wireless network card hasn't set the correct IP address. When the user uses a manual method to set the IP address, if the IP address and the IP address of wireless AP are not in the same network segment, then it would also fail to access the wireless network.

(3) When there's only one computer having this problem, we should consider if there's something wrong with the operation system; especially if the problems existed with browsers like IE, and the wireless client will not connect normally because of this.

e) When the network environment changes, it fails to access normally

Your office and home both have wireless networks. In the office, the laptop accesses the company wireless network normally; but when back at home, it is found that the laptop fails to access the wireless network.

There are a few possible reasons that can cause this failure:

(1) The SSID (Service Set Identifier) configuration is not modified in time. Different wireless networks use different SSIDs, if the SSID configuration is incorrect, then you cannot ping through the AP. The laptop would neglect the AP and find a new AP according to the SSID configuration set.

(2) WEP encryption. If the WEP key used is different, then the wireless client will not connect with the new wireless AP. If the WEP configuration is wrong, then the wireless client cannot get the IP address from DHCP server. If you use a static IP address, then the wireless client cannot ping through the IP address of the AP.

(3) IP address information. Generally speaking, the wireless AP would distribute an IP address for the wireless client automatically, if you set the IP address for the wireless client manually, then the client might not communicate with the new AP.

f) All settings are correct, but still fail to access a wireless network

Failure symptom: the network configuration is the same as with other users of the wireless network, including WEP encryption, SSID and IP address (auto get IP address). The wireless signal shows full grid, which means the signal is strong but it fails to access the wireless network.

There are a few probable causes for the failure:

(1) In order to ensure network security, the network administrator installs MAC address filtering to the wireless AP, only allowing specified MAC addresses to connect to the wireless network, but refusing unauthorized users.

(2) The laptop wireless network card function is not enabled, generally, it's disabled in the BIOS Setup or the enable switch is turned off.

(3) The wireless network card is too far away from the AP or wireless router, exceeding the coverage of the wireless.

(4) The wireless AP or wireless router is not powered on or it doesn't work normally.

g) The laptop does not have a wireless way to access the local network and realize Internet sharing

Failure symptom: the local network uses "ADSL Modem + a Broad band router" to enable Internet sharing without PPPoE dialing. No matter which laptop you use, it always fails to access the wireless network and realize Internet sharing.

These are some probable reasons causing this problem:

(1) You are only using an ADSL Modem, but without wireless AP access, so Internet connection sharing cannot be achieved;

(2) The Broadband router used has no wireless AP function, so cannot provide wireless access for the laptop;

(3) A wireless router failure prevents use of the wireless access function.

h) Other computers within the wireless network cannot not be found

Failure symptom: the laptop wireless Internet is OK, but other computers within the network are not found in the Network Neighborhood. The printer share cannot be achieved.

These are a few probable causes for the failure:

(1) Check the SSID and WEP parameter settings, confirm that the spelling and upper-lower cases are correct;

(2) Check whether the laptop enabled the file and printer sharing or not, confirm whether the checkbox "Microsoft network file and printer share" in the "General" option in the property of the wireless network is selected or not.

i) The laptop wireless Internet speed is slow

Failure symptom:

In a practical network test, there are many laptops, all with a wireless link transmission speed that is too slow. There is no interference and even with a close transmission distance, you cannot reach the specified 54MB/s.

These are a few probable causes for this problem:

(1)   There's something wrong with the operation system, maybe a virus or a Trojan infection;

(2)   Improper wireless network settings, the tolerant broadcast SSID option of the wireless router is not cancelled;

(3)   Someone at nearby locations uses the same frequency segment to send their signal. In this case, based on the signal strength, the two wireless routers interfere with each other, which adversely affects the connection speed of the wireless network and the network browsing speed;

(4)   A default launch frequency segment of the wireless router is used, without any modification, and the frequency channel is affected by other devices.

j)   The wireless client receives a signal but you cannot browse webpages

Failure symptom:

All webpages cannot be opened normally, even though the wireless client is receiving the signal perfectly;

These are a few probable causes for this problem:

(1)   When this laptop is the only one with the problem, probably there's something wrong with the operating system, especially problems with a browser like IE. Incorrect firewall settings can also cause the problem where the wireless client does not connect normally;

(2)   If all laptops have this situation, then it should be the DNS parsing problem of the router. If you set the gateway as DNS address, this is the DNS Proxy, but not a real DNS address, then probably address parsing will be wrong.

k)   In the device manager, the wireless network card or the Bluetooth adapter is not listed.

Failure symptom: in the device manager, the wireless network card or Bluetooth adapter does not appear in the list;

These are a few possible causes for this problem:

(1)   There's a setup function in the BIOS to activate the wireless network card (Bluetooth adapter), or you need to load default security settings, but the function is not enabled;

(2)   No integrated wireless network card or Bluetooth adapter is installed;

(3)   The integrated wireless network card or the Bluetooth adapter is defective;

(4)   There's a fault on the motherboard.

l)   In the operating system, the wireless network card or the Bluetooth adapter icon cannot be found

Failure symptom: on the desktop of the operation system, the wireless network card icon or the Bluetooth adapter icon cannot be found.

There are a few possible causes for the failure as listed below:

(1)   In the device manager, there's no wireless network card or Bluetooth adapter listed;

(2)   The wireless network card driver or the Bluetooth adapter driver is not installed, or installed with the wrong driver;

(3)   No exercisable application software is installed or it is installed but not enabled yet;

(4)   The wireless network is disabled. m) The wireless network card (or Bluetooth adapter) is recognized in the OS (Device Manager or Taskbar), but the wireless network card light is red

Failure symptom: the wireless network card (or Bluetooth adapter) is recognized in the OS (Device Manager or taskbar), but does not connect to the Internet and communicate. It is found that the wireless network card (or Bluetooth adapter) light is red.

There are a few possible causes for the failure as listed below:

(1)   The laptop is too far away from the wireless AP or wireless router, exceeding the coverage of the wireless network, the laptop management system has disabled the wireless network automatically.

(2)   The laptop wireless network is controlled by a hardware switch, red means the wireless network is disabled, and the wireless network function is off.

(3)   There's something wrong with the laptop management system software, after the wireless network is disabled, it cannot recover to a working state automatically, and you need to restart the laptop.

n)   The Bluetooth adapter light is on, but it cannot communicate with other Bluetooth devices or cannot find other Bluetooth devices.

Failure symptom: The Bluetooth adapter light is on, but you cannot enable it through the relevant menu or communicate with other Bluetooth devices.

There are a few possible causes for the failure as listed below:

(1)   You haven't ensured that configuration files are matched, and each device used for communications needs to use one configuration file;

(2)   The Bluetooth function is not enabled yet, because by default, the Bluetooth function is probably disabled, you need to enable it;

(3)   Communicating Bluetooth devices must be matched before they can exchange data;

(4) The match sequence hasn't been finished, because one of the devices is set in matched mode, and then activates the match through another device. Generally, we activate this function to enable a match by the relevant menu;

(5) A connection hasn't been created, because sometimes, the match between the two devices needs to be recreated, then the match operation should be done somewhere safe and secret;

(6) Incorrect host/client and multipoint access mode, because some devices, like the wireless earphone, will not maintain several connections at the same time.

Please refer to the first chapter of this article <<10.1.3 Diagnosis and solution for the failure that laptop wireless network card and Bluetooth could not get to Internet>>.

10.1.3 Diagnosis and solution for a failure of the laptop wireless network card (and Bluetooth adapter) to access the Internet

a) The internal wireless network can communicate normally, but still it fails to communicate with the Ethernet connected by a wireless router.

You can use the following solution for this:

(1) Check if the LAN port and Ethernet connection is correct by checking the LAN indication light, when necessary, you may need to change a cable to test the source of the failure;

(2) Check whether the wireless network and Ethernet are within the same IP address segment, only the hosts within the same IP address can communicate with each other.

(3) Contact the network administrator to accept and authorize the user, and allow the MAC address access to the wireless network.

b) A mixed wireless network often goes offline

(1) Eliminate the Wi-Fi wireless electrical interference, change the launch frequency of the wireless router, and set it to a clear frequency used by no one;

(2) Solve the problem that the coverage area of Wi-Fi network is insufficient by moving the location of the laptop, and changing the launch and receiving frequencies. Try moving the antenna of the wireless router to improve the reception of the laptop. The signal may be blocked by a wall or some other obstruction. If the radiation coverage of the Wi-Fi network itself is insufficient, you can increase the length of the antenna or just change to a new wireless router with better coverage.

(3) Avoid linking to the wrong Wi-Fi network

If someone in your neighbourhood uses their Wi-Fi network with the same network name and frequency, then you might inadvertently connect to his network. Check the wireless router and change the launch frequency setting to a different frequency. Please have a look at Figure 10-1.

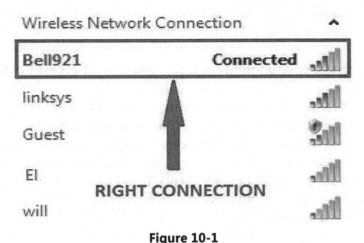

Wireless Network Connection ^

Bell921   **Connected**

linksys

Guest

El   **RIGHT CONNECTION**

will

Figure 10-1

(4)   Avoid incompatible software

Update the drivers for the wireless network card and the network driver.

(5)   Avoid overloading the router (access point). If the computer is playing an online game or BT downloading, and meanwhile, there are several other laptops using the wireless network to access the Internet, then the router might become overloaded. If there's no network password set or the password is too simple, then probably it could be used by anyone, and if they are doing a large batch of data transfer your router could become overloaded.

(6)   Recover the wireless router to the factory settings. Turn off the power of the router, find a such as the tip of sharp objects like a pen head to press the wireless router's reset button; power on the router, wait for 3 to 5 seconds, and then release the reset. That will reset and restore the factory settings. Pay attention to the environment and ventilation of the router; don't let the temperature of the router get too high.

c)   Wireless client does not receive a signal

(1)   Confirm that the distance between the laptop and wireless AP or wireless router is within the effective distance and the coverage area of the wireless network;

(2)   Confirm the wireless AP or wireless router is working normally;

(3)   Confirm that the laptop has enabled the wireless network card, and the switch is already ON;

(4)   confirm that the wireless client has already set the network IP address;

(5)   Confirm that the frequency the laptop wireless network card receives is the same as the launch frequency the wireless router uses.

d)   The wireless client can receive the signal but fails to access the wireless network

(1)   Make sure the wireless AP or wireless router's IP address distribution is complete;

(2)   When the user adopts manual IP address setup, then confirm that the IP address set is within the same network segment of the IP address for the wireless AP;

(3) If only one computer has this problem, confirm that the operating system has no problem and the IE browser has no problem either.

e) When the network environment changes, you cannot access normally

(1) When accessing a new wireless network, change the SSID (Service Set Identifier) configuration and make sure the SSID configuration is correct;

(2) Use the correct WEP key to let the wireless client connect with the new wireless AP;

(3) Disable manually setting IP addressing for the wireless client, use automatic IP address distribution for all wireless clients. If you use static IP addressing, then you must ensure the static IP address is within the same network segment of the IP address of the wireless AP.

f) Settings are all correct, but you cannot access the wireless network

(1) Contact your administrator; add your MAC address to the MAC address list allowing access;

(2) Check the settings and hardware switch in BIOS, make sure the laptop wireless network card function is already enabled;

(3) make sure the laptop is within the coverage of the wireless network.

g) The laptop does not have a wireless system to access the family network and realize Internet sharing

(1) Make sure to use an ADSL Modem to access the wireless router, the wireless router LAN port connects to the host and provides wireless access for the laptop;

(2) reset the wireless router to factory settings;

(3) Reset the ADSL Modem to factory settings;

(4) Repair according to the tutorial <<Laptop wireless network card, Bluetooth and router failures analysis and repair flow>>.

h) Other computers within the wireless network cannot be found

(1) Check the SSID and WEP parameter settings, confirm there's nothing wrong with the spelling and upper-lower case;

(2) Confirm the file and printer share is enabled; make sure the checkbox "Microsoft network file and printer share" is selected in the "General" option page of the wireless network property.

i) The laptop wireless Internet speed is slow

(1) Scan the hard disk with antivirus software, clearing the viruses or Trojans in the operating system;

(2) After recovering the wireless router to factory settings, restart the router;

(3) Logon to the wireless router's management interface; cancel the "Tolerant broadcast SSID" option.

(4)   Change the launch frequency of the wireless router, set it to a clear frequency used by no one;

j)   The wireless client can receive the signal, but will not browse webpages

(1)   Confirm that only your laptop has this problem, reset the firewall; reinstall the operating system;

(2)   If all computers have this problem, then logon to the management interface of the wireless router, change the gateway and set it to DNS address.

K)   In the device manager, the wireless network card or the Bluetooth adapter cannot be inspected. Please have a look at Figure 10-2.

Figure 10-2 Hp Bluetooth

(1)   Confirm that the wireless network card (Bluetooth adapter) setup function in BIOS is already activated, and the hardware switch is already enabled;

(2)   Confirm that the integrated wireless network card or Bluetooth adapter is properly installed and not loose;

(3)   Confirm that the integrated wireless network card or Bluetooth adapter is not damaged;

(4)   Confirm that the motherboard has no faults.

l)   In the operating system, the wireless network card or Bluetooth adapter icon cannot be found

(1)   Confirm that the wireless network is not disabled;

(2)   Confirm that in the device manager, the wireless network card or Bluetooth adapter can be found on the list; if not, return to (k);

(3)   uninstall the wireless network card or Bluetooth adapter driver; reinstall the latest version of the driver;

(4)   Uninstall relevant application software, reinstall the software and then enable it;

m) The wireless network card (or Bluetooth adapter) is recognized by the OS (Device Manage or taskbar), but the wireless network card (Bluetooth adapter) light is red

(1) Confirm that the distance between the laptop and wireless AP or wireless router is within the coverage area of the wireless network;
(2) Confirm that the laptop wireless network is already enabled, and the hardware or BIOS switch is "On";
(3) confirm that the laptop management system software is good;

n) The Bluetooth adapter light is on, but it cannot communicate with other Bluetooth devices or cannot find other Bluetooth devices

(1) Confirm the configuration file is matched;
(2) Confirm the Bluetooth function is enabled;
(3) Confirm the Bluetooth is already matched;
(4) Confirm the match sequence is already finished;
(5) Confirm the connection is already built;
(6) Confirm the host/client and multipoint access way is OK.

As for more detailed operation methods, please refer to the second chapter of the article <<10.2.5 Laptop wireless network card, Bluetooth and router failure analysis and repair flow>>

10.1.4 Analysis and diagnostic table for a Laptop wireless router Internet connection failure or disconnection

ADSL failure treatments		
Failure symptoms	**Possible causes**	**Troubleshooting Method**
Internet offline	**1**. ADSL modem device problem (Mainly heat radiation and plug connection problems) **2**. Share of software settings problem **3**. ADSL circuitry might has some problems; **4**. Router temperature is too high **5**. Router disconnection time is set too short, sometimes goes offline when browsing websites but without any data flux **6**. Disconnection because memory resource is too full **7**. Laptop operating system problem; **8**. Laptop network card problem	**1**. Change ADSL Modem or take the original ADSL modem to a test center to test and debug **2**. Reset share software to default settings; **3**. Check whether circuitry quality is good, whether each point of the circuit is firm enough. Check the filter, check whether the connection indoor is standard; **4**. Enhance heat radiation, put ADSL Modem somewhere ventilated; **5**. Suggest not using auto offline, spring dialing settings, sometimes there's a problem. **6**. Don't use software occupying too much resource or open too many browser pages; **7**. Clean up operating system or reinstall it; **8**. Reinstall driver for the network card and dialer software or replace network card

Webpage could not open	**1.** Browser cause; **2.** DNSvalue setup problem; **3.** Provider circuitry or device problem, provider's DNS server could be found but it will not work normally. It does not parse **4.** Partial website problem	**1.** Recover or change to a higher version of IE, try using Firefox browser, restart computer; **2.** Set the DNS in TCP/IP for network card according to the manual direction; if you use proxy software, then you should also set DNS in DHCP **3.** Call to alert network provider to check the circuitry problem; **4.** Check more websites to see whether the symptom re-occurs;
Connection timeout problem, failure to dial to Internet	**1.** Whether VCI VPI value is filled correctly; **2.** Recently changed password, computer room material, stop port or network card is disabled; Error 629 and 691, network disabled error 692; **3.** Dialer software could not be bound to the DNS server of the provider: error 678; **4.** LAN, gateway is not set correctly; **5.** Device is not connected correctly; **6.** Browser settings problem; **7.** Circuitry issue;	**1.** VPI, VCI are 0,100; **2.** Whether query password is changed successfully or uses the original password to logon again. Try with the test account, judge whether the password is correct. Contact network provider to deal with the problem; **3.** Check the power of the Modem and restart the Modem, and then reconnect the link; **4.** Gateway settings should be corresponding to the Modem network segment, or you can set to get IP setup automatically, but some brands of routers or Modems have no such function and cannot be achieved automatically;

	8. Dialing network is not installed or installed incorrectly; TCP/IP is not installed or installed incorrectly: error 630, 633;	5. Check connection, device and network card; 6. Remove the proxy settings in browser; 7. Call to alert the network provider to check a circuit problem; 8. Delete network protocol hasn't been installed completely and reinstall the network protocol; reinstall network card or dialing software; restart computer several times.
Some indication lights on Modem Router are on or all out	1. Every indication light has meaning, observe the information the light reflects, as for details, please refer to the chapter 10.2.5 in this article, Step: A-3, Step: A-6 2. Hardware failure 3. Power issue; 4. Circuit signal handshake problem	1. Check the failure information the indication light reflects, ADSL, LINE and ACTIVE are circuit lights. Are they OK? 2. Check whether plug is loose, change Modem or Router; 3. Check power and replace the power supply with a new one; 4. Check up the circuitry

10.2   Repair flow chart to eliminate wireless network card, Bluetooth and router failures

10.2.1 Repair shortcuts for Wireless network card, Bluetooth and router problems.

Solve these kinds of problems with the general easy replacement method

Laptop wireless Internet, Bluetooth and router failures require a repair process that is very complicated, the occurrence of the failure might be caused by problems with certain hardware, or more likely, certain software problems. It can also likely be the combination of several software problems or a combination of software and hardware problems.

The reason why they occur usually is focused on incompatible hardware and drivers, issued software and viruses etc; therefore, here-in we offer a quick shortcut solution for you.

When you have this kind of problem, first exclude the problem according to the following solutions:

As 70% of wireless network card, Bluetooth and router failures are from the operating system and network settings, first of all, make sure the ADSL Modem or wireless router are working normally;

1) Connect one known working desktop (or laptop) to the router through a cable, to see if it's the problem with the Modem or wireless router. If the cabled network works all right, and the network speed is stable, then focus on the wireless network problem. Please jump to the sixth step; or if the cabled network doesn't work, continue to step 2;

2) Solve the problem by disconnecting the cable, observing carefully, for damage on the cable connector, and if the cable is distorted or the core is broken. If nothing is identified, then please continue the step 3.

3) Reset the wireless router or the ADSL Modem to factory settings. If you want to completely check the system, then please refer to the second chapter of this article <<10.2.5 Laptop wireless network card, Bluetooth and router failure analysis and repair flow>>, Step: B-2 and Step: A-5; if it's still not solved, then please continue to Step 4;

4) Remove the wireless router, connect an ADSL Modem directly to a known good desktop (or laptop) and access the Internet through a cabled network; if the problem is still not solved, then please continue to Step 5; if solved, then replace the wireless router;

5) Change to a known good working ADSL Modem and test, or contact the Internet service provider to request technical support. Make sure the phone line and Internet network does not have problems;

6) Disable the wireless network of your laptop, connect to the Internet with a cabled network, confirm that there's nothing wrong with the laptop's operation system; if the cabled network does not work normally, then it means the problem must be in the operating system, you need to first solve the software problem and then focus on the wireless network issue. Please continue to Step 7;

7) Check the antenna of the wireless router if it has one, remove the antenna axis, observe whether there's any damage on the antenna interface or not, and make sure the pin of antenna internal core is not distorted or broken. Confirm that the connection between wireless and router is OK? If not solved, then please continue to Step 8;

8) Connect another known working laptop or desktop computer to the wireless router through a wireless network card, confirm that it works normally. If it does, then it means the wireless router's antenna function is OK, otherwise, the wireless router has problems; if not solved, then please continue to Step 9;

9) Disassemble your laptop, and find the wireless network card, there are 2 or 3 connections there, it can be because the connection between the network card interface and the antenna contact is bad. You might solve the problem by pulling and plugging the antenna contact, and retightening the antenna. If that does not solve it, then please continue to Step 10;

10) Update the driver for the wireless network card, reset the firewall, clean up viruses and Trojans; if the problem is still unsolved, then please continue to Step 11;

11) Install a known good working wireless network card, uninstall the old driver, install a new driver, and make sure the wireless card you use is compatible with the laptop; if the problem is not solved, then please continue to Step 12;

12) The internal antenna of the laptop is over distorted or the core is broken, which leads to bad connection, you will need to change it; if the problem is not solved, then please continue checking with a more detailed procedure, please refer to the second chapter of this article <<10.2.5 Laptop wireless network card, Bluetooth and router failure analysis and repair flow>>

10.2.2 70% of wireless network card, Bluetooth and router failures are from operating system, drivers and network settings

Most causes of wireless network card, Bluetooth and router failures are due to the operating system, drivers and network setting errors.

Generally speaking, technicians initially doubt that the failure is caused by software, but eventually they will deal with the operation system, or network settings, or the drivers.

According to the method introduced in <<10.2.1 Repair shortcuts for wireless network card, Bluetooth and router failures>>; first use a cable to connect a known working desktop (or laptop) to the router, and then access the Internet through the cable network. Make sure the Modem and wireless router are working normally, the settings are correct, and then solve the wireless network problem.

If the suspected laptop does not work normally even through a cabled network, we can initially assume it's a problem with the software, (after confirming the network card hardware is OK). Occasionally when you just finish updating the driver for the wireless network card, you get a blue screen failure. You likely have a problem with that driver. In order to solve that kind of problem, usually, we restart the system under safe mode, and then uninstall the driver. It is proven by experience that 70% of wireless network card, Bluetooth and router failures are caused by software or system settings.

a)   Driver failure after installation.

If you install a wireless network card driver that only supports Windows 7 into a Windows XP system, the wireless network card will not work, and a blue screen failure will occur. Occasionally the driver installed is specified for the operating system, but due to a small difference between laptop models, you encounter a problem when installing the driver. Therefore, after installing a driver, you need to check it out in the device manager, and confirm that the driver is installed correctly. Check in the list of wireless network cards, that there are no yellow exclamation marks there; otherwise, it means the driver hasn't been installed correctly and you need to uninstall and reinstall it. Under certain special circumstances, the driver is installed incorrectly and there won't be a yellow exclamation mark, or after re-installing a few times, you ca not get rid of the yellow exclamation mark, and then it's probably a problem in the operating system. You need to consider whether to reinstall operation system or not.

b)   Failures caused by improper "hot swap"

Many people think that the wireless network card's USB interface or PCMCIA interface supports the hot swap function, so they would pull and plug devices randomly. In this case, you can easily damage the wireless network card or other relevant interfaces of the computer, and may also easily lead to a system crash.

After this happens, the only thing to do is to restart the computer system; in this case, the operating system can easily be damaged. Before removing a PCMCIA wireless network card, the best way is to open the property of the network card in the system device manger, find the setup window, and then temporarily disable the network card device. Doing this makes it very safe to pull out the wireless network card.

For a wireless network card using the USB interface, you should enable the function "Safely remove hardware", and then disconnect from the relevant port.

c)   More ways to avoid USB wireless device failure after installation.

If you want to add a USB interface wireless network card, and you forget to uninstall the driver for the previous wireless network card, and as a result, after installing the device, you may find that the wireless network card does not work at all. When you encounter this failure symptom, you should remember: that you needed to uninstall the driver for the old wireless network card first. If you are lucky, you may find that it works anyway.

If this is the first time you use a wireless network card with the USB interface, you will need to install or update the relevant USB controller application. To accomplish this, proceed as follows: open the system device manager, double click the USB controller option, and then enter the tab page of the driver of the controller, afterwards, update the driver for the USB controller to the latest status by pressing the button "Update driver".

On some devices, the installation sequence is quite important, because some USB interface wireless network cards have different steps for driver installation from other common network cards. You need to install the driver first, and then plug the USB network card into computer. The system will configure and install it automatically; otherwise, you may find that the wireless network card fails to work.

d)   Check the wireless network configuration

Check whether the wireless network card device is working OK or not.

Go to the local network connection list window, find the icon of the target wireless network connection, and open the property setup interface of the target wireless network connection. Get to know the strength of the wireless network signal, make sure the wireless network is not being interfered with from an outside source, try moving the laptop to different positions, and see if the signal changes. If there's variance, but when signal is full grid, and it still does not access the wireless network. It is likely due to the operating system, driver or network settings problems. If the signal does not change, then likely it's a problem with the antenna; (assuming you already confirmed the wireless router is working all right)

e) Clear up viruses and Trojans

ISP software can be an inconvenience for users when setting up their computer. However, if the ISP software is corrupted because of infection of viruses or Trojans, then it would cause Internet failure; so here are some steps to deal with it:

(1) Scan the Windows system entirely with antivirus software, clean up viruses or Trojans, if the ISP software is already defective, then you need to uninstall the original software, and then reinstall and configure it;

(2) Virus or Trojan invasion can also change the settings of a Windows system, if the wireless access service, remote call service and some other services are abnormal, then the wireless Internet fails. Even when a virus or Trojan is cleaned, sometimes, you still cannot recover to the original settings, then you need to reinstall operating system to repair it;

f) Recover to factory settings

(1) Recover wireless router to factory settings;
(2) Recover ADSL Modem to factory settings;
(3) Logon to the management interface of the wireless router, cancel the broadcast SSID option;
(4) Change the launch frequency of the wireless router, set a frequency that is not in use; and set the receive frequency of the laptop to the same thing;
(5) Disable the MAC address filtering function and firewall function temporarily

If there's problem with your Bluetooth, and the connection fails, then you can diagnose the problem according to the steps below:

An HP laptop does not recognize the printer, earphone, mouse, keyboard or Bluetooth devices. Pay attention: in the HP laptop, Bluetooth devices and WLAN devices are probably integrated on the same Mini PCI card.

a) Refer to the accessory manual of the laptop, and make sure your laptop is equipped with Bluetooth technology;

b) Check that the Bluetooth devices are installed correctly, and the Bluetooth device is enabled in the Windows system correctly. The method below takes Windows XP Service Pack 2 for an example:

Use HP Wireless Assistant to confirm whether the laptop Bluetooth hardware is already installed and enabled. The HP Wireless Assistant software will check the

Bluetooth hardware and confirm whether the Bluetooth hardware is installed and running correctly. However, this may not be possible with other models of laptops;

1. To enable HP Wireless Assistant software, please double click the HP Wireless Assistant icon on the system taskbar. Jump to Step 2 to check device status;

   a) If the HP Wireless Assistant icon on the system taskbar is not there, then go to the HP official website to download and install the latest HP Wireless Assistant;

   b) If your laptop doesn't support HP Wireless Assistant, then it would display an error message, not allowing you to install it. Then you can proceed to Step: B-8 "Confirm laptop Bluetooth devices are already installed and enabled manually" in this chapter <<10.2.5 Laptop wireless network card, Bluetooth and router failure analysis and repair flow>>.

2. Check the panel of the HP Wireless Assistant to make sure the status of the Bluetooth devices and WLAN (Wireless LAN) devices are OK.

   a) If the status is "Disabled", then enable the WLAN devices and Bluetooth devices according to the operation manual in HP Wireless Assistant.

   b) If the status is "Enabled", then it means the devices are already installed, and you can connect at any time.

If the methods above are of no help, then you can continue to follow more detailed troubleshooting methods contained in the second chapter of this article <<10.2.5 Laptop wireless network card, Bluetooth and router failure analysis and repair flow>>.

10.2.3 22% of wireless network card, Bluetooth and router failures come from this hardware itself

Probably 22% of network failures are caused by bad hardware.

During the repair process, I often find interface cable connection problems with the wireless Internet and router. Generally we can solve it by pulling and plugging in the cable connection. However, if it's a problem of the hardware itself, then you have to patiently find it and repair it. First of all, determine whether the Modem and wireless router works or not.

1) If none of the computers in the network can access the Internet through the cabled or wireless network, then initially we can say: the failure is in the Modem or the wireless router or relevant with the delivery service of the Internet service provider;

2) Recover the wireless router to factory settings; recover the ADSL Modem to factory settings; if it still does not work normally, then please check the indication lights of the Modem and wireless router carefully to identify the failure. For the complete troubleshooting method, please refer to the second chapter of this article <<10.2.5 Laptop wireless network card, Bluetooth and router failure analysis and repair flow>> Step: A-3; Step: A-6;

3) Remove the wireless router, connect an ADSL Modem directly to a known good desktop (or laptop) computer and access the Internet with a cable; if it still does not work, then do continue to the fourth step, if solved, then it means the problem is in the wireless router;

4) Change to a known good working ADSL Modem to test, or contact the Internet service provider, requesting technical support, and see if there's something wrong with the telephone line (or cable) or the Internet network;

5) Router hardware problem. We can check the hardware issue of the router from the boot log. When the router is starting up; it first initiates the hardware power-on self-inspection, executing hardware test applications in ROM in order to test whether all components are working normally or not. After finishing the hardware inspection, it starts the initialization process of the software. During the start-up process the router hardware is inspected and problems are recorded in the system boot log. Occasionally when you enter certain port configurations, the system may prompt an error, then it's quite likely the problem is with the port.

a) System missing

When such a situation occurs, you can use the backup operating system software stored in ROM, which should make the router start and work. Afterwards, download a new IOS operating system to a FLASH memory to use for repair;

b) System faults

Many new routers have an auto attack defending function. IOS system defaults, generally, cannot be repaired by installing patches, so you must replace it with a brand new IOS. If you find a system BUG, the router manufacturer should have released the BUG, with system influenced and relevant new IOS software on their official website. You must choose the proper version for your router model. Use "zero failure" high-level router software.

c) Password missing

Password is the maximum authorization the key administrator has, and there's always someone who forgets it. Common routers provide a very convenient RESET key on the panel, you just need to reset it several times, and then you can recover the original password.

d) Configuration file missing

Start the initialization configuration for the router from the human-machine interface. Please refer to the second chapter of this article <<10.2.5 laptop wireless network card, Bluetooth and router failure analysis and repair flow>> Step: B-2 reset wireless router with the manual method.

6) Wireless network card hardware failure

   a) Install a Mini PCI interface wireless network card, and then enter the laptop operating system. A system down or blurry screen failure may occur and the driver cannot be installed. After removing the wireless network card, you find everything is OK. Generally, it's a quality problem of the wireless network card itself or it is caused by physical damage to all kinds of components or the circuit board or the golden fingers of the wireless network card;

   b) If the Wireless network card is not installed properly in its socket, it creates the problem where the system does not recognize the wireless network card. You can solve it by simply pulling out and properly plugging in the wireless network card;

   c) The connection between the antenna and wireless network card can be a problem. The antenna contact is subject to vibration and tensility, leading to a bad connection between the card and the antenna contact. Generally, we can solve the problem by pulling and plugging in the antenna connector and tightening the antenna;

7) Wireless network card hardware incompatibility

   a) A Wireless network card with the same Mini PCI interface still can have compatibility problems because of different manufacturers. You can't use any wireless network card that fits your computer. Pay attention to the production statement by the manufacturer specifying which laptop models it is compatible with. If the changed wireless network card is not in the compatible list of your laptop, then you cannot use it. Save it, but don't try it;

   b) Wireless network card failures caused by an imperfect wireless network card driver or incompatibility with the hardware take up a large proportion of problems. The best solution is to download the latest and most stable wireless network card driver, install and update, or change to another version of driver and try it.

8) Motherboard hardware failure

   a) Except for the reasons above, an Internet failure can also happen because of a motherboard slot problem or because the motherboard inspection system does not recognize the wireless network card. If the wireless network card list that should be in BIOS, doesn't appear, (some laptops don't have this function), then you can initially come to the conclusion that it is caused by a motherboard hardware problem.

   b) If you changed to a known normal and fully compatible wireless network card, but it still does not access the Internet, please confirm that the model of the HP laptop is DV6000 and DV9000, and then it would be a problem with the motherboard hardware.

If the problem is still not solved, then please continue checking with a more detailed troubleshooting method, the second chapter of the article << Repair the problem that HP DV9000/6000/2000 laptops could not get to Internet >>

10.2.4 5% of Wireless Internet, Bluetooth and router failures come from bad interface wire connections

5% of causes of wireless Internet failure, and Bluetooth, router failures are because of bad cables or connectors.

During the repair process, I often see failures caused by the connecting cables of the wireless Internet and router. Generally, we can solve the problem by pulling and plugging in the connectors. If a wire is broken somewhere or a connector is defective it is much more difficult to locate and repair it. According to the method "first easy and then complicated", start with pulling and plugging-in the cable connectors, and then according to the failure symptoms, take other relevant steps.

Most ISPs now provide a unit with an integrated modem and wireless router. These are much easier to diagnose. Less cables, and if the unit is defective, they will replace it. The following steps deal with an ISP provided modem and your wireless router.

(1) Interconnection failures

a) Observe the status of the ADSL Modem Ethernet☐LAN Link) light:

If the indication light is out, then it means the DMODEM is not connected to the wireless router (or computer network card). If the light is out, and when you move the ADSL Modem or connection cable, the light is on or flickers, then it means there is a connection problem. Start with the cables. You need to carefully check the R45 cable and connectors looking for sharp bends or insulation damage or a broken connector. You can check the cable continuity with a multimeter or try another cable. If you determine the cable is OK and the problem still exists, you know the problem is in the equipment. Before you replace a defective cable, recover the ADSL Modem to the factory settings, and then replace the cable with the good one. Please take a look at Figure 10-3.

Figure 10-3

b) What the wireless router Internet status indication light tells you:

When the LAN port is connected to the Modem or other exchange device correctly, the indication light should be always on, if it's out, then it means the wireless router is not connected to the Modem and is likely a cable problem. You can check your cables according to Step a) above, until the Internet status indication light is always on. Please take a look at Figure 10-4.

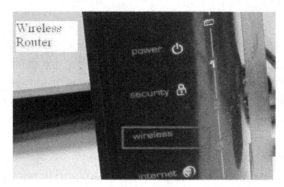

Figure 10-4

c) What the wireless router (WLAN) status indication light tells you:

This light will flash when the wireless function is enabled normally. If the light is out, then it means the wireless function is not enabled yet. You can connect to the wireless router configuration page through the cabled network connection to "Enable" the WLAN (wireless) function, and recover the wireless router to factory settings.

d) Change the ADSL Modem or wireless router

If you know your cables are all OK then you likely have a connector problem. You now need to determine which connector is at fault. The indication light is out, so try wiggling and unplugging and plugging in each connector until the light goes on or flickers. Once you have located the bad connector you need to decide whether it can be repaired or replace the whole device.

e) Repairing the ADSL Modem or wireless router

The modem likely is the property of the ISP and you should not attempt to repair it. They will replace it if it is defective. If you decide to repair the interface of the ADSL Modem (assuming you own it) or wireless router by yourself, then you should open their shell carefully, take it apart to check whether there's some component with a bad connection problem in the internal circuitry. Generally, certain soldered points of the interface can be poorly soldered to the PCB (circuit board), when the crystal head of the cable is plugged into the position; you can obviously tell that the pin soldering is defective and open circuit. For this kind of problem, generally we re-solder the interface pins again, and then this should easily solve the problem.

Any time you encounter this kind of problem, you have to deal with it, either yourself or take it to a repair facility. Hopefully, it will bring you a nice surprise!

(2) Loose antenna or bad connector failure

This instruction deals with wireless routers with an external antenna. Many of them now have internally integrated antennas.

If you have confirmed that your cable interfaces are good, then maybe the antenna connector is loose. This leads to the problem that the laptop wireless Internet often goes offline or even does not connect to the wireless network. Sometimes you may find that your laptop would interrupt the wireless connection, reconnect it automatically, and then the wireless network is working again. This problem will repeat itself causing you much inconvenience and needs to be corrected.

a) Disable your laptop wireless network, and connect a cable directly from your computer to the router. If that works then do the same with the modem. If they both work OK with a cable connection you can proceed to troubleshoot for a wireless problem, otherwise you need to deal with the unit that did not work.

b) First check wireless router antenna, remove the antenna by rotating it about the antenna axis. Now check carefully, for damage in the antenna connector, Determine that the core pin is not distorted or broken, and that the connector on the wireless router is also OK. Please take a look at Figure 10-5.

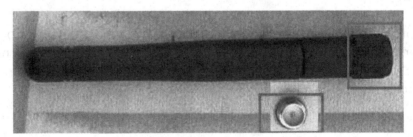

Figure 10-5.

c) If the antenna is OK, reinstall it and try to operate a different computer on the wireless network. If that works your problem is in the other computer, otherwise there is still a problem with the router or antenna.

d) Having isolated the problem to the computer, disassemble it and find the wireless network card. There are 2 to 3 antenna contacts in there but generally, there's bad contact between the network card interface and the antenna contact. Button the antenna tightly in place again to solve the problem.

e) If you find the laptop's integrated antenna is over distorted or the core is broken, and causes a bad connection, you need to change it.

To find more detailed troubleshooting methods, please refer to the second chapter of this article <<10.2.5 Laptop wireless network card, Bluetooth, router failure analysis and repair flow>>

10.2.5 Repair a problem that an HP DV9000/6000/2000 laptop does not access the Internet through the wireless router.

1) After confirming that the wireless router and the ADSL Modem have no problems, remove the problem laptop from the wireless network, and change to a cabled network connection to the router. If the cabled network doesn't work either, then it means the problem must be in the computer operating system, you need to first solve the software problem, and then solve the wireless network problem. Please continue to the second step, if there's no problem with the wireless network, and then please continue to the third step;

2) Under "Safe mode", restart the laptop and clear all issued software, viruses and Trojans. If the problem still is not solved, then you can consider reinstalling the operating system;

3) Try solving bad contact problems by pulling and plugging in the wireless network card. Maybe it was not seated correctly in the first place and this might solve it.

4) Replace the wireless network card with a good one, uninstall the old driver and install a new one, making sure all settings are correct, and the replacement wireless network card is compatible with the laptop;

5) Solve the problem of a bad connection between the antenna and wireless network card by pulling and plugging in the antenna connector and tightening the antenna. Except for reasons above, if the motherboard inspection system fails to recognize the wireless network card, this would also cause the Internet failure. Then we can initially come to the conclusion that a motherboard hardware failure has caused the problem.

If you have not solved the problem, continue checking with a more detailed troubleshooting method. Refer to the second chapter of this article <<10.2.5 Laptop wireless network card, Bluetooth and router failure analysis and repair flow>> Step: D-1 install USB wireless network adapter and solve Internet failure.

10.2.6 Laptop wireless network card and Bluetooth, router failure analysis and repair flows

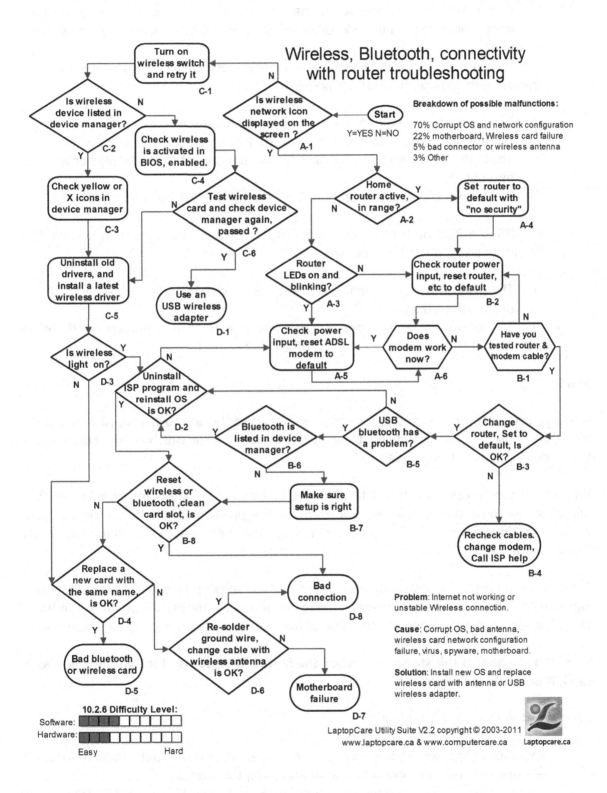

Wireless, Bluetooth, connectivity with router troubleshooting

Turn on wireless switch and retry it C-1

Is wireless device listed in device manager? C-2

Is wireless network icon displayed on the screen? A-1

Start
Y=YES N=NO

Breakdown of possible malfunctions:

70% Corrupt OS and network configuration
22% motherboard, Wireless card failure
5% bad connector or wireless antenna
3% Other

Check wireless is activated in BIOS, enabled. C-4

Check yellow or X icons in device manager C-3

Test wireless card and check device manager again, passed ? C-6

Home router active, in range? A-2

Set router to default with "no security" A-4

Uninstall old drivers, and install a latest wireless driver C-5

Use an USB wireless adapter D-1

Router LEDs on and blinking? A-3

Check router power input, reset router, etc to default B-2

Is wireless light on? D-3

Uninstall ISP program and reinstall OS is OK? D-2

Check power input, reset ADSL modem to default A-5

Does modem work now? A-6

Have you tested router & modem cable? B-1

Bluetooth is listed in device manager? B-6

USB bluetooth has a problem? B-5

Change router, Set to default, Is OK? B-3

Reset wireless or bluetooth, clean card slot, is OK? B-8

Make sure setup is right B-7

Recheck cables. change modem, Call ISP help B-4

Replace a new card with the same name, is OK? D-4

Bad connection D-8

Problem: Internet not working or unstable Wireless connection.

Cause: Corrupt OS, bad antenna, wireless card network configuration failure, virus, spyware, motherboard.

Re-solder ground wire, change cable with wireless antenna is OK? D-6

Bad bluetooth or wireless card D-5

Motherboard failure D-7

Solution: Install new OS and replace wireless card with antenna or USB wireless adapter.

10.2.6 Difficulty Level:

Software: ▓▓▓▓□□□□□□
Hardware: ▓▓▓□□□□□□□

Easy — Hard

This tutorial will help you solve these problems:

1. A wireless client does not receive a signal, or does receive a signal normally but does not access the wireless network, or often goes offline after accessing the wireless network;

2. Settings are all correct, but it fails to access the wireless network, or when the network environment changes, it does not access normally.

   a) The internal wireless network communicates with the wireless router normally, but fails to communicate with the Ethernet connected to the wireless router;

   b) The laptop does not use a wireless system to connect to the family network for Internet sharing;

   c) You cannot check other computers within the wireless network.

3. In BIOS, the Bluetooth card cannot be inspected, or in the operating system, the Bluetooth also cannot be inspected.

   a) The Bluetooth card is identified in the OS (Device Manage or taskbar), but the Bluetooth card light is red;

   b) The Bluetooth light is on, but the laptop cannot communicate with other Bluetooth devices or fails to find other Bluetooth devices.

Start

When you connect the power adapter and press the power button to start up, after entering the system, please check carefully, it should be in accordance with various independent failure descriptions in this tutorial:

When it fails to access the Internet through the wireless, there are many possibilities that might be the cause of the problem. For example, the problem might be on the ISP side. All you can do is call the ISP. If you have that suspicion, call them before doing too much investigation.

For wireless transmission instability and Bluetooth transmission failure it is likely that your laptop transmit power is not sufficient or the external wireless modem/router has problems. This situation does not belong to the range of this tutorial, please check another tutorial.

Step: A-1 the goal of this step is to analyze the failure symptoms of the wireless network card, Bluetooth and router

First of all, here are some problems:

1) Your laptop has worked fine through the wireless connection but suddenly stopped working or drops the connection after accessing the internet.

2) Your laptop is new, and/or has never connected to Internet before; it fails to connect to the Internet or often goes offline after accessing it.

The first situation

A)   The laptop is moved to a new network environment and then it fails to connect? For example, after bringing the laptop home it does not access the wireless network but it did work in the office. One of the following scenarios might be the cause:

(1)   SSID (Service Set Identifier) configuration hasn't been changed, as different wireless networks use different SSIDs. If the SSID configuration is incorrect, then you cannot ping through the AP;

(2)   With WEP encryption, you need the key to access the wireless Internet. If the WEP key used is different, the wireless client cannot connect to the new wireless AP. It will not receive an IP address from the DHCP server.

(3)   Generally speaking, the wireless AP will distribute the IP address for the wireless clients automatically. If in your office, you had set the IP address for wireless client manually, then the client cannot communicate with a new AP at home unless also done manually.

(4)   After excluding the three problems above, find the wireless icon in the right bottom corner of the laptop screen and click on it to see which wireless networks are available. If the icon is present, then please enter Step: A-2; if there's no wireless network card icon, then please enter Step: C-1;

B)   The laptop is not in a new network environment and is not connecting to the internet through the wireless, most likely because it is not receiving the wireless AP signal or there is no signal at all. There are a few possible causes for this failure shown below:

(1)   The wireless network card is too far away from the wireless AP or the wireless router, exceeding the coverage range of the wireless network. The signal received is too weak to achieve a connection.

(2)   The wireless AP or wireless router hasn't been powered on or is malfunctioning,

(3)   If you are using directional antenna technology to enhance the transmission of the wireless signal, you may not be pointed properly and the signal is weak or not there.

(4)   Check the LEDs on the wireless AP or wireless router, if normal, move the laptop closer to them to see if it will receive a strong signal. Then check the laptop to see if it connects correctly but fails to access wireless network, or succeeds to access wireless network but then goes offline, If so please enter Step: A-2; if the laptop cannot receive the signal normally, and you can be sure the network and wireless router is working normally (for example, with the same conditions, another laptop works OK), then please enter Step: C-1

The second situation

1)   The laptop hasn't used a wireless network and on the first attempt does not access the Internet through the wireless. In this case, follow method A) of the first situation above. If there's a wireless network card icon at the right bottom corner of the laptop

screen, then please enter Step: A-2; if there's no wireless network card icon there, then please enter Step: C-1;

2) The laptop hasn't used a wireless network before, and now it receives a signal normally but fails to access the network, or often goes offline after accessing the wireless network; for this situation, please follow the method B) of the first situation to solve the problem. If you still fail to solve it, then please enter Step: A-2. If the laptop does not receive the signal normally, then please enter Step: C-1;

Step: A-2 the goal of this step is to focus on the effective distance of the wireless router

Start by moving your laptop near to the router about.1 to 3 meters away from wireless router will do. See if it works there. Then you know that the router is working. Theoretically speaking, the wireless router's "effective distance" is about within 50 to 100 meters, but the actual effective distance at your location is difficult to confirm. It depends on obstacles that may be present between the laptop and the router. Obstacles such as walls will attenuate the signal and reduce the effective distance. This is because "50~100" meters means line of sight and plane horizontal range. Vertical distance is less than horizontal distance. Wall thickness and material affects attenuation. Metal would be the worst case. Basically a router's signal can pass through a few bricks of about 20CM, and then radiate another 20 meters. If the range seems to be too short it is likely caused by obstructions between the laptop and the router and the signal received is too low to be useful

If the" Effective distance is not enough" the problem could be solved by purchasing an enhanced router, which boosts the signal strength. When you buy one, pay attention to the length of the antenna if it is external. A full wave antenna is the best and should be 12.5 cm long for 2.4 GHz. They also use ½ and ¼ wave antennas, not quite as good. Double antennas are also OK. You should not change the size or type of antenna provided as that would cause an impedance mismatch and a loss of efficiency.

If you are receiving a strong signal and still fail to access the wireless network, or you often lose the connection after accessing the wireless network, you need to investigate some other problems:

(1) Frequent offline may be because of electric wave interferences

Electric wave interference sources can come from many electrical products like a wireless phone, Bluetooth earphone, and microwave oven. Even an electrical garage door opener, air conditioner and numerous other appliances can cause interference. You turn them off, one at a time to discover the source affecting you. Cordless phones often cause problems. You may be able to change channels on your WiFi. Try different channels to find one that is interference free. Keep your telephone base unit at a different vertical level than your WiFi devices. A phone that uses the DECT 6.0 standard will not interfere as long as the base unit is not too close to the router.

(2) Frequent off lines can be caused by router aging that affects the signal radiation pattern or the signal strength. Your WiFi connection may start to become unstable

(3) Frequent offline when linked to the wrong Wi-Fi network

If in the wireless network environment you use, there are two Wi-Fi networks with the same network name, you might link to your neighbor's network incorrectly, (if password protection was not set) and affect your normal Internet access. Likely your neighbours signal will be weaker or at times turned off. Your internet connection will be unreliable.

Frequent off lines can be caused by router (access points) loading that is too heavy.

This would affect the speed and quality of the wireless Internet. The main reasons causing router heavy loading is: online games, BT downloading, or too many computers connecting to the network and so on. According to my few years' computer repair experience, if the router's temperature is too high, probably offline failures would happen.

(4) Failing to access a wireless network is because of software incompatibility.

If since the beginning, the laptop did not connect to the wireless network, then it's quite likely that your laptop has incompatible software, which includes operating system patches, system service components, or other software affecting the system network. It's also possible that the network driver is corrupted, and affects all kinds of functions of the Wi-Fi hardware.

(5) The failure to connect to a wireless network may be because the Wi-Fi hardware itself has problems.

When there are problems or faults in the Wi-Fi hardware, you likely cannot access the wireless network;

Step: A-3 the goal of this step is to investigate the failure from the wireless router indication lights

The wireless router indication lights should not be neglected; it is actually a key clue to the reason for the router failure

1   Power indication light

Marked PWR or Power, then this light should be always on, if it's out, then it means the power is not on and you cannot access the wireless network. Check your ON-OFF switch, power source, cable, and connections.

2   Wired (Ethernet) status lights

It's composed of LAN 1 2 3 4 LEDs showing LAN connection status and the Modem light. LEDs 1 2 3 4 are the port working lights; another is the Modem port light. This light has three types of status: always lighted, flash and out. When cable connected to the Modem correctly or another Internet network, this light would always be on and flashing. If the 1 2 3 4 lights are all out it could be the power switch, otherwise you should focus on checking the connection status of the incoming twisted-pair, or when necessary, you can change a cable or a port and try again.

3   DMZ (Security) system indication light

DMZ is the abbreviation of "Demilitarized Zone". In the computer world, it refers to a buffer zone that separates the Internet and your private LAN. (Note: Microsoft calls this a "Screened Subnet").

It's a buffer between the non-secure and secure areas of your network. The system settings should be checked if the external network does not connect to the internal network server after installing the firewall. This buffer is located within a small network area between the enterprise internal network and the external network. The DMZ area protects the internal network more effectively, because this network deployment adds one more toll-gate for the attacker to overcome as compared to the firewall alone.

Now we consider the data flow from the internet to the local network. It is as follows:

Internet to Modem
Modem to Router
Router to DMZ Hub/Switch
DMZ Switch to WEB/FTP/Game Server
. . . and . . .
DMZ Switch to Firewall External NIC
Firewall Internal NIC to Internal Hub/Switch
Internal Hub/Switch to Internal Systems

The DMZ or Security light on the control panel represents the internal system status. If the router works normally, then this light should be always on or flashing. If it's out, then it means the wireless router hasn't been initialized normally. First you can check that the WAN cable is properly connected. Then turn off the power switch or pull out the power cable, wait for 30 sec and apply the power again. Try it a few times if necessary and hopefully your problem are fixed.

4   Internet status light

The internet status light indicates the connection status with the cabled Modem. This light has three kinds of status: always on, flashing, and out. When the LAN port connects to the Modem or other switch device correctly, the light would be always on; if it's out, then it means the wireless router hasn't connected correctly with the Modem. Check the Wan cable and reset the power as described above until the light activates.

Wireless (WLAN) status light

The wireless function enabled light should be flashing/on when the wireless function is enabled normally. If the light is out, then it means the wireless function is not enabled. You can access the wireless router configuration page through the cabled network card and set the WLAN (wireless) function "Enabled".

Routers made by different manufacturers may label the indication lights differently, but generally speaking, the functions are more or less the same.

The following are detailed explanations of status light functions:

Wireless router: PWR (power, check that the power is ON), SYS (system, checks that the router works normally), WLAN (checks that the wireless network connection is OK), WAN (Wide Area Network, checks that the incoming Internet cable is connected with the router correctly).

The router has indication LEDs 1, 2, 3, and 4; these indication lights represent computer connections to the router. There are four numbered indication lights, indicating the router can connect to four computers. As long as the connection is correct, the light should be on, if not connected or connected incorrectly, then the indication light would be out.

Routers of different brands can have different names for the lights, Generally there are POWER, WAN1, WAN2, DMZ lights, and each LAN port is designated (some would be like LINK (1,2 . . . .)), some more advanced have M1, M2, ACT.

M1 provides one flash every second, implying that system is running. When M2 is on, it means the system is busy at this moment. If M1, M2 are always on, then likely there's something wrong with the router. There's a RESET key available, to recover to factory settings. Try it. Different routers have different steps. Generally, if you power off and then wait for a few seconds and then power on, the M1 flash/second means it succeeds and your problem is solved.

Step: A-4 the goal of this step is to recover the factory settings for the wireless router

One of the most common failures when the network is not working normally is because of improper settings on the router. Typical improper settings for routers are the parameters for the two sides of the circuit of the router that are not matched or wrong parameters, or router mask setting errors. The best solution to solve the problem when the laptop fails to connect to the wireless Internet (or often goes offline) is to reset the router to the factory settings.

A)   Find a small hole at either the front/back panels of the wireless router designated RESET.
B)   Shut down the power of the router, find something pointed like a pen head to press the Reset key;
C)   Power on the router while holding in the reset, wait for about 3 to 5 seconds and then release the reset, the reset is done;

If lucky, the problem is solved, but sometimes, you still cannot reset to the factory settings. If the laptop still does not access the wireless network, or often goes offline once accessing the wireless network, then please enter Step: B-2; Please take a look at Figure 10-6.

Figure 10-6

Step: A-5 the goal of this step is to reset the ADSL Modem to factory settings

One of the most common problems in network failures is when the ADSL Modem is not running properly. Generally, we reset the ADSL Modem back to factory settings to solve the problem.

A)   Find a small hole at either the front/back panels of the wireless router designated RESET.
B)   Cut off the power of the ADSL Modem, find something pointed like a pen head to press the Reset key;
C)   Power on the router while holding in the reset, wait for about 3 to 5 seconds and then release the reset, the reset is done;

If lucky, the problem is solved, but sometimes the problem still is not solved. You should check that all cables are connected correctly, pull out (unplug) all cables, and then plug all cables back. If the laptop still fails to receive the signal, then please enter Step: A-6;

Step: A-6 the goal of this step is to determine the failure cause from the indication lights of the ADSL Modem

Most people now use Broad Band Internet for their service. An ADSL modem is provided and has many LED indication lights that are very useful in diagnosing problems. It is always important to locate the modem so that the lights can be easily seen, rather than hidden away. If you have a problem accessing the internet, a glance at the lights can tell you exactly what is happening, or if you call your service provider they will first ask you the status of the lights.

Most ADSL Modems will have 5 main indication lights, taking the SpeedStream ADSL Modem for an example, the purpose of the lights are discussed below:

(1)   Power light

Designated PWR or Power, A green light means the device is powered on and running normally. If the light is out, then it means the power is not on, or the unit is malfunctioning. Possibly the ADSL modem power inverter has failed. Check the power connection, cable, and switch position. Logically confirm whether the Modem hardware is still in good condition;

(2)   Ethernet (LAN Link) light

The Ethernet link light has three conditions: always on, flashing, and out. A green light means the modem output cable is connected to the wireless router (or computer network card) correctly. If the light is out; it means the MODEM is not connected to the wireless router (or computer network card). If this light is flashing, then it means there's data transmission through the line. If the light is out for a long time, and when you move the ADSL Modem, and the light flickers intermittently or turns on, then it means the cable connection is not good, you should first check the connections of the RJ45 cable and when necessary, install a new one and give it a shot.

(3)   DSL (ADSL Link) light

The ADSL link light has three conditions: always on, flashing, and out. The Green light means that after the ADSL link activates, the signal is synchronized, and telephone line is connected to the MODEM port correctly; now the data gateway is available for use. If the light is flashing quickly, it means the ADSL link is in activation process, and the signal is synchronizing. Wait till that is complete and the light is steady on. If the light flashes and then dies out, or did not turn on then it means the telephone line connection is not working and needs to be checked, Check the cable and connectors and make sure they are not damaged in any way and plugged in properly. Next use a telephone set to check for dial tone from the service cable. If so, the problem can be in the modem. It tells you the connection to the service provider is OK. Make sure you have the modem turned on, then try powering it down for a few seconds and on again and then try a reset. If no dial tone, likely the modem is OK, try changing the cable. If still no dial tones call the service provider. To check and repair the circuit.

(4)   USB light

(5)   Meaning: USB link light, when you use a USB cable to connect a modem to the computer, the function is same as the Ethernet (LAN Link) light, this light has three conditions: always on, flash and out. A green light verifies that the USB cable is connected to the computer from the MODEM correctly. If the light is out; it means the MODEM to computer USB connection is not working. If the light is flashing; it means there's data transmission through the data gateway. If the light is out and when you move the USB cable, the light is on occasionally, then it means the cable connection is not good. Try pulling out and repluging the connectors and changing the cable. If this does not work, the problem can be in the modem or the computer itself. Check the modem as described in steps above and if the modem is OK locate other areas of this manual to troubleshoot the computer

(6)   Activity (ADSL Activity) light

Meaning: ADSL data light, status information: if it's out, it means there's no data transmission on the data gateway; green light flashes, then it means there's data transmission on the gateway. If there's no data transmission for a long time, after halting for a period of time, normal data transmission should be recovered. If not, you need to check whether the signal separator connections are correct or not, Check other devices connected to your telephone line.; is there a fax machine, telephone exchange and other devices, if yes, then:

a)   Disconnect these devices and try again;
b)   Uninstall PPPIE dialing software in use, and then reinstall;
c)   Delete TCP/IP protocol, restart computer and then add TCP/IP again;

If the laptop still does not receive a signal normally, then please enter Step: B-1;

Step: B-1 the goal of this step is to confirm whether your failure is caused by a defective cable

When a laptop fails to access a wireless network or often goes offline after accessing a wireless network; mostly it is, because of a defective cable or connection. You have to know that between the ADSL Modem and wireless router and the computer, there are many connection lines that could be at fault. Many users ignore these cables and just keep them out of sight; they can be placed in corners, and under desks and tables. When they move tables or chairs, a cable may be damaged or pulled out and then a failure occurs. Usually users don't know where to start checking, so just start from the cable port, this would simplify the elimination process of many problems. Pulling out and plugging in connectors might fix the problem. You check each connector for damage while doing this. If you see a problem you cannot fix, change the cable. However, if you have problems similar to the examples below, you will need other solutions to help solve them.

a) After a cable is pressed and extruded or stretched, a conductor can be broken, or a cable connector might start to overheat, or the joint becomes oxidized. A bad contact, will cause a lower quality of circuit transmission or too much attenuation of the signal;

b) Bad connections between the Modem and telephone line and network cable. The joint between the telephone line and a signal separator is in bad condition. Failure solution: find the connection causing the problem and fix it or change the cable. If the laptop still does not receive a signal, then enter Step: B-2; if you already did this, then please enter Step: B-3;

Step: B-2 the goal of this step is to manually reset a wireless router

If with Step: A-4, we cannot recover the factory settings to the wireless router; you need to enter the router management interface. Logon to the management page with an administrator account and password to recover the factory settings, here we take TL-WR541G wireless router for an example as below:

1. **Fail to dial**

    Failure symptom: cannot execute a normal dialing application. These are the correct reset steps:

    (1) Set the IP address for the connection: http://192.168.1.2; subnet mask: 255.255.255.0; default gateway, no need to set for DNS.

    (2) Cut off power, press the Reset button, and then switch on the power, about 3 seconds later, a system indication light first dies out and then lights up later, the configuration is then reset to the default factory settings.

    (3) Open the Web browser, enter the management address of the router to the address bar: such as 192.168.1.1, at this moment, the system would request you to enter a logon password, default user and password are admin/admin; when logon occurs, check the computer's IP address, it should be within the network segment 192.168.1.0. After logon, enter the management interface, choose the "WAN port setup option" under the "Network parameters" Menu, in the right side main window, choose "PPPoE", in the option "WAN port connection type", enter "Internet account" and "Internet password", then click the Connect button.

2. **Fail to browse web pages**

    Failure symptom: the webpage does not open normally, but some applications like the chatting tool QQ works normally.

This situation is the DNS parsing problem on the router, if the gateway is set to the DNS address, this is DNS Proxy, not the actual DNS address, then probably there's an address parsing error.

Solution: open the router setup interface, find "Network parameters"—"WAN port parameter" field, and then set to DNS server address manually. In the setup option "DHCP service", you also need to set to DNS server and backup the DNS server address manually, which you need to get from the ISP supplier.

3. **Fail to logon to the management interface of the router**

Failure symptom: I want to make relevant settings for Internet sharing on the enterprise Broad Band router, but fail to access the management interface.

Solution: if you logon to the router management interface and now that problem occurs, then you should first check the connections between the Broad Band and the router, and close the firewall and monitoring antivirus software. Set the gateway address to the default IP address of the router. Brand Band routers usually provide all Web management, so open "Internet option" dialog, and in the option "Connection", if you've created a connection before, then check the option "Never dial to connect", click the button "LAN setup", cancel all the selected options.

For a more detailed instruction, please refer to another article <<Linksys Router Setup>>

http://laptoprepair.ca/news/1295.html

Step: B-3 the goal of the step is to confirm that your failure is not caused by the wireless router

If you've already worked through Step: B-1, but the result is that the laptop still does not receive a signal normally, then the problem might be in the wireless router. Find another working wireless router to take the place of it and try testing with it. If it also does not work; it confirms that the failure is not caused by the wireless router. Now here I use the setting of a D-Link wireless router for an example:

1. Pull out one end of Ethernet cable and then plug it into the port on the back side of the new D-Link wireless router;
2. Find another Ethernet cable, one end of it is connected to the network card of the desktop computer, the other end is connected to the Ethernet port of the router. Pull out the end of the Ethernet cable and plug it into the port of the new replaced wireless router;

Access the configuration screen of D-Link

3. Open your network interface, enter http://192.168.0.1 to the address bar, and then click "Enter" or "Return".
4. Use the left logon screen when "manage" user name and password are blank.
5. Click "OK". Now you should see the D-Link configuration screen, and then create a general security setup;
6. By clicking the "Tools" label, choose the "Manage" button and choose the "Admin" button. Enter a new password under the "Administrator" heading. Confirm it, and click "Apply."
7. Temporarily disable the wireless area network (LAN), confirm that nobody can access your network. And under the "Home" tab, choose "Wireless" and select the "Off" option. Enable Wireless Encryption Protocol (WEP).
8. Find the "Home" label under the D-Link configuration screen; click the "Wireless" button.
9. Use the "Authentication" beside the "Open system" button, and then choose "WEP" beside the" Enabled" button, set the Encryption key to "128 bit"
10. Set the "Key Type" to "ASCII" and choose a 13-digit password for the "Key 1" field.
12. Write down the password in a secure location. Click "Apply" and change the SSID.
13. Change the SSID to make it more difficult for others to locate and use your network by clicking on the "Home" tab and locating the "Wireless" button
14. Disable SSID broadcast. On the "Advanced" option tab, click "Performance" and select the "Disable" text and click "Apply". Filter MAC address by clicking on the "Advanced" label "Configure" interface on the D-Link. Choose the "Filter" button.
15. Choose "MAC filter" and click "Only allow listing computers below to connect to network with MAC address". Enter the name and MAC; allow accessing network, accorded with the computer address you are configuring at the beginning, click "Apply".

If the problem is still unsolved, then please enter Step: B-4; if you still have a Bluetooth problem, then please enter Step: B-5;

Step: B-4 the goal of this step is to finally determine the source of the failure.

The most common network failure affecting access to the Internet is the ADSL Modem, if Step: A-6 is bypassed; the repair process to recover the ADSL Modem to the factory settings must be added to solve the problem.

a) On the back panel of ADSL Modem, find a small hole designated "Reset";
b) Turn off the power for the ADSL Modem, use a pointed tool like a pen head to press the "Reset" key;
c) Power on for ADSL Modem, wait for about 20 seconds and then release it to activate the, reset;

If the problem is still unsolved, you need to check all cables and connectors for defects. Repair any problems you see or change the cable. Try unplugging and plugging in the connectors. Changing the cables one at a time can identify a defective cable without visible damage.

If the problem is still unsolved, then you need to consider replacing the ADSL Modem. Note that sometimes the indication lights of ADSL Modem may show normally but there still can be a problem with the ADSL Modem. You need to replace the modem with one you know is working to see if it works. That will tell you if the original modem is defective or not

Sometimes network problems can also be at fault. None of your computers will be able to access the internet normally. You should contact the service provider to resolve the problem.

Step: B-5 the goal of this step is to confirm the type of Bluetooth adapter needed

The Bluetooth adapter is an interface switch that enables all kinds of digital products that use Bluetooth devices. The Bluetooth adapter uses a global general short distance wireless connection technology in the 2.4GHz band also used by microwave, remote controls, and some civilian wireless communication equipment that are potential causes of interactive interference. Therefore, the Bluetooth adapter uses 1600 times high-difficulty jump frequency and encryption protection technology.

Bluetooth is one of the wireless network transmission technologies. Bluetooth transmits data for a distance less than 10 meters, but with the help of signal amplification, the communication distance could reach as far as100 meters.

Current Bluetooth adapters use USB interfaces and are "Plug-and-play". They are called Bluetooth USB adapter to differentiate. Besides Bluetooth USB adapters, there is Bluetooth earphone, Bluetooth microphone etc.

The latest Bluetooth adapter design is based on the Bluetooth SIG 2.1 standard, a new generation of high-speed Bluetooth adapter, (free of driver, supporting Win7). It plugs into the USB interface on the desktop computer or laptop and provides Bluetooth communication functions for the computer. Once the computer is Bluetooth equipped, it will communicate with all kinds of Bluetooth devices like the Bluetooth cell phone, Bluetooth keyboard and mouse, Bluetooth earphone, Bluetooth PDA etc.

- Use valid IVT Bluesoleil 5.4 version Bluetooth software, authorized to the Bluetooth address code of the product, so a 5M bytes data transmission limitation would not occur as on cheap Bluetooth adapters.
- In Windows 7/XP/Vista systems, you can use Microsoft Bluetooth software, namely, plug-and-play. The user could also use the matched IVT5.4 Bluetooth software with more powerful functions on the driver disc.
- Be able to connect several Bluetooth devices at the same time, such as cell phone, earphone, keyboard and mouse. Compared to Bluetooth 2.0 adapter, multi-device connections are more fluent. It supports A2DP Bluetooth dimensional sound audio transmission; the audio effect is quite excellent. When transferring dimensional sound, it will also transfer Bluetooth audio through the Bluetooth microphone.

- With the integrated high sensitive professional Bluetooth ceramic antenna, open space communication distance can reach above 10 meters, which can go through walls and communicate through Bluetooth.

If you use new Bluetooth adapter (USB) with Microsoft system Bluetooth software, the likely possibility for a problem would be relevant with the signal network or USB interface. Please enter Step: B-6; if you use the old integrated Bluetooth adapter, then mostly it's relevant with the driver; please enter Step: D-2;

Step: B-6 the goal of this step is to analyze the failure symptoms of a Bluetooth adapter

Building a Bluetooth connection

1.   Make sure the configuration file matches

To match and use the device, every device on communication needs to share the same configuration file. For instance, if you connect an earphone to a cell phone, then you need to confirm that both the earphone and cell phone have a hands-free config. profile HFP. If you need to create a dial session to access the Internet by connecting a cell phone and PDA, then you have to make sure both the cell phone and PDA have a dial network DUN config file. If you want the printer to print out the content on the cell phone, then usually both printer and cell phone should have basic print config file. Generally, you can find the relevant information on which config files are supported in the user manual.

2.   The Bluetooth function must be enabled

For the devices communicating through Bluetooth wireless technology, you need to confirm that the Bluetooth function is enabled. Although the basic design of Bluetooth keeps the power consumption to a minimum, by default, the function can be disabled to save power, or on special occasions (such as in an aircraft or hospital) disabling the wireless function is necessary. For most devices, the Bluetooth function (wireless) has already been enabled by software, then we can choose "Turn Bluetooth radio on" from the menu.

3.   Bluetooth match

On normal occasions, for the sake of security, two Bluetooth devices should always match first, and then exchange data. The term "Match" sometimes is also called binding. Usually, it means that two devices exchange maintenance keys with each other. After matching successfully, all messages sending through the Bluetooth would be encrypted and can only reach the devices that have been matched.

4.   Match sequence

Set one of the devices as match mode, and then activate the match through another device. For example, to match an earphone and cell phone, you can set the earphone as match mode by a series of button operations. Afterwards, activate the function to enable match through the relevant menu on the cell phone.

5. Create connection

Generally, there won't be any problem when devices are matched; but you need to be clear how to start and prompt the initial match. For more detailed information, please refer to "Connect devices". Once a match succeeds, then you can create a connection, and no need to do anything else. If the match between the two devices needs to be rebuilt; the match operation should be carried at somewhere safe.

6. Host/visitor and multipoint access

If you connect several devices on an individual network (one host for several visitors); that is multipoint access. There's always one device as the host, and other devices are visitors. For example, a computer can connect a PDA, camera and cell phone at the same time, and send data to them. However, please be aware: some devices like a wireless earphone, cannot keep several connections at the same time.

7. Disable WiFi wireless Internet temporarily

Bluetooth technology is based on low-cost close distance wireless connections, working at 2.4GHz frequency. As Bluetooth and a WiFi device using the 802.11b standard all work on the 2.4GHz frequency band, there can be interference between them, although some manufacturers explain that new products already conquer this fault. After you send out a command, you may have to spend a long time waiting for the result, even more than 8 seconds, so you should consider disabling the WiFi wireless Internet temporarily (if possible). There's a case indicating that after disabling a WiFi wireless Internet, to a certain extent, this situation could be improved. The Bluetooth data pack loss rate can be significantly reduced; similarly, when you use a 3G satellite wireless broad band Internet, disabling the WiFi on the laptop would also bring you much improvement.

If you haven't disabled the WiFi wireless Internet temporarily, then do so temporarily. If you've already disabled the WiFi wireless Internet or you cannot disable it, and the problem still exists, then please enter Step: B-7;

Step: B-7 the goal of this step is to reset the Bluetooth adapter

1. Cannot find the Bluetooth device

A Bluetooth device is disabled or other devices are not at the "discoverable mode", then enable this mode from the relevant menu or execute a series of button operations on the device with the limited user interface. If you worry about the security problem, then make the device you are looking for match with visible/discoverable. After finishing the match, you can reset the device undiscoverable/invisible.

2.   Match doesn't work out

Match between devices fails. Generally, the reason causing such a situation is because when trying matching, you entered the wrong password or PIN. Confirm that the password entered is correct, then turn off and restart the match device.

3.   Match succeeds but it still doesn't work

If a device cannot match to use it, one of the rarest reasons is that these two devices don't support the same config file; however, support is exactly one of the necessary conditions.

   a)   Generally, the answer for this problem can be found by referring to the manuals that have config file information.
   b)   Another reason is that it's not easy to find out the correct command or menu for the connection. As manufacturer implementation and device user interfaces are too complicated, please contact the product manufacturer directly or browse the manufacturer's website to get technical support.

If you confirm that you've already reset the Bluetooth adapter, and it's completely correct, but still does not work normally, then please enter Step: B-8;

Step: B-8 the goal of this step is to confirm that the failure is not with the Bluetooth adapter (or wireless network card)

Wireless network card

   a)   Check whether the failure disappears by pulling and plugging the integrated wireless network card. Before plugging, you should first clear up dust and clean the gold plated board (edge connector), including the slot. When you install it, you should first pay attention to how well the card fits in the socket. It should be a firm fit, not too loose of too tight. Make sure there is no damage in the socket that would impair the connection.
   b)   If the steps above do no help you, I suggest you put the wireless network card in another working laptop to test it and see if it works. Please take a look at Figure 10-7.

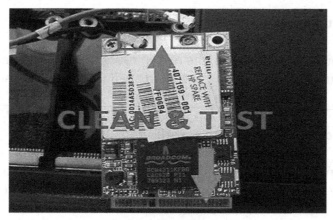

Figure 10-7

Bluetooth adapter

1) If your laptop has two or more USB ports, you should try using another port since the one you are using may be damaged and causing the problem. However, the settings for Bluetooth adapter might need to be reset and then test it again;

2) Check whether the failure disappears by pulling and plugging the integrated Bluetooth adapter. Before plugging, you should first clear up the dust and clean the gold plated board (edge connector), including the slot. Also check how the card fits in the slot as in a) above

3) If the steps above don't help, try the adapter in another laptop as in b) above.

If you still cannot ensure 100% whether your Bluetooth adapter is good or not, you can try another adapter that you know is working properly. However, you need to make sure that the Bluetooth adapter has the same technical standard with the original one. Also change both the earphone and cell phone, with others that are working normally under matched mode;

a) If it works normally, it means the laptop hardware and drivers are compatible. Otherwise, it means the Bluetooth adapter's driver has something wrong with it, but needs to be reinstalled. Another possibility is that there's something wrong with the hardware compatibility, and needs to be checked and corrected.

b) If it works normally, then remove the Bluetooth earphone you are now using, and connect the original Bluetooth earphone to test it. If it works normally; it means the original earphone is good. If it does not, it means the original suspected Bluetooth earphone has a problem and has to be changed. There could also be a compatibility problem with the original earphone that has to be dealt with.

c) You can also follow the same process as the earphone with the Bluetooth cell phone as in a) and b) above.

If the steps above do not help you, then please enter Step: D-4; if you can get to the Internet, but it is not that stable, then please enter Step: D-8;

Step: C-1 the goal of this step is to confirm that wireless network switch is not turned on.

Many HP laptops have a wireless network switch, when the network switch is off, naturally it will not connect to the wireless network, and usually it would behave as below:

a) Can not find the wireless network, sometimes it would prompt that the wireless switch is open;

b) On the operating system desktop, there's a yellow or red mark on the icon representing the wireless network status. If it indicates the wireless is not working, you cannot connect and need to take steps to correct it so you can connect.

c) The wireless network card indication light is always orange; no matter how you press keys it does not turn blue . . . .

If you have any of the problems above, then it's quite likely that your network switch is open. If you can't find the switch, maybe there isn't one. Check your manual.

1) If the wireless switch is off, and you haven't disabled the wireless network card, there's no way it can work.

2) An HP laptop wireless network switch can be a key combination, usually you press Fn and the key with the relevant upper symbol, (little antenna icon), then you can see whether the wireless switch is on or off. There should be an indication light turning blue. The "Fn" key is usually located at the left bottom corner on laptop keyboard. The other key is at the top of the numeric keys, such as with the hp6535b laptop's where the F7 and F8 keys have a little antenna mark; you can give it a shot.

3) Check that your laptop has an integrated wireless network card or just an interface slot where you can plug one in.

If you have an installed wireless network card, and the wireless network switch is turned on, but you still cannot connect to the network, then please enter Step: C-2;

Step: C-2 the goal of this step is to confirm that there's an available wireless network card on the device management list

1. Click "Start"—"Control Panel"—"System"—"Hardware"—"Device Manager"—"Network Adapter", and then double click "Network Adapter", check whether there's an available wireless network card on the list or not. If your "Network adapter" list has no "wireless network card" icon, then it means that you need to reset the wireless network card in CMOS, or you need to check that the laptop actually has an integrated wireless network card, and whether the wireless network switch is on. After that, assuming you do not have the wireless card listed, here's the solution:

2. Reinstall the wireless network card, pull it out and then plug it in again. A failure because of a bad contact of the wireless network card might be eliminated in this way. However, if there's a hardware problem with the wireless network card, then you need to use the replacement method to solve the problem.

If you confirm that the device management list has a wireless network card, then please enter Step: C-3; if there's no available wireless network card in the device management list, then please enter Step: C-4;

Step: C-3 the goal of this step is to confirm that there's a wireless network card with a yellow mark on the device management list.

Open the "Device Manager"; do you see a yellow exclamation mark? If there is, then it means the wireless network card needs a driver, or you need to update the driver, it could also be because of a card contact problem. Please take a look at Figure 10-8.

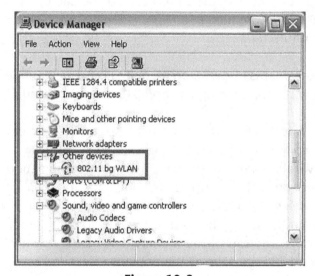

Figure 10-8

If there's a red exclamation mark, then it means the wireless function of the device is disabled you need to start the wireless function so that it can be searched by the wireless client. Generally speaking, there are two sayings about the client:

One is to reinstall the operating system, following that if the yellow exclamation mark appears on the wireless network card listed, obviously it's caused by a driver problem. You just need to reinstall the driver to solve the problem;

Another is that before the failure occurs, your laptop is getting the Internet normally, but when you start again, suddenly there's no local connection and no wireless network icon. You need to restart the laptop again and reinstall the driver if needed. If it doesn't work out, then pull out the network card and reinstall it again.

Sometimes when using a Windows 7 operating system, a recently local connection shows that the network suddenly changes to network 2, while the original network1 has a yellow mark. It's not a system problem, but is caused because the local connection hasn't set the fixed IP address. At this moment, the operating system would auto name network 2, (next time to start up, the number might change), adding another connection for the computer. Of course this is not a failure, but also not within the discussion range of this chapter.

If your laptop has no yellow exclamation mark and you still have a problem, you've already done the method according to the flowchart and it still fails to connect to the network, then please enter Step: C-5;

Step: C-4 the goal of this step is to confirm that the wireless network adapter is activated in BIOS

Few laptops need to set the wireless network adapter in BIOS, or need to load default security settings. If you confirm that the BIOS management has already activated the wireless network adapter settings, then please enable the wireless network adapter function, (if no choice for such a function, then skip it), and then please enter Step: C-6;

Step: C-5 the goal of this step is to install a new wireless network adapter driver

A corrupted driver is a common problem that results in a failure of a device to work. The first thing to do it to uninstall the driver and reboot the computer to automatically reinstall a fresh one already contained it the OS. A driver disc provided with a new laptop is helpful if the previous step did not work. Proceed as follows:

a) Right click on "My computer" and choose "Properties" and then click "Hardware", enter the device manager, and check if there's an interrogation mark on the network card in the list, double click the interrogation mark and click to reinstall driver, and then choose the auto install software, put the driver disc to DVD-ROM/CD-ROM, and click next.

b) If you don't have a driver installation disc use a cable connection to the modem/router to access the internet. Then enter the device manager and choose the network adapter, click the dropdown list, update device driver for the devices with yellow exclamation marks, choose auto connect network to search for the driver.

c) If the auto network connection search fails, then first confirm the brand and model of your new network card, and then go to a relevant website to download the driver and install it. Usually, HP has drivers available for download, most manufacturers do as well;

d) If after connecting a network cable and you cannot access the internet, you can download from another computer and copy it to U disk and then install it in your laptop. If the installation prompts failure; it means the driver downloaded is incorrect, or you should close the antivirus supervision and then install it again.

If you've already installed a new wireless network card driver, and the device with the yellow exclamation mark is fixed, but you still do not get to the network, then please enter Step: D-3;

Step: C-6 the goal of this step is to confirm whether the failure occurs in device manager or wireless network card itself

If there's no wireless network card in the laptop device management list, or no wireless network card with a yellow mark, then the failure is quite likely to be relevant with the wireless network card hardware. Of course it could also be a device manager (motherboard) or controller BIOS problem.

1) Check whether the failure disappears or not by pulling and plugging the wireless network card; before plugging the network card back clean up any dust and clean the card gold plated board (edge connector), including the slot. When you install the card, you should pay attention to whether the network card is too loose, or a jack is too tight or any other problems that would lead you to suspect you are not getting a good connection.

2) If the steps above do not help, I suggest pulling out the wireless network card and then try it in another laptop (of the same manufacturer/brand and same model) and test it. Judge whether the wireless network card works and runs normally; if the wireless network card works normally in another laptop, then it means the problem probably is in the device manager (motherboard), then please enter STEP: D-1;

If the wireless network card being installed on another laptop is tested with some problems, then you must find another wireless network card that you know is working, and install it in the suspected laptop. You need to make sure the technical type of this one is the same as the original wireless network card. For instance, PCI or PCI-E, and has the same manufacturer's name and the model. Then you can confirm the wireless network card is 100% compatible with your laptop, and make sure it can work normally if all else is OK.

It's really a headache when the wireless network card is incompatible with the laptop and leads you to a wrong conclusion. It might even show a wireless network card in the device management list, and even with the correct driver, the incompatible problem is not solved by these methods. If you have changed the wireless network card, but wireless network problem is still unsolved, then please enter STEP: C-5;

Step: D-1 the goal of this step is to install a USB wireless network card to solve the problem of a wireless network failure

If the laptop device management list doesn't show a wireless network card, but the wireless network card is good after testing, then basically the failure might be relevant with the device manager (motherboard), the best solution is to install a USB wireless network card. Please take a look at Figure 10-9.

Figure 10-9

However you might encounter a problem after installing USB wireless network card, finding that the laptop still does not auto connect to the wireless network. You need to perform further operations with the wireless management tool. Generally, there are two wireless management tools on the laptop, one is the wireless management tool in the Windows operating system, and another is the management tool provided by the laptop manufacturer. By default, which management tool works? We can get to know this from the next few steps:

1. "Start"—"Control Panel"—"Network connection", right click "Wireless network connection", and choose "View available wireless connections", as the picture below shows:

2. If the computer uses a Windows wireless management tool currently by default, then the resulting message "searching wireless network" should appear. If the list is empty; it means the laptop hasn't found a wireless network. Please click "Refresh network list" at the right top corner, if the result is still the same, then probably there are a few more situations as below:

   a) There's no wireless network existing within the wireless receivable range of the laptop;

   b) The wireless AP hasn't been enabled or the wireless function is disabled. In fact, if there's a wireless AP around you, for example a D-Link, then check whether that device is already enabled, and whether wireless signal light is on or not. If the device is enabled, but the wireless signal light is out, then it means the device wireless function is disabled and you'd have to enable the wireless function. Then it should be found by the wireless client;

   c) A USB wireless network card driver hasn't been installed yet, then even if there's a wireless network available, the laptop cannot find it;

   d) A wireless AP and laptop wireless work mode problem. If the AP and laptop wireless are all enabled, but the laptop still does not find the wireless network, excluding hardware problems, it should be the problem where the wireless working modes of are not matched. If your laptop is Windows XP SP2, I suggest setting your computer to connect to any available network adaptive state. By default, it already has this setting, you can right click "Wireless network connection" and choose "Properties", enter "Wireless network configuration" and click "Advanced". confirm that the wireless working mode you've chosen is "Any available network", shown as below:

For a more detailed procedure, please refer to an article I wrote earlier <<How to solve the problem that a USB wireless network card cannot find a wireless network>>

Step: D-2 the goal of this step is to confirm that the ISP software (the driver) of the wireless network card (integrated Bluetooth adapter) works all right.

Wireless network card:

What's ISP software?

ISP is short for Internet Service Provider; here primarily the service means Internet access service, namely, to connect your computer or other terminal devices to the Internet through the telephone wire (twisted pair).

PPPoE is short for Point to Point Protocol over Ethernet. Actually this protocol is a relay protocol between the Ethernet and dialing Internet, which inherits the quickness of Ethernet and the simplicity of PPP dialing, user validation, IP distribution and some other advantages. Virtual dialing is to dial on an ADSL digital cable, different from the dialing with a Modem on a simulated telephone wire, but using special PPPoE software. Similarly, cable connection broad band Internet (3G high speed Internet) also uses professional software, of course, if you know LAN technology well, probably you will not use ISP software to set up a computer, but you can achieve the same purpose to get to Internet.

In order to facilitate final users, generally, network service providers all offer ISP software to set up computers. But for final users, there's no need to know embedded LAN technology using this software. With it they can quite easily connect a computer to the Internet. However, if the ISP software is damaged because of viruses or Trojan invasion, then it can cause a problem to access Internet. If a laptop wireless network card works normally before, but suddenly one day there's a problem with it and the network card itself has no problem, then there are probably two reasons that can cause this failure:

(1) It's quite likely that the ISP software cleaned garbage files that are needed, or the ISP software is damaged because of a virus or Trojan invasion. You need to uninstall the original OS software, reinstall it, and configure it to retrieve the deleted files.
(2) After excluding the problem above, check carefully whether the wireless network card works or not, if it still does not work, then you should consider whether you've executed the operation STEP: A-5 of the flow chart during the repair process. If no, then please continue to the STEP: A-5 method. If you've already satisfactorily completed Step: A-5, then please continue the step 3;
(3) Something is wrong with the operating system, you need to format the disk (initialization operation), repair disk problems all caused because of the ISP software, then reinstall WIN XP or Vista (Win 7). If there's not a similar failure after reinstalling the operating system, then it means the laptop is fixed. If the steps above are no help for you, then please continue to STEP: B-8;

Bluetooth adapter:

A) Check that all devices are Bluetooth capable.

Of course, the first condition you should satisfy is that all devices you want to connect have a Bluetooth wireless function. If you cannot ensure whether your laptop has Bluetooth technology or not, then you should contact your device manufacturer or refer to a product technical specification.

1. Make sure all devices have a relevant Bluetooth configuration file;
2. Make sure the device has already been "enabled" for the Bluetooth function;
3. Make sure that the device you want to communicate with is properly matched. If it is still not working, you can find some general prompts for solving potential problems with Bluetooth connections from the content below.
4. Enable communication session functions;
5. Whether all methods are executed correctly or not;

B) If your laptop Bluetooth adapter is working normally, then suddenly there's a problem with it, In this case, then there are few reasons that can cause your failure:

(1) It's quite likely that some software cleaned garbage files that are needed, and then the Bluetooth driver doesn't work. You need to uninstall the original software and then download a new driver, reinstall it and configure;
(2) A device match is disturbed because of other reasons or there's a problem with the hardware itself, then you need to reset the match or replace the issued hardware;
(3) After excluding the two problems above, check carefully whether the laptop Bluetooth adapter works or not. If it still does not work, then you should consider whether you've executed STEP: A-5 flow chart correctly during the repair process. If not, then please repeat STEP: A-5 method to proceed. If you've already satisfactorily completed method Step: A-5, then please continue the fourth step:
(4) Something wrong with operating system, you need to format the disk (initialization operation), repair disk problems caused by the software, then reinstall the WIN XP or Vista (Win 7). If the failure doesn't repeat any more after reinstalling the operating system, then it means the laptop is fixed. If the steps above have not helped you, then please continue to STEP: B-8

Step: D-3 the goal of this step is to determine the failure from wireless network card indication lights

The wireless network card indication lights being neglected are actually an important clue to determine wireless network card failures.

Light would change colors

Here I take the HP540 laptop wireless network card as an example; the light should show blue and red. When you press the switch button, it turns red (also yellow), and when pressed again, turns blue. With these two conditions seen in, the right bottom corner of the display screen, where there's a small computer icon representing the wireless signal, blue means the wireless network works, while red means the wireless network is disabled. You might think that when the wireless network is disabled, there should be no computer icon for the wireless signal showing. This is not always true;

Light flashing

Sometimes a laptop wireless network card would keep flashing, which means the signal is transferring. If the signal is not that stable, and there is a frequent data exchange, or it requests to resend, then the light would often flash. When it keeps flashing, then it means the signal is at a stable transferring status. With the situation that you have no network access, the wireless network card is still connected with the network, so it would flash a few times, it's quite normal.

Light dies out

If the indication light of the wireless network dies out automatically, of course, you cannot connect to the Internet. You must restart computer. But sometimes it's useless even to restart the computer. These are a few reasons:

1)   When wireless network card light dies out, if you can see wireless network card normally in the device manager, it means that network signal could not be found, but it can also be a hardware problem, you need to change the wireless network card;

2)   There's something wrong with the driver of the wireless network card, one is that it's too old; the second is that it's damaged because of a virus or Trojan invasion. So you need to uninstall and reinstall the driver, or next upgrade to the latest version;

3)   The laptop power manager software has lost control because the wireless network card power is cut off by mistake. These are the steps to follow: find the control panel, and then find the device manager, next find the node where wireless network card is, and click to expand it, and then right click the node and choose Properties, next click the last "Power options" tab, remove the check on the checkbox for disabling power, and then save the changes. Then you should be OK!

Light always off:

If the light for the wireless network does not turn on, the following are the likely causes:

1)   The laptop wireless Internet is all OK, just the light is out, which indicates there's something wrong the light itself, you need to change the indication light;

2)   Fail to get the Internet with the wireless network card. The light of the wireless network card is out, and you can see the wireless network card in the device manager. You

uninstall and reinstall the driver, or reset the power manager, but the problem is not solved. Probably there's something wrong with the wireless network card hardware, you need to change it;

3) If after the second test item, it is found that there's nothing wrong with the wireless network card hardware, then it means the laptop power manager hardware has lost control, then you can only change the motherboard. First check the power switch to make sure it is not off;

4) Fail to get to the Internet with the wireless network card, the light is out, and you cannot see wireless network card in the device manager;

   (a) Integrated wireless network card is not installed;
   (b) Integrated wireless network card is not working;
   (c) There's a fault with the motherboard;

If the steps above are of no help for you, then please continue to STEP: D-4;

Step: D-4 the goal of this step is to confirm the failure is in the wireless network card (Bluetooth adapter)

Wireless network card

If you decide to use a new wireless network card to take the place of the suspected one, then you should pay attention to the next few points:

1) Your new wireless network card must be compatible with the interface of the original wireless network card, in other words, if the original wireless card is a mini PCI interface, then the new wireless card interface must also be a mini PCI. If the original wireless card has a PCI-E interface; the replacement should be the same.

2) A new wireless network card manufacturer and model must be the same or specified compatible to the original manufacturer and model, for instance, if the original wireless network card manufacturer is Intel, then the replacement should also be Intel; the models should better be the same too. This will avoid other incompatible problems. Make sure the new wireless network card is working normally;

3) Uninstall the relevant driver for the original wireless network card. In Windows XP system, click "Start"—"Run", to open run window. And then enter "devmgmt.msc" to the text on Run dialog and click "OK". This would open device manager control panel. Click to expand the network adapter and open the list, right click the driver icon, and then click "Uninstall", delete the driver according to the prompt.

4) To install with a wireless network card product installation disc or download a new driver to install; you proceed according to the prompts of the wizard. However, many drivers don't have the validation for Microsoft operating systems, so probably there are prompts like "Incompatible" or "Without digital validation", then just leave them alone and keep installing. Just once if there's some mistake, then you need to restart the operating system in "Safe mode", and then uninstall the driver and install a correct driver.

Bluetooth adapter

If you decide to use a new Bluetooth adapter to take the place of the suspected one, then you should pay attention to the next few points:

1) The manufacturer of the new Bluetooth adapter must be same as the original one, also the model should be the same or compatible;
2) Make sure all devices have the relevant Bluetooth configuration file;
3) As for the methods to uninstall and install the driver, you can follow relevant methods of the wireless network card above.

First make sure the new wireless network card (Bluetooth adapter) is compatible with the laptop, because an incompatible problem could be only be solved by changing the wireless network card (Bluetooth adapter). If you change a compatible wireless network card (Bluetooth adapter), but the problem is still unsolved, then please enter STEP: D-6; but if the problem is solved, then please continue to enter STEP: D-5;

Step: D-5 the goal of this step is to finish the confirmation of the wireless network card (Bluetooth adapter)

If you use a new wireless network card (Bluetooth adapter) to take the place of the suspected wireless network card (Bluetooth adapter), then the result should be the problem is solved. Most people would think that the wireless network card (Bluetooth adapter) that was replaced is defective but, actually the situation is not that simple. Sometimes you will find that the wireless network card (Bluetooth adapter) being replaced will work normally on another computer, this is because:

1) The wireless network card (Bluetooth adapter) being replaced conflicts with the software settings of the original laptop and is disabled;
2) The driver software of the wireless network card (Bluetooth adapter) being replaced has a confliction with the software of the original laptop, which leads to the failure;
3) The interface of the wireless network card (Bluetooth adapter) being replaced has a slight distortion, which prevented it from working.

So it's advisable to check the wireless network card (Bluetooth adapter) being replaced to make sure it was faulty.

Step: D-6 the goal of this step is to confirm the failure is not because of the antenna of the wireless network card (Bluetooth adapter)

After installing a new wireless network card (Bluetooth adapter), test the laptop close to the router. Here's the procedure: put the laptop 1 to 3 meters from the wireless router, and see that it is working, if it still fails to receive a signal normally; then your problem might be because of the "strength of the signal". If excluding the aging of the router or software incompatibility problems, usually, it's caused because the laptop integrated antenna has a bad contact or is broken or the wrong type for the card.;

If you change the antenna of the integrated wireless network card (Bluetooth adapter), but the problem is still unsolved, then please enter STEP: D-7; if the problem is solved, then please enter STEP: D-8;

Step: D-7 the goal of this step is to confirm that the failure is in the laptop motherboard

If you uninstall and reinstall the driver, or replace the wireless network card and the problem is not solved, probably there are some problems in the laptop motherboard and it needs to be replaced. However, before solving this problem, first check up whether the laptop power manager's software has lost control;

For the HP Pavilion DV6000, DV 9000 series; find the control panel, and then find the device manager, reset the power manager, remove the check in the checkbox "Close wireless network card power", and then save the changes.

Update the BIOS application to the latest version. For detailed method, please refer to the second chapter <<2.2.2 Update BIOS steps>>

Considering that the cost of changing a laptop motherboard is too high, the best solution is to install a USB wireless network adapter ($20), as for a more detailed method, please refer to this chapter <<Step: D-1 the goal of this step is to install a USB wireless network adapter, to solve the problem that the wireless Internet cannot be accessed>>

Step: D-8 the goal of this step is to finish the confirmation of the failure

a)   If you eliminate the machine failure by pulling and plugging the integrated wireless network card (Bluetooth adapter), then congratulations you've finished the repair task. What you need to pay attention to is that you should clean up the dust and clean the gold plated board (edge connector), to prevent the failure happening again;

b)   If you eliminate the failure by replacing the antenna of the wireless network card (Bluetooth adapter), a good thing to do is to check the replaced antenna hardware again; it might work OK with other computers so still has value.

In all, the following summarizes the tutorial for the reasons why a laptop cannot access the Internet through the wireless:

Cause: the system is infected by a virus or Trojan, an operating system problem, a wireless network card (Bluetooth adapter) router problem, ADSL, Modem and other hardware is defective or there's a setting error, a bad antenna, or a motherboard with faults.

Solution: reset the network, clean up viruses and Trojans, replace hardware with faults, install a USB wireless network adapter, as for details; please refer to this tutorial, thank you!

10.3   Twenty-seven repair cases of HP laptop Internet connection failures

10.3.1 8 repair cases for the Internet access failure due to wireless card issues

174)   HP laptop has Windows 7 installed—repair case for wireless card issues

Failure symptom:

Client states that his HP DV-4 1428tx laptop originally had windows Vista installed but since he changed it to Windows 7 system, the wireless network card no longer works.

Solution:

This failure symptom obviously belongs to the description of flowchart 10, according to the repair method of sequence: Start->A-1->C-1->C-2->C-3->C-5

Repair summary:

Right click "My Computer" and choose properties—hardware—device manager, and you'll find a yellow exclamation mark next to the network card in the list, which means you need to install the wireless network card driver, or you need to update it. Double click the network card exclamation mark, reinstall the driver, and then choose automatic install, put the CD into the DVD-ROM/CD-ROM, and then click Next; when the driver is finished installing, restart the laptop, and everything returns to normal;

Hint:

1). If there's no driver installation disc, plug in through a wire network to get the internet and update the driver by going to the manufacturers website and download the driver and install it.
2). Find a computer that can access the Internet, and follow the same direction as above and then copy it to a USB flash drive and install it in the PC that requires the driver and the issue is solved.

175)   after HP V3240AU laptop shuts down and restarts, the wireless network card can't be found in hardware device

Failure symptom:

Client states that his HP V3240AU laptop was running great and then one day he shut it down and it hinted him that no wireless network card was found; even in the device manager.

Solution:

This failure symptom obviously belongs to the description of flowchart 10, according to the repair method of sequence: Start->A-1->C-1->C-2->C-4->C-6->C-5->D-3->D-4

Repair summary:

Very few laptops need to a set up for wireless network card in BIOS in order to activate the wireless network card. After confirming there's no such function, uninstall the wireless network card and install into another normal working laptop. As a result, same failure occurs, it seems the wireless network card is the problem, changing the wireless network card and the failure is solved;

Hint:

1) You can check whether the failure disappears by removing and installing the wireless network card backs in the slot; before reinstalling, clean any dust from it and the slots. When installing it back in verify whether it's loose or the jack is too tight, because that could stop it from being installed properly
2) Check whether the wireless button is on or not (lights is blue if enabled).

176) HP PAVILION DV6675US laptop could not connect to wireless network

Failure symptom:

Client states that laptop connected to the wireless network, but now the connection is lost. He tried to open and close the wireless network switch but it didn't change to the connection status.

Solution:

This failure symptom obviously belongs to the description of flowchart 10, according to the repair method of sequence: Start->A-1->C-1

Repair summary:

When turning the wireless network card's switch on or off, you can hear slight sound, you should also feel a small force when opening or closing the switch. If you don't hear anything or there isn't a little resistance then there's probably an issue with the switch therefore change the switch and the issue is solved.

Hint:

The settings for HP Wireless Assistant software could directly affect the usage of the wireless network card. However, only the HP laptops produced in 2005 and later have the software.

1. Enable the HP Wireless Assistant by double clicking the Wireless Assistant icon in the system taskbar. Then jump to step 2 and check the device status;
2. Follow the operating direction of the HP Wireless Assistant and check the status of the wireless device.

  - IF the status is "Disabled", then enable it
  - If the status is "Enabled", then the device has been installed successfully and is ready to be connected.

177) HP PAVILION DV9700 laptop's wireless network frequently goes offline

Failure symptom:

Client states that he was able to connect to the wireless network, but now the connection is lost. If you observe the connection status of the wireless network, you will find that the signal is quite weak.

Solution:

This failure symptom obviously belongs to the description of flowchart 10, according to the repair method of sequence: Start->A-1->C-1->C-2->C-3->C-5->D-3->D-2->B-8->D-4->D-6

Repair summary:

Usually when the distance between the laptop and the wireless router exceeds the coverage range of wireless card this issue will occur. When you place the laptop 1 to 3 meters close to the router, the problem still exists. So the issue has nothing to do with the distance.

It is quite common that drivers get damaged, when you uninstall the old driver, and reinstall the latest one doesn't help the issue either.

Enter repair flow step B-8, rremove and install the internal wireless network card and check whether the failure is gone; before plugging it back, remove any dust but it also doesn't solve the issue. Put the wireless network card into another good known laptop to test. As a result, it works normally. Go to repair step D-6, it seems the issue is with the antenna of the wireless network card, replace it and problem is solved.

Hint:

There are also other reasons that could cause frequent offline failures:

(1) Interference from other electric waves;
(2) Wi-Fi network radiation due to aging router.

(3) Connecting to the network from network neighbourhood incorrectly;

(4) Overloading of the router access point can affects both speed and quality of the wireless Internet.

178) HP PAVILION DV9628CA laptop can't find wireless network card hardware

Failure symptom:

HP Pavilion DV9628CA laptop's internal wireless network card light was on, but now it can't connect to the wireless network. When opening and closing I turn on or off the wireless switch, the orange light status is unchanged

Solution:

This failure symptom obviously belongs to the description of flowchart 10, according to the repair method of sequence: Start->A-1->C-1->C-2->C-4->C-6->D-1

Repair summary:

Right click "My Computer" choose "Properties", "Hardware", enter "Device manager", as a result, there's no wireless network card found in the list, which means CMOS doesn't recognize it. Checking the laptop wirelesses switch again, pulling out the wireless network card and cleaning it and plugging it back in doesn't help the issue.

Put the wireless network card into another good known laptop to test, the result shows it works normally; it seems there's something wrong with the device manager <u>on</u> of the motherboard; Go to step D-1 and after installing a USB wireless network card, the failure is resolved.

Hint:

1) HP Pavilion DV6000 or DV9000 laptops are known for such issues so if the "Wireless network card" icon can't be found in the list of "Network adapters", then you need to check the internal wireless network of the laptop, whether the wireless network switch is on or not; if you put the wireless network card into another known good laptop to test, and it works, then it means the problem is probably with the device manager (on the motherboard).

2) If after installing a USB wireless network adapter, the laptop still can't connect to the wireless network automatically. Then you need to use the proper wireless management tool software. Generally, there are two wireless management tools—one is the Windows operating system's wireless Zero configuration management tool and the other one is that of the manufacturer's tool.

179) HP PAVILION DV2000 laptop's failure that wireless network frequently gets offline

Failure symptom:

When DV2000 laptop connects to wireless network, the connection is lost continually; however, using another laptop it doesn't have this issue.

Solution:

Because other computers use the same wireless network with no issues, this tells us that the failure isn't with the network or the wireless router.

This failure symptom obviously belongs to the description of flowchart 10, according to the repair method of sequence: Start->A-1->C-1->C-2->C-3->C-5->D-3->D-2->B-8

Repair summary:

Enter repair flow step C-5, considering it usually happens that drivers become faulty so uninstall it and replace it with the latest driver, but the result remains the same

Enter repair flow step B-8, Remove and install the internal wireless network card, remove and clean any dust before plugging back and the failure is solved.

Hint:

There are other reasons for frequent offline failures:

1) Usually when the distance between the laptop and the wireless router exceeds the coverage range of wireless card this issue will occur. If the failure disappears, then it means the problem is caused by the "effective distance" of the wireless router;

2) Sometimes in DSL Modem this will also lead to frequent offline issue, which is one of the most common network failures. Usually we can recover the DSL Modem back to factory settings to solve such a problem:

   A) Find the reset hole on the back panel of DSL Modem;
   B) Turn the power off for the DSL Modem, press Reset button;
   C) Power on the DSL Modem, wait about 5 to 10 seconds then release and the reset is done!

180) HP PAVILION DV6939CA laptop wireless card's indication light is on, but can't access the Internet.

Failure symptom:

HP Pavilion DV9628CA laptop's internal wireless network card light is on, when I turn on or turn off the wireless network switch, the orange indication light's status doesn't change; but now it doesn't even connect to the wireless network;

Solution:

This failure symptom obviously belongs to the description of flowchart 10, according to the repair method of sequence: Start->A-1->C-1->C-2->C-4

Repair summary:

Right click "My Computer" choose properties, click on Hardware to enter Device manager, as a result, no wireless network card is displayed in the list, which means CMOS doesn't recognize the wireless network card. Check the wireless network switch again, pull the wireless network card and re plug it back, but it still doesn't work;

HP manufacturer has already confirmed that some HP Pavilion and Compaq Presario V3000/V6000, DV2000/DV6000/DV9000 series laptops have certain hardware problems it also released dv2000/V3000 F.39 BIOS version and 3 D dv6000/dv9000/v6000 versions for those new laptops, download the latest BIOS version, after updating and installation, the failure is solved.

Hint:

1) BIOS refresh process is irreversible, you only have one chance, so make sure that the laptop will not stop or power off! Updating the BIOS has a certain risk, we do not recommend flashing your laptop BIOS, except if you're quite familiar with BIOS; besides, you must have a certain manual ability and experience to do this.
2) Different countries uses different BIOS packages, even if the laptop model is the same they probably use different BIOS software packages. So you must check your laptop's BIOS version to make sure you have the right BIOS version, and then update the BIOS.

181) HP Pavilion DV6700 laptop's wireless light is still orange and fails to connect to Internet.

Failure symptom:

HP Pavilion DV6700 laptop can't connect to the Internet, wireless assistant can't start! HP Wireless Assistant is disabled; even device manager can't change the status.

Solution:

This failure symptom obviously belongs to the description of flowchart 10, according to the repair method of sequence: Start->A-1->C-1->C-2->C-3->C-5->D-3->D-2

Repair summary:

Enter repair flow step C-5, considering now that it's quite common that drivers has failure, first uninstall the old driver, and then install the latest one but the result isn't helpful;

Enter repair flow step D-2, uninstall the HP Wireless Assistant software package, my experience of repairing laptops, the Quick Launch Control Button is also the place which often has problems. So uninstall it altogether, use Windows system's wireless Zero configuration tool, then the failure is solved.

Hint:

1) ISP software can be convenient for users but however, if ISP software is infected and damaged due to viruses or Trojans, then the cause would be Internet failure; therefore, scan the entire system with your antivirus software and remove the viruses and or Trojans;
2) If you installed a similar software package like the HP Power Assistant, then the problem you have to pay attention to is that the software will automatically cut off all movable power interfaces; and may cause Internet failure, so you should also reinstall and set up it again.

10.3.2 5 HP laptop repair cases for non communication of Bluetooth failures

182) HP Nw8440 laptop Bluetooth system displayed error message "Hardware not found"

Failure symptoms:

Client states that the Bluetooth light in the right corner of his HP NW8440 laptop shows blue-red, but not blue-white; clicking it we get an error message "Bluetooth device not found";

Solution:

This failure symptom obviously belongs to the description of flowchart 10, according to the repair method of sequence: Start->B-5->B-6->B-7

Repair summary:

First of all, find the Bluetooth controller in the control panel, if it's not found then usually it is because you haven't enabled the Bluetooth hardware device. The general way to boot is to to enable your Bluetooth device, press FN+F5 or CTRL+ wireless communication key. If after restarting, Bluetooth device is still not recognized. Uninstall and delete the Bluetooth driver, then reinstall the latest driver, and then enter the BIOS recovery setup and the problem is resolved.

Hint:

1) On a machine whose Bluetooth is working normally, there are two drivers displaying on the device manager list._

   a). HP Integrated Module with Bluetooth 2.0 Wireless Technology b). Bluetooth BUS enumerator;
   b). Go to HP official website and download

2) Now with Bluetooth BUS enumerator and the other Bluetooth device, the laptop already has the Bluetooth function; besides, the driver is installed.
3) If the Bluetooth doesn't connect, then you can use the other Bluetooth function devices (such as cell phone) and try it! Two computers could be connected with Bluetooth, and you can set to transfer through IP protocol in "Bluetooth Network"!
4) If the hardware device has no such failure, then after completing the above test, first consider the possibility of a hardware failure; we test it by the replacement method to figure it out.

183) **HP Probook 4416s laptop could not connect with printer, earphone (Bluetooth headset), mouse, keyboard and Bluetooth devices.**

Failure symptoms:

The client states that there's no Bluetooth icon at the right bottom corner of the screen, failing to search the whether the Bluetooth is enabled and the laptop cannot find any enabled Bluetooth devices nearby.

Solution:

This failure symptom obviously belongs to the description of flowchart 10, according to the repair method of sequence: Start->B-5->B-6->B-7

Repair summary:

Since there is no Bluetooth icon at the right bottom corner of the screen, first we need find the Bluetooth controller on control panel or start menu. Unfortunately, we cannot find it.

Then I press the FN+F5 to reboot the laptop, but any Bluetooth device still cannot be recognized by the laptop. Now that most HP laptops have no Bluetooth, in order to confirm, then I go checking the users manual. Then buy an external USB Bluetooth device, and install the driver for it, which should solve the issue.

Hint:

1. Make sure configuration files are paired with the device. Every communication device needs share one same config share the same configuration file. For instance, if you want to connect your headset with your cell phone, then both earphone and cell phone should have Hands-free Cconfiguration File (HFP). If you want to create the dial session by connecting through a cell phone PDA, then both cell phone and PDA should have dial network DUN config file.
2. Bluetooth function must be enabled, you'd have to open Bluetooth card at the same time in BIOS/FN+F5/Bluetooth. Although Bluetooth basic design makes power consumption quite low, the function still might be closed by power management in default settings to save more power;
3. Bluetooth pairs; normally, two Bluetooth devices should always be paired first, and then they can exchange data to each other. The term "pair" sometimes is also called binding which means two devices exchange and repair keys mutually.

184) HP Mini 210 Series laptop can't use Bluetooth devices

Failure symptoms:

A client claims that his laptop could not detect wireless network card or Bluetooth card.

Solution:

This failure symptom obviously belongs to the description of flowchart 10, according to the repair method of sequence: Start->B-5->B-6->D-2->B-8

Repair summary:

1. Check hardware switch;
2. Check FN+F5, whether the wireless network card is disabled;
3. If there's no problem with the settings above, then uninstall all wireless network card drivers and software. Restart, and then install the drivers again, enter repair flow Step: B-8 reset wireless network card and Bluetooth card. Remove and install Bluetooth

card, check whether the failure disappears or not; before pulling and plugging, first clean dust and clean (Edge Connector) gold plated board, including the slots.

Please pay attention when installing, ensure the Bluetooth card isn't loose or whether the jack is too tight, the failure should disappears.

Hint:

Sometimes Bluetooth light is on, but doesn't communicate with other Bluetooth devices; also it can't find other Bluetooth devices.

1. Set up Bluetooth card in operating system correctly; check a few options such as "accessibility", "Find" and "pair";
2. Disable WiFi wireless Internet temporarily. When you send out the command, you have to wait quite a long time for a result, even exceeding 8 seconds. Then you should reconsider temporarily disabling WiFi wireless Internet (if possible). There's some cases that after closing the WiFi wireless Internet, to a certain extent, this condition could be improved, making the data loss rate of Bluetooth data package greatly;
3. In rare situations you need to update the BIOS too.

185)   HP Mini 110 Series laptop cannot use Bluetooth devices

Failure symptoms:

Client states that the laptop has Bluetooth module, but doesn't recognize any Bluetooth device.

Solution:

This failure symptom obviously belongs to the description of flowchart 10, according to the repair method of sequence: Start->B-5->B-6->D-2->B-8->D-4->D-5

Repair summary:

Check FN+F5 to confirm whether Bluetooth was disabled by mistake. Check whether there's an unknown device in system device manager. Uninstall all Bluetooth the laptop. The problem remains and Bluetooth device can't be recognized; enter repair flow Step: B-8, reset Bluetooth card, Remove and install Bluetooth card again, and then restart the laptop. But Bluetooth device still isn't recognized yet; enter Step: D-4, confirm Bluetooth device SPS: 575920-001, which is a compounded adapter, HP Half Wireless Card and Bluetooth 2.1+EDR, the number is: Broadcom 4312b/g WiFi and 2070 Bluetooth 2.1+EDR, replace it with a known working Bluetooth device and test, the failure disappears.

Hint:

If the steps above were of no help to you, suggest putting the Bluetooth adapter on another working normal laptop to test, and then judge whether it starts and runs normally;

a) You'd have to confirm if it's the same technical standard as the original Bluetooth adapter, besides, you should also change the Bluetooth headset and cell phone together, which works normally under the mode of pairing;

b) If it works normally, then it means the laptop Bluetooth device is OK. The problem might be with the driver or settings, you need to confirm and then reinstall it again.

186) HP Probook 4321s laptop Bluetooth adapter doesn't work

Failure symptoms:

Client states that a few days ago, he used the Bluetooth adapter and now he can't;

Solution:

This failure symptom obviously belongs to the description of flowchart 10, according to the repair method of sequence: Start->B-5->B-6->D-2->B-8->D-4->D-6

Repair summary:

Now that it's quite common that a driver malfunctions. First uninstall the old driver, and then re install the new one. As a result, it doesn't help somehow; enter repair flow Step: B-8, Remove and install the internal Bluetooth card again, check whether the failure is gone. Before plugging it back, clean away the dust and also clean the (Edge Connector) gold plated board, but still helpless. Then put Bluetooth 3.0 Module BCM92070MD card on another known working common HP Probook 4325g laptop to test (compatible with Probook 4321s). And the result turns out that it works normally; enter repair step D-6, it seems there's something wrong with the Bluetooth wire on the motherboard, try replacing the connection wire, and the failure is solved.

Hint:

Other causes:

(1) Other electric wave interference

(2) If there are several devices connected on the personal network (one host for several visitors), then it's called mutlipoint access. And one of the devices is taken as the host, the other devices are visitors. For example, computer can connect the PDA camera and cell phone at the same time, and send data to them. But some devices such as wireless Bluetooth headset, could not keep several connections at the same time.

10.3.3 8 repair cases for the failure that HP laptop can't connect to Internet (Router);

187)   HP Presario F700 laptop can't connect to Internet

Failure symptoms:

Client states that there was a power outage at his place and when he restarted his laptop he could no longer connect to the Internet. When going to the office at work everything returned to normal.

Solution:

In this case that the laptop connects to the Internet is work at the office, it means nothings are wrong with the laptop. This failure symptom obviously belongs to the description of flowchart 10, according to the repair method of sequence: Start->A-1->A-2->A-3

Repair summary:

Internet status indication light represents the connection status with the cabled Modem. The light has three statuses: always lit, flashing and dying out. When LAN port connects to Modem or other exchange devices correctly, the indication light would always be on, but now it's dead, which means the wireless router does not connect to the DSL Modem normally. Check whether the WAN wire is fast, pull out the pin and plugs it again, at this moment, the network status light is on; therefore, we can conclude that the connection wire was loose, after removing and installing it again, the problem is solved.

Hint:

Improper setup of router would lead to issues that the network doesn't work normally; it is also one of the most common network failures. Therefore, when resetting the router, you need match the parameters and set the network mask and gateway. The best way is to reset the router to its default value.

188)   COMPAQ PRESARIO CQ71 laptop always gets offline failure when use wireless network Internet

Failure symptoms:

Client states that his laptop always goes offline when using wireless Internet and had to frequently reconnect. What is he supposed to do?

Solution:

This failure symptom obviously belongs to the description of flowchart 10, according to the repair method of sequence Start->A-1->A-2->A-4

Repair summary:

Generally, if the connection between MODEM and wireless router (or computer network card) is not good, then you'll run into these issues. The first place to check is whether the RJ45 wire is damaged or over twisted, if so; enter repair flow Step: A-4, resetting the router.

A) Find the little hole at the front/back side panel of the wireless router, it should read "Reset"
B) Cut the power off with a sharp object like a pen or needle and press on the reset button;
C) Power on the router, wait about 5 to 10 seconds and then let go. The reset is done; restart the wireless router and the problem is resolved.

Hint:

1) When you can't find the reset button on router, refer to the routers manual. Sometimes you need to press the reset button for 20 seconds, which sometimes reset the router back to factory default settings;
2) After changing and restarting several times, user's router configuration file might be damaged. Therefore, you had better configure the Dynamic Host Configuration Protocol (DHCP) through the control panel. Only by doing this will the computer connect automatically.

189) HP HDX X18-1103TX laptop can't connect to the wireless Internet

Failure symptoms:

Client states that his HP HDX laptop works normally with the office network, but once at home, it can't connect through his wireless.

Solution:

This failure symptom obviously belongs to the description of flowchart 10, according to the repair method of sequence Start->A-1->A-2->A-4->B-2

Repair summary:

First reset the router, after restarting, you can find available networks, but even after entering the WEP key, you still can't connect to any available network. In consideration of that under normal circumstance, wireless AP would auto automatically distribute the IP address for the wireless client, but once you've set up the IP address at the office, then this would occur with any new AP. So you need to re set the AP and the problem is resolved

Hint:

(1) Different wireless networks use different SSIDs, if SSID (Service Set Identifier) configuration is incorrect, then you cannot ping through AP;

(2) When connecting to the router to create a wireless Internet, you need to make sure the wireless router's SSID and router name match and chose them to connect.

190) HP G60-238CA laptop gets offline after connecting 30 seconds

Failure symptoms:

Client states that lately his HP laptop goes offline once he connects to the Internet. Wireless router is Linksys wrt54g. There are only two grids of signal, while the HP laptop has no such problem anywhere else.

Solution:

Since the HP laptop has no issues with the Internet in other places, then it indicates the problem isn't with the laptop.

This failure symptom obviously belongs to the description of flowchart 10, according to the repair method of sequence Start->A-1->A-2->A-3->A-5->A-6->B-1->B-3

Repair summary:

First check the line at the client's home, finding that the indoor connection is good, also there's no interference source with the line, and the line is far away from the air condition, fridge and TV set. Enter repair flow Step: B-1, the key is to check the RJ45 wire connection. Check the Crystal head connection, and finding there isn't any damage or twist to it. After replacing the cable the issue remains, then enter Step: B-3, after three years of usage the wireless router has aged; replacing it and the failure disappears;

Hint:

1) Check whether the firewall and IE browser settings are correct, although it's quite impossible for router to get attacked by hackers, we don't exclude the possibility. Once attacked, interruption, cutoff symptom would occur. Check the DMZ link light, if router is normal, then it should always be on or flashing; but if dead, then it means the wireless router could not be initialized normally, check whether the WAN wire is connected correctly, or restart or pull out the power plug and plug it in again until it works normally.

2) Check if the firewall, shared Internet proxy server software, Internet acceleration software has been installed, if they are, stop this kind of software, connect to the Internet and test, check whether the speed recovers to normal;

3) IF Internet is unstable, then you can first try disabling the firewall, test whether it's stable or not. Then start other related settings. Additionally, firewall or IE browser failure will also cause a connection error where it doesn't open the webpage.

191)   HP G62-130ET laptop could not connect to Internet

Failure symptoms:

Client states that it's the first time today that his HP laptop can't connect to the Internet, including the desktop machine.

Solution:

If all laptops and desktops can't connect to the Internet, it means the problem must be irrelevant with the computer itself; the problem is on the router, DSL Modem and related cables, This failure symptom obviously belongs to the description of flowchart 10, according to the repair method of sequence Start->A-1->A-2->A-3->A-5->A-6->B-1->B-2

Repair summary:

For some reason the most common network failure is due to the DSL Modem. Generally, we can reset the DSL Modem to default value to solve laptop failure that laptop can't connect to the wireless Internet.

A)   Find the little reset hole on the DSL Modem.
B)   Cut off the DSL Modem's power; find something thin like a pen head to press the Reset button;
C)   Power on the DSL Modem, wait about 5 to 10 seconds then release, the reset is done; however, this time the problem remains. Enter repair flow Step: B-1, Now check RJ45 wire connection situation, finding that the plastic plug of the cable is distorted; the external insulated tube of the wire is broken and probably damaged internally. After changing the RJ45 wire, the problem still exists; enter Step: B-2; reset the wireless router to default value, as a result, the failure disappears.

Hint:

There's are a lot of connection wires between the DSL Modem, wireless router and computer, while many users don't care about these cables much. Usually these cables would be placed in corners and under chairs and tables. After moving chairs and tables, cables get loose or damaged and then failure occurs and user can do nothing with them anymore. Start from the cable interface, remove plastic plug of the cable from the two ends and then plug it in again. Bad contact between network cables could be eliminated this way. However, if such a problem as below occurs, then change the cable to solve the problem;

a) There might be damage inside, or the cable has a bad contact, the cable's quality of signal transmission is below the average.

b) The connection between DSL Modem and the telephone line or the Ethernet cable is bad, or the connection between the telephone line and the DSL splitter is bad.

192) HP COMPAQ 6735S laptop can't connect to Internet

Failure symptoms:

Client states that the laptop can't connect to the Internet, but after an hour, it goes offline. Even when the indoor temperature is high, offline problem occurs. However, the laptop can surf the Internet for a few hours without any problem in other offices.

Solution:

Now that the laptop can work elsewhere it proves the laptop isn't the issue.

This failure symptom obviously belongs to the description of flowchart 10, according to the repair method of sequence: Start->A-1->A-2->A-4->B-2->A-6->A-5->A-6->B-1->B-3

Repair summary:

Offline failure that usually occurs after an hour usually means it's relevant with temperature. Remove and install the wire connection between wireless router and the Modem, the problem isn't solved; enter repair flow Step: B-3, change the router with one that works and connect according to the factory settings and the failure disappears. We now know the router had overheating problems.

Hint:

Overheating of router and DSL Modem would lead to network failure; it's a quite common.

(1) Router and DSL Modem should be placed somewhere well ventilated;

a) Avoid direct sunshine and ensure good heat radiation;
b) Never put paper, books or something else around the router, which would stop effective air flow.

(2) Set the software to start together with the operating system properly; when surfing on the Internet, don't run software that occupies a large amount of resource or open too many browser pages; otherwise you'll end up going offline because there will be a lack of available memory resource

193)   HP COMPAQ NX6310 laptop could not open webpages

Failure symptoms:

Client states his HP Compaq NX6310 laptop can't not connect to the Internet but yet the desktop is ok.

Solution:

Laptop and desktop computer have issues, which mean the issue regarding the router, DSL Modem and relevant cable. This failure symptom obviously belongs to the description of flowchart 10, according to the repair method of sequence: Start->A-1->A-2->A-3->A-5->A-6->B-1->B-2

Repair summary:

For some reason the most common network failure is due to the DSL Modem. Generally, we can reset the DSL Modem to default value to solve connection issues, however problem still exists. Check the RJ45 wire connection whether the cable is bent but after pulling out and plugging the plastic plug of the cable in again, the problem remains, so enters repair flow Step: B-2, reset the wireless router to default value doesn't change the issue. Then the repair is at a stand still. Looking back the repair process, there's a new symptom attracted my attention, the DSL link light is not always on, but continually flashing and then dies out. After a while, the symptom repeats itself, which indicate the telephone wire connection isn't good. After replacing the telephone wire, the failure disappears.

Hint:

1)   DSL link light has three statuses: on, flashing and out. Green light on means after DSL link is activated, signal is synchronized, data link is also done and ready to use
2)   If the light is flashing quickly, it means the DSL link is being activated, data link is still under construction, and you should be patient;
3)   If the light flashes and then dies out, or it hasn't lit at all, then it means the telephone line connection isn't good, or never connected

   a)   You should check whether the telephone works, if it does then you should contact your network provider and find out whether there's something wrong with the network;
   b)   If the telephone line doesn't work then the telephone line might have a short circuit or circuitry break failure, which you'll need a professional repair technician to check the circuitry.

194) HP ELITEBOOK 8530W laptop could not connect to Internet

Failure symptoms:

Client states that his HP laptop can't connect to the Internet, including the HP ELITEBOOK 8530W laptop, which also can't connect either.

Solution:

Now in this case that all laptops and desktop computers can't connect to the Internet, it means the problem is irrelevant with the computer themselves; the problem is on the router, DSL Modem and relevant cables. This failure symptom obviously belongs to the description of flowchart 10, according to the repair method of sequence: Start->A-1->A-2->A-4->B-2->A-6->A-5->A-6->B-1->B-3->B-4

Repair summary:

The point is to reset the DSL Modem and wireless router to default value to solve the problem. However, after doing this, the problem still exists. Remove and install the plastic plug of the cable again, the problem is still unsolved; however, there's one new symptom drawing my attention that the Ethernet (LAN Link) light is not always on. This DSL Modem has an interface problem. When I move the cable from left to right with my hands, the Ethernet light at the front side of DSL Modem is suddenly comes on and suddenly goes out, which means the wireless router can't connect the Modem normally. Check whether WAN cable is connected tightly, pull out the cable, replace it and plug it back in, when I hold the plastic plug of the cable, at this moment, the Ethernet (LAN Link) light is always on; however, once I take my hands off the cable, the light would go out. It seems obvious that the problem is with the DSL Modem's Ethernet interface; therefore, we are sure the Ethernet interface is loose; after changing DSL Modem, the failure is finally resolved.

Hint:

(1) Ethernet (LAN Link) light is always on, when green light is always on, it means the wireless router or network card is correctly connected with the DSL Modem by the cable and ready to use

(2) If the light flashes, then it means there's data transmission on the data link;

(3) If the light is out for a long time, then it means the MODEM hasn't connected with the wireless router (or computer network card). If when you move the DSL Modem, the light is on occasionally, then it means the cable connection is not that good; you should focus on checking the connection of the RJ45 cable and should consider that the problem is the Modem Ethernet interface is loose;

(4) All other light also has its own meaning, to know the details, please refer to the chapter 10.2.5 of this article, Step: A-3, Step: A-6.

10.3.4 Six repair cases for HP laptop Internet failure caused by other reasons

195) HP COMPAQ NX9105 laptop can't connect to the Internet after changing locations

Failure symptoms:

Client states that both office and home have a wireless network, and when at the office laptop connects to the companies' wireless network but when at home, it fails to connect wirelessly.

Solution:

This failure symptom obviously belongs to the description of flowchart 10, according to the repair method of sequence: Start->A-1->A-2->A-4->B-2

Repair summary:

Probably there are few reasons causing such a failure as below:

(1) SSID (Service Set Identifier) configuration hasn't been updated. Different wireless networks use different SSIDs, if SSID configuration is incorrect, you cannot ping through AP. Laptop neglects this AP and looks for new AP according to SSID configuration.
(2) WEP encryption. If the WEP key used is different, the wireless client will not connect with the new wireless AP. If the WEP configuration is incorrect, wireless client will not get IP address from DHCP server. After resetting it, the problem is resolved.

Hint:

IP address information. Generally speaking, wireless AP would automatically distribute IP address for wireless client. If you set up IP address for wireless client manually, then this client will not communicate with the new AP.

To solve this problem, you can use the solutions below:

(1) When accessing a new wireless network, change the SSID setting of the client.
(2) If it needs a key (password) to access the wireless network, then input that key in to access it.
(3) Generally, it's ok to use the IP address distributed by wireless AP. If you need to use static IP address, then you'd have to ensure the IP addresses of this static IP address and wireless AP are within the same network segment.

196) HP ELITEBOOK 8530P laptop's settings are all correct, but it fails to access the wireless network

Failure symptoms:

Client states that the router at home supports wireless network access, He then sets it up according to the wireless configuration, including WEP encryption, SSID and IP address information (auto get IP address information) and so on but, it still fails to access the wireless network.

Solution:

This failure symptom obviously belongs to the description of flowchart 10, according to the repair method of sequence: Start->A-1->A-2->A-4->B-2

Repair summary:

Through the network we can directly ping the wireless access point, but cannot ping it wirelessly. Basically we can come to the conclusion that the failure is temporary. However, after debugging, the problem remains. Testing the signal strength of the access point, we find that the signal strength is quite weak. The client said that he didn't change anything, so he logged in to the management page of the router with the administrator's account and password. Reset the router to default value, and changed the channel of the wireless access and after testing, the signal increased and the problem is resolved.

Hint:

It is found that during this repair process there's a Wi-Fi network with the same channel in the network neighbourhood. And the signal strength difference is not obvious, so it's quite likely that the laptop links to the network neighbourhood incorrectly, therefore affecting the Internet access. For such a situation, the result is that the signals interfere with each other. The best solution is to change the channel of the wireless access point.

197) HP PRESARIO V3624AU laptop can't connect to the wireless network

Failure symptoms:

Client states that the laptop was connecting to the wireless network, but now the connection is no longer working.

Solution:

This failure symptom obviously belongs to the description of flowchart 10, according to the repair method of sequence: Start->A-1->C-1->C-2->C-3->C-5->D-3->D-2

Repair summary:

Windows XP SP2 can repair a damaged wireless network connection automatically. Execute the operation steps below, using the repair function to fix:

1. Click "Start"—"Connect to", and then click "Display all connections";
2. Right click "Wireless network connection" icon, and then choose "Repair";
3. During the next few minutes, Windows will reset the network adapter and try reconnecting to a preferred network. But the result of this repair process is still unsuccessful.

However, such a problem occurs quite often, laptop doesn't auto connect to wireless network. Generally, computers have two wireless management tools, one is with the Windows operating system and the other is with the one provided by the laptop manufacturer. By default, Windows wireless Zero management tool is used with the following steps:

1. Start—Control Panel—Network connection, and right click "Wireless network connection", choose "View available wireless connections";
2. A list of available network is shown choose the right one, enter the password if required and issue is solved.

Hint:

a) You must first install Windows XP Service Pack 2 before doing these operations. If you aren't sure whether it's updated, then access the HP Windows XP Service Pack 2 for more detailed information.
b) If laptop can't connect to a wireless network, ensure the Windows Wireless Zero Configuration is installed. Afterwards, execute the steps below.

   1. Click "Start";
   2. Click "Run";
   3. Enter "service.msc", but without the quotation marks.
   4. Find Wireless Zero Configuration;
   5. Right click on "Wireless Zero Configuration";
   6. Choose "Properties";
   7. Under "Boot type", choose "Automatic" (If still now chosen yet);
   8. Under "Service status", click "Enabled";
   9. Click "OK" button.
   10. Close "Service" window.

198) PAVILION DV5170US can't find other computers within the same wireless network

Failure symptoms:

Clients states his laptop uses the Vista system at home, also the wireless network established is connected, and chooses "Family" as his preferred network and the "Network discovery" and "Shared Public folder" is also on. "Password protection share" is disabled. Computer firewall is disabled too. All computers within the "network" only see themselves and not the others.

Solution:

This failure symptom obviously belongs to the description of flowchart 10, according to the repair method of sequence: Start->A-1->C-1->C-2->C-3->C-5->D-3->D-2

Repair summary:

When using the XP system, you have to create a new network in the Network Neighbourhood to start the network installation wizard.

a) Enable Guest account;

b) Go to Control Panel—Local Security policies—Local policies—User Rights Assignment, add Guest account to "Access this computer from network", and delete Guest account from "Refuse to access this computer from network";

c) My Computer—Tools—Folder options—View—Remove the hook before the option "Use simple file share (recommended)";

d) Set shared folder;

e) Control Panel—Management tool—Local Security Policies—Local policies—Security options, set "Network access: local account share and safe mode" as "Only validate local Guest user with Guest identity" (**Optional**, this option setup can cancel the dialog asking to enter password when accessing or you can set it as "Classic—local user validate with own identity" according to different situations);

f) Right click "My computer"—"Properties"—"Computer name", whether your LAN work group name appears on the option card, such as "Work" and so on. And then click "Network ID" button, start "Network Identification wizard"; click "Next", choose the option "local host is one part of commercial network, connect to other working computers with it"; click "Next", and choose "Company uses network without domain"; click "Next" button, and then enter the work group name of your LAN, such as "work", and then click "Next" button again; at last, click "Finish" button to finish the settings. Afterwards, connect to wireless network, and then the problem is solved.

Hint:

If the problem isn't solved, then you'd have to check:

1. Check the physical connection between computers. Network card is the basic device for connecting, on desktop computer, every network card's back side light should be on, which indicates normal

2. Make sure all computers have TCP/IP installed to work normally. In Windows XP system, TCP/IP is already installed by default. However, if there's problem with the network, then it would not be easy to reinstall TCP/IP after you uninstall it; if you need to reinstall TCP/IP to recover TCP/IP stack back to original status, then you can use Net Shell Utility to reset TCP/IP stack, letting it recover to the initial status when installing the operating system;

3. Use ping command to test the connection between two computers within the network; ping other computer's IP address, and at command Hint, enter "ping ****" (**** is the IP address of another computer), and then press the enter button and you should be able to see a few replies from the other computer;

4. Use ping command to test the name parsing in the network, whether it could ping computer name successfully, and the computer name is the name of the remote computer. With the ping command, we can test the computer connection.

5. To install the network components correctly, first right click on Network Neighbourhood—Properties, and choose the network card to share. Set the IP within the same network segment of the LAN, such as 192.168.1.x network segment. And then check TCP/IP advanced property, whether NETBIOS is enabled.

199) HP PAVILION DV2505TX laptop's wireless Internet speed is slow

Failure symptoms:

A client state that his HP DV2505TX laptop's wireless speed is quite slow and often goes offline.

Solution:

This failure symptom obviously belongs to the description of flowchart 10, according to the repair method of sequence: Start->A-1->C-1->C-2->C-3->C-5->D-3->D-2

Repair summary:

1. Set up virtual memory; ensure the laptop has enough memory space to support multi-application from running. Here's the setup method: set the initial size 1.5 times the size of your memory capacity to a maximum set of 3 times the memory capacity (for example, if you have 512MB, set it to 768 MB and 1536 MB; if memory capacity is 1GB, then set it 1536 MB and 3072 MB);

2. Windows XP system preserves 20% bandwidth by default. Find "Computer configuration"—"Administrative template"—"Network"—"Quos data package debugger", choose the option "Limit preferable bandwidth" at the right side, and choose "Properties" to open limit preferable bandwidth property dialog, and choose "Enabled", set the original "20" value to "0";

3. Too many webpage cache files will affect network speed obviously. To increase the Internet speed, you'd have to delete temporary files in cache periodically. Here are the concrete operation steps: open IE browser—Tools—Internet options—Delete all Internet records and garbage files.

4. It will affect network speed severely if there are too many applications starting at start-up. In "Start"—"Run", enter "msconfig" to open System Configuration Utility Editor. Find "Start-up" and remove the useless start-up items. Click "OK" and restart the computer.

5. Defragment to accelerate system speed; of course network speed will improve too. Here's the method: right click on drive C—Properties—Tools—Start defragmentation. The defragment time is long, so do this when not using the computer;

6. Good heat radiation is helpful to accelerate network speed. Therefore, you should keep laptop as cool as possible, and adding a USB fan will greatly help.

7. Viruses and Trojans will cause network speed to slow down. First use antivirus software to scan the entire disk. Also you should upgrade the antivirus software everyday.

8. If laptop is running along with the Internet for a long time it can also slow the connection and it is quite normal. The speed will increase if you restart the computer. The problem should now be solved.

Hint:

a) Placing the wireless router or the wireless node device accurately is an effective approach to accelerate network speed. Using Nets tumbler tool, we can find the most ideal node position within the wireless LAN letting the signal of the wireless node device cover every corner.

b) First find and download Nets tumbler from network, after finishing installing the application, enable the wireless network card device installed in movable work station to look for wireless access point within the local wireless LAN. And then find the most ideal place to position it for the wireless router or wireless node device within local wireless LAN.

c) Place the wireless router device (wireless node device) in the best possible area to maximize connection.

200) HP PAVILION DV6700 laptop could not connect to wireless network

Failure symptoms:

Client states HP Pavilion DV6700 laptop has an internal wireless network card, and two days ago, the wireless light went off; however, it still connects to the wireless router. But on this day it fails to connect to the Internet, but the other computers work normally.

Solution:

This failure symptom obviously belongs to the description of flowchart 10, according to the repair method of sequence: Start->Start->A-1->C-1->C-2->C-3->C-5->D-3->D-4->D-5

Repair summary:

Other computers work normally and access to the Internet, which means the wireless router and DSL Modem have no issues, go to repair step C-5 to consider. Given the driver is easy to get damaged, I uninstall the existed driver and then install a new driver, but the problem still remains.

Enter repair flow step D-4, considering that the wireless light is out, then probably the failure is related to the internal wireless network card. Remove and install the internal wireless network card and clean any dust from it, but the failure still exists; try replacing the network card (same as the original one), uninstall the original wireless network's driver, and reinstall and the failure disappears.

Hint:

1) After making sure that the wireless router and DSL Modem have no problem, disable wireless network of all suspected laptops. Change to cable to connect to the router and judge whether there's a problem with the operating system. If the cabled network works normally, then it means the problem is related to the operating system, you need to first solve the software problem, and then solve the wireless network problem.

2) The new wireless network card should be the same or as close to the original one card, if it's an Intel then replace with an Intel. The model should be same, and this is to avoid any incompatible problems caused. Make sure the new wireless network card works normally.

CHAPTER 11

Acoustic system failure repair

11.1 Laptop sound card failure occurrence and treatment

11.1.1 Common failure symptoms of a laptop audio system;

a) Windows prompts that no hardware driver is found;
b) The operating system does not recognize the sound card;
c) The laptop sound distorts or there's no sound and just noise;
d) The laptop sound card makes very loud noises;
e) The internal speaker emits no sound, but the external earphone works normally;
f) The external earphone has no sound, but the internal speaker is OK;
g) One internal speaker has no sound; and the other has no sound or very low sound;
h) The speaker icon controlling volume in the taskbar is missing, and volume cannot be controlled;
i) The laptop internal speaker and the external earphone both have no sound;
j) The laptop will not record audio normally;
k) The laptop will not play wav and midi music;
l) No sound when playing a music CD;
m) No sound when the computer plays movies etc;
n) When you speak into the microphone, the audio level indicator shows no sound at all; when voice chatting, or you cannot hear sound from the other side or the other side cannot hear you;
o) The laptop microphone is noisy or when on voice chat, there are echoes from the microphone;

11.1.2 Laptop sound failure cause and analysis

a)   Windows prompts that no hardware driver is found;

The causes for this failure probably are:

(1)   The first time loading the driver did not complete normally;
(2)   A driver file was deleted, but the driver file remained in the registry table, and did not uninstall completely;
(3)   The sound card driver is too old, and caused a system failure;
(4)   A new problem is caused by updating the operating system, because the update of the driver is not synchronized with the operating system update;
(5)   A failure is caused because the sound card driver is installed incorrectly;

b)   The operating system did not recognize the sound card;

(1)   Possible hardware damage; the sound card does not appear in the device manager, and the operating system does not recognize it;
(2)   There are sound card functions available for choice in the laptop BIOS, but you chose to disable it;
(3)   The laptop has HD Audio technology, but the operating system is too old and does not have the software to handle it. It does not recognize the sound card, the message "Unknown device" appears in the list of the device manager;
(4)   The necessary chip drivers are not installed, and cannot parse the 2 to 3 drive devices included in "Unknown device". This leads to the problem that the sound card driver is not installed, and the failure to recognize it;
(5)   The failure is caused because the wrong sound card driver is installed;

c)   The laptop sound is distorted or there's only noise and no sound

(1)   There's a fault with the sound card chip (hardware);
(2)   The cable for the loudhailer (sound reproduction devices from microphone or other audio generating equipment, through to speaker) has a problem, maybe it is not long enough, possibly damaged, or it cannot be moved to the right position, thus creating poor sound affects;
(3)   The system sound player software has problems or the system audio settings are not correct, possibly on mute or the volume is too low.
(4)   The internal sound output wiring or the internal jack are not making a solid connection causing the audio to be noisy;
(5)   Poor ventilation or internal cooling problems make the laptop internal temperature rise too high, and the sound card is affected by the high heat;
(6)   The failure is caused because the wrong sound card driver is installed;

d) The laptop speaker makes very loud static noise;

(1) There's a fault with the motherboard, the shielding could be defective or grounding no longer effective and interference is generated into the sound card chip;

(2) There are power supply problems on the motherboard; possibly caused by aging capacitors or other components creating noise or not filtering properly, leading to noise in the audio.

(3) A speaker diaphragm is damaged or degraded due to aging, dampness, or volume set too high.

(4) The computer audio output jack is worn or damaged and no longer provides a good connection.

(5) The laptop's anti-jamming ability is diminished, and there is electromagnetic wave

(6) Interference from devices, such as the power adapter, fridge, or speakers that can interfere with it.

(7) The wrong sound card driver is installed, which leads to incompatibility problems.

e) The internal speaker is not working, but the external earphone works fine.

(1) You have a sound card volume control on the keyboard of the laptop, also there's the slide volume adjustment in operating system as well as a mute. You should check and adjust these.

(2) The speaker's diaphragm is damaged as in d)-3 above and maybe a connecting wire are broken.

(3) The sound jack is defective or a bad solder joint prevents the signal from reaching, the internal speaker. The sound jack has contacts that cut out the speaker when the earphones are plugged in.

(4) The operating system (or third party software) sound control panel options are not correctly set and is selecting the external sound rather than the internal loudhailer;

f) The external earphone does not work, but the internal speaker is normal;

(1) The plug of the external earphone is connected to the sound input or some other jack rather than the earphone jack.

(2) The earphone jack is worn, damaged, or the wires to it are open or no longer soldered properly, thus preventing the audio from reaching the earphone.

(3) The earphones themselves are no longer working because the connections in the plug on the external earphones are open circuit or some other problem with it.

(4) There are improper settings in the software audio effects manager.

g) **There is only one internal speaker emitting sound, the other is not working or the sound is extremely low**

(1) There are incorrect settings in the sound control panel in the third party software or operating system, generally, the volume balance adjustment slide should be in the middle position and not adjusted too far left or too far right. This would cause the problem.

(2) One speaker's diaphragm is affected as in e) 2 above.

(3) The audio output jack is defective as in e) 3 above or the wires or solders connections open circuit thus interrupting the flow of the audio signal to one of the speakers.

(4) There's something wrong with the audio chip on the motherboard that causes an absence of signal to the speaker.

h) **The speaker icon in the taskbar is missing, and the audio volume cannot be controlled**

(1) There's a virus or Trojan invasion in the operating system, or the volume control application is missing or corrupted;

(2) The control panel is not set up, which means there are no volume settings for the audio and video devices. You should select the option "put volume icon to taskbar";

(3) The sound card driver is defective, or an updated audio driver is not compatible;

i) **Both the laptop internal speaker and external earphone are not working**

(1) The sound card chip (hardware) has faults, and is not working properly;

(2) The internal loudhailer is not working, because there's a problem with the internal sound output wire or the internal jack is not tight enough;

(3) The system player software has problems or there's a virus or Trojan invasion in the operating system, or the control application file is missing or corrupted;

(4) Poor laptop cooling causes the laptop temperature to be high and the sound card cannot work normally at this temperature;

(5) The sound card driver is not installed or is installed incorrectly, causing the failure.

j) **The laptop does not record audio normally**

(1) The internal microphone may be blocked by tape, or you are speaking too far from the microphone.

(2) Your external microphone is plugged into the wrong jack;

(3) The control panel is not set up, which means you haven't set up the microphone yet. Make sure you check microphone at the option checkbox;

(4)   The audio device is on mute, or the microphone volume is not high enough;

(5)   There's a problem with your microphone hardware;

(6)   The external microphone jack is defective or the internal microphone has been jarred sufficiently to break a solder joint.

(7)   The record function is not started by the third party software or the operating system, or there's a virus or Trojan invasion, or the control application file is missing or corrupted;

k)   **The laptop will not play wav or midi music**

(1)   The sound card driver does not support wav or midi because it is too old or corrupted

(2)   Your windows version is too old and a newer one is needed, the program you edited will not run normally and is not compatible,

(3)   The antivirus software is too old or the version is incompatible with your Windows system. The disk utility or other system applications have conflicts.

(4)   Virus or Trojan damage makes important MIDI files corrupt and then the MIDI music cannot be played;

(5)   The MIDI channel in the Windows volume control is set to mute mode.

l)   **There is no sound when playing a music CD**

(1)   The windows volume control channel is set in mute mode;

(2)   The DVD-ROM has no digital replay function, but it's enabled when setting up;

(3)   The DVD-ROM device should enable digital CD audio, but it was not enabled when setting up;

(4)   The CD itself has some physical faults;

(5)   The part of the DVD-ROM device laser head that reads the CD has aged severely and no longer works;

(6)   The operating system or Windows Media Player files are corrupted.

m)   **There is no sound when the computer is playing movies or video;**

(1)   If you cannot hear a series of system sounds during computer on/off operations, please follow the case solution in << i) Both the laptop internal speaker and external earphone are not working>>;

(2)   The sound card driver is too old or corrupted or maybe has not been installed.

(3)   The antivirus software or disk utility has software conflicts with other system applications;

(4)   Virus or Trojan damage, has corrupted important MIDI playing files and, the MIDI audio cannot be played;

(5)   The player volume control channel is set on mute mode or the volume is turned to the minimum;

n) **There's no sound indication in the speaker sound box when you talk into the microphone, and when doing voice chat, or you cannot hear the other person's voice or they cannot hear your voice**

Both sides should check these points as below:

(1) The internal microphone may be blocked by tape, or you are speaking too far from the microphone.
(2) Your external microphone is plugged into the wrong jack;
(3) The control panel is not set up, which means you haven't set up the microphone yet. Make sure you check microphone at the option checkbox;
(4) The audio device is on mute, or the microphone volume is not high enough;
(5) There's a problem with microphone hardware;
(6) The external microphone jack is defective or the internal microphone has been jarred sufficiently to break a solder joint.
(7) QQ chatting interface software or the operating system voice function is not enabled yet;
(8) There's a virus or Trojan invasion, important files of the audio control application are missing or corrupted;

o) **The laptop microphone itself is noisy or when you are voice chatting, there are echoes from the microphone**

(1) If the computer's noise is continuous, including system sounds, then please follow the solution in the case <<d) The laptop speaker makes static loud noise >>;
(2) The sound mixture setting for the microphone is not correct;
(3) The microphone is set at enhanced status and there's a conflict with other hardware or software;
(4) The external microphone plug or the internal jack are worn and not tight enough, or the internal microphone's connection wire is off and you are picking up power line interference;
(5) The external microphone's setting for the sound box speaker is incorrect and makes the sound replay from the speaker;
(6) The laptop's anti-jamming ability is diminished, and there is electromagnetic wave interference from devices, such as the power adapter, fridge, speakers that interfere with it.
(7) The microphone itself has hardware problems;
(8) Poor ventilation or internal cooling problems make the laptop internal temperature rise too high, and the sound card is affected by the high heat;
(9) The wrong sound card driver is installed, or a virus or Trojan has damaged the driver;
(10) The acoustic environment where the computer is used is not good; there can be sound echo or reverberation causing the problem.
(11) The network or other reasons like missing data, incomplete files, and improper plug-ins are installed, and can all cause these abnormal symptoms;

11.1.3 Diagnosis for common laptop audio failures

In the chapter 1 <<1.4.2 6 "Hardware" methods to repair laptop>>, the method we discuss will be used on the diagnosis for audio failures.

For the diagnosis of a soundless speaker, first of all, we have to use the observation method.

The observation should not only be careful, but also intensive. Make initial diagnoses of the suspected sound card to determine if the failure caused comes from hardware or software or both.

Software problem:

1. Windows prompts no hardware driver is found;
2. There is a yellow mark in the list of the device manager;
3. The failure is caused because the wrong sound card driver is installed;
4. The function to disable the sound card is chosen in laptop BIOS;
5. There is an error with the player software settings, the volume is set too low, or mute is selected.
6. The hardware control switch is not open or the volume is set too low;
7. There's electromagnetic wave interference in the area;
8. There's a virus or Trojan invasion in the operating system and the volume control application is lost or corrupted;

Hardware problem: after excluding the software problems above, look for these symptoms:

(1) The sound card is not in the list of the device manager;
(2) The internal speaker sound distorts or there's only noise but no sound, while the external speaker is OK;
(3) There's only one internal speaker with sound and the two external speakers are functioning OK;
(4) The internal microphone is not working but the external microphone works OK.

It may be related to both software and hardware problems

(1) The laptop internal speakers and external earphone are not working;
(2) The internal speaker and external earphone sound is distorted or there's only noise but no sound.
(3) Only one internal speaker and one external earphone works;
(4) The internal and external microphones are not working;

Next you can use the knocking method

Sometimes certain parts of the laptop may have bad contacts and can cause your sound problems. It is difficult to locate and repair these problems. The knocking method is the easiest way. You knock the suspected component with a rubber hammer, or other insulated tool to make the failure reoccur without damaging it. This can identify the location of the problem.

Next use the replacement method

The replacement method uses a USB sound card to take the place of the suspected sound card on the motherboard. Install it and restart the laptop to see if the failure symptom disappears or changes or not, If it disappears or there's a change, (most cases, XP, Vista, Win 7 all include the driver), you have an important clue. If the USB sound card works, then it means the failure is not in the operating system. We now just follow the sequence "first simple and then complex" to further investigate the problem. You can first consider whether there's a problem with the player software driver compatibility. If that is OK then consider whether the internal speaker or the sound card interface may have a problem or not, and if external speaker and microphone are working normally. Then consider whether the internal speaker, cable and sound card itself has problems. Finally look at the sound card interfacing hardware and circuitry.

At last, cleaning

Too much heat build up due to laptop cooling problems can make the laptop temperature rise too high, and the sound card cannot work normally under this extreme environment;

Mostly it's caused by too much dust in the machine, which needs to be cleaned during the process of repair. This includes dust inside and outside of the machine. You should first clean up the dust before continuing with the following troubleshooting and repair.

When you clean the motherboard, first you must cut off all power supplies, including the motherboard battery; then make sure you don't cause static electricity damage to components while you are doing this. Use a plastic brush or dust collector to clean the dust. When you use a metal tool, you need to ground out static in your body first. Now, observe the sound card integrated circuit chips, other components and connectors, to see if there are bad soldering connections or humidity symptoms. Check for motherboard distortion, and whether components are discoloured or liquid has leaked

A magnifying glass can reveal more problems than with the naked eye.

11.1.4 Troubleshooting common failures of laptop sound

a)   Windows prompts that no hardware driver is found

1)   Check that the driver for the sound card is installed properly, and whether there's an external device or not. Right click "My computer" and choose Properties—hardware—device manager, see if there's a yellow exclamation mark . . .

2)   If there's a yellow exclamation mark, it means no driver is installed, and you need to download and install one;

3)   If there's no yellow exclamation mark, then first uninstall the driver, and then download and install a new driver;

4)   If the driver cannot be uninstalled, then you need a software tool to uninstall it, or first install the driver, and then uninstall the driver. Next install the latest driver;

5)   upgrade the driver for the sound card when you update the operating system;

b)   The operating system does not recognize the sound card;

(1)   Check the laptop BIOS for a sound card function option, if there is one, then enable it;

(2)   Check that the sound card is listed in the device manager, if not, it means the hardware is defective, and you can only use a USB port to replace it with an external one;

(3)   If it is listed in the device manager, then check to see if the laptop uses HD Audio technology. The operating system may be incompatible with it, so consider updating the operating system;

(4)   If it is listed in the device manager, but there are the words "Unknown device" appearing in the list, it means you'd have to install the driver for the chip. Uninstall the 2 to 3 drive devices included in Unknown device, and then install the sound card driver;

(5)   After finishing the job above, if there's still no sound, then it's quite likely that you have installed the wrong sound card driver. Try it again making sure you have the right driver. Uninstall the driver, and then download the latest the driver and install it;

c) The laptop sound distorts or there's only noise but no sound

(1)   Connect an external earphone and check whether it works; if not, then please follow the case << i) the laptop internal speaker and external earphone both have no sound >> to deal with it;

(2)   If the external earphone works normally, then check the system sound player software. If it is not working, just reinstall and update the player. Pay attention to the property settings for the sound, don't set it on mute mode or turn the volume too low.

(3)   After the above steps, if the failure still exists, then you might have the wrong sound card driver installed. Uninstall the driver and then download the latest driver and install it;

(4)   Open the laptop; test it with a known working speaker. Use alligator clips or some other method for a temporary connection, and connect this speaker to the terminals of the existing speaker. Carefully partially reassemble the laptop enough to power it up and listen for sound. If there is no sound then likely the speaker is OK.

(5)   Check to see if the audio input jack is inhibiting the sound. Make a temporary connection directly from the circuit board audio output to the speaker thus bypassing the jack. You might also see a more convenient way to do this.

Assemble and power up the computer as in step 4. Listen for sound. If you have normal sound you know your problem is in the jack. Hearing AC hum may indicate the problem is elsewhere or your temporary connection is not right.

(6) If your laptop is overheated because of defective cooling or reduced ventilation, your sound card is probably affected.

d) Laptop speaker makes very loud noise and you have completed step c) above

(1) Connect the external earphone to check if the noise is still there or very loud; if not, then it's quite likely the problem is in the internal loudhailer system, please replace and test it;

(2) If the external earphone noise is also very loud, then next locate external interfering sources that may be causing it. They can come through your AC connection or by direct radiation. Some of these are a daylight lamp, fridge, dust collector, sound device and so on. Turn them off one at a time and see if the noise disappears.

(3) Boot up the laptop in battery mode, then with just the power adapter and also try another working power adapter;

(4) uninstall the sound card driver, and then download the latest driver and install it;

(5) Disconnect with the internal jack, and connect the sound output wire directly to the internal speaker interface if you haven't already done this in step c);

(6) disconnect the internal microphone temporarily;

(7) Change the laptop motherboard;

e) Internal speaker has no sound, but the external earphone works normally;

(1) If there's a sound card volume option on the keyboard of the laptop, then turn the volume to the maximum;

(2) Check the sound property settings of the player software, don't set it on mute mode or turn the volume too low . . . .

(3) Uninstall audio player software in the system; install Microsoft or other third party player software temporarily;

(4) Open the laptop, and install new or working speakers;

(5) Temporarily bypass the internal jack by connecting the sound output wire directly to the internal speaker interface;

f) The external earphones are not working, but the internal speaker works OK

(1) Try plugging a known working external earphone to the audio output jack;

(2) uninstall the system sound player software, install Microsoft or other third party players temporarily, and set up correctly;

(3) Check the jack connections to the circuit board by bypassing the internal connector on the circuit board, by soldering the sound output wire directly to the external earphone interface;

(4) Change the internal sound connector, or use a USB sound adapter to replace it;

g) There's only one internal speaker having sound, but the other one has nothing or the sound is extremely low.

    (1) reset the sound player and the sound control panel in the operating system, keep the volume balance adjustment slide in the center position;

    (2) uninstall the sound player in the system, install another player temporarily, and set it up correctly;

    (3) Try plugging a known working external earphone to the audio output jack; if the failure disappears, then it means the problem is in the sound connection on the circuit board or the internal loudhailer, refer to the process in item (4), if the failure doesn't disappear, then it means the problem is on the sound jack or the motherboard circuit, you can refer to the process in item (5);

    (4) Disconnect the internal jack, and connect the wires directly to the internal speaker interface; if the problem disappears, then the problem should be a bad solder joint or sound connector, which needs to soldered again or changed; if the failure doesn't disappear, then it means the problem is in the internal loudhailer, you can change it;

    (5) If the internal speaker and external earphone both have the same failure symptom, then under the precondition that you have excluded the problem of the sound jack or connector on the board, you can assume that there's something wrong with the motherboard circuit; just change the motherboard or use a USB sound adapter to replace it;

h) The speaker icon controlling volume in the taskbar is missing and the volume cannot be controlled.

    (1) In the control panel, set the volume for the audio and video devices, put the volume icon into the taskbar, and mark the checkbox before the option frame;

    (2) scan the disk operating system, clear all viruses and Trojans;

    (3) uninstall the sound card driver, and then download the latest driver and install it;

    (4) Consider reinstalling the operating system.

i) The laptop internal speaker and external earphone both have no sound

    (1) Uninstall the sound card driver, and then download the latest driver and install it;

    (2) scan the disk operation system, clear all viruses and Trojans;

    (3) uninstall the system sound players, install other third party player software temporarily, and set it up correctly;

    (4) Disconnect the internal jack, and connect the sound output wire directly to the internal speaker interface, if the failure disappears, then it means the problem is a bad solder connection or a sound jack problem. Re-soldering or install a new jack as required;

    (5) If the internal speaker and external earphone has the same failure symptom, then under the precondition that you have excluded the problem of the sound jack, we can assume there's something wrong with the motherboard circuit, we

can only change the motherboard or use a USB sound adapter to replace the defective circuitry.

j)   The laptop does not record normally

(1)   Check the internal microphone sound input surface for blockage like adhesive tape and putty;
(2)   Check the settings of the control panel, find the microphone column, and then mark the checkbox before the option frame;
(3)   scan the disk operating system, clean up all viruses and Trojans;
(4)   uninstall the recording software, install other recording software temporarily, and set the recording/playing functions correctly;
(5)   Try plugging in a known good external microphone to the sound input jack; if the failure disappears, then it means the problem is in the internal microphone, refer to the process in (6); if the failure happens to record jack or the motherboard circuit, then please refer to the process in
(6)   Disconnect the internal microphone, and install a known good internal microphone to test or replace it, if the failure disappears, then it means the problem was in the internal microphone;
(7)   After changing the internal microphone, if the failure still exists, and the external microphone, also does not work, then we can assume that the problem is on the motherboard. You can use a USB sound adapter to bypass the problem and not have to deal with the motherboard.

k)   The laptop does not play wav and MIDI music

(1)   Check the MIDI channel settings in the Windows volume control, cancel mute mode;
(2)   After uninstalling the sound card driver, download the latest driver and install it;
(3)   scan the operating system on the disk, clean up all viruses and Trojans;
(4)   uninstall the sound player in the system, install another third party player temporarily and set it up correctly;
(5)   Uninstall antivirus software and disk utilities to solve software conflict problems;
(6)   update the application before compatibility becomes an issue as the OS is updated;

m)   There is no sound when playing a music CD;

(1)   Check the MIDI channel settings in the Windows volume control, cancel mute mode;
(2)   Uninstall sound player software in the system, install another third party player temporarily, and set it up correctly;
(3)   Check the settings of the CD, cancelling the digital replay function and use digital CD audio mode;
(4)   Change the DVD-ROM device;
(5)   clean the disk and reinstall the operating system;

n) There's no sound when the laptop is playing movies or other audio.

    (1) If you cannot hear a series of system sounds when the computer is turning on/ off, then please follow the case << I) Both laptop internal speaker and external earphone have no sound>> and deal with the problem;

    (2) Check the player volume control channel settings, cancel mute mode and adjust the volume higher;

    (3) uninstall the sound card driver, and then download the latest driver and install it;

    (4) Scan the operating system on the hard disk, and clean up all viruses and Trojans;

    (5) uninstall the system sound player software, install another third party player temporarily and set it up correctly;

    (6) uninstall the antivirus software and disk utilities to solve software conflict problems;

    (7) clean the disk and reinstall operating system;

p) There is no sound from the speaker sound box when you talk into microphone, and when you are voice chatting, or you cannot hear the other end or the other end does not hear your voice;

Both sides should check these points below:

    (1) Check the internal microphone sound input surface, for blockage like adhesive tape and putty

    (2) Check the control panel settings, find the microphone column, and hook the checkbox before the option frame;

    (3) Check the settings of the control channel in audio device, cancelling mute mode;

    (4) Uninstall QQ chatting software, and reinstall chatting software, then set up the software and the audio function in the operating system correctly;

    (5) Scan the operating system on the disk, and clean all viruses and Trojans;

    (6) Try a known working external microphone; if the failure disappears; then it means the problem is in the internal microphone, and please refer to (7) processing; if the failure doesn't disappear, then it means the problem is on your motherboard circuit, please refer to (8) processing;

    (7) Disconnect the internal microphone, install a working good internal microphone and test it; if the failure disappears, then it means the problem was in the internal microphone;

    (8) After changing the internal microphone, if the problem still exists, or the problem is the same even using the external microphone, then we can assume that the motherboard circuit has problems, you can just use a USB sound adapter to replace it to solve the problem and avoid fixing motherboard problems;

q) The laptop microphone is noisy or has echoes when voice chatting;

(1) If the laptop has continual noise, including system sound, then please follow the case in << d) the laptop speaker makes very loud noise>> to deal with it;

(2) check the microphone settings, set up the mix for the microphone properly;

(3) cancel the enhanced mode in microphone settings, in case it has conflicts with other hardware or software;

(4) Check the audio device control channel settings, adjust the volume properly;

(5) Uninstall the chat software in the system, reinstall new chat software and set up the software and the audio function in the operating system correctly and properly;

(6) Disable external interfering sources temporarily, one at a time, checking each time for noise. Typical sources are daylight lamp, fridge, dust collector, sound device and any others you may suspect. Interference can come through the AC lines or by over the air radiation

(7) Uninstall the sound card driver, and then download the latest driver and install it. Clean up all Trojans and viruses;

(8) replace with a USB sound adapter to solve the problem;

(9) Change the position of the microphone, move away from sound box speaker, in case it is feeding back through the microphone;

(10) Change the location of the laptop to another room. When using the laptop, be away from locations with loud noise, echo and dampness like in the basement;

(11) Try using a known working external microphone;

(12) add one external USB fan radiation unit under the laptop, in case the laptop internal temperature is rising too high;

11.2   Repair flow chart to eliminate Laptop Audio system failure

11.2.1 Repair shortcuts for laptop acoustic failures

You can solve this kind of failure with a routine driver uninstall method, and then reinstall the driver; or use the simple replacement method.

The repair process for laptop acoustic failures can be very complicated, because the occurrence of the failure may be due to hardware problems, driver problems, or software conflicts, or a combination of these.

In most cases incompatible drivers, issued software, viruses, and other software problems will cause these problems. Following are some shortcuts to use to more easily isolate and fix the problem. When you encounter sound problems, first use these steps to eliminate them.

1) 63% of laptop acoustic failures are from the sound card driver and the operating system First you need to determine that you have a sound card driver installed.

a) Right click "My Computer" and choose "Properties"—"Hardware"—"Device manager" and open it, find whether there's a yellow exclamation mark on the sound card driver, if there is yellow exclamation mark, then it means the driver hasn't been installed yet, you need to download and install one; if there is no yellow exclamation mark, then follow a) method to deal with the problem; Please take a look at Figure 11-1.

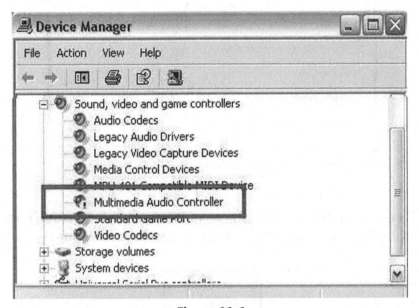

Figure 11-1

b) First uninstall the driver and then download the latest driver and install it;

c) If the driver could not be uninstalled, then you need a professional tool to uninstall the software, or first install the driver and then uninstall the driver again; next install the latest driver;

d) Make sure that the upgrade for the sound card driver is compatible with an operating system upgrade;

2) If there is a sound card listed in the device manager; however, the laptop has HD Audio technology, then the operating system might fail to recognize the sound card; and the words "Unknown device" would appear in the list, meaning that a chip driver needs to be installed. De-install the 2 to 3 drive devices included in Unknown device, and then reinstall the correct sound card driver;

a) After finishing the job above, if it's still soundless, then possibly you installed the wrong sound card driver. Recheck the specs. For the driver and install the right one if need be.

b) Some laptop keyboards have a volume option; increase the volume to the maximum;

Please take a look at Figure 11-2.

Figure 11-2

c) Check the sound property settings of the player software, don't set it to mute or adjust the volume too low . . . Please take a look at Figure 11-3.

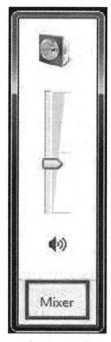

Figure 11-3

d) Uninstall the sound player software you are using; Install Microsoft or another third party player temporarily;
e) Clean all viruses and Trojans and consider reinstalling the operating system;

3) 25% of failures come from the internal sound output connector and the connecting cable of the sound card;

   a) Enter the BIOS Setup page of the laptop, if there's the setup for sound card function, please choose to enable it;
   b) Right click "My Computer" and choose "Properties"—"Hardware"—"Device manager" and open it; if there's no sound card listed, then it means the hardware is damaged, and you can only use a USB sound adapter to take the place of it;
   c) Insert a known good working external earphone into the audio output jack, check that it works in order to isolate the problem to the internal speaker;
   d) If the earphones are working, disconnect the wires from the rear of the sound jack, and connect them directly to the internal speaker interface;
   e) Replace the original internal speaker with a known good working speaker to test it, and resolder the output wire connections;
   f) Use a USB sound adapter if you cannot fix the problem;

If the problem is still not solved, then please continue to check more detailed troubleshooting methods; please refer to the second section of this chapter <<11.2.5 Laptop acoustic failure analysis and repair flow>>

11.2.2 63% of acoustic failures come from the sound card driver and operating system

Most failures, when you are prompted that the hardware driver is not found or does not recognize the sound card are caused by operating system settings and player settings or driver error.

Generally speaking, problems caused by the software include the conflict between drivers and software, and the conflict between hardware and software; usually, in the end, we find it's a problem of the operating system.

According to <<11.2.1 Repair shortcuts for laptop acoustic failures>>, first check the BIOS Setup page of the laptop, if there's the option for sound card function, then choose to enable it.

Next go to the device manager and check that there's a sound card listed; if there is not, then it means the hardware is damaged, please continue to use a more detailed troubleshooting method; please refer to the second section of this chapter <<11.2.5 Laptop sound failure analysis and repair flow>>.

After confirming there is a sound card listed, you can investigate the failure in the software. However, sometimes you will find that the sound card driver you've just installed or updated produces a blue screen failure immediately or the system interface freezes, then the conclusion will become much easier. Definitely it's a problem with the driver. The general solution is to boot the operating system under safe mode, and then uninstall the problem driver.

1)   Eliminate driver failures

If the wireless network card driver is only compatible with the Windows 7 system but is installed in the Windows XP system, then not only the sound card will not work, but also even a blue screen failure may occur, or the system would repeat restarting. Even if the driver installed is compatible with the operation system, but with a tiny difference of laptop models, it's quite possible an error may occur when installing the driver. Therefore, after installing a sound card driver, make sure to go to the device manager to check whether the driver is installed correctly or not; at least there should be no yellow exclamation mark on the sound card list; otherwise, it means that you haven't installed the driver correctly. You just need to uninstall and reinstall it again. Under certain special circumstances, even if driver is installed incorrectly, there would be no yellow exclamation mark appearing to tell you the problem still exists, but actually there's a software conflict happening. Sometimes no matter how you install the driver (including correct and wrong situations), there would always be a yellow exclamation mark, then it's quite possible the operating system has problems. You need to clean the disk and reinstall operation system.

2)   Eliminate the failure that the operating system does not recognize the sound card

Many people think that after opening the device manager, as long as you find that there's a yellow exclamation mark in the sound card list, then directly installing the driver will solve the problem; actually the situation may be like this. If the laptop uses HD Audio technology, while the operating system is too old for it, then it will not recognize the sound card and the words "Unknown device" will appear in the list. You now need to install the correct chip driver; de-install the 2 to 3 drive devices out from the unknown device, and then install the correct sound card driver. If you don't first de-install the 2 to 3 drive devices included, and install the sound card driver, then it would not only fail to solve the problem that the sound card doesn't work, but also the operating system can be easily damaged.

3)   Eliminating the failure of the laptop to produce sound

If after finishing the work above, you still find that sound card does not work, you need to reconsider software settings. You should also remember that there's volume control on the laptop keyboard. Make sure you have adjusted the volume to the maximum, sometimes this is all that is needed.

If the movie the laptop plays has no sound or Wav music, or Midi music cannot be played; then probably you need to check the sound property settings for the player software, don't set it to mute or adjust the volume too low . . . Even if the settings are correct, you should also consider whether there's a software conflict or the sound player is damaged. You can follow the next operation: uninstall the audio player software that you have, install Microsoft or a third party player temporarily; and make sure you set the audio functions for the software and the operating system correctly. If that works you know your original software was causing the problem. Whether you re-install your original software or stay with the new one is up to you.

4)   Clean viruses and Trojans

Usually a new operating system will bring users a greater convenience to set the audio. However, if Win 7 is infected by viruses or Trojans and was damaged, then it would cause even more complicated audio failures; therefore, refer to the next few points:

(1)   Use antivirus software to scan the entire operating system, clean away viruses and Trojans;

(2)   The invasion of viruses or Trojans can also change Windows system settings itself. If some important audio player functions are damaged, then sound playing will have problems and may not play, even after viruses and Trojans are already cleaned. Sometimes you cannot recover to the original factory settings, and then you need to reinstall operating system to repair it and recover the factory settings.

11.2.3 25% of acoustic failures originate with the sound card connections or wiring

About 25% of acoustic failures are caused by hardware interfacing and connector degradation.

1)   During the repair process, I might discover that an audio interface or connecting wire has problems. A good way to make an intermittent failure reappear is by knocking the suspected part with a rubber hammer, or vibrating and pressing in various locations or on a specific part suspected while listening for audio. A noise or short burst of audio can identify where the problem is. Before anything else though, you should make sure the internal speaker is working

2)   If the internal speaker doesn't work, but the internal earphone works OK; after eliminating any software problems we can conclude that there is likely a wiring or connection problem with the audio system.

3)   With step 2) in mind, bypass the internal speaker connector by soldering the wires directly to the internal speaker solder interface; if the failure disappears, you have solved your problem and can either leave it as is or replace the connector. If the failure still exists, then it means the problem is in the internal loudhailer, you should continue to the fifth chapter of this article <<Laptop acoustic failure analysis and repair flow>>; to deal with it.

4)   If the external earphone has no sound, but the internal speaker works OK, then first make sure you earphones are working. Assuming that and, after eliminating any software problems, then we can initially come to the conclusion that the failure is somewhere between the audio output jack and connections to the circuit board. Open the laptop and continue troubleshooting using bypass and shaking/knocking techniques already discussed in step 1). Repair as necessary.

5)   If there's only one internal speaker having sound, and the other has no sound or little sound, then after eliminating any software problems, we can initially come to the conclusion that the failure is in the wiring and connections between the circuit board or the speaker. Try the external earphone audio and if it is working, your conclusion is

confirmed. Assuming it is, disassemble the laptop and continue to troubleshoot using bypass and shaking techniques already discussed in step 1). Repair as necessary.

6) If the laptop internal speaker and external earphone have no sound all, then after eliminating any software problems we can conclude the problem is in the audio output jack or on the motherboard. Recall that the external audio output jack inhibits the speakers when the earphones are plugged in. The simplest thing is to just replace the jack but you can also bypass it once you determine how the inhibit circuit is wired by disconnecting the jack and deactivating the inhibit function. If none of this works then you have a motherboard problem. I would go over all of the solder connections and audio wiring just to be sure of this. Rather than attempting motherboard repairs or replacement, you are better off using an external USB audio adapter to continue having audio

7) If the laptop does not record normally, after eliminating any software problems, we can initially come to the conclusion that the failure is caused by a microphone fault or its associated wiring. Make sure nothing is covering the face of the microphone and then try an external known working microphone, if it works, check the wiring and solder connections or replace the internal microphone.

8) If both the laptop internal and external microphones are not working, first make sure your external microphone is not defective. Then follow step 7) above to check the internal microphone, wiring, and connections. If you have not solved your problem, your only choices are to repair/change the motherboard or replace the audio function with a USB audio adapter.

11.2.4 10% of acoustic failures come from the motherboard sound control integrated circuits and speakers.

Motherboard, south bridge, sound control integrated circuits and speaker problems can also cause acoustic failures, about 10% of the time

During the repair process, I often come to the situation where there's no sound card list in the device manager, the operation system does not recognize it, or the laptop sound is distorted severely, or there's only noise but no sound and so on. Generally, we install a USB sound card adapter and then test and eliminate the operating system problem. We normally proceed by determining whether the BIOS can recognize the sound card integrated circuit or not, and then confirm if it's a software problem or hardware issue. Then we can come to the final solution to the problem. This troubleshooting method is easy and convenient and if it's confirmed there is a problem with the chip itself, then you need patience to isolate and repair the problem. First make sure the internal speakers are working normally;

1) The internal speaker doesn't work, and the external earphone works;

After excluding any software problems, connect the sound output wire directly to the internal speaker interface, if the failure still exists, then it means the problem is on the internal loudhailer; just replace it. If you need a more detailed procedure, please refer to the fifth chapter of this article <<Laptop acoustic failure analysis and repair flow>>.

2) Only one internal speaker has sound, the other has no sound or very little;

After excluding any software problems, try a known working external earphone to test it; if it works, it means the problem may be the internal speaker or its wiring. Check the wiring and connections and if OK replace the speaker. If you have the same problem with the external earphones, then it means the problem is likely on the motherboard. We can initially come to the conclusion that the sound card's chip (hardware) has faults. Follow the detailed procedure in the fifth chapter of the article << Laptop acoustic failure analysis and repair flow>>

3) The laptop sound is distorted severely or there's only noise but no sound

After excluding any software problems, and if the external earphones are working properly, change the internal speaker and connect the sound output wire on the motherboard directly to the internal speaker interface; if the failure still exists, not gone, then it means the problem is on the motherboard. We can initially come to the conclusion that the sound card's chip (hardware) has faults, or the laptop is not cooling properly and causing the temperature to rise too high. The sound card may not work normally under extreme temperatures. Follow the detailed procedure in the fifth chapter of the article << Laptop acoustic failure analysis and repair flow>>

4) The laptop speaker makes very loud noise.

After excluding any software problems, change the internal speaker, connect the sound output wire directly to the internal speaker interface; if the failure still exists, not gone, then it means the problem is on the motherboard. There are 2 probable conclusions we can make:

A) Bad shielding or grounding of the motherboard can cause static noise interference that disturbs the sound card chip;

B) There's a problem with the DC current filtering circuit on the motherboard and noise is not removed. A capacitor has aged and its performance deteriorated so that the noise is getting through to the DC bus and affecting various components. A detailed troubleshooting procedure is found in the fifth chapter of the article << Laptop acoustic failure analysis and repair flow>>

5) The laptop internal speaker and external earphone both have no sound

After excluding the device manager settings and any other software problems, then we can confirm if it's a chip hardware problem by checking whether the BIOS can recognize the sound card integrated circuit or not. If the BIOS does not recognize the sound card chip, then we can come to the conclusion that the sound card chip (hardware) on the motherboard has faults. The detailed troubleshooting procedure is found in the fifth chapter of the article << Laptop acoustic failure analysis and repair flow>>

11.2.5 Laptop Audio failure analysis and repair flow chart

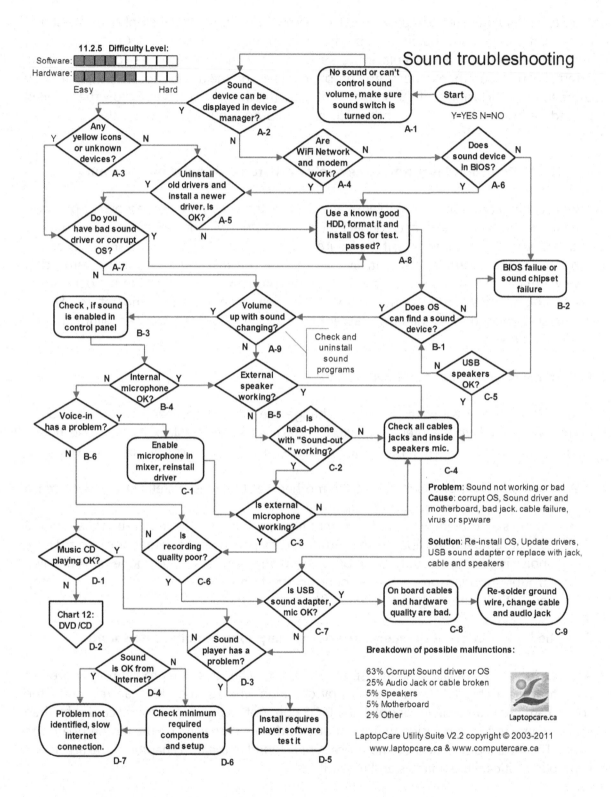

This tutorial will help you solve these problems:

a) Windows prompts that no hardware driver is found;
b) The operating system does not recognize the sound card;
c) The laptop makes very loud noise or the volume cannot be controlled;
d) The internal speaker has no sound, but the external earphone is ok;
e) No sound with the external earphone, but the internal speaker works OK;
f) The laptop sound is distorted or there's only one speaker with sound;
g) The laptop internal speaker and external earphone have no sound at all;
h) The laptop does not record normally or the computer has no sound when playing movies or something else;
i) Other audio problems;

In this article, I will explain how to find the cause of a laptop audio failure. It applies to most laptop brands and models.

Start

When you connect a power adapter, press the power button to start up, and after entering system, you find that there is an audio problem that is in accordance with one or several of the following scenarios:

Please note: there are a lot of reasons that can cause your laptop audio problems. For example, the laptop sound output is set to "mute". Then click on the small sound icon at the right bottom corner of the screen (a little speaker), then a volume adjust slide appears, along with the "Mute" checkbox; if it is checked, click the checkbox to clear it, That should restore your sound but if checked, other installed player software may also be muted. Some laptops have a hardware sound switch that could be turned off. If this was enough to solve your problem, you do not need this tutorial.

When your external environment (temperature) has extreme variations within a short period of time, it can cause an audio failure or other disasters. This situation does not belong to the scope of this article, please check another tutorial article.

Step: A-1

Many laptop owners have come across the situation where a laptop loses audio or volume control. Mostly this kind of failure comes from software, and a lesser percentage is from hardware. As sound card technology improves, especially with the inclusion of HD Audio technology, failure rates also raise because of higher complexity, component count, and software and hardware incompatibility. Comparatively speaking, the failure ratio caused by hardware drops a little but if the hardware is a little more complex, then probably the sound control hardware may develop problems more often than software failures. Therefore, when dealing with an audio failure, eliminate hardware problems first before considering software problems. Generally speaking, there are two types of volume controls. One is with hardware, such as a variable resistance adjustment wheel or a keyboard function, and the other is totally software that you open and use. For example, the speaker icon in the taskbar at the right bottom corner of the screen opens the operating system software sound control or you may have a media player to do the same.

A)   Sound loss failure treatment:

1)   Adjust the speaker volume to the maximum with function key (Fn+), (or adjust the volume to the maximum with the sound adjust control), and then double click the speaker icon at the right bottom corner of the screen and adjust all controllable volume slides to the maximum;

2)   Adjust the speaker volume to the maximum with a shortcut key, meanwhile, adjust the laptop quick play sound control to the maximum;

3)   Uninstall the laptop quick play software packet, disable the shortcut and adjust the volume by adjusting the volume control accessed through the icon at the right bottom corner of system taskbar. Experience proves that this repair method is quite effective, and not only avoids the software losing control, but also takes shortcut hardware faults into consideration. If these methods do not solve the problem, then please enter STEP: A-2;

B)   Volume cannot be controlled

There are three situations where laptop volume cannot be controlled:

1)   The icon to access volume control is not found. If the volume icon is missing, it's likely a setting problem. Deal with the setting problem, according to the sequence: click Start—Control Panel—Sound and Audio device/volume. Choose to put the volume icon into the taskbar, and then click OK. If the volume icon was already checked, then first you need to uncheck it and then click OK. Next check the option for the volume icon, and then click OK. If this method still does not solve the problem, then please enter STEP: A-2;

2)   There's a volume icon on the taskbar, but you fail to control the volume by adjustments accessed through the volume icon. Then you need to check, whether you've chosen the mute option. If you checked mute, then you'd have to uncheck the option first, and then click OK. Otherwise, it won't work when you adjust volume. If this method still does not solve the problem, then please enter STEP: A-2;

C)   The volume icon is present, but the volume icon adjustment button is disabled, and cannot be adjusted. Probably you haven't chosen a play device. You will need to click the property and find the correct option to choose your loudhailer; if this method does not solve this problem, then please enter STEP: A-2;

Step: A-2 the goal of this step is to confirm there's no available sound card in the device manager list

Click "Start"—"Control panel"—"System"—"Hardware"—"Device Manager"—"Sound Video and Game controllers", and then double click "Sound Video and Game Controllers". Check that there's an available sound card in the device manager list. If there's a "Sound card" icon in the list, then you should first check the function choices of the laptop sound card, and enable it. If the device manager has no sound card in the list, then it means:

1) The sound card has a hardware problem, you need to change the motherboard or replace the sound card to solve the problem;
2) The operating system does not recognize the sound card. If the laptop has HD Audio technology, while the operating system is too old and incompatible, there will be the words "Unknown device" appearing in the list. The solution is to install the driver for the chipset;

If in the device manager, there's no sound card listed (including no yellow exclamation mark), or the words "Unknown device", then please enter Step: A-4;

If in the device manager, the sound card is listed (including a yellow exclamation mark), or it is an "Unknown device", then please enter Step: A-3;

Step: A-3 the goal of this step is to solve the issue where the sound card has a yellow exclamation mark in the device management list

Open the "Device Manager", and see if there's a yellow exclamation mark in the sound devices. If there is, then it means the sound card needs a driver or driver upgrade and likely there's a conflict problem.

A red exclamation mark means the sound card function has been disabled; you have to enable the sound card function to use it. Generally speaking, there are two options:

a) One is to reinstall operating system, and if a yellow exclamation mark appears on the sound card; it means the driver did not install and you need to reinstall the driver. You may also encounter the words "Unknown device" and you need to install the driver for the chip, but first de-install the two to three drive devices included in "Unknown device". Next install the sound card driver. If you don't do it like this, and install sound card driver first, it will not solve the problem and may damage the operating system. If the problem is still not solved, then please enter Step: A-7;
b) The next option occurs when, the laptop sound is ok, but when restarting the laptop, suddenly, there's no sound. If you open the "Device manager", and do not see the yellow exclamation mark, then restart the laptop and check again, please enter Step: A-5;

Step: A-4 the goal of this step is to confirm that the WiFi and Modem is listed in the device manager.

Click "Start"—"Control Panel"—"System"—"Hardware"—"Device Manager"—"Network Adapter and Modem", and then double click "Network Adapter and Modem", check that the WiFi, network and Modem card is in the device manager list; if so you know that the control circuit chip is working OK, please enter Step: A-5;

If either the WiFi network or the Modem is not listed, then you have a problem with it. The problem may be on the motherboard in the associated chip or interfacing circuitry. Please enter Step: A-6;

Step: A-5 the goal of this step is to install a new sound card driver

Driver problems are fairly common. If you have a sound problem, the first thing to do is uninstall the sound card driver and install the latest compatible one. If you happen to have a disc with the original driver, give it a try.

a) Right click on "My Computer" and choose "Properties", and click Hardware, enter the device manager, find the sound card icon, double click the interrogation mark and then click to uninstall the driver. Next put the driver disc into the DVD-ROM/ CD-ROM, and choose to auto install the software.

b) If you do not have a driver disc, then use a cabled network connection to access the Internet, and then enter the device manager to choose the sound adapter, click the dropdown list, update the driver for the devices with a yellow exclamation mark, and choose auto connect to internet to find the driver.

c) If the auto network internet search has failed, then you need to find the driver manually. First, confirm your laptop model, and then look for and download the driver from the Internet and install it. Usually the driver can be found in the manufacturer's web site.

d) If your laptop fails to access the Internet temporarily, then you can use another computer to download the driver, and copy to a flash drive or disc, to install it in your laptop. If it prompts a failure during the installation process, then it means the driver you downloaded is not correct, or you should first close the antivirus monitoring and then install it.

If you have installed the new sound card driver, and the icon with yellow exclamation mark is removed, but it still is soundless, then please enter Step: A-7; if the icon with yellow exclamation mark still exists, then please enter Step: A-8;

Step: A-6 the goal of this step is to confirm that the sound card is already enabled in BIOS

Some laptops need to have the sound card set in CMOS, or need to use default settings. If you confirm that the BIOS management page has a sound card setup, then please enable the sound card function, and then enter Step: A-8; If that function does not exist, please skip it and enter Step: B-2;

Step: A-7 the goal of this step is to confirm whether the sound card registry table in the operating system is damaged or not

There are a multitude of sound card drivers available and you have to use the one that is compatible with your operating system, laptop model, and sound card. Even the CPU, whether it is from Intel or AMD, can make a tiny difference which might prompt an error when you install the driver, or even damage the sound card registry table in the operating system. Even worse, some carefree websites may put the wrong drivers for customers to download and install, which finally can cause a serious problem;

For users, it's very important to know the reason why a failure happens:

A) If the laptop sound card is working normally, but after a software update or system reinstallation, a sound failure occurs, then it means the sound card is OK and there are 2 other probable causes for the failure:

    1) If the device manager list has the yellow exclamation mark, then it means the driver is not installed correctly or not updated, you then need to uninstall and reinstall it. If that does not eliminate the yellow exclamation mark, you may have a problem with the operating system, and you need to clean the hard disk and reinstall the operating system again. Please enter Step: A-8;

    2) Under certain special circumstances, when the driver is defective or installed incorrectly and the yellow exclamation mark does not appear but you have a sound problem; there might also be a software conflict. You deal with it by uninstalling, and reinstalling drivers and observing when the conflict disappears.

B) If the laptop sound card has been work normally, and then suddenly one day a problem occurs, one of the situations below may explain it:

    1) A virus or Trojan invasion. You need to use antivirus software to scan the operating system entirely to clean the virus or the Trojan; afterwards, please enter Step: A-9;

    2) Something is wrong with the operating system; a virus or Trojan invasion changed the settings of the operating system, or even corrupted the essential sound player software. Even after you cleaned the virus or Trojan, the original settings are not recovered, then please enter Step: A-8.;

    3) Probably there's something wrong with the sound card hardware, but you need to first confirm whether the operating system has a problem or not, and then continue with the further process in STEP: A-8;

Step: A-8 the goal of this step is to confirm the failure has nothing to do with the operating system

With the repair flow above, we've already determined that the source of these failures is related to the sound card system or the software system on the original disc; now let's take a look at two different situations:

Situation 1: if you need to do "data backup" to a hard disk;

a) Refer to the seventh chapter and the methods in << STEP: C-6: Confirm whether need to back up your data (files)? >> and << STEP: C-7: confirm the backup of the data (files) you need is already finished>>.

b) If you have already finished data backup or did not need it, then you can use the HP "one-key recovery" method. This is the way to do it: connect the power adapter, press the power button to start up, and press F11, and then enter the system recovery software, finish system recovery, and then please enter Step: B-1;

Situation 2: if cannot back up the data, but you don't want to lose the data, then the best way is to replace your disc with a known working hard disk to do your troubleshooting. Install the operating system on it. Please note:

1) The interface of the replaced hard disk must be the same as the original disk, which means if the original disk has an IDE interface, then the new disk interface should also be an IDE interface;

2) The replaced disk's capacity should be close to the capacity of the original disk, it's not advisable to use a larger capacity disk for testing, in case the laptop BIOS does not recognize a disk of larger capacity, and leads to other problems.

Now you can proceed to install the operating system: when installing Win XP, Vista or Win7, it must be under Windows, then format the disk again (initialization operation), which will recreate the logical structure of the disk, and activate the partitions of the disk; next please continue the method of Step: B-1 to do this.

Step: A-9 the goal of this step is to confirm the failure is not with software or hardware settings

During the repair process, I have found that sound failures often happen, and are mostly caused by hardware or software incorrect settings. If after finishing the troubleshooting above, your sound card still fails to work normally, you need to recheck the following items:

Hardware:

1) If there's a volume adjust control on the laptop's operation panel, then please enable the sound and set the volume to maximum;

2) If there's a sound switch at the side panel of the laptop, then turn it on and set the volume at maximum;

Software:

a) Check the sound property settings of the player software, don't set it on mute or adjust the volume too low . . .

b) Check all sound adjust slides in the operating system, don't set the sound output on "Mute";

c)   The sound control panel options are incorrect, external sound is chosen rather than the internal loudhailer;

d)   Uninstall the sound player software you have and temporarily install Microsoft or another third party player and set the software and the audio functions in the operating system correctly;

If the sound property settings are all OK, then please continue to STEP: B-5; if the sound property software is disabled or unchangeable, (like when there's no little speaker icon at the right bottom corner on the screen), then please enter Step: B-3;

Step: B-1 the goal of this step is to confirm whether there's an available sound card after installing a new operating system

Step: B-1 and Step: A-2, the operations are basically the same, the difference is that for Step: B-1, the sound card registry is not damaged, also there's no virus or Trojan in the operating system. Click "Start"—"Control Panel"—"System"—"Hardware"—"Device Manager"—"Sound Video and Game Controllers", and then double click "Sound Video and Game Controllers", check that there's an available sound card in the device manager list. If there's no "sound card" icon in the list, then you should first check the laptop sound card function choices and select "Enabled" If there's no sound card listed in the device manager; then it means:

1)   The sound card has a hardware problem or the motherboard BIOS has problems;

2)   The words "Unknown device" is in the list, and it's because the laptop uses HD Audio technology, which needs the correct chip driver.

If in the device manager, there's no sound card listed (including yellow exclamation mark), and no "Unknown device" then please enter Step: A-9;

Step: B-2 the goal of this step is to confirm that the failure is on the motherboard

If you do not find a "Sound audio device" listed in the "Sound" category of the control panel; in most cases, the failure is in the hardware, but also in a rare situation there may be a conflict between the software and hardware. Many people might neglect the possibility of a BIOS problem on the motherboard. The BIOS is also a program, and can have Bugs that can lead to some indescribable failures. For example, restart without any reason, frequent system down, device confliction, hardware device "missing" without reason and so on. Usually manufacturers will release a new version of BIOS to revise these known BUGS. New versions of the BIOS would enable the shielded functions before adding the ability to recognize other new hardware and whatever other changes are needed.

If you don't like to upgrade your motherboard BIOS or cannot upgrade your motherboard BIOS, then please enter Step: C-5; if after updating the BIOS, the sound still is not recovered to normal, then please enter Step: C-5.

Step: B-3 the goal of this step is to confirm the OS sound settings are correct.

Enter the repair flowchart Step A-9, we can solve most sound problems using this process However, if the problem involves network and chatting aspects, you should confirm the settings for system (OS) sound are correct. If you cannot find the icon controlling the volume, then you can click Start—Control Panel—Sound and Audio Devices, and do a complete setup. Pay attention to the "volume" adjustment slide, and check whether the "Mute" checkbox is selected or not. If it is selected, cancel it and then drag the volume slide up to turn up the volume. It may be all that is needed to make the sound normal. If that does not work, then you need to return to Step: A-1 to repeat the process, until you do get it working normally. Warning: Windows sound does not need to be enabled but you should set up the music CD, video, network telephone, broadcasting and games, next please continue to Step: B-4.

Step: B-4 the target of this step is to confirm the internal microphone works normally

a) The laptop is not recording normally;
b) When speaking into the microphone, you do not get recorded sound from the speaker loudhailer. When voice chatting, you cannot hear the other end, or the other end does not hear you;
c) The laptop microphone is noisy or there's echo from the microphone when you are voice chatting;

If you find your laptop has the above problems, then please enter STEP: B-6; if you don't have these problems, then please continue to next STEP: B-5.

Step: B-5 the goal of this step is to confirm an external speaker is working normally

If an internal speaker does not work, and you are not willing to open the laptop to check it, then the best way is to try using one working external speaker to test it, and then find out the root of the problem.

1) The replacement external speaker cannot be a USB device, because the USB speaker has its own sound card, and you are not using the laptop internal sound card;
2) Check the sound property settings of the player, don't set it to mute or turn the volume too low . . .
3) If the external speaker is plugged in and connected to the correct interface, but still there's no sound, then turn the volume to the maximum, if this still does not solve the problem, then please continue following the next steps, enter STEP: C-2; if the external speaker does work normally, then please continue executing STEP: C-4;

Step: B-6 the goal of this step is to confirm the internal microphone can capture sound;

Mostly internal microphones are located at the top of laptop LCD or LED screen. You can use the following method to test whether sound is captured normally or not:

a) Adjust the screen of the laptop to put the microphone in the best direction to not receive feedback sound from the internal loudhailer;

b) Choose a quiet environment and speak closely into the microphone,

If the microphone does capture sound successfully, then test the computer recording quality. Next please enter STEP: C-6; if the microphone does not capture sound, then please continue to STEP: C-1;

Step: C-1 the goal of this step is to confirm the recording failure has nothing to do with software settings.

A) Check the internal microphone recording head and make sure it is not blocked by tape or dirt, if you cannot record, even when speaking closely into the microphone; check the microphone settings, make sure the microphone settings in the system (Windows Vista/Win 7) are correct.

   a) Right click on the "Sound" icon beside the time clock on the system taskbar. Choose "Record device" from the dropdown menu; please take a look at Figure 11-4.

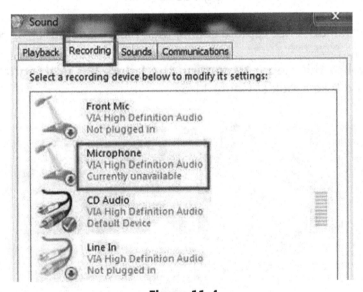

Figure 11-4

   b) After opening the "Sound" window, enter the "Sound" option card, and then choose "Microphone";

   c) Click "Properties", and then, "Microphone property" window will appear;

   d) Make sure on the "General" option card, that the device is already enabled from the "Device use" dropdown menu;

   e) Click the "Level" option card, set the microphone volume to 100.

   f) Click the "Advanced" option card; make sure all checkboxes on the window are chosen.

   g) Click "Apply", and then click "OK" to close the window.

If the problem still is not solved, then please try the method "B" as below.

B) Double click the speaker icon on the screen: choose "Properties"—"Record", and check whether all setup items are correct. Next go to "Control Panel"—"Multimedia"—"Device", select "Mixer device" and "Circuit input device", and set them as "Available" status, so the stereo mix is adjusted by the volume control interface. On the volume control interface, if you chose mute, then the device will not capture sound or mix and means it can only play music but not record anything. If the problem is still not solved, then please try using the method "C" below.

C) Sound card mix problems can be complicated to deal with. Under certain special circumstances, the software function can have problems, for example, "Multimedia—audio"—"Record" option is grey, and then a certain function of the sound card is unavailable. The device management list does not have a yellow exclamation mark, but actually there's a software conflict; then we can process like this:

  a) First uninstall audio effect chip driver accompanied with the machine, and then install an Intel driver for HD Audio.
  b) Compare and test repeatedly, if it still does not work, then you can only recover the factory operating system settings and the original sound card driver, temporarily giving up the upgrade request.

If the microphone still does not capture sound, then please enter STEP: C-3;

Step: C-2 the goal of this step is to confirm the failure has nothing to with the audio output jack; please take a look at Figure 11-5.

Figure 11-5

If external speaker is already plugged and connected with correct interface, but still there's no sound, then please adjust the volume to the maximum, and pull the connector outside about 1 millimeter, letting the connector not plug into the interface too closely. This solution is quite effective for the problems caused by audio output jack distortion and loosening. If still the problem could not be solved yet, then please enter STEP: C-4; if the external speaker works normally, then please continue STEP: C-3;

Step: C-3 the goal of this step is to confirm the recording failure is irrelevant with the internal microphone;

Click the "Device advanced setup" on top right corner of the audio manager, and then you will see two record device options, please choose "External microphone". Now use a known working external microphone to plug into the laptop microphone jack to test it. If you connect to the correct interface, but it still does not work, then pull back the jack slightly (about 1 millimeter), to create a better connection. This method is effective in solving the problems caused by jack distortion and loosening. If the microphone records sound successfully, it means the problem is relevant with the internal microphone and circuits, please test the record function of the computer contained in STEP: C-6; if the external microphone does not work, then please continue following to STEP: C-4; to check for other hardware problems in the laptop.

Step: C-4 the goal of this step is to confirm the failure is relevant with other internal hardware

In the first chapter <<1.4.2 6 "Hard" method to repair laptop>> of this book, once I recommended the "Observation" and "Knock" methods, and now we need them, first, according to the manufacturer's manual, open the laptop shell:

A) troubleshoot using the "Observation" method

Observe the suspected speaker, cable and single connector, pin, jack and connection status, and look for cable/wire damage or bad connections and any other physical irregularities that could be responsible. You also need to inspect for dust build-up in the machine, and especially the CPU thermal system. Dust and dirt must be cleaned up according to techniques discussed elsewhere in this manual. Make sure the ventilation and cooling system for the laptop is perfectly clean.

B) Troubleshooting with the "Knock" method

Knock any suspected parts with a little rubber hammer or other insulated tool, to make the failure disappear or reappear with the vibration of the part. This can identify the defective part;

A simple test to locate the fault is done by: disconnecting the audio output connection on the motherboard so it can be easily reconnected again. Then connect wires directly from the motherboard audio output to the speaker interface. If the failure disappears, then it means the problem is in the audio jack or the wiring you disconnected, if the failure does not disappear, then it means the problem is on the audio circuit of the motherboard. (The precondition is that the internal speaker has already been tested and it does work normally), if this step doesn't help, then please enter STEP: C-7;

Step: C-5 the goal of this step is to replace the internal speaker with a USB speaker

If the internal speaker does not work, then it's quite likely that the problem is on the motherboard; the easiest solution is to try using a known working USB speaker to test this theory.

As the USB speaker has an internal sound card, it does not need the sound system on the motherboard. In Windows XP/Vista/Windows 7 systems, it will install automatically without a special driver. Besides this, there are new types: a 3.5mm Line-in, will connect an MP3or iPod and so on.

If the USB speaker works successfully, then please enter STEP: C-4; if the USB speaker does not work, first try another USB port. If you are sure the USB interface is working, please continue STEP: B-1;

Step: C-6 the goal of this step is to determine the reason for bad recording quality

Let's take a look at these two different situations:

Situation 1: the internal microphone is working, but the audio output on playback is noisy, distorted, and intermittent echoes making it low quality or un-listenable.

If you face such a situation, then you may have added the input sound track to the output sound track. In this case, what you will hear is the microphone input sound and audio parsing sound simultaneously. It's just like a cell phone with echo. Check the sound settings in the OS and reset them if they are incorrect. If the problem is still not solved, then use method 3 to test it;

Situation 2: the internal microphone does work, but when playing the audio obviously there's noise or inflexion. It sounds like an alien talking;

When dealing with this situation, then please lower the microphone output volume and see if it helps. You can also enter the "Microphone effect" option card, reduce the noise by enabling the "Noise restrain" option. If you open the "Noise restrain" option; you may get more sound distortion. You can select the option "Echo elimination" and try that; if the problem is still not solved, then please use method 3 to continue;

Method 3, as many people feel that internal microphone quality is not good enough, they usually use an external MIC. If it is found that the external MIC or earphone does not work when plugged in, you likely need to access the audio settings to enable it. Click the "Device advanced settings" on the top right corner of the audio manager, and then you will see two record device options; just choose "Separate all input jacks as independent input device" or choose "External microphone", then it should work. If it solves your audio problems, then it means there is a problem with the internal microphone, so just continue using the external MIC and earphones; next please continue STEP: D-1; make sure you can play CD music and other audio functions.

If the problem is still unsolved, then it's quite possible that the failure is in the internal sound card hardware. Please continue following STEP: C-7;

Step: C-7 the goal of this step is to confirm the failure is relevant with the internal sound card hardware

If the internal speaker does not work, or the effect is not good even with the external MIC earphone, then the failure is probably in the soundcard on the motherboard. The simplest way to check it is to try using a known good working USB sound card adapter (or USB MIC) to see if it works, If it does, you have confirmed the problem is in the internal sound card. Please take a look Figure 11-6.

Figure 11-6

As a USB sound card adapter has an internal sound card, there is no need for the laptop internal sound card. Your best option is to continue using the USB devices. In Windows XP/Vista/Windows 7 systems, it will auto install without installing a new driver. The new type of interfacing (3.5mm Line-in, Line-out, and MIC) can now connect external speakers, external microphone, MP3 and iPod etc.

If the USB sound card adapter (or USB MIC) test is ok, and it does produce sound successfully when connecting the external speaker, or using an external microphone, then we can confirm the problem is in the internal sound card hardware, please enter STEP: C-8; if after adopting these methods, the problem still exists, then we know the problem is in the software and related applications, please continue STEP: D-3

Step: C-8 the goal of this step is to solve the internal sound card hardware problem

In the first chapter <<1.4.2 6 "Hard" method to repair laptop>> of this book, I recommended the "Cleaning" and "Replacement" methods, and now we need them:

a)   Use the "Cleaning" method to repair the failure

    1)   When there's too much dust accumulating inside the laptop, the loudhailer may be covered with oily dust, which will distort the sound. You need to clean up the dust;

2) When the laptop temperature rises sharply because of bad thermal conditions, the sound card is affected and cannot work normally under high heat conditions; you may hear noise but no sound. The high heat condition has to be lowered and stabilised by cleaning out the dust and dirt that is interfering with the cooling. If that does not solve it, then make sure the fan is clean and is working properly and replace the thermal silica gel between the thermal module and CPU. A USB powered external cooling fan can also help. Finally you need to check that the temperature conditions are normal using your OS software or Speedfan. If you have not cured the problem you should replace the CPU fan if not done already.

b) Use the "Replacement" method to repair the failure

The replacement method is basically changing out suspected parts with new/good ones. While doing this you need to inspect cables, single connection wires, pins, soldering, and connectors to make sure they are not at fault. Also look for discoloured components on the motherboard especially in the audio portion. Replacement proceeds with the easiest first and then the more difficult ones; "first simple and then complex".

1) First consider whether the internal speaker and microphone have problems themselves;
2) And then consider whether there's a problem with pins, jacks and connection wires;
3) Then consider whether there's a failure of the audio chip circuit or not;
4) At last, decide whether to install a USB sound card or change the motherboard.

Step: C-9 the goal of this step is to confirm the failure is irrelevant with the audio plug, jack and pin cable:

Please take a look at Figure 11-7.

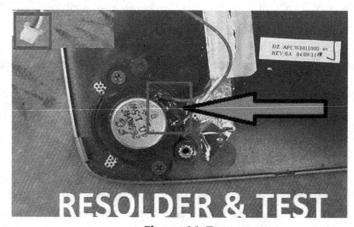

Figure 11-7

If you already used the "Cleaning" way to deal with the motherboard, then you can use "Replacement" way to make further check on the suspected parts and connection cables on the motherboard. Here's the concrete way:

1) Replace with a working normal internal speaker;
2) Weld the suspected cable, plug and jack pins again, at last, consider changing the plug, jack and connection cable;
3) Observe the motherboard audio circuit components; whether they change color, consider whether the audio chip circuit has failures;
4) Confirm to replace the motherboard or keep using USB sound card installed to solve the problem.

Step: D-1 the goal of this step is to confirm a music disc can play normally

When come to the repair flowchart Step C-6, we can say that basically the problems on the acoustic aspects are already solved. However, as the OS and drivers are updated, there may be some strange sound problems introduced. For example, there's no sound when playing a music disc, but the chat and system have sound and when this or other audio problems appear you need to check your system sound settings.

(1) Find the sound card model by clicking your mouse to expand the string of characters and numbers in the "Sound, video and game controller" dropdown menu, that's the model number of your sound card. Next click "Start"—"Run"—enter "dxdiag" to open "DirectX diagnosis tool"—"Sound", find it in the open interface. Please examine these settings:

a) The windows volume control channel is setup in mute mode;
b) The DVD-ROM has no digital playback function, but it's already enabled when set up;
c) The DVD-ROM device should enable the digital CD audio, but it's not enabled when set up;

(2) The driver or Windows Media Player file is damaged

Right click the sound card and choose "Uninstall" to delete it. Then choose "Update driver" to open the "Hardware update wizard", choose "Auto install software". The system will auto search the network and install the sound card driver, if it doesn't work:

a) Enter your sound card model to "GOOGLE search" text, press "Search" button, from the open interface, choose the website where you can download the driver and the driver software, next download it and reinstall the sound card driver;

    b)   "Uninstall" the old Windows Media Player software, next download the latest version of the driver and reinstall the sound card driver. Make sure it is compatible with the operating system.

(3)   The CD disc has physical faults;

Test and confirm whether the music disc play function is OK or not. Test with an original music disc in good shape and not a burned copy.

    a)   Some CD discs will play, some will not. Those not playing may have physical faults;

    b)   To make a CD music disc, use a CD-R disc and make sure the burning method is "Once burning". Lower the burning speed to 4x, 2x even 1x to increase the compatibility of the player;

    c)   If you create your music files with the Windows Media Player, and they do not play after burning the disc, then the problem might be just in settings. In Windows Media Player, click "Tool" menu "Options", and then choose "Copy music" label, cancel "Copy settings"—"Protection content" option.

        If it doesn't solve your problem, then probably have a fault in the laptop CD-ROM/DVD-ROM drive, please continue to execute the following steps.

Enter STEP: D-2; if the music disc plays normally, or please continue to STEP: D-3; to solve the sound problem when playing movie files;

STEP: D-2 the goal of this step is to confirm that the 12 repair flow process is chosen

Your problem is quite likely with the laptop CD-ROM/DVD-ROM hardware, please check another tutorial article (in chapter 12) about the failure analysis and repair flow that a laptop does not recognize the DVD burner or cannot read a disc.

Step: D-3 the goal of this step is to confirm that a sound failure is caused by software

Occasionally both the internal sound card and external USB sound card do not work, when playing movie files; however, the system sounds do work and the driver installation is also OK. Focus on the next few points to deal with this problem:

1)   MIDI player volume control volume; check whether it's set in mute mode or the volume is turned minimum;

2)   WAV, and MIDI music do not play; usually it's because there's more than one "Audio device" under "Multimedia"—"Devices", disable one of them;

3)   The antivirus software or the disk Utility has software conflicts with other applications in the system, try disabling the antivirus software temporarily;

4)   Damage by viruses or Trojans corrupts some important MIDI files, and sound is lost. Scan the disk completely, clear all viruses and Trojans;

5) The sound card driver is too old or corrupted or a driver is not installed. If during the previous repair steps, you haven't updated or reinstalled the driver, then please update or reinstall it now;

If still the problem is not solved, then probably it's the fault of the MIDI player software, please continue executing the following steps. Enter STEP: D-5; if sound is OK when playing movie files, then please continue STEP: D-4; solve the problems that online flash playing and Skype has no sound;

Step: D-4 the goal of this step is to confirm that online flash playing and SKYPE or voice chat sound failure is caused by the software

There's another special audio failure, that is, there's no sound when watching an online FLASH video in the Win7 system. Even the result is the same with IE8 or the Google browser. Meanwhile, SKYPE has no sound either. The sound icon at the right bottom corner of the screen is present and other MP3 or movie playing is all OK. System sound or audio is all normal. I have tried updating the sound card driver, or reinstalling the FLASH plug-in, but all without any effect. You can try the next method:

1) Check "Tools" on the webpage—"Internet options"—"Advanced"—"Multimedia"—"Play the sound in webpage"; click the checkbox again and refresh the page;

2) Change registry:

Start—Run—enter "regedit" and find the branch HKEY_LOCAL_MACHINE\SOFTWARE\Microsoft\Windows NT\CurrentVersion\Drivers32, create a character string value, change the value of the item named "wavemapper" as "msacm32.drv".

3) Confirm the voice function in the SKYPE chatting interface software or the operating system is already enabled;

If the problem cannot be solved, then it's quite likely that the registry in the operating system has faults, please continue executing the next steps. Enter STEP: D-6; if the sound is ok when playing movie files, next please continue to STEP: D-7; solve the problems that the online Flash playing and SKYPE sound are paused and delayed;

Step: D-5 the goal of this step is to reinstall the MIDI player software

Under some circumstances, even after you clear all viruses and Trojans, you cannot make the damaged MIDI player's file recover and it finally leads to the problem that partial MIDI files do not play. Of course, there won't be any prompt or message;

Also in some cases, the MIDI part will not play sound; usually the reason is because antivirus software or a disk utility has software conflicts with system applications. You need to uninstall and reinstall; until the conflict disappears; you should pay attention to the next few points during the repair process:

1) Uninstall the system sound player software, change to another third party player temporarily, and set it up correctly;

2) If you need to install the MIDI player software, then you are better to set the antivirus software as "disabled", and then set the firewall as "Disabled", before reinstalling. After reinstallation, restart the computer and try it again, and enable the antivirus software and firewall functions.

3) If the problem is still unsolved after following the methods above, then probably the operating system registry table is defective, please continue executing the following steps. Enter STEP: D-6;

Step: D-6 the goal of this step is to confirm that the sound failure has something to do with the operating system

There's no sound when watching an online Flash video, even the result is same when using IE8 or the Google browser. If the repair path is from Step: D-4 to Step: D-6; there are a few points you should also pay attention to:

1) The Laptop system memory, CPU speed and display card memory should all accord with the minimum requirements of online Flash playing;

2) The flash version installed must be compatible with the operating system version, not always the latest version is the best;

3) When downloading and installing Flash, you are better to disable antivirus software and the firewall, stopping them from blocking partial Flash plug-ins during download and installation;

After finishing the above work, if there is still no sound, then it's quite likely that the operating system registry table is defective; you need to clean the hard disk and reinstall the operating system. In order to avoid software conflicts and registry breakdown happening again, you can change the IE version or try a Firefox browser. The repair path of this method is from **Step: D-5 to Step: D-6,** which is also quite effective;

Step: D-7 the goal of this step is to confirm the failure is caused by network speed

No matter whether you are online playing or local playing, multimedia playing requests media flow to keep a stable speed rate. When the speed does not reach the playing requirement, the system will get "stuck". No matter whether using computer music player, computer player, computer flash player, you will experience time delay; and sound and video playing will not be stable and smooth. Please test your network speed, if the network speed is too slow, then the only way to solve the problem is to use a reliable high speed network needed by the media playing.

11.3 Twenty-four repair cases of laptop Audio failures

11.3.1 9 repair cases for the acoustic failures caused by driver and software to HP laptops

201) HP PAVILION DV5-1234CA laptop suddenly has no sound

Failure symptoms:

As client reported that HP DV5 laptop suddenly had no sound, after restarting it, there's sound again. But get voice distortion again after a while.

Solution:

This failure symptom obviously belongs to the description of flowchart 11, according to the repair method; confirm the repair path, finding it's accorded with the sequence:

Start->A-1->A-2->A-3->A-5

Repair summary:

(1) Right click "My Computer"—"Properties"—"Hardware"—"Device manager", expand the "Sound, video and game controller" option, there is no yellow "?" mark;

(2) Find the model of the sound card, expand the "Sound, video and game controller" dropdown list, the string of characters and numbers is the model of your sound card, you can also click "Start"—"Run"—enter "dxdiag" to open "DirectX diagnosis tool"—Sound, find it from the opened interface;

(3) Reinstall driver

Right click on the sound card; choose "Uninstall" to delete it. And then choose "Update driver", open the "Hardware update wizard", choose "Yes, at this time"—"Next" click on the—"Auto install software"—and then "Next", the system would auto search and install the sound card driver from the disc; if there's no manufacturer sound card driver disc available, the simplest method is to go to any famous portal websites, enter your sound card model numbers to the "Find" text, press "Find" button, and on the opened interface, you choose the website you can download the driver. Open HP website, if there's no driver software you want, you can use the website search engine to find it. Next download it and reinstall driver for the sound card, then the failure is resolved.

Hint:

1. Pay close attention when downloading driver software: one is, make sure the brand model must be compatible with the version of driver; second is, to check which system does it work on; third is to check the releasing time of the driver, even the latest one would not be proper for use. Yon can download several versions and try;

2. Generally, the driver software downloaded has auto installation function; after opening it, click it to install it automatically. But it would not install automatically, you need to extract the file. Remember the location of the software on disk after decompression extraction, such as C:\ . . . . \ . . . .; and then check the item "Install from the list or specified position"—click "Next", and choose the the location of the software on the disk, system would find the sound card driver from the specified position and install automatically.

202)   HP PAVILION DV3-2050EA laptop's soundless failure

Failure symptoms:

A client reports that this morning, after starting the laptop, there's no sound, when he shut the laptop down last night, operating system auto upgraded the software package, and previously the sound was OK.

Solution:

This failure symptom obviously belongs to the description of flowchart 11, according to the repair method, confirm the repair path, finding it's consistent with the sequence:

Start->A-1->A-2->A-3->A-7->A-9

Repair summary:

First, check whether there is a volume icon on the right side of the taskbar. I find no volume icon, then I click Sound and audio device icon on Control panel and open the "Sound and audio device property" dialog. Then I check one in the "Application event" column, such as application error. I pick one sound type and then check the "Preview" button on the right side whether it is disabled or not. If "Preview" button is grey, then click "Control Panel/ System properties/Hardware/Device manager" command, check "Device manager" window, whether there's any yellow mark. I find there's a yellow "!" exclamation mark. We can come to the conclusion that probably the sound card driver failure is caused because of system confliction or application damage. Therefore, there was no sound. Download the sound card driver again, install it and then restart the computer. Sound comes back again. The failure is resolved.

Hint:

a) Open "Sound and audio device property" dialog, and click "Sound" option card on the dialog, and then in the "Application event" column, click one event, and choose one sound type, if the "Preview" button at the right side is disabled, then mostly it means the sound card driver is OK. Probably the failure is because system volume is too small, or you set mute, or there's something wrong with the volume;

b) If there a s yellow "!" mark, then check whether it's sound card device option (sound card device option usually has "Audio" or "Sound" keyword). If any item with regard to sound card device has a yellow exclamation, then it means the sound card driver is missing or not installed yet. Reinstall the sound card driver, then soundless problem could be resolved.

203) HP PRESARIO V3023AU laptop has no sound, it's useless even to upgrade sound card driver

Failure symptoms:

A client reported that there's no sound after starting the computer, and after downloading and upgrading sound card driver, it does not make any sound.

Solution:

This failure symptom obviously belongs to the description of flowchart 11, according to the repair method, confirm the repair path, finding it is consistent with the sequence:

Start->A-1->A-2->A-3->A-5->A-7->A-9

Repair summary:

Computer suddenly has no sound, even after upgrading the sound card driver and restarting computer, it does not make any sound; since the installation of sound card drivers and the installation of patches for the operating system follow an order, that is, first install patches, and then install sound card driver. Probably you may get the error message "HD Audio BUS driver could not be found", then sound card driver fails to work;

a) Uninstall High Definition Audio driver patch KB835221 & KB888111 (in the option "Add/delete applications" of control panel, uninstall all if you have);
b) Restart computer system;
c) Reinstall sound card driver, (Application would auto enable HD Audio BUS application) and then install the patches whose versions are compatible with the operating system, then it would be ok.

Hint:

Microsoft Universal Audio Architecture (HD Audio) driver is a new generation of AC97 audio standard HD Audio BUS system support driver made by Microsoft mainly for Intel platform. While laptop sound card mostly needs to install HD Audio patches, namely, Microsoft KB835221 and KB888111 patches. However, Microsoft doesn't provide download link officially;

What's the difference between these two patches? Actually Kb835221 is for Microsoft Windows Server 2003/Microsoft Windows XP Service Pack 1 (SP1)/Microsoft Windows 2000 Service Pack 4 (SP4) systems, while KB888111 is the updated version, already supporting Microsoft Windows Server 2003 Service Pack 1 (SP1)/ Microsoft Windows XP Service Pack 2 (SP2) / Microsoft Windows 2000 Service Pack 4 (SP4) systems.

204)   HP PAVILION dv6000 laptop has no sound after reinstalling system, even it doesn't work after reinstalling sound card driver

Failure symptoms:

A client reported that after reinstalling system for HP Pavilion DV6000 laptop, the volume icon at the right bottom corner is missing. "Sound and Audio device" in Control panel has no audio device displayed, device volume and the volume icons are all grey; it doesn't work even reinstalling the sound card driver several times;

Solution:

This failure symptom obviously belongs to the description of flowchart 11, according to the repair method; confirm the repair path, finding it's consistent with the sequence:

Start->A-1->A-2->A-3->A-5->A-8

Repair summary:

It's quite important to know the cause of this problem; previously the laptop's sound card was working normally, while after reinstalling the operating system, the sound failure occurs. This indicates that the sound card hardware has no problem itself, and then probably the cause of the failure might be a wrong driver installed. As expected, there's yellow exclamation mark on the sound card list in the device manager, which means the driver hasn't been installed correctly. You need to uninstall and reinstall the driver again; but it still doesn't work even after reinstalling the sound card driver several times, the yellow exclamation mark would always appears, then it's quite likely that the sound card registry table in operating system has failure you need to clean up the disk, reinstall the operating system again. In order to avoid installing wrong driver, first find the same model of HP laptop, back up the sound card driver, and then install onto the suspected laptop, the problem is solved then.

Hint:

The driver to install should not only be compatible with the operating system, but also be compatible with the model of the laptop. Even you have to know about whether the CPU is Intel or AMD, a tiny difference, might cause error when installing driver, even damages the sound card registry table of the operating system.

205)   HP PAVILION DV2000 laptop's soundless failure

Failure symptoms:

A client reported that his HP Pavilion DV6000 laptop suddenly has no sound when using. The volume icon at the right bottom corner is still there, but there's no adjustment function, even there's no yellow exclamation mark in the device manager.

Solution:

This failure symptom obviously belongs to the description of flowchart 11, according to the repair method, confirm the repair path, finding it's accorded with the sequence:

Start->A-1->A-2->A-3->A-7->A-9->

Repair summary:

According to the failure symptom, system has no sound, but device manager shows everything is ok, without any yellow exclamation mark, system and drivers are all ok.

Check the volume control, whether the volume is adjusted to the minimum range. Double click the volume icon at the right bottom corner, adjust all controllable slides to the maximum, the problem is still not solved. Then turn the volume to the maximum with the function key, meanwhile, adjust the volume in laptop Quick Play to the maximum, still not ok. Since the Quick Play software usually gets problems and sometimes the design of some function keys is defective, then I uninstall the Quick Play software, disable the function keys with regard to controlling sound volume, and only use the sound volume control provided by the operating system. When I restart the laptop, the problem is solved.

Hint:

Under special circumstances, even sound card driver has error, there will be no yellow exclamation mark, but in fact there is software conflict. You need to uninstall and reinstall again; until the confliction disappears.

If you are blocked or there's error message when you installing sound card driver, under the circumstance that the sound card driver is confirmed correct, please set antivirus software as "Disabled", and set firewall "Disabled", please disable your anti-virus software and firewall and then install sound card driver. Sometimes there will be an accidental achievement, if the installation succeeds, then you need to restart computer again to test. Afterwards, enable the anti-virus software and firewall

206) HP PAVILION DV6110US starts up after shutting down, then sound card could not be found in hardware device list

Failure symptoms:

A client reported that his PAVILION DV6110US laptop was already in good condition, but after one shutdown and restart, the screen prompts a message that no sound card can be found, after installing, the volume icon at the right bottom corner is gone. "Sound and Audio device" in Control panel also has no audio device displayed.

Solution:

This failure symptom obviously belongs to the description of flowchart 11, according to the repair method, confirm the repair path, finding it fits the sequence:

Start->A-1->A-2->A-4->A-6->B-2

Repair summary:

According to failure symptom, "Sound and audio device" option in Control Panel doesn't show audio device. Most cases, we would think that the failure comes from hardware, but to neglect related BIOS settings on motherboard. These years, as the technology of sound card has been improved, problems because of motherboard BIOS also increase. In this case, after upgrading motherboard BIOS, sound recovers normally, which means the motherboard BIOS problem is caused because of version issue previously. The sound card confliction failure is solved by upgrading the BIOS.

Hint:

In fact, BIOS is also a program, therefore, it is not perfect and has bugs which can cause unexpected failures. For instances, the computer restarts automatically, the operating system freezes frequently, device conflicts or some hardware devices cannot be recognized. After manufacturer found, they would release new version of BIOS in time to revise these known Bugs, new version of BIOS would also enable the functions blocked before, adding the ability recognizing other new hardware and so on. Finally, those indescribable failures could be solved.

207) HP520 laptop's soundless failure—special case

Failure symptoms:

A client reported that his HP 520 laptop suddenly had no sound, and the volume icon at the right bottom corner also disappeared, and in device manager, there's no yellow exclamation mark.

Solution:

This failure symptom obviously belongs to the description of flowchart 11, according to the repair method, confirm the repair path, finding it's consistent with the sequence:

Start->A-1->A-2->A-3->A-5->A-7->A-8

Repair summary:

According to failure symptom, system has no sound, but everything in device manager is normal without yellow exclamation mark there. Then examine the volume control, adjust all sound slides to the middle range, move volume slide to the maximum, the problem is still not resolved; reset the volume of sound and video device, put volume icon to taskbar, and hook the checkbox; restart the laptop, the failure is still unresolved; scan the disk and operating system with antivirus software entirely, after removing all viruses and Trojans, the failure disappears.

Hint:

This case is typically caused by virus or Trojan, which invaded the operating system, then volume control application is missing or damaged, consequently it could not play sound. If after finishing the job above, it still makes no sound, then it's quite likely viruses has infected the operating system and damaged sound card driver. You can consider the points shown as below:

1) First delete the sound card driver, and then restart the laptop, letting operating system recover automatically;
2) If the problem is severe, then you should first uninstall this driver, next install the latest sound card driver;
3) Considering reinstalling operating system.

208) HP PAVILION DV7-2065EG laptop has no sound when playing movies

Failure symptoms:

A client reported that HP PAVILION DV7-2065EG laptops had always been in good condition, but few days ago, after upgrading software, there was no sound when playing movie, but he could hear sounds when he boot the laptop or shut it down.

Solution:

This failure symptom obviously belongs to the description of flowchart 11, according to the repair method, confirm the repair path, finding it fits the sequence:

Start->A-1->A-2->A-3->A-5->A-7->A-9->B-3->B-4->B-6->C-6->D-1->D-3-E-3

Repair summary:

According to the failure symptom, system has sound; it means the driver is installed normally. Check the sound adjustment slide in operating system, finding that when turn the volume slide to the maximum, system sound is also at maximum, but only when playing movies, there's no sound. Focus on checking the volume control channel of MIDI player, check whether or not the sound volume is muted or turned to the minimum As a result, the settings are OK. Uninstall MIDI player software, temporarily change to other player and confirm the settings are correct. Restart the laptop and play the movie again, finally the sound is normal, the failure disappears.

Hint:

1   Wav, Midi music could not be played, probably it's because the sound card driver is too old or the compatibility is bad. Besides, operating system version might be too old, you need to upgrade it which would also make application compatibility worse;

2   Sometimes certain antivirus software would be incompatible with operating system, which leads to confliction with system applications. At this moment, the failure that there's no sound when playing movie would happen. You can uninstall the original antivirus software, turn to use other different antivirus software to solve the problem, until the confliction disappears; meanwhile, pay attention to the MIDI channel of volume control in the operating system, don't set it to mute mode.

209)   HP PAVILION DV6 has no sound when playing flash

Failure symptoms:

A client reported that his PAVILION DV6 laptop installed Win 7 operating system, and there was no sound when playing Flash online, even the situation was the same when playing with IE8 or Google Browser. Meanwhile, an instant message software had no sound either. There's volume icon at the right bottom corner, other MP3 or movies were playing well, and system sound or audio was OK. Sound card driver had been updated, or Flash plug-in was reinstalled, but it's useless.

Solution:

This failure symptom obviously belongs to the description of flowchart 11, according to the repair method; confirm the repair path, finding it's consistent with the sequence:

Start->A-1->A-2->A-3->A-5->A-7->A-9->B-3->B-4->B-6->C-6->D-1->D-3->E-3

Repair summary:

According to the failure symptom, system has sound; it means the driver has no problem. Check the "Tools" on the page—"Internet options"—"Advanced"—"Multimedia"—"Play the sound in the webpage", Then I open the Internet Explorer, choose Tools—Internet options—Advanced—Multimedia, and find the option "Play sounds in web pages" is checked. After refreshing the website, the problem remains. Then I try regediting:

Start—Run—enter "regedit"

HKEY_LOCAL_MACHINE\SOFTWARE\Microsoft\Windows NT\CurrentVersion\Drivers32, create a character string value, change the value of the string named "wavemapper" as "msacm32. drv". Then restart the computer, the problem is solved.

Hint:

If the problem is still not solved according to the methods above, then it's quite likely that the operating system's registry table is broken; you need to clean up the disk, and then reinstall the operating system. To avoid software conflicts and registry damages, you can try another version of Internet Explorer and then install Flash plug-in.

1) The version of Flash plug-in should not be too old and it should be compatible with the version of the operating system;
2) When downloading and installing the Flash plug-in, you had better disable the anti-virus software and firewall, in case they would block partial flash plug-ins.

11.3.2 7 repair cases for HP laptop acoustic failures caused by hardware

210) HP Envy 15-1103tx Notebook internal speaker has no sound, but the external earphone works all right

Failure symptoms:

As our client reported that the laptop had no sound, and the volume icon is existed at the right bottom corner, but could not adjust the volume. Try listening with a headset, it shows that it works normally.

Solution:

This failure symptom obviously belongs to the description of flowchart 11, according to the repair method; confirm the repair path, finding it fits the sequence:

Start->A-1->A-2->A-3->A-7->A-9->B-3->B-4->B-5->C-4

Repair summary:

After starting up the computer, check the volume icon at the right bottom corner of the screen, it's not muted. Open the volume control and check the sound property settings for the player software, change the volume adjustment slide from the middle position to the maximum; the problem is not solved yet;

Test with a pair of known working external speakers, they work fine. Open the laptop, disconnect the internal speaker, solder the sound output wire directly to the internal speaker interface and add soldering the output wire; restart the laptop, the sound turns normal. It seems the failure is caused because the speaker connection wire is unsoldered;

Hint:

a) As the speaker vibrates frequently so the down-lead of the speaker is easily broken, usually the cable is already broken, but externally it's still connected. So you'd have to check up carefully to find out the problem. You can replace the broken cable with flexible wire.

b) Soundless failure would also cause the problem that speaker voice coil is broken. You can use a multi-meter RX1 range to measure the tab terminal of the speaker, if the resistance is ∞ (infinite), then you can scrape out the sealing wax of the wire both sides of the voice ring with a small knife, letting the bare copper wire exposed and then test again. If the current still cannot pass through, then it means the voice ring voice coil has a broken wire internally; if the current can pass through and make squeaking noise, then it means the voice coil wire is broken. solder tin on the end of the wire and then, solder a section of varnished wire, which is similar to the voice coil, to the

211) HP PAVILION DV7-1137US internal speaker low sound, severely distorted;

Failure symptoms:

A client reported that the laptop internal speaker low sound and he could not use the volume icon to adjust the volume. The problem still remains after resetting Sound and audio devices properties.

Solution:

This failure symptom obviously belongs to the description of flowchart 11, according to the repair method; confirm the repair path, finding it fits the sequence:

Start->A-1->A-2->A-3->A-7->A-9->B-3->B-4->B-5->C-4

Repair summary:

After starting up the laptop, check volume control, I don't find that the volume is set to the minimum. Double click the volume icon at the right bottom corner, to open the volume control dialogue, turn all controllable volume slides to the maximum, but the problem is still not solved yet; turn the volume control slide of the Quick Play software to the maximum the problem is still existed; test with a pair of working normal external speakers, it works well; open the laptop, resolder the output cable of the speaker and add solder to the conduction wire. The problem is still not solved yet; at last, change the volume, the failure disappears.

Hint:

a) Another simple measurement way is to try a known working headset, plug it into the audio output jack; if the failure disappears, it means the problem is on the sound jack or the speaker. If the failure doesn't disappear, then it means the problem is on the sound jack or the motherboard circuit;

b) When there's too much dust accumulated inside the laptop, speaker is stuck with dust or liquid, which would change the frequency when vibrating, finally leading to rustiness. As for few cases, as the laptop cover is deformed, the internal speaker is crushed so that it fails to make sound. You need to clean the dust, disassemble the shell and revise again to recover using again.

212) HP PRESARIO CQ40-325AX only has one internal speaker with sound, another one without any sound.

Failure symptoms:

As our client reported that the laptop only has one internal speaker working, the volume icon at the right bottom corner could adjust volume, open "Sound and audio device property", reset the sound and audio, always there's only one speaker working.

Solution:

This failure symptom obviously belongs to the description of flowchart 11, according to the repair method; confirm the repair path, finding consistent with the sequence:

Start->A-1->A-2->A-3->A-5->A-7->A-9->B-5->C-4

Repair summary:

Double click the volume icon at the right bottom corner, adjust all slides controlling volume to the middle, the problem is not solved; reset the sound player software and the sound control panel in operating system, keep the volume balance adjustment slide at the middle position, including volume balance control, Line in, CD player balance control, reset them all. As a result, the problem is not solved. Test with a pair of working normal external speakers, they works all right. Start the laptop, replace the speaker which does not work, then the problem disappear.

Hint:

   a)   After replacing the internal speaker, if the failure still exists, then you can consider whether it's the problem of the internal jack connection; usually the connection wire is unsoldered or the audio output jack is distorted, then you need to solder or replace it;

   b)   If the internal speaker and external headset have the same failure symptom, after excluding the possibility of the failure of the audio output jack, we can ensure that the sound circuit on the motherboard also has some problems. You can only change the motherboard or replace with USB sound adapter;

213)   HP PAVILION DV6107US laptop's no sound failure

Failure symptoms:

As our client reported that one night he chose the mute in the laptop sound options, then the second morning, after he cancelled mute, start-up and shutdown operating still had no sound, previously everything was OK with the sound; he also tried system recovery, but still not working.

Solution:

This failure symptom obviously belongs to the description of flowchart 11, according to the repair method; confirm the repair path, finding it fits the sequence:

Start->A-1->A-2->A-3->A-5->A-8->B-1->A-9->B-5->C-4->C-7->C-8->E-1

Repair summary:

According to the failure description of the chapter flowchart, system has no sound, check the control panel in system, the sound option has already been enabled, after entering system, use a multimedia program to test. The laptop internal speaker doesn't make sound, even there's no sound after plugging a headset.

Then the cause for the failure is probably wrong driver is installed, but there's no yellow exclamation mark on the sound card list in device manager. To ensure there's nothing wrong with the sound card driver, uninstall the sound card driver and reinstall again; go to HP official website, download the sound card driver for the laptop model, and then install onto the suspected laptop, the problem is still not resolved.

Then it's quite likely that the operating system's the registry with regard to sound card is damaged, you need to clean disk, reinstall operating system again. After resetting the operating system to default value, the problem is still existed. It seems the problem is with the hardware. Disassemble the machine and test, it shows that the audio output is ok, the internal speaker is hot. It is found that the headset jack has a short circuit internally. After changing the plug, the failure is eliminated.

Hint:

In fact, when checking whether the failure is caused by softwares or hardwares, we could have made it simple by omitting one step that formatting the HDD and reinstalling the operating system. If we can make sure confirmed that the sound card driver has no problem, then the next step is to recreate a new account, with such a method, we can solve the soundless problem because of user configuration file error. Usually, after restarting the laptop, there would be sound when starting up and turning off. If there's still no sound, then most cases, there's something wrong with the hardware system.

214) HP PAVILION DV6130 CA laptop internal speaker and external earphone have no sound at all

Failure symptoms:

A client reported that his HP PAVILION DV6130CA laptop suddenly had no sound, right click the volume icon at the right bottom corner; the volume slide cannot change the volume. There is no yellow exclamation mark in device manager.

Solution:

This failure symptom obviously belongs to the description of flowchart 11, according to the repair method; confirm the repair path, finding it fits the sequence:

Start->A-1->A-2->A-3->A-5->A-8->B-1->A-9->B-5->C-4->C-7

Repair summary:

Start from checking system sound tuner, double click the volume icon at the right bottom corner, adjust all slides controlling volume to the maximum, the problem is not resolved; uninstall the software package in the laptop Quick Play, disable shortcut control volume, simply using the sound controller of operating system, but the problem is still not solved; uninstall the original sound card driver, go to HP official website, download the latest sound card driver, and then reinstall onto the laptop, the problem is still not solved yet.

It seems the problem is the hardware, disassemble the machine, and disconnect the connection of the internal jack, solder the sound output wire directly to the internal speaker interface, but the problem is still not solved yet. So far I have excluded the possibility that the speaker has any problems. Then I use an ammeter to examine the output current of the audio device and find the output current is 0, therefore I am certain that the motherboard audio circuit has something wrong, we can only change the motherboard or replace with USB sound adapter, install one USB sound adapter, and then the failure is eliminated.

Hint:

a)   Damp environment would cause great damage to laptop, storing and using under damp environment would cause corruption to the electronic components inside the laptop, accelerating oxidization. If you use the laptop under damp environment (like basement) for a long time, it would accelerate the damage to the laptop, such as not being able to connect to Internet or there's no sound. Even worse, system could not start up;

b)   Severe dust would block the thermal system of the laptop, which would also easily cause short circuit to the internal accessories; finally lead to performance degradation of damage.

215)   HP PAVILION DV9000 laptop could not find sound card after starting up

Failure symptoms:

A client reported that his HP PAVILION DV9000 laptop suddenly had no sound, the volume icon at the right bottom corner also disappeared, there's no sound card list in the device manager.

Solution:

This failure symptom obviously belongs to the description of flowchart 11, according to the repair method; confirm the repair path, finding it fits the sequence:

Start->A-1->A-2->A-4->A-5->A-8->B-1->B-2->C-5->C-4->C-7->C-8

Repair summary:

According to the failure symptoms, "Sound and audio device" in the control panel has no audio device, most cases, the failure is from hardware, rare situation is because of conflict between software and hardware. Test with a pair of external working normal speakers, as a result, there's still no sound. Enter repair flowchart 11 of step A-8, clean hard disk, then reinstall operating system. In order to avoid installing wrong sound card driver, reset the operating system to default value and then restart the laptop to test. The problem is still not solved yet.

Examine the hardware, disassemble the machine, check the connection of the internal jack, everything is ok. I'm certain that the circuit of the audio chip on the motherboard has problems. We can only change the motherboard or replace with USB sound adapter. After installing USB sound adapter, the failure is eliminated.

Hint:

a) When encountering with such problems that your laptop does not make any sound, you should follow the sequence to check and eliminate gradually: from internal to external, from software to hardware. Generally, when installing sound card driver, we would always choose default value to install, but sometimes this default value would have conflicts with other devices, which causes that the sound card fails to make normal sound.

b) It's quite important to check the compatibility of the driver, as Windows XP system's stability is quite high, many people would choose to change system. However, as many manufacturers don't provide drivers of XP system version, which usually disable some new laptops to work well. Although sometimes Windows XP might install driver for sound card automatically, in actual practical use, sound card might fail to work. You should pay attention to such kind of situations.

216) HP PRESARIO V6223EA laptop's sound is distorted severely and makes noises

Failure symptoms:

A client reported that his V6223EA laptop's sound is distorted severely, 20 minutes later, there's only noise but no normal sound. Even the volume icon at the right bottom corner, the turner slide is disabled.

Solution:

This failure symptom obviously belongs to the description of flowchart 11, according to the repair method; confirm the repair path, finding it fits the sequence:

Start->A-1->A-2->A-3->A-5->A-8->A-9->B-5->C-4->C-7->C-8

Repair summary:

According to the failure symptom, sound distortion is quite severe. Check up the device manager, everything is OK, without any yellow exclamation mark; check the volume control in system, the volume slide is in the middle. Turn the volume slide to the maximum, the problem is not solved; reset the sound player software and the sound control panel in operating system. Keep the volume balance turner slide at the middle position. As a result, the problem is not resolved. Test with a pair of working normal external speakers, they are working all right. However, 20 minutes later, there's only noise but no sound. Uninstall the sound card driver, reinstall new sound card driver and make sure that the settings are correct. As a result, the problem is still not resolved.

It seems the laptop has hardware problems; besides, there are more than two failures. Open the cover, and then I find that the internal speakers and the heat sink are blocked by dust severely, which drastically lowers the performance of the speakers. Sound is distorted severely. While after 20 minutes, laptop temperature rises sharply because of bad heat radiation. Sound card could not work normally under extreme status, which causes the failure there's only noise but no sound. Then it's easy to do with knowing the cause for the failure. Test CPU thermal system, clean the thermal system and fan dust, and wipe new thermal silica gel between thermal module and CPU, connect heat sink and restart the laptop. The failure disappears.

Hint:

a) It's quite necessary to keep the laptop working under the environment with as less dust as possible. Severe dust would block laptop's thermal system and would easily cause short circuit to the internal accessories, finally lowering down the performance of the laptop or even causing damage.

b) It's quite necessary to keep the laptop working under suggested temperature. Under over cold or overheated temperature, it would accelerate the internal components' even worse; the laptop would fail to start.

11.3.3 3 repair cases for the noise failures happening to HP laptop

217) HP Pavilion dv5000 laptop "beeps loudly"

Failure symptoms:

A client reported the internal speaker beeps loudly when he was using his laptop. Following the laptop screen froze, after shutting down and restart the laptop again, 5 to 10 minutes later, the failure occurred again.

Solution:

This failure symptom obviously belongs to the description of flowchart 11, according to the repair method; confirm the repair path, finding it fits the sequence:

Start->A-1->A-2->A-5->A-8->B-1->A-9->B-5->C-4->C-7->C-8->E-1

Repair summary:

Check the surrounding environment, no strong sound wave source or strong magnetic field source is found. We can confirm it's not caused by these reasons, considering that when power adapter has problems, probably such a failure would occur. So put suspected laptop power adapter on another HP laptop and try, as a result, everything is OK. Then we can initially judge the failure has nothing to do with the external power supply. Next enter repair flow Step: A-8, reinstall operating system and sound card driver. But the problem is not solved yet; enter repair flow Step: B-5, test with a pair of good external speakers; however, as a result, before long, external speakers still beeps loudly

According to the memory of the client, after shutting down at night, the second morning when it starts up, if you watch YouTube, generally, 40 to 60 minutes later, failure symptom occurs. This message is quite important; at least it indicates two problems:

1) The failure might be related to the temperature, the longer interval between shutting down the laptop and starting the laptop is, the later the failure would happen.
2) The failure might be related to CPU and RAM use status, because when playing video, it would take up a large part of CPU and memory source; by this token, we can say the problem is related to the laptop hardware.

Open the cover, test the CPU thermal system, clean up the dust on thermal system and fan, and then wipe new thermal silica gel between thermal module and CPU/GPU. Make sure the laptop temperature would not rise sharply. Restart the laptop, as a result, the failure symptom is eased up. Failure recovery time would be postponed 80 minutes later, it is suspected that the memory has quality problem, after changing the memory, the problem is resolved.

Hint:

In the seventh chapter of this book, we recommend readers using Memtest86 memory test software, because its test accuracy is quite high, as high as 99.7%, but could not reach 100% accuracy; in this case, previously I already made test to the memory, and it's approved by Memtest86 software, as the laptop could work normally within a short time, while under high running status for a long time (when playing video on YouTube), error occurs. In this case, Memtest86 software would be quite difficult to test out the problem; as for the solution of this problem, we can rely on the Hint and analysis of this flowchart, namely, test memory with replacement method. Change the memory with same brand, same model type and same technical parameters to satisfy the high requirements of the memory for application software, and solve such problems. Replacement method would always be one of the best repair methods forever.

218)   HP Pavilion R3000 laptop speaker has current noise failure

Failure symptoms:

A client reported that after the HP laptop continually worked for 5 hours, suddenly speaker sent quite big current sound, and then shut down automatically. The second time when power was on, the speaker always has current noise; sometimes the sound would become bigger gradually.

Solution:

This failure symptom obviously belongs to the description of flowchart 11, according to the repair method; confirm the repair path, finding it fits the sequence:

Start->A-1->A-2->A-5->A-8->B-1->A-9->B-5->C-4->C-7->C-8->E-1

Repair summary:

According to the case, considering it's quite possible that the external power has interference on laptop, letting the laptop work under battery mode, as a result, the failure basically disappeared, which means the failure must be related to the external power supply. After changing the power adapter, although there's no current noise, the speaker would make other noise from time to time. Enter repair flow Step: B-5, test with a pair of working normal external speakers, as a result, before long, the external speaker also makes quite big noise.

The key point is to check the laptop hardware. Open cover, knock the suspected certain component with a rubber hammer gently, bend the component properly or specific component to make the failure reoccur. Finally it is found that the power jack is unsoldered sometimes there's little spark occurring, which causes interference and makes speakers to have noise from time to time. After tightening resoldering the power jack, the problem is resolved.

Hint:

I warned readers to pay attention in the third chapter of this book that if you have to change the power adapter, then make sure that you use a correct model type, output voltage must be the same as the voltage of the original power adapter. Output current must be same with the original power adapters, or even higher, but could not be lower.

219)   HP Pavilion dv4272US laptop speaker has big noise failure

Failure symptoms:

A client reported that after the laptop was used once, suddenly there's big noise from the speaker, and he found later that as long as the fan was started, the speaker would have noise, sometimes the noise would become louder gradually.

Solution:

This failure symptom obviously belongs to the description of flowchart 11, according to the repair method; confirm the repair path, finding it fits the sequence:

Start->A-1->A-2->A-5->A-8->B-1->A-9->B-5->C-4->C-7->C-8->E-1

Repair summary:

According to the case, directly enter repair flow step B-5, test with a pair of working normal external speakers, as a result, before long, the external speakers make loud noises. The failure still exists. Considering the fan working might have a big interference to the laptop, focus on checking the laptop hardware. Open the cover, make electronic cleaning for the motherboard, first cut off all power, including motherboard battery; (must not use plastic brush or cleaner to clean dust), discharge the static to the metal tool in use. The key point is to check and clean sound card integrated circuit, components, whether the pins are unsoldered or humidity symptom. Whether motherboard distorts, whether component changes color or there's liquid leak. At last, tighten and resolder the suspicious places, after changing the fan, the problem is solved.

Hint:

Most case, it is because the laptop overheating makes the motherboard chip heats up quickly, which makes loading current increasing sharply, while sound card could not work normally under extreme status. Finally such a failure would happen. So after disassembling the laptop, pay attention whether there's much dust inside the machine; if yes, you should first clean up the dust from the thermal system, and then make following assumption

11.3.4 4 Repair cases for HP laptop internal microphone failures

220) HP PAVILION DV4 turns off and then start up again, record software could not record

Failure symptoms:

As our client reported that now his laptop's recorder or record software could not record, could hear the other side, and when he used audio chat software, he could hear others' voices, but could not make himself heard.

Solution:

This failure symptom obviously belongs to the description of flowchart 11, according to the repair method; confirm the repair path, finding it fits the sequence:

Start->A-1->A-2->A-3->A-5->A-7->A-9->B-3->B-4->B-6->C-1

Repair summary:

According to the failure symptoms, we follow the procedures as below:

A) First test the internal microphone; usually, internal microphone is at the top of the laptop LCD screen, or close to the hinge under the LCD screen. With the method below, we can easily capture sound:

1) Adjust the screen of the laptop, place the microphone at the best recording direction;
2) Choose the environment without background noise, speak directly to the microphone, (don't get far away from microphone), but as a result, this method doesn't solve the problem;

B) Test the computer record function; make sure the computer record program is ok. Follow the next operating steps:

1) Click "Start"—"All programs"—"Accessories"—"Recorder";
2) Click "Record" and speak to the microphone. Save the file to the position which could be accessed easily, such as desktop.
3) To play the sound already recorded, you can use Windows Media Player to open the file. As a result, the problem is not resolved;

C) Test the microphone settings, make sure the microphone settings (in Windows Vista/ Win 7) are correct;

1) Right click the "Sound" icon beside time clock in system taskbar. And choose "Record device" from the dropdown menu;
2) After opening "Sound" window, enter "Record" option card, and then choose "Microphone". Usually there should be a indicator beside the option "Microphone";
3) Knock the plastic part on the screen slightly. Then the indicator should jump upper and down to respond to the sound. As a result, the microphone doesn't work, either there's no indicator; then follow the following steps:

   a) Click "Properties", at this moment, "Microphone Property" window would appear;
   b) Make sure that in the "Device Use" dropdown menu from the "General" option card, the device is already enabled;
   c) Click "Level" option card, set microphone volume to 100;
   d) Click "Advanced" option card, make sure that all checkboxes in the window are chosen already;
   e) Click "Apply" and then click "OK" to exit the window.

Then try recording again, make sure that the problem is already solved then.

Hint:

If there is still no sound, then please continue executing the following steps below:

D) Make sure that correct record device is chosen.

Access sound property:

1) Click "Start"—"Control Panel"—"Hardware and Sound"—"Sound", then "Sound" window would appear immediately;
2) On the "Sound play" option card, choose "SPDIF interface" or audio device;
3) On the "Record" option card, choose the audio device already installed on the computer. This device should be same as the device listed in the "Sound play";
4) Click "OK" to close the "Sound" window.

221) HP COMPAQ MINI CQ10-120SE Skype audio chat did not work

Failure symptoms:

A client reported that his laptop's Skype voice function doesn't work, he could hear the other but the sound of his own could not be sent out.

Solution:

This failure symptom obviously belongs to the description of flowchart 11, according to the repair method; confirm the repair path, finding it fits the sequence:

Start->A-1->A-2->A-3->A-7->A-9->B-3->B-4->B-6->C-6

Repair summary:

According to the failure symptom, follow the method of the case above to repair, as a result, the problem is not solved. Open "Device manager", finding there's repeated sound card list, which means they might have conflict. Then execute the next steps, check whether there's exists conflict and delete the repeated item.

1) Click "Start"—"Control Panel"—"Hardware and audio device"—"Device manager;
2) Click the plus (+) beside the option "Sound, video and game controller" in the list and check whether there's sound card option with the same name. If there is, choose them one by one. Right click the repeated item and choose "Delete", until all repeated items are deleted;
3) Click the "Scan hardware change" button the taskbar of "Device manager". Windows Vista/Win 7 would scan system hardware and provide default driver according to the requirement. Then try recording again, make sure the problem is already solved.

Hint:

If there's still no sound, then please continue the following steps:

The software function might have problem, such as the driver is too old, certain function of sound card could not work now, or after operating system update, there's compatible problem with sound card, certain function of sound card is blocked and so on. In all, as for the process of sound card mix problem, it's kind of complex to operate;

a) First uninstall the sound effect chip driver accompanied, and then install HD Audio driver for Intel;
b) Next install the driver whose version must be compatible with the model of your laptop and your operating system. After the installation, test your laptop. If the failure still remains, then you need reset your operating system and sound card driver to default value and do not upgrade your operating system or sound card driver for the moment.

222)   HP Presario CQ61-320ER microphone has current sound, noise and so on.

Failure symptoms:

As our client reported that after he used the laptop one time, suddenly there was big current sound from the microphone. Following shut down and start the laptop again, there was still little noise from the microphone, and then gradually the sound became bigger. After the laptop started and worked at battery mode, the failure still had no change.

Solution:

This failure symptom obviously belongs to the description of flowchart 11, according to the repair method; confirm the repair path, finding it fits with the sequence:

Start->A-1->A-2->A-3->A-5->A-7->A-9->B-3->B-4->B-6->C-6->D-1->D-3->E-3

Repair summary:

According to the case, the laptop works under two different working modes: with battery and external power supply, but the failure symptoms are the same. This indicates that the failure has nothing to do with the external power supply, now there is no strong sound wave source surrounding (sound box and volume etc), either there is no strong magnetic field source (like fridge and TV set etc), so it seems the problem is not caused by these reasons. Check the computer record application, record at the internal display status, the result shows normal. Then check the mix volume slide key of the microphone, finding it's already adjusted to the maximum, readjust the mix volume of the microphone, pull the controllable slide key to the 85% position, try recording; although the noise from the microphone becomes smaller, it's still not perfect, the problem is not solved at all.

Next check the microphone settings, considering that some sound card technology doesn't support the enhanced status of microphone, so remove the enhanced function of the microphone. Then try recording again, the problem is still unresolved.

Next clean up system garbage files in system, at the same time, clear viruses and Trojans, test network speed. As a result, no virus or Trojan is found, either there's nothing abnormal;

Test with external microphone, finding there's the same problem. It seems it's quite likely that the problem is from video mutual chatting software. Because of network or other reason, data is lost, file is incomplete or plug-in is installed improperly, then abnormal symptom would occur too. First back up the important material data (chatting records, mails and so on), and then close chatting application, uninstall it from the control panel, and then download again and install, the failure disappears then.

Hint:

When such kind of failures happens, you should also consider the points as below:

a) Once you and your friends (any side) open the internal play or leave the sound box open (including the surrounding environment is quite noisy), interference or sound abnormality would always occur;

b) You'd better to set both sides' firewall settings same. If one side set too high, or use different bandwidth user (like Telecom or AT&T), then probably some problems on voice would occur. This is quite difficult to solve;

c) Knock or press the plastic part of the screen slightly, check whether the failure symptom changes or not. If the failure symptom changes, then you need to check whether there's bad contact in the microphone;

d) Listen to the computer host carefully, whether there's other abnormality (such as fan sound is too big, bad rotation and so on), under cold status (meaning the fan is not working), check whether the failure symptom changes or not. If the failure symptom change, then it's quite possible that the fan is disturbing the microphone, you need to change it.

223) HP PRESARIO CQ62-200CA laptop could not record; other audio chatting could not work either

Failure symptoms:

A client reported that his laptop's internal microphone could not record, but could hear the others, just the sound of himself could not be sent out.

Solution:

This failure symptom obviously belongs to the description of flowchart 11, according to the repair method; confirm the repair path, finding it fits the sequence:

Start->A-1->A-2->A-3->A-5->A-7->A-9->B-3->B-4->B-6->C-6->C-7->C-8

Repair summary:

According to the failure symptoms, follow the next process as below:

First test the internal microphone, check whether the internal microphone recorder is blocked by some tape or dirt, speak to the microphone closely, as a result, it fails to record; next check up the microphone settings, confirm the microphone settings (in Windows Vista/Win 7) are correct.

a)   Right click the "Sound" icon beside the clock in system taskbar, choose "Record device" from the dropdown menu;

b)   Click "Property", and "Microphone property"

c)   Dialog appears. Make sure in the dropdown "Device use" on the option card "General", the device is already enabled.

d)   Make sure the audio device has not been muted, and turn the microphone volume to the maximum; as a result, the problem is still not resolved;

Enter repair flow Step: B-4, test with a known working external microphone, the result shows everything is all right. It seems that the internal microphone hardware or circuit has some problems. Open the laptop cover, then just understand that the internal microphone is located at the top of the laptop display, the laptop display is opened and closed for many times, which loose connected. Then connection wire is unsoldered or broken. Audio signal could not be sent to the laptop; knowing the failure cause, then it's quite easy to repair. Change the connection wires of the microphone resolder it, then restart the laptop. The failure disappears.

Hint:

The principle of sound setting: when choose microphone in record control window, only the sound captured by microphone would be outputted. Therefore, at this moment, you can only hear speaking voice, but could not heard music sound. When you choose stereo mixed sound in record control, all the sound in the computer would be mixed and output. Then you can hear music sound.

Stereo mixed sound is turned in volume control interface. in the volume control interface, if the device sound volume is muted, its sound will not be recorded and mixed up, which means that you can only play the song but not hear the speaking sound; wave volume and microphone volume adjustment would decide the contrast of the volumes of them two in the mixed sounds. For example, if you feel the music sound is too loud, then you should turn down the wave volume.

11.3.5 One repair case for hp laptop a suddenly outburst of harsh noise

224)   HP PRESARIO CQ60 laptop a suddenly outburst of harsh noise

Failure symptoms:

A client reported that after using one time, his laptop suddenly made quite big current sound from the internal speaker, following shut the laptop down and restarted it again, the laptop suddenly screamed loudly, which is uninterrupted.

Solution:

This failure symptom obviously belongs to the description of flowchart 11, according to the repair method; confirm the repair path, finding it fits the sequence:

Start->A-1->A-2->A-3->A-7->A-9->B-3->B-4->B-6->C-6->C-7->-C-8->E-1->E-2

Repair summary:

First I remove the power adaptor and let the laptop work under battery mode, but the laptop's speaker still screams, which means the failure is not related to the external power. In fact, the possibility of external power's interference is very small. Check up the surrounding environment, no strong sound wave source (sound box and volume etc.) or strong magnetic source (like fridge and TV set and so on) is found; Then check the mixed sound volume controllable slide of the microphone, pull the controllable slide to the 50% position, however, the laptop still loud noise.

Since sometimes the failure of the internal microphone would cause such problems, so I block the internal microphone record mouth with tapes, and then test with a pair of known working external microphones, as a result, the laptop still makes loud noise.

It seems the problem of the laptop hardware or the circuit. Open the laptop cover, cut off the connection between the laptop microphone and motherboard, then the laptop stops the strident screaming, the problem is resolved.

Hint:

Considering when microphone is at enhanced status, such kind of noise like "squeak noise . . ." would occur, annoying noise so you'd better to remove the microphone's enhanced function.

When motherboard circuit has bad contact connection failure, current filter circuit is aging or the quality is bad, then it would cause severe interference to current, and increase the noise volume sound distortion would occur. As internal microphone and external microphone don't use same one circuit, (generally speaking, failure would not occur on external microphone at the same time), so the simplest way is to cut off the connection between internal microphone and motherboard, and then use external microphone.

CHAPTER 12

Optical drive repair

12.1 Causes and analysis for the failure that laptop could not recognize DVD-RW or could not read disk;

12.1.1 Laptop DVD-ROM working principle and internal structure

The laptop DVD-ROM and desktop DVD-ROM is physically different but otherwise identical but with minor differences in the kernel components and working principle aspects. Laptop DVD-ROM development and updates are almost the same as the desktop DVD-ROM because of this.

In December 1995, IBM, HP, Apple and others, convened Sony, Philips, HITACHI, Pioneer and other manufacturers to make and unify the DVD specifications and changed the original Digital Video Disk to the current Digital Versatile Disk.

DVDs use the MPEG-2 standard, and contain 4.7GB of storage capacity (a program of 133 minutes' at a high compression rate, and containing AC-3 5.1 sound track output coding).

1. Main DVD specifications:

Main DVD: DVD-ROM, DVD-Video, DVD-Audio, DVD-R, DVD-RW, DVD-RAM

1) DVD-ROM

DVD-ROM is a DVD spec used to read digital material. They are produced in four storage capacities. The choices are 4.7GB, or 8.5GB, or 9.4GB, or 17GB; this hardware product is called read-only DVD-ROM. Please take a look at Figure 12-1.

Figure 12-1

2) DVD-Video

DVD-Video is a consumer video format used to store and read digital video on DVD discs, it is based on the MPEG2 standard and various audio single and multi-channel formats; the hardware product is called DVD laser video machine (namely DVD-Video).

3) DVD-Audio

DVD-Audio is a DVD spec used to store and read digital music data, now focusing on HD audio performance; the hardware product is called DVD music ROM (DVD-Audio). Some DVD laser video machines also provide DVD-Audio play functions.

4) DVD-R

DVD-R (DVD Recorder)

DVD recorder is an optical disc recorder which records digital materials onto writeable DVD media for one time.

There are mainly two types of DVD recorders.

The first generation of DVD-R (A) (3.95GB) is mainly used for professional production, but it is not compatible with the applications of software productions of DVD-ROM (4.7GB).

The second generation of DVD-R (G) (4.7GB) is mainly used by common customers for DVD production. While DVD-R (A) media cannot be used in DVD-R (G), they are similar to CD-R, and DVD-R discs are compatible with DVD-ROM

DVD-RAM

DVD-RAM is a rewritable optical disc usually encased in a cartridge. Currently available in standard 4.7 GB, it is useful in applications that require quick revisions and rewriting such as a camcorder. In computers the hardware product is called rewritable digital multifunctional drive (DVD-RAM), the second generation 4.7 GB DVD-RAM can be compatible with DVD-ROM.

5) DVD-RW

DVD-RW product that came out after the DVD alliance brought forward DVD-RAM. It is a DVD spec that allows rewriting data; the hardware product is called rewritable digital multifunctional drive (DVD-RW); the writing methods of DVD-RW and DVD-RAM are different, also the application fields are different.

6) Blu-ray DVD

Blu-ray or Blu-ray disc (abbreviation is BD) uses blue laser light with short wavelength (405nm) to read and write data. It gets the name because of this.

So far, Blu-ray is the most advanced large capacity disc format, BD laser technology's giant progress enables you to store 25GB documents on only one disc, which is the 5 times as much as current DVD (single DVD disc).

2. DVD-ROM working principle

The DVD-ROM working principle is almost the same as the CD-ROM's, with both sending out beams of light formed through an optical system from laser diodes onto the disc. The beams of light reflected from the disc irradiate onto the photoelectric receiver, where it is turned into an electrical signal. Finally the signal is parsed into the data we need.

A DVD drive must be compatible with a CD-ROM disc, while the tunnels and densities burned by the different discs are all different; of course the requirements for the laser are also different. The DVD laser head uses different light powers when reading different discs.

To be compatible with a CD-ROM disc, so far the DVD laser head's reading methods are divided into the following 4 types:

1) Single head single-focus lens

Adopting one head and one integrated holographic focusing lens, the laser bean is of 645nm wavelength, but the lens is quite special. The laser beam through the edges of the lens cover the focus points on the CD/VCD information side, while the laser beam in the middle of the lens focuses on the DVD information side only. Since there's only one lens, a lens change is not involved when reading the data, and time is not needed for a lens change. The disc reading speed is fast, but the reading precision is bad, and causes further burden to the laser head.

2) Single head double-focus lens

This system uses two lens's with different focuses, but they share one laser emitter and receiver (namely, they share one laser head) and they get different focus depths by switching the lens to read CD/VCD and DVD information separately. The signal reading quality is quite good, but when reading the disc, it involves the mechanical switching process of the laser head. So it occupies disc reading time, and the reading speed is slower.

3) Double laser heads double-focus lens

This system uses two sets of completely independent laser heads, and two sets of lenses with different focuses. The signals emitted from the receivers use common encoding and playback circuitry for both the CD/VCD and DVD. Therefore, the disc reading performance is good and another advantage is that it can be compatible with CD-R and CD-RW. Since there are double laser heads, the cost is quite high and the servo mechanism has one double-head switch process when selecting disc types, occupying some time, thus the disc reading speed is slower.

4) Single laser head with multi-wavelength

This technology uses one laser head with two different laser emitters integrated together. It is a high technology. Based on keeping the advantage of a single-focus lens of a single laser head; it improves the disc reading performance and disc recognition speed. The compatibility is good, and could be compatible with both the CD-R and CD-RW as well. This is the newest solution available.

12.1.2 Laptop DVD-RW drive common failure symptoms

a) The laptop does not detect the DVD-RW disc, the drive volume disappears;
b) You can hear the DVD-RW disc running but it does not read or play the content on the disc;
c) The DVD-RW drive can only read a CD disc, but not a DVD;
d) The DVD-RW drive can only read a DVD disc, but not a CD;
e) When the DVD-RW drive is reading a disc, it makes a very loud noise;
f) The Disc drawer will not open; you cannot get a CD or DVD out;
g) The DVD-RW drive does not read a disc successfully, and you cannot boot from a disc;
h) The Disc does not auto play;
i) Disc burning always fails; an error prompts during the burning process, exit burning;
j) The system prompts that the disc burning is finished, but there's nothing on the disc;
k) Burned CD music does not play normally;
l) DVD burning machine will only burn a CD but not a DVD;
m) DVD burning machine can only read a disc but not burn a CD/DVD;
n) After upgrading a DVD burning machine, it does not burn;
o) A DVD-RW drive may sometimes not read parts of a DVD-RW disc or may provide a corrupted result.

12.1.3 Laptop DVD burning failure causes and analysis

a)   Open "My Computer" on the desktop and notice that the DVD-ROM volume icon is missing;

Probable causes for this failure are:

(1)   An important drive file is damaged or there's conflicts between software, which prevents the operating system from finishing the DVD-RW icon loading;

(2)   The DVD-RW drive is damaged, preventing the operating system from recognizing it.

(3)   The interface on the motherboard connecting the DVD-RW drive is loose or damaged;

(4)   A problem with the South Bridge circuit controlling the DVD-RW drive prevents the motherboard BIOS from detecting the existence of it;

b)   DVD-RW disc running sound is heard, but it is not playing or reading out the content on the disc;

Probable causes for this failure are:

(1)   Some software installed conflicts with the DVD-RW operation;

(2)   The laser head of the DVD-RW has severely aged, or the laptop has been jarred sufficiently to knock the laser head out of position;

(3)   The disc is not inserted correctly or the surface of the disc has severe scratches and disables normal reading;

(4)   There's an incompatibility problem between the format of the disc and operating system;

c)   The DVD-RW drive can only read a CD, but not a DVD;

Probable causes for this failure are:

(1)   If the DVD-RW drive uses "Single laser head with double wavelength" or "Double laser heads" technology, then one laser emitter (used for reading the DVD) doesn't work or the laser head has severely aged;

(2)   If the DVD-RW drive uses "Single laser head double-focus lens" technology, then one focus lens (for reading a DVD) accumulated too much dust or the focus lens is out of position and the DVD reading fails.

(3)   The DVD disc surface has severe scratches or the format is incompatible with the operating system and prevents normal reading;

d)   The DVD-RW drive can only read a DVD, but not a CD

Probable causes for the failure are:

(1)   If the DVD-RW drive uses "Single laser head double wavelength" or "Double heads" technology, then one laser emitter (for reading the CD) is not working or the laser head has aged severely;

(2)   If the DVD-RW drive uses "Single laser head double-focus lens" technology, then one focus lens (reading the CD disc) accumulated too much dust or the focus lens is out of position and prevents the reading process.

(3)   The CD disc surface has severe scratches or there's an incompatibility problem between the format and the operating system preventing reading;

e)   When the DVD-RW drive is reading a disc, a loud noise is heard;

Probable causes of the failure are:

(1)   If the DVD-RW drive uses "Single laser head double-focus lens" technology, then converting the focus lens when reading the disc, so the disc reading speed is slow with quite big noise;

(2)   The laptop has been jarred sufficiently to damage the DVD-RW drive so it is slightly distorted and out of balance. When the DVD-RW drive is running at high speed, the disc wobbles slightly;

(3)   The DVD/CD surface has too many scratches on it and when the laser head is reading the data, it would continually convert the rotating speed to try to improve the disc reading performance.

f)   The disc drawer does not open to eject the CD or DVD;

Probable causes for the failure are:

(1)   For occasional failures, certain software has temporary conflicts with the DVD-RW drive;

(2)   After the laptop has been jarred, the shell is distorted slightly and stops the disc drawer from opening;

(3)   There's something stuck inside the DVD-RW drive preventing it from ejecting;

(4)   Faults with the DVD-RW itself, mechanical or electronic, prevent the normal eject process;

g)   The DVD-RW drive reads a disc successfully, but the system will not boot up from the drive

(1)   For various reasons, the CMOS was not set to select the first boot device as the CD-ROM drive;

(2) The DVD-RW laser head accumulated too much dust, which lowers the penetration ability of the laser beam;

(3) The DVD-RW drive has aged or is not fully compatible with the motherboard;

(4) The DVD-RW drive BIOS (Firmware) is too old to be fully compatible with the disc.

h) The disc does not play automatically

Probable causes for the failure are:

(1) You haven't applied AutoPlay for all media and devices, the checkbox option is unchecked;

(2) The operating system has viruses or Trojan invasion and the AutoPlay function is affected;

i) Disc burning always fails, there's always an error prompt during the burning process, exit burning;

Probable causes for the failure are:

(1) There's a problem with the disc itself, or the disc used is not blank;

(2) A wrong format is chosen when burning, for example, to burn a DVD you chose CD in the burning software;

(3) There's other software running when burning that causes a conflict;

(4) The laptop enables system power management functions when burning, such as disk shutdown, sleep mode, and so on;

(5) You haven't disconnected the network from the computer and there's another network member accessing your machine resources or other network activity occurs when burning;

(6) The burning software has problems itself, which affects the stability of the burning process, and possibly caused by the invasion of a virus or Trojan;

(7) The disc used for burning has problems, it is bad quality or a non-standard format;

(8) A large amount of heat is generated when burning and occupies too much of the resources to deal with it, as a result, insufficient resources are available.

j) The system prompts that disc burning is finished, but there's nothing on the disc

Probable causes for the failure are:

(1) The laser head of the burning machine is severely aged or there's too much dust accumulated on it and makes the disc burn with poor readability;

(2) The burning machine has a severe deflection fault, this means that DVD burner can burn two types of discs: +R and -R; but after burning, it will only read one type of disc;

(3) A problem with the burning software itself, such as software with a virus or Trojan invasion;

(4) The disc used for burning, is of bad quality or non standard format;

k) CD music burned does not play normally

Probable causes for the failure are:

(1) You haven't chosen "data disc" to burn the music on the CD-R disc, namely the music CD burned must be accorded with the CD-DA file format;

(2) The disc has copyright protection, failures will occur like cannot copy, or cannot play normally after copying it;

(3) The burning software itself has problems, such as a virus or Trojan invasion;

(4) There's problems with the disc used for burning, it's of bad quality or it's not CD-R standard formatting;

l) A DVD burning drive will only burn a CD but not a DVD

Probable causes for the failure are:

(1) The DVD-RW drive uses single laser head double beams of light (lasers of two different wavelengths) to burn and play a CD and DVD. It will recognize the type of disc automatically and auto adjusts the laser wavelength when reading and burning. If one of the beams has problems (including its decoding circuit), then one function would be missing, but it would not affect the other function;

(2) The laser beam power on one of the devices is too low due to aging, or there's too much dust accumulated on it;

(3) A burning software setting error; you want to burn a DVD, but you chose CD in the burning software, or the burning speed is set higher than the marked speed of the disc;

(4) The burning software has faults itself, the DVD burning function is not working;

(5) Too much resource support is needed during the DVD burning process, and there's a temporary shortage of resources;

m) The DVD-RW drive can only read a disc but not burn a CD/DVD

Probable causes for the failure are:

(1) The laser beam power needed to burn the disc is higher than the laser beam power available but sufficient to play a disc; when the laser head has aged or there's too much dust accumulated, then it will only read a disc but not burn it;

(2) Burning software faults, the CD/DVD burning function is corrupted;

(3) There's other software running when burning and causes a conflict;

(4) Operating system problems, such as caused by virus or Trojan invasion;

n)   After upgrading to a DVD-RW drive, it does not burn

Upgrading to a DVD-RW drive means that originally the laptop used CD-RW discs, now it's upgraded to use DVD-RW discs;

(1)   The newly installed DVD-RW drive is incompatible with the motherboard, even the BIOS cannot recognize it;

(2)   The DVD-RW drive shell body has a small difference with the original CD-RW drive shell body and causes a slight distortion after installing the new DVD-RW drive, when it is running at high speed, eccentricity would occur and it shakes too much to burn successfully;

(3)   The burning software is too old, out of date, and can only burn a CD;

(4)   Burning software faults, the DVD burning function is corrupted;

(5)   There's insufficient resources supporting DVD burning, or there's a software conflict, which causes the DVD burning failure;

o)   "DVD-RW picks up disc" can only read the data of some discs, but fails to read out the data on some other discs;

What is the so-called "DVD-RW picks up disc"? it means that the DVD-RW can read the data on some discs correctly, but is quite sensitive to some other discs and cannot recognize or read the data on the disc normally;

(1)   It is caused by a DVD-RW drive mechanical failure. The mechanical part of the DVD-RW drive is abraded, moved and distorted, the mechanical part shakes too much or it's directly damaged and leads to the problem that some discs do not run or the laser cannot be emitted or focused onto the track of the disc;

(2)   The laser head has aged and emits less power or the laser head is covered by dust; when this situation appears, the penetration ability of the laser beams is lower, also the power is lower, therefore, some new discs will be read, while some older discs cannot be read;

(3)   The failure might be caused because there's a scratch on the disc or partial information on the disc is damaged. When the penetration ability of the laser beams lowers and power is also lowered, the error correction ability of the disc reading firmware would also be less and some discs that could be read before might not be read now;

(4)   Failure caused by the partial bad quality of the discs used. With some disc manufacturing processes the disc quality is not good; the distance of each track on the disc differs greatly, when the distance is far enough, the data can be read; but when the distance is too close, the laser beam focusing on the tracks is not correct and then it can easily jump tracks or the signal picked up is drifting and you cannot be sure of it.

12.1.4 Treatments for laptop DVD-RW drive failures

a)   Open "My computer" on the desktop, and finding that the DVD-RW drive icon is missing

Here's the treatment method:

Put one pure DOS disc or other professional Windows PE system disc (notice: not operation system installation disc) into the laptop DVD-RW drive to boot, the effect of it is primarily to see whether the laptop DVD-RW can finish a normal start-up and run process. If the DVD-RW drive starts from the disc and runs normally, then it means there's nothing wrong with the hardware, and the failure can only be software related. If it fails to boot from disc and run, then it indicates the problem is with the hardware, (DVD or motherboard), but it's also possible that it is a combination of hardware and software.

A)   If a DVD-RW drive does boot the computer from a disc normally, then the key point is to check for a conflict problem with it. Right click "My Computer" and choose Properties—Hardware—Device manager, and check for a yellow exclamation mark;

1)   If there is a yellow exclamation mark there, it means that an important driver file is defective or there's a conflict between software, that prevents the operating system from finishing the DVD-RW icon loading successfully;

2)   If there is no yellow exclamation mark, then the situation might be more complex. You should first clear viruses, and then try disabling firewall and update the operating system and drivers; if the problem is still unsolved, then you should consider reinstalling the operating system.

B)   If the DVD-RW drive does not boot the computer from a disc, then the key point is to check for a DVD-RW drive hardware problem.

(1)   Check whether the plug-in interface between the motherboard and the DVD-RW is loose or damaged or not;

(2)   Try installing a known working DVD-RW drive that is compatible to boot from the disc.

(3)   If the motherboard BIOS does not detect the existence of the DVD-RW drive, then your options are to change the motherboard or use a USB DVD-RW drive.

b)   The DVD-RW drive running sound is heard, but it will not play or read out the contents on the disc;

Here's the treatment method:

Use a known working DVD to see if it will work in the drive. If the DVD-RW drive works with that disc and runs normally, it means the failure must be in the software or the disc was defective or not compatible. If you cannot boot the computer from a disc and run, then it indicates the problem is with the DVD-RW drive hardware, assuming it has nothing to do with the disc format or scratches on the surface.

A) If the DVD-RW drive does boot up the computer from a disc, then the key point is to check for viruses; also you can update the operating system and drivers; if the problem is still unsolved, then you can consider reinstalling operation system;

B) If the DVD-RW drive does not boot the computer from a disc, then the key point is to check for a drive hardware problem;

    (1) Clean the laser head of the drive and see if that clears the problem;

    (2) Install a known working DVD-RW drive that is compatible or use a USB DVD-RW to replace it.

c) A DVD-RW drive can only read a CD, or a DVD, not both;

Here's the treatment method:

Follow the same procedure as b) above except do it with a good CD/DVD and then with the other.

d) deleted

e) When a DVD-RW drive is reading a disc; it makes an unusual loud noise;

Here's the treatment method:

    (1) Change the DVD/CD disc to a new unblemished high quality type which will make it DVD-RW drive principle axis motor accelerate to the data reading speed easily;

    (2) Install a known working DVD-RW drive that is compatible or use a USB DVD-RW to replace the old one.

f) DVD-RW drawer does not open and you cannot get the CD or DVD out

Here's the treatment method:

    1) If this only happens occasionally, then you should first try rebooting the computer;

    2) There might be a slight distortion of the drive case or something stuck in the drive and you need to uninstall the drive from the laptop and clean it. If you find the case is slightly distorted and maybe a difficult fit when it is plugged in, you need to repair or change it;

    3) If it's internal mechanical damage because the DVD-RW drive developed a fault itself or possibly an electronic failure, then you should change the DVD-RW drive or use a USB DVD-RW drive to replace the old one;

g)   DVD-RW drive can successfully read the disk, but you cannot boot from a CD /DVD disk

Here's the treatment method:

1)   You need to remove the main battery and pull out the external power adapter; press power button above 30 seconds, and then separately connect the power adapter to start up the laptop. Set the first boot device as DVD/CD.

2)   Clean the laser head of the DVD-RW deck, if there is too much dust accumulated on the laser head it lowers the penetration ability of the laser beam;

3)   The DVD-RW deck has aged or is completely incompatible with the motherboard; you can consider updating the DVD-RW BIOS (Firmware) or change the DVD-RW deck.

h)   A disc does not play automatically

You know the disc will run automatically but it does not auto-run in your DVD-RW deck. This is the treatment:

Method 1)

A DVD-RW disc auto runs if it has the autorun.inf file on it; after the system detects the file, it would call up AutoPlay to run the file. Write the path of the disc application you need to run to the file autorun.inf.

Method 2)

In REGEDIT subkey "HKEY_CURRENT_USER\Software\Microsoft\Windows\Current version\Policies\Explorer", there's one key with value "NoDriveTypeAutoRun" on the right side pane, the data should be set as "95 00 00 00". You can also set the subkey "NoDriveTypeAutoRun" on the right side panel of "HKEY_USER\.DEFAULT\Software\ Microsoft\Windows\Currentversion\Policies\Explorer", by changing the data of the key as "95 00 00 00".

Method 3)

In the DVD-RW drive property or the control panel, on the page for AutoPlay, there are dropdown menus. For different file formats, there are different selections. You must first choose the dropdown men for "Music CD" (notice: not "Music file"), and then click "Every time remind me to choose one operation". If after setting it like this, it still does not auto play, then click "Start"—"Run", and then enter "gpedit.msc", click OK and run "Group Policy", on the left side, find "Local computer policies—Computer configurations(or user configuration)—Administrative template—System", and then double click "Disable AutoPlay" on the right side, choose "Not configured" and then click OK to exit. There's "Disable AutoPlay" settings both in these two configurations, but under the circumstances that it's all configured, "Computer Configuration" is of higher priority than "User configurations".

Method 4)

If it still does not auto play, then the key point is to check for viruses; also update the operating system; if it still does not solve the problem, then you should consider reinstalling the operating system.

i)   Disc burning always fails, during the burning process; it always prompts an error, and then exits burning.

1)   The disc itself has a problem, try another disc, and please confirm that the disc you put in is blank;

2)   Make sure that the burning format you choose is correct. If you are going to burn a DVD, and the disc is a DVD, select DVD burn, but not CD burn.

3)   Burn with a low speed, such as below 16x (4X) speed. And use "First read disc and then burn" method to make sure the disc has no error;

4)   You could have a burning software issue, you can try uninstalling the burning software and reinstalling it, here I recommend Nero;

5)   Disc burning always fails; you should pay attention to these scenarios:

(1)   Close the applications not needed for burning

During the burning process, any other computer activity can interfere with the burning process and cause it to fail. Therefore, before burning a disc, you should temporarily close the screensaver, power management, firewall, antivirus software, music player, movie watching software, game software, internet connection and so on. You can use them after burning finishes successfully;

(2)   Close power management and disk shutdown service

Before burning, if you already have enabled the system power management function, disk shutdown function, BIOS system hibernation and other relevant options, then the entire burning process would face a great threat, you should close all of these;

(3)   Power off or pull out peripheral devices not needed for burning

If there is a printer, digital camera, USB disk, movable disk or other peripherals connected, then even they are not activated, a signal would be sent onto the SCSI Bus. Any error data occurring on the SCSI Bus will influence the entire disc burning process.

(4)   Disconnect the LAN and ISP

Before burning, you should disconnect the MODEM and telephone line, in case the host responds to the communication signal of the MODEM and cause a burning failure. The best way is to shut down the entire network, in case other members can access your computer resources through the network causing a burning failure;

(5)   Choose a burning software with stable performance and powerful functions.

The performance of burning software and tools, to a great extent, impacts the stability of the burning process. I suggest using the burning software Nero series.

(6)   Use a disc with reliable quality

Use a good quality disc, in order to ensure the burning accuracy and success rate to the maximum extent. I suggest you choose Sony, BenQ, Philips, LG and other well known brands.

(7)   Laptop overheating consumes resources needed for burning

   a)   Heat is generated by the burning process. Make sure you are using the laptop on a hard flat surface and not blocking ventilation.
   b)   Make sure the laptop CPU fan is working normally and the intake air can flow smoothly. If temperature becomes too high during the burning process, you may need to add an additional USB radiator to accelerate heat radiation.

j)   The system prompts disc burning finishes, but there's nothing on the disc

First put the burned disc in another computer to try it, check that it can read out the content. If it can, then the failure should be as mentioned above in b) "DVD-RW disc running sound can be heard, but will not play or read the disc content" Use the method of b) to deal with it.

(1)   Clean the laser head of the DVD-RW drive; make sure there's not too much dust accumulated on the laser head of the DVD-RW drive.
(2)   Try another type of disc, such as the current +R disc. Then try using a—R disc. Make sure it is a good quality disc in case the burning machine has a deflection fault, which means after burning, it can only read one type of disc.
(3)   Install a good working DVD-RW drive or use a USB DVD-RW instead. If the failure disappears, then the problem is in the original DVD-RW drive; if the problem still exists, you have a software problem or the settings are wrong.
(4)   If the burning still fails to work successfully, the key point is to scan for viruses, clean them, and update operating system applications; if this does not solve the problem, then you should consider reinstalling the operating system.

k) The CD music disc burned does not play normally

1) First check whether the source disc has copyright protection, if yes, then do not copy it, probably it will not work normally even if you duplicate;

2) Choose a CD-R disc of high quality; I suggest using Sony, BenQ, Philips, LG and other well known brands;

3) Choose the correct file burning method, use data disc burning (sound track) to burn on the CD-R, namely, what we often say is "CD-DA file format", Do not use the CD burning method;

4) Use another computer and try it again, in case the burning software of the original laptop has problems.

l) DVD burning drive could only burn a CD, but not a DVD

1) Clean the laser head of the DVD-RW drive; check that there is not too much dust accumulated on the laser head of the DVD-RW drive causing a problem.

2) Uninstall the original burning software; I suggest reinstalling the burning application Nero series software. Make sure the settings are correct, when burning the DVD disc, don't choose CD in the burning software; meanwhile, pay attention to the speed settings of the burning, which should be lower than the marked speed of the disc;

3) Install a known working DVD-RW drive or use a USB DVD-RW instead; if the failure disappears, then it means the problem is in the original DVD-RW drive; if the problem still exists, then it means the problem is in the software or a resource shortage;

m) A DVD burning drive can only read a disc but not burn a CD/DVD

1) Clean the laser head of the DVD-RW drive; check that there is not too much dust accumulated on the laser head of the DVD-RW drive causing the problem.

2) Uninstall the original burning software; I suggest reinstalling the burning application Nero series software. Make sure the settings are correct, when burning a DVD disc, don't choose CD in the burning software; meanwhile, pay attention to the speed settings of the burning, which should be lower than the marked speed of the disc;

3) Refer to the method in h), namely "Disc burning always fails; it always prompts an error during the burning process and exits burning".

4) Install a known working DVD-RW drive or use a USB DVD-RW instead; if the failure disappears, then it means the problem is in the original DVD-RW drive; if the failure still exists, then it means the problem is in the software or settings.

n) After installing a new DVD-RW drive, it fails to burn

It means the original laptop was set up for CD-RW, and now needs to be updated to DVD-RW.

1) First check up whether the laptop BIOS can recognize the updated DVD-RW drive, if the type installed is not the DVD-RW drive in the list, then it means the installed

DVD-RW drive is incompatible with the motherboard. You need to use a type that the BIOS can recognize;

2) If the BIOS does recognize the updated DVD-RW drive, then you should put one working DVD disc into the drive and check if that there is no reading problem. If it has a problem with disc reading, it means the laptop still has software or hardware problems, you need to eliminate these problems and then go on to solve the problem that the DVD-RW drive fails to burn;

3) Uninstall the original burning software; I suggest reinstalling the burning application Nero series software. Make sure the settings are correct, choose discs of higher quality, meanwhile, pay attention to the speed settings of the burning, which should be lower than the marked speed of the disc;

4) Refer to the method (h), "namely "Disc burning always fails, it always prompts error during the burning process and exits burning".

5) Install a known working DVD-RW drive to replace the original one; if the failure disappears, then it means the problem is in the original DVD-RW drive; if the failure still exists, then it means the problem is in the software or settings.

o) "DVD-RW picks up disc" means it can only read the data of some discs, but cannot read for some other discs;

This so-called "DVD-RW picks up disc" means a DVD-RW drive can read the data of some discs correctly, but for other discs, it's still quite sensitive and cannot recognize or read the data on the disc normally;

1) Clean the laser head of the DVD-RW and check that there's not too much dust accumulated on the DVD-RW head, which will lower the penetration ability of the laser beam;

2) Install a USB DVD-RW to replace the old one; if the failure disappears, it means the problem is in the original DVD-RW drive; if the problem still exists, then it means the problem is in the software or settings.

12.2 Repair flow chart to Eliminate laptop DVD-RW failures

12.2.1 Repair shortcuts for the failure that a DVD cannot be recognized or a disk cannot read.

This problem occurs when a DVD-ROM volume icon disappears or when it cannot read a disk or burn discs, which bring much trouble to the users. When you deal with this kind of failure, the method many people would adopt is "First hardware and then software", namely, first consider the DVD-ROM hardware; and then consider other problems. The best operation is to find a similar DVD-ROM and install it in the laptop to find out the reason. Please take a look at Figure 12-2

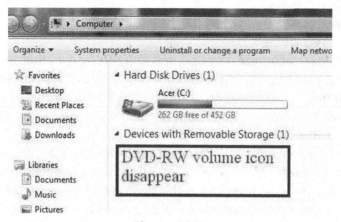

Figure 12-2

As there are many kinds of DVD-ROMs, the shell shapes are often different and this test method would not have a useful effect, wasting much time. Actually the method to determine a laptop DVD-ROM problem quickly is quite simple; with the method below, within 1 to 2 minutes you can quickly find out the reason why the laptop DVD-ROM doesn't work. It immediately lets you know whether the problem comes from software or hardware. You can also find out if the problem is caused by both software and hardware aspects at the same time!

Troubleshooting shortcuts:

A) Put one bootable pure DOS disc into the DVD-ROM to boot up; after the laptop starts up, tap any key on the keyboard to test the typing. If there's no system crash symptom, then it means the DVD-ROM failure has nothing to do with the laptop hardware. At this moment, the suspected points for the failure are the operation system, application software, viruses, hacker software, and other drivers related to the hardware.

B) If the laptop does not finish a DOS boot or after finishing a DOS boot, a system crash happens when tapping on the keyboard; it means the DVD-ROM failure is related to the laptop hardware. The key points to determine the failure are: whether the interface between motherboard and the DVD-ROM is loose or damaged, or the DVD-ROM itself, power adapter, memory stick and the operating temperature also are creating a problem.

Sometimes, both software and hardware combined can cause a laptop DVD-ROM failure. This means that after the hardware passes through testing, (there's no system down symptom happening under DOS operation system), but probably under the Windows operating system, the DVD-ROM volume control would also disappear or the DVD-ROM will not read or burn discs. You need to repair the laptop again according to the methods that eliminate software failure.

12.2.2 43% of failures where a laptop will not recognize or burn a DVD is from the DVD burning machine itself

When we deal with such a failure, the first thing many people would think of is to find an identical DVD-RW drive to replace the faulty drive and see if it will work. If you happen to have one on hand, then probably it's a pretty good idea, but if you decide to buy a new DVD-RW drive, then do you know how much the risk there is? There is a 57%, or more chance it may not be compatible with your laptop; there are many kinds of drives and even the shell shapes are different. You can cause a more serious failure while trying to fit it or get it working. Please take a look at Figure 12-3.

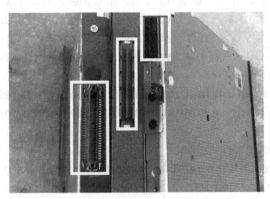

Figure 12-3

So before you decide to buy a new DVD-RW drive, it's necessary to carry out a few important tests on the suspected laptop DVD-RW drive.

Now let's take a look at the next four situations:

A) Try to boot the laptop using alternately a bootable CD and DVD. If the laptop boots up, it means the drive can read and burn with the disc you used. Likely the failure is only in the laptop software, so focus on checking: operating system, application software, viruses, hacker software and drivers for the hardware.

B) If the laptop completes a CD boot up, but fails to boot with a DVD, then it means the failure might be in the DVD-RW drive hardware, and probably also in the software. The solution is to refer to the chapter <<12.1.4 Treatments with laptop DVD-RW failures>>.

C) If the laptop finishes a DVD boot, but fails to finish a CD boot, then it means the laptop failure is in the DVD-RW drive hardware, but also might be in both the software and hardware. The solution is to the chapter <<12.1.4 Treatments with laptop DVD-RW failures>>.

D) If the laptop does not finish either a CD/DVD disc boot, then it means the failure is in the hardware, (DVD or motherboard), but it's also likely to be connected with both the hardware and software (BIOS). The key points to check are: whether the interface between the motherboard and DVD-RW is loose or damaged, the internal laptop temperature is normal, and so on.

12.2.3 25% of DVD recognition or DVD burning failures is from the DVD driver and the operating system

25% of DVD-RW volume disappearance or disc read failures are from software conflicts or because the executive application file of the operating system is damaged; check whether the DVD-RW drive has a conflict problem or not, right click "My Computer"—"Properties"—"Hardware"—"Device manager", look for a yellow exclamation mark . . .

1) If there's a yellow exclamation mark, it means there's a conflict between software, which prevents the operating system from finishing DVD-RW icon loading;

2) Even if there's no yellow exclamation mark there, it's also likely there's a conflict between the software and the DVD-RW drive, put a boot disc into the laptop drive, if the DVD-RW does not start from the disc normally, then it means there is not a problem with the DVD-RW hardware, the failure is only caused by the software.

12.2.4 25% of DVD recognition failures or DVD burning failures are from the motherboard, DVD drive connection interface and connection cable

25% of DVD-RW volume disappearance or disc reading failures are from the DVD drive interface no longer connecting properly, loosening, interfaces distortion, or a screw missing used to solidly install the drive and a cracked plastic lock and so on.

The solution is also quite simple; you can uninstall the DVD-RW drive, repair the interface and then install it carefully. Next add the proper screws or change the plastic lock, until the problem is solved.

12.2.5 Analysis for a DVD recognition failure or a DVD burning failure and repair flow to deal with it.

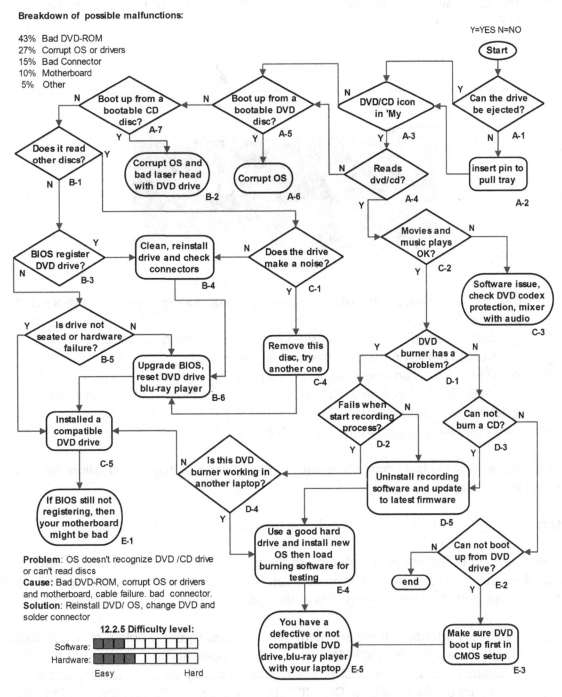

This tutorial will help you solve these problems:

a) The laptop does not detect a DVD-RW disc, or the DVD-RW drive volume control disappears;

b) A DVD-RW disc running sound is heard, but it cannot play or read out the content of the disc;

c) The DVD-RW drive can read either a CD or a DVD, but not both;

d) The disc drawer does not open, and it cannot read a CD or DVD; please take a look at Figure 12-4.

Figure 12-4

e) Disc burning always fails, there's an error prompt during the burning process, exit burning;

f) System prompts disc burning finished, but there's nothing on the disc;

g) The burned music on the CD does not play normally;

h) A DVD-RW drive can only burn a CD or a DVD disc but not both;

i) The DVD-RW drive can only read out some of the disc data, but for some other discs, it doesn't read out at all;

j) Other problems related to the DVD-RW drive;

In this article, I will explain how to find out the reason for a laptop sound failure when it is related to the disc drive.

Start

When you plug in the power adapter, press the power button to start the computer, and enter the system; please observe the process carefully. What happens will be covered by one or a few independent failure descriptions of this tutorial:

1) Please pay attention: there are many reasons causing the problem of laptop sound loss. For example, the DVD-RW drawer will not open and you cannot get the CD or DVD out; if it's an occasional problem, then probably certain software might have temporary conflicts with the DVD-RW drive. Use a paperclip to plug into the access hole on the front of the drawer and press it, then by force, the DVD-RW drawer will

pop out. This might be all that is needed to solve the sound problem and the rest of the tutorial is not required;

2) The external environment (temperature) has an extreme change within a short period, and causes a DVD-RW drive failure. This situation doesn't belong to the context of this tutorial, please check another tutorial article.

Step: A-1

First of all, please check whether the laptop DVD-RW drive can open normally?

If it does, then enter Step: A-3;

If it doesn't, then enter Step: A-2

Step: A-2

The laptop does not open the DVD-RW drive drawer and you cannot remove the CD or DVD disc.

Here's the treatment process:

If this is just an occasional failure, then you need to first shut down, and restart the laptop; if after restarting the laptop, it still does not open the DVD-RW drawer, then there are two ways to pop out DVD-RW drawer; these are "Hard popout" and "Soft popout";

1) "Hard popout": means the use of a thin pinpoint inserted in the emergency popout hole on the DVD-RW drive front. to let the drawer pop out; Please take a look at Figure 12-5.

Figure 12-5

"Soft popout": means to enter the laptop system, enter "My Computer"—right click on "DVD-RW/CD-RW drive", and in the option list, choose eject;

2) If after reinserting a disc, the problem still exists, then check whether you have used a utility software package similar to Drive Letter Access (DLA) or not. It lets the DVD-RW stay at "Wait for burning" status. If so, please try deleting the file;

3) If you have a mechanical failure because the shell has a slight distortion or there's something stuck inside the DVD-RW drive, then you disassemble the DVD-RW drive from the laptop, and repair it;

4) If the DVD-RW drive shell has a slight distortion, then you need to heat, revise or change it, to make the disc drawer open successfully; if there's another problem, please enter Step: A-3;

Step: A-3 checks whether "My Computer" has a "DVD-RW/CD-RW" device icon.

If there is an icon, then please enter Step: A-4

If you open "My Computer" on the desktop, and finding the DVD-RW drive volume disappeared, then the failure cause might be:

(1) An important driver file is damaged or there's a software conflict, which prevents the operating system from loading the disc drive icon;

(2) The DVD-RW drive is damaged and the operating system cannot recognize it;

(3) The motherboard interface connecting the drive is defective;

(4) The South Bridge circuit controlling the DVD-RW drive has a problem, which results in the motherboard BIOS not detecting the existence of the DVD-RW drive. When there's no icon, then enter Step: A-5;

Step: A-4 checks that the DVD-RW drive will read a disc;

If it does read a disc, then enter Step: C-2;

If you can hear the disc running in the DVD-RW drive, but it cannot play or read the contents of the disc;

Then you should consider the few reasons below:

(1) Some of the software installed may have conflicts with the DVD-RW drive; you can restart the operating system, under safe mode, and try the DVD-RW drive again. If it does read the disc content, we know there is a software conflict;

(2) The DVD-RW drive laser head has aged severely, or is dislodged due to rough handling of the laptop; then enter Step: A-5 to continue;

(3) The disc surface has severe scratches, and cannot be read; use a new disc, and try again;

(4) The disc format has incompatibility problems with the operating system; try using another disc; if the problem is not solved, then please enter Step: A-5 to continue detection;

Step: A-5 checks that the DVD-RW drive will boot the laptop from a DVD disc;

Use one bootable DVD or a professional Windows PE system disc to boot from the drive and see if it works or not:

A)   If the laptop boots successfully from the DVD, and completes the process, without an error message; you know the problem is in the OS software only and not the hardware: please enter Step: A-6;

B)   If the laptop cannot boot from the DVD-RW drive, then the probable the causes of the failure are shown below:

   (1)   If DVD-RW drive uses "Single head and dual wave-wavelength" or "Dual heads" technology, then there's one laser emitter (reading the DVD) not working or the laser head has aged severely; you will need to electrically clean the laser emitter or change the drive;

   (2)   If DVD-RW uses "Single head and dual focusing lens" technology, then one focusing lens (reading the DVD) has accumulated too much dust or the focusing lens is skewed off target, which leads to a DVD reading failure. You need to electrically clean the laser emitter or change the drive;

   (3)   There's a severe scratch on the surface of the DVD or the format is incompatible with operating system, which leads to a reading failure; if this is the situation, then your problem might be relevant with the CD you are using, please enter Step: A-7;

Step: A-6 Check the operating system and the hard disk

After putting a boot DVD into the DVD-RW drive, next start the computer and if the process completes the inspection successfully, it means the failure is in the operating system on the original hard disk or the current hard disk. There's likely a conflict problem, right click "My Computer"—"Properties"—"Hardware"—"Device manager"; after opening it, observe if there's a yellow exclamation mark there.

1)   If there's a yellow exclamation mark, it means that a certain important driver file is damaged or there's a conflict between software, which leads to a problem that the operating system cannot finish loading the icon of the DVD-RW drive; you need to uninstall antivirus software, and then try disabling the firewall;

2)   If there's no yellow exclamation mark there, then the situation might be more complex. You should first clear viruses and hacker software. Then update the operating system and drivers; and if the problem still is not solved (assuming the client doesn't request to save the original data), then the implementation approach is simple, that is, after formatting the disk, reinstall the operation system. Generally, this problem will be solved. However, when installing the operating system, if there's an error prompt or a blue screen failure, indicating the operating system reinstallation and repair does not work, and does not finish operating system installation, then this failure symptom

belongs to the description of flowchart 07. Please follow the flowchart 07 to solve the problem;

If you haven't formatted the hard disk, and the failure is still there after reinstalling the OS, then the system is probably infected by viruses or hacker software. Simple reinstallation did not solve the problem completely, and you will need to format hard disk with DOS, and then the viruses can be cleared 100%;

Step: A-7 Check whether the DVD-RW drive can boot from a CD or not;

A) If the laptop boots from a CD successfully, and the failure disappears, then it means the original failure is with the laser emitter (reading DVD disc) of the DVD-RW drive, or the focusing lens (reading DVD disc) has accumulated too much dust or is skewed off target, leading to a DVD reading failure. The solution is to clean the laser emitter or change the drive; please enter Step: B-2;

B) If the laptop does boot up from a CD, but the CD did not be read in the operating system, then the causes for the failure probably are:

A CD surface might have severe scratches or the format is incompatible with the operating system, and causes the reading failure. If it is the case, then your problem might be with the CD disc, please enter Step: B-1;

Step: B-1 the goal of this step is to confirm the failure is not with the CD

1) Change to a known good working CD disc, check whether the disc reading failure disappears or not. If it doesn't read the CD disc, then check that the disc drive is inserted and connects properly. Make sure the central jack of the CD-ROM is tight and the drive is securely plugged in and fitted flush to the case as it should be. Then try the disc again.

2) After loading a CD disc, you are better off to close the opened "My Computer" window, and then open it again, in this case, it can accelerate the reading speed of the CD disc;

If the steps above do you no favour, or we can say that the failure still exists, then please enter STEP: B-3; if the failure disappears, then for the next problem you need to solve, please enter STEP: C-1;

Step: B-2 Check the operating system and change the DVD-RW drive

After putting a CD disc in the DVD-RW drive, start up the machine, and the inspection passes successfully, then it means the failure is with the laser emitter (reading DVD disc) of the DVD-RW drive; however, it is not that simple as it looks, because the DVD-RW volume control in "My Computer" on the desktop is missing. The reason probably is because certain important driver files are damaged or there's a conflict between software, preventing the operating system from finishing loading the icon for the DVD-RW drive. This failure can be the combination of two problems, first of all, investigate problems with the operation system, then follow the method in "Step: A-6 Check the operating system and the hard disk" of this chapter, and then decide whether to change the DVD-RW drive;

Step: B-3 the goal of this step is to confirm the failure is not with the laptop motherboard

By the repair flow Start->A-1->A-3->A-5->A-7->B-1, I can confirm that the failure probably comes from these two points:

(1) The DVD-RW drive is damaged and the operating system cannot recognize its existence or does not read the disc;
(2) The interface connector of the DVD-RW drive on the motherboard is damaged, and prevents the drive from connecting properly.

The solution is to remove the drive and check the interface and slots before re-installing it, Inspect it thoroughly for any damage. When installing the drive, the interface should feel smooth and snug but not be too loose or too tight, plugged into the right position and not extruded out. Next open the BIOS Setup page of the laptop, check that there's a DVD-RW drive listed in the registry table, if there is, please enter Step: B-4; if it is not listed, then please enter Step: B-5;

Step: B-4 this step provides maintenance hints that may solve the drive problems

If the laptop DVD-RW drive has not been a problem over time, eventually it will fail to read discs. Likely the laser head has dirt on it and needs cleaning to restore it to working order. It is important to know that the laser head of DVD-RW drive is much more fragile than a CD laser head so gentle care is needed. A tiny physical deviation of the laser head will move the DVD-RW laser off focus so be very careful not to do this,

The best way is to use a glass washing liquid with cotton. Dip the cotton in the liquid and wash the cotton under a clean water supply to get rid of any tiny particles. Use the cotton with the remaining washing liquid to wipe the laser lens. The cotton should be wet but not dripping, (you'd have to twist dry it) clean the laser head of the DVD-RW drive, until the laser head looks crystal with no liquid left on it.

If your laser head is very dirty, (for example, there's smoke oil on the surface), one try at cleaning may not be enough, Repeat until clean. Never clean a laser head with some mordant liquid like alcohol, otherwise, not only DVD-RW drive is not repaired, but you might damage it more.

If the steps above do not help for you, or the failure still occurs, then please enter Step: B-5; if the failure disappears, congratulations, you've succeeded to repairing your laptop.

Step: B-5 the goal of this step is to confirm the screws securing the DVD-RW drive are properly installed

If you remove the DVD-RW drive and reinstall it, make sure you also reinstall the one or two screws that secure it. Failing to do so can affect the system BIOS recognition of the DVD-RW drive, or prevent it from working normally. If the steps above have not helped you, or the failure still occurs, then please enter Step: C-5; if the fixture screws are properly installed, then please enter Step: B-6;

Step: B-6 the goal of this step is to update the BIOS version for the laptop

The biggest advantage to updating the BIOS is to get more new functions without any cost. For example, with previous HP Pavilion dv2000/dv6000/dv9000 laptops, after updating the motherboard BIOS, it updates the system algorithm controlling the fan and provides a more precise measurement of the temperature, enabling new functions not available before. After a BIOS update, the DVD-RW drive problem might be solved and it works normally again.

If you decide to update the motherboard BIOS, please refer to the second chapter <<2.2.3 BIOS update steps>> in this book, if your laptop BIOS version is the latest or you are not planning to update the BIOS, then please enter Step: C-5;

If after the steps above, the failure still exists, then please enter Step: E-1; if the failure disappears, congratulations; your laptop has been repaired successfully.

Step: C-1 when a DVD-RW drive is reading a disc, it makes a loud noise

Here's the solution:

1) When playing a movie with the DVD-ROM drive, sometimes it would make annoying noises, and this is because of the motor's high-speed rotation inside the DVD-ROM drive. This symptom usually happens on high-speed DVD-ROM drives. When a disc is put in and ejected, the noise is unusually loud, and there's a mechanical friction cacophony. The disc shelf in and out speed is not stable or it may not open at all. The noise might be caused because the disc rotates unstably or by mechanical friction. It is likely the rotation gear in the motor servo assembly is worn out or damaged.
2) If you notice that the shell of the drive is slightly distorted or there's something stuck inside the DVD-ROM drive, you need to first disassemble it from the laptop, clean and remove the obstruction and then try to correct or change the distorted shell.
3) If you have a mechanical or electronic fault in the drive, it is mostly not worth repairing; you should change the DVD-ROM drive or use a USB DVD-RW drive to replace it.

After the above steps, if you are still dealing with your drive problem: Step: C-4; if the noise has disappeared but you want to ensure the problem is completely eliminated, please enter Step: B-4;

Step: C-2 Treatment for a laptop failure to play a DVD movie

1) First you need to confirm that the DVD drive supports a DVD format. It should support DVD-ROM, COMBO, and DVD-RW formats. Then you need to confirm that the hardware is functioning properly and the DVD drive is reading the disc (DVD format), and then focus on software problems;

2) If you install a DVD player, such as POWERDVD, WINDVD, WINDOWS MEDIA PLAYER and REAL PLAYER, etc but it still cannot play, it's because you still need to download a plug-in to install;

3) Playing a DVD with software is different from playing directly with a DVD machine player. During its playing process; it uses the CPU, display card and other hardware, cooperating together to finish the soft decompression process. An operating system free of all problems and running smoothly is also quite important. If important files are missing, or there's a virus or Trojan in the system, it can affect the normal operation of your drive.

If the steps above have not helped you, or the failure still exists, then please enter STEP: C-3; if the failure disappears, you need to solve the next problem, please enter STEP: D-1;

Step: C-3 a laptop cannot play a DVD or there's no DVD decoder

Hardware issues:

If it is a CD-ROM drive you are using, of course it will not play a DVD. You can play CDs and VCDs. Your only options are to replace the drive with a DVD capable drive or use a USB DVD drive

Software issues:

If you use WINDOWS MEDIA PLAYER and REAL PLAYER, and they do not play, it is because you still need to download a plug-in to install. How do you check the DVD decoder in Vista system?

1) Click on the Windows orb logo at the bottom of the desktop to show the Start menu. Type "windows media player" in the search box at the bottom of the menu and press the "Enter" key to open the Windows Media Player (WMP) application

2) Click WMP top "Help" menu, there's one drop down menu shown. And choose "About Windows media player" menu;

3) Click the link on "Technical support information" dialog. Let it open a webpage on the Internet browser.

4) Find the "Video Codecs" and "MPEG/DVD Filters" sections on the Web page to see the DVD decoder for Vista.

If the steps above have not helped you, or the failure still exists, then please enter Step: B-3; if the failure disappears, you will need to solve the next problem, please enter Step: C-1;

Step: C-4 the goal of this step is to use a disc without scratches on the surface

A DVD-ROM drive might make a loud noise when playing or reading a disc, if it is an occasional failure, you need to first shut down the laptop, change the DVD/CD disc, but use a high quality disc without scratches on the surface, and then restart the laptop. This will make the DVD-ROM drive principle axis accelerate to the data reading speed, lowering down the noise.

If the steps above are of no help for you, or the failure still occurs, then please enter Step: C-5

Step: C-5 the goal of this step is to change a DVD-RW drive

1) If you change a working DVD-RW drive, then first check whether the laptop BIOS will recognize the DVD-RW drive, if it is not in the list, then it means the DVD-RW drive installed is incompatible with the motherboard, or possibly the motherboard has faults itself;

2) If the BIOS recognize the new DVD-RW drive, try a DVD disc you know is good and see if it reads. If there's still a problem with disc reading, then it means the laptop has other software problems that need to be eliminated.

If the steps above have not helped you, or the failure still occurs, then please enter Step: E-1

Step: D-1 this step is to check whether the DVD-RW has problems when burning a DVD disc.

If there's no problem, then enter Step: D-3, if there is, then you can follow the next method to deal with it;

1. As the disc itself may have a problem, you can try changing it for another blank disc.

2. Please confirm the burning software format you choose is correct and the DVD should be blank; the burning file format must also be chosen as DVD, and not CD.

3. Burn with a low burning speed, below 16x (4X), and use the "First read disc and then burn" method, to confirm the source disc has no error;

If the steps above have not helped you, please continue by entering STEP: D-2;

Step: D-2

If disc burning always fails, and error prompts during the burning process: then you can follow the next method to solve it;

If it's another problem, such as the disc burning is finished, but there's nothing that can be read on the disc, then enter Step: D-5;

1. Close all applications not needed for burning

    During the burning process, any operation disturbing or stopping the burning data transmission will lead to failure. After finishing data burning, then run these applications;

2. Close power management and disk shutdown service;

    Before burning, don't enable the system power management function, the disk shutdown function or the BIOS system hibernation and various other relevant options.

3. Power off or pull out the devices not needed for burning;

    Disconnect the printer, digital camera, USB storage disk or movable disk and all other peripherals from the laptop that could affect the entire disc burning process.

4. Disconnect the LAN and ISP

    Shut down the entire network, stopping other members from visiting your machine resources through the network and causing a burning failure;

5. Choose the burning software Nero series since it has very stable performance and powerful functions;

6. Use a writable disc of reliable quality

    I suggest choosing the products of well known brands like Sony, BenQ, Philips, LG and so on.

7. Prevent machine overheating that uses up resources

    a) High heat will be produced when burning. Do not do anything to interfere with the laptop ventilation such as using it on a soft surface like your lap or a bed.

b) Make sure the laptop "Fan" works normally and the intake's airflow is smooth and not obstructed. You can add a USB radiator to accelerate the heat radiation.

Step: D-3 This step is to check whether your DVD-RW drive will also burn a CD disc or not

If there is no problem, then please enter Step: E-2; if there's problem, you can follow the next steps to deal with it;

1) Try changing the disc, and please confirm the CD disc you put in is blank;
2) Clean the laser head of the DVD-RW drive, check that the laser head (controlling the CD disc) has not accumulated too much dust, which would lead to a disc burning failure;
3) Make sure the settings are correct, when burning a CD disc, don't choose the DVD format in the burning software and make sure that the burning speed setting is lower than the marked speed of the disc;
4) Use the method "First read disc and then burn", to make sure the disc has no errors;

If the steps above have not helped you, please continue to enter STEP: D-5;

Step: D-4

After the treatment of Step: D-2, if the problem still occurs, then try removing the suspected DVD-RW drive and test it in a laptop that you know works properly with a similar drive. Make sure the interfacing in the test unit is compatible and not damaged in any way. It should not be too loose or plugged in too tight and fits properly like the one that was there. If the problem still occurs, then it means the problem is definitely in the hardware and maybe also the software of the original unit, please enter STEP: C-5; if the failure disappears, then it means the problem is in the original laptop software, please enter STEP: E-4;

Step: D-5

Uninstall the original burning software; and I recommend using the Nero series burning software. Make sure the settings are correct; choose discs of high quality; and make sure that the burning speed setting is lower than the marked speed of the disc;

The DVD-RW drives update BIOS (Firmware) is fixed in the memory hardware of the drive. It determines the running mode and the database of the reading or writing capability for various discs used in the drive. The user could refresh to the latest DVD-RW drive BIOS to increase the compatibility for different discs.

If the steps above have not helped you, please continue to enter STEP: E-4;

Step: E-1

If after you have installed a known working DVD-RW, the problem still exists, then you must check the next few points:

1) If you have not checked for viruses and Trojans, then the key point is to clear the viruses and Trojans, and also update the operating system applications; keep the operating system in good running condition;

2) If this has not solved the problem, then you should consider that there might be a conflict between software. Try uninstalling relevant applications, you could also decide to format the hard disk, and reinstall the operation system;

3) After completing the repair flow above, if the BIOS or the operating system still does not recognize the existence of the DVD-RW drive or cannot read a disc, then you can consider that it is a problem on the motherboard, and the only solution is to change the motherboard or use a USB DVD-RW drive.

Step: E-2

If the DVD-RW drive does not start; it means the drive cannot read the data of the disc correctly. It might also be difficult to boot from a disc. If the system does not recognize the disc or read the data on the disc, then please follow the next method:

1) Clean the laser head of the DVD-RW drive if there is too much dust accumulated on the laser head, which lowers the penetration ability of the laser beam;

2) The DVD-RW drive is too old, deteriorated due to aging, or is completely incompatible with the motherboard; you can consider updating the DVD-RW drive BIOS (Firmware) or change the DVD-RW drive.

If the steps above have not helped you, please continue to enter Step: E-3;

Step: E-3

The CMOS is used to store system information, such as time and boot sequence relevant data. If the CMOS cannot save the modified page for some reason, then probably the laptop would fail to boot up from a disc. Before continuing, you need to remove the main battery and pull out the external power adapter; press power on button for 30 seconds, and then connect power adapter only to start up the laptop. Set the first boot device as DVD/CD.

If the steps above have not helped, then your problem is quite likely in the hardware, please enter Step: E-5;

Step: E-4

After following through the repair flow above, we already know approximately where the problem is. The sources of these failures are likely the original hard disk itself or the software in the original hard disk. If you haven't started a DOS disk formatting job, then you can first test the hard disk and after confirming the hardware itself does not have a problem, consider repairing the system software.

Generally speaking, a HP laptop has one tool in the software for detecting hard disk problems. Usually you can find it in the system BIOS. The detailed troubleshooting is found in Step: D-5 in the book <<7.2.5 Laptop cannot load Windows or repeat restarting and blue screen failure analysis and repair>>.

If the disk passes through this test, we can now consider repairing the system software;

You are better off to reinstall operating system. In HP laptops, usually, you can use the "system recovery" function (F11) to recover the system, and then install Nero series burning software. At this point we can say the laptop problem should be solved completely. After the "Recovery installation" process, the success rate for a DVD-RW drive to work normally is above 99%; there are a few other considerations to conclude the process, please continue to enter STEP: E-5;

Step: E-5

1) In the extreme case where the DVD-RW drive is still not working normally, possibly the shell is distorted slightly or there's something stuck inside. You need to remove the DVD-RW drive from the laptop, clean it up, and if not ok, then change it.
2) The DVD-RW drive sometimes works and sometimes not, which is a fault in itself, such as a mechanical distortion or electronic failure, you should just install a new DVD-RW drive;
3) There are some other possibilities, like a motherboard fault in the laptop, a loose interface or laptop overheating, which would lead to a DVD-RW drive failure to work. When the internal temperature is lowered, the DVD-RW drive might recover back to a working status. The simplest solution is to use an external USB DVD-RW drive;

To summarize this tutorial, on problems with your DVD drive we can basically state the following:

Causes: A DVD burning system hardware failure, a failed DVD driver, system damage, connection problems between the drive and the system motherboard, and motherboard problems;

Solutions: reinstall the driver for the DVD-RW drive or system, change the DVD-RW drive hardware, fix the problems on the motherboard or install a new one, use a USB DVD-RW drive and so on.

As for details, please refer to this tutorial, thank you!

12.3   Twenty-two repair cases of laptop DVD failures

12.3.1 Two repair cases for DVD-RW/CD-RW tray could not eject out failure

225)   HP PAVILION DV5—after putting one CD or DVD disc, plan to open the DVD drive, but it would not eject out normally.

Failure symptom: after putting one CD or DVD disc into his HP laptop, it would not come out no matter to use right-click D:/ to eject the DVD-RW to come out, or press the button manually!

Solution:

This failure obviously belongs to the description of flowchart 11, according to the repair method; confirm the repair path, finding it accords with the sequence:

Start->A-1->A-2->

Repair summary:

When press the button manually, the drive light is on, and could hear DVD-RW sound, which is similar to the sound when it eject before. But actually it could not eject out.

Use a paperclip and to insert into the pin hole, then DVD-RW could eject out. But after installing the DVD RW, problem still exists. Iinspect the DVD-RW inside, finding there are too much dust accumulating at the door, which blocks the tray's coming out. After disassembling the DVD-RW, dip some alcohol onto a piece of cloth to wipe. Don't wipe with any corrosive material. After DVD-RW eject, there's one track slot at the in/out door close to the front, dip some lubricant onto the track slot. Then it's OK!

Hint:

When such kind of failure happens, you should still consider that after the laptop is crushed strongly, the shell distorts slightly, which would also block DVD-RW tray's coming out.

226)   HP PAVILION DV7—after putting one CD or DVD disc, sometimes DVD-RW could not eject out.

Failure symptom: after putting one CD or DVD disc into his HP laptop, sometimes it could not eject out by right click on the DVD-RW volume, even the result is same by pressing the button.

Solution:

This failure obviously belongs to the description of flowchart 11, according to the repair method; confirm the repair path, finding it accords with the sequence:

Start->A-1->A-2->

Repair summary:

Use a paperclip and insert into compulsory eject hole, then DVD-RW could eject out. But after installing, connection problem still occurs before long! Inspect the DVD-RW inside, finding it's quite clean at the door, even there's no dust in the track slot of the DVD-RW door. Then inject some lubricant into the track slot, this has no effect since it is possible that some software temporarily has conflicts with the DVD-RW; check it carefully, the result is as expected. The client used one utility, named Drive Letter Access (DLA), few files were dragged moved to the DVD-RW. After the application starts, DVD-RW is always at "Wait for burning" status, which sometimes blocks DVD-RW tray's coming out. After deleting the files, the problem is resolved.

Hint:

When such kind of failures occurs, you should also consider the DVD-RW has faults itself, mechanical or electronic problems, which can cause the failure that DVD-RW's tray could not eject out at this moment, you could only change.

12.3.2 8 repair instances of disc reading failure caused by HP DVD-RW failure

227) HP DV4-1540us reading disc failure

Failure symptom:

The laptop sometimes could read disc but sometimes cannot, the laser head has is already been wiped, but still could not read disc normally;

Solution:

This failure obviously belongs to the description of 12 flowchart, according to the repair method, confirm the repair path, finding it accords with the sequence:

Start->A-1->A-3->A-5->A-6

Repair summary:

According to the flowchart tutorial, first of all, you should check whether the DVD-RW icon in "My Computer" is displayed normally, as a result, you find that the DVD-RW volume disappears; so probably the reasons causing the failure are:

(1) Certain important driver file is damaged or there's conflict between software;
(2) DVD-RW is already damaged, operating system could not recognize the existence of the DVD-RW;

Test with one bootable DVD disc, or use other professional Windows PE system disc to boot, then to analyze and check whether the laptop DVD-RW would work normally or not. As a result, laptop succeeded in booting up from the DVD disc, it means the original failure is unrelated to the DVD-RW, but only related to operating system. After formatting disk, reinstall operating system, then the failure disappears.

Hint:

When DVD-RW icon in "My Computer" is not displayed, usually we would think that the DVD-RW is not good itself, at this moment, even if you change to a new compatible DVD-RW, the icon would not display there. Therefore, before changing the DVD-RW, pay attention that you must confirm the original DVD-RW really doesn't work (hardware problem), otherwise, it would cause unnecessary waste.

228) HP HDX16 laptop reading disc failure

Failure symptom:

Laptop could not read disc, operating system prompts "as I/O device error, the request could not run", but it could boot up from disc.

Solution:

This failure obviously belongs to the description of flowchart 12, according to the repair method, confirm the repair path, finding it accords with the sequence:

Start->A-1->A-3->A-4->A-5->

Repair summary:

We can know from the failure symptom that the laptop could not recognize or read the disc, but could boot up from the disc. According to the tutorial direction, probably there are reasons causing such a failure:

(1) Certain software installed have conflicts with DVD-RW;

(2)   The surface of the disc has severe scratches, which causes the reading problem;

(3)   Incompatible problem between disc format and operating system;

After changing the disc and test again, as a result, DVD-RW could read normally, then failure disappears.

Hint:

This case is caused because disc failure that system could not recognize normally, which leads to disc reading failure. However, if system prompts error: I/O device error, and could not load operating system, then after excluding connection failure, this symptom would occur only when motherboard or DVD-RW device is not good.

229)   HP CQ61-310US reading disc failure

Failure symptom:

Laptop DVD-RW failure, after putting a disc, there is a creak sound when reading the disc, but finally system fails to read the disc, no content is displayed.

Solution:

This failure obviously belongs to the description of flowchart 12, according to the repair method; confirm the repair path, finding it accords with the sequence:

Start->A-1->A-3->A-4->A-5->A-7->B-1->B-3->B-4->C-5

Repair summary:

According to flowchart tutorial, confirm there's DVD-RW icon in "My Computer", put one DVD disc, testing whether the DVD-RW could read and boot up normally. As a result, it failed to boot up. Then put one CD disc to test the DVD-RW, if there is a rotating action, but still could boot up, then remove the DVD-RW from the laptop, check whether there's any problem with the connection, and then install the DVD-RW again. However, as a result, it still fails to read the disc. Then, test another DVD-RW. After replacing it with aanother new DVD-RW, the failure is eliminated. It now could read disc normally; besides, the system could boot up from the disc. The failure is because the laser head of the DVD-RW is old, or after the laptop in it causes displacement of the laser head;

Hint:

When there's disc reading failure in a DVD-RW, but system could still boot up from disc, then you should pay attention to some software in the laptop, they may have conflicts with the DVD-RW.

230) HP Pavilion DV7 laptop DVD-RW could not reading disc

Failure symptom:

The laptop could not read any disc, even there's no any DVD-RW icon displayed in "My Computer".

Solution:

This failure obviously belongs to the description of flowchart 12, according to the repair method, confirm the repair path, finding it accords with the sequence:

Start->A-1->A-3->A-5->A-7->B-1->B-3->B-5->C-5

Repair summary:

According to the flowchart tutorial, check whether system could boot up from disc, and the result shows that it could not. Meanwhile, test whether DVD-RW is able to be displayed normally in BIOS, if no DVD-RW could be detected, then continue checking; when you put one disc, and there is no rotation or vibration sound when reading the disc; replace the DVD-RW with another DVD-RW which you are certain works fine, then the result shows that the DVD-RW could read disc normally.

Hint:

When there's no DVD-RW icon displayed in "My Computer", you should consider the possible reason for the failure: certain important driver file is damaged or there are conflicts with software;

231) HP CQ61-313US laptop reading disc failure

Failure symptom:

Laptop could read disc normally before, but recently it started failing to read discs, the DVD-RW has no reaction.

Solution:

This failure obviously belongs to the description of flowchart 12, according to the repair method; confirm the repair path, finding it accords with the sequence:

Start->A-1->A-3->A-4->A-5->A-7->B-3->B-4

Repair summary:

According to the flowchart tutorial, check whether the DVD-RW could be displayed in "My Computer" normally. And it shows normal, but there is an error message when you double click on it. Then put one DVD and CD disc separately, continue testing whether system would boot up normally from DVD-RW, as a result, it could not boot from disc, at the moment when you put one disc into the DVD-RW, the DVD-RW would rotation in high speed and read the disc, in this case step to repair flow B-4. After cleaning the laser head of the DVD-RW, the DVD-RW could read the disc normally, all functions are OK.

Hint:

If DVD-RW could not be recognized in BIOS, generally speaking, we can come to the conclusion that the DVD-RW itself has some problems, you will need to change the DVD-RW, then the failure would be resolved.

232) HP Pavilion DV6000 laptop could only read DVD disc but not CD disc

Failure symptom:

Laptop could not read CD disc, there's no any content displayed when reading CD disc, but there's no problem reading DVD.

Solution:

This failure obviously belongs to the description of flowchart 12, according to the repair method, confirm the repair path, finding it accords with the sequence:

Start->A-1->A-3->A-4->A-5->A-7->B-2

Repair summary:

Test with one known CD disc would boot normally, if the DVD-RW could boot up from disc normally and run, then it means the failure is only related to software; if it fails to boot up from CD disc, then it means the failure is related to the DVD-RW hardware, then clean the laser head of the DVD-RW, at last, the DVD-RW still could not boot from disc; after changing the DVD-RW, the failure is eliminated;

Hint:

When DVD-RW could only read CD disc but fail to read DVD, you can use the same method to test, just use a DVD disc to test.

233) HP DV9000 laptop—finding DVD-RW volume disappears when entering "My Computer" on the desktop.

Failure symptom:

Laptop doesn't display DVD-RW volume, after putting one disc, DVD-RW could not rotate or read disc at all, of course, there's no any content displayed either.

Solution:

This failure obviously belongs to the description of flowchart 12, according to the repair method, confirm the repair path, finding it accords with the sequence:

Start->A-1->A-3->A-5->A-7->B-1->B-3->B-5->C-5->E-1

Repair summary:

According to the flowchart tutorial, put one DVD disc, test whether the DVD-RW could read and boot up, at last, it fails to boot up. Check whether there's DVD-RW listed in BIOS, the result shows that no DVD-RW is detected, then please continue checking up, remove the DVD-RW from the laptop, and then reassemble the laptop, the result is the same, it still could not read any disc. Therefore, change the DVD-RW to test, but still it could not read disc normally. It seems the problem is on the motherboard, the solution could only be to change the motherboard or use external USB DVD-RW.

Hint:

When the failure above occurs, you can try updating BIOS. Sometimes it could solve the problem of the motherboard failing to recognize the DVD-RW.

234) HP G62 laptop could not play DVD movie disc

Failure symptom:

Laptop could not play DVD movie disc, but could read the file on the disc.

Solution:

This failure obviously belongs to the description of flowchart 12, according to the repair method, confirm the repair path, finding it accords with the sequence:

Start->A-1->A-3->A-4->C-2->C-3

Repair summary:

According to the flowchart tutorial, put one DVD disc, test whether the DVD-RW could read or not. After confirming the DVD-RW supports DVD format and there's no problem with hardware, then you need inspect software; if you find that the client has installed Windows Media Player, then it seems the reason it could not play is because you still need to download a plug-in and install. After downloading and installing the plug in, the failure could be eliminated.

Hint:

Playing DVD with PC software is different from playing with DVD machine directly. The displaying of PC software is supported by the calculation of CPU, the display card and other hardware' cooperation. Therefore, it's quite important to have one good operating system with good running conditions. If some important files are missing, or there's virus or Trojan in system, failure like laptop fails to play DVD would also occur.

12.3.3 HP laptop cannot burn disc—7 failure repair cases

235) HP CQ60-204NR laptop DVD-RW could not burn disc failure

Failure symptom:

Laptop DVD-RW could not finish burning disc. After starting the burning application, within few minutes, error prompts that it could not continue burning, but it can read discs.

Solution:

This failure obviously belongs to the description of flowchart 12, according to the repair method, confirm the repair path, finding it accords with the sequence:

Start->A-1->A-3->A-4->C-2->D-1->D-2->D-4->E-4

Repair summary:

According to the flowchart tutorial, the DVD-RW could read disc normally, but when burning applications starts, it would stop burning automatically, then test whether the burning DVD-RW could work normally on other type of laptops. If the result shows that it could burn normally, then put the DVD-RW into the laptop again, continue testing the system. After passing through the steps above, we can come to the conclusion that the failure source is from software problem or software setting problem:

1) First close the applications unrelated to burning, then restart system and test whether DVD-RW could recover the burning. At last, the failure still exists;

2) Disable power management and HDD service, and then test the DVD-RW, finding the burning function recovers, and then the failure disappears.

Hint:

During the burning process, any interference or pause operation for burning data transmission would lead to burning failure. So during the burning process, you'd have to close these applications. Similarly, don't enable system power management function, disk shutdown function and BIOS system sleep and some other related options.

236) HP Pavilion dv6-1361sb Entertainment laptop DVD-RW cannot read the discs which was burnt by the DVD-RW itself

Failure symptom:

The DVD-RW cannot read the discs which was burnt by the DVD-RW itself. The laser head has already been cleaned, but still could not read disc normally;

Solution:

This failure obviously belongs to the description of flowchart 12, according to the repair method, confirm the repair path, finding it accords with the sequence:

Start->A-1->A-3->A-4->C-2->D-1->D-2->D-5

Repair summary:

DVD-RW could not burn normally, but DVD-RW could read other disc as usual, then put the burnt disc in another laptops. As a result, it still could not display, then check the burning software settings, no any error found, the burning speed is lower than the marked speed on the disc; change the burning disc with high quality (Philips), check whether the DVD-RW could burn normally or not. As a result, the failure still exists. At last, according to the flowchart tutorial, uninstall the burning software, and then reinstall burning software Nero series. Make sure the settings are correct and then the failure is eliminated.

Hint:

a) Problems like this probably are because the disc is of bad quality or not standard format, and there are too many scratches on the disc surface;
b) DVD-RW might have severe deflection fault, which means that DVD burning disc has two types: +R and -R. But after burning, there's only one type of disc.

237)   When HP PAVILION DV5-1050ER laptop burns disc, there's error message

Failure symptom:

Recently when laptop burnt disc, there's error message "xxxxxx reading error", with such kind of error message, the disc burnt could not be read normally, the DVD-RW makes "squeaking . . ." sound, but it could read other CD/DVD normally.

Solution:

This failure obviously belongs to the description of flowchart 12, according to the repair method, confirm the repair path, finding it accords with the sequence:

Start->A-1->A-3->A-4->C-2->D-1->D-2->D-5->E-4

Repair summary:

DVD-RW could not burn normally, but it could still read other discs as usual. Install this DVD-RW on other laptop to read disc, as a result, error messages. After installing one working normal DVD-RW into the suspected laptop, check whether the DVD-RW could burn normally, unexpectedly, the failure still happens. It seems the problem of the software. Then uninstall the burning software and reinstall Nero series burning software, the problem still couldn't be solved; at last, according to the flowchart tutorial, reinstall the operating system, after changing to Nero series software, the DVD-RW could burn normally, which indicates the failure is caused because of the problem with the operating system.

Hint:

You can solve similar problems if you could improve the compatibility of the DVD-RW for different types of discs. The method is to update BIOS (Firmware), which is the memory body inside the DVD-RW, software integrated in the hardware; by refreshing BIOS, we can improve the running mode of the DVD-RW device and the reading/writing compatibility for different discs.

238)   HP HDX X16-1007TX laptop DVD-RW could not burn DVD discs, but could burn CD discs

Failure symptom:

Laptop DVD-RW could not burn, after starting the burning software, error messages, burning could not continue, but could read the disc.

Solution:

This failure obviously belongs to the description of flowchart 12, according to the repair method, confirm the repair path, finding it accords with the sequence:

Start->A-1->A-3->A-4->C-2->D-1->D-2->D-4->C-5

Repair summary:

According to the flowchart tutorial, DVD-RW could read disc normally, but when burning software starts, it would auto stop burning, we should remove the suspected DVD-RW, put it in another same type of laptops to test. As a result, it still could not burn DVD normally, so we can come to the conclusion that the DVD-RW has some problems, after changing the DVD-RW and test, the failure is eliminated.

Hint:

If this kind of failure that DVD-RW could not burn happens, sometimes, except the problem of the DVD-RW itself, it's related to the conflicts between system software, which leads to the failure that DVD-RW fails to read disc normally and burning failure. Therefore, when solving the failure, you should pay attention after changing the DVD-RW; there might be software conflicts problem still.

239) HP tx2-1370us laptop DVD-RW could not burn CD discs

Failure symptom:

After changing laptop burning DVD-RW, the problem happens, and every time burning progress is around 40%, they would get a message that the burning could not continue.

Solution:

This failure obviously belongs to the description of flowchart 12, according to the repair method, confirm the repair path, finding it accords with the sequence:

Start->A-1->A-3->A-4->A-6->D-1->D-3->D-5

Repair summary:

According to the flowchart tutorial, remove the DVD-RW, and change it onto other HP laptops, check whether the burning function is OK or not. As a result, they could burn CD normally. Thereafter, we can come to the conclusion that the failure source is from a software issue. Then reinstall operating system, change to Nero series software, and then check whether DVD-RW could burn as usual.

Unexpectedly, the failure remains. It seems the DVD-RW is incompatible with system, which leads to the failure that DVD-RW could not burn normally. At last, after updating DVD-RW firmware, the DVD-RW could burn normally.

Hint:

There are many kinds of advantages to updating the firmware for DVD-RW. The DVD-RW would improve error revise ability, increase performance and so on. But firmware update also has certain risk; please take this it into consideration before updating.

240) HP G62-A10EV laptop DVD-RW could not finish burning CD/DVD disc.

Failure symptom:

Laptop DVD-RW could not finish burning, after starting the burning software, from time to time, it would have error message that burning could not be finished, but the DVD-RW could read disc.

Solution:

This failure obviously belongs to the description of flowchart 12, according to the repair method, confirm the repair path, finding it accords with the sequence:

Start->A-1->A-3->A-4->C-2->D-1->D-2->D-4->E-4

Repair summary:

DVD-RW could read disc normally, but during burning process, it would auto stop burning, put the DVD-RW in another type of laptop to test, as a result, it could burn normally. And then put the DVD-RW back onto the suspected laptop, continue testing software and software settings, finding that all processes unrelated to burning are all closed, power management and disk shutdown service are also disabled. However, inspect carefully, finding the network is enabled, meanwhile, resource share is also enabled, so we can say the problem is here. Disconnect LAN and ISP, and then test the DVD-RW, finding the burning function recovers, the failure is eliminated.

Hint:

During the burning process, stop other members from accessing your machine resources through the network, meanwhile; disconnect the printer, digital camera, USB storage disk or movable disk and other peripheral devices connecting to the laptop, which would influence the entire disc burning process.

241)   HP DV6-2150us laptop DVD-RW could not burns disc

Failure symptom:

During the process when laptop DVD-RW burns disc, you get s error message "Buffer Underrun", it could burn as normal.

Solution:

This failure obviously belongs to the description of flowchart 12, according to the repair method, confirm the repair path, finding it accords with the sequence:

Start->A-1->A-3->A-4->C-2->D-1->D-2->D-5

Repair summary:

It's confirmed that the disc could be burnt normally on other laptop DVD-RW, and then put the disc back to the suspected laptop, focus on checking software problem. Uninstall the burning software, and then reinstall burning application Nero series software, the problem still could not be solved; scan the system entirely, clear up virus and Trojan, at last, disable antivirus software, Windows task manager and plan task application and screensaver. Later continue to test, then the DVD-RW could burn normally.

Hint:

The meaning of the error message "Buffer Underrun" is that the buffer is under running. Generally, during burning process, the data to burn need to be sent to the host from hard disk, and then send to the high buffer (BufferMemory) of the DVD-RW. In the end, burn the data stored in BufferMemory onto CD-R or CD-RW disc. The process must be continuous but not intermittent. If there's intermittent problem at some segments of during the process, then the burning machine could not write data on normally, and there will be error message that the buffer is under running, which would make the disc unusable.

12.3.4 5 repair instances for HP laptop CD, DVD disc failure and other cases

242)   HP DV5117CA notebook has a big noise, when DVD driver to read disk

Failure symptom:

When laptop is reading, disc would rotate in high speed continuously, which makes loud noises; sometimes, the disc content could not be read or displayed.

Solution:

This failure obviously belongs to the description of flowchart 12, according to the repair method, confirm the repair path, finding it accords with the sequence:

Start->A-1->A-3->A-4->C-2->D-1->D-2->D-4->C-5

Repair summary:

Put one movie disc on the tray. When laptop DVD-ROM, runs in high speed, it makes annoying noises. This is produced from the inside of the DVD-ROM. Even there's big noise when disc goes inside or outside, seems there's mechanical friction noise. The disc in/out speed is not stable either. Even it would stop drive door from popping out. Remove the DVD-ROM from the laptop, and clean it. However, there's nothing found stuck inside the DVD-ROM, it seems the failure noise is probably because disc rotation is unstable or there's mechanical friction. After observing carefully, the DVD-ROM has physically deformed, probably the laptop was strongly crushed before, the DVD-ROM has slight distortion and central deviation, when the DVD-ROM is in high speed rotation, and the disc could not keep balance; after changing a new DVD-ROM, the failure disappears.

Hint:

As the failure there's big noise when reading disc, except the factors above, it's also related to the uses.

(1) If DVD-ROM uses "Single laser head and double focus lens" technology, then you need to switch focus lens when reading disc; therefore, the disc reading speed is slow, and there's big noise.
(2) There are too many scratches on the surface of the DVD/CD disc, when laser head is reading data, it would change rotation speed continually, which makes the disc reading increases.

243) HP DV4-2170US laptop could not play burnt disks of music normally

Failure symptom:

The laptop could read disc normally, even music file could be played well on hard disk, but the burnt CD music disc could not be played.

Solution:

This failure obviously belongs to the description of flowchart 12, according to the repair method, confirm the repair path, finding it accords with the sequence:

Start->A-1->A-3->A-4->C-2->D-1->D-2->D-4->C-5

Repair summary:

Music CD burnt by DVD-RW could not be played normally, but DVD-RW could still read other discs normally, then put the burnt music CD on other laptop to play, as a result, it still could not play, then uninstall the burning software and reinstall burning application Nero series software. But the problem still could not be resolved. At last, after checking the entire operation of the client, we found where the problem is. The burning disc he uses d is not CD-R standard format, and he chose "Make Audio CD" incorrectly, then the failure is caused because of setting error. Choose to burn on CD-R disc with data disc way, namely, the burnt music CD is accorded with CD-DA file format. The failure disappears then.

Hint:

Probably there are other reasons causing such a failure:

1) During the duplication process of the disc with copyright, problem would happen that duplication fails, or after copy, it could not work normally;
2) Burning software problem, for example, it uses the burning software with virus or Trojan infected.

244) HP COMPAQ NC6400 laptop could not play DVD, or there's no DVD decoder! But it could play CD.

Failure symptom:

The laptop could not play DVD, and after putting one DVD in, double click the DVD drive volume, then error messages, saying there's no DVD decoder!

Solution:

This failure obviously belongs to the description of flowchart 12, according to the repair method, confirm the repair path, finding it accords with the sequence:

Start->A-1->A-3->A-4->C-2->D-1->D-2->D-4->C-5

Repair summary:

Since the operating system has problems, then it would cause the failure that DVD-ROM could not read disc. So use one bootable DVD disc to test, or use other professional Windows PE system disc to boot up, then analyze and check whether the laptop DVD-ROM could run normally. As a result, it fails to boot up from DVD disc. Then remove the suspected DVD-ROM, and then install it in another same type of laptops to test, the result shows that it still could not read DVD disc normally, so we can come to the conclusion that probably the DVD-ROM has some problems. After changing the DVD-ROM to test, the failure is eliminated.

Ashok liu

Hint:

Probably there are some other reasons causing such a failure as below:

If you use CD-ROM, such a situation would occur, which means the drive could only play CD, VCD, but could not play DVD. When to play DVD, you'd have to convert the CD-ROM to DVD-ROM.

245)   HP dv4-2160us laptop DVD-RW sometimes could not read disc

Failure symptom:

Laptop DVD-RW sometimes could read disc but sometimes could not. When fails to read disc, it could not boot up from disc either.

Solution:

This failure obviously belongs to the description of flowchart 12, according to the repair method, confirm the repair path, finding it accords with the sequence:

Start->A-1->A-3->A-5->A-7->B-1->B-3->B-5

Repair summary:

Because under the situation that operating system has problems itself, it would lead to the problem that DVD-RW could not read disc. So when such a failure occurs, enter the laptop BIOS and inspect, finding there's no DVD-RW listed. Therefore, I'm certain that there is bad connection or hardware failure. Then remove the suspected disc, clean and then reassemble again. Besides, change the DVD-RW interface's fixing screws, and test it again. Then finally it could read disc normally.

Hint:

If you remove the DVD-RW and reassemble again, then please pay attention that usually, there are two screws to fasten the DVD-RW/CD-RW. If the fixture screws are not assembled, then please assemble immediately, because it might affect system BIOS to recognizing the DVD-RW, or we can say the loosing DVD-RW affects our normal work;

246)   HP G71-340US laptop DVD-RW read disc successfully, but could not boot up from disc

Failure symptom:

Laptop DVD-RW driver read disc no problem, but it could not boot up from disc.

Solution:

This failure obviously belongs to the description of flowchart 12, according to the repair method, confirm the repair path, finding it accords with the sequence:

Start->A-1->A-3->A-4->C-2->D-1->D-3->E-2->E-3-E-5

Repair summary:

Because under the situation that operating system has problems itself, it would lead to the problem that DVD-RW could not read disc. Then remove the suspected DVD-RW and put in another type of laptops to test. As a result, it could boot up from disc, so we can come to the conclusion that the DVD-RW has no problem. Then reassemble the DVD-RW back onto the suspected laptop, focus on checking BIOS software problem. Then set the first boot device as disc, and then test again. As a result, it fails to boot up from DVD disc, Try another disc, but the failure remains. Since it is possible that CMOS could not save the modified page. So, afterwards, refresh BIOS, then the failure is eliminated.

Hint:

There are other possible reasons causing the problem:

1) DVD-RW is not compatible with the motherboard completely;
2) DVD-RW BIOS (Firmware) is too old, which is not compatible with disc completely.

CHAPTER 13

Touchpad, keyboard and USB port repair

13.1 Causes for laptop touchpad, keyboard and USB port failures

13.1.1 Common failure symptoms for a laptop touchpad, keyboard and USB port.

Keyboard

1. Some keys on a Keyboard fail or all keys don't work;
2. The Keyboard test fails, the laptop makes a series of beeps during the start process;
3. The Keyboard has a sticky key problem, if you type every letter, then another letter or character would also appear;
4. The Keyboard has a serial key failure (key connected), you press key A, but it posts the letter "S";
5. A Laptop key does not pop up after striking it;
6. The Laptop auto repeats letters after pressing a key, it posts a string of letters;
7. A Laptop keyboard key cap falls off, the bracket has cracked and there is too much dust accumulated, or liquid has entered it;
8. An abnormal sound failure happens when typing on a laptop keyboard;
9. The Laptop keyboard circuit has a short circuit failure;

Touchpad

10. A Laptop touchpad lock failure;
11. The Laptop touchpad fails or a mouse cursor floating failure;
12. A Laptop touchpad double-click failure;
13. The Laptop touchpad only has one key working;
14. The Laptop touchpad works, but a key doesn't work;

USB

15. A Laptop USB interface is defective, the interface is damaged;
16. a Laptop USB interface power supply current-limiting resistor or chip has failed;

17. A Laptop USB interface is loose;

13.1.2 Touchpad, keyboard and USB port common failure causes and analysis

Keyboard

1. Some keys on the Keyboard fail or all the keys don't work;

    Likely causes for the failure are:

    (1) There's dirt on the keyboard rubber cup, which stops circuits from connecting to each other normally;
    (2) There's a bad contact between a key and its circuit contacts;
    (3) A plastic scissor-shaped spring (Retainer clip) is broken or is obstructed by something, which prevents the key cap from being pressed down;
    (4) Liquid entered the keyboard, and dissolved the keyboard rubber cup;
    (5) Long term use of the keyboard breaks or degrades the rubber cup under it; Please take a look at Figure 13-1.

Figure 13-1

    (7) The interface between the keyboard data cable plug and the motherboard connector is corroded or damaged;
    (8) A keyboard hardware problem;
    (9) The driver or software switcher changes the keyboard saving function;

2. The keyboard test fails and the laptop makes a series of beeps during the start process

    The likely causes for the failure are:

    (1) Certain keys on the keyboard are stuck down and do not pop up;
    (2) Liquid has entered the keyboard, and ruined the keyboard conductive performance;
    (3) A partial circuit for the keyboard has short circuited or is open circuit;

3. The keyboard has a sticky key failure, when you type a letter, another letter or character would also appear

    The likely causes for the failure are:

    (1) A logic circuit failure;
    (2) Certain parts of the keyboard circuit line cable or row cable is open circuit or short circuit;
    (3) There's something stuck between two keys;
    (4) Operating system failure;
    (5) Application failure;

4. The keyboard has a serial key failure (key connected), and the keyboard outputs incorrect letters;

    The likely causes for the failure are:

    (1) A PCB filter capacitor has a short circuit;
    (2) The keyboard data cable interface has a short circuit;
    (3) A south bridge I/O management chip failure;
    (4) Operating system failure;
    (5) Application failure;
    (6) Keyboard language settings are changed;
    (7) A digital lockup key is activated;

5. A laptop key does not pop up

    The likely causes for the failure are:

    (1) The rubber cup under the key cap or the plastic scissor-shaped spring (Retainer clip) position is offset, which makes the key shell stick after pressing the key cap, and then not pop up; Please take a look at Figure 13-2.

Figure 13-2

(2) After a key has been used for a long time, the plastic scissor-shaped spring distorts (Retainer clip) or the rubber cup has aged and increases the frictional resistance making the key harder to press;

(3) The plastic scissor-shape spring (Retainer clip) under the key cap is damaged, and looses the flexibility;

6. The laptop auto repeats letters after a single key stroke.

The likely causes for the failure are:

(1) Because of system bugs, keys repeat too fast when inputting a password;
(2) The keyboard delay in the system setup is too short;
(3) A key sticks
(4) Trojan or virus infection.

7. A laptop keyboard key cap falls off, the bracket underneath the cap is cracked or broken, too much dust has accumulated, and liquid entry has caused problems

The likely causes for the failure are:

(1) Playing too many games, normal wear and tear;
(2) The lock buckle under the key cap is damaged; please take a look at Figure 13-3.

Figure 13-3

(3) Liquid enters the keyboard, and damages the lock buckle;
(4) Improper cleaning of the keyboard;
(5) Bad laptop use habits;

8. An abnormal sound is heard when typing on the laptop keyboard

Probably the causes for the failure are:

(1) A key cap is loose;

(2) The plastic scissor-shaped spring (Retainer clip) under the key cap is loose or broken;

(3) Operating system or application failure;

9. A laptop keyboard circuit has a short circuit failure;

The likely causes for the failure are:

(1) Liquid enters the keyboard, and dissolves the keyboard rubber cup;
(2) The keyboard rubber cup or PCB is dirty;
(3) The keyboard motherboard circuit is oxidized;
(4) Keyboard overheating leads to the aging of the rubber cup.

Touchpad

10. Laptop touchpad failure;

The likely causes for the failure are:

(1) The touchpad device in BIOS is disabled;
(2) There's something wrong with the touchpad driver;
(3) You pressed the touchpad switch shortcut key by mistake;
(4) The interface between the touchpad data cable and motherboard is loose or open;
(5) Components of the touchpad circuit have failed.

11. The laptop touchpad fails or the mouse cursor is floating

The likely causes for the failure are:

(1) Liquid has entered touchpad, and changed the conductive performance;
(2) The connecting cable between the touchpad and motherboard is loose;
(3) There's dirt on the touchpad;
(4) There's dust, liquid, grease or food on your fingers;
(5) Improper setting of the mouse cursor movement speed;
(6) Touchpad driver error;
(7) Improper setting of the touchpad touch sensitivity;
(8) An internal device directly contacts a touchpad component, making the touchpad surface temperature too high;
(9) More than one finger used on the touchpad causes confused information;
(10) Components on the PCB for the touchpad have failed.

12. A laptop touchpad click problem or double-click failure

    The likely causes for the failure are:

    (1) The mouse double-click speed is set too fast;
    (2) "Replace keystroke with touch" is disabled;
    (3) Operating system failure;
    (4) Virus or Trojan infection;

13. The laptop touchpad only has one key working

    The likely causes for the failure are:

    (1) The PCB under the failed key is aged or damaged;
    (2) The failed key has encountered heavy pressure and the scissor-shape spring (Retainer clip) under the keys is broken;
    (3) The interface between a failed key data cable and the motherboard is loose or damaged;
    (4) The micro switch of the failed key is damaged;

14. The laptop touchpad works, but a key doesn't work;

    The likely causes for the failure are:

    (1) The interface between the touchpad and relevant data cables for the left and right keys is loose or damaged;
    (2) The micro switch controlling the left and right keys has failed;
    (3) The PCB under the left and right keys is damaged;
    (4) The scissor-shape springs (Retainer clip) under the left and right keys are all defective;
    (5) The touchpad keys are set at disabled;

USB

15. A laptop USB port is unavailable, the interface is damaged

    The likely causes for the failure are:

    (1) Attempting to plug in the wrong way or using too much force has damaged the internal contact surfaces or pushed the interface into the computer.
    (2) The USB interface pin is bent, cracked or short circuited;
    (3) The USB interface board is distorted because of heavy pressure when plugging in, which can also damage the plastic case of the USB cable jack;
    (4) The USB driver is corrupted; the laptop USB interface +5V power supply has failed;

The likely causes for the failure are:

(1)   The USB power supply overcurrent protection circuit resistor is burnt;
(2)   The South Bridge I/O management chip has failed;

17.   the laptop USB interface is loose

The likely causes for the failure are:

(1)   Imprudent plugging in of USB devices can move the contact copper plate in the USB interface;
(2)   The USB port is forced enough to break solder connections on the USB PCB or the motherboard.

13.1.3 Laptop touchpad, keyboard and USB port failure solutions

a)   Some or all keyboard keys fail to function

Here's the solution:

Put one pure DOS disc or other special Windows PE system disc into laptop DVD-ROM to start up. The function of this is mainly to analyze whether the laptop keyboard will type normally or not. When the laptop finishes start-up, tap any key on the keyboard to test the typing. If the keyboard types and works normally, then it means the keyboard hardware has no problem and the failure is only in the software. if some keys fail or all keys do not type, then the failure is in the hardware, (keyboard or motherboard); but its also likely to be both a software and hardware problem.

1)   If all keys do not type, then the failure is relevant with the keyboard itself or the connection of the keyboard data cable to the motherboard. The key to solving the problem is to reset the keyboard. Remove the keyboard, re-assemble it and check whether there's still a typing failure or not; when you assemble a keyboard, pay close attention to the data cable and make sure it is plugged into the motherboard jack properly. If you found it not seated properly, you likely have solved your problem. Please take a look at Figure 13-4.

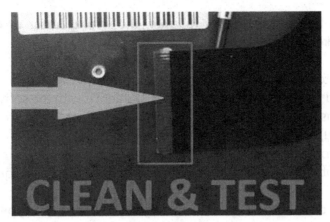

Figure 13-4

3) After reseating the keyboard data cable, if the failure doesn't disappear, then you should try changing the keyboard; also disconnect the touchpad connection to the motherboard to test the possibility that a touchpad circuit problem might be affecting the keyboard.

4) After proceeding according to the method of step B, if the problem still is not solved, then you should consider that the problem is with the motherboard hardware.

b) Keyboard test fails, the laptop makes a series of beeps during the boot process

Here's the solution:

After removing the keyboard, use a USB keyboard instead, and then start the laptop. If the beeps disappear, then it means the original keyboard hardware has problems; if it still makes a series of beeps, then it means the failure is in the memory;

(1) A key on the keyboard is stuck and does not pop up;

To remove the defective key, you press down the key and pry up with a blade and then push it forward slightly and then you can remove the key cap. Next change the plastic scissor-shaped spring (Retainer clip) or the conductive rubber cap;

(2) Liquid has entered keyboard and ruins the keyboard conductive performance

Remove the defective keys, remove the conductive rubber cap, and check the conductive layer below it. It should be a bright metal layer. If there's a color change, water trace, or oil and dirt, then you must clean it up with alcohol without water content;

(3) A partial keyboard circuit has a short circuit problem of is open circuit. Install a new keyboard and have a try.

c) The keyboard has continual key failures, the wrong letter or character appears when you strike a key.

1) Start the laptop with one pure DOS disc or other special Windows PE system disc. If the keyboard types normally, it means the problem is with the software; if the problem only happens with some of the keys, it is likely a hardware problem (keyboard or motherboard);
2) Hardware problem, install a new keyboard;
3) Software problem, reinstall the operating system or the office software;

d) Keyboard has disordered keys failure, keyboard could not type correct letters or characters;

1) Start the laptop with one pure DOS disc or other special Windows PE system disc. If the keyboard could type normally, then it means the problem is relevant with the software; if partial keys still could not type correct letters or characters, then the failure is relevant with the hardware, (keyboard or motherboard);
2) Confirm to recover keyboard language settings to factory settings, meanwhile, and confirm whether the digital lockup key is changed and activated;
3) After removing the keyboard, assemble it back again, pay attention whether the data cable is plugged to the motherboard jack tightly or not, in case data cable is not plugged right to the position or get extruded out; remember to fix up the data cable;
4) Change a new keyboard and try;
5) Motherboard hardware issue;

e) Laptop keys could not pop up;

Remove the issued keys and key hats. Change the plastic scissor-shape spring (Retainer clip) or the conductive rubber cup;

f) Laptop auto key repeating failure, showing countless same letters;

1) Start the laptop with one pure DOS disc or other special Windows PE system disc, and then test the typing, if keyboard failure disappears, then it means the problem is relevant with software; if partial keys still auto repeats typing the same letter, then the problem is relevant with hardware, (keyboard or motherboard);
2) Remove the issued keys and key hats. Change the plastic scissor-shape spring (Retainer clip) or the conductive rubber cup;
3) Confirm the keyboard system settings is reset to factory settings, meanwhile, confirm the delay time could not be set too short;
4) Clear Trojan or virus infection, meanwhile, update system programs to avoid bugs;

g) Laptop keyboard hats fall off, plastic scissor-shape spring (Retainer clip) cracks, too much dust accumulate and water enters keyboard;

1) Remove the issued keys and key hats. Change the plastic scissor-shape spring (Retainer clip) or the conductive rubber cup;
2) If the key is difficult to be fount out, then you can disassemble a key not used a lot on the original keyboard, such as the key "Home", replace the damaged key often used with it, including the plastic scissor-shape spring (Retainer clip) and the conductive rubber cup;
3) As for the solution after water enters laptop keyboard, please refer to the first chapter of the book <<1.3.1 what to do after water enters laptop? >>;
4) Clean the keyboard with a correct way, rectify bad laptop use habits;

h) Laptop makes strange noise when typing on keyboard

1) Start the laptop with one pure DOS disc or other special Windows PE system disc, and then test the key typing, if the strange noise failure disappears, then it means the problem is relevant with the software; if partial keys still make strange noises when typing, then the problem must be relevant with keyboard hardware;
2) Hardware issue, then change a new keyboard;
3) If software problem, then reinstall operation system or the office software;

i) Laptop keyboard circuit has short circuit failure

Sometimes keyboard circuit would have short circuit failure, mostly is because liquid enters keyboard. Rare situation is that laptop overheating causes the rubber cup aging and circuit oxidization. Bad situation, it would not work, operation system interface freezes, black screen and so on; but worse, it would get the motherboard burnt, totally scrapping the laptop. Solution is to change a working normal keyboard right away. Please take a look at Figure 13-5.

Figure 13-5

j) Laptop touchpad lockup failure

1) First enter motherboard BIOS Setup page, confirm the touchpad device is already enabled; if there's no such a function setup, then please check whether there's switch shortcut for the touchpad, and confirm it's already enabled;
2) First uninstall the touchpad driver, and then download and install new touchpad driver;
3) After removing the touchpad, reinstall it back; confirm the data cable works normally, when plug to motherboard jack, avoid not plugging it to the right position or get it extruded out; at last, don't forget to fix up the data cable;
4) Change a working normal touchpad, or use one USB mouse to replace it.

k) Laptop touchpad failure or cursor floating failure

1) Reset the mouse cursor's moving speed, until the mouse cursor could work normally;
2) First uninstall touchpad driver, and then download and install new touchpad driver;
3) After removing the touchpad, reassemble it back, confirm the data cable could work normally, when necessary, change the data cable too;
4) Clean the touchpad and circuit board, the key is dust, liquid dirt, grease; and then recover the touchpad to the factory settings and performance;
5) Assemble touchpad components correctly, in case steel parcel and some devices would touch the circuit components directly;
6) Change a working normal touchpad, or use one USB mouse to replace the touchpad.

l) Laptop touchpad's click failure or double-click failure

1) Reset touchpad double-click speed time, enable "Replace tapping key with touch" function;
2) First uninstall touchpad driver, and then download and install the new touchpad driver;
3) I would scan the disk entirely for one time to clear virus or Trojan infection;
4) Reinstall operation system, or use USB mouse to take the place of it.

m) Laptop touchpad has only one working key;

1) Remove the touchpad (including the failed key), confirm the data cable could work normally, then reassemble it back to the laptop, confirm the interface between data cable and motherboard would not be loose;
2) Change the aging data cable or cracked scissor-shape spring (Retainer clip);
3) Change the damaged jiggle switch under the failed key;
4) Change the key circuit board or the entire touchpad circuit;
5) Use one USB mouse to take the place of the touchpad.

n) Laptop touchpad works, but key doesn't work

1) Confirm the touchpad keys are already enabled; if there's no such application function setup, then check whether there's switch shortcut, and confirm it's already enabled;
2) Remove the touchpad (including the failed keys), after confirming the data cable could work normally, assemble it back to the laptop, and make sure the interface between data cable and motherboard would not be loose;
3) Change the aging data cable;
4) Change the damaged jiggle switch or the cracked scissor-shape spring (Retainer clip);
5) Change the entire touchpad circuit board, including the key circuit board;
6) Use one USB mouse to take the place.

o) Laptop USB interface has power but could not work, or the interface is damaged

1) Confirmed the USB interface sinks inside and moves, then plug one working normal USB mouse to the USB interface, and start the laptop with one professional Windows PE system disc, and then test whether the USB mouse could work or not; if works, then it means the problem is relevant with the original operation system; if not work, then the problem is relevant with the USB hardware;
2) First uninstall the USB driver, and then restart the laptop. Let the laptop auto install the new USB driver, meanwhile, update operation system service packages;
3) Revise and repair already bended USB interface pins, in case the pins crack or short circuit occurs;
4) Use one USB hub with 4 interfaces, plug to the distorted USB interface or the USB port with damaged plastic flake, and then fix with glue. Then later on, just use the USB interface on the hub;
5) Change the USB interface on the motherboard; please take a look at Figure 13-6.

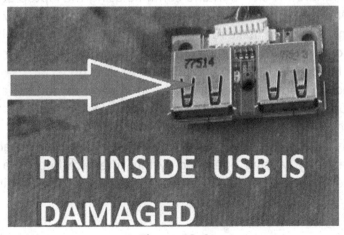

Figure 13-6

p)   Laptop USB interface doesn't supply power, +5V power disappears

1)   Disassemble the laptop and remove the laptop motherboard, change a same USB power supply protection circuit resistor;
2)   Find the issued South Bridge I/O management chip, and change a same chip;
3)   Install one PCMCIA USB adapter to take the place of the USB interface fixed on motherboard;
4)   Change the laptop motherboard.

q)   Laptop USB interface is loose

1)   Disassemble the laptop and remove the laptop motherboard, change a same USB interface;
2)   Find the issued USB interface, and weld the pins additionally to fix up the USB bracket.

13.1.4 Laptop black screen and boot failures caused by touchpad, keyboard and USB port short circuit failures

-Failure symptom:

Laptop black screen and start-up failure

Touchpad and keyboard

a)   Liquid enters the touchpad or keyboard, and then a black screen failure occurs. It is an especially severe situation when the liquid is not pure water. When an accidence happens, generally, you should open the laptop and don't use it for 72 hours. You can assist the drying process by using a low velocity fan to blow over the keyboard. Many users ignore the situation and continue using the laptop at their peril hoping nothing will happen. In this case, the laptop works under a very damp conductive environment, which can make rubber components melt, and circuits corrode leading to a short circuit failure, if it did not already happen soon after the liquid spill. It results in a laptop black screen and a failure to start up.
b)   The connection cable connector between the motherboard and the keyboard becomes loose over time and after long-term pressure, or an internal wire breaks causing a short circuit failure and a black screen.
c)   Occasionally laptop overheating can cause the rubber cup to age and circuits to oxidize, eventually causing operating system interface freezes, a black screen and so on, but even worse, it can cause the motherboard to fail, entirely scrapping the laptop.

USB

A black screen failure is caused by a short circuit in the USB interface. This is commonly caused in the following 2 ways:

a) One is when a flash memory falls into water or is impacted causing the internal parts of the device to be short circuited; when it is plugged into the laptop USB interface, the power supply for the USB ports is immediately short circuited and if not over current protected, the power supply and/or the motherboard is damaged.

b) Frequent pull-and-plug operations for USB devices, done forcefully, or attempts to plug in with the connector upside down, can bend the reed inside the USB interface so it touches the shell of the USB interface and causes a short circuited power supply. Generally speaking, motherboards have a USB interface auto protection circuit design, when the USB interface has a short circuit, the computer will auto shut down. However, if the manufacturer simplifies or omits this part of the protection circuit, then the South Bridge chip would directly get burnt.

13.2 Repair flow chart to eliminate touchpad, keyboard and USB port failures

13.2.1 Touchpad, keyboard and USB port failure repair shortcuts

Put a DOS disc (with USB and touchpad drivers) or professional Windows PE system disc into the laptop DVD-ROM to start up. If the failed device now works normally (the keyboard typing is ok, touchpad and external USB mouse work all right), then it means these hardware devices have no problem. The failure is only in the original laptop software. Please check solution A. If the failure still cannot be solved; it means the failure is in the hardware. Please check solution B:

A: First uninstall the suspected driver, and then restart the laptop, letting it auto install a new driver. Next update the operating system service package. After completing these steps, if the failure is still unsolved, then you need to reinstall operating system. A detailed solution can be found in the chapter 13.2.5 of this article <<Laptop touchpad, keyboard and USB port failure analysis and repair flow>>

B: Second to do the following tasks:

1) Internal connections or cables can be open circuit. Remove the keyboard and disassemble the cover over the touchpad to check the condition of their related cable and connectors. Repair or replace anything that looks damaged, clean areas that need it including corroded connectors, and reassemble the laptop making sure the connectors are securely in place. Now see if that has solved the problem.

2) Disconnect the touchpad from the motherboard as circuit problems on the touchpad can affect the keyboard. If that has not helped try installing a new keyboard.

3) The USB port can be damaged. Inspect it carefully and if contacts appear to be bent, try to straighten them. The best bet is to just replace the USB port hardware.

4) Check the motherboard interface connection for the failed device. If you find the interface connection is open, just resolder it. However, if the motherboard South Bridge chip is burnt because of a short circuit, then you need to change the

motherboard. For a detailed solution, please refer to the chapter 13 of the 13.2.5 <<Laptop touchpad, keyboard and USB port failure analysis and repair flow>>

13.2.2 60% of touchpad or keyboard failures are from the touchpad and keyboard hardware itself

There is about a 60% failure rate caused by the scissor-shape spring (Retainer clip) under the key button, rubber cup, keyboard circuit, touchpad circuit board, keyboard data cable interface and motherboard South Bridge.

During the repair process, I often encounter problems where the keyboard or touchpad fails; or the keyboard test fails. During the boot process the laptop makes a series of beeps or there are connected keys, crossed keys, stuck keys, and abnormal sounds when typing on the keyboard. Generally, we would put a pure DOS disc or other special Windows PE system disc in the laptop DVD-ROM to boot; and then confirm whether the failure cause is from software or hardware and finally come to a solution. Some hardware failures are obvious like a keyboard cap that falls off, and you can immediately repair it or install a replacement.

(1) Keyboard failure

After excluding a software problem, if partial keys or all keys do not work, then you need to reinstall the keyboard; if just some individual keys fail, then you need to clean the dirt under the keys or change the scissor-shape spring (Retainer clip) or the rubber cup. If after changing the keyboard, the failure still exists, then it means the problem is likely on a motherboard circuit. For detailed troubleshooting and repair, please refer to the chapter 3 of this article <<Laptop touchpad, keyboard and USB port failures analysis and repair flow>>.

(2) The keyboard test fails and the laptop makes a series of beeps during the start process;

Removing the keyboard and connect a USB keyboard, then start the laptop, if the beeps disappear, then it means the original keyboard hardware has some problems; if beeps still exist, then it means the failure might be in the memory. For detailed troubleshooting and repair, please refer to the chapter 3 of this article << Laptop touchpad, keyboard and USB port failures analysis and repair flow>>.

(3) Connected keys, crossed keys, stuck keys, abnormal sounds happen when typing on the keyboard

After excluding software problems, disassemble the failed keys, remove the key cap, clean the dirt under the key cap or change the plastic scissor-shape spring (Retainer clip) or the rubber cup, and reinstall the keyboard. If after reinstalling the keyboard the failure still exists; then change the keyboard. If after changing the keyboard, the problem still is not solved, then it means the problem is in a motherboard circuit or chip; then changes the motherboard. For the detailed methods, please refer to the chapter 3 of this article << Laptop touchpad, keyboard and USB port failures analysis and repair flow>>.

(4) The laptop keyboard circuit has a short circuit failure;

A keyboard circuit can sometimes have a short circuit, mostly it is because liquid enters the keyboard and then the failure occurs. A rare situation is when laptop overheating leads to rubber cup aging and circuit oxidization. The best solution is to install a new keyboard.

(5) The touchpad is locked, cursor moves, or a key fails

After excluding software problems, remove the touchpad, clean the dirt under the touchpad, inspect the touchpad or the external circuit of the failed keys and jiggle the switch; reinstall the touchpad. If after reinstalling the touchpad, the failure still exists, then you can use a USB mouse or change the touchpad. If after changing the touchpad, the problem still cannot be solved, then it means the problems is likely on the motherboard circuit or the chip, then just change the motherboard. For a detailed method, please refer to chapter 3 of this article << Laptop touchpad, keyboard and USB port failures analysis and repair flow>>.

13.2.3 25% of Touchpad, keyboard and USB port failures are from the driver and operating system

There are about 25% of touchpad, keyboard and USB port failures that are caused by drivers and the operating system

Put a pure DOS disc or other special Windows PE system disc into laptop DVD-ROM to boot up. If the failed device runs normally, it means the hardware is not a problem; the failure is in the software.

Here's the solution: first uninstall the suspect driver, and then restart the laptop, letting it auto install a new driver; then update the operating system service package. After repairing according to these steps, if the failure is still unsolved, then you need to reinstall the operating system. For a detailed solution, please refer to the chapter13 of this article 13.2.5 <<Laptop touchpad, keyboard and USB port failure analysis and repair flow>>.

13.2.4 12% of touchpad, keyboard and USB port failures are from interface connections, open circuit, and short circuit

There is about a 12% proportion of touchpad, keyboard and USB port failures that are caused by interface connections, open circuit, and short circuit.

Excluding driver and operating system software problems, you need to work on the hardware itself, Start by removing the touchpad and keyboard and their connections and re-install them to see if the failure disappears. During this process inspect connectors and parts for damage and repair or replace as necessary. If you notice a connector not firmly in place, you likely have found your problem.

If the failure doesn't disappear, then you should try installing a new keyboard, but before that make sure a touchpad problem is not affecting the keyboard by disconnecting it and seeing if the keyboard will work.

For USB interface failures, carefully inspect the port for bent or distorted components. Repair or replace the USB port.

If the failure is still unsolved, then you need to check the motherboard USB interface connection circuit. If you find the interface connection cable open, then just solder it. However, if the motherboard South Bridge chip is burnt because of a short circuit, then you need to change the motherboard. For a detailed solution, please refer to the chapter 13.2.5 of this article <<Laptop touchpad, keyboard and USB port failure analysis and repair flow>>.

13.2.5 Laptop keyboard, touchpad, and USB port failure analysis and repair flow

The laptop repair shop workbooks—

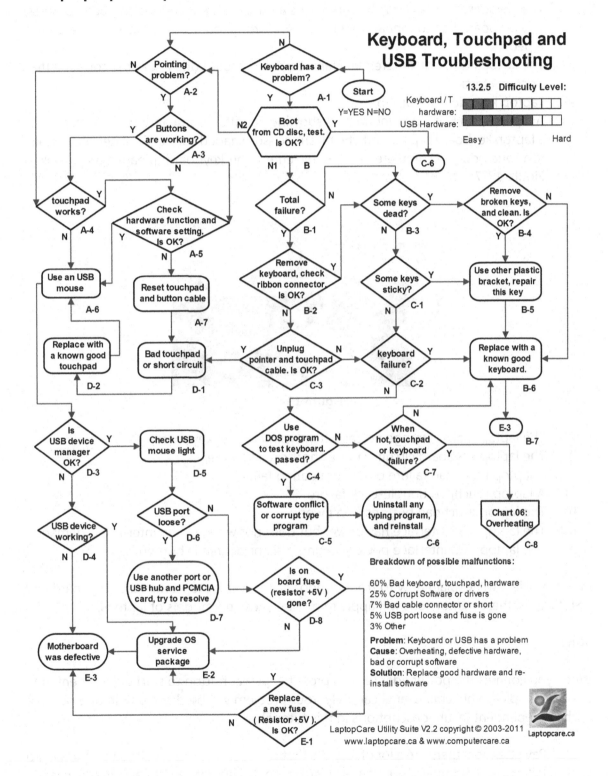

Keyboard, Touchpad and USB Troubleshooting

13.2.5 Difficulty Level:

Keyboard / T hardware:
USB Hardware:

Easy   Hard

Y=YES N=NO

Start

Keyboard has a problem? A-1

Pointing problem? A-2

Buttons are working? A-3

touchpad works? A-4

Check hardware function and software setting. Is OK? A-5

Use an USB mouse A-6

Reset touchpad and button cable A-7

Replace with a known good touchpad D-2

Bad touchpad or short circuit D-1

Boot from CD disc, test. Is OK? B

Total failure? B-1

Remove keyboard, check ribbon connector. Is OK? B-2

Unplug pointer and touchpad cable. Is OK? C-3

Some keys dead? B-3

Some keys sticky? C-1

keyboard failure? C-2

Remove broken keys, and clean. Is OK? B-4

Use other plastic bracket, repair this key B-5

Replace with a known good keyboard. B-6

C-6

E-3

B-7

Use DOS program to test keyboard. passed? C-4

When hot, touchpad or keyboard failure? C-7

Software conflict or corrupt type program C-5

Uninstall any typing program, and reinstall C-6

Chart 06: Overheating C-8

Is USB device manager OK? D-3

Check USB mouse light D-5

USB device working? D-4

USB port loose? D-6

Use another port or USB hub and PCMCIA card, try to resolve D-7

Is on board fuse (resistor +5V) gone? D-8

Motherboard was defective E-3

Upgrade OS service package E-2

Replace a new fuse (Resistor +5V). Is OK? E-1

Breakdown of possible malfunctions:

60% Bad keyboard, touchpad, hardware
25% Corrupt Software or drivers
7% Bad cable connector or short
5% USB port loose and fuse is gone
3% Other

Problem: Keyboard or USB has a problem
Cause: Overheating, defective hardware, bad or corrupt software
Solution: Replace good hardware and re-install software

LaptopCare Utility Suite V2.2 copyright © 2003-2011
www.laptopcare.ca & www.computercare.ca

Laptopcare.ca

This tutorial will help you solve the following problems:

a) Some keyboard keys fail or all keys do not type;
b) The keyboard test fails, the laptop makes a series of beeps during the boot process;
c) The keyboard has continual key failures, the wrong letter or character appears when typed;
d) The keyboard has disordered key failures, the keyboard does not post correct letters or characters;
e) Laptop keys do not pop up;
f) A laptop auto key repeating failure, showing countless same letters;
g) a laptop keyboard cap falls off, the plastic scissor-shaped spring (Retainer clip) breaks, too much dust accumulates and water enters the keyboard; please take a look at Figure 13-7.

Figure 13-7

h) The laptop makes strange noises when typing on the keyboard;
i) The laptop keyboard circuitry has a short circuit failure;
j) A laptop touchpad failure or cursor floating failure
k) A laptop touchpad double-click failure
l) The laptop touchpad buttons don't work;
m) The laptop USB interface has power but does not work, or the interface is damaged
n) The laptop USB interface power limiting resistor or chip is burned;

In this article, I will explain how to troubleshoot and repair laptop touchpad, keyboard and USB failures, these instructions will apply to most makes and models of laptops.

Start

When you connect the power adapter and press the power button to start up, after entering the system, please observe events carefully. Your problem will be dealt with in one or more of the independent failure descriptions in this tutorial:

1) Pay attention: there are a lot of reasons that can cause laptop touchpad and keyboard failures. For example, the external environment (temperature) has an extreme change

within a short time, or striking the keys too hard causes a cap to fall off or a spring or bracket to be broken; these kind of simple problems can be solved without the direction of this tutorial;

2)   Please also pay attention to another type of laptop USB port failure, which might be caused by insufficient laptop power or a USB peripheral device that is not good and so on. These kinds of situations are not covered by the range of this tutorial; please refer to another tutorial.

Step: A-1

First of all, does the laptop keyboard have a failure?

If there is a failure, then please enter Step: B;

If there is no failure, then please enter Step: A-2;

Step: A-2

Check the pointer of the touch-pad. If the pointer does not work, please enter Step: A-4. If the speed of the pointer is not proper, please follow the procedures below:

1)   Reset the speed of the mouse pointer, until the mouse pointer works normally;
2)   First uninstall the driver for the mouse, and then download and install the latest mouse driver for your laptop;

If the problem is still not solved, then please enter Step: A-3 to continue;

Step: A-3

Now check whether the touchpad buttons are working normally or not; if the buttons do not work, then please confirm that the touchpad buttons are not disabled; if there's no program function for this, then you should check the touchpad disable device to confirm it is enabled. Laptops have either a key, touchpad switch, or a software method to disable the touchpad. Refer to your manual for the correct method. If your laptop touchpad buttons are working normally, then please enter Step: A-4; if your touchpad buttons have a problem, please enter Step: A-5 to continue;

Step: A-4

If the laptop touchpad fails or does not work normally, then please confirm that the touchpad disable device is not disabled as in step A3 above; you may have pressed a switch shortcut key to disable the touchpad by mistake. If your laptop touchpad still does not work normally, then first uninstall the touchpad driver, and then download and install the latest touchpad driver for your laptop; then set up the pointer speed for the touchpad;

If the problem is not solved, follow the instructions below:

1) Remove the touchpad, and then re-install it. Confirm the data cable is not damaged and works all right, and make sure the interface between data cable and motherboard is not loose;
2) Clean the touchpad and its circuit board of mainly dust, liquid, dirt and grease etc; make sure you clean any liquid that entered the touchpad, and caused the performance to be affected;
3) Install the touchpad component correctly; don't let the steel parcel directly contact any circuit components. It can lead to the problem where the touchpad surface temperature is heated;

Step: A-5

Please follow the method below to solve the button problem:

1) Remove the touchpad (including failed buttons); make sure the data cable works normally, then re-install the touchpad and buttons; make sure the interface between the data cable and motherboard is not loose;
2) If the data cable is damaged or aged, then you should change it immediately;
3) If found that the jiggle switch under the failed buttons or the plastic scissor-shape spring (Retainer clip) have sustained damage, then you should also change them immediately;
4) If any components on the touchpad (or buttons) circuit board look burned or damaged, then you should change the circuit board;

Step: A-6

To use a know working USB laser mouse, and plugged into the Issue laptop to test its work or not, please go to Step D-3;

Step: A-7

After excluding driver, operating system and software issues, if the failure still exists, then you should check the interface connection cable between the touchpad and the motherboard for damage.

Check the solder joints of the connection cable, and look for cable distortion, severe bending, or the core is broken? Check the plastic lock on the motherboard connection cable slot and make sure it is not cracked or broken; if so, you must change or repair it right away. If it's a motherboard problem, such as the South Bridge chip burnt, then the touchpad will not work and you should use a USB mouse or change the motherboard.

Start: B

Use a DOS disc (to load USB and touchpad drivers) or a professional Windows PE system disc to boot the laptop from the DVD-ROM. If the failed devices now run normally including the keyboard, touchpad and external USB mouse, then it means the hardware devices are good. The failure is in the original laptop software. Please check the solution in Step: C-6; if the failure is still unsolved, then the problem is the hardware. Please check the solution in Step: B-1; if Touchpad and external USB mouse have problems only, please checks the solution in Step: A-2;

Step: B-1

During the repair process, I found that there are two types of keyboard problems: one is where an individual key or group of keys do not type; another is where all keys on the keyboard do not type; if the problem belongs to the former, then please enter Step: B-3; if belongs to the latter issue, then please enter Step: B-2;

Step: B-2

If all keys do not type, then the failure must be in the keyboard itself or the keyboard cable connection to the motherboard. Start by removing and re-installing the keyboard. During this process closely inspect the keyboard cable, the connector on it, and the connector on the mother board. Look for bent or discoloured pins, cracks in the plastic shell, or a broken connector lock. Look for damage to the cable and make sure it is plugged in properly and the connector lock closed. Any defects noticed should be repaired or the component replaced.

After completing Step: B-2, if the problem still is not solved, then please enter Step: C-3; if the problem is not completely solved, and there are still a few other problems, then please enter Step: B-3 to continue;

Step: B-3

In my experience I found there are two types of button problems: one is when the key does not type when pressed; the other is when a key sticks and is a little difficult to use; this is covered in Step: B-4; for the other case refer to Step: C-1;

Step: B-4

The most common problems with laptop keyboards are key cap fallen off and cannot be put back, broken bracket or mechanism below the cap, and dirt or liquid in the keyboard. The situation where the key cap falls off and cannot be put back is quite common for laptop users.

First, make sure the cap bracket is assembled correctly, you can pick the bracket gently with your fingernail; if it moves up and down normally, then there's no problem. If it sticks, first shut down the laptop and the remove battery, remove all faulty keys, clean the attached dirt under the key caps. The brush used for cleaning should be completely dry. After finishing, reassemble the keys, you first install the bracket assembly and be careful to do it properly; if the cap does not easily snap on don't force it; you can easily break the bracket

If water enters the keyboard accidently, the first thing you should do is turn over the laptop and pull out the battery, then pull out the adapter jack. Leave it turned over to prevent the water from getting to the motherboard then let the water drip out as much as possible. This sequence is important in case the battery is short circuited

Afterwards, absorb any water on the surface of the keyboard with a dry cloth; try disassembling the keyboard and drying the water at the back side of the keyboard. If you find that some keys no longer work, then recheck and make sure all the liquid has been thoroughly dried. You might have to remove the keyboard but take more care for this step, because many keyboards have a "hidden lock" you have to find otherwise something might get broken. A keyboard circuit board is usually made of two to three layers of thin plastic; you can wipe it carefully with a cotton swab with strong water absorption ability, but not something harder that might ruin the circuit board. After wiping the keyboard, you need to dry it for a few hours in a warm sunny location (don't use a hair dryer or any other hot air blower that could ruin the plastic parts), and then re-install it.

After doing all of this and the problem has been solved. Enter Step: B-6; if the problem is solved partially, but there's some other key problem, then please enter Step: B-5 to continue;

Step: B-5

Disassemble the failed or broken keys, remove the key caps, clean the dirt under the key cap and check whether the plastic scissor-shaped spring (Retainer clip), conductive rubber cap and circuit under the key cap are aged, broken, somehow damaged, or not. If the bracket is broken and does not work any more, then you can consider changing it with a bracket from another key you don't use. Be careful, they are easy to break.

After assembling the bracket, you attach the key cap. This is how it is done.

There is a bulge in the center part of the key cap that must fit into the, concave part in the middle of the flexible rubber on the bracket center. Orient the key properly and put the key cap on the bracket gently, then move it back and forth, up and down slowly, until you feel the bulged part at the back of the key is fitting into the concave part in the middle of the flexible rubber, you will feel when you move the key cap, a resistance from the flexible rubber. At this moment, you can press down the key hat, and the clip on the key cap will auto clamp the bracket, making a "Ka da . . ." sound meaning it is the right position. Now press the four corners of the key cap to make sure the four clip tendons have latched on to the bracket correctly. The key should be working now.

After finishing the jobs above, reinstall and try the keyboard. If the failure still exists then enter Step: B-6;

Step: B-6

Steps to change a laptop keyboard:

1) Pull out the power adapter jack;
2) Remove the battery;
3) Raise the laptop keyboard bezel with a flat screwdriver, and then remove it;
4) loosen the two screws, one on each side of the keyboard;
5) Take the keyboard out carefully, unlock the plastic lock on motherboard slot and release the flat cable and then remove the keyboard;
6) Insert the flat cable of the new keyboard into the slot, and lock the plastic lock;
7) Tighten the two screws used to hold the keyboard;
8) Install the bezel.

Notice: be very careful not to damage the plastic lock mechanism on the motherboard slot. It would result in having to change the entire motherboard, it is hard to repair.

After completing step B-6, if the problem still is not solved, enter Step: B-7;

Step: B-7

After changing the new keyboard, if the failure still exists, then we can say it's a problem on the motherboard. Usually a South Bridge management chip failure causes the keyboard (keys) to fail. The South Bridge chip is in charge of the communication over the I/O bus, for the PCI Bus, USB, LAN, ATA, SATA, audio controller, keyboard controller, and real-time clock controller, advanced power management and so on. A South Bridge chip change is a professional job and even if you can find the right chip replacement, you might not be able to handle it if you have not experienced in board repair. The best thing is to just replace the entire motherboard instead.

Step: C-1

There are a lot of factors causing keyboard key sticking problems making it difficult to type. The common reasons are: the plastic scissor-shape spring (Retainer clip) under the key cap is broken, the conductive rubber is aged and, loses flexibility, or there's something stuck between two keys. You might also have a keyboard circuit failure or software failure which makes the letter appear after a time lag. If you have a key sticking problem, enter Step: B-5; for the key typing lag problem, enter Step: C-2 to continue;

Step: C-2

It's a complex job to repair the circuits inside the keyboard, you should be careful to disassemble the keyboard. The circuit board is made of two to three layers of thin plastic, and the tracks are composed of plastic film of high flexibility with a few very thin metal threads in the middle. Check the tracks carefully to see where there are obvious rust traces or abrasion. Broken tracks are totally caused by these two factors. Wipe the metal threads carefully with absorbent cotton with strong water absorbent ability, until there is no rust trace and the metal threads shine. Then repair with a special PCB copperplate circuit repair pen (Silver Microtip Conductive PEN). The broken circuit part after repair has an anti-corrupt function.

If there is no circuit failure found, then please enter Step: C-4. If you find an open circuit failure, but have no special tool, or after repair, it still doesn't work. Please enter Step: B-6;

Step: C-3

If the data cable between the touchpad and motherboard is not positioned properly, after long-term pressure, the cable can break or a short circuit failure develops. A worse situation happens after liquid enters the touchpad, the laptop is then under a very damp conductive environment and still working, the circuit might rust or rot, and then a short circuit failure occurs. If there is only slight moisture penetration, the, laptop may still not work normally, the operating system interface freezes or black screen and other issues occur; but worse, the motherboard may get burnt, totally scrapping the laptop. Therefore, disconnect the touchpad from the motherboard; in case of a touchpad circuit problem which would affect the keyboard normal function. If you still have not solved out problem, please enter Step: C-2; if the problem is solved, but still there's a touchpad problem, then please enter Step: D-1 to continue;

Step: C-4

If you have reinstalled the keyboard data cable or cleaned and repaired the keyboard circuits, you then restart the laptop to test the keyboard. I suggest testing the keyboard with it working under a DOS system. We can then avoid making a mistaken diagnosis because of a software conflict; if using the DOS system, the original failed keys all recover normally, then please enter Step: C-5; if the failure still exists, then please enter Step: C-7;

Step: C-5

Under DOS system, if the keyboard typing is ok, and the touchpad works fine, we know there is no hardware problem. The failure will be in the original laptop software and likely a software conflict or the typing software is corrupted. Please check the solution in Step: C-6;

Step: C-6

First uninstall the typing software, and then restart the laptop to reinstall new typing software. Next you can update the service package for operating system. After these repair steps, if the failure still exists, then you should consider reinstalling a new operating system.

Step: C-7

Test whether the laptop has an overheating problem with software. Refer to section 2 of chapter 6 of this book <<6.2.6 Laptop system crash caused by overheating or auto shutdown failure analysis and repair flow>> to carry out this process.

If the laptop has an overheating problem, I suggest buying a USB Cooler Fan, and install temperature monitor software. When the temperature is high, don't open too many applications at the same time, and don't let the laptop continually work. You are better to shutdown the laptop once every few hours to cool it down. For a complete procedure, please enter Step: C-8;

If the laptop doesn't have an overheating problem, then possibly liquid has entered the touchpad or keyboard, or a key button failure intermittently causes a sudden short circuit when in use, then please enter Step: B-6;

Step: C-8

Please check another tutorial (in chapter 06) for curing laptop overheating failures.

Step: D-1

1) Please refer to the solution in Step: A-4;
2) A rare situation is when a touchpad short circuit failure causes a keyboard failure; if you disconnect the touchpad data cable from the motherboard, the keyboard would recover and work normally, the operating system interface would not freeze or there is no black screen or other problems, then you can confirm the touchpad has a short circuit failure. If the problem is still not solved, then please enter Step: D-2;

Step: D-2

Change the aged touchpad data cable, broken jiggle switch or defective scissor-shape spring (Retainer clip), or change the entire touchpad circuit board, including the key circuit board;

Here are the steps to follow to change the touchpad:

1. Remove the touchpad using Step: C-3;
2. Plug the cables of the new touchpad into the motherboard slot, slide the plastic lock into position;
3. Tighten the 6 screws to mount the touchpad;
4. Install the fan and hard disk;
5. Reassemble the shell.

Step: D-3

1) Open the "Control Panel"; check that the "Device manager" has recognized the USB device correctly. If USB device has an item with a yellow interrogation mark, it means the USB device was not recognized correctly. A USB device driver failure, USB port failure, motherboard failure all might cause the problem where the system fails to recognize a USB device correctly;

2) Try uninstalling the USB driver, and then restart the laptop, letting it auto install a new USB driver.

Step: D-4

Plug a working USB mouse to the USB interface, and put a DOS disc (needed to load the USB and touchpad drivers) or a special Windows PE system disc into the laptop DVD-ROM to start up. Check whether the USB mouse works or not; if it works, then it means the failure is in the original operating system. Proceed to Step: E-2;

If it does not work, then the problem is in the USB hardware, please enter Step: E-3;

Step: D-5

Plug a working USB mouse into the USB interface; check whether USB mouse light is on or not.

If the mouse light is on, then we can basically say the USB port power supply is OK, the problem might be in the driver or OS software service package, which needs to be updated. Please enter Step: E-2; if the mouse light is out, then we can assume that the problem must be the USB port power supply, please enter Step: D-6;

Step: D-6

There are various reasons that can cause a USB port bad contact:

(1) An attempt to plug into the interface the wrong way and/or too much force plugging in pushed the socket into the laptop shell and broke the retaining tabs.
(2) The USB interface pins are bent, cracked or there's a short circuit failure inside;
(3) The USB interface board is pressed from outside, which causes serious distortion or damage to the plastic parts;

If your laptop has suffered any of these symptoms, please enter Step: D-7; if the USB interface is perfect, it means the problem is in the motherboard hardware, please enter Step: D-8;

Step: D-7

Method 1: stop using that USB port, and change to another one;

Method 2: use a USB hub with four ports. If you only have one port to plug into and it is damaged you may still be able to use it if you are careful and maybe glue the hub plug in place.

Method 3: install a PCMCIA USB adapter to take the place of the USB interface fixed on the motherboard;

Method 4: The bended USB interface pins can be bent back to normal and soldering the contact pin break may be possible.

Step: D-8

Measure the USB port power supply voltage with a multimeter; the USB port power supply protection circuit resistor should have +5V voltage (negative pen connects to the ground, while positive pen connects USB port 1). If there is no voltage, it means the USB port is not getting voltage from the power supply, a USB device will not work. It could be either the USB power supply protection resistor is burnt or the power supply on the motherboard has failed. If +5V voltage has disappeared, please enter Step: E-1; if the voltage is normal, then please enter Step: E-2;

Step: E-1

Open the laptop and remove the laptop motherboard, change out the USB power protection resistor and reassemble the laptop.

After changing the resistor, if the failure disappears, then please enter Step: E-2, and also update the service package for the operating system; if the failure is still unsolved, then it means a motherboard failure, please enter Step: E-3;

Step: E-2

Check that you have the latest driver and system service packages.

Solution: first uninstall the USB driver, and then restart the laptop, letting the laptop auto install a new USB driver. Then update the service package for the operating system if needed.

Step: E-3

Find the South Bridge I/O management chip, try replacing the chip; you can also install a PCMCIA USB adapter to replace the USB interface fixed on the motherboard or you can directly change the motherboard of the laptop.

In all, summarizing this tutorial for laptop touchpad, keyboard and USB port failures:

Probable causes are: system overheating, liquid spills, too much accumulated dust, bad hardware system software damage, and other factors.

Solutions: cleaning, changing out hardware and reinstalling the operating system and drivers should solve most problems.

13.3 19 repair cases for Laptop touchpad, keyboard and USB port failures

13.3.1 8 repair cases for functional failures caused because HP laptop touchpad, keyboard and USB port are not good;

247) HP Pavilion DM3-1040US laptop touchpad failure

Failure symptom:

Laptop touchpad suddenly failed to work, you cannot move cursor to do anything, it still could not work even after reinstalling the driver.

Solution:

This failure obviously belongs to the description of flowchart 13, according to the repair method; confirm the repair path, finding it accords with the sequence:

Start->A-1->A-2->A-4->A-5->A-7->D-1->D-2

Repair summary:

According to flowchart tutorial, first put one DOS disc or other professional Windows PE system disc into the laptop DVD-ROM to start up, and then test the working status of the touchpad, as a result, the failure still exists. Open the laptop, remove the touchpad, check the cables, there's no short circuit problem there; besides, the cable is good, clean the cable slot and reinstall the touchpad. However, the startup failure still exists. Remove the touchpad, replace it with a good touchpad, and start up to test again, the failure is gone. Then we can confirm the failure is caused because of bad touchpad hardware.

Hint:

Sometimes when you assemble touchpad, probably system might fail to recognize new hardware; at this moment, you need to delete the old driver and reinstall the latest driver. Restart the laptop and the problem is solved.

248)   HP Compaq 6531s laptop touchpad failure

Failure symptom:

Recently laptop touchpad failed, cannot do any operation. Water was accidentally poured on the laptop, and it could work normally after drying it, the laptop worked fine.

Solution:

This failure obviously belongs to the description of flowchart 13, according to the repair method, confirm the repair path, finding it accords with the sequence:

Start->A-1-> A-2->A-4->A-5->A-7

Repair summary:

According to the failure symptom, touchpad fails work, first of all, remove the old driver, and install the latest driver. Restart the laptop, the failure still exists, and because once water enters laptop, it's quite likely that after touchpad gets damp, the internal electrical circuit is already damaged. Therefore, open the laptop, remove the touchpad, and check up the cable plug, finding the interface had green mildew points. Try cleaning and then replace the cable. At last, fold the lockup to fix up the cable. Restart the laptop and then failure is eliminated.

Hint:

Laptop touchpad is a precious component, which is quite easy to get affected by outside factor, then failure occurs. When external liquid enters inside, you'd have to do proper dispose immediately, otherwise, it is likely to cause other failures.

249)   HP Pavilion DV6-2105ea laptop touchpad failure

Failure symptom:

Laptop touchpad's right-click key could not work, but the right-click key and move function are all right.

Solution:

This failure obviously belongs to the description of flowchart 13, according to the repair method, confirm the repair path, finding it accords with the sequence:

Start->A-1-> A-2->A-3->A-5->A-7->D-1->D-2

Repair summary:

According to flowchart tutorial, reinstall the touchpad driver. Restart the laptop, the failure is not eliminated. Open the laptop, remove the touchpad, finding the left-key's plastic key retainer under the touchpad is already aged and broken, the key retainer ability is weak. Change a new plastic reed with good elasticity, (or paste one proper thick plastic piece under the failed key, the thickness should accord with the actual need),

Hint:

After excluding the software problem, remove the touchpad, clean the dirt under the touchpad, if after reinstalling the touchpad, the failure still exists, it's kind of difficult to repair, then you can use USB mouse or change the touchpad.

250)   HP dv7-3080US laptop keyboard function failure

Failure symptom:

Laptop keyboard "S" key fails, cannot enter anything.

Solution:

This failure obviously belongs to the description of flowchart 13, according to the repair method, confirm the repair path, finding it accords with the sequence:

Start->A-1->B->B-1->B-3->B-4

Repair summary:

According to flowchart tutorial, first put one DOS disc or other professional Windows PE system disc to the laptop DVD-ROM to start up, the failure still exists. Remove the failed key hat, clean the dust attached on the conductive rubber and the circuit board. After putting on key, the button recovers function, and then you can enter normally.

Hint:

Laptop keyboard construct is quite delicate, internal electronic circuits are quite intensive, if there's dirt on circuit board or silicon membrane that these two could not be connected normally, then keyboard failure and function problem would be caused. Therefore, usually you should pay attention to avoid too much dust entering laptop keyboard, which might cause functional failure.

251)   HP dv4-1547sb laptop keyboard functional failure

Failure symptom:

Laptop keyboard button enters A, but screen always shows AS.

Solution:

This failure obviously belongs to the description of flowchart 13, according to the repair method, confirm the repair path, finding it accords with the sequence:

Start->A-1-> B->B-1->B-3->B-4

Repair summary:

According to flowchart tutorial, first put one DOS disc or professional Windows PE system disc to the laptop DVD-ROM to start up, test the keyboard, finding the failure still exists. Then remove the keyboard, finding there's something stuck between keys A and B. After cleaning it, then test the keyboard again, the failure is eliminated.

Hint:

a)   There are also some possibilities causing the sticky keys problem: logical circuit failure, line or row cable of keyboard circuit has certain broken somewhere or short circuit.

b)   This kind of failure symptom might be caused because of typing software problem, you need to uninstall and reinstall typing software, generally speaking, the problem could be solved. If still not, then you need to reinstall operation system.

252)   HP ProBook 4310s laptop keyboard stuck key failure

Failure symptom:

Laptop keyboard space bar key doesn't work, sometimes you need to press countless times to enter, after pressing "K" button, it won't pop up again, screen shows countless "K", at this moment, keyboard other letters could not enter, you need to press "K" once again, then it key cannot come up

Solution:

This failure obviously belongs to the description of flowchart 13, according to the repair method, confirm the repair path, finding it accords with the sequence:

Start->A-1->B->B-1->B-3->C-1->B-5

Repair summary:

According to flowchart tutorial, first put one DOS disc or other professional Windows PE system disc to laptop DVD-ROM to start up. The failure still exits. Then pull out the key hat of "K" button, finding the stuck key failure is caused because the scissor-shape key retainer is cracked. Then change a new plastic key retainer to reduce the friction, finally recovering the K key. Afterwards, remove the space bar key hat, finding the silicon membrane is already aged, then change a new silicon membrane, then the space bar key could work normally.

Hint:

a)   This failure is keyboard "Stuck key" failure, not only happening on the old keyboard used for a long time, but also sometimes keyboard failure would also happen to new individual keyboard not being used a long time yet. Keyboard stuck key failure mainly have two causes as below:

1)   One reason is that the pole position under the key hat is moved, which stops the key body shell cover stuck after pressing the button down, It usually happens to new keyboards or keyboards not used for a long time;

2)   After the keys are used for a long time, reset key retainer's elasticity becomes worse, the friction between key retainer and the pole increases that key button could not flip up again, then cause the key stuck. This failure is mostly happening to the keyboards working for a long time.

b)   If buttons are difficult to be found, then you can remove one key not used a lot on the original keyboard, such as "Home", to replace the damaged common key used a lot, including the plastic scissor-shape key retainer and silicon membrane hat.

253)   HP Pavilion dv5-1235dx laptop keyboard failure

Failure symptom:

On laptop keyboard, there are several keys not in one line, nor in the same row, could not enter . . . .

Solution:

This failure obviously belongs to the description of flowchart 13, according to the repair method, confirm the repair path, finding it accords with the sequence:

Start->A-1-> B->B-1->B-3->B-4->B-6

Repair summary:

According to flowchart tutorial, first put one DOS disc or professional Windows PE system disc to laptop DVD-ROM to start up, then test the keyboard, finding the problem still exists. Then remove all failed key hats, clean the dirt attached under the key hats, the failure still exists. After changing the keyboard, the failure disappears. It means the original keyboard circuit has problem.

Hint:

If you cannot find same model of keyboard, then suggest removing the keyboard, test with 100MHz high frequency oscilloscope find the failed component and unsoldered position, and then resolder it.

254) HP 4310S laptop keyboard test failure

Failure symptom:

Laptop keyboard test fails, during the process laptop starts up, there's a series of beeps from the laptop.

Solution:

This failure obviously belongs to the description of flowchart 13, according to the repair method, confirm the repair path, finding it accords with the sequence:

Start->A-1-> B->B-1->B-3->B-4->B-5->B-6

Repair summary:

According to flowchart tutorial, first put one DOS disc or professional Windows PE system disc to laptop DVD-ROM to start up, test the keyboard, finding the failure still exists. Then check up the keyboard, finding there's certain key stuck, and could not pop up again. Then press down the issued key, meanwhile, remove the key cap and then push forward slightly, then you can remove the key hat. Afterwards, change the aged silicon membrane, then put the key hat on, there's still a series of beeps made when machine starts up, which means the keyboard partial circuit has a short circuit or is already broken, you need to change the keyboard.

Hint:

a)   Sometimes liquid enters keyboard, which might ruin the key conductive performance, then you need to remove the issued keys, remove the conductive rubber hat, check the conductive layer under there, it should be bright metal layer; if there's color change, water trace, like oil mud, then you must clean with absolute alcohol.

b)   If after changing a new keyboard, the failure still exists, then it means the motherboard or the memory has problem.

13.3.2 four repair cases for HP laptop touchpad, keyboard and USB port functional failures caused by software conflicts and program errors

255)   HP dv6-1360us laptop keyboard buttons have no response

Failure symptom:

Recently few buttons on laptop keyboard failed, having no response.

Solution:

This failure obviously belongs to the description of flowchart 13, according to the repair method, confirm the repair path, finding it accords with the sequence:

Start->A-1->B->C-6

Repair summary:

According to flowchart tutorial, first of all, put one DOS disc or other professional Windows PE system disc to the laptop DVD-ROM to start up, and then test whether the keyboard could work normally or not. If it works all right, then it should be the software problem. Then uninstall and reinstall typing software, and then the failure is eliminated.

Hint:

Laptop keyboard hardware failures caused because of software conflicts, if you cannot ensure the failure is caused because certain one or several software, then generally speaking, you can reinstall operation system for the laptop or recover the system back to factory settings to solve the problem.

256)   HP Compaq cq60 laptop touchpad failure

Failure symptom:

Laptop touchpad fails, cursor could not move, even the left and right buttons lose the function too.

Solution:

This failure obviously belongs to the description of flowchart 13, according to the repair method, confirm the repair path, finding it accords with the sequence:

Start->A-1->B->C-6

Repair summary:

According to flowchart tutorial, first of all, make sure the switch shortcut key of the touchpad is already enabled, and then put one DOS disc (with touchpad driver loaded) or professional Windows PE system disc to laptop DVD-ROM to start up, and then it tests the touchpad could would work normally, then we can be certain that it's caused by software problem. Uninstall and reinstall typing software, then the failure is eliminated.

Hint:

a)   As for such kind of touchpad failure, under the circumstance excluding hardware problem, generally, we can reinstall operation system to solve system incompatibility problem, letting it recover to the initial system state.

b)   Some typing software have touchpad switch, which could enable and disable touchpad function, you need to first check whether the software already enabled the touchpad function.

257)   HP dv4-1547sb laptop USB interface failure

Failure symptom:

Recently laptop USB interfaces suddenly all failed, any external USB device could not be recognized by system.

Solution:

This failure obviously belongs to the description of flowchart 13, according to the repair method, confirm the repair path, finding it accords with the sequence:

Start->A-1->A-2->A-4->A-6->D-3->D-5->E-2

Repair summary:

According to flowchart tutorial, put one DOS disc (USB mouse driver loaded) or other professional Windows PE system disc to laptop DVD-ROM to start up, and then test the USB mouse, finding it works normally. Now I am certain that the operating system has problems. Then I plug in a USB mouse to test, finding the problem of the original operation the mouse light is on. Next update Windows Service Package, restart the laptop and then the failure disappears.

Hint:

First uninstall USB driver, and then restart the laptop, letting laptop auto install the new USB driver. Meanwhile, update operation system service package.

258) HP dm3-1040us laptop touchpad failure

Failure symptom:

Laptop touchpad failed, both click and double click do not work, and the cursor does not move at all.

Solution:

This failure obviously belongs to the description of flowchart 13, according to the repair method, confirm the repair path, finding it accords with the sequence:

Start->A-1->B->C-6

Repair summary:

According to flowchart tutorial, first of all, make sure the touchpad switch shortcut key is already enabled, and then put one DOS disc (with touchpad driver loaded) or other professional Windows PE system disc to laptop DVD-ROM to start up; next test it, finding the touchpad could work normally; so it should be software problem. Open the device manager list, finding the device manager could not recognize touchpad program correctly, so uninstall the existed driver, install the latest version of driver, then the failure is eliminated.

Hint:

If touchpad settings are incorrect, such kind of failure would happen. Suggest downloading HP touchpad control software, set up the touchpad correctly.

13.3.3 Three repair cases of HP laptop touchpad, keyboard and USB port functional failures caused by of cable plug badness or short circuit

259) HP dv7-3080us laptop keyboard functional failure

Failure symptom:

Laptop keyboard has no response at all, cannot enter, device manager shows no abnormality, USB external keyboard could work.

Solution:

This failure obviously belongs to the description of flowchart 13, according to the repair method; confirm the repair path, finding it accords with the sequence:

Start->A-1-> B->B-1->B-2

Repair summary:

According to flowchart tutorial, first of all, put one DOS disc or professional Windows PE system disc to laptop DVD-ROM to start up, test the keyboard, finding the failure still exists. After confirming the keyboard has no function reaction at all, and then removes the keyboard, check the keyboard circuit lines, finding there are two tiny cracks on the cable, then we know it caused the keyboard functional failure. Repair the cracked cable with conductive pen, or directly change the keyboard.

Hint:

When assembling the keyboard, pay attention to the status whether cable is plugged to the motherboard jack tightly or not, in case the cable is not plugged into the right position or get a loose connection; at last, remember to lock up the cable.

260)   HP dv6-1360us laptop touchpad failure

Failure symptom:

Laptop touchpad failed, it's useless no matter how to slide the touchpad, and button also failed.

Solution:

This failure obviously belongs to the description of flowchart 13, according to the repair method; confirm the repair path, finding it accords with the sequence:

Start->A-1-> A-2->A-3->A-5->A-7->D-1

Repair summary:

According to flowchart tutorial, first of all, check whether touchpad is disabled normally because of wrong operation; confirm it's at enabled status. And then check the device manager, there's yellow exclamation mark on the touchpad driver. Then remove the original driver immediately, install the latest version of driver, restart it, but the failure still exists. Then remove the touchpad, check the touchpad circuit on the motherboard, after testing the signal, finding the interface has short circuit problem, you need to use USB mouse to replace.

Hint:

Pay attention that laptop system has touchpad switch program; generally, we can accomplish through combination function keys. Some users know little about the function keys. When come to similar touchpad no response failure, they thought the touchpad hardware failure; actually just the switch is off.

261)   HP dm3-1040us laptop keyboard failure

Failure symptom:

Laptop keyboard suddenly failed and could not do any operation. Device manager could not recognize keyboard correctly.

Solution:

This failure obviously belongs to the description of flowchart 13, according to the repair method; confirm the repair path, finding it accords with the sequence:

Start->A-1-> A-2->A-3->A-5->A-7

Repair summary:

According to flowchart tutorial, first of all, put one pure DOS disc or other professional Windows PE system disc to laptop DVD-ROM to start up, test it and find the failure still exists. Remove the keyboard and check up, finding the cables are perfect, but the plastic lockup is already broken. Then plug the cable to the motherboard slots again, then stick the damaged plastic lockup with strong glue, lock up the plastic lockup, next fix up the plastic lockup with tapes. Wait for the next day, after the plastic lockup is completely fixed tightly, and then assemble the keyboard, and then restart the laptop, the failure is eliminated then.

Hint:

If you find the plastic lock and cables are both good after disassembling the keyboard, it still could not work, then you should consider whether the motherboard hardware have something wrong.

13.3.4 Two repair cases of HP laptop USB functional failures caused by USB interface is loose or fuse is melt

262) HP 5310m laptop USB failure

Failure symptom:

There are two USB ports do not work; any USB device plugged in these USB ports cannot be recognized. The other two USB ports work fine.

Solution:

This failure obviously belongs to the description of flowchart 13, according to the repair method, confirm the repair path, finding it accords with the sequence:

Start->A-1->A-2->A-4->A-6->D-3->D-5->D-6

Repair summary:

According to flowchart tutorial, USB interface has no response symptom, first of all, you need make sure the USB device has no problems, then enter device manager, check whether USB interface device state is normal, finding the device works well, there is no yellow exclamation mark shown in the device manager list, then continue checking up the USB interface, remove the motherboard, check up the failed USB interface status carefully. At this moment, finding the USB interface is unsoldered, then when there's device connecting to USB interface, it would get loose, which could not connect to motherboard normally. And finally leading to the problem that device could not be recognized correctly. Resolder the USB interface to fix up on the motherboard, and then USB interface function is OK, any USB device could be recognized.

Hint:

If there's no soldering tool, you can use an USB hub with 4 interfaces, plug to the distorted or the USB interface with damaged plastic piece carefully, and then fix up with glue. Later you can only use the USB interface on the hub.

263) HP pavilion V5000 laptop USB interface could not be recognized

Failure symptom:

Certain USB interface of laptop keyboard could not recognize USB device, then plug USB mouse to the interface, the mouse light is not on.

Solution:

This failure obviously belongs to the description of flowchart 13, according to the repair method, confirm the repair path, finding it accords with the sequence:

Start->A-1-> A-2->A-4->A-6->D-3->D-5->D-6->D-8->E-1

Repair summary:

According to the failure symptom that USB mouse light is not on, first check up the USB interface. Make sure the USB interface is not loose; besides, the metal contact pins inside the interface are not cracked or bent. Then measure the USB port power supply protection circuit's resistance and voltage with a multimeter. Normally, USB port power supply protection circuit resistor should have +5V voltage. Test and find that the +5V voltage disappears, which means the USB port could not supply power, which leads to the problem that USB device could not work. Open the laptop cover, remove the laptop motherboard, and check the USB control circuit on the motherboard, whether there's some failure existed. After measuring the voltage between each point, finding there's one resistor broken, which causes USB power supply voltage interruption, directly affect USB interface's normal function. After changing a same USB power supply protection circuit resistor, the USB interface function could be recovered.

Hint:

(1) USB interface device has a comparatively strict requirement for voltage, if USB interface could not provide enough voltage, then any device could not be recognized;

(2) USB power supply protection circuit resistor is already burnt or the motherboard failure might cause the problem that USB port could not supply power. If the failure still exists after changing USB power protection circuit resistor, then you need to consider changing South Bridge I/O management chip or the entire motherboard.

13.3.5 Two repair cases of HP laptop touchpad, keyboard and USB port functional failures caused because of overheating

264) HP ProBook 4510s laptop keyboard functional failure

Failure symptom:

Laptop keyboard has some buttons could not type letters, and mostly focusing on the left area on the keyboard, typing function is missing.

706

Solution:

This failure obviously belongs to the description of flowchart 13, according to the repair method; confirm the repair path, finding it accords with the sequence:

Start->A-1-> B-1->B-3->C-1->C-2->C-4->C-7->C-8

Repair summary:

According to flowchart tutorial, check up the keyboard buttons without letter typing function, and analyze these few letters on the left area. First of all, change a new keyboard with known normal functions, as a result, it shows ok, which means the keyboard has failure, but the problem is why the keys without functions all gather around the left part of the keyboard? Observe and find the keyboard left part and salver part are quite heated, even too hot to touch. Then check further, as a result, the system is already much overheated, there's problem with heat dissipation. As heat was not able to be released, thus mostly accumulating surrounding the heat sink, which is located beneath the left part of the keyboard, Overheating caused the circuit under several keys to have failures. You may go to Chapter 06 to know more details about troubleshooting overheating problems.

Hint:

a)   As for system overheating symptom, you should pay attention and take some measures in time, in case it overheats continually, because it would make keyboard button circuit damaged because of overheating. Similarly, it would also affect touchpad and USB interface working normally.

b)   Suggest using one USB cooling fan to facilitate the heat dissipation of the laptop

265)   Compaq Presario CQ45-101TU laptop USB interface recognition failure

Failure symptom:

Laptop keyboard has certain USB interface failing to recognize USB device, then connect USB mouse to the interface, the mouse light is on.

Solution:

This failure obviously belongs to the description of flowchart 13, according to the repair method; confirm the repair path, finding it accords with the sequence:

Start->A-1-> A-2->A-4->A-6->D-3->D-5->D-6->D-8->E-2->E-3

Repair summary:

According to the failure symptom that USB mouse light is on, first of all, check whether device manager could recognize USB interface correctly. After updating operation system software package, the failure still exists. Make sure the USB interface is not loose and the metal contact pins inside the interface are not cracked or bent. At last, I am certain that the motherboard has failure.

Hint:

You do not have to replace the motherboard. You can also find out the defective South Bridge I/O management chip, and change same chip. If your laptop has PCMCIA interface, then you can install one PCMCIA USB adapter to replace the USB interface fixed on the motherboard.

CHAPTER 14

Wired Internet access (ethernet) failure repair

14.1 Laptop wired Internet access failure repair

14.1.1 Common failure symptoms for the laptop cable network card

a) ADSL Modem does not dial or connect;

b) Settings are all correct, but the laptop does not access the cable network;

c) It goes offline frequently when on the Internet;

d) Pick up the phone and then dial to connect, then it does connect the to Internet normally;

e) First shut down the computer and then power off the DSL Modem, the laptop then auto restarts;

f) You cannot use a cable to connect to the family network to realize Internet sharing;

g) Other computers within the network cannot be seen;

h) The speed is slow when the laptop connects to the Internet with an RJ45 cable;

i) A DSL Modem connects, but does not browse webpages; Please take a look at Figure 14-1.

 Server not found

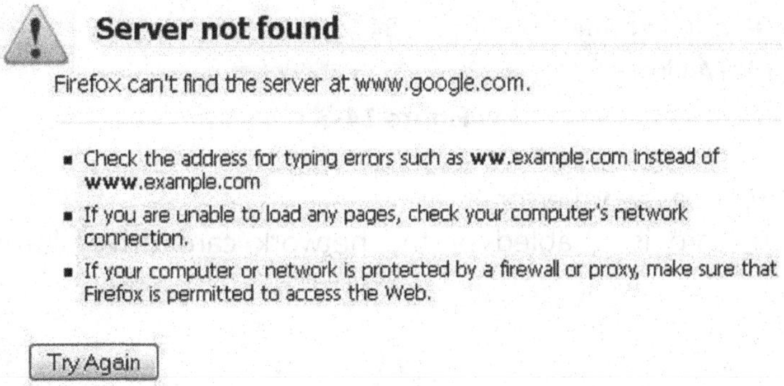

Firefox can't find the server at www.google.com.

- Check the address for typing errors such as **ww**.example.com instead of **www**.example.com
- If you are unable to load any pages, check your computer's network connection.
- If your computer or network is protected by a firewall or proxy, make sure that Firefox is permitted to access the Web.

[Try Again]

Figure 14-1

j)   In the device manager, a network card icon cannot be found;

k)   The network card doesn't work, the indication light status is incorrect;

l)   Sometimes the network is on but sometimes off; please take a look at Figure 14-2.

Figure 14-2

14.1.2 Laptop cable network card Internet failure and cause analysis

a)   The DSL Modem does not dial or connect

The causes of the failure probably are as below:

(1)   RJ45 cable or a server failure, which disables the modem that creates a connection with the ISP server;

(2)   Remote computer error—no response;

(3)   A dialing software failure or after installing the software, the relevant protocol is not bound correctly;

(4)   An IP distribution problem;

(5)   The operating system is incompatible with the dialing network relevant components;

(6)   A network protocol error caused by an abnormal shutdown;

(7)   The PPPoE is not installed completely or correctly; please take a look at Figure 14-3.

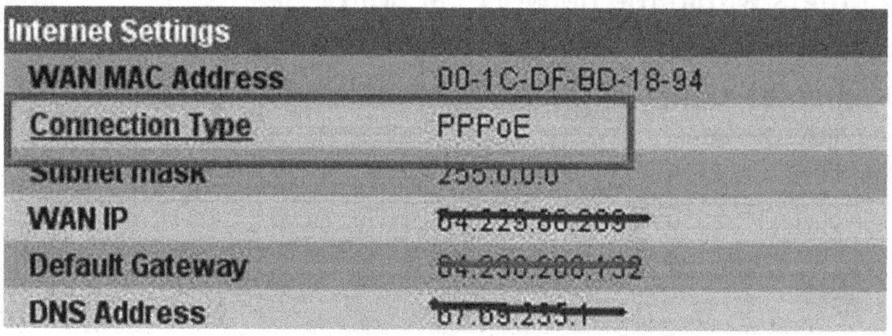

Internet Settings	
WAN MAC Address	00-1C-DF-BD-18-94
Connection Type	PPPoE
Subnet mask	255.0.0.0
WAN IP	84.223.80.209
Default Gateway	84.230.200.132
DNS Address	87.09.233.1

Figure 14-3

(8)   A user name or password error;

(9)   The network card is disabled or the network card driver hasn't been installed correctly.

b) Settings are all correct, but does not access the cable network;

The causes of the failure probably are as below:

(1) Certain connections between the DSL modem and the computer are abnormal;

(2) The IP address settings are incorrect;

(3) The operating system has viruses and Trojan infections, which causes problems to the IE browser;

(4) The firewall settings are incorrect or the user installed several firewalls at one time;

(5) The PPPoE is not installed completely or correctly;

(6) Check the BIOS setup and hardware switch; make sure the laptop's cable network card function is enabled.

c) The laptop goes offline frequently when on the Internet;

The causes of the failure probably are as below:

(1) A TCP/IP protocol installation or settings error;

(2) A device conflict occurs;

(3) The RJ45 cable connectors have a contact problem;

(4) The cable connector has patina because of humidity and causes a bad contact;

(5) The insulation of the cable is broken or the internal conductor is exposed; Please take a look at Figure 14-4

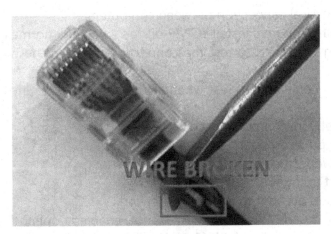

Figure 14-4

(6) A DSL MODEM or network card thermal problem;

(7) If the Data Terminal Ready (DTR) signal's invalid, the time to connect exceeds the default value of Modem, and it goes offline.

d) First shut down the computer and then power off the DSL Modem; the laptop then auto restarts

The BIOS power management enables the modem wake-up function

e) You cannot use a cable to connect to the family network to realize Internet sharing;

The causes of the failure probably are as below:

(1) Make sure the DSL Modem LAN port connects to the host (if using a router, then check the router interface), and confirm you are using the correct RJ45 cable;
(2) Recover the router to factory settings;
(3) Recover the DSL Modem to factory settings;
(4) Repair according to <<Laptop cable network card Internet failure analysis and repair flow>>.

f) Other computers within the network cannot be seen;

The causes of the failure probably are as below:

(1) Make sure the File and Printer share is enabled, and the cable network property "General" option card has the checkbox "Microsoft network file and printer share" checked;
(2) Check the physical connection between computers;
(3) Make sure all computers install TCP/IP protocol, to work normally together;
(4) Use the ping command to test the connection between the two computers in the network;
(5) Use the ping command to test whether the name parsing in the network is ok or not;
(6) Install the network components correctly;
(7) Enable "Computer browser" service;
(8) Run the network mark wizard;
(9) Enable Guest account;
(10) Allow the guest account to access the network;
(11) Firewall: make sure WinXP firewall is not enabled, open the local connection property—advanced, disable the Internet connection firewall;
(12) Check that the RPC, Plug and Play service is enabled, check the authorization of the relevant system folder, and register the dynamic link libraries below again:

    (a) Set the account and password;
    (b) Several ways to access "network computers".

g)   The speed is slow when the laptop connects to the Internet with an RJ45 cable;

The causes of the failure probably are as below:

(1)   The laptop does not have enough memory;

(2)   Too many line connectors, a bad contact in the connector or not connected properly, the plug oxidization is severe; all these can cause the low quality of the line transmission by adding signal attenuation, which affects the Internet speed;

(3)   The modem operates for a long time without shutting down to rest, a chip overheats and influences the Internet speed;

(4)   A bad contact between the device and the phone cable or the network cable lowers the Internet speed;

(5)   A bad contact occurs on the interface between phone cable and the tone segregator (DSL line conditioner);

(6)   A bad contact occurs on the interface between the modem and the computer Ethernet card;

(7)   The computer has a virus infection that occupies a large amount of bandwidth, or the user did not set a wireless network password to prevent use by others;

(8)   The bandwidth is too small;

(9)   The computer configuration is too low;

(10) There's a loop in the network that causes network speed slowness;

(11) A problem caused because of the network itself.

h)   The DSL Modem connects, but cannot browse webpages;

The causes of the failure probably are as below:

(1)   A network setup problem;

(2)   A DNS server issue;

(3)   An IE browser problem;

(4)   A network firewall problem;

(5)   A network protocol and network driver problem;

(6)   HOSTS file issue;

(7)   A system file problem;

(8)   An application Management service problem;

(9)   A virus infection issue.

i)   In the device manager, a network card icon cannot be found;

The causes of the failure probably are as below:

(1)   The network card is not plugged in tightly;

(2)   Make sure the relevant services are enabled;

(3)   Make sure the TCP/IP components are installed;

(4) Make sure the DCOM authorization settings are correct;
(5) Make sure the Network Neighborhood is not hidden;
(6) Make sure the existing connection is deleted;
(7) The device manager does not display in the device list normally because of a virus infection;
(8) The network card is set as a hidden device.

j) The network card doesn't work, the indication light status is incorrect;

The causes of the failure probably are as below:

(1) A network port failure;
(2) A modem power failure or power converter issue;
(3) A hardware failure that makes the self-inspection fail;
(4) The communication signal on the current circuit is not stable;
(5) The communication line has short circuit or open circuit failure.

k) Sometimes is network is on but sometimes it is off;

The causes of the failure probably are as below:

(1) The network port has a bad contact problem;
(2) The network card is not plugged in tightly;
(3) The RJ45 interface plastic connector is damaged or the holding clip is broken and it cannot be inserted properly or is loose. Please take a look at Figure 14-5.

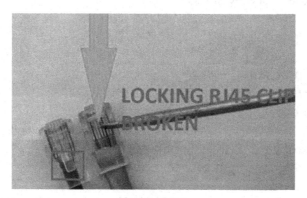

Figure 14-5

(4) The external protection cover of the RJ45 network cable is not inserted inside the plastic connector, and does not properly support the conductor termination causing intermittent disconnects.

Please note: RJ45 cables and standard telephone cables can look similar to a lay person. The RJ45 cable connector is larger. Trying to plug a standard telephone cable into an RJ45 port can damage it. Make sure you know which to use.

There are 2 types of RJ45 cables, one is a crossover cable and one is standard. The crossover cable is used to connect 2 computers directly together. If you use it to connect to a modem or router, nothing will work.

14.1.3 Solutions for a laptop cable network card causing an Internet connection (or system crash) failure

a)   The DSL Modem does not dial or connect;

Solution:

Confirm the user name and password entries are correct. Check the DSL Modem power and connection cables. Check the network property; whether the PPPoE relevant protocols are installed correctly and bound correctly (relevant protocols) or not. Check whether the network card has "?" or "!" mark on it and set it as "Enabled". After attempting the steps above, if the failure is still unsolved, then please try the next steps below:

(1)   Change the RJ45 network cable for one you know is good;
(2)   Call the ISP, to see if the problem is on their side and provide assistance;
(3)   Uninstall the original dialing software, reinstall the dialing software;
(4)   Reinstall the PPPoE network protocol;
(5)   Set the system as "Auto distribute IP address";
(6)   Reinstall the operating system;
(7)   Reinstall the network card driver;

b)   The PPPoE network protocols settings are all correct, but you cannot access the cable network;

Solution:

(1)   Pull out the DSL Modem power cable, then reconnect it after 1 min and restart the DSL Modem;
(2)   Remove the telephone cable and the RJ45 network cable; examine them carefully for damage to the connectors or the cables. Change any cable that is damaged. Re-insert the cables and make sure they snap into place smoothly and without abnormal force. Be sure you are using the correct cable when plugging in. The RJ45 cable with the larger connectors goes between the computer and modem.
(3)   Reset the IP address correctly;
(4)   Scan the hard disk entirely with antivirus software and clear all virus and Trojan infections, and then reinstall IE browser;
(5)   Set up the firewall correctly. If you have installed several firewalls, pick one and uninstall the others;
(6)   Check the device manager settings; make sure the laptop cable network card function is enabled.

c) The laptop goes offline frequently when on the Internet;

Solution:

(1) Make sure the line connections are correct and the line conditioners provided are installed correctly. (different types of tone segregators/ line conditioners can connect differently; so please make sure they are connected correctly according to the instructions provided) Make sure the line communication quality is good, without any interference and not interconnected with other devices that cause line interference.

(2) Remove the network card, clean the dust off the golden fingers and motherboard slots and reinstall it. If the failure still exists, then I suggest you replace the network card;

(3) Install new patches released in the Microsoft Update site. Select auto-update or Windows update in Tools. Wait until you finish installing the patches, then install the virtual dialing software;

(4) Use the operating system PPPoE (Point-To-Point Protocol over Ethernet) dialing software, then the offline symptom should only happen rarely. However, you should pay attention not to install several PPPoE settings at one time, in case a conflict occurs;

(5) Setting error: the most common one is to set ADSL network card IP address or the DNS server incorrectly. Please reset as auto distribution. For TCP/IP and the gateway, generally, there's no need to set anything;

(6) If you suddenly find that the browsing becomes abnormal, then you can try deleting the TCP/IP protocol and then add the TCP/IP protocol again, as TCP/IP problems can easily cause these issues;

(7) Uninstall all possible software that might cause you to go offline. If an offline occurs when certain software starts and then everything becomes normal again after closing the software, you should try uninstalling and not using that software;

(8) Temporarily pause the running firewall, the Internet share proxy server software, and the Internet acceleration software and so on. Now test whether it still goes offline frequently;

(9) Check the plugs on the RJ45 network cable for abnormalities such as patina on the plug because of humidity, the insulation of the cable is damaged or internal conductors are exposed, or a plug latch is broken etc. If these kinds of symptoms exist, you need to change the RJ45 network cable.

d) When you shut down the computer and then turn off the DSL Modem power, the computer auto restarts;

Solution:

Choose the "Power Management Setup" item in the BIOS setup, set "Power On by Ring" as "Disable", then save the settings; afterwards, the computer will not restart.

e) **You cannot use a cable to connect to the family network to realize Internet sharing;**

Solution:

1) Pull and plug the RJ45 network cable, make sure the DSL Modem LAN port and the laptop port are ok; check the interface of the router and make sure the router's network indication light and RJ45 interface lights are all on. If the lights are all out, then you need to change the RJ45 network cable or the router;

2) Recover the router to the factory settings;

   a) Find one little hole on the front/back panel of the router identified by the word "Reset";
   b) Shut down the power of the router, find a thin probe like a pen head to press and hold the Reset key inside the hole;
   c) Power on the router, wait for 3 to 5 seconds and then release the reset key, the reset is done;

3) Recover the DSL Modem to factory settings;
   a) Find one little hole at the back panel of the ADSL Modem, identified by the word "Reset";
   b) Shut down the power of the ADSL Modem, find a thin probe like a pen head to press and hold the Reset key;
   c) Power on the ADSL Modem, release the reset after 5 to 10 seconds', the reset is finished;

4) Repair according to <<Laptop cable network card Internet connection failure analysis and repair flow>>;

f) **Other computers within the network cannot be seen;**

Solution:

Make sure File and Printer Share is enabled, and ensure on the "General" option card of the cable network property, the checkbox "Microsoft network File and Printer share" is checked.

If you can see your own computer in the Network Neighborhood, then it means the network card and software installation have no problems; you can try finding the cause with the following steps:

1) Hardware issue

   (1) Ping the IP address of the other hosts, check whether the connection speed of other computers is normal or not; if ok, then jump to the step (4) of 2), otherwise, continue to the next step:
   (2) Check the indication lights on the hub ports and other computer ports for normal status. Check that both ends of the network cable are properly plugged in;

2) Software setup issue

(1) If the network card light is not on, then probably the network card is not installed correctly, also it might not be connected to the network device correctly. Reinstall the driver for the network card;

(2) Choose "Control Panel"—"Network"—"Configuration" and check that each computer has installed TCP/IP protocols and NetBEUI protocol and IPX/SPX protocol. If not, then add the protocols mentioned above;

(3) IP address settings may be incorrect. Check that the IP address is at the same network segment with other computers'. The computers needing to visit each other should be unified in the same workgroup, otherwise, it would not be displayed in the Network Neighborhood;

(4) Open "Control Panel"—"Network"—"Configuration"—"File and Printing share", check whether the checkboxes "Allow other users visiting my file" and "Allow other computers using my printer" are chosen or not; if not, then choose these options;

(5) Make sure the operating system has set the user name and password correctly. Check the authorization of relevant system folders and register the dynamic link library again;

(6) Enable the Print and File Share. In the Network Neighborhood and local connection property, you can see whether the Printer and File share is installed or not. If you cannot see your own machine in the Network Neighborhood, then it means you haven't installed the Printer and File share;

(7) Make sure the WinXP system firewall is not enabled, open the local connection "Property"—"Advanced", and disable the Internet connection firewall.

g) The speed is slow when the laptop connects to the Internet with an RJ45 cable;

Solution:

(1) Update the laptop. Add physical memory, replace the memory with a higher quality one, set the virtual memory properly; add disk capacitance; update the drivers and the operating system software package;

(2) Change the indoor phone lines and the RJ45 network cable; make sure of the good condition of each plug on the lines by pulling out, inspecting, and plugging back in, and use cables with high transmission quality of and minimal signal attenuation. Make sure the RJ45 interface and network cable interface are not distorted and the internal metal contact pins are not bent or broken and change the RJ45 interface or the network cable if necessary;

(3) If the DSL Modem is used for more than two hours, then I suggest shutting down the power for a while to let it cool down, in case the DSL Modem has an overheating problem;

(4) Call the telephone company to check the condition of the DSL line and the incoming phone cable;

(5) Pull out the phone cable plug and the tone segregator plugs and make sure the interface is OK. You can also consider using a new tone segregator of higher quality;

(6) Viruses in computers occupy a large amount of bandwidth; the most common symptom is after downloading certain software the Internet speed suddenly slows down. Your anti-virus did not catch it. You should update it or use a better one. Try scanning your computer and eliminate the virus. If you can't clear it or your OS is corrupted then consider reinstalling the operating system;

(7) During the peak periods of Internet surfing, when there are too many people on the Internet, the entire network becomes comparatively slow. If the bandwidth you use is small, then you should avoid being online during the peak period;

(8) When the network constructs a loop, then the Internet speed slows down; in some complex networks, frequently there are extra backup lines, if you somehow connected one, it would construct a loop and finally affect the entire network speed. If you doubt this has happened, you can use the elimination method and partition and segment step by step.

h) The DSL Modem connects, but you cannot browse WebPages;

Solution:

(1) Network setup issue

This problem usually happens on the occasion that you need to manually specify the IP, gateway and the DNS server the online way, and use a proxy server to connect the Internet. Check your network settings on the computer carefully;

(2) DNS server issue

When the IE fails to browse a webpage, you can first try visiting it with the IP address; if it's available for access, then it should be a DNS problem, sometimes it could also be a problem with the router or the network card not connecting with the ISP DNS Server; in this case, you can shut down the router for a while, and then turn it on again, or reset the router.

(3) IE browser issue

When IE browser has a failure itself, then of course, it would affect the browsing. If the IE is damaged maliciously, it would also lead to the problem that the webpage does not open. At this moment, you can try using antivirus software to repair it.

(4)   Network firewall issue

If the network firewall settings are not right, then it would hold up all network connections. The simplest way to troubleshoot is to disable the firewall and see if it clears up the problem. That will tell you if the firewall is causing the problem.

(5)   Network protocol and network driver issues

If the IE does not browse, probably it's because the network protocol (especially TCP/IP protocols) or the network card driver is corrupted, and you can try reinstalling the network card driver and network protocols.

(6)   HOSTS file issue

If the HOSTS file was modified, it might cause browsing abnormality. The solution for it, of course, is to clear the content in the HOSTS file.

(7)   System file issue

When the system file for the IE is changed or corrupted, it will affect the IE normal functions.

i)   In the device manager, the network card icon cannot be found;

Solution:

(1)   Check the network card status

Make sure the network card is not disabled. If the network card working status is abnormal or there's something damaged, then open the network and dial connection window and you might not see the icon "Local connection". That will confirm your suspicion

Pull out the network card, and change to a new slot, and then restart the computer again to check it. Assuming that the system now recognizes the network card correctly; open the network and dial connection window again, then the "Local connection" icon might appear.

(2)   Check whether the relevant service is enabled or not

Many individual users might disable some unfamiliar system services or not used temporarily right now, in order to make sure that his/her own server would not be damaged by hacker attacks or invalid invaders. They are not aware that once some of the system services are disabled, then the local connection icon in "Network and dial connection" cannot display normally. Therefore, when you encounter the situation where the Local Connection icon cannot be found, then you can follow the next methods and check that every relevant service is enabled.

(3) Check whether simple TCP/IP components are installed

If the simple TCP/IP service components in the network service are not installed, then on the Network and Dial connection window, the Local Connection icon might not display.

(4) Check whether the DCOM authorization settings are correct or not

If the system distributed DCOM simulated level authorization is not set properly, then it would also cause the problem that the Local Connection icon on the Network and Dial connection window would disappear.

(5) Check whether the Network Neighborhood is hidden or not

This is also an important method to find the missing "Local Connection" icon.

(6) Check whether the existing connection is deleted or not

Check whether the option "Delete the existing dialing connection settings" is selected; if it is then please cancel the selection. Now click "OK" button. And restart the computer system, then the local connection icon might appear again.

j) The network card doesn't work and the indication light status is incorrect;

Solution:

(1) Change the RJ45 cable;
(2) Reset the DSL Modem power or the power converter;
(3) Pull out the network card to check the contacts, clean the rust on the golden fingers, plug it back in and retest it.
(4) Change the network card and update the driver.

k) Sometimes network is on but sometimes off;

Solution:

(1) The laptop RJ45 port has a bad contact, you need to change it;
(2) Reset the network card or change it for one you know that works;
(3) The condition of the RJ45 interface port is bad; the little plastic card is of poor quality, and even cracked, you need to replace it;
(4) The RJ45 cable plug has a crack inside, you need to install a new one;
(5) The RJ45 port on the modem has a bad contact, you need to use another port or change the Modem entirely;
(6) The Modem overheats or is aged, and needs to be replaced.

14.1.4 Laptop cable network card problem, causing Internet freezing or restart failure

There are mainly two reasons:

1) Cable network card hardware issue

   a) When the cable outside covering is damaged and the conductor is exposed or partially broken, or the cable connector rusts (patina) because of humidity and causes signal attenuation; or the network card plug's lockup is broken or the RJ45 interface distorts and so on, you should change or repair these as soon as possible;

   b) Plugging the RJ45 cable into the interface by force, can make the lock cracked or the plug distorted, then the port contact pins can be distorted or heaved, and can cause a short circuit in the interface. This problem can cause a failure to dial or a black screen when on the Internet. Please take a look at Figure 14-6.

Figure 14-6

   c) The connection cable between cable network card and motherboard develops a problem after long-term vibration, or the connection between cable network card and its slot might be loose, or there's too much accumulated dust, and causes the internet operation to become unstable or inoperable.;

   d) Another situation is caused by laptop overheating, which can make the internal connection cable age, and the oxidized cable adversely affects the RJ45 port, leading to an operation system freeze. It might also cause a cable network card or motherboard failure.

2) Drivers and software issues

   a) Operating system problems caused by virus or Trojan infection can cause problems with the IE browser. You must clean the virus or Trojan infection, and reset the network protocol again;

   b) If several antivirus software are installed, it would cause an Internet freezing problem and even if you don't connect to the Internet, a freezing failure can happen;

c) Incorrect settings for the firewall, or there are several firewalls installed, can make a freezing failure. Please disable and uninstall the extra firewall.

d) Uninstall and reinstall the driver for the cable network card;

e) Replace the issued laptop cable network card with a working normal one and if the failure disappears, it means the original network card has a problem;

f) Reinstall the operating system;

g) Call the ISP service and make sure they are not having a problem; then check the outdoor phone plug and the connection cable quality.

14.2 Repair flow chart to eliminate laptop wired internet access failure

14.2.1 Repair shortcuts for a cable network card Internet connection failure

Solve these kinds of failures with the general simple replacement method

The repair process for a laptop cable network card failure to connect to the Internet can be complex. It could be a hardware or a software problem or a combination of both.

Usually the causes are focused on an old driver needing updating, installed software, viruses and some other aspects (70% probability), a cable network card hardware issue (15%), and a RJ45 interface issue or bad connection of cables (10%) and so on. Totally the failure rate would occupy 95%, and the following are the shortcuts solutions. First make sure that the RJ45 interface and connection cable is working normally and the ISP is not at fault.

1) Pull out the RJ45 network cable, and then plug it into the interface again.

2) Inspect the RJ45 cable for defects. Check the connectors and the ports for damage such as bent, broken, or discoloured contacts and broken plastic housings. Check the cable itself for exposed conductors, damaged insulation, tight bends, and impacts that may have broken a conductor. Any significant damage discovered probably means you should change the cable.

3) Try another laptop you know is working properly to access the internet; if it does not work either, repeat steps 1) and 2); if the problem is solved, then we know the failure has nothing to do with the network cable and Internet network.

4) Open the laptop where the cable network card connects to the motherboard. Look for bad contacts on the cable connectors and RJ-45 interface. You can usually solve it when you pullout and plug in a connection as that can be enough to clean the contacts. Fasten the connection cable tightly, as it originally was, before re-assembling When necessary, change the RJ-45 interface and cable, if the problem is not solved, then please continue to step 5);

5) Remove the cable network card and clean any oxidization layer you find on the golden fingers and the accumulated dust in the slots of cable network card as well, and then re-install the cable network card. Plug it in again and see if that solves the problem. If the problem is not solved, then please continue to step 6);

6) Update the driver for the cable network card, reset the firewall, and clean viruses and Trojans; if the problem is not solved, then please continue to step 7);

7) Install a cable network card you know is good, uninstall the old driver and install the latest driver, make sure the cable network card used is compatible with the laptop. If the problem is not solved, then please continue to step 8);

8) Do full viruses scan of the laptop, clean all viruses and Trojans, uninstall the original software, and then reinstall the protocol configuration; after cleaning viruses and Trojans, if it still does not resume to the original settings, you will need to reinstall operation system. If the problem is not gone, then please continue to step 9);

9) After confirming the cable network card works normally, if the cable network card with the original operating system, is not recognized, and also is not recognized in a new operating system, then it means the motherboard hardware has problems. After installing the cable network card, if the laptop does not start up, but after removing it, it starts normally again, usually this is because of motherboard hardware issues or damages in the slot. You need to repair damages or replace the USB network card, and then reinstall a new driver.

10) If in the end there is nothing wrong with your laptop and you cannot connect to the internet, usually it's because of a remote computer error, or the server is too busy. You should contact the Internet provider for help. Hopefully you did this before any of the more drastic steps. As for a more detailed repair method, please refer to the second chapter <<14.2.5 Laptop cable network card Internet dialing failure analysis and repair flow>>.

14.2.2 70% of cable network card failures are from the operating system and network settings

The cable network card does not connect to the Internet; it goes offline frequently, or there's frequent data stops and system crashes, the internet speed is slow, a webpage cannot be opened, the operating system does not recognize the cable network card correctly and so on, about 70% of these failures are from the operating system and network settings.

According to <<14.2.1 Repair shortcuts for cable network card Internet connection failure>>, generally, first eliminate the external causes of the failure, like the RJ45 network cable plug is loose, the DSL Modem is too old or there's electromagnetic interference, and then try the network with a computer you know is good. That will tell you if the problem is either in the network or in the computer. Assuming you now know it is a computer problem and you have determined you do not have a hardware problem, the following steps will help you eliminate software problems:

Generally speaking, a technician would always first suspect the failure is caused by software, but after confirming the network settings, drivers and hardware have no problems, then you assume an operating system failure;

Start by making sure the RJ45 network cable plug's plastic lock is not cracked or broken, and then open the "Control Panel", enter the "Device manager" list to check whether there's a cable network card in the list, and showing it's recognized correctly.

Eliminate the driver failure:

- a) If the cable network card and the port are not displayed in the list or is not recognized correctly, then the likely reasons follow:

    (1) Virus and Trojan invasion has damaged the operating system or the driver of the cable network card;
    (2) The IP address setup is incorrect.; find the IP address in the TCP/IP property, set up the IP address, subnet mask and gateway, if you need, you can also set the DNS and WINS server address;
    (3) Cable network card hardware and laptop motherboard problems.

- b) If the cable network card driver can only be used in Windows 7 and is installed under a Windows XP system, then the cable network card will not work; there might be a blue screen failure or a software conflict. Check the list in the device manager, there should be no yellow exclamation mark there, if there is, the driver hasn't been installed correctly yet, you need to uninstall and reinstall it again. If the yellow exclamation mark can not be erased, then the port setup and IP address setup error might be the cause of the failure. If there is an operating system failure, then probably the cable network card and the port would not be displayed in the list or not recognized correctly.

- c) If the cable network card is displayed and recognized correctly in the list, but still cannot connect to the Internet, then after excluding the hardware problem, you should clean the disk, and reinstall the operating system; for more detailed solutions, please refer to the chapter 2 <<14.2.5 Laptop cable network card Internet connection failure analysis and repair flow>>.

How to eliminate a webpage failure to open problem

If the operating system is infected by viruses or Trojans and damaged, then the Internet connection failure would occur; therefore:

(1) Scan the Windows system entirely with antivirus software, clean viruses or Trojans; if the dialing software is corrupted, then you need to uninstall the original software and reinstall and configure it;
(2) Make sure the firewall settings are correct, disable extra firewalls;
(3) Virus or Trojan invasion can change Windows system settings itself; after reinstalling and setting the TCP/IP protocol, and it still does not solve the Internet problem, then even though the viruses and Trojans have already been cleaned, sometimes you still cannot recover the original settings. You will need to reinstall operating system to repair the laptop;

How to eliminate the problem when the Internet speed is slow

Check the hardware:

1. Check the laptop system memory and display card memory, make sure they meet the basic requirements of the Internet;
2. Make sure the proxy server settings are correct, and it's capable of reaching an even faster speed;
3. Check the used space on the disk, make sure there's at least 10% free disk space; otherwise, you will need a larger capacity hard disk;
4. Adjust the cable network card to full speed, if that does not work, try replacing the cable network card with a good and compatible one to take the place of the suspected one, if the failure disappears, then it means the original cable network card had problems.

Check the software

1. Remove irrelevant boot applications in the system;
2. Remove irrelevant protocols;
3. Don't open too many WebPages or run several applications at the same time when you surf on the Internet;
4. Disable the online antivirus software. Remove extra antivirus software, make sure there's only one antivirus software running;
5. Uninstall and reinstall the driver for the cable network card;
6. Cancel the firewall;
7. Clean virus or Trojan infections in the operating system, or reinstall the operating system;
8. Call an ISP service provider for help. Ask them to confirm the DSL connection to your modem is working up to spec . . .

14.2.3 15% of cable network failures are from the network card hardware itself

Bad hardware can cause a failure to connect to the Internet, with about a 15% probability.

During the repair process, I often first check whether the metal contact pins inside the RJ45 port are distorted, bent or short circuited and if the plug's plastic lock is cracked or broken; if not, then the problem might be solved just by pulling and plugging the RJ45 cable. The next step is to use a known working computer to replace the suspect one and see if it works.

If the test laptop works OK, while the original laptop does not connect to the Internet, next open the "Control Panel" to enter "Device manager" list to check it.

1) If the cable network card and port are not displayed in the "Device manager" list, (if displayed in the list, then enter step 3); you need to install a known working normal cable network card. While doing so make sure to clean the dust in the slot for the cable network card on the motherboard. Make sure the golden fingers of the cable

network card and the connection inside the slots are all OK, and then pay attention to full compatibility.

2) After changing a cable network card, if it's still not displayed in the "Device manager" list, then the motherboard slot or the motherboard would be the most probable cause of the failure. The problem could also be caused by an operating system failure.

3) Reinstall the latest driver and carry out a dialing connection test. If it still doesn't work, then the likely reasons for the failure would be an operating system problem or a laptop motherboard hardware issue. Reinstall the operating system and the latest driver, and then carry out the dialing connection test.

4) If the cable network card in the original operating system was not recognized, while similarly it still is not recognized with a new operating system and there's no way the cable network card will dial to the Internet and work; then it indicates the motherboard hardware has problems. You need to use a USB network card to replace it, and reinstall a new driver;

If the problem is still unsolved, then please continue checking with more detailed solutions, in chapter 2 <<14.2.5 Laptop cable network card Internet connection failure analysis and repair flow>>.

A modem does not connect to the Internet, there are frequent offlines when on the Internet, the modem indication lights flash abnormally, the modem connects online but the webpage cannot be opened and so on, about 24% of these cable network Internet failures are from the network card hardware itself

During the repair process, I often encounter these problems. Generally, we can put a professional Windows PE system disc into the laptop DVD-ROM to start up and finally make a conclusion that the Internet dialing failure cause is because of the operating system and network setting problems, or the network card hardware itself. If there's a Windows PE system disc at hand, then you can use a USB network card to connect to the Internet and then find the failure cause.

Excluding the operating system and network settings problems, I suggest using a USB network card to replace it, or open the laptop shell, remove the cable network card, and install a new one. For a more detailed method, please refer to the chapter 3 <<Laptop Internet dialing failure analysis and repair flow>>.

14.2.4 10% of cable network failures are from an RJ45 interface failure or interface bad connection

During the repair process, I often find a cable network card Internet connection failure; usually, the problem is easily solved by pulling and plugging in the RJ45 network cable, but if network cable plug has a crack internally or the RJ45 interface has an internal problem, then it's not that easy to find and repair it. Usually it is because of pulling and plugging in the cable with too much force and damaging the RJ45 interface so it no longer works.

According to the basic method "First simple and then complex", the first to do is pull out and plug in the network cable without having to force it, and then continue according to the failure symptom.

(1) Solving RJ45 network cable interface problems;

A) Pull out RJ45 network cable, and then plug it into interface again. Carefully inspect the RJ45 cable plug and the RJ45 cable for damage If you notice that the RJ45 interface is distorted or the metal contact pins bent or broken, then you should just change it, and then replace the RJ45 cable with a new one;

B) Test whether the RJ45 network cable and the phone interfaces have problems or not: pull out the RJ45 cable from the cable network card interface and test it with a working computer. If it does not connect to the Internet, then please repeat the step (A) again to make sure it is OK. If the failure still is not solved, then please contact the DSL service provider and request a check of the DSL line to make sure it is not giving you the problem.

(2) Repair the RJ45 interface

A) If you decide to repair the RJ45 interface by yourself, then you must be careful when opening the suspect laptop, disassemble it and examine the components carefully, maybe certain pin soldering points at the interface to the motherboard are open circuit because of bad soldering and you can often see that a badly soldered connection looks different or is obviously open. You can usually touch the joint with the heated soldering iron with a little paste on it, and melt the solder which will flow into the connection or maybe add a tiny bit of solder if necessary.

B) If the RJ45 interface is distorted and the metal contact pins are damaged, then you need to remove the RJ45 interface, and install a new one.

(3) Cable network card with internal bad contacts

A) If you have confirmed the RJ45 interface and cable is good, then next check the cable network card. If it feels loose in its slot, that could be the source of the problem. Remove the cable network card, clean the oxidization layer on the golden fingers and the accumulated dust in the network card slot, and then put the cable network card back in the original position and make sure the cable network card is properly inserted in its slot;

B) Inspect the cable that connects the network card to the RJ45 interface. Pull out and plug in connectors to establish a better contact and look for any signs of degradation that should be repaired. Re-install the cable as it originally was including any ties or fasteners.

If the problem is still not solved, then please continue checking with the more detailed process, please refer to the chapter 2 <<14.2.5 Laptop cable network cad Internet connection failure analysis and repair flow>>.

14.2.5 Laptop cable LAN failure analysis and repair flow

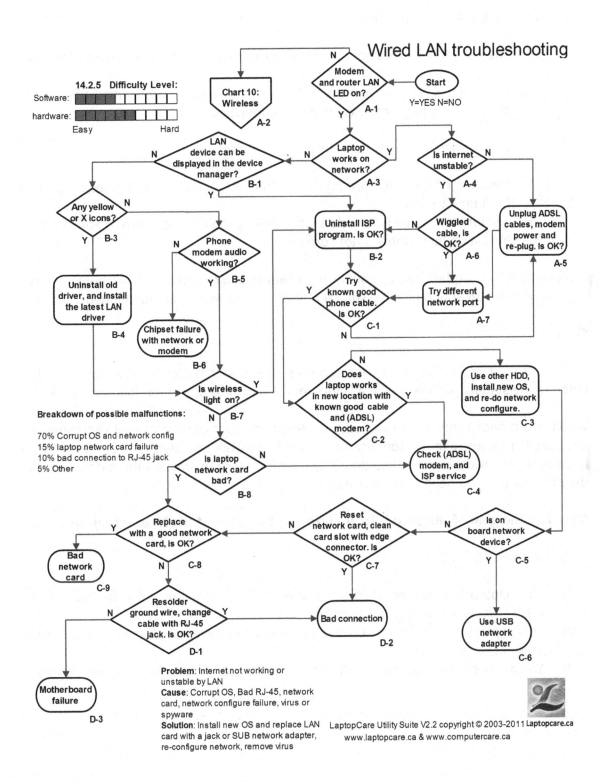

14.2.5 Difficulty Level:

Software: ▮▮▮▮□□□□□□

hardware: ▮▮▮▮▮□□□□

Easy   Hard

Wired LAN troubleshooting

Start
Y=YES N=NO

Modem and router LAN LED on? A-1

Chart 10: Wireless A-2

Laptop works on network? A-3

Is internet unstable? A-4

Unplug ADSL cables, modem power and re-plug. Is OK? A-5

Wiggled cable, is OK? A-6

Try different network port A-7

LAN device can be displayed in the device manager? B-1

Uninstall ISP program. Is OK? B-2

Any yellow or X icons? B-3

Phone modem audio working? B-5

Uninstall old driver, and install the latest LAN driver B-4

Chipset failure with network or modem B-6

Try known good phone cable. Is OK? C-1

Is wireless light on? B-7

Does laptop works in new location with known good cable and (ADSL) modem? C-2

Use other HDD, install new OS, and re-do network configure. C-3

Breakdown of possible malfunctions:

70% Corrupt OS and network config
15% laptop network card failure
10% bad connection to RJ-45 jack
5% Other

Is laptop network card bad? B-8

Check (ADSL) modem, and ISP service C-4

Replace with a good network card, is OK? C-8

Reset network card, clean card slot with edge connector. Is OK? C-7

Is on board network device? C-5

Bad network card C-9

Resolder ground wire, change cable with RJ-45 jack. Is OK? D-1

Bad connection D-2

Use USB network adapter C-6

Motherboard failure D-3

Problem: Internet not working or unstable by LAN
Cause: Corrupt OS, Bad RJ-45, network card, network configure failure, virus or spyware
Solution: Install new OS and replace LAN card with a jack or SUB network adapter, re-configure network, remove virus

LaptopCare Utility Suite V2.2 copyright © 2003-2011 **Laptopcare.ca**
www.laptopcare.ca & www.computercare.ca

This tutorial will help you solve these problems and laptop issues:

a)   The cable LAN does not work

    1)   The DSL Modem does not connect to the network or does not browse WebPages when online;

    2)   The settings are all correct, but it does not connect to the wired network or cannot see other computers within the network;

b)   Unstable connection problems with a cabled-network

    1)   Frequent offline when surfing on the Internet, or the network goes off and on from time to time;

    2)   The Internet speed is very slow when the laptop connects with an RJ45 cable;

    3)   Indication light status is not correct;

In this article, I will explain how to troubleshoot failures in a cabled LAN. It will apply to most laptops with the exception of some special brands or models that are mentioned

Start

When you plug in the power adapter and press the power button to start up, and after entering the system, you encounter a failure that is similar to one in the following tutorial:

When you cannot connect to a cabled LAN, there are a lot of reasons that can cause the problem. For instance, the laptop external network (network provider) device is defective. If it is a service provider problem, we do not go any further than advising the problem is with the provider and you need to contact them.

Step: A-1 the goal of this step is to analyze the character of the Internet failure

Problems to be dealt with:

1)   Your laptop has connected to the Internet before, but now it has Internet access problems like frequently going offline;

2)   Your laptop is accessing a new network, or it has never been used to surf on the Internet.

3)   You are not able to connect to the internet or it goes offline after connecting to it.

You first check the status lights on the modem and router to see where the problem is.

a)   Check the router

(If you don't use a router, then you can jump to the next Modem chapter)

(1)   Power indication light

This light designated PWR or Power should be always lighted. If not on, then it means the power is not on. Check the ON/OFF switch and the source of your power

(2)   Wired (Ethernet) status indication lights on the router

A router has 5 lights; LAN 1, 2, 3, 4 showing LAN connection status, and a Modem status light. The 1, 2, 3, 4 lights are port connection/working lights; the other is the Modem port light which has three status conditions; always on, flashing, and off. When connected properly to the Modem or other Internet network, this light would be always on or flashing. If all of the lights for ports 1, 2, 3, 4 are out, then you should focus on checking the twisted-pair service connection; you can try changing the cable or try another port if the other 3 are not used.

b)   Check Modem

(1)   Power indication light

This light is designated PWR or Power; the green light always on means the device is powered on and working normally. If the light is out; it means the power is not on, or the device is not working. Possibly the ADSL power converter or your wall outlet has problems. Check them out to see whether the Modem hardware is ok or not.

(2)   Ethernet (LAN Link) light

The Ethernet link indication light has three conditions: always on, flashing, and off. The light always on means that the cable is connected correctly from the Modem to the router (or computer network card). If the light is out, it means the Modem and router (or computer network card) are not connected. If the light is flashing; there's data transmission through the data connection. If the light is out for a long time, and when you move ADSL Modem or the cable, the light might flicker or turn on; it means the cable connection is not good, so focus on checking the RJ45 connection. Change the cable if all else fails.

After excluding the problems above; if the laptop still does not access the network, and under the same circumstances, another computer cannot access the wired network either; then please enter Step: A-2; the goal is to recover the router and ADSL Modem to factory settings. For a more detailed instruction, please refer to the chapter 10 <<10.2.6 Laptop wireless network card and Bluetooth, router failure analysis and repair flow>>, check the two sections Step: A-4, Step: A-5;

Under the same conditions, if another computer does connect to the wired Internet, then please enter Step: A-3; and check the right bottom corner of the laptop screen carefully, there should be a wired network card icon, please confirm the network card is not disabled.

Step: A-2

Please check another article <<10.2.6 Laptop wireless network card and Bluetooth, router failure analysis>> tutorial.

Step: A-3 the goal of this step is to confirm that your failure is not caused by the network card

The first situation:

A) A laptop is moved to a new network environment, and then does not connect. For example, after taking a working office laptop home, and it won't work on your wired network; you can try finding the reason from the following situations:

(1) Connections between the RJ45 cable or the DSL Modem are not ok, and causes a failure to access the network;

(2) The router is not powered on or not configured yet or the network card is disabled;

The user name or password is wrong;

(3) PPPoE is not completed or installed incorrectly;

After excluding the 3 items above, then check the wired network card icon at the right bottom corner of the laptop screen; if there's an icon, generally, after clicking it, you can find the network connection status. If it goes offline frequently after accessing the network, then please enter Step: A-4; if there is no network card icon, or under the same circumstance, another computer does access the Internet through the wired network, then please enter Step: B-1;

B) You haven't moved to a new network environment, and the symptom that it does not work normally occurs; you should start checking the following items to find out the causes of the failure:

(1) An RJ45 cable or router failure causes the problem that the Modem does not connect with the ISP server to access the Internet;
(2) A router error, there's no response;
(3) The operating system has a virus or Trojan infection, including the IE browser;
(4) The PPPoE is not installed correctly;
(5) A dialling software problem;
(6) An IP distribution issue;
(7) The network card driver has problems;
(8) An invalid shutdown, which creates a network protocol error.

After excluding the 8 problems above, then check the wired network card icon at the right bottom corner of the laptop screen. After clicking it, check the signal received status, If it often goes offline after accessing the network, then please enter Step: A-4; if there's no network card icon at the right bottom corner of the laptop screen, or under the same situation, another computer does access the Internet through wired network, then please enter Step: B-1;

The second situation:

1) The first time a laptop is used on a wired network it does not connect even though the network is working. To deal with this, start with A) of the first situation.
2) A laptop often goes offline after accessing a wired network; if this happens, please follow method B) above in the first situation to deal with it.

Step: A-4 the goal of this step is to find the cause for unstable Internet or frequent offline

Consider the 6 situations following:

(1) Failure to access a wired network because of software setup errors or virus infection;

If a laptop hasn't been used on a wired network yet, then it's quite possible that the installed and running TCP/IP protocol settings are wrong, including software and operating system patches, operating system service components, or other software settings affecting the system network. It is also possible that the operating system is infected by viruses.

(2) A wired network card driver has failed, and affects the all kinds of functions of the hardware;
(3) The network card hardware has defects or there's a defect with a motherboard chip;

(4) Frequent offline caused by the RJ45 cable connecting to the Modem or Router has a problem that causes serious signal attenuation. Then the circuit transmission quality is quite bad and the network is unstable.

   a) The cable outside cover is damaged and the internal core is exposed causing a short or open circuit. There's patina forming on connection plugs due to dampness, which leads to a bad contact;
   b) A network interface failure because the RJ45 cable plug is damaged, the interface is deformed or distorted, or the metal contact pins are bent or even broken and there is a bad connection.

(5) Because of an aging router, there is network instability. The router temperature is too high, and the device quality has deteriorated;
(6) Router (access points) loading is too heavy and affects the Internet speed and quality. It can cause frequent offline. The main causes of over loading on the router are online games, BT downloading, or there are too many computers connecting to the network simultaneously.

If the problem still cannot be solved, then please enter Step: A-5; if the laptop does access the Internet sometimes, but sometimes does not; then please enter Step: A-6;

Step: A-5 the goal of this step is to confirm the failure has nothing to do with the ADSL Modem

Recovery of an ADSL Modem to factory settings will most often solve your internet access problems assuming the service is not down. Incorrect settings is one of the most common causes of network failures.

   A) Find the small hole at the backside panel of ADSL Modem designated "Reset";
   B) Cut off the ADSL Modem power, find something pointed like a pen head to press the Reset button inside of the hole;
   C) Power on the ADSL Modem, wait for about 5 to 10 seconds and then release the button; the reset is done.

If lucky, the problem can be solved by this; but sometimes, it doesn't help and you should proceed to check the cables. Start by unplugging and replugging the connectors and inspecting them for damage and check the condition of the cables. Make sure they are plugged into the correct port. If you are using a router; use the same method to recover the router to factory settings, or if available replace the modem and the router one at a time to see if that identifies a defective device. If the laptop still does not access the Internet through the cabled network, then please enter Step: A-7;

Step: A-6 the goal of this step is to make sure that your failure is not caused by a cable.

If a laptop does not access a wired network, or goes offline frequently; it could be a cable problem. Between the ADSL Modem and router, and computers, there are many connection cables, and users can be careless and cause problems with them. Usually, these cables are placed in locations that conceal them as much as possible rather than protecting them from damage.

When a desk or chair is moved a cable can be stretched or crushed and creates a failure. To deal with it, all cables and connectors need to be inspected for damage and replaced where necessary. You might find damaged connectors or broken conductors where a cable has been damaged. Watch for intermittent flashes of indication lights on the equipment as you work as it will indicate where the problem exists. The cables should be routed properly to ensure they are protected and the user made aware of the importance of caring for them.

After excluding the problems above, click the network card icon at the right bottom corner of the screen to confirm you are receiving a strong signal. If the laptop still does not connect to the Internet through the wired network but under the same situation, another computer does, then please enter Step: B-2; if another computer cannot access the Internet with the wired network, then please enter Step: A-7;

Step: A-7 the goal of this step is to confirm that the failure is caused by the router

If you've already followed the method above by resetting the router back to factory settings, but the laptop still does not access the wired Internet, then the problem might be in the router:

1) Try another port on the router. Pull out one end of the Ethernet cable (connect to router), and then plug it into the another port of the router;
2) Replace the router with a good one and if it works, your router is definitely at fault. If it also does not work; please enter Step: C-1;

Step: B-1 the goal of this step is to confirm that there's an available "wired network card" in the device manage list

1. Click "Start"—"Control Panel"—"System"—"Hardware"—"Device Manager"—"Network Adapter";

   And then double click "Network Adapter", check that there's an available wired network card in the list. If not; you need to check whether the laptop has an internal wired network card or whether it is disabled or not. Here's the method:

   Reinstall the wired network card, pull it out and then plug it back in. A bad contact can be eliminated with this way. However, if there's a hardware problem with the network card, and in many cases, a chip has failed on the motherboard; then you have to use the replacement method to resolve it.

2. If you confirm there is a "wired network card" in the device manager list, then please enter Step: B-2; if the device manager list has no "Wired network card" or the "wired

network card" is marked with yellow/red interrogation mark, then please enter Step: B-3;

Step: B-2 the goal of this step is to confirm the ISP software works normally

In order to facilitate the final users, generally, network service providers will provide free ISP software to setup computers for their service. It contains complex settings that most users are not familiar with, to make it easy to access the service and the internet. However, if the ISP software is damaged because of a virus or Trojan invasion, then it may fail to access the service or the internet.

If a laptop wireless network card has worked normally before, and suddenly one day it has something wrong, but you know the network card hardware itself is OK; the following scenarios are likely the cause:

(1) It's quite possible that software recently installed has cleaned junk that is not junk, or because of a virus or Trojan invasion, which might have come from the ISP or other software, has caused damage. You need to uninstall the original software, and then try reinstalling and configuring again;

(2) After excluding the problems above, then check carefully whether the wired network card is working or not; if it still does not work, then you should consider whether the repair process includes the STEP: B-4 procedure. If not, please continue to STEP: B-4 to continue. If you already did that, then please continue to the third step;

(3) There's something wrong with the operating system, and you need to format the hard disk (initialization operation), repair all disk problems caused by the software, and reinstall Win XP or Vista/Win 7 system; If that fixes your problem, your repair is complete; if the steps above have not helped you, then please continue to STEP: C-1;

Step: B-3 the goal of this step is to confirm whether the device manager list (network card) has a yellow mark or not;

Open the "Device manager", and check for a yellow interrogation mark on Network devices. If there is, then it likely means the wired network card needs a new or updated driver. It can also indicate the network card is not connected properly due to a bad contact in the slot for the card.

If there's red interrogation mark, then it means the network card device function is disabled, you have to enable the function to use it. There are two more situations we can be faced with:

a) One is to reinstall the operating system, and if the wireless network card has a yellow interrogation mark; obviously this is because the driver is not correct or not installed, you'd just need to reinstall the proper driver;

b)   Another is that the laptop did access the Internet normally but when you start again, suddenly there's no local connection. You need to restart the laptop or if that does not work; reinstall the driver. If it still does not work, try pulling out the network card and reinstalling it again.

If there is no yellow interrogation mark in the Device Manager list, you still have a problem accessing the Internet, and already worked through the flowcharts; then please enter Step: B-4;

Step: B-4 the goal of this step is to install a new network card driver

Driver damage is a common problem; the result is that you cannot access the Internet. To deal with it, you, first uninstall the old driver, and then reinstall the latest driver. When you buy a laptop, if the manufacturer also provided a driver disc, it can be very helpful:

a)   Right click "My Computer" and choose "Properties", then click "Hardware" to enter Device manager, check if there's an interrogation mark beside the network card; double click the interrogation mark and reinstall the driver, and then choose auto install the software. Put the driver disc in and click "Next".

b)   If there's no driver installation disc available and you can still access the Internet by wireless, then enter the Device Manager and choose the Network Adapter, click the dropdown list, update the driver for the device with the yellow exclamation mark, and choose to connect to the network automatically to find the driver;

c)   If it fails to find a driver automatically, identify the make and model of the network card and go to the website of the manufacturer to download the driver and install it. Most manufacturers have drivers available for download.

d)   If you have another computer available that does access the Internet, you can use it to download a driver and transfer it to the problem computer by disc or flash drive. If the installation prompts failure, then it means the driver downloaded is not correct, or you should close the antivirus software supervision and reinstall it again.

If you've already installed a new wired network card driver, and previously the device with the yellow exclamation mark is already gone; however, it still cannot access Internet, then please enter Step: B-7;

Step: B-5 the goal of this step is to confirm whether the device manager list has an available Modem and Audio

Open the laptop and pull and plug the internal wired network card, check whether the failure disappears or not; before plugging again, you should first clean up the dust and clean the gold plated board (edge connector), including in the slot.

Then click "Start"—"Control Panel"—"System"—"Hardware"—"Device Manager"—"Network Adapter" and "Modem", and then double click Network Adapter and Modem, to check if there are an available Network Adapter and Modem in the Device Manager list; if there are, then it means the control circuit chip works all right, then please enter Step: B-7;

If in the Device Manager, there's no Network listed (including no yellow exclamation mark), nor Modem card, even there is no Audio, then it's quite likely that the control circuit chip on the motherboard has failed, please enter Step: B-6;

Step: B-6 the goal of this step is to confirm the failure is on the motherboard

According to the failure symptom, go to Control Panel—Device Manager—Network Adapter, and there's no network device displayed. Then in most cases, the failure comes from hardware, but also in a few cases it's caused by a conflict between software and hardware. There can also be a problem with the BIOS on the motherboard which causes a device conflict or a hardware device is "missing" without any reason, and so on. Generally, we would try solving the problem by updating the motherboard BIOS or installing a USB network adapter. Finally if the failure cannot be eliminated, you are faced with replacing the motherboard.

Step: B-7 the goal of this step is to confirm the wired (Ethernet) status indication light works all right

An HP laptop has no indication light for the network card, so we can only use the router Wired (Ethernet) status lights, consisting of the LAN 1, 2, 3, 4 connection status lights and the Modem light. When the wired connections to the Modem and router are correct the LAN 1, 2, 3, 4 ports should always be on; if not, then you should focus on checking the RJ45 cable connection, and you can try using another LAN interface on the router.

Users not using a router can directly observe the Modem Ethernet (LAN) status light, when you are connected to the Modem correctly, an Ethernet (LAN) status light should be always on; but if not on, then you should focus on checking the RJ45 connection and cable.

Step: B-8 the goal of this step is to confirm the failure is not in the network card

If you don't see a wired network card in the device manager, or you do see it and after uninstalling and reinstalling driver, your problem is not solved; probably there's something wrong with the hardware, you need to confirm the two points below:

a) Whether the internal wired network card is installed or not;
b) Whether the internal wired network card is damaged or not;

Open the laptop, confirm the network card is installed, and then remove it; then put the network card in the same model of laptop to test it. If it is good then next continue to STEP: C-4; if the network card does not work normally in another laptop, then please continue STEP: C-8;

Step: C-1 the goal of this step is to confirm that your failure is not caused by the cable

Not accessing a wired network, or going offline frequently after accessing the wireless network; is often caused by a bad cable connection, or a virus or Trojan invasion, which damaged the ISP software. Try pulling out both ends of the RJ45 cable and plug them back in again, exclude any virus or Trojan invasions, and confirm the ISP software works all right. If the problem is still not solved; then you should consider the possibilities below:

a)   A cable is pressed or stretched, and there's a break internally, or the cable itself has connector problems. A connector is oxidized or damaged and there is a bad contact, which causes a low quality circuit transmission, because the signal attenuation is too large;

b)   Bad contacts influence the connection between the Modem, telephone line and the tone segregator.

The solution is to temporarily replace the cables one at a time to locate the defective one and then replace it. If none of the cables are defective and your problem is not solved then continue to Step: A-5 but if you have already done that enter Step: C-2;

Step: C-2 the goal of this step is to change the network environment to test the computer

If your laptop does not access a network normally at home, but you can take it to your office and test it there; if the laptop still does not access the wired Internet, then please enter Step: C-3; if it does access the network and work normally, then please enter Step: C-4;

Step: C-3 the goal of this step is to confirm the problem is in the software

Make sure you know whether the failure comes from software in the original matched hard disk or the software on the original supplied disk; otherwise, it's impossible to make the correct judgment. After finishing installing the operating system, go to the relevant website to download the driver for the network card and then reset the wired network. If your problem is not solved; then please continue to STEP: C-5 to carry on troubleshooting.

Step: C-4 the goal of this step is to confirm the source of the failure

One of the most common network failure modes is due to problems with the ADSL Modem. If Step: A-5 has been bypassed you should now work through it in order to reset the ADSL Modem and Router back to factory settings and possibly resolve your problem.

After the operation above, if the problem is still not solved yet and you have not worked through Step: C-1, then do so now in order to check the condition of your cables and connections.

After finishing all of these steps and a problem still exist, then you need to consider changing the ADSL Modem but please note:

If within the same period of time, you find none of your computers are accessing the Internet, it may be a service provider problem and you need to contact them to resolve it or confirm they do not have a problem

Step: C-5 the goal of this step is to confirm the failure is happening on the motherboard or the network card

The laptop device manager list does not show a wired network card or shows a wired network card without the yellow mark or even displays a network card normally, and you have tried uninstalling and reinstalling the driver without success. Likely the network card hardware has problems; of course, it's also possible the motherboard controller or the BIOS may be at fault.

If the laptop wired network card is integrated on the motherboard, then please enter

Step: C-6; if wired network card can be uninstalled from the motherboard; then please enter Step: C-7;

Step: C-6 the goal of this step is to install a USB network adapter to solve a wired network access failure

If the laptop Device Manager List does not show a network card, while you know the network card is good after testing it, then basically the failure can be assumed to be on the motherboard. The best solution is to install a USB network adapter, however, if it does not auto connect and does not give you network access, do the following:

a)   Confirm the USB network adapter driver is already installed;
b)   Set the computer to access any available network with auto adaptation status;

Step: C-7 the goal of this step is to confirm the failure is due to the network card connection

See whether the failure disappears by pulling out and plugging in the wired network card but before plugging it back in, you should first clean the dust and clean the gold plated board (edge connector), including in the slot. When installing the card make sure if feels right, not too loose, or too tight and is seated properly. If the problem is still not solved, then you can choose either Step C-6 or enter Step: C-8;

Step: C-8 the goal of this step is to confirm the failure is in the network card

If you decide to use a new network card to take the place of the suspected network card, then you should pay attention to the next two points:

1)   The new network card must be the same as the interface of the original matched network card; if the original network card is the mini PCI interface, then the new one must also be a mini PCI interface;
2)   The new network card's model and manufacturer should be the same or close to the original one and specified to be compatible. It would be better to use to use the exact same type to avoid compatibility problems.

3) Uninstall the relevant drivers for the original network card. In Windows XP system, click "Start"—"Run", open "Run" dialog, and then enter "devmgmt.msc" to open "Run text in window", and then click "OK" button. Then the Device Manager Control Panel would be displayed. Click to expand the network adapter and open the list, right click the drive icon, and then click "Uninstall", and then follow the prompt to delete the driver;

4) Install with the original matched installer disc or download a new network card driver, follow the prompt in the wizard; however, many drivers haven't passed through the Microsoft operation system validation, which might have "incompatible" or "no digital validation" kind of prompts, just neglect it and keep on installing. If there's an error, then you need to restart the operating system under "safe mode", and then uninstall the driver. Next install the correct driver, and make sure the new network card is compatible with the laptop otherwise it is not going to work. If you installed a compatible network card, but your problem is still not solved, then please enter STEP: D-1; if the problem is solved, then please enter STEP: C-9;

Step: C-9 the goal of this step is to finish the confirmation of the network card failure

If the problem is solved with a new network card taking the place of the suspected one, then most people would think that the replaced network card is faulty. Actually, the situation is not that simple, sometimes you will find that the replaced network card will work normally in another laptop; these are some of the reasons to consider:

1) The network card replaced has a conflict with the software settings in the original laptop, and caused the failure;

2) The network card drive software replaced has something wrong and causes the failure;

3) The interface for the network card on the computer had a slight distortion preventing both cards from working;

Therefore, check the network card that was replaced, there may be nothing wrong with it.

Step: D-1 the goal of this step is to confirm the failure has nothing to do with the RJ45 interface

Disassemble the suspected laptop, and inspect the RJ45 interface connections. You may find a bad solder connection at the interface or on the motherboard. The solder point on the motherboard may have come loose. Resolder any defects found to solve your problem. Please take a look at Figure 14-7.

Figure 14-7

A) If the RJ45 interface is distorted, or the metal pins cracked, then you need to install a new RJ45 interface. If you confirmed the RJ45 interface is good, then next check whether the wired network card's internal cable is loose or not and repair as necessary.

B) Find the wired network card, which has the connection wire to the RJ45 interface. Usually, there's bad contact between the cable and the RJ45 interface. You need to pull and plug the connection cable, and tie up the connection cable tightly. If the problem is still not solved, then you can consider changing the cable.

If the Internet access problem is still not solved, then please enter STEP: D-3;

Step: D-2 the goal of this step is to finish the confirmation of the failure

If you solved the machine failure by pulling and plugging the internal network card, then congratulations, you've finished the repair job. You should clean the dust and clean the gold plated board (edge connector), to prevent the failure happening again;

If you solved the machine failure by replacing the network card or the network card cable, make sure you check the replaced card as it may still be good and work in another computer.

Step: D-3 the goal of this step is to confirm the failure is in the laptop motherboard

After you uninstall or reinstall the driver, or change the network card, the problem is still not solved. Probably the laptop motherboard has a defect and needs to be replaced. Considering that the cost of changing the laptop motherboard is too high, the best solution is to install a USB network adapter, ($15). For the detailed method to do so, please refer to this chapter Step: C-6 how to install a USB network adapter, to solve the problem of a wired Internet access failure.

In all, summarizing this tutorial when a laptop fails to access a wired network:

Cause: the system is infected by a virus or Trojan, the operating system has problems, or the wired network card, router, ADSL Modem, and hardware had failed or have setting errors, bad connections, motherboard defects, and so on.

Solution: reset the network, clean viruses, change the defective hardware, install a USB network adapter, and all other instructions contained in this tutorial, thank you!

14.3   18 repair cases of HP laptop cable LAN failures

14.3.1 8 repair cases of HP laptop wired LAN failures caused by network configuration and system badness

266)   HP Pavilion zd8230us laptop cable network connection failure

Failure symptom:

Laptop could not connect to the Internet, always showing error message "could not browse Network. Network is inaccessible. For more information, please check 'Help Index'—'Network troubleshooting' subject error message"

Solution:

This failure obviously belongs to the description of flowchart 14, according to the repair method; confirm the repair path, finding it accords with the sequence:

Start->A-1-> A-3->B-1->B-2->C-1->C-2-> C-3

Repair summary:

According to the flowchart tutorial, as LAN network is not working normally, first of all, check that the LAN network device is displayed normally in device manager. Try uninstalling the ISP application and then reinstall, after reinstalling, the failure is still the same, then try changing the network cable with a new cable, then test whether the network is OK or not. From the above, it shows that the problem is still the same. Then change the ADSL Modem, and still could not connect to the network. Finally, reinstall the operating system, after that, set the network configurations to a s default, then try reconnecting, now the network is back to normal again, the failure is eliminated.

Hint:

Sometimes the LAN would not work normally because of system application change or software modification, or conflicts. This is because the original network configuration is damaged, this then cause the connection failure. In generally, you just need to reinstall the operating system again, or recover your system to a specific initial point.

267) HP Compaq 2710p laptop cable network connection failure

Failure symptom:

Laptop could not connect to network, always showing error message when connecting "Connection error, please check network configuration".

Solution:

This failure obviously belongs to the description of flowchart 14, according to the repair method; confirm the repair path, finding it accords with the sequence:

Start->A-1-> A-3->B-1->B-3->B-4

Repair summary:

According to the flowchart tutorial, first open the device manager and check, the network interface card in the laptop device manager is working abnormally Then uninstall the existing LAN driver, then reinstall the latest version of the driver, then the failure is eliminated.

Hint:

Network configuration change would directly cause such network connection failures. Generally speaking, if after network configuration changes, you can try to restore the operating system to a previous state. Therefore, you need make system restore point before and then later it will be very convenient for you to use GHOST software to restore the operating system to a previous state.

268) HP Compaq 2510p laptop cable network connection failure

Failure symptom:

When laptop connects to network, the speed is extremely slow; there is a stagnancy symptom when connecting.

Solution:

This failure obviously belongs to the description of flowchart 14, according to the repair method; confirm the repair path, finding it accords with the sequence:

Start->A-1-> A-3->B-1->B-2->C-1->C-2-> C-3

Repair summary:

According to the flowchart tutorial, first of all, make sure that the network interface card is working ok or not, as the laptop could connect to the network, but network speed is extremely slow, and there's stagnancy symptom, which means the network connection signal is bad. As for this symptom, the failure might be caused because of system software conflicts or system configuration file error, which makes network interface card working abnormally Therefore, do a system recovery or format the entire hard drive and reinstall, so that the operating system and the network interface card can work without any conflicts or interferences. Later when connecting network, the speed and responding speed would be fast. The problem is solved then.

Hint:

System software conflicts usually would lead to many problems, including hardware, software failures. In general the solution is to recover the system and reinstall the operating system, as for the network failure here; resetting the system means to reset network configuration protocol, which makes it more accurate.

269)   HP Pavilion dv1650us laptop cable network connection failure

Failure symptom:

Laptop goes offline frequently when surfing on the Internet, besides, the speed is extremely slow.

Solution:

This failure obviously belongs to the description of flowchart 14, according to the repair method; confirm the repair path, finding it accords with the sequence:

Start->A-1-> A-3->B-1->B-2->C-1->C-2-> C-3

Repair summary:

According to the flowchart tutorial, this failure symptom is the network connection abnormality by system software conflicts. According to the tutorial, we suggest doing a system recovery and resetting the network configuration; after recovering the system, then try reconnecting to the network again, then there's no offline situation occurring when on the Internet.

Hint:

Use system recovery method to let system and all configuration information recover back to a normal status, which is kind of a useful method. Of course, this also includes recovering the network configuration, and then we could the network connection would be back to at normal status.

270) HP Pavilion dv1440us laptop cable network connection failure

Failure symptom:

When laptop connects to the Internet, it always fails, Modem light doesn't flash at all.

Solution:

This failure obviously belongs to the description of flowchart 14, according to the repair method; confirm the repair path, finding it accords with the sequence:

Start->A-1-> A-3->B-1->B-2

Repair summary:

According to the flowchart tutorial, as LAN could not work normally, first of all, check that the LAN device is displayed normally in device manager. Try uninstalling the ISP application, and reinstall again, then the failure disappears.

Hint:

ISP application would sometimes cause a failure whereby the ADSL Modem indication light is out.

271) HP Pavilion zd8230us laptop network connection failure

Failure symptom:

When the laptop is trying to connect to the Internet, there is always an error message "Already disconnect with your computer, double click "Connect" to retry". But could not connect network normally.

Solution:

This failure obviously belongs to the description of flowchart 14, according to the repair method; confirm the repair path, finding it accords with the sequence:

Start->A-1-> A-3->B-1->B-2->C-1->C-2-> C-3

Repair summary:

According to the flowchart tutorial, first of all, for this failure symptom, reconfigure the network interface card software, after reinstallation, start the connection, the connection still has no response. It would not exit normally. System has no responses. I assume that the system has been infected by virus. Then I format the HDD and reinstall the operating system. According to the sequence to install network interface card and other software, restart the machine and connect the network. The failure is eliminated.

Hint:

When system has been infected by virus, virus would change system parameters, it would even affect the network interface card, by changing the configuration information, boot time sequence and so on, which causes network connection to malfunction.

272) HP Pavilion dv1150us laptop network connection failure

Failure symptom:

When laptop connects to network, it shows the error message "Network could not deal with the specific compatible network protocol set in 'Server type'".

Solution:

This failure obviously belongs to the description of flowchart 14, according to the repair method; confirm the repair path, finding it accords with the sequence:

Start->A-1-> A-3->B-1->B-2->C-1->C-2-> C-3

Repair summary:

According to the failure symptom, system shows error message "Compatible" problem, and according to the flowchart tutorial, the failure might be caused because system software conflicts or virus infection, which causes configuration setup invalidation and so on. To solve such failures, reinstall the network adapter application, recover the configuration settings, but the failure still exists after recovery, next reinstall the operating system, recovering system completely, then connect to the network, the failure is eliminated.

Hint:

When it comes to network software incompatibility or conflicts, the most effective way of recovering the system initial settings is to format the entire disk and reinstall the operating system.

273) HP Pavilion dv1150us laptop network connection failure

Failure symptom:

Laptop has problem when connecting to the network. Although computer displays bandwidth connection is normal, it could not open any webpage, could not realize network access. All LED lights on Modem show normally.

Solution:

This failure obviously belongs to the description of flowchart 14, according to the repair method; confirm the repair path, finding it accords with the sequence:

Start->A-1-> A-3->B-1->B-2->C-1->C-2-> C-3

Repair summary:

According to the flowchart tutorial, for such kind of failure symptom, network has "die away" status, probably there's some driver that hasn't been installed correctly. Uninstall the network interface card application, delete all history records before, later then reinstall the application, restart and then connect to the network, the failure is eliminated, the connection is now normal, webpage could be opened.

Hint:

When network connection has abnormal status, reinstall network hardware, reset network configuration information, this is an effective way of solving the problem.

14.3.2 Three repair cases of HP laptop cable LAN failures caused by network interface card problem

274) HP Compaq 515 laptop could not connect network

Failure symptom:

Laptop could not connect to the Internet, network cable has no any response, and the connection icon on the taskbar has no change.

Solution:

This failure obviously belongs to the description of flowchart 14, according to the repair method; confirm the repair path, finding it accords with the sequence:

Start->A-1->A-3->B-1->B-3->B-5->B-7->B-8->C-8

Repair summary:

According to the flowchart tutorial, check whether there's network interface card listed in the device manager, finding WiFi and sound card device work normally. But, ADSL Modem light is out, then removes the network interface card, finding the circuit board of the network interface card is old, which needs to be replaced immediately. Then the failure disappears.

Hint:

Sometimes, except the network interface card hardware failure itself, it would also have hardware conflicts. Then you need to check what hardware it in conflicts with. And then change the related interrupt signal and I/O address to avoid conflicts. Some network interface cards need to be set up in CMOS, then would work normally again.

275) HP Elitebook 6930p laptop frequent offline failure

Failure symptom:

The laptop always goes offline frequently, which is quite unstable, network connection is abnormal.

Solution:

This failure obviously belongs to the description of flowchart 14, according to the repair method; confirm the repair path, finding it accords with the sequence:

Start->A-1-> A-3->B-1->B-3->B-5->B-7-> B-8->C-8

Repair summary:

According to the failure symptoms of always going offline frequently, unstable connection etc, according to the flowchart tutorial, check whether there is software conflicts in the system, reinstall the network interface card software, update the driver, restart and try connecting again, the failure still exists. Then we can exclude the software as the cause. Remove the laptop network interface card, check the network interface card status, you will noticed that the (Edge Connector) gold plated board of the network interface card are dark. Then change the a network interface card with a known good one, then the network connection is OK, and then it means the failure is caused because network interface card is often removed and installed, which causes bad connection, finally leading to the unstable network connection failure.

Hint:

Network interface card is loose connected; generally, wiping the (Edge Connector) gold plated board of the network interface card may help enhance the connection. As for the problem that network interface card has bad connection failure, then you can replace it, if the network interface card is loose soldered, then resolder it.

(276)   HP Elitebook 2530p laptop network connection failure

Failure symptom:

Laptop could not connect to the Internet, webpage would not open, we reinstall the network interface card, the failure is still the same.

Solution:

This failure obviously belongs to the description of flowchart 14, according to the repair method; confirm the repair path, finding it accords with the sequence:

Start->A-1-> A-3->B-1->B-3->B-5->B-7-> B-8->C-8

Repair summary:

According to the failure symptom, system could not open a webpage normally; even reinstalling network interface card driver would not solve the problem. Check the network interface card status in device manager, we find there's a yellow exclamation mark on the device, uninstall the network interface card device again, install the driver again, restart and try connecting again, the failure is still same. Continue checking up, open the laptop, check the network interface card hardware connection failure, uninstall the network interface card, observe the network interface card, it seems that it's not plugged into the slot completely. After cleaning the (Edge Connector) gold plated board, plug it correctly again, start up and try connecting, the failure is cleared, this indicates that the Internet connection failure is caused because of bad connection on the network interface card.

Hint:

The network interface card may get loose connected when you carry with the laptop or the surroundings are vibrating.

14.3.3 Two repair cases of HP laptop cable LAN failures caused by network interface badness

277) HP Compaq 6530b laptop network connection failure

Failure symptom:

When laptop connects to the network, it would go offline frequently, system always shows that the connection is already cut, please check the network status.

Solution:

This failure obviously belongs to the description of flowchart 14, according to the repair method; confirm the repair path, finding it accords with the sequence:

Start->A-1-> A-3->B-1->B-3->B-5->B-7-> B-8->C-8->D-1-> D-2

Repair summary:

According to the flowchart tutorial, check and we find that the network interface card is not displayed normally in device manager, then reinstall the driver for the network interface card, restart and then test again, the failure still exists. Then test the original network cable, finding that the cable plug has no problem, and then change other network cable to test, the failure is still the same, then continue testing, check up the network interface status. Touch the interface with fingers, finding it's loose, and then remove the motherboard, finding that the network interface is loose, which is the root cause of the network going offline. After adding the solder, the failure is eliminated, the network connection returns to normal again.

Hint:

Network interface often become gets loose, bad solder symptom is quite common. This has certain relationship with laptop mobile portability; you should pay attention to the maintenance of the network interface daily. When removing and installing network cable, you must make sure the cable is connected stably, don't plug from other angle by force; if there's external force to the interface, then it's quite easy to get the network interface broken.

278) HP Compaq 6730b laptop network connection failure

Failure symptom:

Laptop could not connect network, network cable connection is normal, but system always shows: Please plug network cable.

Solution:

This failure obviously belongs to the description of flowchart 14, according to the repair method; confirm the repair path, finding it accords with the sequence:

Start->A-1-> A-3->B-1->B-3->B-5->B-7-> B-8->C-8->D-1-> D-2

Repair summary:

According to the failure symptom, system prompts to plug network cable, which indicates system cannot recognize the network cable you plugged into the jack, then there are two possibilities: one is that the network cable you plug is not good, laptop could not recognize; the second one is that laptop network interface is bad, therefore, the motherboard cannot communicate with the network interface, system could not recognize network signal either. Replace network cable, the failure still exists. Check up the network interface status; observe the situation, finding the interface has bad solder. Then add solder and plug network cable again, the connection is normal again.

Hint:

When system shows : please plug network cable, it means that system hasn't inspected network signal, when come to such kind of symptom, you should pay attention whether network cable and interface have some problems or not, then the root of the problem could be found directly and effectively.

14.3.4 Three repair cases of HP laptop wired LAN failures caused by ISP service provider or network cable problem

279) HP Pavilion dv1130us laptop network connection failure

Failure symptom:

Laptop could not connect network, always showing: Error! Could not configure network connection.

Solution:

This failure obviously belongs to the description of flowchart 14, according to the repair method; confirm the repair path, finding it accords with the sequence:

Start->A-1-> A-3->B-1->B-2->C-1->C-2-> C-4

Repair summary:

According to the flowchart tutorial, first of all, check whether there's yellow exclamation mark on the network interface card status in the device manager; if there is, then reinstall it again, make sure it could display normally in device manager, after confirming its status is normal again, the failure still exists, then check the network connection, replace network cable to test; after changing it and try reconnecting, everything is all right, the failure is eliminated, so the problem is caused because of the bad network cable.

Hint:

When it comes to such kind of failure symptom, after isolating all system and software aspects problem, the next important link is to consider the external network cable connection condition.

280) HP Pavilion dv4-2141nr laptop could not connect network

Failure symptom:

Laptop network connection has no response, showing that could not connect normally, please check up the network configuration.

Solution:

This failure obviously belongs to the description of flowchart 14, according to the repair method; confirm the repair path, finding it accords with the sequence:

Start->A-1-> A-3->B-1->B-2->C-1->C-2-> C-4

Repair summary:

According to the flowchart tutorial, first of all, check and find that there's no yellow exclamation mark on the network interface card in device manager. Then change the network cable and test the original place. After changing it, the failure is still the same. Then take the laptop to another place to test, the failure is eliminated. Then call your ISP that the original place's network state is not normal.

Hint:

You can also take another laptop that could connect Internet normally to the original place to test.

281)   HP Compaq 6730b laptop network connection failure

Failure symptom:

Laptop could not connect to the network, network cable connects normally, but system always shows: Please insert network cable.

Solution:

This failure obviously belongs to the description of flowchart 14, according to the repair method; confirm the repair path, finding it accords with the sequence:

Start->A-1-> A-3->B-1->B-2->C-1->A-5

Repair summary:

According to the failure symptom, check the network cable, finding the network cable plug's plastic lock is cracked, the plug could not connect to the RJ45 port successfully. Then disassemble the cracked plastic lock, change the plug and then insert the port again, the failure disappears.

Hint:

When system shows "Please plug network cable", it means that system hasn't inspected network signal yet, when it comes to such a symptom, you should pay attention to the network cable, or port, whether there's something bad, then the problem root could be found directly and effectively.

14.3.5 Two repair cases of HP laptop cable LAN failures caused by motherboard

280) HP Pavilion dv4-2141nr laptop could not connect network

Failure symptom:

Laptop network connection has no response, showing that it could not connect normally, please check the network configuration.

Solution:

This failure obviously belongs to the description of flowchart 14, according to the repair method; confirm the repair path, finding it accords with the sequence:

Start->A-1-> A-3->B-1->B-3->B-5->B-7-> B-8->C-8->D-1-> D-3

Repair summary:

According to the flowchart tutorial, first of all, check whether the network device is displayed normally in device manager, finding there's no any yellow exclamation mark there, check whether system wireless signal works normally, the connection indication light shows abnormal, then replace the network interface card device, but the failure still exists. Then change the network cable slot, then try connecting again, still the problem could not be solved. Then you need to disassemble the motherboard, repair and change the motherboard.

Hint:

You can add one USB network interface card device to take the place of the cable network interface card for Internet connection.

281) HP Compaq 6730b laptop network connection failure

Failure symptom:

Laptop network connection has no response; sound card and WiFi does not work.

Solution:

This failure obviously belongs to the description of flowchart 14, according to the repair method; confirm the repair path, finding it accords with the sequence:

Start->A-1-> A-3->B-1->B-3->B-5->B-6

Repair summary:

According to the flowchart tutorial, first open device manager, check and you will find there's no network interface card, sound card and WiFi device in the list, then check the motherboard, it is likely that the South Bridge I/O management chip has something wrong, we need to change the South Bridge chip or the entire motherboard.

Hint:

You can add one USB network interface card device to take the place of the cable network interface card for Internet connection.

CHAPTER 15

Dial up Internet failure repair

15.1 Laptop dial-up Internet access failure repair

15.1.1 Laptop (Internal dial-up Modem) Internet common failure symptoms

1. Internal phone Modem dialing failure;
2. Internal phone Modem could dial-up, but could not connect;
3. Internal phone Modem often gets offline when surfing on the Internet;
4. Internal phone Modem has no dialing tone when dialing, or there's only "squeaking." noise;
5. Internal phone Modem indication light flashes abnormally, continually making "beeping." sounds;
6. Internal phone Modem's data flow is cutoff and end up with a system crash;
7. Internal phone Modem Internet speed is slow;
8. All settings are correct, but could not open webpage after getting on the Internet;
9. OS could not recognize internal Modem correctly;
10. When there is incoming calls, the laptop gets offline
11. Laptop could not start up normally after connecting to the Modem.

15.1.2 Laptop Internet dialling failure and cause analysis

(1) Internal Modem dialling failure

The following reasons may cause this failure:

(1) Telephone wire problem would cause Phone Modem dialling failure;
(2) Dialling software failure;
(3) I/O address is used repeatedly, conflicting with another COM port;
(4) Operation system has virus or Trojan infection;
(5) Internal Modem is disabled or the driver is not installed correctly;
(6) Internal Modem hardware is damaged, for example, in a thunder storm, it could get damage by strike;

(7) Circuit connection gets electromagnetic interference from extension telephone, electrograph and other devices;

(8) RJ11 port connection is not good

(2) Internal Modem could dial, but could not connect

The following reasons may cause this failure:

(1) Remote computer has no response, then the Internal Modem could not connect with ISP;

(2) After installing the dialling software, the requested relevant protocol hasn't been bounded correctly;

(3) Operating system has virus or Trojan infection, which leads to network protocol error;

(4) User name or password error;

(5) Circuit connection gets electromagnetic interference from extension telephone, electrograph and other devices;

(6) Internal Modem I/O address has a conflict with another COM port;

(3) Internal Modem often disconnected when surfing on Internet

The following reasons may cause this failure:

(1) Operation system has virus or Trojan infection, which leads to network protocol error;

(2) The insulation cover is broken or the internal core is exposed or partially cracked;

(3) One or more plugs have a loose connection.

(4) As outside circuit is affected with damp, then connection plug and others are rusted (patina), which leads to signal attenuation;

(5) Indoor extension telephone and other devices have no voice separation filter, the circuit gets electromagnetic interference;

(6) Internal Modem hardware is defective, would not work properly;

(7) Internal Modem slot accumulates too much dust, gold plated board (edge connector) is oxidized;

(8) Internal Modem, internal connection with RJ11 port is loose.

(9) Internal Modem overheats, would not work properly;

(10) The Data terminal ready (DTR) signal is invalid and the continual time exceeds the Modem default value, and then it would go offline.

(4) Internal Modem has no dialling tone when dialling, or there's only "squeaking" noise

The following reasons may cause this failure:

(1) Internal Modem dialling sound is disabled or the sound property is set as mute or the volume is turned down low;

(2)   Internal Modem hardware is damaged;

(3)   Telephone line is not connected properly, for example, Internal Modem RJ11 port is not connected, but connecting to the phone port;

(4)   RJ11 port's pin is bent or broken, then there is a failure with port;

(5)   Telephone line's plug plastic lock is cracked or the plug is damaged, internal core contact pin connection is loose;

(5)   Internal Modem indication light flashes abnormally, continually making "beeping." sounds;

The following reasons may cause this failure:

(1)   Remote computer error, or the server is too busy, which leads to the failure of the Internal Modem could not connect with the ISP server, there is always a busy tone;

(2)   Dialling software failure or wrong input ISP number, which leads to the problem of the that Internal Modem not connecting with ISP server;

(3)   Internal Modem hardware failure, which makes the laptop self-checking to fail;

(4)   The communication signal on current circuit is not stable, sometimes there's short circuit problem;

(5)   The extended phone or fax machine connected with the phone line is in use, which leads to the problem that Internal Modem could not connect ISP server, there's busy tone;

(6) The security device connected with the phone line is in use.

(6)   Internal Modem often goes off line and system crash;

The following reasons may cause this failure:

(1)   Outdoor telephone line is iron, there are too many circuit splices, on which oxidization is quite severe, or the phone circuit quality is low, which causes the performance of signal transmission becomes bad, signal attenuation consumption is too big;

(2)   Operation system failure, there are virus and Trojan infections;

(3)   The online antivirus software is running while the user is surfing the Internet, or several antivirus software have been installed.

(4)   The firewall used is set incorrectly or too many installed several firewalls;

(5)   Internal Modem has defects, running error or the driver is not installed correctly;

(6)   Internal Modem heat radiation is not good, there's overheating problem;

(7)   There is bad connection between telephone line and tone separator interface, there's electromagnetic interference;

(8)   TCP/IP protocol is not bounded or installed incorrectly;

(7) Internal Modem Internet speed is slow;

The following reasons may cause this failure:

(1) Phone line circuit quality is bad, which makes circuit transmission quality bad, signal attenuation consumption is too big;
(2) Operation system failure, there are virus and Trojan infects;
(3) Too many software running on computer at the same time, or the memory is too low, which causes slow running speed;
(4) When the user is surfing the Internet, the online antivirus software is running.
(5) User installs several firewalls;
(6) Internal Modem has been running for a long time without shutdown, there's overheating symptom, which lowers the performance;
(7) Network card hardware has defect, or the driver is not installed properly
(8) Proxy server settings is improper or the capacity of the ISP is limited
(9) The network card binds to too many protocols, and is different from the protocols used by the ISP;
(10) After connected to the Internet, there are too many WebPages opened, then system is overloaded

(8) All settings are correct, but could not open webpage after connected to Internet;

The following reasons may cause this failure:

(1) Certain connection between Modem and computer is abnormal;
(2) TCP/IP protocol installation or IP address setting is incorrect;
(3) Operation system has virus and Trojan infections, which leads to problem with IE browser;
(4) Firewall setting is incorrect or user installs too many firewalls;

(9) OS could not recognize internal Modem correctly;

The following reasons may cause this failure:

(1) Internal Modem driver is not installed correctly;
(2) I/O address is distributed, conflicting with another COM port, which leads to the problem that COM port could not be recognize correctly;
(3) Internal Modem hardware is damaged or burnt out;
(4) Internal Modem slot accumulates too much dust, which makes gold plated board (edge connector) or slot inside pins to be oxidized;
(5) Bent RJ11 port pins cause short circuit;
(6) Internal Modem internal insulation cover is broken or the internal core is exposed, which leads to a short circuit;
(7) Motherboard's South Bridge chip is damaged, which makes the problem that Internal Modem could not be recognized correctly.

(10) Coming calling rings and then disconnected;

The following reasons may cause this failure:

(1)   Splitter error
(2)   Tone separator failure;
(3)   Phone message or tone software setting error;

(11) Laptop could not start up normally after connecting Modem.

The following reasons may cause this failure:

(1)   Bent RJ11 port pins cause a short circuit;
(2)   Internal Modem internal connection wire's insulation cover is broken or the internal core is exposed, which leads to a short circuit;
(3)   The pins inside slot are bent, when plug Internal Modem, the pins inside slot have a short circuit.

15.1.3 Laptop internal Modem Internet dialing failure solution

1.   Internal Modem dialing failure

Check the outside circuit, whether there's failure:

a)   Pull out the phone cable, and plug it into the jack again, make sure the phone cable is to RJ-11 jack, but not RJ-45 jack. Please take a look at Figure 15-1.

RJ-11 jack (Modem jack)   RJ-45 jack (Network card jack)

Figure 15-1

b)   Check whether phone line and phone jack have problems: remove the telephone line out from internal Modem jack, and then directly plug it into the phone to test;
c)   Disconnect other devices temporarily, like phone set, phone responder beacon (RSP), fax machine and extension box.

Make sure there are no other software conflicts

d)   Open "Control panel", enter "Device manager" list, check whether Internal Modem and COM port are displayed in the list and recognized correctly. If Internal Modem and COM port are not in the list or could not be recognized correctly, then you need to change the internal Modem to test;

(e) Reinstall operation system and the latest drivers, and then dial the connection and test;

(f) Change the USB Phone Modem and reinstall the latest driver.

2. Internal phone Modem could dial, but could not connect

1) Make sure the user name and password are correct;
2) Make sure the ISP number is entered correctly;
3) Disconnect other devices temporarily, like telephone, phone responder beacon (RSP), fax machine and extension box.
4) Make sure there's no other software accessing COM port (such as fax software, communication software, device resources using the COM port, which might cause laptop Internet dialing failure or Internet freezing failure);
5) Disable the COM port not used, release extra I/O addresses, and then restart the computer to let I/O address redistributed;
6) Reinstall operation system and Internal Modem driver;
7) Call Internet provider for help.

3. Internal phone Modem often gets offline when surfing on the Internet;

1) Remove and plug all phone connections once again, replace all suspected telephone lines or distorted RJ11 jacks;
2) Clear viruses or Trojan infected operation system, reset network protocol;
3) Reinstall operation system and the latest driver for the internal Modem;
4) Add tone separation filter for indoor extension telephone and other devices, in case circuit gets electromagnetic interference;
5) Reset Internal Modem, clean the dust in the slot of the internal Modem, make sure the connection between gold plated board (edge connector) of the internal Modem and the slots are good and fasten;
6) make sure it doesn't overheat when the internal Modem is working;
7) Change with another normal working internal Modem and test;
8) Change to another ISP with larger capacity and test

4. There's no dialing sound when internal modem dials, or there's only "squeaking" noise;

1) Make sure the dialing tone function of the internal Modem is enabled, the volume property is set properly;
2) Make sure the telephone line is connected to RJ11 jack correctly, but not to the phone port;
3) Check whether RJ11 port is distorted, whether the metal pins inside the jack are bent or cracked;
4) Change to another telephone line with good plug, make sure the pin plastic lockup is not cracked or broken;
5) Change to another normal working Internal Modem.

5. the indication lights of Internal Modem flash abnormally, continually making "beeping" sounds;

1) Disconnect other devices temporarily, like phone set, phone responder beacon (RSP), fax machine and extension box;
2) Turn off the security devices connected to the telephone line
3) Add tone separation filter for indoor extension telephone and other devices, in case circuit gets electromagnetic interference
4) Try dialing known numbers, if still could not connect, then uninstall and reinstall the dialing software;
5) Change to another working Internal Modem;
6) Call Internet provider for help.

6. Internal Modem data flow is cut off and system crash;

1) Clear the virus and Trojan in operation system reset the network protocol;
2) Reset tone separation filter. If the telephone cable plug's lockup is cracked or the RJ11 jack is distorted, then change in time;
3) Close online antivirus software. Remove extra antivirus software, make sure there's only one antivirus software in system;
4) Uninstall and reinstall the driver for Internal Modem;
5) Make sure the firewall setting is correct, disable extra firewalls;
6) Replace the issued internal Modem in laptop with a normal working internal Modem, if the failure disappears, then it means the original Internal Modem has failed itself;
7) Reinstall the operation system;
8) Call telephone provider for help, check the outdoor phone line plug and the line quality.

7. Internal Modem's Internet speed is slow

1) Add system memories, check the memory of the display card, make sure all these accord with Internet basic requirements;
2) Make sure the proxy server is set correctly;
3) Make sure disk has 10% spare space;
4) Clear virus or Trojan infection in operation system, reinstall operation system again;
5) When surfing on Internet, notice not to open too many WebPages or run too many software;
6) Disable online antivirus software. Remove extra antivirus software, make sure there's only one antivirus software in system;
7) Uninstall and then reinstall the driver for the internal Modem;
8) Make sure the firewall setting is correct, close extra firewalls;
9) Replace the issued laptop Internal Modem with a working Internal Modem, if the failure disappears, then it means the original Internal Modem has problem itself;

10) Call telephone provider for help, check the outdoor phone line plug and the line quality;
11) Change to another Internet server company with better and stronger processing ability;

8. Settings are all correct, but webpage could not be opened after connecting to the Internet;

1) Reset Internal Modem, make sure the connection of the gold plated board (edge connector) of the Internal Modem and slots is in good condition and reliable;
2) Reset TCP/IP protocol, make sure the IP address distribution is correct;
3) Uninstall and reinstall browser;
4) Remove all the virus and Trojan from the operating system and reinstall the operation system;
5) Make sure the firewall setting is correct, disable extra firewalls;

9. OS could not recognize Internal Modem correctly

1) Uninstall and reinstall the driver for the Internal Modem;
2) Disable the COM ports not used, release extra I/O addresses, and then restart the computer, I/O address would be redistributed;
3) Reset Internal Modem, clean the dust inside motherboard slot, check and confirm the connection between Internal Modem's gold plated board (edge connector) and slots is good;
4) Check whether the metal pins inside RJ11 port are bent or cracked and if there's short circuit, change the RJ11 jack;
5) Change to another working Internal Modem;
6) Change another working USB Modem.

10. Coming calling rings, then Internet goes offline;

1) Install user tone separation filter correctly;
2) Disconnect other devices temporarily, like phone set, phone responder beacon (RSP), fax machine and extension box.
3) Set phone message software correctly, if your phone has "calling wait" phone control function, then please disable it temporarily;

11. Laptop could not start up normally after connecting with Internal Modem

1) Check whether the metal pins inside RJ11 port are bent or cracked and if there's short circuit, change the RJ11 jack;
2) Change to a working Internal Modem and internal connection cable;
3) Clean the dust inside the slot of the Internal Modem, make sure the pins inside the slot of the Internal Modem has no short circuit;
4) Change to a working normal USB Modem.

As for laptop internal Modem Internal dialing failure, there are more and more detailed solutions, please refer to "15.2.5 Laptop Internal Modem Internet Dialing Failure Analysis and Repair Flowchart"

15.1.4 Laptop Internet dialling freezing failure analysis

There are two main aspects of the reasons:

1) Internal Modem hardware problem

a) There is extension telephone, fax machine and other devices without tone separation filter on the circuit connection, the circuit gets electromagnetic interference, especially the insulation cover is broken or the internal core is exposed or partially cracked. Because of humidity, circuit connection plug rusts (patina), which causes signal attenuation;

b) Insert the phone line plug into the interface by force, which might make the lockup to cracked or plug bent or cracked, finally causing the pins of RJ11 port, while the bent pins would get bent, which might causes a slight short circuit. At last, laptop could not dial up or you get Internet freezing;

c) The connection cable between internal Mode and motherboard is not fixed tightly, after long-term vibration, the connection between internal Modem and slot would get loose, or there's too much dust accumulated, then it would not work correctly stably;

d) And rare situation is that laptop overheating also causes the internal cable aging and circuit oxidization, finally leading to bad contact with RJ11 port. The operation system might get frozen, but what's worse, it would get the internal Modem or motherboard burnt.

2) Driver and other software problems

a) Operation system failure, there are virus and Trojan infections, which damages IE browser; If you enabled online auto antivirus software or installed several antivirus software, then probably it would also cause Internet freezing failure, even if you don't connect the Internet, freezing failure would also happen too;

b) Incorrect firewall settings, or installed several firewalls, then freezing failure would also occur;

c) If the internal Modem driver is aged, damaged or TCP/IP protocol is not bind or IP address setting is not correct, then freezing failure would occur too;

d) After connecting to Internet, too many WebPages are opened, operation system loading is too heavy, or ISP server processing ability is limited, then freezing failure happens;

e) If your phone has "calling wait" phone control function, then every time when there's a call coming in, the Modem would disconnect because of interference.

15.2   Repair flow chart to eliminate dial-up Internet failure

15.2.1 Repair shortcuts for Internal Modem Internet dialling failures

Solve such kind of failures with common simple replacement method

During the repair process, it's a kind of complicated thing to solve the problem that laptop internal Modem would not dial to the Internet, because of the occurrence of the failure; probably it is caused by certain hardware, or some other software, or even probably the combination of software or software and hardware together.

But the cause of the failure usually is focused on aging driver, issued software, virus and some other aspects (60%), Internal Modem hardware problem (24%), and RJ11 Interface or cable failure (14%) etc. In all, the failure rate would occupy 98%, here I provide some shortcut solutions for you, when it comes to suck kind of problems, first compare to this solution and then to solve the problem;

First confirm whether the RJ11 interface and cable work normally:

(1)   Pull out the telephone cable and then plug it into the interface again. Make sure the telephone cable is plugged to RJ-11 interface, but not RJ-45. RJ-11 interface (Modem) and RJ-45 interface (network card);

(2)   Test whether telephone cable and phone interface has problems: pull out the phone cable from the Internal Modem interface, and then directly plug to phone to test. If it could call normally, work stably, then solve the Internet problem; come to step 5, if the phone calling still has problem, then please continue step 3;

(3)   Pull out the phone cable to check carefully, check whether the phone cable plug is broken or not, whether the phone cable is over twisted or the core is cracked. After replacing it with a section of new phone cable, if the problem is still unsolved, then please continue step 4;

(4)   Disconnect other devices temporarily, such as telephone set, phone responder (RSP), extension box, make sure plug plastic lockup is not cracked or broken, if the dialing test fails, then it means the issue should be on the telephone lines, you should contact phone service provider to request checking the outdoor phone circuit;

(5)   Remove the suspected laptop, find one known good working desktop (or laptop) computer and connect to the Internal by dialling through the Internal Modem; if the problem is not resolved, then please continue to step 5, if the problem is solved, then you can confirm the failure is not related to the phone cable and Internet network;

(6)   Open the suspected laptop and find the internal Modem, there are 2 or 3 cable contacts upper there, usually there will be bad contact symptom between the cable and RJ-11 interface. Remove the cable and then make sure it is plugged into the interface tightly, then it should be resolve. If necessary, change the RJ-11 interface and connection cable, if the problem is still not solved, then please continue step 7;

(7)   Remove the internal Modem, clean the oxidization layer on the gold plated board (edge connector) and the accumulated dust inside Modem slots, and then reset the internal Modem back to the original position. We can solve the problem that system

could not recognize the Internal Modem by removing and reinstalling, or solve the failure of bad contact between the Modem and motherboard slots. If the problem is not resolved, then please continue step 8;

(8) Update the driver for the internal Modem, reset firewall, clear viruses and Trojans, if the problem is still not resolved, then please continue the step 9;

(9) Change to a known working internal Modem, uninstall the old driver and install the new driver. Make sure the replaced internal Modem is compatible with the laptop. If the problem is not resolved, then please continue step 10;

(10) Scan the Windows system entirely and completely, remove viruses and Trojans, remove the original software, and then reinstall protocols and configurations; after removing viruses and Trojans, if still could not recover the original settings, at this moment, you need to reinstall the operation system to repair. If the problem is not resolved, then please continue step 11;

(11) After confirming the internal Modem works normally, if the Internal Modem still would not be recognized in the original operation system, and could not be recognized in the new operation system, either, then it means the motherboard hardware has problems. If after connecting the internal Modem, laptop it still could not start up, while after removing it, laptop could start up normally, then usually it should be the problem of the motherboard hardware issue or the physical damage in slot. You need to replace with another USB phone Modem, and then reinstall the new driver;

(12) If everything tested is all right, then just the internal Modem could not create connection with ISP server, or there's busy tone from the speaker, then usually it should be the remote computer error, or the server is too busy. You should contact the Internet provider for help. As for more and more detailed repair methods, please refer to "15.2.5 Laptop Internal Modem Internet dialling Failure Analysis and Repair Flowchart".

15.2.2 60% of Internal Modem Internet dialling failures are from operating system and network settings

Internal Modem could not dial, or could dial but fail to connect to Internet, frequently getting offline error, or data stop frequently and system crash, Internet speed slowness, webpage could not be opened, and operating system could not recognize Internal Modem correctly and so on. About 60% of this kind of failures is from operating system and network settings.

Generally speaking, technicians would always first doubt whether the failure is caused by software, but usually after confirming that network settings, drivers and hardware are ok, then could finally determine whether the problem is the operating system;

According to the method in "15.2.5 Laptop Internal Modem Internet dialling Failure Analysis and Repair Flowchart". First exclude the external causes of the failure caused by loose telephone line plug, old telephone cable or electromagnetic interference, and then use one known working phone set to test calling, the purpose is to confirm whether the phone cable is loose. Next solve the Internet problem.

If the phone calling is ok, while the laptop could not get to Internet with Internal Modem dialling, then after confirming, disconnect other peripheral phones, fax machines and so on, open "Control Panel" go into "Device manager" list to check.

(1) Check whether the driver has failures

a) If Internal Modem and port are not displayed in the list or could not be recognized correctly, then probably the causes as listed below (occupying 74%):

      i. Virus and Trojan infection breaks down the operating system or the internal Modem driver;

      ii. Repeated distribution of I/O address might also cause the failure of the port not be recognized correctly. You can disable the COM ports not being used, release extra I/O addresses, and then restart the computer. Afterwards, I/O address would be reassigned;

      iii. Internal Modem hardware and laptop motherboard problems (occupying 24%).

b) If you install a driver which is only compatible with Window 7 into a Window XP system, then not only the Internal Modem would not work, but even there's blue screen failure or software conflicts. Check the list in the device manager, there should be no yellow exclamation mark anymore; otherwise, the driver is still not installed correctly. Then you need to uninstall and reinstall again. However, if the yellow exclamation mark could not be remove, then the port setting and I/O address repeated distribution would be the most possible reason causing the failure. It's could also likely be the operating system problem.

c) If the Internal Modem could be displayed in the list and recognized correctly, but still could not connect to the Internet after dialling, then after excluding hardware problem, you should format the HDD, reinstall operating system; to find more detailed solutions, please refer to "15.2.5 Laptop Internal Modem Internet dialling Failure Analysis and Repair Flowchart".

(2) Solve the failure that webpage could not open;

Operating system is damaged because of virus or Trojan infection, which would cause Internet failure; therefore:

a) Scan Windows system entirely with antivirus software, clean viruses or Trojans; if the dialling software is already damaged, then you need to uninstall the original software, and then reinstall and configure;

b) Confirm the firewall setting is correct, disable extra firewalls;

c) Virus or Trojan infection would also change Windows system settings, if reinstall and set up TCP/IP protocol, the Internet problem is still not solved, even if you've already cleaned the virus or Trojan, sometimes it still could not recover the original settings, at this moment, you need to reinstall the operating system to repair;

(3) Solve the Internet slow speed failure

(1) Examine the hhardwares

    a) Check the laptop system memory and display card memory, make sure it accords with the basic Internet requirements;

    b) Make sure the proxy server settings are correct and capable of reaching a faster speed;

    c) Check the occupied space of the disk, make sure there's 10% disk space free; otherwise, you need to change to a bigger disk;

    d) Adjust the Internal Modem to full speed, if not ok, then replace the suspected Internal Modem with a normal working one; if the failure disappears, then it means the original Internal Modem has failure itself.

(2) Examine the software

    e) Remove unrelated random start-up applications;

    f) Remove unrelated protocols;

    g) When surfing on the Internet, pay attention not to open too many WebPages or several software at the same time;

    h) Disable online antivirus software, uninstall extra antivirus software, make sure there's only one antivirus software running;

    i) Uninstall and reinstall Internal Modem driver;

    j) Cancel firewall;

    k) Clean virus or Trojan infection in operating system, reinstall operating system;

    l) Call telephone service provider for help, check the outdoor telephone cable and circuit quality.

15.2.3 24% of Internal Modem Internet dialling failures are from the Modem hardware

24% Internet failures are caused by hardware failures.

During the repair process, I often first check whether the metal contact pins inside RJ11 port are cracked, bent or have short circuit. Whether the plastic lockup on the plug is cracked or broken; if not, then generally, we can remove and plug the phone cable to solve the problem, and then test the phone cable by making a call with the phone set.

If calling is ok, while the laptop could not connect to the Internet with Internal Modem dialling, then you should first disconnect the outside devices, such as telephone set, fax machine, then open "Control Panel" to enter "Device manager" to check the list.

1) If internal Modem and port are not displayed in "Device manager" list, (if not display, then enter step 3), then you need to change to a known working internal Modem, please pay attention to cleaning up the dust inside the Internal Modem slots, make

sure the internal Modem's gold plated board (edge connector) are well connected with the slots, and pay attention to the compatibility;

2) After changing to a new Internal Modem, if it is still not displayed in "Device manager" list, then the port setting and I/O address repeatedly assigned might be the cause of the failure. Also it's likely the operating system;

3) Reinstall the latest driver, disable the COM ports not used, release extra I/O address, next restart the computer. Then I/O addresses would be reassigned. And then dial connection to test;

4) If the Internal Modem still doesn't work, then the most possible cause of the failure might be the operating system or the laptop motherboard hardware problem. Reinstall the operating system and the latest driver, and then dial the connection to test;

5) If the Internal Modem could not be recognized either by the original operating system or by the new operating system, then it means the motherboard or hardwares have problems. You need to replace with an USB phone Modem and reinstall new driver.

If the problem remains, please refer to "15.2.5 Laptop Internal Modem Internet dialling Failure Analysis and Repair Flowchart." to get more detailed instructions.

15.2.4 14% of Internal Modem Internet dialling failures are from RJ11 interface problem or interface cable failure

During the repair process, I often come upon the failures that Internal Modem could not dial to Internet; generally, we can solve it by removing and reinstalling the phone cable again, but if the cable plug has an internal crack or the RJ11interface has problem internally, then it would be difficult to find out and repair. Usually, user might remove and plug the phone cable too hard or plug the phone to RJ45 interface by mistake, which would damage the phone cable. Finally causing Internet dialling failure. And after Internal Modem connection cable is loose, it could not work normally either.

According to the process method "First simple and then complex", first consider and then remove and plug the phone cable, and then follow the instructions as below according to the failure symptom.

(1) Check whether the phone cable interface has problems

A) Pull out the phone cable and plug it into the interface again. Make sure the phone cable is connected to the RJ-11 interface but not RJ-45 interface. Pull out the phone cable and then observe carefully, checking whether the plug of the phone cable is broken, whether the cable is over twisted or the core is broken? Whether RJ11 interface is distorted or not, whether contact pins are bent or cracked. If there's such situation happening, then you must change, and then replace with a known working phone cable step by step to check the user circuit;

B) Check whether the phone cable and interface have problems: pull out the phone cable out of the Internal Modem interface, directly plugging into phone set and test the line. If the calling could not work, then please repeat the first step, or contact phone service provider to check the phone line, until calling is normal again.

(2) Repair RJ11 interface

A) If you decide to repair RJ11 interface by yourself, then you'd have to be careful to open the suspected laptop, disassemble it to test; usually, there's bad solder between certain pin spot solder of the RJ11 interface and the motherboard. Sometimes you can tell the pin stick is already off the solder point obviously. For such kind of failures, generally, you can add spot solder to the pin again, then the problem could be solved easily;

B) If RJ11 interface is distorted or the metal contact pin cracks, then you need to get rid of solder and remove the issued RJ11 interface, and then reinstall a new RJ11 interface;

(3) Internal Modem and internal bad contact failures

A) If confirmed the RJ11 interface is good, then next is to exclude the cause of loose Internal Modem, which may cause frequent offline to the laptop or Internet connection failure. Remove the internal Modem, clean the oxidization layer on the gold plated board (edge connector) and the accumulated dust in the Modem slots, and then assemble the Internal Modem back to the original position. Make sure the Internal Modem is well connected with the slots;

B) Remove the Internal Modem; (there are two or three pins). Usually, there will be bad connection between the cable and RJ-11 interface. You need to remove and then plug the pins again and make sure the cable can be plugged in tightly.

If the problem remains, please refer to "15.2.5 Laptop Internal Modem Internet dialling Failure Analysis and Repair Flowchart" to get more detailed instructions.

15.2.5 Laptop Internal Modem dial-up Internet failure analysis and repair flow chart

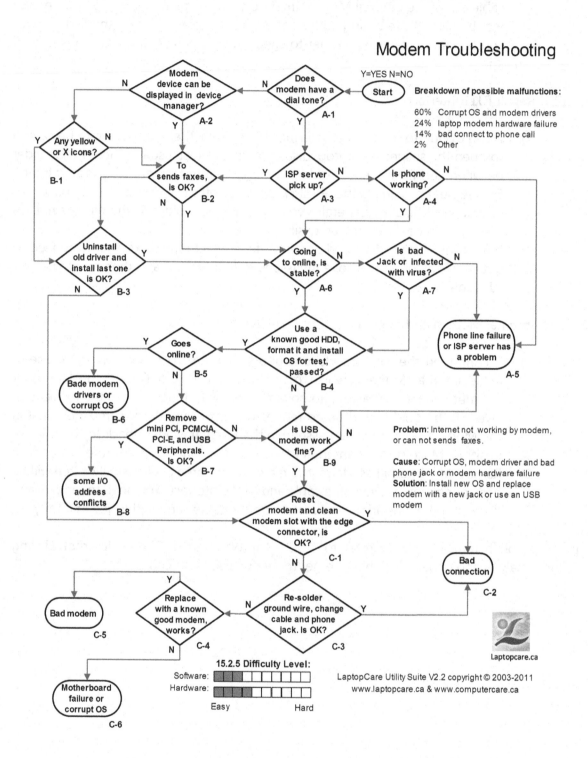

Modem Troubleshooting

Y=YES N=NO

Start

Breakdown of possible malfunctions:

60% Corrupt OS and modem drivers
24% laptop modem hardware failure
14% bad connect to phone call
2% Other

Does modem have a dial tone? A-1

Modem device can be displayed in device manager? A-2

Any yellow or X icons? B-1

ISP server pick up? A-3

Is phone working? A-4

To sends faxes, is OK? B-2

Uninstall old driver and install last one is OK? B-3

Going to online, is stable? A-6

Is bad Jack or infected with virus? A-7

Phone line failure or ISP server has a problem A-5

Use a known good HDD, format it and install OS for test, passed? B-4

Goes online? B-5

Bade modem drivers or corrupt OS B-6

Remove mini PCI, PCMCIA, PCI-E, and USB Peripherals. Is OK? B-7

Is USB modem work fine? B-9

some I/O address conflicts B-8

Problem: Internet not working by modem, or can not sends faxes.

Cause: Corrupt OS, modem driver and bad phone jack or modem hardware failure
Solution: Install new OS and replace modem with a new jack or use an USB modem

Reset modem and clean modem slot with the edge connector, is OK? C-1

Bad connection C-2

Replace with a known good modem, works? C-4

Re-solder ground wire, change cable and phone jack. Is OK? C-3

Bad modem C-5

Motherboard failure or corrupt OS C-6

15.2.5 Difficulty Level:

Software:
Hardware:

Easy   Hard

Laptopcare.ca

LaptopCare Utility Suite V2.2 copyright © 2003-2011
www.laptopcare.ca & www.computercare.ca

This tutorial will help you solve these problems: laptop

1. Internal Modem could not dial;
2. Internal Modem could dial, but could not connect;
3. Internal Modem frequently gets offline when connects to Internet;
4. Internal Modem has no dialing tone when dial, or there's only "Cici . . ." noise;
5. Internal Modem indication light flashes abnormally, continually making "Dudu . . ." sound;
6. Internal Modem often gets data stop and crash down;
7. Internal Modem Internet speed is slow;
8. Settings are all correct, but webpage could not open after connecting to Internet;
9. Operation system could not recognize Internal Internet Modem correctly
10. Coming calling rings, then phone gets offline;
11. Laptop could not start up normally after connecting Internal Modem.

In this article, I will explain how to find the failure cause—Laptop Internal Modem Internal Dialing failure, and the prompt is special for certain special brand or model, it should be applied for most part of laptops.

Start

Step: A-1

Check whether Internal Modem could dial successfully, if dialing tone could be heard, then please enter Step: A-2; if not, then please enter Step: A-3.

Step: A-2

Open "Control Panel" and check whether "Device manager" could recognize Internal Modem device correctly. If the Internal Modem has yellow interrogation mark on the item, or there's no Internal Modem in the list at all, then it means the Internal Modem could not be recognized correctly. If it belongs to this case, then please enter Step: B-1; if the Internal Modem could be displayed normally in the list, then please enter Step: B-2;

Step: A-3

Start acoustic device, start dialing and checking whether ISP server is responding or not.

If Internal Modem could not dial, then uninstall and reinstall system accompanied dialing software.

If Internal Modem has no dialing tone when dials, or there's only "Cici . . ." noise, then check up whether the plug of the phone cable is good or not, whether phone cable is connected to RJ11 port correctly, whether RJ11 interface has failure existed.

If acoustic device makes similar high-frequency sound like when fax machine is working, then it means ISP server has response, please enter Step: A-6; if dialing tone is busy tone, then please enter Step: A-4.

Step: A-4

First check whether the internal metal contact pins of the RJ11 port are distorted, heaved or of short circuit problem. whether plug's plastic lock is cracked or broken; if not, then please pull and plug the phone cable to continue testing; if you doubt the phone cable has problem, then please change a normal telephone cable, then use the phone to test ISP server, and confirm the ISP number is input correctly; if phone test is not ok, then please enter Step: A-5; if phone test succeeds, then please enter Step: A-6;

Step: A-5

Test whether the Internal Modem could connect to Internet normally; if not, then you should check as below:

(1) After setting dialing software, then relevant protocol requested is not bound correctly;
(2) Operation system has virus or Trojan infection, which causes network protocol error;
(3) User name or password error;
(4) There is electromagnetic interference on the line from extension phone, fax machine and other devices;
(5) Internal Modem's I/O address is conflicted with another COM port;

Step: A-6

If the problem could not be solved or is solved, but it still gets offline frequently, then please enter Step: A-7; if could connect to Internet stably, but webpage could not open, then please enter Step: B-4;

Step: A-7

Probably there are these factors causing the failure:

(1) Operation system has virus or Trojan infection, which causes network protocol error;
(2) The scarfskin of the cable is broken or the inside core is exposed or partial cracked;
(3) There's at least one of the connection plugs of the phone cable is of bad contact;
(4) Connection plug rusts (patina) because humidity to the cable, which causes signal attenuation;
(5) Indoor extension phone and other devices haven't added tone separation filter, the line gets electromagnetic interference;

(6)   Internal Modem hardware defects, it could not work stably;

(7)   Internal Modem slots have too much accumulated dust, gold plated board (edge connector) are oxidized;

(8)   Internal Modem's internal line has bad contact with RJ11 port;

(9)   Internal Modem overheats, stopping it working stably;

(10) Data terminal ready (DTR) signal's invalid durative time exceeds the default value of the Modem, then offline problem would happen;

(11) Software confliction;

If the problem still could not be solved, then return to Step: A-5; if the problem is solved, but still could not open webpage, then please enter Step: B-4;

Step: B-1

Open "Device Manage", whether there's any yellow exclamation mark existed? If in device manager, there is no Internal Modem list (including the one without yellow exclamation mark) or unknown device letters, then please enter Step: B-2; if in device manager, there's Internal Modem list (including the one with yellow exclamation mark), then it means needing to install driver, or if there's X mark, it means "Disabled", then you need to click to enable, next please enter Step: B-3;

Step: B-2

Call the electrograph with the Internal Modem, check whether there's high-frequency sound made like when electrograph is working? Or send faxing to test whether telecom network is ok or not; if ok, then please enter Step: A-6; if not ok, then please enter Step: B-3;

Step: B-3

Uninstall old internal Modem driver, after installing the latest driver, if "Device manager" could recognize the Internal Modem correctly, then please enter Step: A-6; if system still could not recognize the device correctly, then please enter Step: B-4;

Step: B-4

If you don't mind the data on the original disk is deleted, then you can also format the original disk, reinstall operation system and the latest driver, and then test dialling connection. If there's important data on the original disk couldn't be deleted, then you can remove the hard disk of the original laptop, change another working normal disk, and install new operation system and the latest driver, and then test dial connection again.

If "Device manager" could recognize the Internal Modem correctly, then please enter Step: B-5; if system still could not recognize Internal Modem correctly, then please enter Step: B-9;

Step: B-5

Test whether the Internal Modem could connect to Internet; if could not, then you should check as below:

(1) After setting up the dial software, the relevant protocol requested is not bound correctly;
(2) User name or password error;
(3) Internal Modem I/O address is conflicted with another COM port;

If the problem is solved, then please enter Step: B-6; if the problem could not be solved, then please enter Step: B-7;

Step: B-6

Make sure the failure cause is because the driver or operation system has failures.

Step: B-7

Remove PCI, PCMCIA card reader, PCI-E and USB peripherals. Make sure there is no other software could access COM port (such as faxing software, sync software, communication software, peripherals need to remove COM port).

If the failure is eliminated, then please enter Step: B-8; if the failure still exists, then please enter Step: B-9.

Step: B-8

Make sure the failure cause is because of I/O address confliction.

Open system "Start" menu, enter "cmd" to the "Run" dialog and click OK button. In DOS system, enter the command "netstat—ano", test and find there's COM port address confliction. Disable the COM ports user not use, release extra I/O address, and then restart the computer, let I/O address redistributed. And then click "Start"—"Control Panel"—"Phone and Modem options", choose "Properties/Connection page/Advanced options" from Modem, click "Advanced port settings", and in COM port number setup, choose one COM port number different from before, and then continue laptop Internet testing.

Step: B-9

USB Modem just needs to connect USB port, then it could start working, no need extra power supply. In Windows XP/Vista/Windows 7, it could auto install, no special driver needed!

If USB Modem could get to Internet and work successfully, then next please enter STEP: C-1; if USB Modem could not work, then please change another USB interface to try, under the circumstance that confirmed the USB interface has no problem, please continue to STEP: A-5;

Step: C-1

Remove the Internal Modem, clean the accumulated dust on the edge connector and the metal pins inside motherboard slots, and reset the Internal Modem. If the failure is eliminated, then please enter Step: C-2; if the failure still exists, then please enter Step: C-3.

Step: C-2

Confirm the cause of the failure is because hardware connection is loose.

Step: C-3

Weld grounding wire, change phone cable and phone interface.

If the failure is eliminated, then please enter Step: C-2; if the failure still exists, then please enter Step: C-4;

Step: C-4

Replace the suspected user Modem with a known working Internal Modem to test; if the failure is eliminated, then please enter Step: C-6; if the failure still exists, then please enter Step: C-5;

Step: C-5

Make sure the failure cause is because of motherboard problem, or the problem of operation system, you need to clean disk or reinstall operation system.

Step: C-6

Make sure the cause of the failure is because of the hardware problem of the Internal Modem itself.

15.3   18 repair cases for HP laptop dial-up Internet failure

15.3.1 8 repair cases for dial-up Internet failure caused by HP laptop Modem driver failure or OS failure

284)   HP PAVILION DV4-1166CA laptop Internet dialling failure

Failure symptom:

The Modem laptop could not dial-up to Internet; MODEM could not dial-up normally, always prompting "No dialling tone, please check whether MODEM is connected to telephone line correctly".

Solution:

This failure obviously belongs to the description of flowchart 15, according to the repair method; confirm the repair path, finding it's consistent with the sequence:

Start->A-1->A-2->B-1->B-2->B-3

Repair summary:

According to the flowchart tutorial, first of all you need to confirm that the phone plug plastic lockup is OK and connected to the RJ11 port correctly. And then open control panel, finding that device manager list has Internal Modem item with a yellow exclamation mark. We should uninstall the driver right away, and then install the latest version of driver. After restarting, device manager was able to recognize the Internal Modem correctly; at this point the Internet dialling test was successful.

Hint:

Generally, when we have the situation that laptop Internet dialling failure occurs, the first you should do is to check the driver of the Modem, whether it is normal; if the driver has failed, then you'd have to reinstall or update to solve the problem.

285)   HP G60 laptop dial-up Internet failure

Failure symptom:

Laptop could not dial-up to the Internet, no dialling tone.

Solution:

This failure obviously belongs to the description of flowchart 15, according to the repair method; confirm the repair path, finding it's consistent with the sequence:

Start->A-1->A-2->B-1->B-2->B-3->A-6->B-4

Repair summary:

According to flowchart tutorial, first go to device manager and check whether the device in this case the Modem is in normal state, you will find there is a yellow exclamation mark on the Modem, which means the Internal Modem device has a problem. Uninstall the driver, and install the latest version of the driver. After restarting, device manager still would not recognize the Internal Modem correctly. Format the original hard disk; then reinstall the operating system and the latest driver. And then test, finding the failure is resolved; this means the original operating system failure causes the Internet dialling failure.

Hint:

If there's important data on the original hard disk, which could not be deleted, then you can remove the hard disk from the original laptop, change with another working hard disk, and then install new operating system and the latest driver. And then dialling to test. If after reinstalling operating system, the failure still exists, then it means the Internal Modem or the motherboard hardware has problem.

286)   HP G50-108NR laptop Internet dialling failure

Failure symptom:

Laptop could not dial-up to Internet, showing the message no dialling tone, it would auto disconnect when trying to connect, showing that the dialling program has no response.

Solution:

This failure obviously belongs to the description of flowchart 15, according to the repair method; confirm the repair path, finding it's consistent with the sequence:

Start->A-1->A-2->B-2->B-3->A-6->A-7

Repair summary:

According to the flowchart tutorial, first of all, make sure the telephone cable's plug's plastic lockup is OK and connected to RJ11 port correctly. And then open control panel, we find that the laptop has more than two Modem drivers installed, in this case the system could not recognize which Modem is the one being used currently. As a result, dialling failure symptom occurs. The solution is to delete the extra driver, specify the current driver. However, as we could not confirm which driver is the right one, so just delete any one of them, and then test again. The result shows that we still could not dial-up; now delete the second Modem driver, and then install the correct driver accompanied with the machine. After that, the failure disappears.

Hint:

1. If you install a modem driver which is not compatible with the model of your Modem or is general version, the modem would fail to dial-up.
2. The dialing program and the driver for the Modem might be damaged during the operating system are running. This is probably because of other software conflicts, also possible because some related software or drivers were deleted by mistake when you dialed with other programs. Then although there's no yellow exclamation mark; the driver is really damaged already. The solution is to reinstall the driver.

287) HP DV6910us laptop could not open webpage when dialling Internet

Failure symptom:

After laptop dials, it shows normal connection state, but when you open a Web Page, it always shows "This page could not be displayed".

Solution:

This failure obviously belongs to the description of flowchart 15s, according to the repair method; confirm the repair path, finding it's consistent with the sequence:

Start->A-1->A-2->B-2->A-6->B-4->B-5->B-6

Repair summary:

According to the failure symptom analysis, there are a lot of reasons causing such a problem. First of all, check whether TCP/IP protocol is installed and whether the settings are correct or not. Open "Control Panel"—"Network", double click the property of TCP/IP, and check the IP address, we find no problem. Then we reset the network, set IP address as dynamic IP address distribution, as for other settings, set them as default value. The problem is not solved, then we delete the working dialling connection, and create a new dialling connection and try again. But the test result is still the same; the webpage still could not open. As we know from this chapter flowchart tutorial, definitely the operating system has a problem, reinstall stable "Firefox" browser, the problem is readily resolved.

Hint:

As for this case, the symptom of the failure is that the modem cannot connect with the Internet. Such a failure is usually caused by the operating system's problems and also has other kinds of symptoms. You just need to reinstall the operating system, recovering to the initial status, be careful of uninstalling or deleting the files or programs provided by the operating system, then you can solve such network connection failures.

288)   HP Presario F500 laptop Internet dialling breakdown failure

Failure symptom:

Laptop Internal Modem Internet dialling often goes offline or crash.

Solution:

This failure obviously belongs to the description of flowchart 15, according to the repair method, confirm the repair path, finding it's consistent with the sequence:

Start->A-1->A-3->A-4->A-6->A-7

Repair summary:

According to the flowchart tutorial, first of all, test whether ISP server has response or not by dialling. As a result, after dialling, the server reply with working signal sound, and then it means the ISP server is all right; reconnect the telephone cable to RJ11 port. Next open the operating system click the "Start" menu, and enter "cmd" on the "Run" dialog and click OK. In DOS system, enter "netstat—ano" command, finding that COM port has conflicts. First disable the COM ports that the client doesn't use, release the extra I/O addresses, and then restart the computer, letting I/O address redistributed. Next uninstall the MODEM driver, reinstall the latest driver, and then click "Start—Control Panel—Phone and Modem options", choose "Properties/connection page/Advanced options" from Modem, click Advanced port settings, in COM port number settings, choose one COM port number different from the previous one, then continue the laptop Internet test. As a result, the failure disappears.

Hint:

1)   Make sure there's no other software accessing the COM port (such as: fax software, sync software, communication, or any device resources using the COM port), which might cause laptop dialling failure or Internet freezing.

2)   Sometimes, there's an error message appearing on the screen "The Modem is being used by another Dial-up Networking connection or another program□Disconnect the other connection or close the program, and then try again". Probably I/O addresses are distributed repeatedly, which causes conflict with another COM port. But the

conflicts between the operating system and some software are also likely to cause such failures. If the method above could not solve the problem, then you could only format the original hard disk, reinstall operating system and the latest driver.

289)   HP DV6823US laptop Internet dialling failure

Failure symptom:

After the laptop starts up, Internet dialling always fails no matter what, man can hear the dialing sound but after waiting for a long period of time, screen prompts "Computer has no response".

Solution:

This failure obviously belongs to the description of flowchart 15, according to the repair method, confirm the repair path, finding it's consistent with the sequence:

Start->A-1->A-3->A-4->A-5

Repair summary:

According the flowchart tutorial, test whether the interface between telephone line and phone has a problem or not: remove the telephone line out off the Internal Modem interface, and then directly plug it into the telephone jack and dial the telephone to test the quality of the Internet service. As a result, after dialling, the server sends similar busy tone signal sounds, temporarily disconnect with other devices, such as telephone, phone responder, fax machine and extension box. The dialing test proves the Internet service is fine, then seems the network server has problem, then call ISP network Server Company for help, until the problem is solved.

Hint:

1)   If the dialing test fails, then you should change another phone interface and a new phone cable, until the calling could work normally; otherwise, you'd have to call the telephone company for help to check the telephone lines;
2)   If you remove and plug the phone plug by force, then it would make the lockup cracked or RJ11 interface distorted. Then the internal port metal contact pins would distort and bent. If there's such a situation happening, you need to change RJ11 interface and a new phone cable;

290)   HP DV2832se laptop Internal Modem often gets offline after dialling

Failure symptom:

Laptop internal Modem could dial-up, but could not connect the network stably, it goes s offline frequently.

Solution:

This failure obviously belongs to the description of flowchart 15, according to the repair method, confirm the repair path, finding it's consistent with the sequence:

Start->A-1->A-3->B-2->A-6->A-7->A-5

Repair summary:

Telephone line quality is not good, there's frequent disconnection problem, which would affect the browsing speed seriously. If there are many interfering sources near the telephone line, (for example, extension phones, composite phones, encrypted phones, would affect Modem performance.) Even it would affect the computer port stability; usually, we lower down the serial port speed rate to solve the problem.

However, when check up telephone line, finding the plug lockup was cracked, replaced a new telephone line, and directly connected the line to the Modem. After confirming there's no problem, then dial-up to Internet again. Afterwards, the failure is eliminated.

Hint:

Set up answering machine correctly, if your phone has "Call waiting" telephone control function, then please temporarily disable; otherwise, once incoming calling rings, offline failure would happen right away.

291)   PRESARIO CQ50-100CA laptop Internet speed is very slow after Internal Modem dial-up to Internet, even screen freezes

Failure symptom:

Laptop Internal Modem could dial to Internet, but the speed is very slow, some webpage get timeout and could not open.

Solution:

This failure obviously belongs to the description of flowchart 15, according to the repair method, confirm the repair path, finding it's consistent with the sequence:

Start->A-1->A-3->B-2->A-6->B-4

Repair summary:

As the laptop Internal Modem could dial-up to Internet connection normally, then directly enter Step B-2. Use a fax machine to check, and find the network signal is OK. Then I assume the failure might be caused by software conflicts. First of all, remove too much start-up software with system starting, and then add some memory, laptop speed would increase much obviously. However, when check whether operating system has virus and Trojan infection or not, it is found that the client installs two different antivirus software at the same time. Then this is the main cause of the problem. Because two different antivirus software would cause conflicts, even make operating system frozen. Uninstall one of the antivirus software, and then test dialling to Internet, the speed is normal again.

Hint:

a)   Internet dialling speed is very slow, here are some reasons below: operating system have virus and Trojan infections, IE browser is damaged partially;
b)   Firewall settings are incorrect, or user installs several firewalls;

After connecting to Internet, too many webpages are opened, which causes too much loading to system.

15.3.2 Three repair cases for HP laptop Modem badness failure causes Internet dialing failure

292)   HP Presario F7000 laptop could not dial to Internet

Failure symptom:

Laptop could not dial to Internet; connection status is always no response. Click dialing program to run, the system freezes. After closing the application, then system restore to normal.

Solution:

This failure obviously belongs to the description of flowchart 15, according to the repair method; confirm the repair path, finding it's consistent with the sequence:

Start->A-1-> A-2->B-2->B-3-> C-1->C-3->C-4->C-6

Repair summary:

According to flowchart tutorial, open the device manager list, finding there's no Modem installed. Considering probably I/O address is distributed repeatedly, which causes conflicts with another COM port, then adjust COM port number, and then reinstall the driver, reconfigure network and each parameter again, then probably the failure is caused because other software conflicts in system. After changing a Modem with confirmed normal function, install and dial to Internet, the result shows the connection is OK, then the failure is eliminated, which means the cause of dialing failure is because the Modem itself has some problems.

Hint:

After changing the Modem, if device manager has the list, then probably the cause is because some other software conflicts in system. If no need to preserve the data, you can format the disk, reinstall operating system, then the problem could be solved.

293)   HP Pavilion DV6833US laptop could not dial to Internet

Failure symptom:

Laptop has no dial tone, could not dial to Internet, no any error message.

Solution:

This failure obviously belongs to the description of flowchart 15, according to the repair method, confirm the repair path, finding it's consistent with the sequence:

Start->A-1-> A-2->B-2->B-3->C-1

Repair summary:

Laptop could not dial to Internet, according to this chapter flowchart tutorial, open the device manager list, finding there's Modem listed, and driver shows normal. Then test with fax software to dial, still no dialing tone, open the laptop, redial the internal Modem, and before assembling back to the original position, first clean the dust and (Edge Connector) gold plated board, including slots. Afterwards, make sure the Modem has already been plugged to the right position and not get loose; restart the laptop, dial to Internet and everything shows OK.

Hint:

Under some circumstances, it could recover connection if reinstall Modem. However, if the problem still exists after reinstalling again, then you need to delete the current driver, and then reinstall the driver again. If the problem still could not be solved like this way, then you need to make a decision whether it is because of the Modem hardware problem.

294) HP Presario C500 laptop could not dial to Internet

Failure symptom:

Laptop could not dial to Internet, no dialing tone. Error message when connecting "could not connect to network . . . ."

Solution:

This failure obviously belongs to the description of flowchart 15, according to the repair method, confirm the repair path, finding it's consistent with the sequence:

Start->A-1-> A-2->B-2->B-3->A-6->A-7

Repair summary:

According to this chapter flowchart tutorial, open the device manager, finding the Modem is in the list. Open the laptop and pull out the Internal Modem, as a result, system still shows that it could not connect to network. According to the process principle that first simple and then complex, first consider removing and then plugging the phone cable, however, as a result, the failure doesn't disappear; pull out the Internal Modem, test on another same model of HP laptop, the result is OK, which means the Internal Modem has no problem. It seems the problem is with the RJ11 interface and the data cable connecting it. After replacing them and testing again, the failure disappears.

Hint:

Test whether the telephone line has problem or not; you can pull out the telephone line off from the Internal Modem interface, and directly plug the phone line to the telephone to test the dialing. If the dialing test fails, then it means the phone line has a problems, you need to pull and plug the phone cable again; however, if the cable has crack inside or the outdoor cable has problem, then, you need ask the telephone service provider to check the phone line.

15.3.3 Four repair cases for dial-up Internet failure caused by HP laptop phone port bad contact problem or COM port conflicts

295) HP PAVILION DV6-3114CA laptop Internet dialing failure

Failure symptom:

Laptop Modem could not dial-up to Internet.

Solution:

This failure obviously belongs to the description of flowchart 15, according to the repair method; confirm the repair path, finding it's consistent with the sequence:

Start->A-1->A-3->A-4->A-6->A-7

Repair summary:

According to flowchart tutorial, first of all, make sure the plastic lockup at the phone cable joint is OK and connected correctly to RJ11 port. And then open control panel, finding that the device list could recognize the Internal Modem. Then test the line with a phone, ISP has response, also fax machine signal is working ok. Open "Start" menu, enter "cmd" on the "Run" dialog, and click OK. In DOS system, enter the command "netstat—ano", test and find that COM port has conflicts. After removing all peripherals, COM port still has conflicts. Then disable the COM ports that the client doesn't use, release extra I/O address and restart the computer, then I/O address would be redistributed. After restarting, it could dial-up to Internet normally.

Hint:

If wizard tests that there is COM port conflicts, then Modem and physical COM port might configure and use same COM port. Then you need to set the Modem to another COM port not being used, or disable physical COM port. Pay attention that you'd have to restart Windows, try Modem, whether it already recovers normal. And click "Start"—"Control Panel"—"Phone and Modem options", choose "Properties/Connection page/Advanced options" from Modem, click Advanced port settings, and in COM port number settings, choose one COM port number different from before, and continue laptop Internet test.

296)   Compaq Presario F761US laptop Internet dialing failure

Failure symptom:

Laptop could not dial-up to Internet; speaker continually making beeping noise; it stays at the status failing to connect.

Solution:

This failure obviously belongs to the description of flowchart 15, according to the repair method, confirm the repair path, finding it's consistent with the sequence:

Start->A-1->A-3->B-2->A-6->A-7-> A-5

Repair summary:

According to flowchart tutorial, when it comes to such kind of dialing failure, first of all, remove and then plug the telephone cable to test dialing, next test the line with the phone, ISP has a response, fax machine signal is OK. Remove the extension phone, answering machines, fax machine, extension box and some other devices, and then restart to continue validation, the failure still exists. Then I find out there's one line connecting telephone alarm system device; besides, there's no splitter, in case circuit might get electromagnetic interference; after reinstallation, the failure is eliminated.

Hint:

1) If the failure still exists, then you should change to another phone interface and a new phone cable, until it could work normally again;
2) If there is still a problem, then you should call telephone service provider for help, check out the outdoor telephone line plug and the quality of the line.

297) Compaq Presario CQ45-125TX laptop Internet dialing failure

Failure symptom:

Laptop could not dial-up to Internet; no dialing tone when dials, but there's slight "squeaks;

Solution:

This failure obviously belongs to the description of flowchart 15, according to the repair method, confirm the repair path, finding it's consistent with the sequence:

Start->A-1-> A-2->A-3->B-2->A-6->B-4-> B-9-> C-1-> C-2

Repair summary:

According to flowchart tutorial, first test whether ISP server line is normal, after confirming OK, then check the phone connection interface. When I try to plug the phone cable into the RJ11 jack, I find the plastic plug of the cable is broken and the RJ11 jack is loose connected with the motherboard. Remove the motherboard, finding the metal contact pins inside RJ11 interface are already bent, and unsoldered to the motherboard. After resoldering the RJ11 jack to the motherboard and replacing a plastic plug of the phone line, I plug the phone line into the jack and make sure the connection is fine. Finally the dialing test passes.

Hint:

Sometimes laptop could not dial-up to Internet; this is because of phone interface failure. Usually, when dial-up to Internet; you should pay attention to the position plugging to interface correctly. Make sure telephone line is connected to RJ11 interface but not RJ-45 interface.

298)   HP PAVILION DV6105TX laptop Internet dialing failure

Failure symptom:

Laptop could not dial-up to Internet; no dialing tone, no any message prompts.

Solution:

This failure obviously belongs to the description of flowchart 15, according to the repair method; confirm the repair path, finding it's consistent with the sequence:

Start->A-1-> A-2->B-2->B-3->A-6-> A-7->B-4->B-9-> C-1-> C-3

Repair summary:

According to flowchart tutorial, open the device manager, make sure that device manager could recognize the Internal Modem. Then uninstall the Internal Modem's old driver, reinstall the latest driver, and then the failure still exists. After changing to USB Modem, it could dial-up to Internet normally. Then we can assume it's the problem with the hardware. Open the laptop cover, remove the Internal Modem, finding the data cable between Internal Modem and RJ11 interface is broken. Then change the data cable and reinstall the Internal Modem. After restarting the laptop, the failure is eliminated.

Hint:

Humidity, overheating, lightning strike and others might cause the problem that the internal copper wire of the data cable or the insulating tube is broken.

15.3.4 Three repair cases for the Internet dialing failure caused because of HP laptop motherboard problem

299)   Compaq Perasrio C500 laptop could not dial to Internet

Failure symptom:

Laptop could not dial to Internet; no any dialing tone, connection auto cut off and could not connect to network again.

Solution:

This failure obviously belongs to the description of flowchart 15, according to the repair method; confirm the repair path, finding it's consistent with the sequence:

Start->A-1-> A-2->B-1->B-3->C-1->C-3->C-4->C-5

Repair summary:

According to flowchart tutorial, first of all, open device manager; check whether there's Internet Modem item displayed in the device manager list. Reinstall the latest version of driver, then open the device manager again, but there's still no Internal Modem displayed in the list. Open the laptop cover, remove the Internal Modem and reinstall it, the failure is still existed. Next check RJ11 interface, no problem is found. Then change another known working Internal Modem, and after reinstalling operating system, the laptop still could not recognize the Internal Modem. So I am certain that this failure is caused by the motherboard failure. Install one known working normal USB Phone Modem to replace the Internal Modem, then the failure is gone.

Hint:

There are a lot of reasons causing system Internet dialing failure caused because of motherboard, for example, motherboard interface is badly soldered, distorted RJ11 jack, cracked pins, electronic components' failure, and short circuit and so on. You should analyze and figure out the problem according to your real circumstances.

300) HP Presario CQ40-506TX laptop could not dial to Internet

Failure symptom:

Laptop could not start normally.

Repair summary:

According to repair experience, try to narrow the range of the failed parts with the method "Minimum system judgment", locating the failed part accurately. First remove battery, wireless network card, network card, Modem, card reader, hard disk and so on. As a result, under the minimum system, laptop could start up normally, which indicates the problem is on the removed part, next assemble the removed parts one by one. When plug the internal Modem and restart the laptop, black screen failure shows again, finally, we are certain it is the internal modem that causes black screen. Plug one known working Internal Modem to the laptop to test, the result is still black screen! It seems the motherboard has a defect. Install one USB phone Modem to

Replace the Internal Modem, and then the failure disappears.

Hint:

a) After installing the Internal Modem, laptop could not start up, while after removing the Internal Modem, it could start normally. Usually, its motherboard hardware problem or the physical damage of the slot, also probably it is because the South Bridge chip has defect.

b) When the connection between the Internal Modem and motherboard is loose, or there's hardware problem with the Internal Modem, probably laptop could not start up either.

301) HP Presario V6109EA laptop could not dial to Internet

Failure symptom:

Laptop could not dial to Internet, no any dialing tone, connection auto cuts off, could not connect to the network.

Solution:

This failure obviously belongs to the description of flowchart 15, according to the repair method; confirm the repair path, finding it's consistent with the sequence:

Start->A-1-> A-2->B-1->B-3->C-1->C-3->C-4->C-5

Repair summary:

According to flowchart tutorial, first of all, open device manager; finding there's no Internet Modem item displayed in the device manager list. Reinstall the latest version of driver, then open the device manager again, but there's still no Internal Modem displayed in the list. Open the laptop cover, check hardware, finding the Internal Modem slots (on motherboard) have several obvious mildew spots, probably is affected with damp for a long term. Clean with alcohol, and then the failure disappears.

Hint:

Some users put laptop in basement when working, because the humidity in basement is usually high, so that machine is quite easy to get damaged by humidity, so it's quite easy for this or that failure happening.

AUTHOR BIOGRAPHY

Ashok Liu (Xiaochun Liu) has co-founded Computer Care Center, a laptop repairing and service firm, which has entered the 18 years of operation in North America. He has over 35 years of experience in related electronic troubleshooting. In 1982, he was completing a B.S degree in Electrical and Electronic Engineering.

Printed in the United States
By Bookmasters